Boomer'sTree

by Toma

Contents

ISBN-13: 978-1533051325

ISBN-10: 1533051321

Dedication

To all my forefathers, without whom I would never have existed.

Generation No. 1

1. Thomas Aldwyn "Tom" Allsworth was born 17 Nov 1946, in London, Middlesex, England, christened 15 Dec 1946, in Harrow, Middlesex, England. He was the son of Thomas William Allsworth and Yvonne Rowland. He married Janet Beasley 14 Mar 1964, in Oxford, Oxfordshire, England.
Notes for Thomas Aldwyn "Tom" Allsworth:

Personal history found in published autobiography - Boomer's Walk.

Generation No. 2

2. Thomas William Allsworth was born 23 Sep 1905, in Headington, Oxfordshire, England,[1] christened 5 Nov 1905, in Headington, Oxfordshire, England,[2,3] died 12 May 1992, in Jeffreyston, Pembrokeshire, Wales,[1] buried May 1992, in Jeffreyston, Pembrokeshire, Wales.[1] He was the son of Walter William Allsworth and Annie Newell. He married (1) Yvonne Rowland[5,6,7] 21 Jul 1945, in Harrow, Middlesex, England.[4] She was the daughter of George William Rowland and Sarah Lucas. He married (2) Agness Moran. He married (3) Edith Mary Carter 23 Jan 1932, in Darlington, County Durham, England.[8] Notes for Thomas William Allsworth:

Born in Headington 1905 (High Street, New Headington - now known as New High Street, Headington.) Christened in St Andrew's Church, Headington - 5 November 1905 (HEADINGTON St. Andrew PARISH REGISTERS Baptisms Page 144) Moved to 2 Deans Row, St Aldwyns, Gloucester during 1906 Lived at Woodbine cottage, 99 Lime Walk, Headington, Oxford from 1914 Lived in Church Street, New Headington, in 1918 (where his brother Ernest died) until he joined Army. Army # RCS2321127 (Royal Corps of Signals) Married Edith Carter 23 JAN 1932 - USED NAME OF THOMAS WILLIAM ALDWYN-ALLSWORTH Report of her being already married was not true. At start of war 1939 he appears on registration as being Thomas William Aldwyn-Allsworth a name he contrived based on the place he lived as a small child. Address 19 Camden Road, St Pancras, London, where he lodged with the STRATTON family.

Children of Thomas William Allsworth and Yvonne Rowland:

    i.   **Thomas Aldwyn "Tom" Allsworth**, born 17 Nov 1946, in London, Middlesex, England.

    ii.   **Anne Allsworth**, born 10 Feb 1948, in Oxford, Oxfordshire, England, christened 28 Mar 1948, in Headington, Oxfordshire, England. She married Michael Richard Hill 10 Sep 1966, in Headington, Oxfordshire, England. Michael Richard Hill was born 23 Mar 1943, in England.

    iii.   **Richard Allsworth**, born 6 May 1951, in Oxford, Oxfordshire, England. He married (1) Karen L. Westbrook Apr 1990, in Pembrokeshire, Wales. Karen L. Westbrook was born about 1955, in United States. They were divorced. He married (2) Lesley Karen Shepherd 21 Apr 1990, in Haverfordwest, Pembrokeshire, Wales. Lesley Karen Shepherd was born 2 Dec 1948, in Salt Lake, Utah, United States. They were divorced. He married (3) Sorrel Gossert 26 Jun 1993, in Pembrokeshire, Wales. Sorrel Gossert was born 25 Jul 1955, in Santa Monica, Los Angeles, California, United States. They were divorced. He married (4) Cheryl Cartwright 21 Oct 1978, in Swansea, Glamorganshire, Wales. Cheryl Cartwright was born about 1952, in Pembrokeshire, Wales. They were divorced.

    iv.   **Helen Aldwyn-Allsworth**, born 9 Sep 1952, in Oxford, Oxfordshire, England. She married (1) John G. Walker Feb 2002, in Neath, Glamorganshire, Wales. John G.

Walker was born about 1945, in England. She married (2) Phillip Francis Mackin 3 Nov 1973, in St Florence, Pembrokeshire, Wales. Phillip Francis Mackin was born about 1950, in England.

v. **Joan Aldwyn-Allsworth**, born 21 Apr 1958, in Oxford, Oxfordshire, England. She married Raymond Eric Evans 1 May 1976, in St Florence, Pembrokeshire, Wales. Raymond Eric Evans was born about 1950, in St Florence, Pembrokeshire, Wales.

vi. **David Allsworth**,[9] born Jun 1967, in Oxford, Oxfordshire, England, died Jun 1967, in Oxford, Oxfordshire, England.
David Allsworth Birth: Jun 1967 - Oxfordshire, England Death: Jun 1967 - Oxfordshire, England Parents: Thomas William Allsworth, Yvonne Rowland

Children of Thomas William Allsworth and Agness Moran:

i. **Patricia Agness Moran**, born 28 Jan 1935, in Aldershot, Hampshire, England. She married Albert William "Bill" Coles 27 Apr 1954, in Bristol, Gloucestershire, England. Albert William "Bill" Coles was born 1928, in Bristol, Gloucestershire, England, died 2 Apr 2014, in Bristol, Gloucestershire, England.
Notes for Patricia Agness Moran and Albert William "Bill" Coles: ref: Marriages Jun 1954 - Moran Patricia A. & Coles, Albert W (Bill) Bristol 7b 81

3. Yvonne Rowland was born 25 May 1926, in Lambeth, London, England, died 2 Sep 2008, in Pencoed, Wooden, Saundersfoot, Pembrokeshire, Wales, buried 11 Sep 2008, in Pembrokeshire, Wales. She was the daughter of George William Rowland and Sarah Lucas. She married Thomas William Allsworth[5,6,7,10] 21 Jul 1945, in Harrow, Middlesex, England.[4] He was the son of Walter William Allsworth and Annie Newell.
Notes for Yvonne Rowland:

Birth Cert shows she was born at Lambeth Hospital and her parents (GW Rowland) lived at 12 Holland Road, Brixton. This road was re-named = MINET road many years later. It is interesting to note that Mum was brought up just two miles from where my future wife, Jan, was brought up years later. Married: - Our Lady and St Thomas of Canterbury, Catholic Church, Harrow, Middlesex PERSONAL KNOWLEDGE registration district - Lambeth, vol. 1d page 465

Generation No. 3

4. Walter William Allsworth was born 6 Jun 1879, in St Thomas, Oxford, Oxfordshire, England, christened 7 Sep 1879, in St Thomas, Oxford, Oxfordshire, England, died 6 Sep 1965, in Oxford, Oxfordshire, England, buried after 7 Sep 1965, in Oxford, Oxfordshire, England. He was the son of Thomas Allsworth and Sarah Morgan. Residences: 1881, Oxford St Thomas, Oxfordshire, England; 1891, Oxford, Oxfordshire, England. He married Annie Newell[10,12,13,14] 26 Dec 1903, in St Frideswide's, Oxford, Oxfordshire, England, United Kingdom.[11] She was the daughter of Eliseus Clark Newell and Elizabeth Allsworth.

Notes for Walter William Allsworth:

Born: 6 Jun 1879, St Thomas, Oxford. Baptised: 7 Jun 1879, St Thomas's Church, Oxford Married: 26 Dec 1903, St Frideswide's Church, Oxford Died: 6 Sep 1965, Cutteslow, Oxford residences Ayres Yard, St Thomas, Oxford Church Street, Headington Coln St Aldwyns Lime Walk, Headington Cutteslowe, Oxford. Background information Walter was born at 3 Ayres Yard, St Thomas in Oxford. He was the son of Thomas and Sara ALLSWORTH and one of their 8 children. He started work at the age of 14 at the Clarendon Press and then worked at Simmonds brewery. In 1897, at the age of 18, he joined the first battalion of the Royal Berkshire regiment; he was in South Africa for the whole of the Boer war and returned home in 1902. (Explains why he does not appear in the 1901 census.) On Boxing Day 1903, he married Annie NEWELL (his cousin) from Stanton St John at St Frideswide's Church in Oxford. He returned to the battalion before the First World War. In 1914, he was with Worcestershire regiment where he remained until 1919. Walter worked at the Pressed Steel factory and then the Radcliffe Infirmary as a painter and decorator. Walter and Annie had 9 children and 23 Grandchildren. They lived near the famous Cutteslow wall. British Army Service Records 1760-1915 Transcription Print Close First name(s): Walter William Last name: ALLSWORTH Calculated year of birth: 1879 Parish of birth: St Thomas Town of birth: Oxford County of birth: Oxfordshire Age at attestation: 18 years 4 months Attestation date: 28 October 1897 Attestation corps: Princess Charlotte of Wales's (Royal Berkshire Regiment) Attestation soldier number: 5183 Discharge rank: Discharge corps: Discharge soldier number: The National Archives reference: WO97 / 4253 / 52

Children of Walter William Allsworth and Annie Newell:

i.   **Thomas William Allsworth**,[5,6,7,10] born 23 Sep 1905, in Headington, Oxfordshire, England,[1] died 12 May 1992, in Jeffreyston, Pembrokeshire, Wales.[1]

ii.   **Lydia Amy Allsworth**,[15] born 6 Jan 1907, in Coln Saint Aldwyn, Gloucestershire, England, christened 7 Feb 1907, in Oxford, Oxfordshire, England, died Apr 1989, in Westergate, Sussex, England, buried Apr 1989, in Sussex, England. She married Albert Ronald Portman 1929, in Headington, Oxfordshire, England. Albert Ronald Portman was born 1905, in Headington, Oxfordshire, England, died 1941, in England.
born 2 Deans Row, Coln St Aldwyns, Gloucestershire, England, United

Kingdomland Lydia Amy Allsworth; Female; Birth: 06 JAN 1907 2 Deans Row Coln St Aldwyns, , Oxford, England, United Kingdomland; Christening: 07 FEB 1907 St Frideswide'S, , Oxford, England, United Kingdomland; Death: Before 2000 Westergate, Sussex, England, United Kingdomland; Father: Walter William Allsworth; Mother: Annie Newell Registered at Northleach Gloucestershire Christened 1907 - St Frideswide, Oxford Marriage 1929 - Oxford - Albert Ronald Portman Marriage 1964 - Oxford - Albert G Wood Died 1989 - Westergate, Sussex Burial 1989 - Chichester crem.

iii. **Edith Florence Allsworth**,[16] born 28 Oct 1908, in Coln Saint Aldwyn, Gloucestershire, England,[16] died 26 Jun 1998, in London, England.[16]
Born: 28 oct 1908 - 2 Deans Row, Coln St. Aldwyns, Gloucestershire, England Christened : Marriage: Died: 12 jun 1998 - Camden, London Burial: NEVER married

iv. **Reginald Walter Allsworth**,[17] born 18 Aug 1910, in Coln Saint Aldwyn, Gloucestershire, England,[17] christened 2 Oct 1910, in Coln St Aldwyn, Gloucestershire, England, died 17 Aug 1979, in Felpham, Sussex, England,[17] buried Sep 1979, in Felpham, Sussex, England.[17] He married Maria Zilda Gloria Vaz about 1931, in England. Maria Zilda Gloria Vaz was born 24 Dec 1908, in Recife, Pernambuco, Brazil, christened 21 Jul 1912, in Recife, Pernambuco, Brazil, died 16 Dec 1977, in Felpham, Sussex, England, buried Dec 1977, in Felpham, Sussex, England.
Reginald Walter Allsworth; Male; Birth: 18 AUG 1910 2 Deans Row, Coln St Aldwyns, Gloucestershire, England, United Kingdom marriage Death: 17 AUG 1979 Felpham, Sussex, England, United Kingdomland; Burial: St Mary'S, Felpham, Sussex, England, United Kingdomland; Father: Walter William Allsworth; Mother: Annie Newell

v. **Annie Elizabeth Allsworth**, born 4 Apr 1913, in Coln St Aldwyns Gloucestershire, England, died 26 Dec 1983, in Rose Hill, Oxford, Oxfordshire, England, buried Jan 1984, in Iffley, Oxfordshire, England. She married Edward A. Rawlings Jul 1935, in Oxford, Oxfordshire, England. Edward A. Rawlings was born 2 Apr 1914, in St Thomas, Oxfordshire, England, christened 10 May 1914, in St Pauls, Oxford, Oxfordshire, England, died 23 Dec 1983, in Rose Hill, Oxford, Oxfordshire, England, buried 4 Jan 1984, in Iffley, Oxford, Oxfordshire, England. born 2 Deans Row, Coln St Aldwyns, Gloucestershire, England

vi. **Mildred Dorothy Allsworth**,[18] born 17 Nov 1914, in Headington, Oxfordshire, England, died Mar 1993, in Braintree, Essex, England. She married Reginald Charles Looker[19] 1 Oct 1938, in Summertown, Oxfordshire, England. Reginald Charles Looker was born 26 Oct 1906, in Islington, London, England, died Sep 1989, in Redbridge, Greater London, England.
Born: 17 nov 1914 - Woodbine cottage, headington, oxford Christened : Marriage: 1938 - oxford - Reginald Charles looker Died: March1993 - Braintree, essex Burial:

vii. **Ernest R. George Allsworth**, born Oct 1917, in Headington, Oxfordshire,

England, died Nov 1918, in Headington, Oxfordshire, England, buried 11 Nov 1918, in Headington, Oxfordshire, England.
HEADINGTON CEMETERY REGISTERS Burials Page 31 1918 11 Nov ALLSWORTH Ernest Robert .G. 13m Church St New Headington son of Walter Wm.

viii. **Emily Grace Allsworth**,[20] born 28 Mar 1921, in Headington, Oxfordshire, England, died 26 Jan 2002, in Oxfordshire, England, buried 4 Feb 2002, in Headington, Oxfordshire, England. She married Leslie Charles Ernest Cox[21] 15 Dec 1951, in Summertown, Oxfordshire, England. Leslie Charles Ernest Cox was born 14 Sep 1919, in Ledwell, Oxfordshire, England, died 3 Jul 1981, in Churchill, Oxfordshire, England, buried 9 Jul 1981, in Oxford, Oxfordshire, England.

ix. **John Frederick Allsworth**,[22] born 28 Mar 1921, in Headington, Oxfordshire, England, died Dec 1978, in Oxford, Oxfordshire, England, buried Dec 1978, in Oxford, Oxfordshire, England. He married Esther Lillian Gibbins[22] 9 May 1942, in Summertown, Oxfordshire, England. Esther Lillian Gibbins was born Jul 1921, in Bethnal Green, London, England, died Apr 2010, in Oxfordshire, England. They were divorced.
Known as Uncle Jack - lived in Barton East, Headington, Oxford Born: 28 march 1921 - Woodbine cottage, Headington Oxford Christened : Marriage: 1942 - Oxford Died: 1978 - Oxford Burial: 1978 - Oxford Crem. Bayswater Road, Headington.
Notes for Esther Lillian Gibbins: Re-married - BROWN

5. Annie Newell was born 4 Apr 1882, in Stanton St John, Oxfordshire, England, christened 2 Jul 1882, in Beckley, Oxfordshire, England, died 6 Aug 1969, in Littlemore, Oxfordshire, England, buried Aug 1969, in Oxford Crematorium, Oxford, Oxfordshire, England. She was the daughter of Eliseus Clark Newell and Elizabeth Allsworth. She married Walter William Allsworth[10,13,14,23,24,25] 26 Dec 1903, in St Frideswide's, Oxford, Oxfordshire, England, United Kingdom.[11] He was the son of Thomas Allsworth and Sarah Morgan.
Notes for Annie Newell:

Occupation Scullery maid until her marriage dates Born: 4 Apr 1882, Bayswater Farm, Headington, Oxfordshire, England Married: 26 Dec 1903, St Frideswide's Church, Oxford Died: 6 Aug 1969 residence Stanton St John; Water Eaton; Church Street, Headington; Cutteslowe, Oxfordshire Background information Annie was the daughter of Elezeus who was a carter at Stowford Farm and Elizabeth NEWELL. The NEWELL family comes from Beckley and Cuxham. They were mainly blacksmiths. Annie was one of seven children. In 1891, they all lived in a small cottage in Water Eaton. In the 1901 census, she was a scullery maid at the Warneford Hospital and she continued in this job until she married Walter. They had 9 children and 23 grandchildren. They lived near the famous Cutteslowe wall.

6. George William Rowland was born 8 Jul 1901, in Fulham, Middlesex, England, died 29 Jun 1959, in Surrey, England, buried 6 Jul 1959, in Surrey, England. He was the son of George Stephen Rowland and

Augusta Mary Humber. He married (1) Sarah Lucas[26,27,28] 4 May 1921, in Dublin, Ireland. She was the daughter of Charles Lucas and Mary Ann Giles. He married (2) Emily Mildred Mary Brewer[29,30,31] Sep 1958, in Surrey, England. He married (3) Agnes Elizabeth McGovan[32,33,34] May 1939, in Surrey, England. Notes for George William Rowland:

Registration district: Dublin North Record type: MARRIAGES Registration date - quarter and year: Jan - Mar 1922 Estimated birth year: Age: Mother surnames: Film number: 101575 Volume: 2 Page: 339 Digital GS number: 4199367 Image number: 00032 Collection: Ireland, Civil Registration Indexes 1845-1958 Served in MALLOW BARRACKS IRELAND - was there when he married Sarah Lucas she was living at 11 Upper Abbey Street, Dublin, Ireland Will - address: 6 Cavendish Avenue, New Malden, Surrey died 29 June 1959 - will administered London, 6 August to Emily Mildred Mary Rowland (widow). Effects 1193 8s 10d. General info: George's wife (Sarah) had died the year before the start of the war . The children were placed in the charge of various family members, and into 'care.' He took his youngest daughter, Winifred, to Hammersmith in London. It was there he met and married his 2nd wife, Agnes. She died in 1957 and he married his 3rd wife Emily. He died one year later. Emily survived him until 1990. Surry District, vol. 2a, page 1231. Mary Lucas & Albert Edward Duckworth - witnesses to the marriage Married on 4th May 1921 but the marriage was not registered until 5th Feb 1922 Registration district: Dublin North Record type: MARRIAGES Registration date - quarter and year: Jan - Mar 1922 Estimated birth year: Age: Mother surnames: Film number: 101575 Volume: 2 Page: 339 Digital GS number: 4199367 Image number: 00032 Collection: Ireland, Civil Registration Indexes 1845-1958 Served in MALLOW BARRACKS IRELAND - was there when he married Sarah Lucas she was living at 11 Upper Abbey Street, Dublin, Ireland Will - address: 6 Cavendish Avenue, New Malden, Surrey died 29 June 1959 - will administered London, 6 August to Emily Mildred Mary Rowland (widow). Effects 1193 8s 10d. Mary Lucas & Albert Edward Duckworth - witnesses to the marriage Married on 4th May 1921 but the marriage was not registered until 5th Feb 1922 Surry District, vol. 2a, page 1231. http://search.findmypast.co.uk/record?id=gbor%2fs choool%2fp3%2fgbor%2fschoool%2fp3%2f6720661

Children of George William Rowland and Sarah Lucas:

i. **George Stephen Rowland**,[35] born 21 Sep 1921, in Wandsworth, London, England, died Sep 2003, in Downham, Norfolk, England. He married Pearl H. Pym Jun 1947, in Hendon, Middlesex, England. She was the daughter of Pym and House. Pearl H. Pym was born 1929, in Willesden, Middlesex, England, died 7 Jan 2014, in Downham Market, Norfolk, England, buried 22 Jan 2014, in Downham Market, Norfolk, England.
Surname Given Name District Volume Page Rowland George S Wandsworth 1d 1030 Mother's Maiden Name - Lucas wifes name is Pearl...........? possible emigrated to australia 1957 Name: George Stephen Rowland Birth Date: 21 Sep 1921 Death Registration Month/Year: Sep 2003 Age at death (estimated): 82 Registration district: Downham Inferred County: Cambridgeshire, Norfolk Register number: 19D Entry Number: 95 First name(s) GEORGE STEPHEN Last name ROWLAND Gender Male Birth day 21 Birth month 9 Birth year 1921 Age - Death

quarter 3 Death year 2003 District DOWNHAM District number 6331 Register number 19D Entry number 095 Date of registration mm/yy 0903 County Norfolk Country England Record set England & Wales deaths 1837-2007 Category Birth, Marriage, Death & Parish Records Subcategory Deaths & burials Collections from Great Britain

Notes for Pearl H. Pym: First name(s) PEARL H Last name PYM Birth year 1929 Birth quarter 1 Registration month - Mother's last name HOUSE District WILLESDEN County Middlesex Country England Volume 3A Page 380 Record set England & Wales births 1837-2006 Category Birth, Marriage, Death & Parish Records Subcategory Births & baptisms Collections from Great Britain First name(s) Pearl H Last name Rowland Age guide 65+ Address 11, Gallow Drive, Downham Market, Norfolk, PE38 9RD Town Downham Market District Downham Market County Norfolk Country England Year 2002-13 Electoral rolls 2002, 2004, 2005, 2006, 2007, 2008, 2013 Occupancy (years) 15 Other occupants George Rowland Record set UK electoral registers 2002-2014 Category Census, land & surveys Subcategory Electoral Rolls Collections from Great Britain Pearl Rowland : Obituary Published in the Lynn News on 17th January 2014 ROWLAND On January 7th 2014 peacefully at the Queen Elizabeth Hospital, Pearl aged 85 years of Downham Market. dearly loved wife of George (deceased). Funeral service at Mintlyn Crematorium on Wednesday 22nd January at 3.15 pm. Family flowers only, donations for Macmillan Cancer Support may be given at the service or sent to A.J. Coggles Funeral Directors, 69 Bridge Street Downham Market. Pearl H Pym England and Wales Birth Registration Index Name   Pearl H Pym Event Type Birth Registration Registration Quarter Jan-Feb-Mar Registration Year 1929 Registration District Willesden County Middlesex Event Place Willesden, Middlesex, England Mother's Maiden Name (not available before 1911 Q3)   House <https://familysearch.org/ark:/61903/1:1:QV3L-S6G6> Volume 3A Page 380 Line Number   5 Citing this Record "England and Wales Birth Registration Index, 1837-2008," database, FamilySearch (https://familysearch.org/ark:/61903/1:1:QV3L-S6GD : accessed 2 December 2015), Pearl H Pym, 1929; from "England & Wales Births, 1837-2006," database, findmypast (http://www.findmypast.com : 2012); citing Birth Registration, Willesden, Middlesex, England, citing General Register Office, Southport, England.

Notes for George Stephen Rowland and Pearl H. Pym: First name(s) PEARL H Last name PYM Marriage quarter 2 Marriage year 1947 Registration month - GEORGE S ROWLAND Spouse's last name ROWLAND District HENDON District number - County Middlesex Country England Volume 5F Page 300 Record set England & Wales marriages 1837-2008 Category Birth, Marriage, Death & Parish Records Subcategory Marriages & divorces

ii.   **Pauline Stella Rowland**,[36] born 24 Oct 1922, in Wandsworth, London, England, died Jan 1952, in Hendon, Middlesex, England. She married William C. J. Stanley Feb 1944, in Hendon, Middlesex, England. William C. J. Stanley was born 1923, in

Aylesbury, Buckinghamshire, England, died Dec 1986, in Brent, London, England. Aunt Pauline

iii.   **Raymond Rowland**,[37] born 29 Sep 1924, in Wandsworth, London, England, died 26 Feb 2004, in Johnston, Pembrokeshire, Wales. He married Mildred Molly Allison[38] Apr 1947, in Durham, England. Mildred Molly Allison was born May 1926, in Durham, England, died before 2000, in England.
Registered as Raymond Always known as John
Notes for Mildred Molly Allison: aka: Molly

iv.   **Yvonne Rowland**,[5,6,7] born 25 May 1926, in Lambeth, London, England, died 2 Sep 2008, in Pencoed, Wooden, Saundersfoot, Pembrokeshire, Wales.

v.   **Winifred Agatha Rowland**,[39] born 20 Apr 1932, in Harrow, Middlesex, England, died 18 Feb 1987, in Harrow, Middlesex, England, buried 24 Feb 1987, in Harrow, Middlesex, England. She married Robert F. Stanley Oct 1948, in Harlow, Essex, England. Robert F. Stanley was born 2 May 1927, in Willesden, Middlesex, England, died Apr 1997, in Hillingdon, London, England.

Children of George William Rowland and Agnes Elizabeth McGovan:

i.   **Caroline F. Rowland**,[40] born 30 Nov 1941, in Surrey, England, died Jan 2003, in Sussex, England. She married Alan J. Green Jul 1964, in Surrey, England. Alan J. Green was born 1937, in Surrey, England.

ii.   **Nicolette M. Rowland**, born 1945, in Surrey, England. She married Brian J. Lucas Feb 1966, in Surrey, England. Brian J. Lucas was born 1941, in Surrey, England.

7. Sarah Lucas was born Jan 1897, in West Ham, Essex, England, died 19 Feb 1938, in Harefield, Middlesex, England. She was the daughter of Charles Lucas and Mary Ann Giles. Residence: 31 Mar 1901, West Ham, Essex, England. She married George William Rowland[10,28,41,42] 4 May 1921, in Dublin, Ireland. He was the son of George Stephen Rowland and Augusta Mary Humber.
Notes for Sarah Lucas:

Died in Harefield Hospital, Harefield, Middlesex, England Surname shown as 'ROWLANDS' on Death cert - UxbridgeDistrict, Vol. 3 a, Page: 94 Died from TB in Harefield Hospital, Harefield, Uxbridge, Middlesex, England, United Kingdom 19-Feb-1938 Appears on 1911 census with family : LUCAS SARAH F 1897 14 West Ham Essex 1911 address: 42 Woodstock St, Canning Town, Essex. Age 14 occupation: Cigarette stripper. Name: Sarah Lucas Registration district: Dublin North Record type: MARRIAGES Registration date - quarter and year: Jan - Mar 1922 Film number: 101575, Volume: 2, Page: 339 Digital GS number: 4199367, Image number: 00023 Collection: Ireland, Civil Registration Indexes 1845-1958 Surname shown as 'ROWLANDS' on Death cert - UxbridgeDistrict, Vol. 3 a, Page: 94

Generation No. 4

8. Thomas Allsworth was born Dec 1849, in Stanton Harcourt, Oxfordshire, England, christened 17 Feb 1850, in Stanton Harcourt, Oxfordshire, England, died Sep 1908, in St Thomas, Oxford, Oxfordshire, England, buried 30 Sep 1908, in St Thomas, Oxford, Oxfordshire, England. He was the son of Thomas Allsworth and Ellen Drinkwater. Residences: 1871, St Thomas, Oxfordshire, England; 1881, Oxford St Thomas, Oxfordshire, England; 1891, Oxford, Oxfordshire, England; 31 Mar 1901, Oxford St Thomas, Oxfordshire, England. He married Sarah Morgan[44,45,46,47,48,49,50,51,52] 19 Mar 1871, in St Thomas, Oxford, Oxfordshire, England.[43] She was the daughter of Charles Morgan and Martha Foster.
Notes for Thomas Allsworth:

At time of marriage he was living on the Botley Road, Oxford (1871). Note spelling on parish christening records - ALDSWORTH 17 Feb 1850 masons laborer went to live at 3 Ayers yard, oxford 1861 census Name: Thomas Allsworth Age in years: 11 Gender: Male Birth place: Stanton Harcourt, Oxfordshire Relationship to head-of-household: Son Record type: Household Collection: 1861 England and Wales Census masons laborer 1891 census Brewers labourer age 51 masons laborer Died at 11 Hollybush Row, St Thomas, Oxford - buried on 30 Sep 1908

Children of Thomas Allsworth and Sarah Morgan:

    i.   **Charles Thomas Victor Allsworth,**[53] born Nov 1872, in St Thomas, Oxford, Oxfordshire, England, christened 24 Nov 1872, in St Thomas, Oxford, Oxfordshire, England, died Oct 1926, in Headington, Oxfordshire, England, buried 26 Oct 1926, in Headington, Oxfordshire, England. Residence: 1881, Oxford St Thomas, Oxfordshire, England. He married Emily Newell[54] 26 Jun 1897, in Headington Quarry, Oxfordshire, England. She was the daughter of Eliseus Clark Newell and Elizabeth Allsworth. Emily Newell was born May 1876, in Stanton St John, Oxfordshire, England, christened 21 May 1876, in Stanton St John, Oxfordshire, England, died Jul 1947, in Headington, Oxfordshire, England, buried 12 Jul 1947, in Headington, Oxfordshire, England. Cause of death: Died in fire.
26 Oct ALLSWORTH Charles Thomas age: 54 address: William St New Headington Brewery Workman
Notes for Emily Newell: Died in house fire at 12 William St, Headington, Oxford, Oxfordshire, England, United Kingdom. 12 July 1947.

    ii.   **Fredrick Joseph Allsworth,**[55,56] born Dec 1873, in 3 Ayres Yard, St Thomas, Oxford, Oxfordshire, England, christened 8 Feb 1874, in St Thomas, Oxford, Oxfordshire, England, died 1 Jul 1916, in Somme, Picardie, France, buried Jul 1916, in Redan Ridge, Beaumont-Hamel, France. Residences: 1881, Oxford St Thomas, Oxfordshire, England; 1891, Oxford, Oxfordshire, England. He married Ellen Elizabeth Thurston 18 Dec 1902, in St Frideswide, Oxford, Oxfordshire, England.[57] Ellen Elizabeth Thurston was born about 1880, in Somers Town,

London, England, died Sep 1943, in Abingdon, Berkshire, England.

Parents living in New Osney when he was christened. In Memory of Serjeant FREDERICK JOSEPH ALLSWORTH MM 16387,

iii. **Martha Ellen Allsworth**,[58,59,60] born Apr 1875, in St Thomas, Oxford, Oxfordshire, England, christened 6 May 1875, in St Thomas, Oxford, Oxfordshire, England, died Aug 1875, in St Thomas, Oxford, Oxfordshire, England, buried 15 Aug 1875, in St Thomas, Oxford, Oxfordshire, England.

This entry was created from the following transcription: Surname Given Name Age District Volume Page Transcriber Deaths Sep 1875 Allsworth Martha Ellen 0 Oxford 3a 403

iv. **Alice Rose Allsworth**,[61,62,63] born Dec 1876, in St Thomas, Oxford, Oxfordshire, England, christened 8 Apr 1877, in St Thomas, Oxford, Oxfordshire, England, died Nov 1877, in St Thomas, Oxford, Oxfordshire, England, buried 29 Nov 1877, in St Thomas, Oxford, Oxfordshire, England.

This entry was created from the following transcription: Surname Given Name District Volume Page Transcriber Births Mar 1877 ALLSWORTH Alice Rose Oxford 3a 691 England, United Kingdomland

v. **Lily Allsworth**,[64,65,66] born Mar 1878, in St Thomas, Oxford, Oxfordshire, England, christened 9 Jun 1878, in St Thomas, Oxford, Oxfordshire, England, died Oct 1957, in Oxford, Oxfordshire, England, buried Oct 1957, in Oxford, Oxfordshire, England. She married Henry Wilkins[66] 10 Jul 1897, in St Thomas, Oxford, Oxfordshire, England. Henry Wilkins was born 1877, in St Thomas, Oxford, Oxfordshire, England, died Jun 1936, in Oxford, Oxfordshire, England, buried Jun 1936, in Oxford, Oxfordshire, England.

Father shown as MALTSER on christening record Thomas born before she was married . Both she and Thomas Wilkins were living at #5 Ayres Yard, Oxford. Lily was born at 3 Ayres Yard, St Thomas, Oxford, Oxfordshire, England Entry of death: Surname Given Name District Volume Page Transcriber Births Mar 1878 Allsworth Lily Oxford 3a 704-Civil Registration event: Death Name: WILKINS, Lily Registration District: Oxford, Oxfordshire Year of Registration: 1957 Quarter of Registration: Oct-Nov-Dec Age at death: 79 Volume No: 6B Page No: 1107.

vi. **Walter William Allsworth**,[10,13,14,23,24,25] born 6 Jun 1879, in St Thomas, Oxford, Oxfordshire, England, died 6 Sep 1965, in Oxford, Oxfordshire, England.

vii. **Mary Elizabeth Allsworth**,[67,68,69] born Oct 1881, in St Thomas, Oxford, Oxfordshire, England, christened 5 Dec 1881, in St Thomas, Oxford, Oxfordshire, England, died Jan 1882, in St Thomas, Oxford, Oxfordshire, England, buried 15 Jan 1882, in St Thomas, Oxford, Oxfordshire, England.

This entry was created from the following transcription: Surname Given Name District Volume Page Transcriber Births Dec 1881 Allsworth Mary Elizabeth Oxford 3a 735 Born at 3 Ayres Yard, St Thomas, Oxford, Oxfordshire, England

viii. **Amy Allsworth**,[10,70] born Dec 1884, in St Thomas, Oxford, Oxfordshire, England, christened 25 Jan 1885, in St Thomas, Oxford, Oxfordshire, England, died Feb 1959, in Oxford, Oxfordshire, England. Residences: 1891, Oxford, Oxfordshire,

England; 31 Mar 1901, Oxford St Thomas, Oxfordshire, England. She married John Reginald Maisey 25 Dec 1911, in Oxford, Oxfordshire, England. John Reginald Maisey was born Nov 1884, in Oxford, Oxfordshire, England, died Oct 1956, in Banbury, Oxfordshire, England.

Amy gave birth to Harry in 1898 when she was aged 13 and unmarried. Albert in 1905 when she was aged 20 and unmarried. Thomas in 1907 when she was aged 22 and unmarried. Florence in 1910 when she was aged 25 and unmarried. Amy married John Maisey 25 Dec 1911. 1911 CENSUS Address: 11 Holly Bush Row Oxford , Oxfordshire Name Relation Sex Age Birth Year Occupation Born ALDWORTH, Sarah Head Widow F 61 1850 Oxford ALDWORTH, Amy Daughter Single F 27 1884 Machinest Tailoring Oxford ALDWORTH, Harry Grandson M 13 1898 Machine Boy Printers Oxford ALDWORTH, Albert E Grandson M 6 1905 School Boy Oxford ALDWORTH, Thomas William Grandson M 4 1907 Oxford ALDWORTH, Florence Rose Granddaughter F 0 1911 Oxford Marriage banns 3, 10

Notes for John Reginald Maisey: spelt MASSEY on death reg

9. Sarah Morgan was born Apr 1850, in St Thomas, Oxford, Oxfordshire, England, christened 14 Apr 1850, in St Thomas, Oxford, Oxfordshire, England, died 27 Jul 1917, in St Thomas, Oxford, Oxfordshire, England,[71] buried 27 Jul 1917, in St Thomas, Oxford, Oxfordshire, England. She was the daughter of Charles Morgan and Martha Foster. Residences: 1871, St Thomas, Oxfordshire, England; 1881, Oxford St Thomas, Oxfordshire, England; 1891, Oxford, Oxfordshire, England; 31 Mar 1901, Oxford St Thomas, Oxfordshire, England. She married Thomas Allsworth[46,47,48,51,72,73,74,75,76] 19 Mar 1871, in St Thomas, Oxford, Oxfordshire, England.[43] He was the son of Thomas Allsworth and Ellen Drinkwater. Notes for Sarah Morgan:

At time of marriage she was living on the High Street, Oxford. (1871). Sarah lived 2 doors away from her future husband Dwelling: 1 Ayers Yard Census Place: Oxford St Thomas, Oxford, England Living at 11 Hollybush Row at time of death

10. Eliseus Clark Newell was born 10 May 1844, in Stanton St John, Oxfordshire, England, christened 9 Jun 1844, in Stanton St John, Oxfordshire, England, died 14 Apr 1899, in Headington, Oxfordshire, England, buried Apr 1899, in Headington, Oxfordshire, England. He was the son of Michael Newell and Eliza Hinton. He married Elizabeth Allsworth[48,78,79,80,81,82,83,84] 4 Jan 1874, in St Barnabas, Oxford, Oxfordshire, England.[77] She was the daughter of Thomas Allsworth and Ellen Drinkwater. Notes for Eliseus Clark Newell:

He was shown as a deceased labourer on Annie's marriage cert. 1903 The marriage cert. gives his name as Elias Newell - 29 - farm labourer - 8 Cranham Street, oxford. Father Michael Newell - black-smith. Thomas Allsworth (Elizabeth's brother)and Hannah Floyd (Hannah Allsworth - Elizabeth's sister) were witnesses. He was shown as a labourer on daughter Annie's marriage cert. 1903 1881 census shows him as a labourer on Stafford Farm, Woodperry, Stanton St John. Oxfordshire. Working for Farmer Collett VARIOUS FIRST NAME SPELLINGS USED: Elias / Eliseus / Elezeus / Elezius Civil Registration event: Birth Name: NEWELL, Elezius Registration District: Headington County: Oxfordshire Year of Registration: 1844 Quarter of Registration: Apr-May-Jun Volume No: Help 16 Page No:Help 73 Death register - Name: NEWELL, Elezeus Registration District: Headington County: Oxfordshire Year of Registration: 1899 Quarter of Registration: Apr-May-Jun Age at death: 53 Volume No: 3A Page No: 481 Living with family 7 Water eaton Lane, Water Eaton, Oxfordshire - 1891 census

Children of Eliseus Clark Newell and Elizabeth Allsworth:

i. **Walter Edward Allsworth**,[85] born 17 Nov 1863, in Cumnor, Berkshire, England, died 5 Nov 1949, in Marlow, Buckinghamshire, England. He married Sarah Herodias Wakelin 17 Nov 1885, in Oxford, Oxfordshire, England. Sarah Herodias Wakelin was born 16 Apr 1864, in England, died 1929, in Marlow, Buckinghamshire, England.
recorded as Walter Allsworth on 1881 census GSon Dwelling: 12 Duke St Census Place: Oxford St Thomas, Oxford, England Source: FHL Film 1341363 PRO Ref RG11 Piece 1504 Folio 67 Page 80 Marr Age Sex Birthplace Thos. ALLSWORTH M 59 M Stanton Harcourt, Oxford, England Rel: Head Occ: Labourer Helen ALLSWORTH M 58 F Brize Norton Rel: Wife Walter ALLSWORTH 17 M Cumnor, Oxford, England Rel: Grandson Occ: Labourer Married as Walter Edward Alsworth - Oxford 3a page 1039 - 1885 2/4 Birth mother is Elizabeth Allsworth b1846 Father? but assumed to be Eliseus Clerk Newell b1846 prior to marriage

ii. **Elisa Lavinia Allsworth**,[54] born Jun 1869, in North Hinksey, Berkshire, England, christened 20 Jun 1869, in North Hinksey, Berkshire, England, died Apr 1909, in Headington, Oxfordshire, England, buried Apr 1909, in Headington, Oxfordshire, England. Residence: 31 Mar 1901, Cumnor, Berkshire, England. She married David Gomm 15 Apr 1895, in Headington, Oxfordshire, England. David Gomm was born 1869, in Charlton on Otmoor, Oxfordshire, England.
Child born to her before she was married Birth INCORRECTLY given as Abingdon, Berkshire on 1901 census Name given as ELIZABETH GOMM on death reg. Reg District: Headington, Oxfordshire 1909 Apr-May-Jun Age at death 39 Vol: 3a; Page:522
Notes for David Gomm: Private soldier on marriage licence. Father's name - William Gomm employed as a shepherd

iii. **Arthur Newell**,[54] born May 1874, in Stanton St John, Oxfordshire, England, christened 24 May 1874, in Stanton St John, Oxfordshire, England, died Jan 1951, in Oxford, Oxfordshire, England, buried Jan 1951, in Oxford, Oxfordshire, England. Residence: 31 Mar 1901, Headington, Oxfordshire, England.
Name: NEWELL, Arthur Registration District: Oxford County: Oxfordshire Year of Registration: 1951 Quarter of Registration: Jan-Feb-Mar Age at death: 76 Volume No: 6B Page No: 1283

iv. **Emily Newell**,[54] born May 1876, in Stanton St John, Oxfordshire, England, christened 21 May 1876, in Stanton St John, Oxfordshire, England, died Jul 1947, in Headington, Oxfordshire, England, buried 12 Jul 1947, in Headington,

Oxfordshire, England. Cause of death: Died in fire. She married Charles Thomas Victor Allsworth[53] 26 Jun 1897, in Headington Quarry, Oxfordshire, England. He was the son of Thomas Allsworth and Sarah Morgan. Charles Thomas Victor Allsworth was born Nov 1872, in St Thomas, Oxford, Oxfordshire, England, christened 24 Nov 1872, in St Thomas, Oxford, Oxfordshire, England, died Oct 1926, in Headington, Oxfordshire, England, buried 26 Oct 1926, in Headington, Oxfordshire, England.

Died in house fire at 12 William St, Headington, Oxford, Oxfordshire, England, United Kingdom. 12 July 1947.

Notes for Charles Thomas Victor Allsworth: 26 Oct ALLSWORTH Charles Thomas age: 54 address: William St New Headington Brewery Workman

v.   **Annie Newell**, born 14 Apr 1878, in Forest Hill, Oxfordshire, England, christened 15 Apr 1878, in Forest Hill, Oxfordshire, England, died 20 Apr 1878, in Forest Hill, Oxfordshire, England, buried 21 Apr 1878, in Forest Hill, Oxfordshire, England.

vi.   **Fredrick Newell**,[54] born Sep 1879, in Forest Hill, Oxfordshire, England, christened 14 Sep 1879, in Forest Hill, Oxfordshire, England, died Nov 1948, in Thrup, Oxfordshire, England, buried 19 Nov 1948, in Kidlington, Oxfordshire, England.

vii.   **Annie Newell**,[10,12,13,14] born 4 Apr 1882, in Stanton St John, Oxfordshire, England, died 6 Aug 1969, in Littlemore, Oxfordshire, England.

viii.   **William Newell**, born 30 Aug 1885, in Tackley, Oxfordshire, England, died Nov 1941, in Oxford, Oxfordshire, England, buried Nov 1941, in Oxford, Oxfordshire, England. He married May Annie Chandler about Sep 1908, in Oxford, Oxfordshire, England. May Annie Chandler was born Jun 1877, in Summertown, Oxfordshire, England, christened 24 Jun 1877, in Summertown, Oxfordshire, England.

At the time of his marriage to May Annie, William was a gunner in the Royal Garrison Artillery DEATH reg: Name: NEWELL, William Registration District: Oxford County: Oxfordshire Year of Registration: 1941 Quarter of Registration: Oct-Nov-Dec Age at death: 57 Volume No: 3A Page No: 2348

ix.   **Ada Newell**, born Sep 1888, in Tackley, Oxfordshire, England, christened 2 Sep 1888, in Tackley, Oxfordshire, England, died Jul 1954, in Surrey, England. She married William Henry Thatcher[86] Aug 1920, in Maidenhead, Berkshire, England. William Henry Thatcher was born 1889, in Ckkham, Berkshire, England, died Dec 1950, in Eton, Buckinghamshire, England.

Gave birth to Ada (UNMARRIED) then departed to London. 1911 census she was a servant in the ANTHONY house 46 Woodland Rise Muswell Hill , Middlesex Marriage: Name: THATCHER, William Registration District: Maidenhead, Berkshire Year of Registration: 1920 Quarter of Registration: Jul-Aug-Sep Spouse's last name: Newell Volume No: 2C Page No: 1265 Living with family 7 Water eaton Lane, Water Eaton, Oxfordshire - 1891 census Living with mother (Widow) & brother William in Headington - 1901 census Servant in 46 Woodland Riad Muswell Hill, London - 1911 census

11. Elizabeth Allsworth was born 27 Dec 1846, in Northmoor, Oxfordshire, England, died Jan 1904, in Oxford, Oxfordshire, England. She was the daughter of Thomas Allsworth and Ellen Drinkwater. She married Eliseus Clark Newell[54,87,88,89,90] 4 Jan 1874, in St Barnabas, Oxford, Oxfordshire, England.[77] He was the son of Michael Newell and Eliza Hinton.
Notes for Elizabeth Allsworth:

Births Sep 1846 ALLSWORTH Elizabeth Witney XVI 135 1901 census shows she was widowed and working as a Laundress (taking im laundry to make ends meet) Living in Windsor street, Headington, Oxford with Walter and Ada Marriage Reg Married after first two cildren born England

12. George Stephen Rowland was born Jan 1879, in Poplar, London, England, died Jan 1929, in Hendon, Middlesex, England. He was the son of Stephen Rowland and Mary Ann Elleston. He married Augusta Mary Humber[6,91,92,93,94,95] 6 Apr 1899, in Chelsea, London, England. She was the daughter of Thomas Humber and Fanny Humphreys.
Notes for George Stephen Rowland:

Wife lied about her age to get married - she claimed to be 21 years old when she was in fact only 17 years old - married in Register Office at Chelsea by certificate with NO family members attending. 1911 - address: 131 Tylecroft Road, Norbury, Surrey, England. His age shown as 32 on 1911 census - CORRECT His age shown as 32 on 1901 census - INCORRECT 1901 Census Occupation Inscription (filer?) S Ken Musuem living at 18 Rosebury Road Fulham 1911 Census Occupation Writer Incription living at 131 Tylecroft Road Norbury Croydon married 12 years 2 children born both living WW1 service record states joined up 24/09/1914 aged 34 years job Inscription Writer Victoria. Probate shows he left 1620.11s 5d when he died in 1929 = about 66,000 in 2015

Children of George Stephen Rowland and Augusta Mary Humber:

    i.   **George William Rowland**,[10,28,41,42] born 8 Jul 1901, in Fulham, Middlesex, England, died 29 Jun 1959, in Surrey, England.

    ii.   **Winifred Alice Rowland**, born Apr 1903, in Fulham, Middlesex, England, died Feb 1959, in London, England. She married Francis G. Mitchell Jul 1925, in Wandsworth, London, England. Francis G. Mitchell was born Sep 1893, in Edmonton, Middlesex, England, died 1944, in Europe.
Reported to had owned a sweet shop in Eastcote Lane, Harrow, England
Notes for Francis G. Mitchell: Registration event: Death Name:MITCHELL, Francis G Unit:Royal Berkshire Regiment Rank:2nd Lieutenant Year:1944 Volume:3; Page:77 Record source: GRO War Death Army Officers Indices (1939 to 1948)

13. Augusta Mary Humber was born 1 Aug 1881, in Poplar, London, England, christened 7 Aug 1881, in Tower Hamlets, Middlesex, England,[96] died Apr 1952, in Surrey, England.[92] She was the daughter of Thomas Humber and Fanny Humphreys. She married George Stephen Rowland[6,94,95,97,98,99] 6 Apr 1899, in Chelsea, London, England. He was the son of Stephen Rowland and Mary Ann Elleston.

Notes for Augusta Mary Humber:

Christening place, Christ Church, Manchester Road, Tower Hamlets, Middlesex, England, United Kingdom lied about her age to get married - she claimed to be 21 years old when she was in fact only 17 years old - married in Register Office at Chelsea by certificate with NO family members attending. Baptism only Augusta Humber on Ancestry is Augusta Mary Humber daughter of Thomas

14. Charles Lucas was born 11 Jun 1857, in Barking, Essex, England, christened 6 Sep 1857, in Barking, Essex, England, died Mar 1920, in Whitechapel, London, England. He was the son of Thomas Lucas and Mary Ann Stringer. He married Mary Ann Giles[100,101,102,103,104,105,106,107] 21 Mar 1881, in Mile End, London, England. She was the daughter of George Giles and Ann Wine.
Notes for Charles Lucas:

1881 census - living at : 3 Baston Street, London, Middlesex, England Brother-in-law shown as living with them as a lodger in 1901 Charles LUCAS 23 Barking, Essex, England Labourer Mary LUCAS Wife 20 Limehouse, Middlesex, England 1881 census - living at : 3 Baston Street, London, Middlesex, England 1861 Census, Class: RG9; Piece: 1070; Folio: 16; Page: 28; GSU roll: 542747. 1871 Census, RG10 piece 1647 folio 44 page 8 1881 Census, RG11 piece 468 folio 17 page 27. 1891 Census, RG12 piece 210 folio 99 page 20. 1901 Census, RG13 Piece 1585 Folio 20 Page 31. 1911 Census, RG14 piece 9506 ref# RG78PN508 RD188 SD4 ED36 SN75.

Children of Charles Lucas and Mary Ann Giles:

    i.   **Mary Ann Lucas,**[108,109] born 22 Dec 1881, in Stepney, Middlesex, England, christened 15 Jan 1882, in Limehouse, Middlesex, England, died Jul 1882, in Stepney, Middlesex, England.

    ii.   **Charles William Lucas,**[110] born 11 Dec 1882, in Limehouse, Middlesex, England, christened 31 Dec 1882, in Limehouse, Middlesex, England, died Aug 1953, in Poplar, London, England. He married Louisa J. Bird Dec 1904, in West Ham, Essex, England. Louisa J. Bird was born Jun 1880, in Whitechapel, London, England.
Bap St Anne's Church, Limehouse, West Ham Civil Registration event: Marriage Name: LUCAS, Charles Registration District: West Ham County: Essex Year of Registration: 1904 Quarter of Registration: Oct-Nov-Dec Spouse's name: BIRD, Louisa Jane Volume No: 4A Page No: 308 1911 Census living at 28 Durham Road, Canning Town, Essex Death index Name: Charles Lucas Birth Date: abt 1883 Date of Registration: Jul-Aug-Sep 1953 Age at Death: 70 Registration district: Poplar, London Volume: 5d Page: 191
Notes for Louisa J. Bird: address 1911 census 28 Durham Road, Canning Town, London Civil Registration event: Marriage Name: LUCAS, Charles Registration District: West Ham County: Essex Year of Registration: 1904 Quarter of Registration: Oct-Nov-Dec Spouse's name: BIRD, Louisa Jane Volume No: 4A Page No: 308

iii. **George Lucas**, born Jun 1888, in West Ham, Essex, England, died Jun 1937, in West Ham, Essex, England.

iv. **Thomas Lucas**, born Dec 1889, in West Ham, Essex, England, died Jan 1958, in West Ham, Essex, England.
Incorrectly given name of AMOS by enuminator of the 1891 English census.

v. **Harriet Lucas**, born 7 May 1891, in West Ham, Essex, England, died Oct 1974, in London, England. She married Thomas Matthew Cross 1912, in West Ham, Essex, England. Thomas Matthew Cross was born 25 Jul 1889, in West Ham, Essex, England, died 18 Jan 1958, in Plaistow St Mary, Essex, England.

vi. **Sarah Lucas**,[26,27,28] born Jan 1897, in West Ham, Essex, England, died 19 Feb 1938, in Harefield, Middlesex, England.

vii. **James Lucas**,[111,112] born Sep 1899, in West Ham, Essex, England, died Aug 1903, in West Ham, Essex, England.

viii. **Elizabeth Lucas**, born 7 Jun 1901, in West Ham, Essex, England, died Jun 1975, in Lambeth, London, England. She married Albert Edward Winslade 17 Dec 1922, in West Ham, Essex, England. Albert Edward Winslade was born 1898, in Middlesex, England.

ix. **Marie Lucas**,[113] born May 1903, in Camden Town, London, England, died 15 Jun 1903, in Camden Town, London, England.

x. **Henry John Lucas**,[114] born 14 May 1906, in Southwark, Surrey, England, christened 26 May 1906, in Southwark, Surrey, England, died Jul 1906, in West Ham, Essex, England.
Born in Newington Workhouse

xi. **Edith Catherine Lucas**,[115] born 10 Oct 1907, in West Ham, Essex, England, died Feb 1980, in Brent, London, England. She married Walter Griggs[115] Jul 1930, in Hendon, Middlesex, England.[115] Walter Griggs was born 1902, in London, England, died Feb 1966, in Harrow, Middlesex, England.
Married as Kathleen in Hendon Death reg as Kathleen Griggs.

15. Mary Ann Giles was born 5 Aug 1860, in Limehouse, Middlesex, England, christened 2 Sep 1860, in Limehouse, Middlesex, England, died Dec 1943, in Croydon, Surrey, England. She was the daughter of George Giles and Ann Wine. Residence: 1871, St Ann Limehouse, London, Middlesex, England. She married Charles Lucas[102,103,104,116,117,118] 21 Mar 1881, in Mile End, London, England. He was the son of Thomas Lucas and Mary Ann Stringer.

Generation No. 5

16. Thomas Allsworth was born 17 Jan 1822, in Stanton Harcourt, Oxfordshire, England, christened 10 Feb 1822, in Stanton Harcourt, Oxfordshire, England, died Oct 1906, in Oxford, Oxfordshire, England, buried 29 Oct 1906, in St Thomas, Oxford, Oxfordshire, England. He was the son of William Aldsworth and Jane Turner. He married Ellen Drinkwater[119,120] 21 Nov 1841, in Brize Norton, Oxfordshire, England. She was the daughter of William Drinkwater and Hannah Haydon.
Notes for Thomas Allsworth:

Note spelling on parish records - ALDSWORTH Spelling on Brize Norton marriage register transcripts - HALLSWORTH Surname spelled - ALSWORTH on the 1851 census Living at 12 duke street St thomas oxford 1881 census died:5 Christ Church Buildings, Oxford, Oxfordshire, England

Children of Thomas Allsworth and Ellen Drinkwater:

      i.   **Elizabeth Allsworth**, born May 1842, in Northmoor, Oxfordshire, England, christened 29 May 1842, in Northmoor, Oxfordshire, England, died 7 Aug 1842, in Brize Norton, Oxfordshire, England.
           parish records give name as ALDSWORTH

     ii.   **Hannah Allsworth**,[121] born 31 Aug 1844, in Northmoor, Oxfordshire, England, died 27 May 1924, in London, Middlesex, Ontario, Canada, buried 29 May 1924, in Mount Pleasant Cemetery, London, Middlesex, Ontario, Canada. She married William Floyd Oct 1862, in Abingdon, Berkshire, England. William Floyd was born 4 Aug 1833, in Cumnor, Berkshire, England, died 25 Jan 1922, in Ontario, Canada.
           1861 census Name: Hannah Aldsworth Age in years: 18 Gender: Female Birth place: Northmoor, Oxfordshire Relationship to head-of-household: Servant Record type: Household Collection: 1861 England and Wales Census

    iii. **Elizabeth Allsworth**,[48,78,79,80,81,82,83,84] born 27 Dec 1846, in Northmoor, Oxfordshire, England, died Jan 1904, in Oxford, Oxfordshire, England.

    iv. **Eliza Ann Allsworth**, born 29 Dec 1847, in Stanton Harcourt, Oxfordshire, England, christened 29 Dec 1847, in Stanton Harcourt, Oxfordshire, England. She married James Wharton 7 Sep 1867, in Cumnor, Berkshire, England. James Wharton was born about 1845, in Stanton St Jahn, Oxfordshire, England.
           Note spelling on parish records - ALDSWORTH
           Notes for James Wharton: Parish reg Marriages - Cumnor, Berkshire 1867 7 Sep. Witnesses: Thomas Allsworth & Elizabeth Allsworth

     v.   **Thomas Allsworth**,[46,47,48,51,72,73,74,75,76] born Dec 1849, in Stanton Harcourt, Oxfordshire, England, died Sep 1908, in St Thomas, Oxford, Oxfordshire, England.

    vi. **Noah Allsworth**,[122] born Mar 1852, in Stanton Harcourt, Oxfordshire, England, died 11 Feb 1942, in Cumnor, Berkshire, England, buried 11 Feb 1942, in Cumnor,

Berkshire, England. Residence: 1891, Cumnor, Berkshire, England. He married Ruth Lilly Pricket 14 Aug 1876, in Stanton St John, Oxfordshire, England. Ruth Lilly Pricket was born 1857, in Cumnor, Berkshire, England, died 16 Mar 1942, in Cumnor, Berkshire, England, buried 16 Mar 1942, in Cumnor, Berkshire, England. Timeline(View details) 1852 Birth Stanton Harcourt, Oxforshire 1 source citation 1901 England Census 1861 Age: 9 Residence Cumnor, Berkshire, England 1 source citation 1861 England Census 1871 Age: 19 Residence St Thomas, Oxfordshire, England 1 source citation 1871 England Census 1876 14 AugAge: 24 Marriage to Ruth Lilly Pricket Stanton St John 1881 Age: 29 Residence Oxford St Thomas, Oxfordshire, England 1 source citation 1881 England Census 1891 Age: 39 Residence Cumnor, Berkshire, England 1 source citation 1891 England Census 1901 Age: 49 Residence Cumnor, Berkshire, England 1 source citation 1901 England Census 1942 Age: 90 Death Cumnor Cem This entry was created from the following transcription: Surname Given Name District Volume Page Transcriber Births Mar 1852 Allsworth Noah Witney 3a 572 dwelling 13 duke st, st thomas, oxford 1881 census Appear on 1930 Cumnor Polling District Electoral Register as Allsworth, Noah-Botley Pound Allsworth, Ruth Lily-Do. http://www.bodley.ox.ac.uk/external/cumnor/documents/census-1901.htm Botley Pound, ALLSWORTH Noah, 49, sawyer, b.S.Hinksey,Oxon. Wife: Ruth, 44, b. Cumnor Chn: Edith, 15, b.Cumnor; Cyril, 13, b.Cumnor; Arthur, 11, b.Cumnor; Leonard, 9, b.Cumnor Gertrude, 7, b.Cumnor; Hilda, 6, b.Cumnor; Ida, 4, b.Cumnor; Daisy, 3, b.Cumnor; Nelson, 10m. b.Cumnor. Grandson: Thomas, 1, b.Oxted,Surrey. 1861 census Name: Noah Allsworth Age in years. 9 Gender: Male Birth place: Stanton Harcourt, Oxfordshire Relationship to head-of-household: Son Record type: Household Collection: 1861 England and Wales Census 1891 Census - Labourer in Saw Mill. Living at Swinford Lodge1901 Census - Sawyer (Employer) - son Owen Cyril a labourer in Saw Works. Living at Botley Pound1911 Census - Sawyer (worker). Living at Botley Pound. Form completed and signed by Ruth. 14 children born alive, 2 deceased: married 34 years
Notes for Ruth Lilly Pricket: Name: Ruth Lilly Pricket Birth 1857 Cumnor -Alternates 1857 Stanton St John, , Oxfordshire, England OneWorldTree abt 1857 Cumnor, Berkshire, England Marriage14 Aug 1876 (Age: 19) Stanton St John to Noah Allsworth 1881 England Census Residence (Age: 24) Oxford St Thomas, Oxfordshire, England 1891 England Census Residence (Age: 34) Cumnor, Berkshire, England 1891 England Census

vii. **Fredrick Allsworth**,[123] born Aug 1854, in Stanton Harcourt, Oxfordshire, England, christened 3 Sep 1854, in Stanton Harcourt, Oxfordshire, England, died before 1950, in England.
Appear on 1930 Cumnor Polling District Electoral Register as Allsworth, Frederick-Do. (Swinford)

17. Ellen Drinkwater was born 25 Jun 1820, in Brize Norton, Oxfordshire, England, christened 25 Jun 1820, in Brize Norton, Oxfordshire, England, died 25 May 1899, in St Thomas, Oxford, Oxfordshire,

England, buried 25 May 1899, in St Thomas, Oxford, Oxfordshire, England. She was the daughter of William Drinkwater and Hannah Haydon. She married Thomas Allsworth[124,125,126,127,128] 21 Nov 1841, in Brize Norton, Oxfordshire, England. He was the son of William Aldsworth and Jane Turner.

Notes for Ellen Drinkwater:

Living at 42 High Street, Oxford at time of death. . Also known as Helen and Eleanor died: 42 Hight St, St Thomas, Oxford, Oxfordshire, England 1861 census Name: Ellen Allsworth Age in years: 39 Gender: Female Birth place: Brize Norton, Oxfordshire Relationship to head-of-household: Wife Record type: Household Collection: 1861 England and Wales Census also known as Helen

18. Charles Morgan was born 1803, in Kidlington, Oxfordshire, England, died 30 Jun 1884, in Oxford, Oxfordshire, England.[129] He was the son of John Morgan and Sarah Hartlett. He married (1) Martha Foster[130] 7 Sep 1834, in St Thomas, Oxford, Oxfordshire, England. She was the daughter of John Foster and Ann King. He married (2) Mary Foster[133] 14 Oct 1826, in Stanton Harcourt, Oxfordshire, England.[131,132]

Notes for Charles Morgan:

1851 census - lived at #64 High Street, St Thomas, Oxford #1 St. Thomas Street By 1861, Martha and some of the children were living in Ayres Yard #1 St. Thomas Street Charles married Mary Foster 14 Oct 1826 at Stanton Harcourt.

Children of Charles Morgan and Martha Foster:

i. **Henry Morgan**,[134] born Jan 1835, in St Thomas, Oxford, Oxfordshire, England, christened 25 Jan 1835, in St Thomas, Oxford, Oxfordshire, England, died 1890, in Oxfordshire, England. Residences: 1871, St Thomas, Oxfordshire, England; 1881, Oxford St Ebbe, Oxfordshire, England. He married Mrs Mary Morgan about 1858, in Oxfordshire, England. Mrs Mary Morgan was born 1838, in Witney, Oxfordshire, England.

ii. **Mary Anne Morgan**,[135] born Oct 1836, in St Thomas, Oxford, Oxfordshire, England, christened 23 Oct 1836, in St Thomas, Oxford, Oxfordshire, England.

iii. **Charles Morgan**,[136] born Nov 1838, in St Thomas, Oxford, Oxfordshire, England, christened 18 Nov 1838, in St Thomas, Oxford, Oxfordshire, England, died 1901, in England.

iv. **George Morgan**, born Apr 1841, in St Thomas, Oxford, Oxfordshire, England, christened 11 Apr 1841, in St Thomas, Oxford, Oxfordshire, England, died 29 Sep 1854, in St Thomas, Oxford, Oxfordshire, England.
Christening: St Thomas, Oxford, Oxfordshire, England, United Kingdom

v. **Arthur Morgan**,[137] born May 1843, in St Thomas, Oxford, Oxfordshire, England, christened 14 May 1843, in St Thomas, Oxford, Oxfordshire, England.

vi. **Alfred Morgan**, born 1844, in England, died 5 Feb 1915, in Oxford, Oxfordshire, England.

vii. **Fredrick Morgan**,[138] born Sep 1845, in St Thomas, Oxford, Oxfordshire, England, christened 14 Sep 1845, in St Thomas, Oxford, Oxfordshire, England, died 11 May 1894, in Oxfordshire, England.

viii. **John Morgan**,[139] born 4 Apr 1848, in Oxford, Oxfordshire, England, christened 9 Apr 1848, in St Thomas, Oxford, Oxfordshire, England, died 16 Aug 1857, in St Thomas, Oxford, Oxfordshire, England.

ix. **Sarah Morgan**,[44,45,46,47,48,49,50,51,52] born Apr 1850, in St Thomas, Oxford, Oxfordshire, England, died 27 Jul 1917, in St Thomas, Oxford, Oxfordshire, England.[71]

x. **George Thomas Morgan**, born 26 Dec 1852, in Oxfordshire, England, christened 26 Dec 1852, in Oxfordshire, England, died 29 Sep 1854, in Oxfordshire, England. Christening: St Thomas, Oxford, Oxfordshire, England, United Kingdom

xi. **Joseph Morgan**,[140] born Mar 1855, in St Thomas, Oxford, Oxfordshire, England, christened 11 Mar 1855, in St Thomas, Oxford, Oxfordshire, England, died Sep 1932, in Oxford, Oxfordshire, England, buried Sep 1932, in Oxford, Oxfordshire, England.

Children of Charles Morgan and Mary Foster:

i. **William Morgan**, born 1828, in Oxfordshire, England, died 1914, in Maidenhead, Berkshire, England.
1861 census William Morgan - groom and gardener

19. Martha Foster was born 1813, in Stanton Harcourt, Oxfordshire, England, died Mar 1881, in Oxford, Oxfordshire, England, buried 20 Mar 1881, in Oxford, Oxfordshire, England. She was the daughter of John Foster and Ann King. She married Charles Morgan[44,141] 7 Sep 1834, in St Thomas, Oxford, Oxfordshire, England. He was the son of John Morgan and Sarah Hartlett.
Notes for Martha Foster:

1841 England Census Name: Martha Morgan Age: 25 Estimated Birth Year: abt 1816 Gender: Female Where born: Oxfordshire, England Civil Parish: St Thomas Hundred: Oxford County/Island: Oxfordshire Country: England Household Members: Name Age Charles Morgan 35 Charles Morgan 2 George Morgan 6 Mo Henry Morgan 6 Martha Morgan 25 William Morgan 13 Hannah (sister of Martha) was a witness at Martha's wedding (Banns) to Charles Morgan 7 Sep 1834 St Thomas Oxford Martha was born at Stanton Harcourt but no record of her baptism has been found as yet.

20. Michael Newell was born 5 Jun 1811, in Beckley, Oxfordshire, England, christened 5 Jun 1811, in Beckley, Oxfordshire, England, died Aug 1878, in Headington, Oxfordshire, England, buried 6 Aug 1878, in Headington, Oxfordshire, England. He was the son of Richard Newell and Elizabeth Jones. He married Eliza Hinton 12 Feb 1844, in Stanton St John, Oxfordshire, England. She was the daughter of John Hinton and Ann Clarke.
Notes for Michael Newell:

1841 census - worked as a Smith living with his future in-laws and wife. Declared he was 25 years old - infact he was 30. 1851 census - Not shown on with his family - but shown with Richard (father)

Children of Michael Newell and Eliza Hinton:

    i.   **Eliseus Clark Newell**,[54,87,88,89,90] born 10 May 1844, in Stanton St John, Oxfordshire, England, died 14 Apr 1899, in Headington, Oxfordshire, England.

    ii.   **William Newell**, born Dec 1846, in Stanton St John, Oxfordshire, England, christened 25 Dec 1846, in Stanton St John, Oxfordshire, England, died Dec 1920, in Stanton St John, Oxfordshire, England, buried 16 Dec 1920, in Stanton St John, Oxfordshire, England.
Never married

21. Eliza Hinton was born Aug 1820, in Stanton St John, Oxfordshire, England, christened 6 Aug 1820, in Stanton St John, Oxfordshire, England, died Jan 1907, in Stanton St John, Oxfordshire, England, buried 31 Jan 1907, in Stanton St John, Oxfordshire, England. She was the daughter of John Hinton and Ann Clarke. She married Michael Newell 12 Feb 1844, in Stanton St John, Oxfordshire, England. He was the son of Richard Newell and Elizabeth Jones.
Notes for Eliza Hinton:

Marriages from quarter Jan-Feb-Mar 1844 Name:Eliza Hinton District:Oxford Ref:Volume 16 Page 122; Hinton, Eliza Shown living in Headington 1841 census On the 1891 cencus Eliza was living at Stanton st john William hinton head 64 elizabeth hinton wife 58 eliza newell 70 william newell 44 1871 census - Husband (Michael is in the Headington Workhouse - Eliza is living with sons at 44 Village Street, Stanton St John She is shown as a Nurse. 1851 Census shown living at parents home with 2 children

22. Stephen Rowland was born 17 Apr 1842, in Hanham, Gloucestershire, England, christened 17 Jul 1842, in Bitton, Gloucestershire, England, died 19 Jun 1934, in Reigate, Surrey, England.[142] He was the son of George Rowland and Ann Rogers. He married (1) Mary Ann Elleston[144] 3 Oct 1867, in Greenwich, Kent, England.[143] She was the daughter of George Elleston and Mary Langley. He married (2) Mary Ann Garland 1893, in Islington, London, England.
Notes for Stephen Rowland:

1911 Census Occupation Police Pensioner Widower living at 1 Quarry Crescent Hastings Sussex 1901 Census Occupation Retired Police Inspector living at 44 Alfred Road Hastings Sussex 1891 Census Occupation Police Inspector Met Police living at 64 Harwood Road Fulham05/01/1890 Occupation Police Inspector living at 64 Harwood Road per baptism of daughter Nellie Rowland 14/12/1881 Occupation Police Inspector living at 33 Spey Street per baptism of daughters Mary Ann

Children of Stephen Rowland and Mary Ann Elleston:

    i.   **Walter Henry Rowland**,[144,145] born 8 Nov 1870, in East Dulwich, Surrey, England, christened 24 Sep 1871, in East Dulwich, Surrey, England, died Apr 1942, in Uxbridge, London, England.
1871 address: East Dulwich, London 1881 address: Bromley St Leonard, London

1891 address: 59 Ponsonby Place, Westminster, London 1901 address: 56 Rosebury Road, Fulham, London 1911 address: 6 Dalebury Road, Fulham, London 1911 Census Occupation Police Constable living at 6 Dalebury Road Fulham states married 20 years 5 children all living 1908 Occupation Police Constable living at 105 Edith Grove Chelsea per Ediths birth certifcate, 1901 Census Occupation Police Constable living at 56 Rosebury Road Fulham 1891 Census Occupation Cellerman living at 59 Posonby Place Fulham Born 08/11/1870 joined Met Police on 09/05/1892 Warrant No 77658. Last Employer Mr S Raven Windsor Castle Victoria (found on internet Publican Mr Samuel Raven Windsor Castle Tavern 333 Vauxhall Bridge Road Post Office Directory 1891). Was living at 3 Rochester Street Rochester Row Married no children. Started at J Division Bethnal Green 09/05/1892 transfered to B Division Westminster 20/09/1899. 5 foot 8 inches tall 10st 4Lb Light brown hair Blue eyes fair complexion. Resigned 21/10/1918 C82487 medically incapable Police Sergeant. From Old Bailey records Third court Wednesday 11th January 1893 CHARLES SMITH, Violent Theft

ii. **Alice Rowland**,[144] born 12 Aug 1872, in West Ham, Essex, England, christened 12 Mar 1876, in Bethnal Green, London, England.

iii. **Harry Rowland**,[144] born Jan 1877, in Poplar, London, England, died Jan 1898, in Chelsea, London, England.

iv. **George Stephen Rowland**,[6,94,95,97,98,99] born Jan 1879, in Poplar, London, England, died Jan 1929, in Hendon, Middlesex, England.

v. **Elizabeth Rowland**, born Sep 1880, in Bromley, Kent, England, christened 2 Oct 1880, in Bromley, Kent, England.
Not found on any census with Stephen Rowland possible death Oct - Dec 1880 Poplar 1c 399

vi. **Mary Ann Rowland**,[144,146] born 1881, in Poplar, London, England, christened 14 Dec 1881, in Bromley, Kent, England.
1901 Census Occupation Shop Assistant Confectionery living at 44 Alfred Road Hastings Sussex If Mary Ann Rowland did not marry then her birth is Apr - Jun 1881 Barton Regis 6a 156 and a matching death Apr - Jun 1981 Bristol 22 0312 gives date of birth as 18 May 1881 1911 census has a Mary Ann Rowland aged 29 living in Bristol with widowed mother Ellen Rowland. Mary born St Philips Bristol so the birth and death of the above Mary is probably not right Birth Jul - Sep 1880 Poplar 1c 656 Mary Ann Rowland may have been baptised twice see other Mary Ann once in 1880 and again in 1881 there is only 1 birth that fits and no deaths of a Mary Ann Rowland between 1880 and 1881. 1901 Census Occupation Shop Assistant Confectionery living at 44 Alfred Road Hastings Sussex No Mary Rowland on 1911 census living in Sussex

vii. **Ada Rowland**,[146] born 1881, in Poplar, London, England, christened 14 Dec 1881, in Bromley, Kent, England.
Birth Jan - Mar 1882 Poplar 1c 664 1901 Census Occupation Financial Clerk living at 44 Alfred Road Hastings Sussex 1911 Census Occupation Clerk Advertising Jewellers living at 1 Quarry Crescent Hastings Sussex Possible death 1923 aged 41

Brentford Middlesex 3a 211 registered as Ada I Rowland Death is wrong Ada is the informant on Stephen's death in 1934 Possible death Jan - Mar 1961 Wandsworth aged 79 5d 1041

viii.   **Nellie Rowland**,[146] born Jan 1884, in Pimlico, London, England, christened 5 Jan 1890, in Fulham, Middlesex, England.
1901 Census No occupation living at 44 Alfred Road Hastings Sussex 1911 Census Occupation Fathers Housekeeper living at 1 Quarry Crescent Hastings Sussex Only death for a Nellie M Benzie is 1959 Hove Sussex aged 65 makes birth year 1894 10 years out

23. Mary Ann Elleston was born 7 Mar 1843, in Greenwich, Kent, England, christened 5 Apr 1843, in Greenwich, Kent, England, died Oct 1891, in Fulham, Middlesex, England.[147] She was the daughter of George Elleston and Mary Langley. She married Stephen Rowland[144,148,149] 3 Oct 1867, in Greenwich, Kent, England.[143] He was the son of George Rowland and Ann Rogers.
Notes for Mary Ann Elleston:

Birth Jan - Mar 1843 Greenwich 5 216 (Birth recorded as Mary Ann Elliston) Birth year from death Death Oct-Dec 1891 Fulham aged 48 1a 226

24. Thomas Humber was born 4 Nov 1851, in Leigh, Dorset, England, christened 7 Dec 1851, in Yetminster, Dorset, England,[150] died about 1885, in Poplar, London, England, United Kingdom. He was the son of John Churchill Humber and Julia E. Hunt. He married Fanny Humphreys[152,153,154,155,156] 23 Dec 1877, in Millwall, London, England.[151] She was the daughter of James Humphreys and Sarah Chester.
Notes for Thomas Humber:

Birth Record: Original data: Dorset Parish Registers. Dorchester, England. Births and Baptisms, 1813-1906 Name: Thomas Humber Baptism Date: 7 Dec 1851 Parish: Leigh Father's name: John Humber Mother's name: Julia Humber address - 409 West Ferry Rd, Millwall, Middlesex Extract from Marriage record: Name: Fanny Humphreys Spouse Name: Thomas Humber Spouse Age: Full Age Record Type: Marriage Event Date: 23 Dec 1877 Parish: St Luke, Millwall County: Middlesex Borough: Tower Hamlets Father Name: James Humphreys Spouse Father Name: John Humber 1899 - shown as deceased carpenter journyman on Augusta's marriage certificate to George Stephen Rowland

Children of Thomas Humber and Fanny Humphreys:

i.   **John Humphries Humber**,[157] born 1879, in Poplar, London, England, christened 6 Apr 1879, in Poplar, London, England.[158]
ii. **Augusta Mary Humber**,[6,91,92,93,94,95] born 1 Aug 1881, in Poplar, London, England, died Apr 1952, in Surrey, England.[92]
iii. **Frances Hilda Humber**,[159] born 2 Jun 1884, in Poplar, London, England, christened 29 Jun 1884, in Poplar, London, England.
born after father died

Children by subsequent marriage of Fanny Humphreys to James Tennant:

     i.   **James Tennant**,[160] born 1890, in Chelsea, London, England. Residence: 31 Mar 1901, Chelsea, London, Middlesex, England.

25. Fanny Humphreys was born 5 Feb 1853, in Northamptonshire, England, christened 22 Feb 1854, in Marston St Lawrence, Northamptonshire, England, died 1930, in Saint Pancras, London, England. She was the daughter of James Humphreys and Sarah Chester. Residence: 31 Mar 1901, Chelsea, London, Middlesex, England. She married (1) Thomas Humber[161,162,163,164] 23 Dec 1877, in Millwall, London, England.[151] He was the son of John Churchill Humber and Julia E. Hunt. She married (2) James Tennant[160] Jan 1890, in Chelsea, London, England.
Notes for Fanny Humphreys:

Extract from Marriage record: Name: Fanny Humphreys Spouse Name: Thomas Humber Spouse Age: Full Age Record Type: Marriage Event Date: 23 Dec 1877 Parish: St Luke, Millwall County: Middlesex Borough: Tower Hamlets Father Name: James Humphreys Spouse Father Name: John Humber Following death of Thomas Humber she re-married with the name of Frances Humber a James Tennant of Chelsea in 1890.

26. Thomas Lucas was born 1816, in Barking, Essex, England, died 1870, in Romford, Essex, England, buried 1 Jun 1870, in Barkingside, Essex, England. He was the son of Thomas Lucas and Sarah Young. He married Mary Ann Stringer[165,166,167,168,169] 5 May 1844, in Barkingside, Essex, England. She was the daughter of James Stringer and Mary Elizabeth Hyde.
Notes for Thomas Lucas:

Thomas

Children of Thomas Lucas and Mary Ann Stringer:

     i.   **George Lucas**, born 1845, in Barking, Essex, England, christened 15 Jan 1918, in Barkingside, Essex, England. Occupation: General Labourer, 1881; Agricultural Labourer, 1891; General Labourer, 1901; Labourer, 1911. Census: 1871, Chigwell, Essex, England; 1881, 6, Hainault Road, Chigwell, Essex, England; 1891, Chigwell, Essex, England; 1891, High Road, Chigwell, Chingford, Essex, England; 1901, Manor Cottages, Chigwell Village, Essex, England; 1911, Chigwell, Essex, England. He married Ellen Dawkins Dec 1868, in Stepney, Middlesex, England. Ellen Dawkins was born 1845, in Guildford, Surrey, England. Census: 1851, King William, Chigwell Horse Lane, Essex, England; 1861, Chigwell, Essex, England; 1871, Hainault Road, Chigwell, Essex, England; 1881, 6, Hainault Road, Chigwell, Essex, England; 1891, High Road, Chigwell, Chingford, Essex, England; 1901, Manor Cottages, Chigwell Village, Essex, England; 1911, Savills Cottages, Chigwell, Essex, England.

    ii.   **Henry Lucas**, born 20 Aug 1847, in Barking, Essex, England, christened 5 Sep

1847, in Barkingside, Essex, England, died before 1940, in England.

   iii.   **Mary Ann Lucas**, born 15 Nov 1849, in Barkingside, Essex, England, christened 6 Jan 1850, in Barkingside, Essex, England.

   iv.   **Sarah Lucas**, born 1852, in Barking, Essex, England, christened 1 Aug 1852, in Barking, Essex, England.

   v.   **Thomas Lucas**, born 28 Feb 1855, in Barkingside, Essex, England, christened 3 Jun 1855, in Barkingside, Essex, England, died before 1940, in England. Residence: 1881, West Ham, Essex, England.

   vi.   **Charles Lucas**,[102,103,104,116,117,118] born 11 Jun 1857, in Barking, Essex, England, died Mar 1920, in Whitechapel, London, England.

   vii.   **Elizabeth Lucas**, born 31 Oct 1859, in Barkingside, Essex, England, christened 1 Jan 1860, in Barkingside, Essex, England.

   viii.   **Emily Lucas**, born 1862, in Barking, Essex, England, christened 7 Dec 1862, in Barking, Essex, England.

   ix.   **Eliza Lucas**, born 1 Jan 1865, in Barkingside, Essex, England, christened 5 Mar 1865, in Barkingside, Essex, England.

27. Mary Ann Stringer was born 13 Feb 1826, in Barking, Essex, England, christened 3 Mar 1826, in Barking, Essex, England, died 26 Dec 1901, in West Ham, Essex, England. She was the daughter of James Stringer and Mary Elizabeth Hyde. She married Thomas Lucas[170,171] 5 May 1844, in Barkingside, Essex, England. He was the son of Thomas Lucas and Sarah Young.
Notes for Mary Ann Stringer:

Sarah and Mary married two of the Lucas brothers 1861 census living with family in 1841 census shown to be living at Willis Cottages and her Family next door at Yardleys Cottages - both in Chequers Lane. 1871 census - Mary now widowed and living next door to her younger brother, Henry - 31

28. George Giles was born 15 Dec 1833, in Cork, Ireland, died 16 Aug 1911, in West Ham, Essex, England. He was the son of Thomas Giles and Hannah Maria Baldwin. Residence: 1871, St Ann Limehouse, London, Middlesex, England. He married (1) Ann Wine[173,174,175,176] 14 Jan 1856, in Bethnal Green, London, England.[172] She was the daughter of James Vanner Wine and Mary Ann Rapp. He married (2) Harriet Cousins 1883, in Mile End, London, England.
Notes for George Giles:

1881 Census give occupation as lighterman living at 17 St Ann's Street, Limehouse, Stephney, London 1861 Census, 1871 Census Geo Giles b. abt 1833 Ireland Living in 29 St Anne Street, Limehouse, London 1901 Census GILES, George WEST HAM, Essex RG13 piece 1584 folio 52 page 41 His mother Hannah Giles was a witness at his marriage to Ann Wine in St Philip's Church, Bethnal Green, Midx Thomas Giles was born before parents were married Deaths 16 Aug 1911 at 43 Trinity Street, West Ham Name:George Giles District:West Ham Ref:Volume 4A Page 165 aka: George Baldwin Giles

Children of George Giles and Ann Wine:

    i.   **Thomas Giles**, born 3 Jan 1854, in Poplar, London, England, christened 19 Mar 1854, in Stepney, Middlesex, England, died 1888, in Poplar, London, England. Residence: 1871, St Ann Limehouse, London, Middlesex, England.

    ii.   **Hannah Giles**,[177] born 26 Jan 1856, in Limehouse, Middlesex, England, christened 24 Feb 1856, in Limehouse, Middlesex, England, died Feb 1858, in Limehouse, Middlesex, England.
Parish Records Collection - baptism Day: 24 Month: 2 Year: 1856 Forename: Hannah Othernames: Surname: Giles Fathers forenames: George Fathers occupation: Labourer Mothers forenames: Ann Birth date: 26 January 1856 Address: Merchants Row Location of church: Limehouse Parish: St Anne Church address: Commercial Road Entry No: 651 Source Ref: X069/002

    iii.   **Hannah Giles**, born 30 Sep 1858, in Stepney, Middlesex, England, christened 31 Oct 1858, in Limehouse, Middlesex, England, died Dec 1943, in Croydon, Surrey, England. Residence: 1871, St Ann Limehouse, London, Middlesex, England.
Parish Records Collection - baptism Day: 31 Month: 10 Year: 1858 Forename: Hannah Othernames: Surname: Giles Fathers forenames: George Fathers occupation: Labourer Mothers forenames: Ann Birth date: 30 September 1858 Address: St Anne St Location of church: Limehouse Parish: St Anne Church address: Commercial Road Entry No: 1976 Source Ref: X069/002

    iv.   **Mary Ann Giles**,[100,101,102,103,104,105,106,107] born 5 Aug 1860, in Limehouse, Middlesex, England, died Dec 1943, in Croydon, Surrey, England.

    v.   **George Giles**, born 13 Oct 1862, in Stepney, Middlesex, England, christened 2 Nov 1862, in Limehouse, Middlesex, England, died 1911, in England. Residence: 1871, St Ann Limehouse, London, Middlesex, England.

    vi.   **Sarah Ann Giles**, born 27 Dec 1864, in Stepney, Middlesex, England, christened 22 Jan 1865, in Stepney, Middlesex, England. Residence: 1871, St Ann Limehouse, London, Middlesex, England.

    vii.   **Frances Giles**, born 20 May 1867, in Stepney, Middlesex, England, christened 9 Jun 1867, in Limehouse, Middlesex, England. Residence: 1871, St Ann Limehouse, London, Middlesex, England.

    viii.   **Maria Giles**, born 9 Jun 1869, in Limehouse, Middlesex, England, christened 20 Jun 1869, in Limehouse, Middlesex, England, died 1870, in England.

    ix.   **James Giles**, born 10 Oct 1870, in Limehouse, Middlesex, England, christened 30 Oct 1870, in Limehouse, Middlesex, England, died 1935, in England. Residence: 1871, St Ann Limehouse, London, Middlesex, England.
appears in the 1901 census as a lodger at his sister MARY's home Prisoner of war in Germany 1915 Second marriage to Mrs R. Sharp. First marriage to Alice Emma Goddard.

    x.   **Nancy Giles**, born 10 Dec 1874, in Stepney, Middlesex, England, christened 10 Jan 1875, in Limehouse, Middlesex, England, died 1877, in Stepney, Middlesex, England.

xi.   **Ellen Giles**, born 4 Aug 1878, in Stepney, Middlesex, England, died 21 Jan 1943, in Southampton, Hampshire, England.

xii. **Elizabeth Giles**, born Oct 1880, in Limehouse, Middlesex, England, christened 7 Oct 1880, in Limehouse, Middlesex, England.
Limehouse, Stepney, London, England, United Kingdom

29. Ann Wine was born 14 Jul 1834, in Limehouse, Middlesex, England, died Apr 1882, in England. She was the daughter of James Vanner Wine and Mary Ann Rapp. Residence: 1871, St Ann Limehouse, London, Middlesex, England. She married George Giles[175,178,179,180] 14 Jan 1856, in Bethnal Green, London, England.[172] He was the son of Thomas Giles and Hannah Maria Baldwin.
Notes for Ann Wine:

1871 Census St Ann St, St Ann Limehouse Stepney RG10 piece 552 folio 23 page 40 1881 Census GILES, Ann STEPNEY, London, Middlesex RG11 piece 468 folio 120 page 29 1861 Census Wife shown as NANCY and not Ann St. Dunstan, Stepney Deaths from quarter Apr-May-Jun 1882 Name:Ann Giles District:Stepney Ref:Volume 1C Page 296 1881 census Name: Ann Giles Age: 48 Estimated Birth Year: abt 1833 Relationship to Head: Wife Spouse: George Giles Gender: Female Where born: Limehouse, Middlesex, England Civil Parish: Limehouse County/Island: London Country: England Street address: 17 St Anns Street Marital Status: Married Registration district: Stepney ED, institution, or vessel: 20 Piece: 468 Folio: 120 Page Number: 29 Household Members: Name Age George Giles 48 Ann Giles 48 George Giles 18 Sarah Giles 15 Francis Giles 14 James Giles 11 Ellen Giles 3 Elisabeth Giles 6

Generation No. 6

30. William Aldsworth was born Sep 1781, in Stanton Harcourt, Oxfordshire, England, christened 30 Sep 1781, in Stanton Harcourt, Oxfordshire, England, died Feb 1862, in Northmoor, Oxfordshire, England, buried 25 Feb 1862, in Northmoor, Oxfordshire, England. He was the son of William Aldsworth and Hannah Townsend. He married Jane Turner[183] 1 Apr 1805, in Stanton Harcourt, Oxfordshire, England.[181,182] She was the daughter of Giles Turner and Mary Timms.
Notes for William Aldsworth:

1851 census - living with his wife at James Trinder's house as lodgers (PAUPER)

Children of William Aldsworth and Jane Turner:

    i.   **Mary Ann Allsworth**, born 22 Oct 1806, in Stanton Harcourt, Oxfordshire, England, christened 26 Oct 1806, in Stanton Harcourt, Oxfordshire, England, died Sep 1892, in Stanton Harcourt, Oxfordshire, England. She married Isaac Wake 14 Nov 1825, in Stanton Harcourt, Oxfordshire, England. Isaac Wake was born 13 Jul 1806, in Northmoor, Oxfordshire, England, christened 20 Jul 1806, in Northmoor, Oxfordshire, England, died Sep 1869, in Witney, Oxfordshire, England, buried Sep 1869, in Witney, Oxfordshire, England.
Note - spelling on parish records as ALLDSWORTH 1881 census Dwelling: 95 Leighton Rd Census Place: St Pancras, London, Middlesex, England Source: FHL Film 1341049 PRO Ref RG11 Piece 0223 Folio 55 Page 21 Marr Age Sex Birthplace George GOOD M 37 M Cholsey, Berkshire, England Rel: Head Occ: Cheesemonger Journeyman Elizabeth GOOD M 35 F Longboro, Gloucester, England Rel: Wife Florence GOOD 3 F St Pancras, Middlesex, England Rel: Daur Mary Ann ALSWORTH U 75 F Oxford City, Oxford, England Rel: Lodger Occ: Annuitant 1881 census 1881 census Dwelling: 95 Leighton Rd Census Place: St Pancras, London, Middlesex, England Source: FHL Film 1341049 PRO Ref RG11 Piece 0223 Folio 55 Page 21 Marr Age Sex Birthplace George GOOD M 37 M Cholsey, Berkshire, England Rel: Head Occ: Cheesemonger Journeyman Elizabeth GOOD M 35 F Longboro, Gloucester, England Rel: Wife Florence GOOD 3 F St Pancras, Middlesex, England Rel: Daur Mary Ann ALSWORTH U 75 F Oxford City, Oxford, England Rel: Lodger Occ: Annuitant 1881 census

    ii.   **Elizabeth Allsworth**,[184,185] born 11 Jan 1808, in Stanton Harcourt, Oxfordshire, England, christened 17 Jan 1808, in Stanton Harcourt, Oxfordshire, England, died Aug 1838, in Stanton Harcourt, Oxfordshire, England, buried 1 Sep 1838, in Stanton Harcourt, Oxfordshire, England. She married James Robbins[184] 17 Nov 1834, in England. James Robbins was born May 1805, in Standlake, Oxfordshire, England, christened 12 May 1805, in Standlake, Oxfordshire, England, died Dec 1863, in Stanton Harcourt, Oxfordshire, England, buried 24 Dec 1863, in Stanton

Harcourt, Oxfordshire, England.

Note spelling on parish records as ALLDSWORTH

iii.   **Hannah Allsworth**, born 1 Dec 1809, in Stanton Harcourt, Oxfordshire, England, christened 3 Dec 1809, in Stanton Harcourt, Oxfordshire, England.

Note spelling on parish records - First individual with current spelling of family name

iv.   **William Allsworth**,[186,187] born 16 Sep 1811, in Stanton Harcourt, Oxfordshire, England, christened 29 Sep 1811, in Stanton Harcourt, Oxfordshire, England. He married Hannah Turner[189] 23 May 1836, in Ascott Under Wychwood, Oxfordshire, England.[188] Hannah Turner was born 1817, in Ascott Under Wychwood, Oxfordshire, England, christened 8 Dec 1817, in Ascott Under Wychwood, Oxfordshire, England, died 14 Feb 1877, in Cumnor, Berkshire, England, buried 14 Feb 1877, in Cumnor, Berkshire, England.

name spelled Alsworth on parish records for christening

Notes for Hannah Turner: Hannah TURNER and William ALLSWORTH are 1st cousins. Their common ancestors are Giles TURNER and Mrs TURNER.

HUSBAND William Allsworth b.1811 Jane Turner b.1783 Giles Turner b.1755

WIFE Hannah Turner b.1817 Thomas Turner b.1783 Giles Turner b.1755

v.   **Martha Allsworth**, born Jan 1813, in Stanton Harcourt, Oxfordshire, England, christened 10 Jan 1813, in Stanton Harcourt, Oxfordshire, England, died 1817, in Stanton Harcourt, Oxfordshire, England, buried in Stanton Harcourt, Oxfordshire, England.

Note spelling on parish records ALDSWORTH

vi.   **Ann Allsworth**, born Mar 1815, in Stanton Harcourt, Oxfordshire, England, christened 19 Mar 1815, in Stanton Harcourt, Oxfordshire, England, died Sep 1819, in Stanton Harcourt, Oxfordshire, England, buried 8 Sep 1819, in Stanton Harcourt, Oxfordshire, England.

Note spelling on parish records - ALDSWORTH

vii.   **Robert Allsworth**,[190] born 5 Jul 1818, in Stanton Harcourt, Oxfordshire, England, christened 26 Jul 1818, in Stanton Harcourt, Oxfordshire, England, died 25 May 1897, in Witney, Oxfordshire, England, buried 28 May 1897, in Stanton Harcourt, Oxfordshire, England. He married (1) Martha Alder 6 Mar 1873, in Stanton Harcourt, Oxfordshire, England. Martha Alder was born Jun 1827, in Stanton Harcourt, Oxfordshire, England, christened 24 Jun 1827, in Stanton Harcourt, Oxfordshire, England, died 1886, in Stanton Harcourt, Oxfordshire, England. He married (2) Jane Batts 5 Jul 1842, in Stanton Harcourt, Oxfordshire, England. Jane Batts was born 1825, in Stanton Harcourt, Oxfordshire, England, christened 3 Dec 1825, in Stanton Harcourt, Oxfordshire, England, died Jun 1861, in Stanton Harcourt, Oxfordshire, England, buried 30 Jun 1861, in Stanton Harcourt, Oxfordshire, England.

Note spelling on parish records - ALSWORTH Surname spelled - ALSWORTH on the 1851 census Surname spelled - ALLSWORTH on the 1861 census Name: Robert Allsworth Age in years: 42 Gender: Male Birth place: Stanton Harcourt

Relationship to head-of-household: Head Record type: Household Collection: 1861
England and Wales Census Surname spelled - ALSWORTH on the 1851 census
Surname spelled - ALSWORTH on the 1851 census Surname spelled -
ALSWORTH on the 1851 census Surname spelled - ALSWORTH on the 1851
census Surname spelled - ALSWORTH on the 1851 census
Notes for Martha Alder: 1871 aged 42 Ag.Lab.unmarried with widowed father.

viii. **Thomas Allsworth,**[124,125,126,127,128] born 17 Jan 1822, in Stanton Harcourt, Oxfordshire,
England, died Oct 1906, in Oxford, Oxfordshire, England.

ix.   **Eliza Allsworth**, born 21 Jan 1824, in Stanton Harcourt, Oxfordshire, England,
christened 29 Feb 1824, in Stanton Harcourt, Oxfordshire, England, died Nov 1856,
in Northmoor, Oxfordshire, England, buried 16 Nov 1856, in Northmoor,
Oxfordshire, England.
Note spelling on parish records - ALDSWORTH This entry was created from the
following transcription: Surname Given Name Age District Volume Page
Transcriber Deaths Dec 1856 Allsworth Eliza Witney 3a 341 This entry was
created from the following transcription: Surname Given Name Age District
Volume Page Transcriber Deaths Dec 1856 Allsworth Eliza Witney 3a 341

x.   **Charlotte Aldsworth**, born 1 Nov 1829, in Stanton Harcourt, Oxfordshire,
England, christened 27 Dec 1829, in Stanton Harcourt, Oxfordshire, England, died
before 1920, in England. She married George Newman 1876, in Woodstock,
Oxfordshire, England. George Newman was born about 1830, in England, died
after 1876, in England.
Note spelling on parish records - ALDSWORTH - Illegit b 1 nov

31. Jane Turner was born 22 May 1783, in Ascott Under Wychwood, Oxfordshire, England, christened
22 May 1783, in Ascott Under Wychwood, Oxfordshire, England, died Apr 1862, in Northmoor,
Oxfordshire, England, buried 5 Apr 1862, in Northmoor, Oxfordshire, England. She was the daughter of
Giles Turner and Mary Timms. She married William Aldsworth[191,192] 1 Apr 1805, in Stanton Harcourt,
Oxfordshire, England.[181,182] He was the son of William Aldsworth and Hannah Townsend.

32. William Drinkwater was born Oct 1784, in Little Coxwell, Berkshire, England, christened 24 Oct
1784, in Faringdon, Berkshire, England, died 1868, in Witney, Oxfordshire, England. He was the son of
John Drinkwater and Lucy Hawkins. He married Hannah Haydon 30 Oct 1804, in Hinton Waldrist,
Berkshire, England. She was the daughter of William Haydon and Elizabeth "Betty" Hawkins.
Notes for William Drinkwater:

residence: Appleton, Berkshire, England parents: William Drinkwater, Jane record title: England Births
and Christenings, 1538-1975 name: William Drinkwater gender: Male baptism/christening date: 15 Apr
1770 baptism/christening place: Appleton, Berkshire, England father's name: William Drinkwater
mother's name: Jane indexing project (batch) number: C02175-2 system origin: England. source film
number: 1279444 1851 census Name: William Drinkwater Age: 68 Estimated birth year: abt 1783
Relation: Head Spouse's name: Hannah Gender: Male Where born: Little Coxwell, Berkshire, England
Civil parish: Brize Norton County/Island: Oxfordshire Country: England

Children of William Drinkwater and Hannah Haydon:

i. **Cornelius Drinkwater**, born 1805, in Brize Norton, Oxfordshire, England, christened 29 Dec 1805, in Brize Norton, Oxfordshire, England, died Oct 1889, in Brize Norton, Oxfordshire, England, buried 28 Oct 1889, in Brize Norton, Oxfordshire, England. He married (1) Hesther Harley 20 Nov 1831, in Swinbrook, Oxfordshire, England. Hesther Harley was born about 1807, in Oxfordshire, England, christened 5 Apr 1807, in Swinbrook, Oxfordshire, England, died Apr 1851, in Brize Norton, Oxfordshire, England, buried 8 Apr 1851, in Brize Norton, Oxfordshire, England. He married (2) Harriet Price 31 Jul 1869, in Brize Norton, Oxfordshire, England. Harriet Price was born 1809, in Brize Norton, Oxfordshire, England.
Burial found in Brize Norton Parish records - Oct 28, 1889. aged 85 Brize Norton, Oxfordshire, England parish records show he married Harriet Price (2nd wife)
Notes for Hesther Harley: Swinbrook parish records 5 April 1807 Christening Hesther d. of Charles and Ann Burial records for Brize Norton, Oxfordshire show burial 8 Apr 1851 (First name given as Esther)
Notes for Cornelius Drinkwater and Hesther Harley: Swinbrook parish records shows married with consent of parents
Notes for Harriet Price: married 31 jul 1869 Brize Norton, Oxfordshire, England

ii. **John Drinkwater**, born 1807, in Brize Norton, Oxfordshire, England, christened 27 Dec 1807, in Brize Norton, Oxfordshire, England, died 1880, in England.

iii. **James Drinkwater**,[193] born Dec 1809, in Brize Norton, Oxfordshire, England, christened 17 Dec 1809, in Brize Norton, Oxfordshire, England, died 1881, in Witney, Oxfordshire, England, buried 1881, in Witney, Oxfordshire, England. He married Maria Hodkins 21 Feb 1831, in Brize Norton, Oxfordshire, England. Maria Hodkins was born before 1810, in England.
placed into Witney Union Workhouse

iv. **Sophia Drinkwater**, born 1811, in Brize Norton, Oxfordshire, England, christened 8 Dec 1811, in Brize Norton, Oxfordshire, England. She married George Cook 1831, in Brize Norton, Oxfordshire, England. George Cook was born before 1810, in England.

v. **William Drinkwater**,[194] born 1813, in Brize Norton, Oxfordshire, England, christened 26 Sep 1813, in Brize Norton, Oxfordshire, England. He married Rosanna Hayden[194] 23 Nov 1834, in West Hanney, Berkshire, England. Rosanna Hayden was born 1814, in Lyford, Berkshire, England, died 26 Jul 1883, in Oxfordshire, England.

vi. **Elizabeth Drinkwater**, born Jun 1815, in Curbridge, Oxfordshire, England, christened 25 Jun 1815, in Brize Norton, Oxfordshire, England, died 1900, in Oxfordshire, England. She married John Cox about 1838, in Curbridge, Oxfordshire, England. John Cox was born about 1815, in Curbridge, Oxfordshire, England.

vii. **Thomas Drinkwater**, born 1817, in Brize Norton, Oxfordshire, England, christened 20 Apr 1817, in Brize Norton, Oxfordshire, England.

    viii.   **Ellen Drinkwater**,[119,120] born 25 Jun 1820, in Brize Norton, Oxfordshire, England, died 25 May 1899, in St Thomas, Oxford, Oxfordshire, England.

    ix.   **Diana Drinkwater**, born Aug 1822, in Brize Norton, Oxfordshire, England, christened 18 Aug 1822, in Brize Norton, Oxfordshire, England.

    x.   **David Drinkwater**, born 1826, in Brize Norton, Oxfordshire, England, christened 24 Sep 1826, in Brize Norton, Oxfordshire, England, died Apr 1905, in Witney, Oxfordshire, England.

33. Hannah Haydon was born Nov 1782, in Northmoor, Oxfordshire, England, christened 17 Nov 1782, in Northmoor, Oxfordshire, England, died 1860, in Witney, Oxfordshire, England. She was the daughter of William Haydon and Elizabeth "Betty" Hawkins. She married William Drinkwater[195,196] 30 Oct 1804, in Hinton Waldrist, Berkshire, England. He was the son of John Drinkwater and Lucy Hawkins.

Notes for Hannah Haydon:

1851 census Hannah Drinkwater William abt 1780 Moreton, Berkshire, England Wife Brize Norton Oxfordshire

34. John Morgan was born about 1776, in Yarnton, Oxfordshire, England, died 1846, in Oxfordshire, England, buried 1846, in Oxfordshire, England. He was the son of William Veasy Morgan and Mary Stone. He married Sarah Hartlett[198,199] 6 Feb 1797, in Cassington, Oxfordshire, England.[197] She was the daughter of John Hartlett and Mary Gilkes.

Notes for John Morgan:

Pallot's Marriage index MORGAN John 6-Feb-1797 HARTLETT [B. HARTLET] Sarah Oxfordshire Cassington Pallot marriage registry for Oxfordshire Groom's Name - MORGAN John County - Oxfordshire Parish - Cassington Date of Marriage 6-Feb-1797 Bride's Name - HARTLETT [B. HARTLET] Sarah parishrecords_indi.php id=252097 -morgan_country=Oxfordshire. 1841 census Class: HO107; Piece 877; Book: 11; Civil Parish: Sandford; County: Oxfordshire; Enumeration District: 1; Folio: ; Page: 17; Line: 6; GSU roll: 474573. Shown as working on Murral's farm with his son Charles

Children of John Morgan and Sarah Hartlett:

    i.   **Charles Morgan**,[44,141] born 1803, in Kidlington, Oxfordshire, England, died 30 Jun 1884, in Oxford, Oxfordshire, England.[129]

35. Sarah Hartlett was born Aug 1776, in Adderbury, Oxfordshire, England, christened 18 Aug 1776, in Adderbury, Oxfordshire, England, died before 1837, in Oxfordshire, England. She was the daughter of John Hartlett and Mary Gilkes. She married John Morgan[199,200] 6 Feb 1797, in Cassington, Oxfordshire, England.[197] He was the son of William Veasy Morgan and Mary Stone.

Notes for Sarah Hartlett:

Sarah were TWINS Pallot marriage registry for Oxfordshire Groom's Name - MORGAN John County - Oxfordshire Parish - Cassington Date of Marriage 6-Feb-1797 Bride's Name - HARTLETT [B. HARTLET] Sarah parishrecords_indi.php id=252097 -morgan_country=Oxfordshire.

36. John Foster was born 27 Dec 1790, in Stanton Harcourt, Oxfordshire, England, christened 2 Jan 1791, in Stanton Harcourt, Oxfordshire, England, died 18 May 1864, in Witney, Oxfordshire, England.[201] He was the son of John Foster and Mary Or Elizabeth Duffin. He married Ann King[203] 5 Nov 1810, in Stanton Harcourt, Oxfordshire, England.[202] She was the daughter of Daniel King and Sarah Probats.

Notes for John Foster:

Stanton Harcourt parish baptism register

Children of John Foster and Ann King:

i. **Thomas Foster**, born Jan 1811, in Stanton Harcourt, Oxfordshire, England, christened 13 Jan 1811, in Stanton Harcourt, Oxfordshire, England.
Stanton Harcourt parish reg.

ii. **Martha Foster**,[130] born 1813, in Stanton Harcourt, Oxfordshire, England, died Mar 1881, in Oxford, Oxfordshire, England.

iii. **Hannah Foster**,[204] born 10 Jul 1815, in Stanton Harcourt, Oxfordshire, England, christened 30 Jul 1815, in Stanton Harcourt, Oxfordshire, England, died Sep 1844, in Stanton Harcourt, Oxfordshire, England, buried 29 Sep 1844, in Stanton Harcourt, Oxfordshire, England. She married Joseph Belcher 31 Oct 1837, in Stanton Harcourt, Oxfordshire, England. Joseph Belcher was born 15 May 1803, in Stanton Harcourt, Oxfordshire, England, christened 15 May 1803, in Stanton Harcourt, Oxfordshire, England.
Hannah was a witness at Martha's wedding (Banns) to Charles Morgan 7 Sep 1834 St Thomas Oxford

iv. **William Foster**, born Dec 1817, in Stanton Harcourt, Oxfordshire, England, christened 25 Dec 1817, in Stanton Harcourt, Oxfordshire, England.
Stanton Harcourt parish reg.

v. **Esther Foster**, born Feb 1819, in Stanton Harcourt, Oxfordshire, England, christened 7 Feb 1819, in Stanton Harcourt, Oxfordshire, England.
Stanton Harcourt parish reg.

vi. **Eliza Foster**, born Aug 1820, in Stanton Harcourt, Oxfordshire, England, christened 27 Aug 1820, in Stanton Harcourt, Oxfordshire, England. She married Richard Robins 21 Jun 1840, in Stanton Harcourt, Oxfordshire, England. Richard Robins was born about 1818, in Stanton Harcourt, Oxfordshire, England. Married as a minor Stanton Harcourt parish reg.
Notes for Richard Robins: Stanton Harcourt parish marriage register

vii. **Mary Foster**, born Mar 1823, in Stanton Harcourt, Oxfordshire, England, christened 9 Mar 1823, in Stanton Harcourt, Oxfordshire, England.

Stanton Harcourt parish reg.

viii. **Robert Foster**, born Nov 1825, in Stanton Harcourt, Oxfordshire, England, christened 4 Dec 1825, in Stanton Harcourt, Oxfordshire, England. Stanton Harcourt parish reg.

ix. **Ann Foster**, born Dec 1829, in Stanton Harcourt, Oxfordshire, England, christened 20 Dec 1829, in Stanton Harcourt, Oxfordshire, England. Appears in 1841 census with mother

37. Ann King was born 1789, in Bletchingdon, Oxfordshire, England, died 1853, in Witney, Oxfordshire, England.[205] She was the daughter of Daniel King and Sarah Probats. She married John Foster[206,207,208] 5 Nov 1810, in Stanton Harcourt, Oxfordshire, England.[202] He was the son of John Foster and Mary Or Elizabeth Duffin.

38. Richard Newell was born 18 May 1782, in Cuxham, Oxfordshire, England, christened 18 May 1782, in Cuxham, Oxfordshire, England, died 29 Aug 1852, in Beckley, Oxfordshire, England. He was the son of William Newell and Ann Broadway. He married Elizabeth Jones[210,211] 2 Sep 1810, in Beckley, Oxfordshire, England.[209] She was the daughter of James Jones and Ann Giles.
Notes for Richard Newell:

1841Census shows him living in Headington, Oxford, England

Children of Richard Newell and Elizabeth Jones:

i. **Michael Newell**, born 5 Jun 1811, in Beckley, Oxfordshire, England, died Aug 1878, in Headington, Oxfordshire, England.

ii. **John Newell**, born 7 Mar 1813, in Beckley, Oxfordshire, England, christened 7 Mar 1813, in Beckley, Oxfordshire, England, died Oct 1869, in Beckley, Oxfordshire, England, buried 17 Oct 1869, in Beckley, Oxfordshire, England. He married (1) Jane Clay about 1839, in Oxfordshire, England. Jane Clay was born about 1820, in Oxfordshire, England. He married (2) Elizabeth Hedges 14 Nov 1854, in Marston, Oxfordshire, England. Elizabeth Hedges was born 1815, in Beckley, Oxfordshire, England, died Oct 1855, in Beckley, Oxfordshire, England, buried 4 Oct 1855, in Marston, Oxfordshire, England. He married (3) Louisa Whitehead 23 Oct 1852, in Beckley, Oxfordshire, England. Louisa Whitehead was born 31 Mar 1822, in Beckley, Oxfordshire, England, christened 31 Mar 1822, in Beckley, Oxfordshire, England, died 27 Aug 1902, in Beckley, Oxfordshire, England.
Whilst living in Marston, Oxfordshire, had an affair with Jane CLAY (spinster) baby girl (Hannah) born July 1839 and baptised at Elsfield 21 Jul 1839. Parish record:-

iii. **Samuel Newell**, born 1817, in Stanton St John, Oxfordshire, England, died Mar 1891, in Headington, Oxfordshire, England, buried 27 Mar 1891, in Stanton St John, Oxfordshire, England. He married Mary Allen[212] Jan 1840, in Oxford,

Oxfordshire, England. Mary Allen was born Sep 1816, in Great Milton, Oxfordshire, England, christened 15 Sep 1816, in Great Milton, Oxfordshire, England, died Oct 1893, in Headington, Oxfordshire, England, buried 10 Oct 1893, in Stanton St John, Oxfordshire, England.
1851 census - working as gardener to Rev Wilson at Waterperry Village

iv. **Elizabeth Ann Newell**, born 22 Jan 1832, in Beckley, Oxfordshire, England, christened 22 Jan 1832, in Beckley, Oxfordshire, England, died before 1911, in England. She married James Charlett 16 Oct 1853, in Beckley, Oxfordshire, England. James Charlett was born May 1832, in Beckley, Oxfordshire, England, christened 13 May 1832, in Beckley, Oxfordshire, England, died before 1911, in England.
1851 census - living at home
Notes for James Charlett: 1891 census - living in St Pancras, London Wife show as Ann - should be Elizabeth Ann. 1901 census - ditto - Address: 72 Mansfield Pl Railway porter name "CHARLOTT"

39. Elizabeth Jones was born Dec 1794, in Murcot, Oxfordshire, England, christened 25 Dec 1794, in Charlton on Otmoor, Oxfordshire, England, died 15 May 1842, in Beckley, Oxfordshire, England. She was the daughter of James Jones and Ann Giles. She married Richard Newell[210] 2 Sep 1810, in Beckley, Oxfordshire, England.[209] He was the son of William Newell and Ann Broadway.

40. John Hinton was born 1780, in Fencot, Oxfordshire, England,[213] christened 1780, in Fencot, Oxfordshire, England, died Sep 1857, in Stanton St John, Oxfordshire, England,[214] buried 6 Sep 1857, in Stanton St John, Oxfordshire, England.[215] He was the son of John Hinton and Martha Kirby. Census: ; He married Ann Clarke[217] 26 Mar 1815, in Oxford, Oxfordshire, England.[216] She was the daughter of Elezeus Clark and Martha Grant.
Notes for John Hinton:

Class: HO107; Piece 877; Book: 13; Civil Parish: St John Stanton; County: Oxfordshire; Enumeration District: 3; Folio: 12; Page: 10; Line: 14; GSU roll: 474573. 1841 census Name: John Hinton Age: 60 Estimated Birth Year: abt 1781 Gender: Male Where born: Oxfordshire, England Civil Parish: St John Stanton Hundred: Bullingdon County/Island: Oxfordshire Country: England Registration district: Headington Sub registration district: Wheatley Household Members: Name Age John Hinton 60 Ann Hinton 50 Eliza Hinton 20 Elezens Hinton 15 William Hinton 14 Michael Newell 25 1851 census his age was given as 77 (should be 70) Name: John Hinton Age: 77 Estimated Birth Year: abt 1774 Relation: Head Spouse's Name: Ann Gender: Male Where born: Fencott, Oxfordshire, England Civil Parish: Stanton St John County/Island: Oxfordshire Country: England Household Members: Name Age John Hinton 77 Ann Hinton 58 William Hinton 24 Eliza Newell 30 Elezens Newell 7 William Newell 4 Class: HO107; Piece 877; Book: 13; Civil Parish: St John Stanton; County: Oxfordshire; Enumeration District: 3; Folio: 12; Page: 10; Line: 14; GSU roll: 474573.

Contents

Children of John Hinton and Ann Clarke:

    i.   **William Hinton**, born Sep 1816, in Stanton St John, Oxfordshire, England, christened 22 Sep 1816, in Stanton St John, Oxfordshire, England, died Jun 1817, in Stanton St John, Oxfordshire, England, buried 8 Jun 1817, in Stanton St John, Oxfordshire, England.

    ii.   **Eliza Hinton**, born Aug 1820, in Stanton St John, Oxfordshire, England, died Jan 1907, in Stanton St John, Oxfordshire, England.

    iii.   **Eliseus Hinton**, born Sep 1823, in Stanton St John, Oxfordshire, England, christened 9 Sep 1823, in Stanton St John, Oxfordshire, England, died Nov 1863, in Stanton St John, Oxfordshire, England, buried 1 Dec 1863, in Stanton St John, Oxfordshire, England. He married Hannah Morbey Jul 1845, in Oxfordshire, England. Hannah Morbey was born 1827, in Stanton St John, Oxfordshire, England, died Jul 1853, in Stanton St John, Oxfordshire, England, buried 5 Jul 1853, in Stanton St John, Oxfordshire, England.
Stanton St John Parish Baptism records 9 Sep 1923 - Hinton, Eliseus - parents: John

    iv.   **William Hinton**, born Aug 1826, in Stanton St John, Oxfordshire, England, christened 20 Aug 1826, in Stanton St John, Oxfordshire, England, died Aug 1893, in Stanton St John, Oxfordshire, England, buried 30 Aug 1893, in Stanton St John, Oxfordshire, England. He married Elizabeth James 24 Dec 1854, in Stanton St John, Oxfordshire, England. Elizabeth James was born 1831, in Launton, Oxfordshire, England, died Jul 1914, in Stanton St John, Oxfordshire, England, buried 25 Jul 1914, in Stanton St John, Oxfordshire, England.

    v.   **Joseph Hinton**, born 1832, in Stanton St John, Oxfordshire, England, died before 1881, in Stanton St John, Oxfordshire, England. He married Phobe Adams 24 Apr 1859, in England. Phobe Adams was born 1835, in Great Haseley, Oxfordshire, England, christened 17 Jul 1836, in Great Haseley, Oxfordshire, England, died about 1876, in England.
Does not appear on 1841 census Does not appear on 1841 census Does not appear on 1841 census Does not appear on 1841 census Does not appear on 1841 census Does not appear on 1841 census Does not appear on 1841 census Does not appear on 1841 census Does not appear on 1841 census Does not appear on 1841 census Does not appear on 1841 census

41. Ann Clarke was born 3 Dec 1792, in Waterperry, Oxfordshire, England, christened 7 Jan 1793, in Waterperry, Oxfordshire, England, died Feb 1878, in Stanton St John, Oxfordshire, England, buried 17 Feb 1878, in Stanton St John, Oxfordshire, England. She was the daughter of Elezeus Clark and Martha Grant. She married John Hinton[217] 26 Mar 1815, in Oxford, Oxfordshire, England.[216] He was the son of John Hinton and Martha Kirby.
Notes for Ann Clarke:

aka: CLARK 1841 census Name: Ann Hinton Age: 50 Estimated birth year: abt 1791 Gender: Female Where born: Oxfordshire, England Civil parish: St John Stanton Hundred: Bullingdon County/Island:

Contents

Oxfordshire Country: England Name

42. George Rowland was born Apr 1799, in Bristol, Gloucestershire, England, christened 7 Apr 1799, in Bristol, Gloucestershire, England, died 28 Jun 1874, in Hanham, Gloucestershire, England.[218] He was the son of John Rowland and Mary Ann Watkins. He married Ann Rogers[219,220,221,222] 8 Jun 1819, in St James, Bristol, Gloucestershire, England. She was the daughter of Leonard Rogers and Ann Burges.
Notes for George Rowland:

England Births and Christenings, 1538-1975 residence: Bristol, Gloucester, England parents: John Rowland, Mary record title: England Births and Christenings, 1538-1975 name: George Rowland gender: Male baptism/christening date: 07 Apr 1799 baptism/christening place: Bristol, Gloucester, England father's name: John Rowland mother's name: Mary indexing project (batch) number: C01718-6 system origin: England. source film number: 1596677 1871 Census Occupation Retired Labourer living in Hanham Village next door to son Jabez 1861 Census Occupation Quarryman living at Jefferies Hill Hamlet Of Hanham Gloucestershire 1851 Census Occupation Quarry Labourer living at Jefferies Hill Village Of Hanham Gloucestershire 1841 Census Occupation Labourer living at Jefferies Hill Hamlet Of Hanham Gloucestershire Langley And Swinehead (Upper Division) Death Apr-Jun 1874 Keynsham 5c 477 Death certificate received 03/04/10 Aged 75 years Stone Quarrying Cause of death Old Age Debility Informant Aaron Peacock in attendance registered 29/06/1874

Children of George Rowland and Ann Rogers:

 i. **William Rowland**, born 1819, in Hanham, Gloucestershire, England, christened 7 Nov 1819, in Oldland, Gloucestershire, England. He married Hannah Williams 13 Feb 1844, in Aldgate, London, England. Hannah Williams was born 1821, in Bath, Somerset, England.
baptised in Oldland living in Hanham 1851 Census Occupation Metal Refiner living at 7 Bridgend East in Mile End Town Tower Hamlets
 ii. **Joseph Rowland**, born 1822, in Hanham, Gloucestershire, England, christened 11 Aug 1822, in Oldland, Gloucestershire, England, died 1828, in Bitton, Gloucestershire, England, buried 20 Jan 1828, in Bitton, Gloucestershire, England.
 iii. **Ann Rowland**, born 1825, in Hanham, Gloucestershire, England, christened 9 Nov 1825, in Hanham, Gloucestershire, England, died 1826, in Hanham, Gloucestershire, England.
 iv. **Ann Rowland**,[223] born 1826, in Hanham, Gloucestershire, England, christened 19 Nov 1826, in Clifton, Gloucestershire, England. She married George Harris 4 Jun 1854, in Bristol, Gloucestershire, England.[224] George Harris was born 1832, in Gloucestershire, England, christened 22 Jan 1832, in Bristol, Gloucestershire, England.
 v. **Luke Rowland**, born 1827, in Bitton, Gloucestershire, England, christened 8 Nov 1827, in Oldland, Gloucestershire, England. He married Elizabeth Callow Jan 1853, in Keynsham, Somerset, England. Elizabeth Callow was born 1836, in Hanham, Gloucestershire, England, christened 22 Jan 1837, in Stepney, Middlesex,

England.

vi.   **Joseph Rowland**, born 1830, in Hanham, Gloucestershire, England, christened 25 Apr 1830, in Hanham, Gloucestershire, England. He married Sarah Howard 5 Feb 1854, in Bristol, Gloucestershire, England. Sarah Howard was born 1831, in Gloucestershire, England.

vii. **Elizabeth Rowland**,[223] born 1832, in Gloucestershire, England, christened 28 Oct 1832, in Hanham, Gloucestershire, England, died Jan 1905, in Bristol, Gloucestershire, England. She married Stephen Churchill 6 Feb 1862, in Bristol, Gloucestershire, England. Stephen Churchill was born 1833, in Mangotsfield, Gloucestershire, England, died Jul 1897, in Bristol, Gloucestershire, England. Notes for Stephen Churchill: 1871 Census Occupation Pit Labourer living in Staple Hill Road Stapleton Bristol 1891 Census no occupation living in Alexandra Park Fishponds Bristol Death Jul - Sep 1897 Barton Regis 6a 102

viii. **Hannah Rowland**,[223] born 1835, in Hanham, Gloucestershire, England, christened 15 Mar 1835, in Oldland, Gloucestershire, England, died Jan 1925, in Bristol, Gloucestershire, England. She married Charles Talbot 12 Feb 1865, in Bristol, Gloucestershire, England. Charles Talbot was born 1844, in Hungerford, Berkshire, England, christened 20 Sep 1844, in Hungerford, Berkshire, England, died Oct 1894, in Bristol, Gloucestershire, England.
Baptism from Marcelle Winghurst through Genes Reunited 04/04/08 On familysearch.org pilot there is a marriage St Philip and Jacob 1865 Hannah Rowland aged 30 Father George Rowland to Charles Talbot aged 21 Father Charles Talbot Batch M17288-5 1901 Census Widow aged 66 no occupation living at 4 Victoria Road Westbury On Trym 1911 Census Widow aged 76 no occupation on own living at 39 Shadwell Road Bishopston Bristol states 6 children born 5 living 1 died Death Jan - Mar 1925 Bristol 6a 5
Notes for Charles Talbot: 1881 Census Occupation Gardener Servant living at Box Field Cottages Box Wiltshire 1891 Census Occupation Gardener living at Drinach Lodge Sneyd Park Westbury On Trym Bristol Death aged 50 Oct - Dec 1894 Barton Regis 6a 74

ix.   **Emma Rowland**,[221] born 1837, in Hanham, Gloucestershire, England, christened 6 Aug 1837, in Hanham, Gloucestershire, England, died Dec 1886, in England.

x.   **Jabez Rowland**,[221,225] born Oct 1839, in Hanham, Gloucestershire, England, died 15 Dec 1895, in Birmingham, Warwickshire, England. He married Ellen Britton[226,227] Apr 1868, in Gloucestershire, England. Ellen Britton was born 1847, in Bath, Somerset, England, died Dec 1881, in Hanham, Gloucestershire, England. birth Oct-Dec 1839 Keynsham Gloucestershire 11 104 1861 Census Occuption Foreman Paper Mill living in Hanham Mount 1871 Census Occupation Railway Accountant living in Hanham Village next door to Father and Mother 1881 Census Occupation Accountant living in Bitton Gloucestershire near Crown and Horsehoe Inn 1891 Census Occupation Commercial Traveller living at 155 Pershore Road Edgbaston Birmingham also has a servant Betha Gouldsbury aged 22 and Carrie A France aged 13 Nurse Jabez Rowland died Oct-Dec 1895 Kings Norton 6c 265

From Bristol Mercury and Daily Post Thursday 19th December 1895 Rowland - December 15 at Pershore Road Birmingham Jabez Rowland late of Hanham Bristol aged 55. 1st wife - Mary (Bevan or Jeffries) Married 1859 - Daughter 2nd wife Elllen

Notes for Ellen Britton: Birth Oct-Dec 1844 Bath 11 9 1871 Census Ocupation Milliner living in Hanham Village Death Oct-Dec 1881 Keynsham 5c 399 Jabez' 2nd wife

xi.   **Stephen Rowland**,[144,148,149] born 17 Apr 1842, in Hanham, Gloucestershire, England, died 19 Jun 1934, in Reigate, Surrey, England.[142]

43. Ann Rogers was born Dec 1795, in Hanham, Gloucestershire, England, christened 25 Dec 1795, in Bristol, Gloucestershire, England, died about 1882, in Gloucestershire, England. She was the daughter of Leonard Rogers and Ann Burges. She married George Rowland[148,218,221,228] 8 Jun 1819, in St James, Bristol, Gloucestershire, England. He was the son of John Rowland and Mary Ann Watkins.
Notes for Ann Rogers:

1881 Census living with son Jabez in Bitton Gloucestershire aged 86 widow

44. George Elleston was born 1816, in Greenwich, Kent, England, died Dec 1849, in Lewisham, Kent, England. He was the son of Joseph Elleston and Elizabeth Jennings. He married Mary Langley[231] 28 Aug 1836, in Shoreditch, London, England.[229,230] She was the daughter of Abraham Langley and Elizabeth Bayse.
Notes for George Elleston:

Death index - Name: George Elleston Year of Registration: 1849 Quarter of Registration: Oct-Nov-Dec District: Lewisham; Volume: 5; Page: 219 County: Greater London, Kent. aka: ELLERTON 23/01/1839 Occupation Labourer living at Blackheath Hill per baptism of daughter Emma Elleston 27/12/1840 Occupation Labourer living at Church Row per baptism of daughter Martha Elleston 05/04/1843 Occupation Labourer living at Maidinstone Hill per baptism of daughter Mary Ann Elleston 05/03/1845 Occupation Coachman living at Essex Place Lewisham per baptism of daughter Elizabeth Ann Elleston 07/05/1847 Occupation Milkman living at Church Street St Paul Deptford per baptism of daughter Georgina Elleston 06/05/1849 Occupation Milkman living at East Street per baptism of son George Edwin Elleston 1841 Census Occupation Labourer aged 25 living at 18 Straights Mouth Greenwich born in county on Ancestry down as Elston actual image says Elleston. Green Grocer on Marriage Certificate of daughter Mary Ann Elleston 03 October 1867 Death Oct - Dec 1849 Lewisham 5 219

Children of George Elleston and Mary Langley:

i.   **Emma Elleston**, born 31 Dec 1838, in Greenwich, Kent, England, christened 23 Jan 1839, in Greenwich, Kent, England. She married Thomas Thrussell 5 Aug 1855, in Deptford, Kent, England. Thomas Thrussell was born about 1835, in Kent, England.
Birth Jan - Mar 1839 Greenwich 5 197 1911 Census Widow aged 72 no occupation

living at 71 Calvert Road Greenwich states 7 children born 4 living 3 died

ii. **Martha Elleston**, born 29 Nov 1840, in Greenwich, Kent, England, christened 27 Dec 1840, in Greenwich, Kent, England, died Dec 1844, in Lewisham, Kent, England, buried 11 Dec 1844, in Lewisham, Kent, England.
Birth Oct - Dec 1840 Greenwich 5 222 6 months old on 1841 census Not on 1851 census with family at Bennett Street Greenwich - died 1844 Death index: Name: Martha Elleston Year of Registration: 1844 Quarter of Registration: Oct-Nov-Dec District: Lewisham County: Greater London, Kent, London Volume: 5 Page: 230

iii. **Mary Ann Elleston**,[144] born 7 Mar 1843, in Greenwich, Kent, England, died Oct 1891, in Fulham, Middlesex, England.[147]

iv. **Elizabeth Elleston**, born 9 Feb 1845, in Greenwich, Kent, England, christened 5 Mar 1845, in Greenwich, Kent, England.
Birth Jul - Sep 1844 Greenwich 5 234 Witness on Mary Ann Elleston's Marriage to Stephen Rowland 03/10/1867 1861 Census visitor aged 17 visiting Joseph aged 53 Shoemaker born Greenwich Kent and Sophia Elleston aged 48 born Canterbury Kent at 4 Avenue Place Lewisham

v. **Georgiana Elleston**, born 10 Apr 1847, in Greenwich, Kent, England, christened 7 May 1847, in Greenwich, Kent, England, died Nov 1848, in Greenwich, Kent, England.
Birth record Name Georgiana ELLISTON (ELLESTON) Reg Dist- Greenwich Vol - 5 Page - 204 Died Oct-Dec 1848 Greenwich Reg Dist Vol - 5 Page - 176

vi. **George Edwin Elleston**, born 11 Apr 1849, in Greenwich, Kent, England, christened 6 May 1849, in Greenwich, Kent, England, died Jul 1898, in Greenwich, Kent, England. He married Caroline Day Jan 1873, in Woolwich, Kent, England. Caroline Day was born Apr 1854, in Upper Norwood, Surrey, England, died Jan 1912, in Hampstead, London, England.
Birth Apr - Jun 1849 Greenwich 5 239 1861 Census Occupation Scholar living with widowed Mother in St Alphage Greenwich 1871 Census Occupation Metropolitan Police living at 2 Myrtle Cottages Upper Norwood Croydon Surrey 17/09/1873 Occupation Labourer living at 15 ?hidworth Street per baptism of daughter Caroline Elleston 1881 Census Occupation General Labourer living at 4 William Street Greenwich On census as Elliston 1891 Census Occupation General Labourer living at 105 Vanbrugh Hill Greenwich on census as Elliston Death Aged 49 Jul - Sep 1898 Greenwich 1d 712 - (NB: shown as George Edward not Edwin) 07/10/1916 deceased Occupation Time Keeper per marriage of daughter Mary Maud Elleston
Notes for Caroline Day: Birth Apr - Jun 1854 Guildford 2a 58 1901 Census Occupation none Widow living at 105 Vanburgh Hill Greenwich London also has boarder Austin J Dodd Aged 56 Occupation Telegraph Labourer (Submarine) born Marylebone London Death Jan - Mar 1912 Hampstead 1a 774 1911 Census Widow living at 33 Fingal Street East Greenwich states married 39 years 10 children born 7 living 3 died

Contents

45. Mary Langley was born 1816, in Stepney, Middlesex, England, christened 1816, in St George in The East, Stepney, London, England, died Sep 1891, in Greenwich, Kent, England. She was the daughter of Abraham Langley and Elizabeth Bayse. She married George Elleston[231] 28 Aug 1836, in Shoreditch, London, England.[229,230] He was the son of Joseph Elleston and Elizabeth Jennings.
Notes for Mary Langley:

1891 Census Occupation Serviving on own means 59 Beaconsfield , Greewich, Kent 1881 Census Occupation Monthly Nurse 39 London Street Greenwich Kent 1871 Census Occupation Supported ? 2 Myrtle Cottages Upper Norwood Croydon Surrey 1861 Census Occupation widow Charwoman living in Lower Bennett Street, St Alphage, Greenwich 1851 Census Occupation Marine Store Dealer Widow and deaf living at 14 Bennet Street Greenwich

46. John Churchill Humber was born Aug 1813, in Litton Cheney, Dorset, England, christened 15 Aug 1813, in Litton Cheney, Dorset, England, died Mar 1892, in Sherborne, Dorset, England. He was the son of Thomas Humber and Elizabeth Churchill. He married (1) Julia E. Hunt[162,232,233] 10 Apr 1849, in Sherborne, Dorset, England. She was the daughter of William Hunt and Sarah Matthews. He married (2) Mary Frampton Dec 1840, in Sherborne, Dorset, England.
Notes for John Churchill Humber:

1891 Census, he has his granddaughters Augusta Mary and Gertrude Mary and his grandson Harry George Shrimpton staying with them. On Thomas' birth cert shows John to be a sawyer

Children of John Churchill Humber and Julia E. Hunt:

    i.   **Charles Humber,**[162] born May 1849, in Leigh, Dorset, England, christened 27 May 1849, in Leigh, Dorset, England. He married Mrs Mary Ann Humber about 1870, in England. Mrs Mary Ann Humber was born about 1849, in Leigh, Dorset, England.
       on 1881 single and staying with parents. On 1891 with wife.

    ii. **Thomas Humber,**[161,162,163,164] born 4 Nov 1851, in Leigh, Dorset, England, died about 1885, in Poplar, London, England, United Kingdom.

    iii. **Elizabeth Humber,**[162] born 1855, in Leigh, Dorset, England, died 1928, in England.
       on 'vitals'. 1881 she is unmarried 26yrs old, working as a servant to Herbert Batten

    iv. **Mary Hunt Humber,**[162] born 1858, in Leigh, Dorset, England, christened 18 Jul 1858, in Yetminster, Dorset, England. She married Thomas George Travers 15 Oct 1891, in Leigh, Dorset, England. Thomas George Travers was born about 1870, in Chetnole, Dorset, England.

Children of John Churchill Humber and Mary Frampton:

    i.   **Harriet Humber**, born Dec 1841, in Sherborne, Dorset, England, christened 2 Jan 1842, in Yetminster, Dorset, England.

47. Julia E. Hunt was born 1829, in Leigh, Dorset, England, died 1893, in Leigh, Dorset, England. She was the daughter of William Hunt and Sarah Matthews. She married John Churchill Humber[162,233,234,235,236] 10 Apr 1849, in Sherborne, Dorset, England. He was the son of Thomas Humber and Elizabeth Churchill.
Notes for Julia E. Hunt:

on 1881, on 1891 says born 1826 Occupation 1881 Glover Witnessed death cert for her son Thomas in 1884 believed to be born before parents married

48. James Humphreys was born 1808, in Greatworth, Northamptonshire, England, christened 4 Mar 1808, in Marston St Lawrence, Northamptonshire, England, died 1886, in Brackley, Northamptonshire, England.[237] He was the son of William Humphry and Ann Coleman. He married Sarah Chester[153,238] 24 Feb 1831, in Marston St Lawrence, Northamptonshire, England. She was the daughter of Edward Chester and Lydia Savage.
Notes for James Humphreys:

Name spelled HUMPHRY, HUMPHRIS, HUMPHRES HUMPHREYS

Children of James Humphreys and Sarah Chester:

      i.   **William Humphreys**, born 1832, in Marston St Lawrence, Northamptonshire, England, christened 1832, in Marston St Lawrence, Northamptonshire, England.

     ii.   **Harriett Marie Humphreys**, born 6 Jul 1834, in Marston St Lawrence, Northamptonshire, England, christened 13 Jul 1834, in Marston St Lawrence, Northamptonshire, England, died Mar 1902, in Marston St Lawrence, Northamptonshire, England. She married John Mayo 29 May 1859, in Marston St Lawrence, Northamptonshire, England. John Mayo was born 1 Apr 1832, in Marston St Lawrence, Northamptonshire, England, christened Apr 1832, in Marston St Lawrence, Northamptonshire, England, died about 1911, in Marston St Lawrence, Northamptonshire, England.

    iii.   **George Humphreys**, born 1835, in Marston St Lawrence, Northamptonshire, England, christened 25 Dec 1835, in Marston St Lawrence, Northamptonshire, England.

    iv.   **Selina Humphreys**, born 1838, in Marston St Lawrence, Northamptonshire, England, christened 27 May 1838, in Marston St Lawrence, Northamptonshire, England.
Various spellings for given name FamilySearch showed this additional information: Name - Description: Selina Humphreys

     v.   **Edward Humphreys**, born Jan 1841, in Marston St Lawrence, Northamptonshire, England, christened 7 Feb 1841, in Marston St Lawrence, Northamptonshire, England.
FamilySearch showed this additional information: Name - Description: Edward Humphreys

    vi.   **Caroline Humphreys**, born Nov 1841, in Marston St Lawrence, Northamptonshire, England, christened 18 Nov 1841, in Marston St Lawrence, Northamptonshire, England.

    vii. **Mary Ann Humphreys**, born Oct 1844, in Marston St Lawrence, Northamptonshire, England, christened 13 Oct 1844, in Marston St Lawrence, Northamptonshire, England.
FamilySearch showed this additional information: Name - Description: Mary Ann Humphreys

    viii. **John Humphreys**, born 1847, in Greatworth, Northamptonshire, England, christened 19 Aug 1849, in Marston St Lawrence, Northamptonshire, England. He married Catherine Bazeley about Mar 1873, in Marston St Lawrence, Northamptonshire, England. Catherine Bazeley was born about 1854, in West Thorpe, Lincolnshire, England.

    ix. **Leonard Humphreys**, born 1848, in Greatworth, Northamptonshire, England.

    x. **Charles Humphreys**, born 1849, in Northamptonshire, England.

    xi. **Fanny Humphreys**,[152,153,154,155,156] born 5 Feb 1853, in Northamptonshire, England, died 1930, in Saint Pancras, London, England.

    xii. **Henry Humphreys**, born Feb 1854, in Marston St Lawrence, Northamptonshire, England, christened 22 Feb 1854, in Marston St Lawrence, Northamptonshire, England.

49. Sarah Chester was born Mar 1814, in Greatworth, Northamptonshire, England, christened 20 Mar 1814, in Marston St Lawrence, Northamptonshire, England, died 1879, in Brackley, Northamptonshire, England.[239] She was the daughter of Edward Chester and Lydia Savage. She married James Humphreys[153,240] 24 Feb 1831, in Marston St Lawrence, Northamptonshire, England. He was the son of William Humphry and Ann Coleman.
Notes for Sarah Chester:

Married Name spelled HUMPHRIS, HUMPHRES

50. Thomas Lucas was born 1787, in Leytonstone, Essex, England, died Jul 1869, in Epping, Essex, England. He was the son of Thomas Lucas and Jane Mayes. He married Sarah Young[171,241,242] 19 Sep 1809, in Wanstead, Essex, England. She was the daughter of William Young and Ann Elizabeth Turner.
Notes for Thomas Lucas:

1841 census - Source Citation: Class: HO107; Piece 323; Book: 4; Civil Parish: Barking; County: Essex; Enumeration District: 4; Folio: 51; Page: 2; Line: 14; GSU roll: 241362. 1851 census - Source Citation: Class: HO107; Piece: 1769; Folio: 391; Page: 43; GSU roll: 207415. 1861 census - Source Citation: Class: RG9; Piece: 1063; Folio: 83; Page: 9; GSU roll: 542745.

Children of Thomas Lucas and Sarah Young:

    i.   **William Lucas**,[171] born Aug 1813, in Barking, Essex, England, christened 22 Aug

1813, in Wanstead, Essex, England.
William

ii. **Thomas Lucas**,[170,171] born 1816, in Barking, Essex, England, died 1870, in Romford, Essex, England.

iii. **John Lucas**,[243,244] born 1821, in Barking, Essex, England. He married Sarah Stringer 26 Nov 1843, in Stepney, Middlesex, England. She was the daughter of James Stringer and Mary Elizabeth Hyde. Sarah Stringer was born 21 Mar 1821, in Barking, Essex, England, christened 25 Mar 1821, in Barking, Essex, England. 1861 England Census about John Lucas Name: John Lucas Age: 42 Estimated Birth Year: abt 1819 Relation: Head Spouse's Name: Sarah Gender: Male Where born: Barking Side, Essex, England Civil Parish: Barking Ecclesiastical parish: Barking Side County/Island: Essex Country: England Registration district: Romford Sub registration district: Ilford ED, institution, or vessel: 1 Household schedule number: 91 Household Members: Name Age John Lucas 42 Sarah Lucas 46 James Lucas 20 Thomas Lucas 17 Henry Lucas 15 John Lucas 12 Eliza Lucas 10 Sarah Lucas 8 William Lucas 4 Charlotte Lucas 1 James Stringer 62 Notes for Sarah Stringer: Sarah and Mary married two of the Lucas brothers

iv. **Sarah Lucas**,[244] born 1826, in Barking, Essex, England, christened 8 Jan 1826, in Wanstead, Essex, England.

v. **Jane Lucas**,[244] born 1827, in Barking, Essex, England, christened 28 Aug 1827, in Wanstead, Essex, England.

vi. **Matilda Lucas**,[245] born 1829, in Barking, Essex, England, christened 13 Sep 1829, in Barking, Essex, England.

vii. **Mary Ann Lucas**,[245] born Jul 1831, in Barking, Essex, England, christened 10 Jul 1831, in Great Ilford, Essex, England.

viii. **Martha Lucas**,[245] born 1835, in Barking, Essex, England, christened 16 Aug 1835, in Great Ilford, Essex, England.

51. Sarah Young was born 20 Feb 1790, in Wanstead, Essex, England, christened 21 Mar 1790, in West Ham, Essex, England, died 1861, in West Ham, Essex, England. She was the daughter of William Young and Ann Elizabeth Turner. She married Thomas Lucas[171,246,247] 19 Sep 1809, in Wanstead, Essex, England. He was the son of Thomas Lucas and Jane Mayes.
Notes for Sarah Young:

Source Citation: Class: HO107; Piece 323; Book: 4; Civil Parish: Barking; County: Essex; Enumeration District: 4; Folio: 51; Page: 2; Line: 14; GSU roll: 241362.

52. James Stringer was born 22 Jan 1800, in Wanstead, Essex, England, christened 26 Jan 1800, in Wanstead, Essex, England, died Dec 1887, in Romford, Essex, England,[248] buried 18 Dec 1887, in Barkingside, Essex, England. He was the son of James Stringer and Elizabeth Sarah Wyten. He married Mary Elizabeth Hyde[249] 12 Oct 1818, in Barking, Essex, England. She was the daughter of Richard Hyde and Sarah Briggs.
Notes for James Stringer:

1841 census Shows him with his family 1851 census 1861 census shows him living with daughter Sarah

Children of James Stringer and Mary Elizabeth Hyde:

    i.   **Sarah Stringer**, born 21 Mar 1821, in Barking, Essex, England, christened 25 Mar 1821, in Barking, Essex, England. She married John Lucas[243,244] 26 Nov 1843, in Stepney, Middlesex, England. He was the son of Thomas Lucas and Sarah Young. John Lucas was born 1821, in Barking, Essex, England.
Sarah and Mary married two of the Lucas brothers
Notes for John Lucas: 1861 England Census about John Lucas Name: John Lucas Age: 42 Estimated Birth Year: abt 1819 Relation: Head Spouse's Name: Sarah Gender: Male Where born: Barking Side, Essex, England Civil Parish: Barking Ecclesiastical parish: Barking Side County/Island: Essex Country: England Registration district: Romford Sub registration district: Ilford ED, institution, or vessel: 1 Household schedule number: 91 Household Members: Name Age John Lucas 42 Sarah Lucas 46 James Lucas 20 Thomas Lucas 17 Henry Lucas 15 John Lucas 12 Eliza Lucas 10 Sarah Lucas 8 William Lucas 4 Charlotte Lucas 1 James Stringer 62

    ii.   **Mary Ann Stringer,**[165,166,167,168,169] born 13 Feb 1826, in Barking, Essex, England, died 26 Dec 1901, in West Ham, Essex, England.

53. Mary Elizabeth Hyde was born Nov 1798, in Barking, Essex, England, christened 30 Nov 1798, in Barking, Essex, England, died 14 Feb 1854, in Romford, Essex, England.[250] She was the daughter of Richard Hyde and Sarah Briggs. She married James Stringer[251,252,253] 12 Oct 1818, in Barking, Essex, England. He was the son of James Stringer and Elizabeth Sarah Wyten.
Notes for Mary Elizabeth Hyde:

851 Census - aged 79. Widow, Market Gardner (Mossford Green, Barking Side, Essex) 1851 Census - aged 79. Widow, Market Gardner (Mossford Green, Barking Side, Essex) 1851 Census - aged 79. Widow, Market Gardner (Mossford Green, Barking Side, Essex)

54. Thomas Giles was born 1800, in Dover, Kent, England, christened 1 Jun 1800, in Dover, Kent, England, died 1 Mar 1872, in Stepney, Middlesex, England. He was the son of Thomas Giles and Sarah Holmes. He married Hannah Maria Baldwin[254,255] 21 Jun 1821, in North Shoebury, Essex, England. She was the daughter of John Baldwin and Rebecca Dixon.
Notes for Thomas Giles:

1800 - Birth Christening: St. Mary the Virgin, Dover, Kent 1821 - Marriage: 21 Jun Age: 21 Marriage to Hannah Baldwin of Shoebury, Essex. 1841 - census Age: 41 Residence: Ireland 1851 - England Census Age: 51 Residence: Limehouse, Middlesex, England Thomas at the time was a Custom House Pensioner1861 1861 - England Census Age: 61 Residence: 17 James Place, Stepney, Middlesex Thomas, a Coast Guard Pensioner 1871 - England Census Age: 71 Residence: 23 Stepney Causeway, Stepney, London, England 1872 - Death Age: 72 Stepney. Info: Thomas was a coastguard and he did a tour of duty In Ireland. The areas on his record include Sherkin, Ventry, Baltimore in County Cork. He returned to England in 1841. They had at least five Irish born Children.

Children of Thomas Giles and Hannah Maria Baldwin:

    i. **William Giles**, born 1831, in Ireland.
    ii. **George Giles**,[175,178,179,180] born 15 Dec 1833, in Cork, Ireland, died 16 Aug 1911, in West Ham, Essex, England.
    iii. **Joseph Giles**, born 1836, in Ireland.
    iv. **John Morgan Giles**,[256] born 1839, in Ireland.
    v. **Ann Marie Giles**,[256] born 1841, in Ireland. She married Benjamin Charles Dugall about 1860, in Kent, England. Benjamin Charles Dugall was born 1841, in Ratcliffe St James, Middlesex, England.
    1881 Residence: Limehouse Stepney, London Description: 12 Cayley Street. Ann Maria
    vi. **James Giles**, born 1844, in Stepney, Middlesex, England, christened 21 Mar 1844, in Limehouse, Middlesex, England.
    Limehouse, Stepney, London, England, United Kingdom
    vii. **Elizabeth Giles**,[257] born 1847, in Stepney, Middlesex, England.
    Limehouse, Stepney, London, England, United Kingdom

55. Hannah Maria Baldwin was born May 1805, in North Shoebury, Essex, England, christened 9 Jun 1805, in St Sepulchre, London, England, died 13 Jan 1883, in Stepney, Middlesex, England. She was the daughter of John Baldwin and Rebecca Dixon. She married Thomas Giles[254,255,258,259] 21 Jun 1821, in North Shoebury, Essex, England. He was the son of Thomas Giles and Sarah Holmes.
Notes for Hannah Maria Baldwin:

1881 Age: 76 Residence: Limehouse Stepney, London Description: 12 Cayley Street. Hannah was living with her daughter Ann Maria, Anna's husband Benjamin Charles Dugall and children. Died 1883 - 12 Cayley Street. Known as 'Good Mother Giles' East End Pictures: Being More Leaves from My Log of Twenty- Five Years' Christian Work Among Sailors and Others (1885)by Thomas Charles Garland Chapter 7 (Good Mother Giles), from page 54 Contains a preface to the good woman. She was Hannah Baldwin who married Thomas Giles. She gave of herself and tried to bring decency to otherwise sordid and violent lives.

56. James Vanner Wine was born 7 Oct 1817, in Hackney, Middlesex, England, christened 26 Oct 1817, in Hackney, Middlesex, England, died Dec 1838, in St Luke, Middlesex, England. He was the son of William Wine and Sarah Richardson. He married Mary Ann Rapp[262,263,264] 19 May 1834, in St Dunstan, Stepney, London, England.[260,261] She was the daughter of William Thomas Rapley and Martha Steel Mott.

Children of James Vanner Wine and Mary Ann Rapp:

    i. **Ann Wine**,[173,174,175,176] born 14 Jul 1834, in Limehouse, Middlesex, England, died Apr

1882, in England.

57. Mary Ann Rapp was born 25 Aug 1811, in Stepney, Middlesex, England, christened 1 Sep 1811, in Stepney, Middlesex, England, died Apr 1839, in Stepney, Middlesex, England. She was the daughter of William Thomas Rapley and Martha Steel Mott. She married James Vanner Wine[262,265] 19 May 1834, in St Dunstan, Stepney, London, England.[260,261] He was the son of William Wine and Sarah Richardson. Notes for Mary Ann Rapp:

Christened in St Dunstan Stepney 1 September 1811 (also shows date of birth - 25 Aug 1811) Name shown as WINN on death register.

Generation No. 7

58. William Aldsworth was born Aug 1760, in Stanton Harcourt, Oxfordshire, England, christened 6 Sep 1760, in Stanton Harcourt, Oxfordshire, England, died Oct 1796, in Stanton Harcourt, Oxfordshire, England, buried 12 Oct 1796, in Stanton Harcourt, Oxfordshire, England. He was the son of William Aldesworth and Mary Tynedall. He married Hannah Townsend[266,268] 17 Dec 1781, in Stanton Harcourt, Oxfordshire, England.[266,267] She was the daughter of John Townshend and Elizabeth Hopcraft.

Children of William Aldsworth and Hannah Townsend:

    i.   **William Aldsworth**,[191,192] born Sep 1781, in Stanton Harcourt, Oxfordshire, England, died Feb 1862, in Northmoor, Oxfordshire, England.

    ii.   **Mary Aldsworth**, born 1783, in Stanton Harcourt, Oxfordshire, England, christened 23 Feb 1783, in Stanton Harcourt, Oxfordshire, England, died before 1883, in England.

   iii.   **Hanna Aldsworth**, born 14 Feb 1785, in Stanton Harcourt, Oxfordshire, England, christened 20 Feb 1785, in Stanton Harcourt, Oxfordshire, England, died before 1841, in England. She married William West about 1803, in Oxfordshire, England. William West was born about 1780, in Oxfordshire, England.

   iv.   **Martha Aldsworth**, born 23 Nov 1787, in Stanton Harcourt, Oxfordshire, England, christened 2 Dec 1787, in Stanton Harcourt, Oxfordshire, England, died 11 Jan 1788, in Stanton Harcourt, Oxfordshire, England, buried 15 Jan 1788, in Stanton Harcourt, Oxfordshire, England.
             7 wks old at death

    v.   **Martha Alsworth**, born 4 Dec 1787, in Stanton Harcourt, Oxfordshire, England, christened 15 Jan 1788, in Stanton Harcourt, Oxfordshire, England, died 17 Nov 1792, in Stanton Harcourt, Oxfordshire, England, buried 4 Dec 1792, in Stanton Harcourt, Oxfordshire, England.
             Buried: St Michael, Stanton Harcourt, Oxfordshire, England, United Kingdom Note name spelling change from Aldsworth to Alsworth in parish records

59. Hannah Townsend was born Mar 1761, in Bletchingdon, Oxfordshire, England, christened 24 Mar 1761, in Bletchingdon, Oxfordshire, England, died May 1819, in Stanton Harcourt, Oxfordshire, England, buried 31 May 1819, in Stanton Harcourt, Oxfordshire, England. She was the daughter of John Townshend and Elizabeth Hopcraft. She married William Aldsworth[269] 17 Dec 1781, in Stanton Harcourt, Oxfordshire, England.[266,267] He was the son of William Aldesworth and Mary Tynedall.
Notes for Hannah Townsend:

residence: Oxford, England parents: John Townshend, Elizabeth record title: England Births and Christenings, 1538-1975 name: Hannah Townshand gender: Female baptism/christening date: 24 Mar 1761 baptism/christening place: BLETCHINGDON,OXFORD,ENGLAND father's name: John

Townshand mother's name: Elizabeth indexing project (batch) number: C02431-2 system origin: England-ODM source film number: 95216

60. Giles Turner was born about 1743, in Witney, Oxfordshire, England, died Oct 1818, in Ascott Under Wychwood, Oxfordshire, England, buried 1 Nov 1818, in Ascott Under Wychwood, Oxfordshire, England. He was the son of Charles Turner and Ann Cox. He married Mary Timms[270,271] 6 Oct 1777, in Ascott Under Wychwood, Oxfordshire, England.[270] She was the daughter of John Timms and Elenor Cockins.
Notes for Giles Turner:

Name recorded as TANNER on the Parish reg transcription - Oxfordshire Marriages witnesses George Moss

Children of Giles Turner and Mary Timms:

    i.   **Elizabeth Turner**,[271] born Jan 1778, in Ascott Under Wychwood, Oxfordshire, England, christened 4 Jan 1778, in Ascott Under Wychwood, Oxfordshire, England.

    ii.   **Mary Turner**,[271] born Jan 1779, in Ascott Under Wychwood, Oxfordshire, England, christened 31 Jan 1779, in Ascott Under Wychwood, Oxfordshire, England.

    iii.   **Ann Turner**,[271] born Jul 1780, in Ascott Under Wychwood, Oxfordshire, England, christened 23 Jul 1780, in Ascott Under Wychwood, Oxfordshire, England.

    iv.   **Thomas Turner**,[272] born Jan 1782, in Ascott Under Wychwood, Oxfordshire, England, christened 13 Jan 1782, in Ascott Under Wychwood, Oxfordshire, England.
Do not confuse with another with same name from next village

    v.   **Jane Turner**,[183] born 22 May 1783, in Ascott Under Wychwood, Oxfordshire, England, died Apr 1862, in Northmoor, Oxfordshire, England.

61. Mary Timms was born 24 Feb 1744, in Ascott Under Wychwood, Oxfordshire, England, christened 24 Feb 1744, in Ascott Under Wychwood, Oxfordshire, England, died 22 Jun 1828, in Ascott Under Wychwood, Oxfordshire, England. She was the daughter of John Timms and Elenor Cockins. She married Giles Turner[270] 6 Oct 1777, in Ascott Under Wychwood, Oxfordshire, England.[270] He was the son of Charles Turner and Ann Cox.

62. John Drinkwater was born Mar 1759, in Bampton, Oxfordshire, England, christened 24 Mar 1759, in Bampton, Oxfordshire, England, buried 27 Dec 1836, in Brize Norton, Oxfordshire, England. He was the son of John Drinkwater and Ann Windows. He married Lucy Hawkins[273] 25 May 1783, in Faringdon, Berkshire, England. She was the daughter of John Hawkins and Mary Alder.

Children of John Drinkwater and Lucy Hawkins:

    i.   **William Drinkwater**,[195,196] born Oct 1784, in Little Coxwell, Berkshire, England, died 1868, in Witney, Oxfordshire, England.
    ii.   **John Drinkwater**, born May 1786, in Little Coxwell, Berkshire, England, christened 28 May 1786, in Brize Norton, Oxfordshire, England.
    iii.   **Elizabeth Drinkwater**, born Apr 1788, in Little Coxwell, Berkshire, England, christened 6 Apr 1788, in Brize Norton, Oxfordshire, England.
    iv.   **Ann Drinkwater**, born May 1790, in Little Coxwell, Berkshire, England, christened 23 May 1790, in Brize Norton, Oxfordshire, England.
    v.   **James Drinkwater**, born Apr 1793, in Little Coxwell, Berkshire, England, christened 21 Apr 1793, in Brize Norton, Oxfordshire, England.

63. Lucy Hawkins was born Oct 1759, in Little Coxwell, Berkshire, England, christened 29 Oct 1759, in Faringdon, Berkshire, England, buried 7 May 1841, in Brize Norton, Oxfordshire, England. She was the daughter of John Hawkins and Mary Alder. She married John Drinkwater[274] 25 May 1783, in Faringdon, Berkshire, England. He was the son of John Drinkwater and Ann Windows.

64. William Haydon was born Mar 1752, in Buckland, Oxfordshire, England, christened 15 Mar 1752, in Buckland, Oxfordshire, England, died before 1850, in England. He was the son of Richard Haydon and Sarah Smith. He married Elizabeth "Betty" Hawkins[275] 28 Sep 1778, in Northmoor, Oxfordshire, England. She was the daughter of William Hawkins and Mary Gee.
Notes for William Haydon:

residence: Buckland, Berkshire, England parents: Richard Haydon, Sarah record title: England Births and Christenings, 1538-1975 name: William Haydon gender: Male baptism/christening date: 15 Mar 1752 baptism/christening place: Buckland, Berkshire, England father's name: Richard Haydon mother's name: Sarah indexing project (batch) number: C01766-3 source film number: 1279452 In 1781 a removal order under the poor laws William and his family were ordered to move from Northmoor back to Lyford. Marriage Banns read in LYFORD (Berkshire) on Sept 13, 20

Children of William Haydon and Elizabeth "Betty" Hawkins:

    i.   **James Haydon**, born Feb 1781, in Northmoor, Oxfordshire, England, christened 11 Feb 1781, in Northmoor, Oxfordshire, England, died 14 Feb 1781, in Northmoor, Oxfordshire, England, buried 16 Feb 1781, in Northmoor, Oxfordshire, England.
    ii.   **Hannah Haydon**, born Nov 1782, in Northmoor, Oxfordshire, England, died 1860, in Witney, Oxfordshire, England.
    iii.   **John Haydon**, born 1786, in Lyford, Berkshire, England, christened 12 Feb 1786, in West Hanney, Berkshire, England, died 1860, in Garford, Berkshire, England.

65. Elizabeth "Betty" Hawkins was born Apr 1755, in Northmoor, Oxfordshire, England, christened 8

Apr 1755, in Northmoor, Oxfordshire, England, died before 1850, in England. She was the daughter of William Hawkins and Mary Gee. She married William Haydon[276,277,278] 28 Sep 1778, in Northmoor, Oxfordshire, England. He was the son of Richard Haydon and Sarah Smith.
Notes for Elizabeth "Betty" Hawkins:

1. Parish Records Collection - Marriage, Northmoor Parish, Oxfordshire, 1778.

66. William Veasy Morgan was born Nov 1717, in Standlake, Oxfordshire, England, christened 17 Nov 1717, in Standlake, Oxfordshire, England, died before 1817, in England. He was the son of William Morgan and Catherine Veasy. He married Mary Stone[279,280] 24 Apr 1750, in Standlake, Oxfordshire, England. She was the daughter of William Stone and Martha Onion.

Children of William Veasy Morgan and Mary Stone:

    i.   **William V. Morgan**, born Dec 1750, in Standlake, Oxfordshire, England, christened 16 Dec 1750, in Standlake, Oxfordshire, England. He married Martha Edwards 12 Apr 1778, in Standlake, Oxfordshire, England. Martha Edwards was born about 1752, in Oxfordshire, England.

    ii.   **Mary Morgan**, born Nov 1752, in Standlake, Oxfordshire, England, christened 5 Nov 1752, in Standlake, Oxfordshire, England.

    iii.   **Moses Morgan**, born Sep 1754, in Standlake, Oxfordshire, England, christened 15 Sep 1754, in Standlake, Oxfordshire, England.

    iv.   **Matthew Morgan**, born Mar 1757, in Standlake, Oxfordshire, England, christened 6 Mar 1757, in Standlake, Oxfordshire, England, died Oct 1761, in Standlake, Oxfordshire, England, buried 22 Oct 1761, in Standlake, Oxfordshire, England.

    v.   **Frances Morgan**, born Jul 1759, in Standlake, Oxfordshire, England, christened 29 Jul 1759, in Standlake, Oxfordshire, England, died Nov 1759, in Standlake, Oxfordshire, England, buried 12 Nov 1759, in Standlake, Oxfordshire, England.

    vi.   **Dinah Morgan**, born Aug 1760, in Standlake, Oxfordshire, England, christened 24 Aug 1760, in Standlake, Oxfordshire, England, died Aug 1764, in Standlake, Oxfordshire, England, buried 16 Aug 1764, in Standlake, Oxfordshire, England.

    vii.   **Sarah Morgan**, born Apr 1763, in Standlake, Oxfordshire, England, christened 21 Apr 1763, in Standlake, Oxfordshire, England.

    viii.   **Hannah Morgan**, born Feb 1766, in Standlake, Oxfordshire, England, christened 23 Feb 1766, in Standlake, Oxfordshire, England. She married Thomas Mitchell 13 Nov 1790, in Standlake, Oxfordshire, England. Thomas Mitchell was born about 1765, in Oxfordshire, England.

    ix.   **Ann Morgan**, born Mar 1769, in Standlake, Oxfordshire, England, christened 28 Mar 1769, in Standlake, Oxfordshire, England.

    x.   **John Morgan**,[199,200] born about 1776, in Yarnton, Oxfordshire, England, died 1846, in Oxfordshire, England.

67. Mary Stone was born Apr 1725, in Standlake, Oxfordshire, England, christened 4 Apr 1725, in

Standlake, Oxfordshire, England, died Jul 1790, in Standlake, Oxfordshire, England, buried 17 Jul 1790, in Standlake, Oxfordshire, England. She was the daughter of William Stone and Martha Onion. She married William Veasy Morgan[281] 24 Apr 1750, in Standlake, Oxfordshire, England. He was the son of William Morgan and Catherine Veasy.

68. John Hartlett was born Jan 1728, in Middle Barton, Oxfordshire, England, christened 21 Jan 1728, in Enstone, Oxfordshire, England, died before 1810, in England. He was the son of Richard Hartlett and Elizabeth King. He married Mary Gilkes[282] 20 Sep 1761, in Steeple Barton, Oxfordshire, England. She was the daughter of Tobias Gilkes and Sarah Price.
Notes for John Hartlett:

aka: HARTLEY on Oxfordshire marriages 1538-1837 (page 71)

Children of John Hartlett and Mary Gilkes:

i. **Mary Hartlett**, born 4 Jul 1762, in Steeple Barton, Oxfordshire, England, christened 4 Jul 1762, in Steeple Barton, Oxfordshire, England, died 14 Jul 1762, in Steeple Barton, Oxfordshire, England.

ii. **John Hartlett**,[283] born Oct 1763, in Steeple Barton, Oxfordshire, England, christened 23 Oct 1763, in Steeple Barton, Oxfordshire, England, died Nov 1763, in Steeple Barton, Oxfordshire, England, buried 6 Nov 1763, in Steeple Barton, Oxfordshire, England.
record title: England Births and Christenings, 1538-1975 name: John Hartlett gender: Male baptism/christening date: 23 Oct 1763 baptism/christening place: STEEPLE BARTON,OXFORD,ENGLAND death date: 06 Nov 1763 father's name: John Hartlett mother's name: Mary indexing project (batch) number: C02422-2 system origin: England-ODM source film number: 95211 death: 06 Nov 1763 residence: Oxford, England parents: John Hartlett, Mary

iii. **John Hartlett**,[283] born Oct 1764, in Steeple Barton, Oxfordshire, England, christened 21 Oct 1764, in Steeple Barton, Oxfordshire, England.

iv. **Ann Hartlett**,[284] born Jan 1767, in Adderbury, Oxfordshire, England, christened 1 Feb 1767, in Adderbury, Oxfordshire, England.

v. **James Hartlett**,[285] born Jun 1769, in Glympton, Oxfordshire, England, christened 19 Jun 1769, in Glympton, Oxfordshire, England.

vi. **Mary Hartlett**,[286] born May 1771, in Glympton, Oxfordshire, England, christened 26 May 1771, in Glympton, Oxfordshire, England.

vii. **William Hartlett**,[285] born 11 Mar 1773, in Oxfordshire, England, christened 4 Apr 1773, in Glympton, Oxfordshire, England.

viii. **Sarah Hartlett**,[198,199] born Aug 1776, in Adderbury, Oxfordshire, England, died before 1837, in Oxfordshire, England.

ix. **Hannah Hartlett**,[287] born Aug 1776, in Adderbury, Oxfordshire, England, christened 18 Aug 1776, in Adderbury, Oxfordshire, England, died before 1837, in Oxfordshire, England.

Hannah and Sarah were TWINS

69. Mary Gilkes was born Nov 1741, in Middle Barton, Oxfordshire, England, christened 13 Nov 1741, in Chipping Norton, Oxfordshire, England, died before 1838, in England. She was the daughter of Tobias Gilkes and Sarah Price. She married John Hartlett[288,289] 20 Sep 1761, in Steeple Barton, Oxfordshire, England. He was the son of Richard Hartlett and Elizabeth King.

70. John Foster was born 21 Aug 1757, in Standlake, Oxfordshire, England, died 1 Feb 1836, in Sutton, Oxfordshire, England, buried 9 Feb 1836, in Stanton Harcourt, Oxfordshire, England. He was the son of Yeoman John Foster and Sarah Harris. He married Mary Or Elizabeth Duffin[290] 15 May 1780, in Stanton Harcourt, Oxfordshire, England. She was the daughter of John Duffen and Sarah Clark.
Notes for John Foster:

Parish records

Children of John Foster and Mary Or Elizabeth Duffin:

    i.   **James Foster**,[291] born May 1782, in Stanton Harcourt, Oxfordshire, England, christened 2 Jun 1782, in Stanton Harcourt, Oxfordshire, England.

    ii.   **Mary Foster**, born 9 Feb 1785, in Stanton Harcourt, Oxfordshire, England, christened 13 Feb 1785, in Stanton Harcourt, Oxfordshire, England, died May 1787, in Stanton Harcourt, Oxfordshire, England, buried 28 May 1787, in Stanton Harcourt, Oxfordshire, England.
           Stanton Harcourt parish baptism register

    iii.   **Elizabeth Foster**, born 12 Apr 1788, in Stanton Harcourt, Oxfordshire, England, christened 27 Apr 1788, in Stanton Harcourt, Oxfordshire, England. She married William Potter 29 Jan 1810. William Potter was born about 1790, in Stanton Harcourt, Oxfordshire, England.
           Stanton Harcourt parish baptism register
           Notes for William Potter: Stanton Harcourt parish marriage register

    iv.   **John Foster**,[206,207,208] born 27 Dec 1790, in Stanton Harcourt, Oxfordshire, England, died 18 May 1864, in Witney, Oxfordshire, England.[201]

    v.   **Thomas Foster**, born 28 Sep 1793, in Stanton Harcourt, Oxfordshire, England, christened 6 Oct 1793, in Stanton Harcourt, Oxfordshire, England.
           Stanton Harcourt parish baptism register

    vi.   **William Foster**, born 20 Nov 1796, in Stanton Harcourt, Oxfordshire, England, christened 27 Nov 1796, in Stanton Harcourt, Oxfordshire, England.
           Stanton Harcourt parish baptism register

    vii.   **Mary Foster**, born 8 Dec 1799, in Stanton Harcourt, Oxfordshire, England, christened 22 Dec 1799, in Stanton Harcourt, Oxfordshire, England.
           Stanton Harcourt parish baptism register

71. Mary Or Elizabeth Duffin was born May 1766, in Abingdon, Berkshire, England, christened 18

May 1766, in St Helen's, Abingdon, Berkshire, England, died Jul 1820, in Sutton, Oxfordshire, England, buried 7 Jul 1820, in Stanton Harcourt, Oxfordshire, England. She was the daughter of John Duffen and Sarah Clark. She married John Foster[290,292] 15 May 1780, in Stanton Harcourt, Oxfordshire, England. He was the son of Yeoman John Foster and Sarah Harris.
Notes for Mary Or Elizabeth Duffin:

Use of both names in various registers Stanton Harcourt parish marriage register incorrectly transcribed as Puffin

72. Daniel King was born 16 May 1762, in Kidlington, Oxfordshire, England, christened 16 May 1762, in Kidlington, Oxfordshire, England, died before 1860, in England. He was the son of William King and Elizabeth Bartlet. He married Sarah Probats[294,295,296] 5 Oct 1783, in Cassington, Oxfordshire, England.[293] She was the daughter of William Probatts and Sarah Bayly.

Children of Daniel King and Sarah Probats:

     i.   **Ann King**,[203] born 1789, in Bletchingdon, Oxfordshire, England, died 1853, in Witney, Oxfordshire, England.[205]

73. Sarah Probats was born Jul 1763, in Caversham, Oxfordshire, England, christened 17 Jul 1763, in Caversham, Oxfordshire, England, died before 1860, in England. She was the daughter of William Probatts and Sarah Bayly. She married Daniel King[295,296,297,298] 5 Oct 1783, in Cassington, Oxfordshire, England.[293] He was the son of William King and Elizabeth Bartlet.
Notes for Sarah Probats:

Spellings: Proboat, Probats, Probuts

74. William Newell was born 24 Jan 1739, in Brightwell Baldwin, Oxfordshire, England, christened 29 Apr 1739, in Brightwell Baldwin, Oxfordshire, England, died 1788, in England. He was the son of Henry Newell and Ann Oxlade. He married Ann Broadway 5 Jan 1770, in Cuxham, Oxfordshire, England.[299] She was the daughter of John Broadway and Jane Hinde.
Notes for William Newell:

Taken from parish records Witnesses at wedding - John Broadway

Children of William Newell and Ann Broadway:

     i.   **Michael Newell**, born 4 Nov 1770, in Cuxham, Oxfordshire, England, christened 4 Nov 1770, in Cuxham, Oxfordshire, England, died before 1841, in Oxfordshire, England.
    ii.   **Mary Newell**, born 5 Apr 1772, in Cuxham, Oxfordshire, England, christened 5 Apr 1772, in Cuxham, Oxfordshire, England, died before 1841, in England.
   iii.   **Henry Newell**, born 15 Sep 1775, in Cuxham, Oxfordshire, England, christened 15

Oct 1775, in Cuxham, Oxfordshire, England, died 1 Apr 1829, in England. He married Anne King 25 Dec 1812, in Cuxham, Oxfordshire, England. Anne King was born 1788, in Watlington, Oxfordshire, England, christened 24 Jun 1788, in Watlington, Oxfordshire, England, died before 1851, in Oxfordshire, England. Notes for Anne King: Watlington Parish records - baptism 24 june 1788

iv.   **Jane Newell**, born 12 Jan 1777, in Cuxham, Oxfordshire, England, christened 12 Jan 1777, in Cuxham, Oxfordshire, England.

v.   **John Newell**, born 21 Feb 1779, in Cuxham, Oxfordshire, England, christened 21 Feb 1779, in Cuxham, Oxfordshire, England.

vi.   **Richard Newell**,[210] born 18 May 1782, in Cuxham, Oxfordshire, England, died 29 Aug 1852, in Beckley, Oxfordshire, England.

vii. **Thomas Newell**, born 23 Feb 1784, in Cuxham, Oxfordshire, England, christened 23 Feb 1784, in Cuxham, Oxfordshire, England.

viii. **Samuel Newell**, born 19 Jun 1785, in Cuxham, Oxfordshire, England, christened 19 Jun 1785, in Cuxham, Oxfordshire, England, died Mar 1844, in Stanton St John, Oxfordshire, England, buried 10 Mar 1844, in Stanton St John, Oxfordshire, England. He married Mary Waterman 17 Oct 1810, in Hatfield Broad Oak, Essex, England. Mary Waterman was born about 1789, in Hatfield Broad Oak, Essex, England.

ix.   **Ann Newell**, born 1788, in Cuxham, Oxfordshire, England.

75. Ann Broadway was born 13 Jan 1744, in Cuxham, Oxfordshire, England, christened 17 Jan 1744, in Cuxham, Oxfordshire, England, died before 1840, in England. She was the daughter of John Broadway and Jane Hinde. She married William Newell 5 Jan 1770, in Cuxham, Oxfordshire, England.[299] He was the son of Henry Newell and Ann Oxlade.

Notes for Ann Broadway:

Taken from parish records Witnesses at wedding - John Broadway

76. James Jones was born Feb 1762, in Headington, Oxfordshire, England, christened 21 Feb 1762, in Headington, Oxfordshire, England, died before 1830, in England. He was the son of Richard Jones and Mary Green. He married Ann Giles[300,301] 20 Oct 1788, in Charlton on Otmoor, Oxfordshire, England. She was the daughter of Richard Giles and Mary Jackson.

Children of James Jones and Ann Giles:

i.   **Elizabeth Jones**,[210,211] born Dec 1794, in Murcot, Oxfordshire, England, died 15 May 1842, in Beckley, Oxfordshire, England.

77. Ann Giles was born Feb 1769, in Charlton on Otmoor, Oxfordshire, England, christened 12 Feb 1769, in Charlton on Otmoor, Oxfordshire, England. She was the daughter of Richard Giles and Mary Jackson. She married James Jones[300,302] 20 Oct 1788, in Charlton on Otmoor, Oxfordshire, England. He was the son of Richard Jones and Mary Green.

78. John Hinton was born Mar 1742, in Denton, Oxfordshire, England, christened 20 Mar 1742, in Cuddesdon, Oxfordshire, England, died about 1780, in Oxfordshire, England. He was the son of Thomas Hinton and Mary Slaughter. He married Martha Kirby[303,304] 16 Jul 1769, in Charlton on Otmoor, Oxfordshire, England. She was the daughter of Ralph Kirby and Martha Howlett.

Children of John Hinton and Martha Kirby:

    i.   **John Hinton,**[217] born 1780, in Fencot, Oxfordshire, England,[213] died Sep 1857, in Stanton St John, Oxfordshire, England.[214]

79. Martha Kirby was born Jun 1747, in Charlton on Otmoor, Oxfordshire, England, christened 16 Jun 1747, in Charlton on Otmoor, Oxfordshire, England, died before 1840, in England. She was the daughter of Ralph Kirby and Martha Howlett. She married John Hinton[303] 16 Jul 1769, in Charlton on Otmoor, Oxfordshire, England. He was the son of Thomas Hinton and Mary Slaughter.

80. Elezeus Clark was born Dec 1746, in Lillingstone Dayrell, Buckinghamshire, England, christened 7 Dec 1746, in Lillingstone Dayrell, Buckinghamshire, England, died Oct 1804, in Waterperry, Oxfordshire, England, buried 1 Nov 1804, in Waterperry, Oxfordshire, England. He was the son of William Clark and Sarah Rogers. He married Martha Grant[306,307,308] 1 Dec 1785, in Oxford, Oxfordshire, England.[305] She was the daughter of Johannes Grant and Martha Young.
Notes for Elezeus Clark:

Oxfordshire Marriages 1559-1837, listed by husband name, 1785. Clark, Elezeus; of Waterperry; Married Ox St Martin; Grant, Martha (a minor) 1785 1st Dec.

Children of Elezeus Clark and Martha Grant:

    i.   **Ann Clarke,**[217] born 3 Dec 1792, in Waterperry, Oxfordshire, England, died Feb 1878, in Stanton St John, Oxfordshire, England.

81. Martha Grant was born 17 Nov 1751, in Worminghall, Buckinghamshire, England, died Jun 1812, in Waterperry, Oxfordshire, England, buried 12 Jun 1812, in Waterperry, Oxfordshire, England. She was the daughter of Johannes Grant and Martha Young. She married Elezeus Clark[307,309,310] 1 Dec 1785, in Oxford, Oxfordshire, England.[305] He was the son of William Clark and Sarah Rogers.
Notes for Martha Grant:

Oxfordshire Marriages 1559-1837, listed by husband name, 1785. Clark, Elezeus; of Waterperry; Married Ox St Martin; Grant, Martha (a minor) 1785 1st Dec. also shown under her own name in same publication

82. John Rowland was born 1761, in Gloucestershire, England, christened 5 May 1761, in Gloucestershire, England, died 1829, in Easton, Somerset, England. He was the son of George Rowland and Jane Skinner. He married Mary Ann Watkins 2 Apr 1782, in Bristol, Gloucestershire, England. She

was the daughter of John Watkins and Mary Kelly.
Notes for John Rowland:

Name: John Rowland Gender: Male Baptism/Christening Date: 01 Jan 1753 Baptism/Christening Place: Bristol, Gloucester, England Father's Name: George Rowland Mother's Name: Jane Indexing Project (Batch) Number: I04146-2 Source Film Number: 1595986 Reference Number: item 3

Children of John Rowland and Mary Ann Watkins:

i.   **Ann Rowland**, born Jul 1784, in Bristol, Gloucestershire, England, christened 25 Jul 1784, in Bristol, Gloucestershire, England, died Sep 1789, in Bristol, Gloucestershire, England, buried 10 Sep 1789, in Bristol, Gloucestershire, England. England Births and Christenings, 1538-1975 residence: Bristol, Gloucester, England parents: John Rowland, Mary record title: England Births and Christenings, 1538-1975 name: Ann Rowland gender: Female baptism/christening date: 25 Jul 1784 baptism/christening place: Bristol, Gloucester, England father's name: John Rowland mother's name: Mary indexing project (batch) number: C01717-8 system origin: England. source film number: 1596677 England Deaths and Burials, 1538-1991 burial: 10 Sep 1789 Bristol, Gloucester, England record title: England Deaths and Burials, 1538-1991 name: Ann Rowland gender: Female burial date: 10 Sep 1789 burial place: Bristol, Gloucester, England indexing project (batch) number: I04146-4 system origin: England. source film number: 1595986

ii. **Mary Rowland**, born Oct 1794, in Bristol, Gloucestershire, England, christened 8 Oct 1794, in Bristol, Gloucestershire, England.
     England Births and Christenings, 1538-1975 residence: Bristol, Gloucester, England parents: John Rowland, Mary record title: England Births and Christenings, 1538-1975 name: Mary Rowland gender: Female baptism/christening date: 08 Oct 1794 baptism/christening place: Temple Church, Bristol, Gloucester, England father's name: John Rowland mother's name: Mary indexing project (batch) number: C01747-2 system origin: England. source film number: 1596178

iii. **John Rowland**, born about Aug 1796, in Bristol, Gloucestershire, England, christened 4 Sep 1797, in Bristol, Gloucestershire, England.
     England Births and Christenings, 1538-1975 residence: Bristol, Gloucester, England parents: John Rowland, Mary record title: England Births and Christenings, 1538-1975 name: John Rowland gender: Male baptism/christening date: 04 Sep 1797 baptism/christening place: Temple Church, Bristol, Gloucester, England father's name: John Rowland mother's name: Mary indexing project (batch) number: C01747-2 system origin: England. source film number: 1596178

iv. **Ann Catharine Rowland**, born Dec 1797, in Bristol, Gloucestershire, England, christened 25 Dec 1797, in Bristol, Gloucestershire, England.
     England Births and Christenings, 1538-1975 residence: Bristol, Gloucester, England parents: John Rowland, Mary record title: England Births and Christenings, 1538-1975 name: Ann Catharine Rowland gender: Female

baptism/christening date: 25 Dec 1797 baptism/christening place: St James, Bristol, Gloucester, England father's name: John Rowland mother's name: Mary indexing project (batch) number: C00887-7 system origin: England. source film number: 1596534

 v. **George Rowland**,[148,218,221,228] born Apr 1799, in Bristol, Gloucestershire, England, died 28 Jun 1874, in Hanham, Gloucestershire, England.[218]

83. Mary Ann Watkins was born Mar 1761, in Bristol, Gloucestershire, England, christened 17 Mar 1761, in Bristol, Gloucestershire, England, died Feb 1806, in Westerleigh, Gloucestershire, England, buried 26 Feb 1806, in Westerleigh, Gloucestershire, England. She was the daughter of John Watkins and Mary Kelly. She married John Rowland 2 Apr 1782, in Bristol, Gloucestershire, England. He was the son of George Rowland and Jane Skinner.
Notes for Mary Ann Watkins:

residence: Gloucester, England parents: John Watkins, Mary record title: England Births and Christenings, 1538-1975 name: Mary Ann Watkins gender: Female baptism/christening date: 17 Mar 1761 baptism/christening place: ST MARYS REDCLIFFE, BRISTOL, GLOUCESTER, ENGLAND father's name: John Watkins mother's name: Mary indexing project (batch) number: C17254-1 system origin: England-ODM source film number: 1595678

84. Leonard Rogers was born Jun 1759, in Bristol, Gloucestershire, England, christened 4 Jun 1759, in Bitton, Gloucestershire, England, died before 1841, in England. He was the son of Isaac Rogers and Silvester Stone. He married Ann Burges[311] 13 May 1787, in Bitton, Gloucestershire, England. She was the daughter of Ebenezer Burges and Diana Reynolds.
Notes for Leonard Rogers:

Ann

Children of Leonard Rogers and Ann Burges:

 i. **Leonard Tilly Rogers**, born Aug 1787, in Bristol, Gloucestershire, England, christened 26 Aug 1787, in St George, Bristol, Gloucestershire, England, died Jul 1789, in Bristol, Gloucestershire, England, buried 23 Jul 1789, in St George, Bristol, Gloucestershire, England.
England Births and Christenings, 1538-1975 residence: Bristol, Gloucester, England parents: Leonard Rogers, Ann record title: England Births and Christenings, 1538-1975 name: Leonard-Tilly Rogers gender: Male baptism/christening date: 26 Aug 1787 baptism/christening place: St. George's, Bristol, Gloucester, England father's name: Leonard Rogers mother's name: Ann indexing project (batch) number: C00893-5 system origin: England. source film number: 1596488 England Deaths and Burials, 1538-1991 burial: 23 Jul 1789 St. George, Bristol, Gloucester, England parents: Leonard Rogers, Ann record title: England Deaths and Burials, 1538-1991 name: Leonard Rogers gender: Male burial

date: 23 Jul 1789 burial place: St. George, Bristol, Gloucester, England father's name: Leonard Rogers mother's name: Ann indexing project (batch) number: I03976-9 system origin: England. source film number: 1595532

ii.   **Ann Rogers,**[219,220,221,222] born Dec 1795, in Hanham, Gloucestershire, England, died about 1882, in Gloucestershire, England.

85. Ann Burges was born Oct 1766, in Bristol, Gloucestershire, England, christened 29 Oct 1766, in Bristol, Gloucestershire, England, died before 1860, in England. She was the daughter of Ebenezer Burges and Diana Reynolds. She married Leonard Rogers 13 May 1787, in Bitton, Gloucestershire, England. He was the son of Isaac Rogers and Silvester Stone.
Notes for Ann Burges:

England Births and Christenings, 1538-1975 residence: Bristol, Gloucester, England parents: Ebinezer Burges record title: England Births and Christenings, 1538-1975 name: Ann Burges gender: Female baptism/christening date: 29 Oct 1766 baptism/christening place: Bristol, Gloucester, England father's name: Ebinezer Burges indexing project (batch) number: C01716-9 system origin: England. source film number: 1596677 England Marriages, 1538-1973 marriage: 13 May 1787 -Bitton, Gloucester, England spouse: Ann Burges record title: England Marriages, 1538-1973 groom's name: Leonard Rogers bride's name: Ann Burges marriage date: 13 May 1787 marriage place: Bitton, Gloucester, England indexing project (batch) number: I03618-9 system origin: England. source film number: 1595499

86. Joseph Elleston was born 27 Jan 1788, in Harpenden, Hertfordshire, England, christened 31 May 1788, in Harpenden, Hertfordshire, England, died 3 Jun 1854, in Greenwich, Kent, England, buried 8 Jun 1854, in Greenwich, Kent, England. He was the son of Joseph Ellerd and Lydia Mealing. He married Elizabeth Jennings[312,313] 31 May 1806, in Kent, England. She was the daughter of Stephen Jennings and Elizabeth Taylor.
Notes for Joseph Elleston:

Spelt : ELLESTON, ELLISTON, ELLERTON, ELLERD A shoemaker Death registration: Greenwich County: London Year of Registration: 1854 Quarter of Registration: june 3 1854 Volume No: Buried 8 Jun 1854 St Alphege, Greenwich Saint Alfege, Greenwich, Register of burials, P78/ALF, Item 076, P78/ALF/076. 1841 census (Elliston) shows family living at Maidenstone Hill, Greenwich (Not George) 1851 census 17, Maidenstone Hill, Greenwich

Children of Joseph Elleston and Elizabeth Jennings:

i.   **Joseph Elleston**, born Feb 1807, in Greenwich, Kent, England, christened 22 Feb 1807, in Greenwich St Alfege, Kent, England.
ii.   **George Elleston,**[231] born 1816, in Greenwich, Kent, England, died Dec 1849, in Lewisham, Kent, England.
iii.   **Martha Elleston**, born 26 Oct 1817, in Greenwich, Kent, England, christened 21 Nov 1817, in Greenwich, Kent, England.
       Christened in St Alphage, Greenwich ref: Birth: 26 Oct 1817 Christening: 21 Nov

1817 St Alphage, Greenwich, Kent Father: Joseph Elliston Mother: Elizabeth Index project #: C00632-3; Film #: 254592 1851 census she was visiting her parents

    iv.   **Samuel Elleston**, born 1826, in Greenwich, Kent, England.

    v.   **Abigail Elleston**, born 1829, in Greenwich, Kent, England, christened 13 Apr 1829, in Greenwich St Alfege, Kent, England.

87. Elizabeth Jennings was born Jan 1790, in Greenwich, Kent, England, christened 24 Jan 1790, in Greenwich, Kent, England, died Jul 1848, in Greenwich, Kent, England. She was the daughter of Stephen Jennings and Elizabeth Taylor. She married Joseph Elleston[314] 31 May 1806, in Kent, England. He was the son of Joseph Ellerd and Lydia Mealing.

Notes for Elizabeth Jennings:

spellings varied - Elleston - Elliston

88. Abraham Langley was born 25 Feb 1789, in Marylebone, London, England, christened 3 Apr 1789, in St Marylebone, London, England, died before 1880, in England. He was the son of Isaac Langley and Elizabeth Day. He married Elizabeth Bayse[315] 23 Apr 1815, in London, England. She was the daughter of Frederick Bayse and Mary Diman Pike.

Children of Abraham Langley and Elizabeth Bayse:

    i.   **Mary Langley**,[231] born 1816, in Stepney, Middlesex, England, died Sep 1891, in Greenwich, Kent, England.

89. Elizabeth Bayse was born Nov 1789, in London, England, christened 15 Nov 1789, in St George in The East, Stepney, London, England, died before 1880, in England. She was the daughter of Frederick Bayse and Mary Diman Pike. She married Abraham Langley[316,317] 23 Apr 1815, in London, England. He was the son of Isaac Langley and Elizabeth Day.

90. Thomas Humber was born Jul 1793, in Kingston Russell, Dorset, England, christened 28 Jul 1793, in Long Bredy, Dorset, England, died 4 Feb 1865, in Litton Cheney, Dorset, England. He was the son of Joseph Humber and Margaret Tidby. He married Elizabeth Churchill[318,319] 8 Mar 1813, in Litton Cheney, Dorset, England. She was the daughter of John Churchill and Elizabeth Jacob.

Children of Thomas Humber and Elizabeth Churchill:

    i.   **John Churchill Humber**,[162,233,234,235,236] born Aug 1813, in Litton Cheney, Dorset, England, died Mar 1892, in Sherborne, Dorset, England.

    ii.   **Robert Humber**,[320] born Mar 1817, in Litton Cheney, Dorset, England, christened 16 Mar 1817, in Litton Cheney, Dorset, England.

    iii.   **Anne Humber**,[321] born Mar 1819, in Litton Cheney, Dorset, England, christened 28 Mar 1819, in Litton Cheney, Dorset, England.

    iv.   **Mary Humber**,[322] born May 1824, in Long Bredy, Dorset, England, christened 5

Jun 1824, in Long Bredy, Dorset, England.

    v.   **Elizabeth Humber**,[323] born Oct 1829, in Long Bredy, Dorset, England, christened 1 Nov 1829, in Long Bredy, Dorset, England.

    vi.   **Maria Humber**,[324] born Jun 1832, in Long Bredy, Dorset, England, christened 1 Jul 1832, in Long Bredy, Dorset, England.

91. Elizabeth Churchill was born Aug 1791, in Litton Cheney, Dorset, England, christened 4 Sep 1791, in Litton Cheney, Dorset, England, died about 1834, in Bridport, Dorset, England. She was the daughter of John Churchill and Elizabeth Jacob. She married Thomas Humber[325,326] 8 Mar 1813, in Litton Cheney, Dorset, England. He was the son of Joseph Humber and Margaret Tidby.

92. William Hunt was born 1807, in Leigh, Dorset, England, died 1851, in Thornford, Dorset, England. He was the son of John Hunt and Grace Burt. He married Sarah Matthews[327] 14 Sep 1826, in Stour Provost, Dorset, England. She was the daughter of John Matthews and Sarah Fowler.

Children of William Hunt and Sarah Matthews:

    i.   **Julia E. Hunt**,[162,232,233] born 1829, in Leigh, Dorset, England, died 1893, in Leigh, Dorset, England.

    ii.   **Silas Hunt**, born 1830, in Leigh, Dorset, England.

    iii.   **Emily Hunt**, born 1840, in Leigh, Dorset, England, christened 16 Aug 1840, in Yetminster, Dorset, England.

93. Sarah Matthews was born Jun 1803, in Leigh, Dorset, England, christened 11 Jun 1803, in Sherborne, Dorset, England, died 8 Nov 1854, in Thornford, Dorset, England. She was the daughter of John Matthews and Sarah Fowler. She married William Hunt 14 Sep 1826, in Stour Provost, Dorset, England. He was the son of John Hunt and Grace Burt.

94. William Humphry was born 1777, in Greatworth, Northamptonshire, England, christened 13 Jul 1777, in Greatworth, Northamptonshire, England, died 1834, in Marston St Lawrence, Northamptonshire, England, buried 16 Dec 1834, in Marston St Lawrence, Northamptonshire, England. He was the son of William Humphry and Ann Basely. He married Ann Coleman[328] 5 Aug 1800, in Blakesley, Northamptonshire, England. She was the daughter of John Coleman and Elizabeth Franklin.

Children of William Humphry and Ann Coleman:

    i.   **John Humphrey**, born 1802, in Marston St Lawrence, Northamptonshire, England, christened 2 Sep 1802, in Marston St Lawrence, Northamptonshire, England, died 1872, in Fritwell, Oxfordshire, England, buried 17 Dec 1872, in Fritwell, Oxfordshire, England. He married Mary Stanton about 1825, in Greatworth, Northamptonshire, England. Mary Stanton was born about 1803, in Greatworth, Northamptonshire, England, christened 28 Aug 1808, in Marston St Lawrence, Northamptonshire, England.

    ii.   **Elizabeth Humphreys**, born 1804, in Marston St Lawrence, Northamptonshire, England, christened 4 May 1804, in Marston St Lawrence, Northamptonshire, England.

    iii.   **James Humphreys**,[153,240] born 1808, in Greatworth, Northamptonshire, England, died 1886, in Brackley, Northamptonshire, England.[237]

    iv.   **Anne Humphrys**, born 1810, in Marston St Lawrence, Northamptonshire, England, christened 13 Jun 1810, in Marston St Lawrence, Northamptonshire, England, died 1811, in Marston St Lawrence, Northamptonshire, England, buried 24 Apr 1811, in Marston St Lawrence, Northamptonshire, England.

95. Ann Coleman was born 1 Nov 1778, in Rushton, Northamptonshire, England, christened 9 Nov 1778, in Rushton, Northamptonshire, England, died Aug 1842, in Marston St Lawrence, Northamptonshire, England, buried 4 Sep 1842, in Marston St Lawrence, Northamptonshire, England. She was the daughter of John Coleman and Elizabeth Franklin. She married William Humphry 5 Aug 1800, in Blakesley, Northamptonshire, England. He was the son of William Humphry and Ann Basely.

96. Edward Chester was born 1779, in Marston St Lawrence, Northamptonshire, England, died Oct 1842, in Brackley, Northamptonshire, England. He was the son of William Chester and Susannah Calloway. He married Lydia Savage[329,330,331] 1813, in Marston St Lawrence, Northamptonshire, England. She was the daughter of Samuel Savage and Sarah Bodily.

Children of Edward Chester and Lydia Savage:

    i.   **Sarah Chester**,[155,258] born Mar 1814, in Greatworth, Northamptonshire, England, died 1879, in Brackley, Northamptonshire, England.[239]

    ii.   **Edward Chester**, born 1815, in Greatworth, Northamptonshire, England, died 1842.

    iii.   **George Chester**, born Mar 1816, in Greatworth, Northamptonshire, England, christened 11 Mar 1816, in Marston St Lawrence, Northamptonshire, England.

97. Lydia Savage was born 9 Jan 1783, in Green's Norton, Northamptonshire, England, died before 1861, in England. She was the daughter of Samuel Savage and Sarah Bodily. She married Edward Chester[238,332,333] 1813, in Marston St Lawrence, Northamptonshire, England. He was the son of William Chester and Susannah Calloway.
Notes for Lydia Savage:

Appears on 1841 Census

98. Thomas Lucas was born 21 Dec 1757, in Bygrave, Hertfordshire, England, christened 1762, in Bygrave, Hertfordshire, England, died 20 Dec 1862, in Wanstead, Essex, England. He was the son of Thomas Lucas and Mary Broyors. He married Jane Mayes[334,335] 29 Jan 1787, in Ilford, Essex, England. She was the daughter of Nathaniel Mayes and Jane Stevens.
Notes for Thomas Lucas:

CHELMSFORD CHRONICAL - FRIDAY 2ND JANUARY 1863 EXTRODINARY CASE OF LONGEVITY - On the 20th. Mr Thomas Lucas a native of Hertfordshire expired at Wanstead in this county, in his 105th year. He retained the use of all his faculties up to the period of his dissolution. His mother lived to the advanced age of 101. Deceased had been confined to his room only a few weeks previously to his demise, up to which period he enjoyed excellent health. The following interesting particulars connected with this centenarian are from the pen of Rev W.P. Wigram, rector of Wanstead, who was a very kind friend to the aged deceased for many years - Thomas Lucas was born in Bygrave in Hertfordshire and was baptised in 1762. The certificate of his baptism, obtained a few years ago. According to what his mother told him he was either 4 or 5 years old when baptised, and he assured me he remembered walking to church on that occasion when a younger brother was baptised with him. The old man's memory was so good there seems to be no reason to doubt the accuracy of his statements. His family consider him to be 105, he was formally a Bailiff to Mr Long Wellesley at Wanstead House. Had been married and had several children of whom some at advanced age are still living. He had a remarkable healthy appetite and clear grey eyes, was of courteous manners and of a very cheerful temper and retained excellent health and the complete use of his faculties including his memory hearing and eyesight till almost the end. Until a few months of his death he chopped his own firewood, was conversational and agreeable to visitors, and was generally in full enjoyment of life. He received much fondness from many of my parishioners which contributed doubtless to the prolongation of his days. As he died on the 20th December (the day before his birthday which was 21st December) I understand that he had, in point of law, completed 105 years. He suffered considerably during the last 6 weeks but his end was tranquil and happy.

Children of Thomas Lucas and Jane Mayes:

     i.   **Thomas Lucas**,[171,246,247] born 1787, in Leytonstone, Essex, England, died Jul 1869, in Epping, Essex, England.

99. Jane Mayes was born Mar 1769, in Hornchurch, Essex, England, christened 12 Mar 1769, in Hornchurch, Essex, England, died 1843, in West Ham, Essex, England. She was the daughter of Nathaniel Mayes and Jane Stevens. She married Thomas Lucas[334,336,337,338,339] 29 Jan 1787, in Ilford, Essex, England. He was the son of Thomas Lucas and Mary Broyors.

100. William Young was born Mar 1763, in Wanstead, Essex, England, christened 13 Mar 1763, in St Botolph, Bishopsgate, London, England, died before 1851, in England. He was the son of Richard Young and Elizabeth Merigest. He married Ann Elizabeth Turner[340] 21 May 1783, in Wanstead, Essex, England. She was the daughter of Francis Turner and Anne Horsley.
Notes for William Young:

aka YONGE

Children of William Young and Ann Elizabeth Turner:

     i.   **Elizabeth Young**, born Mar 1784, in Wanstead, Essex, England, christened 28 Mar

1784, in Wanstead, Essex, England.

ii. **Anne Young**, born Apr 1785, in Wanstead, Essex, England, christened 8 May 1785, in Wanstead, Essex, England.

iii. **William Young**, born Dec 1786, in Wanstead, Essex, England, christened 17 Dec 1786, in Wanstead, Essex, England.

iv. **Mary Young**, born Sep 1788, in Wanstead, Essex, England, christened 14 Sep 1788, in Wanstead, Essex, England.

v. **Sarah Young**,[171,241,242] born 20 Feb 1790, in Wanstead, Essex, England, died 1861, in West Ham, Essex, England.

vi. **Maria Young**, born Aug 1791, in Wanstead, Essex, England, christened 21 Aug 1791, in Wanstead, Essex, England, died Mar 1792, in Wanstead, Essex, England, buried 17 Mar 1792, in Wanstead, Essex, England.

vii. **John Young**, born Feb 1793, in Wanstead, Essex, England, christened 24 Feb 1793, in Wanstead, Essex, England.

viii. **Frances Young**, born Jan 1795, in Wanstead, Essex, England, christened 18 Jan 1795, in Wanstead, Essex, England.

ix. **Thomas Young**, born Apr 1796, in Wanstead, Essex, England, christened 17 Apr 1796, in Wanstead, Essex, England.

x. **Grace Young**, born Aug 1797, in Wanstead, Essex, England, christened 20 Aug 1797, in Wanstead, Essex, England.

xi. **Susanna Young**, born 11 Aug 1799, in Wanstead, Essex, England, christened 29 Aug 1799, in Wanstead, Essex, England, died 1877, in Edmonton, Middlesex, England.

xii. **Joseph Young**, born 22 Feb 1802, in Wanstead, Essex, England, christened 23 Feb 1802, in Wanstead, Essex, England, died 23 Jul 1875, in Peterson, Morgan, Utah, United States, buried 25 Jul 1875, in Peterson, Morgan, Utah, United States. Residences: 1802, Wanstead, Essex, England; 1870, Utah, United States. He married Jane Fleming 17 Jul 1823, in Essex, England. Jane Fleming was born 12 Apr 1804, in Wanstead, Essex, England, christened 5 May 1805, in Barking, Essex, England, died 17 Mar 1878, in Peterson, Morgan, Utah, United States, buried in Peterson, Morgan, Utah, United States.
Mormon Pioneer Overland Travel, 1847–1868 Young, Joseph Birth Date: 22 Feb. 1802 Death Date: 23 July 1875 Gender: Male Age: 64 Company: John D. Holladay Company (1866) Pioneer Information: wife and 2 children Company Information: 350 individuals and 69 wagons were in the company when it began its journey from the outfitting post at Wyoming, Nebraska (the west bank of the Missouri River about 40 miles south of Omaha) Burial Information: YOUNG, Joseph Birth: 2/22/1802 Death: 7/23/1875 Burial:// Place of Birth: Wanstead, Essex, England Place of Death: Peterson, Morgan, Utah Grave Location: Peterson Cemetery Source: Veloy T. Dickson Comments: Relatives: YOUNG, Jane Flemming (Spouse)
Notes for Jane Fleming: Burial Information: YOUNG, Joseph Birth: 2/22/1802 Death: 7/23/1875 Burial:// Place of Birth: Wanstead, Essex, England Place of

Death: Peterson, Morgan, Utah Grave Location: Peterson Cemetery Source: Veloy T. Dickson Comments: Relatives: YOUNG, Jane Flemming (Spouse)

xiii. **Loay Young**, born 10 Jul 1803, in Wanstead, Essex, England, christened 11 Sep 1803, in Wanstead, Essex, England.

xiv. **Samuel Young**, born Feb 1806, in Wanstead, Essex, England, christened 14 Feb 1806, in Wanstead, Essex, England.

101. Ann Elizabeth Turner was born 1765, in West Ham, Essex, England, christened 10 Mar 1765, in West Ham, Essex, England, died before 1865, in England. She was the daughter of Francis Turner and Anne Horsley. She married William Young[340,341] 21 May 1783, in Wanstead, Essex, England. He was the son of Richard Young and Elizabeth Merigest.

102. James Stringer was born 1770, in Barking, Essex, England, died 7 Jun 1853, in Barking, Essex, England, buried 11 Jun 1853, in Barking, Essex, England. He was the son of Charles Stringer and Martha Blandford. He married Elizabeth Sarah Wyten[342,343] 8 Apr 1799, in Barking, Essex, England. She was the daughter of William Witton and Elizabeth Mayor.

Children of James Stringer and Elizabeth Sarah Wyten:

i. **James Stringer**,[251,252,253] born 22 Jan 1800, in Wanstead, Essex, England, died Dec 1887, in Romford, Essex, England.[248]

ii. **George Stringer**, born 1 Nov 1800, in Stratford, Essex, England, christened 26 Jan 1801, in Wanstead, Essex, England, died Dec 1887, in Romford, Essex, England, buried 8 Dec 1887, in Barkingside, Essex, England. He married Mary Jacobs 13 Nov 1822, in Barking, Essex, England. Mary Jacobs was born 2 Oct 1799, in Bildeston, Suffolk, England, christened 10 Jun 1810, in Bildeston, Suffolk, England, died Jun 1890, in Romford, Essex, England.

iii. **Charles Stringer**, born 30 Sep 1803, in Barking, Essex, England, christened 23 Oct 1803, in Barking, Essex, England, died 16 Apr 1838, in Barking, Essex, England.

iv. **Hannah Stringer**, born 14 May 1805, in Barking, Essex, England, christened 9 Jun 1805, in Barking, Essex, England, died before 1809, in Barking, Essex, England.

v. **William Stringer**, born 4 Jun 1807, in Barking, Essex, England, christened 28 Jun 1807, in Barking, Essex, England.

103. Elizabeth Sarah Wyten was born 3 Sep 1781, in Barking, Essex, England, christened 3 Oct 1781, in Barking, Essex, England, died May 1855, in Barking, Essex, England, buried 27 May 1855, in Barking, Essex, England. She was the daughter of William Witton and Elizabeth Mayor. She married James Stringer[344,345,346] 8 Apr 1799, in Barking, Essex, England. He was the son of Charles Stringer and Martha Blandford.

Notes for Elizabeth Sarah Wyten:

Name spelled WHITTON Parish Record Collection - Baptism Record Day: 3 Month: 10 Year: 1781

Forename: Elizabeth Othernames: Sarah Surname: Whitton Fathers forenames: Fathers occupation: Victualler Mothers forenames: Elizabeth Birth date: Address: Brick Lane Location of church: Spitalfields Parish: Christ Church Church address: Commercial Street Source Ref: X095/621 Original Note: 30 days old Record source: Docklands Ancestors 1851 Census - aged 79. Widow, Market Gardner (Mossford Green, Barking Side, Essex)

104. Richard Hyde was born about 1778, in Barking, Essex, England, died before 1840, in England. He was the son of Richard Hyde and Ann Rainbird. He married Sarah Briggs[347] 28 Mar 1796, in St Dunstan, Stepney, London, England. She was the daughter of John Briggs and Sarah Timbrell.
Notes for Richard Hyde:

aka - William, William Richard, Richard William HYDE

Children of Richard Hyde and Sarah Briggs:

     i.   **Mary Elizabeth Hyde**,[249] born Nov 1798, in Barking, Essex, England, died 14 Feb 1854, in Romford, Essex, England.[250]

105. Sarah Briggs was born 21 Jan 1773, in Shoreditch, London, England, christened 23 Feb 1773, in St Leonard's Shoreditch, London, England, died before 1840, in England. She was the daughter of John Briggs and Sarah Timbrell. She married Richard Hyde[348,349,350] 28 Mar 1796, in St Dunstan, Stepney, London, England. He was the son of Richard Hyde and Ann Rainbird.

106. Thomas Giles was born 1772, in Dover, Kent, England, christened 2 Jan 1773, in Lamberhurst, Kent, England, died Nov 1859, in Kent, England. He was the son of George Giles and Martha Stevens. He married Sarah Holmes[351] 12 Jul 1799, in Dover, Kent, England.[351] She was the daughter of William Holmes and Elizabeth Read.
Notes for Thomas Giles:

Name: Thomas GILES Surname: Giles Given Name: Thomas Sex: M Christening: 2 Jan 1773 Lamberhurst, Kent Death: ABT Nov 1859 in Medway area, Kent Residence: 1851 Borstal Lane, Rochester, Kent Occupation: an agricultural labourer 1851

Children of Thomas Giles and Sarah Holmes:

     i.   **Thomas Giles**,[254,255,258,259] born 1800, in Dover, Kent, England, died 1 Mar 1872, in Stepney, Middlesex, England.
     ii.   **Sarah Giles**, born 29 Mar 1802, in Dover, Kent, England, christened 11 Apr 1802, in Dover, Kent, England.
     iii. **William Holmes Giles**, born 1804, in Dover, Kent, England, christened 22 Jan 1804, in Dover, Kent, England.
     iv. **Elizabeth Giles**, born 1805, in Dover, Kent, England, christened 29 Dec 1805, in Dover, Kent, England.

70

v.   **George Giles**, born 1808, in Dover, Kent, England, christened 17 Oct 1808, in Dover, Kent, England, died 1809, in Dover, Kent, England.

vi.   **George Collison Giles**, born 7 Nov 1809, in Dover, Kent, England, christened 28 Nov 1809, in Dover, Kent, England.

107. Sarah Holmes was born 5 Oct 1779, in Dover, Kent, England, christened 31 Oct 1779, in Dover, Kent, England, died 1870, in Hollingbourne, Kent, England. She was the daughter of William Holmes and Elizabeth Read. She married Thomas Giles[351] 12 Jul 1799, in Dover, Kent, England.[351] He was the son of George Giles and Martha Stevens.

108. John Baldwin was born 2 Mar 1767, in Whitechapel, London, England, christened 23 Mar 1767, in Queenhithe, London, England, died before 1860, in England. He was the son of Henry Baldwin and Rebecca Smith. He married Rebecca Dixon[352] 18 Jan 1802, in St Sepulchre, London, England.[352] She was the daughter of William Scofield Dixon and Mary Ann Miller.
Notes for John Baldwin:

(Batch) Number: M00061-7; Source Film Number: 375005; Reference Number: v 4 Baptism records show as living in Montague Street, Whitechapel, London. Christened at: St Michael Queenhithe, London, England

Children of John Baldwin and Rebecca Dixon:

i.   **Hannah Maria Baldwin**,[254,255] born May 1805, in North Shoebury, Essex, England, died 13 Jan 1883, in Stepney, Middlesex, England.

109. Rebecca Dixon was born Apr 1770, in Whitechapel, London, England, christened 1 May 1770, in Whitechapel, London, England, died before 1860, in England. She was the daughter of William Scofield Dixon and Mary Ann Miller. She married John Baldwin[353] 18 Jan 1802, in St Sepulchre, London, England.[352] He was the son of Henry Baldwin and Rebecca Smith.

110. William Wine was born 13 Oct 1782, in Bethnal Green, London, England,[354] christened 8 Dec 1782, in Bethnal Green, London, England,[354] died before 1880, in England. He was the son of William Wine and Martha Vennor. He married Sarah Richardson[355,356,357] about 1803, in Stepney, Middlesex, England.[355] She was the daughter of William Richardson and Ann Yeates.
Notes for William Wine:

Occupation on James birth cert - Wire drawer - 1817 Christening at St Matthews

Children of William Wine and Sarah Richardson:

i.   **William Wine**, born 18 Mar 1804, in Shoreditch, London, England, christened 29 Apr 1804, in Shoreditch, London, England. He married Mary Cleghorn 9 Feb 1824, in Stepney, Middlesex, England. Mary Cleghorn was born about 1804, in Stepney,

Middlesex, England.

ii. **Henry Charles Wine**, born 9 Apr 1814, in Hackney, Middlesex, England, christened 13 Nov 1814, in Hackney, Middlesex, England.

iii. **Joseph Richard Wine**,[358] born 25 Oct 1815, in Shoreditch, London, England, christened 24 Dec 1815, in Hackney, Middlesex, England.

iv. **James Vanner Wine**,[262,265] born 7 Oct 1817, in Hackney, Middlesex, England, died Dec 1838, in St Luke, Middlesex, England.

v. **Mary Ann Wine**,[359] born 15 Nov 1819, in Shoreditch, London, England, christened 25 Dec 1819, in Hackney, Middlesex, England. She married William Henry Lilly 20 Feb 1837, in Shoreditch, London, England. William Henry Lilly was born 22 Apr 1808, in Bethnal Green, London, England, christened 30 Nov 1808, in Shoreditch, London, England, died 1873, in Bethnal Green, London, England. She was a Pastry Cook
Notes for William Henry Lilly: He was a Baker They appeared in the census on 6 June 1841 in Bethnal Green. They appeared in the census on 30 March 1851 in Mile End Old Town. They appeared in the census on 7 April 1861 in Bethnal Green

111. Sarah Richardson was born 11 Nov 1782, in Westminster, London, England, christened 1 Dec 1782, in Westminster, London, England, died 15 Oct 1854, in Hackney, Middlesex, England. She was the daughter of William Richardson and Ann Yeates. She married William Wine[354,355] about 1803, in Stepney, Middlesex, England.[355] He was the son of William Wine and Martha Vennor.
Notes for Sarah Richardson:

Name: Sarah Richardson Gender: Female Baptism/Christening Date: 1 Dec 1782 Baptism/Christening Place: SAINT Clement Danes, Westminster, London, England

112. William Thomas Rapley was born Jan 1784, in Rotherhithe, London, England, christened 25 Jan 1784, in St Mary, Rotherhithe, London, England, died Mar 1852, in Stepney, Middlesex, England, buried 14 Mar 1852, in Tower Hamlets, Middlesex, England. He was the son of Thomas Rapley and Mary Ann Roberts. He married Martha Steel Mott[361,362] 14 Mar 1808, in St Clement Danes, Westminster, London, England.[360] She was the daughter of Stephen Mott and Ann Steel.
Notes for William Thomas Rapley:

aka RAP, RAPP, RAPLEY, RAPPLY, RAPPLEY 1851 census shows him living in the Workhouse Buried at St Dunstan and All Saints

Children of William Thomas Rapley and Martha Steel Mott:

i. **Elizabeth Rapp**,[363] born 5 Dec 1808, in Stepney, Middlesex, England, christened 12 Feb 1809, in Stepney, Middlesex, England.

ii. **Mary Ann Rapp**,[262,263,264] born 25 Aug 1811, in Stepney, Middlesex, England, died Apr 1839, in Stepney, Middlesex, England.

iii. **William Rapp**,[364] born 15 Jan 1814, in Stepney, Middlesex, England, christened 16

Jan 1814, in Stepney, Middlesex, England.

    iv.   **Joseph Rapp,**[365] born 29 Oct 1816, in Stepney, Middlesex, England, christened 6 Apr 1817, in Stepney, Middlesex, England.

    v.   **Martha Rapp,**[366] born 17 Dec 1818, in Stepney, Middlesex, England, christened 29 Dec 1818, in Stepney, Middlesex, England.

113. Martha Steel Mott was born 18 Jan 1779, in Rotherhithe, London, England, christened 14 Mar 1779, in St Mary, Rotherhithe, London, England, died 1842, in Stepney, Middlesex, England. She was the daughter of Stephen Mott and Ann Steel. She married William Thomas Rapley[367] 14 Mar 1808, in St Clement Danes, Westminster, London, England.[360] He was the son of Thomas Rapley and Mary Ann Roberts.
Notes for Martha Steel Mott:

aka: Motts on Bap register Shown as 8 weeks old at baptism

Generation No. 8

114. William Aldesworth was born about 1736, in Stanton Harcourt, Oxfordshire, England, died Feb 1781, in Stanton Harcourt, Oxfordshire, England, buried 21 Feb 1781, in Stanton Harcourt, Oxfordshire, England. He was the son of William Aldesworth and Mary Baker. He married Mary Tynedall[368,369] 19 Feb 1759, in Stanton Harcourt, Oxfordshire, England.[267] She was the daughter of Nathaniel Tindal and Mary Hanzel.
Notes for William Aldesworth:

Name spelt : Aldsworth

Children of William Aldesworth and Mary Tynedall:

  i.   **Mary Aldesworth**,[370] born Jul 1759, in Stanton Harcourt, Oxfordshire, England, died Jul 1759, in Stanton Harcourt, Oxfordshire, England, buried 14 Jul 1759, in Stanton Harcourt, Oxfordshire, England.

  ii. **William Aldsworth**,[269] born Aug 1760, in Stanton Harcourt, Oxfordshire, England, died Oct 1796, in Stanton Harcourt, Oxfordshire, England.

  iii. **John Aldsworth**,[371] born 6 Oct 1762, in Stanton Harcourt, Oxfordshire, England, christened 10 Oct 1762, in Stanton Harcourt, Oxfordshire, England, died 10 Nov 1833, in Northmoor, Oxfordshire, England, buried 15 Nov 1833, in Northmoor, Oxfordshire, England. He married Anne Weeks[372] 15 Aug 1790, in Northmoor, Oxfordshire, England. Anne Weeks was born 25 Aug 1763, in Northmoor, Oxfordshire, England, died 24 Jun 1829, in Northmoor, Oxfordshire, England.

  iv. **Mary Aldsworth**,[373] born Jul 1764, in Stanton Harcourt, Oxfordshire, England, christened 24 Jul 1764, in Stanton Harcourt, Oxfordshire, England, died 1785, in Witney, Oxfordshire, England, buried in Witney, Oxfordshire, England.

  v.   **Hannah Aldsworth**, born Sep 1766, in Stanton Harcourt, Oxfordshire, England, christened 21 Sep 1766, in Stanton Harcourt, Oxfordshire, England, died Oct 1783, in Stanton Harcourt, Oxfordshire, England, buried 9 Oct 1783, in Stanton Harcourt, Oxfordshire, England.
       Possibly died from inhalation of fumes/vapours/toxic gasses resulting from the Volcano Laki, Iceland'

  vi. **Ann Aldsworth**,[374] born Jan 1769, in Stanton Harcourt, Oxfordshire, England, christened 30 Jan 1769, in Stanton Harcourt, Oxfordshire, England, died 1850, in Bicester, Oxfordshire, England. She married John Shepherd 7 Feb 1785, in Stanton Harcourt, Oxfordshire, England. John Shepherd was born 1765, in Stanton Harcourt, Oxfordshire, England, christened 3 Jul 1765, in Stanton Harcourt, Oxfordshire, England, died 1850, in Bicester, Oxfordshire, England, buried 1850, in Bicester, Oxfordshire, England.
       Notes for John Shepherd: Huntsman also spelled /Shepherd?

vii. **Martha Aldsworth**,[375] born Dec 1770, in Stanton Harcourt, Oxfordshire, England, christened 20 Dec 1770, in Stanton Harcourt, Oxfordshire, England, died Mar 1786, in Stanton Harcourt, Oxfordshire, England, buried 14 Mar 1786, in Stanton Harcourt, Oxfordshire, England.

viii. **Robert Aldsworth**,[376] born Oct 1775, in Stanton Harcourt, Oxfordshire, England, christened 6 Oct 1775, in Stanton Harcourt, Oxfordshire, England, died Oct 1798, in Stanton Harcourt, Oxfordshire, England, buried 25 Oct 1798, in Stanton Harcourt, Oxfordshire, England.

115. Mary Tynedall was born about 1738, in Stanton Harcourt, Oxfordshire, England, died Aug 1781, in Stanton Harcourt, Oxfordshire, England, buried 2 Sep 1781, in Stanton Harcourt, Oxfordshire, England. She was the daughter of Nathaniel Tindal and Mary Hanzel. She married William Aldesworth[377] 19 Feb 1759, in Stanton Harcourt, Oxfordshire, England.[267] He was the son of William Aldesworth and Mary Baker.
Notes for Mary Tynedall:

aka TYNDALL, TYNDELL

116. John Townshend was born Apr 1733, in Witney, Oxfordshire, England, christened 6 Apr 1733, in Witney, Oxfordshire, England, died before 1820, in England. He was the son of Henry Townshend and Sarah Tewksbury. He married Elizabeth Hopcraft[378] 2 Dec 1759, in Stonesfield, Oxfordshire, England. She was the daughter of Robert Hopcraft and Mary Barton.
Notes for John Townshend:

Name spelt TOWNSHEND on Oxford Marriage bond1759

Children of John Townshend and Elizabeth Hopcraft:

i. **Hannah Townsend**,[266,268] born Mar 1761, in Bletchingdon, Oxfordshire, England, died May 1819, in Stanton Harcourt, Oxfordshire, England.

ii. **Edward Townsend**,[379] born Mar 1764, in Bletchingdon, Oxfordshire, England, christened 1 Apr 1764, in Bletchingdon, Oxfordshire, England.

iii. **John Townshend**,[380] born Jan 1767, in Bletchingdon, Oxfordshire, England, christened 1 Feb 1767, in Bletchingdon, Oxfordshire, England.

iv. **Mary Townsend**,[381] born 24 Apr 1770, in Bletchingdon, Oxfordshire, England, christened 29 Apr 1770, in Bletchingdon, Oxfordshire, England.

v. **William Townsend**,[382] born Aug 1773, in Bletchingdon, Oxfordshire, England, christened 15 Aug 1773, in Bletchingdon, Oxfordshire, England.
William and Susanna were twins

vi. **Susanna Townsend**,[382] born Aug 1773, in Bletchingdon, Oxfordshire, England, christened 15 Aug 1773, in Bletchingdon, Oxfordshire, England.
William and Susanna were twins

117. Elizabeth Hopcraft was born about 1742, in Bucknell, Oxfordshire, England, died before 1821, in England. She was the daughter of Robert Hopcraft and Mary Barton. She married John Townshend[378] 2 Dec 1759, in Stonesfield, Oxfordshire, England. He was the son of Henry Townshend and Sarah Tewksbury.

118. Charles Turner was born Dec 1720, in Hailey, Oxfordshire, England, christened 29 Dec 1720, in Witney, Oxfordshire, England, died Jan 1769, in Witney, Oxfordshire, England, buried 5 Feb 1769, in Witney, Oxfordshire, England. He was the son of Thomas Turner and Joane Hix. He married Ann Cox[383,384] 11 Sep 1738, in Ascott Under Wychwood, Oxfordshire, England. She was the daughter of Thomas Cox and Rose Ebsworth.

Children of Charles Turner and Ann Cox:

    i.   **Mary Turner,**[385,386] born Jan 1742, in Hailey, Oxfordshire, England, christened 22 Jan 1742, in Witney, Oxfordshire, England, died Oct 1746, in Hailey, Oxfordshire, England, buried 13 Oct 1746, in Witney, Oxfordshire, England.

    ii.   **Giles Turner,**[270] born about 1743, in Witney, Oxfordshire, England, died Oct 1818, in Ascott Under Wychwood, Oxfordshire, England.

    iii.   **John Turner,**[387] born Jun 1744, in Hailey, Oxfordshire, England, christened 29 Jun 1744, in Witney, Oxfordshire, England.

    iv.   **Richard Turner,**[388,389] born Jun 1746, in Hailey, Oxfordshire, England, christened 29 Jun 1746, in Witney, Oxfordshire, England, died Mar 1760, in Hailey, Oxfordshire, England, buried 23 Mar 1760, in Witney, Oxfordshire, England.

    v.   **Edward Turner,**[390] born Jun 1748, in Haily, Oxfordshire, England, christened 29 Jun 1748, in Witney, Oxfordshire, England.

    vi.   **Mary Turner,**[391,392] born Apr 1750, in Hailey, Oxfordshire, England, christened 16 Apr 1750, in Witney, Oxfordshire, England, died Apr 1753, in Hailey, Oxfordshire, England, buried 1 May 1753, in Witney, Oxfordshire, England.

    vii.   **Elizabeth Turner,**[392,393] born Aug 1752, in Hailey, Oxfordshire, England, christened 16 Aug 1752, in Witney, Oxfordshire, England, died Jul 1753, in Hailey, Oxfordshire, England, buried 19 Jul 1753, in Witney, Oxfordshire, England.

    viii.   **Sarah Turner,**[393] born Aug 1752, in Haily, Oxfordshire, England, christened 16 Aug 1752, in Witney, Oxfordshire, England.

    ix.   **Charles Turner,**[394] born Feb 1755, in Haily, Oxfordshire, England, christened 23 Feb 1755, in Haily, Oxfordshire, England.

119. Ann Cox was born about 1718, in Ramsden, Oxfordshire, England, christened 11 Feb 1718, in Langford, Oxfordshire, England, died Nov 1769, in Witney, Oxfordshire, England, buried 22 Nov 1769, in Witney, Oxfordshire, England. She was the daughter of Thomas Cox and Rose Ebsworth. She married Charles Turner[383,384,395] 11 Sep 1738, in Ascott Under Wychwood, Oxfordshire, England. He was the son of Thomas Turner and Joane Hix.

120. John Timms was born Dec 1705, in Ascott Under Wychwood, Oxfordshire, England, christened

28 Dec 1705, in Ascott Under Wychwood, Oxfordshire, England, died Nov 1777, in Ascott Under Wychwood, Oxfordshire, England, buried 30 Nov 1777, in Ascott Under Wychwood, Oxfordshire, England. He was the son of George Tims and Elizabeth Ferrimen. He married Elenor Cockins[396] 10 Nov 1731, in Steeple Aston, Oxfordshire, England. She was the daughter of John Cockins and Elizabeth Vennimore.

Children of John Timms and Elenor Cockins:

    i.   **John Timms**, born May 1733, in Ascott Under Wychwood, Oxfordshire, England, christened 3 Jun 1733, in Ascott Under Wychwood, Oxfordshire, England.

    ii.   **William Timms**, born Mar 1736, in Ascott Under Wychwood, Oxfordshire, England, christened 13 Mar 1736, in Ascott Under Wychwood, Oxfordshire, England.

    iii.   **Richard Timms**,[271] born 8 Jul 1739, in Ascott Under Wychwood, Oxfordshire, England, christened 8 Jul 1739, in Ascott Under Wychwood, Oxfordshire, England.

    iv.   **Thomas Timms**,[271] born 5 Feb 1741, in Ascott Under Wychwood, Oxfordshire, England, christened 5 Feb 1741, in Ascott Under Wychwood, Oxfordshire, England.

    v.   **Mary Timms**,[270,271] born 24 Feb 1744, in Ascott Under Wychwood, Oxfordshire, England, died 22 Jun 1828, in Ascott Under Wychwood, Oxfordshire, England.

121. Elenor Cockins was born 13 Oct 1699, in Upper Heyford, Oxfordshire, England, christened 29 Oct 1699, in Upper Heyford, Oxfordshire, England, died Jun 1759, in Steeple Aston, Oxfordshire, England, buried 28 Jun 1759, in Steeple Aston, Oxfordshire, England. She was the daughter of John Cockins and Elizabeth Vennimore. She married John Timms[396] 10 Nov 1731, in Steeple Aston, Oxfordshire, England. He was the son of George Tims and Elizabeth Ferrimen.

122. John Drinkwater was born Apr 1733, in Bampton, Oxfordshire, England, christened 25 Apr 1733, in Bampton, Oxfordshire, England. He was the son of John Drinkwater and Ann Lapper. He married Ann Windows 5 Feb 1754, in Bampton, Oxfordshire, England. She was the daughter of William Windows and Mary Grimsher.

Children of John Drinkwater and Ann Windows:

    i.   **Elizabeth Drinkwater**,[397] born Sep 1754, in Bampton, Oxfordshire, England, christened 19 Sep 1754, in Bampton, Oxfordshire, England, died Mar 1756, in Bampton, Oxfordshire, England, buried 12 Mar 1756, in Bampton, Oxfordshire, England.

    ii.   **William Drinkwater**,[398] born May 1756, in Bampton, Oxfordshire, England, christened 6 Jun 1756, in Bampton, Oxfordshire, England, died Feb 1769, in Bampton, Oxfordshire, England, buried 25 Feb 1769, in Bampton, Oxfordshire, England.

    iii.   **John Drinkwater**,[274] born Mar 1759, in Bampton, Oxfordshire, England.

iv. **James Drinkwater**,[399] born Jul 1761, in Bampton, Oxfordshire, England, christened 6 Aug 1761, in Bampton, Oxfordshire, England, died Dec 1764, in Bampton, Oxfordshire, England, buried 9 Dec 1764, in Bampton, Oxfordshire, England.
Recorded as private baptism

v. **Elizabeth Drinkwater**,[400] born Jan 1765, in Bampton, Oxfordshire, England, christened 16 Jan 1765, in Bampton, Oxfordshire, England, died Aug 1766, in Bampton, Oxfordshire, England, buried 4 Sep 1766, in Bampton, Oxfordshire, England.

123. Ann Windows was born Jul 1725, in Bampton, Oxfordshire, England, christened 21 Jul 1725, in Bampton, Oxfordshire, England, died Jun 1768, in Bampton, Oxfordshire, England, buried 25 Jun 1768, in Bampton, Oxfordshire, England. She was the daughter of William Windows and Mary Grimsher. She married John Drinkwater[401] 5 Feb 1754, in Bampton, Oxfordshire, England. He was the son of John Drinkwater and Ann Lapper.
Notes for Ann Windows:

or ANNA

124. John Hawkins was born 13 Dec 1733, in Faringdon, Berkshire, England, christened 18 Dec 1733, in Faringdon, Berkshire, England, died about 1789, buried 30 Dec 1792, in Faringdon, Berkshire, England. He was the son of Edward Hawkins and Mary Cockhead. He married Mary Alder[402,403] 25 Oct 1756, in Faringdon, Berkshire, England. She was the daughter of John Alder and Ann Phelps.

Children of John Hawkins and Mary Alder:

i. **Lucy Hawkins**,[273] born Oct 1759, in Little Coxwell, Berkshire, England.

125. Mary Alder was born Feb 1736, in Great Coxwell, Berkshire, England, christened 6 Mar 1736, in Great Coxwell, Berkshire, England, died Apr 1782, in Little Coxwell, Berkshire, England. She was the daughter of John Alder and Ann Phelps. She married John Hawkins[402,404,405] 25 Oct 1756, in Faringdon, Berkshire, England. He was the son of Edward Hawkins and Mary Cockhead.

126. Richard Haydon was born Jul 1726, in Coleshill, Oxfordshire, England, christened 24 Jul 1726, in Coleshill, Oxfordshire, England, died Mar 1785, in Buckland, Oxfordshire, England, buried 14 Mar 1785, in Buckland, Oxfordshire, England. He was the son of Richard Heydon and Eleanor Young. He married Sarah Smith[406,407,408,409] 30 Sep 1750, in Clewer, Berkshire, England. She was the daughter of Richard Smith and Mary Newton.
Notes for Richard Haydon:

IMPORTANT: Coleshill registry - page 21 Baptisms - 24 July 1726 copy: HAYDON Richard s Ric.d (corrected from Joss.p for every entry)

Children of Richard Haydon and Sarah Smith:

    i.   **William Haydon**,[276,277,278] born Mar 1752, in Buckland, Oxfordshire, England, died before 1850, in England.

    ii.   **Richard Haydon**,[410] born Jan 1754, in Buckland, Oxfordshire, England, christened 6 Jan 1754, in Buckland, Oxfordshire, England.
residence: Buckland, Berkshire, England parents: Richard Haydon, Sarah record title: England Births and Christenings, 1538-1975 name: Richard Haydon gender: Male baptism/christening date: 06 Jan 1754 baptism/christening place: Buckland, Berkshire, England father's name: Richard Haydon mother's name: Sarah indexing project (batch) number: C01766-3 source film number: 1279452

    iii.   **Acreman Haydon**,[411] born Sep 1755, in Buckland, Oxfordshire, England, christened 14 Sep 1755, in Buckland, Oxfordshire, England.
aka: Haidon (spelling error)

    iv.   **Mary Haydon**,[412] born Sep 1757, in Buckland, Oxfordshire, England, christened 18 Sep 1757, in Buckland, Oxfordshire, England, died Apr 1760, in Buckland, Oxfordshire, England, buried 10 Apr 1760, in Buckland, Oxfordshire, England.
residence: Buckland, Berkshire, England parents: Richard Haydon, Sarah record title: England Births and Christenings, 1538-1975 name: Mary Haydon gender: Female baptism/christening date: 18 Sep 1757 baptism/christening place: Buckland, Berkshire, England father's name: Richard Haydon mother's name: Sarah indexing project (batch) number: C01766-3 source film number: 1279452 burial: 10 Apr 1760 Buckland, Berkshire, England record title: England Deaths and Burials, 1538-1991 name: Mary Haydon gender: Female burial date: 10 Apr 1760 burial place: Buckland, Berkshire, England indexing project (batch) number: B01766-3 source film number: 1279452

    v.   **Ann Haydon**,[413] born Mar 1759, in Buckland, Oxfordshire, England, christened 1 Apr 1759, in Buckland, Oxfordshire, England.
residence: Buckland, Berkshire, England parents: Richard Haydon, Sarah record title: England Births and Christenings, 1538-1975 name: Ann Haydon gender: Female baptism/christening date: 01 Apr 1759 baptism/christening place: Buckland, Berkshire, England father's name: Richard Haydon mother's name: Sarah indexing project (batch) number: C01766-3 source film number: 1279452

    vi.   **John Haydon**,[414] born Apr 1761, in Buckland, Oxfordshire, England, christened 12 Apr 1761, in Buckland, Oxfordshire, England, died Nov 1773, in Buckland, Oxfordshire, England, buried 14 Nov 1773, in Buckland, Oxfordshire, England.
residence: Buckland, Berkshire, England parents: Richard Haydon, Sarah record title: England Births and Christenings, 1538-1975 name: John Haydon gender: Male baptism/christening date: 12 Apr 1761 baptism/christening place: Buckland, Berkshire, England father's name: Richard Haydon mother's name: Sarah indexing project (batch) number: C01766-3 source film number: 1279452 burial: 14 Nov 1773 Buckland, Berkshire, England record title: England Deaths and Burials, 1538-1991 name: John Haydon gender: Male burial date: 14 Nov 1773 burial place:

Buckland, Berkshire, England indexing project (batch) number: B01766-3 source film number: 1279452

vii.   **James Haydon**,[415] born Nov 1767, in Buckland, Oxfordshire, England, christened 29 Nov 1767, in Buckland, Oxfordshire, England.
residence: Buckland, Berkshire, England parents: Richard Haydon, Sarah record title: England Births and Christenings, 1538-1975 name: James Haydon gender: Male baptism/christening date: 29 Nov 1767 baptism/christening place: Buckland, Berkshire, England father's name: Richard Haydon mother's name: Sarah indexing project (batch) number: C01766-3 source film number: 1279452

viii.   **Thomas Haydon**,[416] born May 1771, in Buckland, Oxfordshire, England, christened 2 Jun 1771, in Buckland, Oxfordshire, England.
residence: Buckland, Berkshire, England parents: Richard Haydon, Sarah record title: England Births and Christenings, 1538-1975 name: Thomas Haydon gender: Male baptism/christening date: 02 Jun 1771 baptism/christening place: Buckland, Berkshire, England father's name: Richard Haydon mother's name: Sarah indexing project (batch) number: C01766-3 source film number: 1279452

127. Sarah Smith was born Nov 1720, in Iver, Buckinghamshire, England, christened 26 Nov 1720, in Iver, Buckinghamshire, England, died Feb 1785, in Buckland, Oxfordshire, England, buried 15 Feb 1785, in Buckland, Oxfordshire, England. She was the daughter of Richard Smith and Mary Newton. She married Richard Haydon[407,417] 30 Sep 1750, in Clewer, Berkshire, England. He was the son of Richard Heydon and Eleanor Young.

128. William Hawkins was born Nov 1694, in Northmoor, Oxfordshire, England, christened 29 Nov 1694, in Northmoor, Oxfordshire, England, died Oct 1779, in Northmoor, Oxfordshire, England, buried 3 Oct 1779, in Northmoor, Oxfordshire, England. He was the son of Hugh Hawkyns and Martha Fairbeard. He married Mary Gee[418] 20 Feb 1742, in Northmoor, Oxfordshire, England. She was the daughter of Ambrose Gee and Mary Ekley.

Children of William Hawkins and Mary Gee:

i.   **William Hawkins**, born Sep 1744, in Northmoor, Oxfordshire, England, christened 9 Sep 1744, in Northmoor, Oxfordshire, England, died Nov 1744, in Northmoor, Oxfordshire, England, buried 27 Nov 1744, in Northmoor, Oxfordshire, England.

ii.   **John Hawkins**, born Jan 1746, in Northmoor, Oxfordshire, England, christened 2 Feb 1746, in Northmoor, Oxfordshire, England.

iii.   **Anne Hawkins**, born Nov 1748, in Northmoor, Oxfordshire, England, christened 4 Dec 1748, in Northmoor, Oxfordshire, England, died Jun 1750, in Northmoor, Oxfordshire, England, buried 24 Jun 1750, in Northmoor, Oxfordshire, England.

iv.   **William Hawkins**, born Mar 1750, in Northmoor, Oxfordshire, England, christened 18 Mar 1750, in Northmoor, Oxfordshire, England, died 20 Mar 1750, in Northmoor, Oxfordshire, England, buried 25 Mar 1750, in Northmoor, Oxfordshire, England.

    v.   **Mary Hawkins**, born Jun 1751, in Northmoor, Oxfordshire, England, christened 16 Jun 1751, in Northmoor, Oxfordshire, England.

    vi.   **William Hawkins**,[419] born Apr 1753, in Northmoor, Oxfordshire, England, christened 8 Apr 1753, in Northmoor, Oxfordshire, England. He married Ann Gardner[419] 6 Apr 1777, in Northmoor, Oxfordshire, England. Ann Gardner was born Jun 1756, in Brize Norton, Oxfordshire, England, christened 13 Jun 1756, in Brize Norton, Oxfordshire, England.

    vii.   **Elizabeth "Betty" Hawkins**,[275] born Apr 1755, in Northmoor, Oxfordshire, England, died before 1850, in England.

    viii.   **Sarah Hawkins**, born Oct 1756, in Northmoor, Oxfordshire, England, christened 24 Oct 1756, in Northmoor, Oxfordshire, England, died Apr 1758, in Northmoor, Oxfordshire, England, buried 14 Apr 1758, in Northmoor, Oxfordshire, England.

    ix.   **Ann Hawkins**, born Jan 1758, in Northmoor, Oxfordshire, England, christened 8 Jan 1758, in Northmoor, Oxfordshire, England.

    x.   **Jenny Hawkins**, born Apr 1759, in Northmoor, Oxfordshire, England, christened 22 Apr 1759, in Northmoor, Oxfordshire, England.

    xi.   **James Hawkins**, born Nov 1760, in Northmoor, Oxfordshire, England, christened 23 Nov 1760, in Northmoor, Oxfordshire, England.

    xii.   **Hannah Hawkins**, born Jun 1762, in Northmoor, Oxfordshire, England, christened 6 Jun 1762, in Northmoor, Oxfordshire, England.

129. Mary Gee was born 8 Feb 1718, in Chipping Norton, Oxfordshire, England, died Oct 1784, in Northmoor, Oxfordshire, England, buried 10 Oct 1784, in Northmoor, Oxfordshire, England. She was the daughter of Ambrose Gee and Mary Ekley. She married William Hawkins[418,420] 20 Feb 1742, in Northmoor, Oxfordshire, England. He was the son of Hugh Hawkyns and Martha Fairbeard.

130. William Morgan was born Jan 1690, in South Hinksey, Berkshire, England, christened 8 Feb 1690, in South Hinksey, Berkshire, England, died Oct 1719, in Standlake, Oxfordshire, England, buried 28 Oct 1719, in Standlake, Oxfordshire, England. He was the son of William Morgan and Allenora Adkin Or Adkyn.[421] He married Catherine Veasy 25 Sep 1711, in Oxford, Oxfordshire, England. She was the daughter of Richard Veasy and Ann Hunt.
Notes for William Morgan:

Married at St John, Oxford

Children of William Morgan and Catherine Veasy:

    i.   **Mary Morgan**, born Sep 1712, in Standlake, Oxfordshire, England, christened 22 Sep 1712, in Standlake, Oxfordshire, England, died Sep 1717, in Standlake, Oxfordshire, England, buried 10 Sep 1717, in Standlake, Oxfordshire, England.

    ii.   **Elizabeth Morgan**, born Oct 1715, in Standlake, Oxfordshire, England, christened 9 Oct 1715, in Standlake, Oxfordshire, England.

    iii.   **William Veasy Morgan**,[281] born Nov 1717, in Standlake, Oxfordshire, England, died before 1817, in England.

131. Catherine Veasy was born about 1692, in Shifford, Oxfordshire, England. She was the daughter of Richard Veasy and Ann Hunt. She married William Morgan[421,422] 25 Sep 1711, in Oxford, Oxfordshire, England. He was the son of William Morgan and Allenora Adkin Or Adkyn.

132. William Stone was born Mar 1681, in Standlake, Oxfordshire, England, christened 20 Mar 1681, in Standlake, Oxfordshire, England, died Jul 1725, in Standlake, Oxfordshire, England, buried 30 Jul 1725, in Standlake, Oxfordshire, England. He was the son of Richard Stone and Ann Browne. He married Martha Onion[280,423,424] 19 May 1707, in Abingdon, Berkshire, England. She was the daughter of Thomas Onion and Anne Umberstone.

Children of William Stone and Martha Onion:

    i.   **William Stone**, born Jan 1711, in Standlake, Oxfordshire, England, christened 11 Jan 1711, in Standlake, Oxfordshire, England, died May 1712, in Standlake, Oxfordshire, England, buried 24 May 1712, in Standlake, Oxfordshire, England.

    ii.   **Ann Stone**, born Mar 1713, in Standlake, Oxfordshire, England, christened 21 Mar 1713, in Standlake, Oxfordshire, England, died Jan 1715, in Standlake, Oxfordshire, England, buried 1 Jan 1715, in Standlake, Oxfordshire, England.

    iii.   **Thomas Stone**, born Feb 1716, in Standlake, Oxfordshire, England, christened 8 Feb 1716, in Standlake, Oxfordshire, England.

    iv.   **William Stone**, born Dec 1721, in Standlake, Oxfordshire, England, christened 24 Dec 1721, in Standlake, Oxfordshire, England, died Jan 1722, in Standlake, Oxfordshire, England, buried 22 Jan 1722, in Standlake, Oxfordshire, England.

    v.   **Mary Stone**, born Feb 1723, in Standlake, Oxfordshire, England, christened 22 Feb 1723, in Standlake, Oxfordshire, England, died Mar 1723, in Standlake, Oxfordshire, England, buried 1 Mar 1723, in Standlake, Oxfordshire, England.

    vi.   **Mary Stone**,[279,280] born Apr 1725, in Standlake, Oxfordshire, England, died Jul 1790, in Standlake, Oxfordshire, England.

133. Martha Onion was born Mar 1675, in Hinton Waldrist, Berkshire, England, christened 1 Apr 1675, in Hinton Waldrist, Berkshire, England, died before 1750, in England. She was the daughter of Thomas Onion and Anne Umberstone. She married William Stone[280,424,425] 19 May 1707, in Abingdon, Berkshire, England. He was the son of Richard Stone and Ann Browne.
Notes for Martha Onion:

aka: ANN aka ONEUN

134. Richard Hartlett was born about 1708, in Deddington, Oxfordshire, England. He was the son of Richard Hartlett and Mary Stone. He married Elizabeth King[289,426,427] 16 Aug 1735, in Great Rollright, Oxfordshire, England. She was the daughter of Richard King and Elizabeth Barris.
Notes for Richard Hartlett:

aka: HARTLEY

Children of Richard Hartlett and Elizabeth King:

      i.   **John Hartlett**,[288,289] born Jan 1728, in Middle Barton, Oxfordshire, England, died before 1810, in England.

      ii.   **Richard Hartlett**,[428] born Jun 1737, in Deddington, Oxfordshire, England, christened 3 Jul 1737, in Deddington, Oxfordshire, England.

      iii. **Elizabeth Hartlett**,[429] born Sep 1739, in Deddington, Oxfordshire, England, christened 5 Sep 1739, in Deddington, Oxfordshire, England.

135. Elizabeth King was born 3 Mar 1709, in Banbury, Oxfordshire, England. She was the daughter of Richard King and Elizabeth Barris. She married Richard Hartlett[289,426] 16 Aug 1735, in Great Rollright, Oxfordshire, England. He was the son of Richard Hartlett and Mary Stone.
Notes for Elizabeth King:

aka: Betty, Bety, Elizabeth

136. Tobias Gilkes was born about 1718, in Oxfordshire, England, died May 1747, in Chipping Norton, Oxfordshire, England, buried 27 May 1747, in Chipping Norton, Oxfordshire, England. He was the son of John Gilkes and Mary Swift. He married Sarah Price[430] 10 Aug 1744, in Hook Norton, Oxfordshire, England. She was the daughter of Thomas Price and Bridget Berry.

Children of Tobias Gilkes and Sarah Price:

      i.   **Mary Gilkes**,[282] born Nov 1741, in Middle Barton, Oxfordshire, England, died before 1838, in England.

      ii.   **Daniel Gilkes**, born Jul 1745, in Chipping Norton, Oxfordshire, England, christened 3 Aug 1745, in Chipping Norton, Oxfordshire, England.

137. Sarah Price was born about 1720, in Oxfordshire, England. She was the daughter of Thomas Price and Bridget Berry. She married Tobias Gilkes[430] 10 Aug 1744, in Hook Norton, Oxfordshire, England. He was the son of John Gilkes and Mary Swift.
Notes for Sarah Price:

Aka: MARY

138. Yeoman John Foster was born Apr 1731, in South Leigh, Oxfordshire, England, christened 18 Apr 1731, in South Leigh, Oxfordshire, England, died Mar 1822, in Standlake, Oxfordshire, England, buried 19 Mar 1822, in Standlake, Oxfordshire, England. He was the son of John Foster and Mary Spier. He married Sarah Harris[431,432,433] 4 Nov 1756, in Standlake, Oxfordshire, England. She was the daughter of John Harris and Catherine Brooks.

Children of Yeoman John Foster and Sarah Harris:

     i.   **John Foster**,[290,292] born 21 Aug 1757, in Standlake, Oxfordshire, England, died 1 Feb 1836, in Sutton, Oxfordshire, England.

    ii.   **Mary Foster**,[434] born 18 Nov 1759, in Standlake, Oxfordshire, England, died Jan 1778, in Standlake, Oxfordshire, England, buried 8 Feb 1778, in Standlake, Oxfordshire, England.

   iii.   **Ann Foster**,[435,436] born 10 May 1761, in Standlake, Oxfordshire, England, died 21 Nov 1762, in Standlake, Oxfordshire, England.

   iv.   **William Foster**,[437] born 17 Feb 1765, in Standlake, Oxfordshire, England.

    v.   **Sarah Foster**,[438] born 24 May 1767, in Standlake, Oxfordshire, England.

   vi.   **Catherine Foster**,[439] born 8 Feb 1770, in Standlake, Oxfordshire, England.

   vii.   **Thomas Foster**,[440,441] born 14 Jun 1772, in Standlake, Oxfordshire, England, died Feb 1773, in Standlake, Oxfordshire, England, buried 3 Mar 1773, in Standlake, Oxfordshire, England.

  viii.   **Anne Foster**,[442] born 17 Mar 1776, in Standlake, Oxfordshire, England.

139. Sarah Harris was born 25 Apr 1736, in Standlake, Oxfordshire, England, died Mar 1804, in Standlake, Oxfordshire, England, buried 4 Apr 1804, in Standlake, Oxfordshire, England. She was the daughter of John Harris and Catherine Brooks. She married Yeoman John Foster[443,444,445] 4 Nov 1756, in Standlake, Oxfordshire, England. He was the son of John Foster and Mary Spier.

140. John Duffen was born about 1725, in Abingdon, Berkshire, England, died Nov 1787, in Abingdon, Berkshire, England, buried 27 Nov 1787, in Abingdon, Berkshire, England. He was the son of John Duffen and Alice Ludler. He married Sarah Clark[446,447] 7 May 1751, in Abingdon, Berkshire, England. She was the daughter of Robert Clark and Mary Smith.
Notes for John Duffen:

St Helen's records - burials

Children of John Duffen and Sarah Clark:

     i.   **Unnamed Duffen**,[448] born Dec 1752, in Abingdon, Berkshire, England, died 14 Dec 1752, in Abingdon, Berkshire, England, buried 14 Dec 1752, in Abingdon, Berkshire, England.
           St Helen's records - burials

    ii.   **Elizabeth Duffen**,[449] born Nov 1753, in Abingdon, Berkshire, England, christened 18 Nov 1753, in Abingdon, Berkshire, England, died Oct 1755, in Abingdon, Berkshire, England, buried 5 Nov 1755, in Abingdon, Berkshire, England.

   iii.   **John Duffen**,[450] born Mar 1756, in Abingdon, Berkshire, England, christened 21 Mar 1756, in Abingdon, Berkshire, England. He married Rebecca Couling about 1780, in Abingdon, Berkshire, England. Rebecca Couling was born about 1756, in Abingdon, Berkshire, England.

Notes for Rebecca Couling: St Mary church records

    iv.   **Richard Duffen**,[451] born Jun 1761, in Abingdon, Berkshire, England, christened 7 Jul 1761, in Abingdon, Berkshire, England.

    v.   **Thomas Duffen**,[452] born May 1764, in Abingdon, Berkshire, England, christened 3 Jun 1764, in Abingdon, Berkshire, England, died 24 Nov 1764, in Abingdon, Berkshire, England, buried 24 Nov 1764, in Abingdon, Berkshire, England. St Helen's records - burials

    vi.   **Mary Or Elizabeth Duffin**,[290] born May 1766, in Abingdon, Berkshire, England, died Jul 1820, in Sutton, Oxfordshire, England.

    vii.   **Thomas Duffen**,[453] born Dec 1770, in Abingdon, Berkshire, England, christened 26 Dec 1770, in Abingdon, Berkshire, England, died Jan 1773, in Abingdon, Berkshire, England, buried 12 Jan 1773, in Abingdon, Berkshire, England. St Helen's records - burials

141. Sarah Clark was born Dec 1725, in South Hinksey, Berkshire, England, christened 12 Dec 1725, in South Hinksey, Berkshire, England, died Dec 1772, in Abingdon, Berkshire, England, buried 26 Dec 1772, in Abingdon, Berkshire, England. She was the daughter of Robert Clark and Mary Smith. She married John Duffen[446,447] 7 May 1751, in Abingdon, Berkshire, England. He was the son of John Duffen and Alice Ludler.

Notes for Sarah Clark:

St Helen's records - burials

142. William King was born Feb 1716, in Witney, Oxfordshire, England, christened 19 Feb 1716, in Witney, Oxfordshire, England, died before 1800, in England. He was the son of Wiliam King and Elizabeth Ewin. He married Elizabeth Bartlet[298] 28 Aug 1750, in Witney, Oxfordshire, England. She was the daughter of Carew Bartlet and Elizabeth Casey.

Children of William King and Elizabeth Bartlet:

    i.   **Elizabeth King**, born Aug 1751, in Witney, Oxfordshire, England, christened 22 Aug 1751, in Witney, Oxfordshire, England.
          aka: BETTY

    ii.   **Martha King**,[298] born 7 Jan 1760, in Kidlington, Oxfordshire, England, christened 7 Jan 1760, in Kidlington, Oxfordshire, England.

    iii.   **Daniel King**,[295,296,297,298] born 16 May 1762, in Kidlington, Oxfordshire, England, died before 1860, in England.

143. Elizabeth Bartlet was born about 1730, in Witney, Oxfordshire, England, died before 1830, in England. She was the daughter of Carew Bartlet and Elizabeth Casey. She married William King[298,454] 28 Aug 1750, in Witney, Oxfordshire, England. He was the son of Wiliam King and Elizabeth Ewin.

144. William Probatts was born 12 Dec 1705, in Ashbury, Berkshire, England, christened 26 Dec 1705, in Ashbury, Berkshire, England. He was the son of John Probatts and Elizabeth Wilson. He married Sarah Bayly[455] 1743, in Caversham, Oxfordshire, England. She was the daughter of William Bayly and Susannah Lancaster.
Notes for William Probatts:

aka: PROBATS, PROBETTS

Children of William Probatts and Sarah Bayly:

      i.   **Joseph Probats**, born Feb 1745, in Caversham, Oxfordshire, England, christened 9 Feb 1745, in Caversham, Oxfordshire, England.
             aka; PROBUTS on records
     ii.   **Elizabeth Probats**, born Oct 1750, in Caversham, Oxfordshire, England, christened 7 Oct 1750, in Caversham, Oxfordshire, England.
    iii.   **Sarah Probats**, born Mar 1757, in Caversham, Oxfordshire, England, christened 3 Apr 1757, in Caversham, Oxfordshire, England, died before 1763, in Caversham, Oxfordshire, England.
    iv.   **William Probats**, born Sep 1758, in Caversham, Oxfordshire, England, christened 17 Sep 1758, in Caversham, Oxfordshire, England.
     v.   **John Probats**, born Jan 1761, in Caversham, Oxfordshire, England, christened 13 Jan 1761, in Caversham, Oxfordshire, England.
             John & Mary were Twins
    vi.   **Mary Probats**, born Jan 1761, in Caversham, Oxfordshire, England, christened 13 Jan 1761, in Caversham, Oxfordshire, England.
             John & Mary were Twins
   vii.   **Sarah Probats**,[294,295,296] born Jul 1763, in Caversham, Oxfordshire, England, died before 1860, in England.
  viii.   **James Probats**, born Nov 1765, in Caversham, Oxfordshire, England, christened 24 Nov 1765, in Caversham, Oxfordshire, England.

145. Sarah Bayly was born Apr 1724, in Faringdon, Berkshire, England, christened 8 Apr 1724, in Faringdon, Berkshire, England. She was the daughter of William Bayly and Susannah Lancaster. She married William Probatts[456] 1743, in Caversham, Oxfordshire, England. He was the son of John Probatts and Elizabeth Wilson.

146. Henry Newell was born 1708, in Oxfordshire, England, died 1745, in England. He was the son of Henry Newell and Anne Hunt. He married Ann Oxlade[458] 23 Nov 1738, in Lewknor, Oxfordshire, England.[457] She was the daughter of William Oxlade and Mary Salter.

Children of Henry Newell and Ann Oxlade:

      i.   **William Newell**, born 24 Jan 1739, in Brightwell Baldwin, Oxfordshire, England,

died 1788, in England.
 ii.   **Ann Newell**, born 1740, in England.
 iii. **Henry Newell**, born 1742, in England.

147. Ann Oxlade was born Jun 1716, in Great Marlow, Buckinghamshire, England, christened 11 Jun 1716, in Great Marlow, Buckinghamshire, England, died before 1800, in England. She was the daughter of William Oxlade and Mary Salter. She married Henry Newell[458] 23 Nov 1738, in Lewknor, Oxfordshire, England.[457] He was the son of Henry Newell and Anne Hunt.

148. John Broadway was born 6 Sep 1702, in Cuxham, Oxfordshire, England, christened 6 Sep 1702, in Cuxham, Oxfordshire, England, died 10 Mar 1768, in Cuxham, Oxfordshire, England. He was the son of John Broadway and Alice Bolter. He married Jane Hinde[459,460] 1730, in Cuxham, Oxfordshire, England. She was the daughter of Michael Hinde and Elizabeth Scholes.

Children of John Broadway and Jane Hinde:

 i.   **John Broadway**, born 21 Mar 1730, in Cuxham, Oxfordshire, England, christened 26 Jun 1748, in Cuxham, Oxfordshire, England, died after 1755, in Oxfordshire, England.
 ii. **Thomas Broadway**, born 25 Mar 1733, in Cuxham, Oxfordshire, England, christened 1733, in Cuxham, Oxfordshire, England, died 4 Jan 1803, in Cuxham, Oxfordshire, England. He married Sarah Knapper 24 Nov 1753, in Cuxham, Oxfordshire, England. Sarah Knapper was born 1734, in Cuxham, Oxfordshire, England.
 iii. **Jane Broadway**, born 28 Sep 1735, in Cuxham, Oxfordshire, England, christened 30 Nov 1735, in Cuxham, Oxfordshire, England.
 iv. **Joseph Broadway**, born 1736, in England, christened 13 Mar 1736, in Cuxham, Oxfordshire, England. He married Elizabeth Lloyd about 1758, in England. Elizabeth Lloyd was born about 1738, in England.
 v.   **Martha Broadway**, born 12 Feb 1737, in Cuxham, Oxfordshire, England.
 vi. **Hannah Broadway**, born 1739, in Cuxham, Oxfordshire, England, christened 15 Jul 1739, in Cuxham, Oxfordshire, England.
 vii. **Elizabeth Broadway**, born 1741, in Cuxham, Oxfordshire, England, christened 8 Jun 1741, in Cuxham, Oxfordshire, England. She married John Jarrat 14 Jul 1761, in Oxfordshire, England. John Jarrat was born about 1740, in Oxfordshire, England.
 viii. **Michael Broadway**, born 5 Dec 1742, in Cuxham, Oxfordshire, England, christened 5 Dec 1742, in Cuxham, Oxfordshire, England, died 6 Sep 1809, in England.
 ix. **Ann Broadway**, born 13 Jan 1744, in Cuxham, Oxfordshire, England, died before 1840, in England.
 x.   **Edward Broadway**, born 1751, in Cuxham, Oxfordshire, England.
 xi. **Mary Broadway**, born 1 Dec 1751, in Cuxham, Oxfordshire, England, christened 1 Dec 1751, in Cuxham, Oxfordshire, England, died 6 Jul 1830, in England.

    xii.   **Joseph Broadway**, born 12 Sep 1754, in Cuxham, Oxfordshire, England.
    xiii.   **Henry Broadway**, born 18 Dec 1756, in Cuxham, Oxfordshire, England, christened 27 Feb 1757, in Cuxham, Oxfordshire, England.

149. Jane Hinde was born May 1709, in Cuxham, Oxfordshire, England, christened 29 May 1709, in Cuxham, Oxfordshire, England, died 1 Sep 1801, in Cuxham, Oxfordshire, England, buried 3 Sep 1801, in Cuxham, Oxfordshire, England. She was the daughter of Michael Hinde and Elizabeth Scholes. She married John Broadway[460] 1730, in Cuxham, Oxfordshire, England. He was the son of John Broadway and Alice Bolter.
Notes for Jane Hinde:

Christened in Church of the Holy Rood, Cuxham, Oxfordshire, England Sources: (From Cuxham Marriages Registers 1579-1979. Details from OxFHSoc: CD OXF-SO02) (From Cuxham Baptisms Registers 1578-1982, transcriptions page 10, CD page 11) Burial in Church of the Holy Rood, Cuxham, Oxfordshire, England

150. Richard Jones was born Dec 1722, in Oxford, Oxfordshire, England, christened 23 Dec 1722, in St Thomas, Oxford, Oxfordshire, England. He was the son of William Jones and Elizabeth Cligdale. He married Mary Green[461] 6 Mar 1754, in Oxford, Oxfordshire, England. She was the daughter of Thomas Green and Elizabeth Snow.

Children of Richard Jones and Mary Green:

    i.   **James Jones**,[300,302] born Feb 1762, in Headington, Oxfordshire, England, died before 1830, in England.

151. Mary Green was born about 1735, in Headington, Oxfordshire, England, died about 1810, in England. She was the daughter of Thomas Green and Elizabeth Snow. She married Richard Jones[461,462] 6 Mar 1754, in Oxford, Oxfordshire, England. He was the son of William Jones and Elizabeth Cligdale.

152. Richard Giles was born Jun 1739, in Islip, Oxfordshire, England, christened 15 Jun 1739, in Islip, Oxfordshire, England. He was the son of Richard Giles and Susannah Allen. He married Mary Jackson[463,464] 23 Nov 1760, in Kirtlington, Oxfordshire, England. She was the daughter of Joseph Jackson and Sarah Howse.

Children of Richard Giles and Mary Jackson:

    i.   **Ann Giles**,[300,301] born Feb 1769, in Charlton on Otmoor, Oxfordshire, England.

153. Mary Jackson was born Oct 1738, in Bicester, Oxfordshire, England, christened 12 Oct 1738, in Bicester, Oxfordshire, England. She was the daughter of Joseph Jackson and Sarah Howse. She married Richard Giles[465,466] 23 Nov 1760, in Kirtlington, Oxfordshire, England. He was the son of Richard Giles and Susannah Allen.

154. Thomas Hinton was born about 1711, in Denton, Oxfordshire, England, died 1790, in England. He was the son of William Hinton and Hannah Latham. He married Mary Slaughter[467] Sep 1736, in Cuddesdon, Oxfordshire, England. She was the daughter of Edward Slaughter and Mary Holyman.

Children of Thomas Hinton and Mary Slaughter:

  i. **Charles Hinton**,[468] born Feb 1737, in Cuddesdon, Oxfordshire, England, christened 27 Feb 1737, in Cuddesdon, Oxfordshire, England.
  ii. **Thomas Hinton**,[469] born Jul 1738, in Denton, Oxfordshire, England, christened 7 Jul 1738, in Cuddesdon, Oxfordshire, England.
  iii. **John Hinton**,[303] born Mar 1742, in Denton, Oxfordshire, England, died about 1780, in Oxfordshire, England.
  iv. **Richard Hinton**,[470] born Dec 1744, in Denton, Oxfordshire, England, christened 19 Dec 1744, in Cuddesdon, Oxfordshire, England.
  v. **Mary Hinton**,[471] born Apr 1747, in Denton, Oxfordshire, England, christened 12 Apr 1747, in Cuddesdon, Oxfordshire, England.
  vi. **Henry Hinton**,[472] born Dec 1749, in Denton, Oxfordshire, England, christened 26 Dec 1749, in Cuddesdon, Oxfordshire, England.

155. Mary Slaughter was born 1718, in Cuddesdon, Oxfordshire, England, died Oct 1795, in Cuddesdon, Oxfordshire, England, buried 9 Oct 1795, in Cuddesdon, Oxfordshire, England. She was the daughter of Edward Slaughter and Mary Holyman. She married Thomas Hinton[467,473] Sep 1736, in Cuddesdon, Oxfordshire, England. He was the son of William Hinton and Hannah Latham.

156. Ralph Kirby was born Dec 1724, in Charlton on Otmoor, Oxfordshire, England, christened 13 Dec 1724, in Charlton on Otmoor, Oxfordshire, England, died Nov 1800, in Charlton on Otmoor, Oxfordshire, England, buried 4 Dec 1800, in Charlton on Otmoor, Oxfordshire, England. He was the son of Henry Kirby and Mabel West. He married Martha Howlett[474] 5 Nov 1746, in Charlton on Otmoor, Oxfordshire, England. She was the daughter of Robert Howlett and Mary King.

Children of Ralph Kirby and Martha Howlett:

  i. **Martha Kirby**,[303,304] born Jun 1747, in Charlton on Otmoor, Oxfordshire, England, died before 1840, in England.
  ii. **Mary Kirby**, born Jan 1750, in Charlton on Otmoor, Oxfordshire, England, christened 31 Jan 1750, in Charlton on Otmoor, Oxfordshire, England, buried 4 Aug 1782, in Charlton on Otmoor, Oxfordshire, England.
  iii. **Ann Kirby**, born Jan 1763, in Charlton on Otmoor, Oxfordshire, England, christened 13 Jan 1763, in Charlton on Otmoor, Oxfordshire, England.

157. Martha Howlett was born 11 Jun 1722, in Charlton on Otmoor, Oxfordshire, England, christened

24 Jun 1722, in Charlton on Otmoor, Oxfordshire, England, died Sep 1805, in Charlton on Otmoor, Oxfordshire, England, buried 8 Sep 1805, in Charlton on Otmoor, Oxfordshire, England. She was the daughter of Robert Howlett and Mary King. She married Ralph Kirby[304] 5 Nov 1746, in Charlton on Otmoor, Oxfordshire, England. He was the son of Henry Kirby and Mabel West.

158. William Clark was born 1710, in Dinton, Buckinghamshire, England, died before 1810, in England. He was the son of Richard Clarcke and Ester Hallon. He married Sarah Rogers[309,475] about 1743, in Monks Risborough, Buckinghamshire, England.[475] She was the daughter of Thomas Rogers and Mary Clark.

Children of William Clark and Sarah Rogers:

    i.   **Elizabeth Clark**,[476,477] born Dec 1744, in Long Crendon, Buckinghamshire, England, christened 23 Dec 1744, in Long Crendon, Buckinghamshire, England. Long Crendon, Buckingham parish records.

    ii.   **Elezeus Clark**,[307,309,310] born Dec 1746, in Lillingstone Dayrell, Buckinghamshire, England, died Oct 1804, in Waterperry, Oxfordshire, England.

159. Sarah Rogers was born Jan 1717, in Dinton, Buckinghamshire, England, christened 2 Feb 1717, in Dinton, Buckinghamshire, England, died before 1800, in England. She was the daughter of Thomas Rogers and Mary Clark. She married William Clark[475,478] about 1743, in Monks Risborough, Buckinghamshire, England.[475] He was the son of Richard Clarcke and Ester Hallon.

160. Johannes Grant was born 11 Nov 1716, in Worminghall, Buckinghamshire, England, died before 1800, in England. He was the son of Edvardi Grant and Mariae Hawes. He married Martha Young[480] 1 Oct 1738, in Worminghall, Buckinghamshire, England.[479] She was the daughter of John Yong and Martha Stevens.

Children of Johannes Grant and Martha Young:

    i.   **Mary Grant**,[481] born 17 Oct 1739, in Worminghall, Buckinghamshire, England.
    ii.   **Christopher Grant**,[482] born 18 Jan 1741, in Worminghall, Buckinghamshire, England.
    iii.   **Ann Grant**,[483] born 23 Jan 1742, in Worminghall, Buckinghamshire, England.
    iv.   **Frances Grant**,[484] born 16 Dec 1744, in Worminghall, Buckinghamshire, England.
    v.   **Sarah Grant**,[485] born 9 Mar 1745, in Worminghall, Buckinghamshire, England.
    vi.   **John Grant**,[486] born 24 Apr 1748, in Worminghall, Buckinghamshire, England.
    vii.   **Edward Grant**,[487] born 10 Jun 1750, in Worminghall, Buckinghamshire, England.
    viii.   **Martha Grant**,[306,307,308] born 17 Nov 1751, in Worminghall, Buckinghamshire, England, died Jun 1812, in Waterperry, Oxfordshire, England.
    ix.   **William Grant**,[488] born 12 May 1754, in Worminghall, Buckinghamshire, England.

161. Martha Young was born about 1717, in Buckinghamshire, England, died before 1800, in England.

She was the daughter of John Yong and Martha Stevens. She married Johannes Grant[479,489] 1 Oct 1738, in Worminghall, Buckinghamshire, England.[479] He was the son of Edvardi Grant and Mariae Hawes.

162. George Rowland was born Nov 1723, in Fairford, Gloucestershire, England, christened 8 Nov 1723, in Fairford, Gloucestershire, England, died before 1820, in England. He was the son of William Rowland and Martha Bowles. He married Jane Skinner[490] 31 Mar 1749, in Bristol, Gloucestershire, England. She was the daughter of Edward Skinner and Elizabeth Tarrant.
Notes for George Rowland:

England Births and Christenings, 1538-1975," database, FamilySearch (https://familysearch.org/ark:/61903/1:1:JMLR-F6L : accessed 28 November 2015), William Rowland in entry for George Rowland, 08 Nov 1723; citing FAIRFORD,GLOUCESTER,ENGLAND, reference ; FHL microfilm 856,942.

Children of George Rowland and Jane Skinner:

     i.   **John Rowland**, born 1761, in Gloucestershire, England, died 1829, in Easton, Somerset, England.

163. Jane Skinner was born 1719, in Kempsford, Gloucestershire, England, christened 8 Jan 1719, in Kempsford, Gloucestershire, England, died before 1800, in England. She was the daughter of Edward Skinner and Elizabeth Tarrant. She married George Rowland[490] 31 Mar 1749, in Bristol, Gloucestershire, England. He was the son of William Rowland and Martha Bowles.

164. John Watkins was born 1739, in Bristol, Gloucestershire, England, christened 6 May 1739, in Bristol, Gloucestershire, England, died before 1820, in England. He was the son of William Watkins and Sarah Watkins. He married Mary Kelly 12 Oct 1762, in Bristol, Gloucestershire, England. She was the daughter of Martin Kelly and Anne Parry.
Notes for John Watkins:

residence: Bristol, Gloucester, England parents: Wm. Watkins, Sarah record title: England Births and Christenings, 1538-1975 name: John Watkins gender: Male baptism/christening date: 06 May 1739 baptism/christening place: St. Nicholas, Bristol, Gloucester, England father's name: Wm. Watkins mother's name: Sarah indexing project (batch) number: I05747-0 source film number: 1595889

Children of John Watkins and Mary Kelly:

     i.   **Mary Ann Watkins**, born Mar 1761, in Bristol, Gloucestershire, England, died Feb 1806, in Westerleigh, Gloucestershire, England.

165. Mary Kelly was born 1738, in Bristol, Gloucestershire, England, christened 22 Jan 1738, in Bristol, Gloucestershire, England, died before 1820, in England. She was the daughter of Martin Kelly and Anne Parry. She married John Watkins 12 Oct 1762, in Bristol, Gloucestershire, England. He was

the son of William Watkins and Sarah Watkins.
Notes for Mary Kelly:

residence: Bristol, Gloucester, England parents: Martin, Anne record title: England Births and Christenings, 1538-1975 name: Mary Kelly gender: Female baptism/christening date: 22 Jan 1738 baptism/christening place: St. Nicholas, Bristol, Gloucester, England father's name: Martin mother's name: Anne indexing project (batch) number: I05747-0 source film number: 1595889

166. Isaac Rogers was born Sep 1727, in Bitton, Gloucestershire, England, christened 2 Oct 1727, in Bitton, Gloucestershire, England, died Jul 1776, in Bitton, Gloucestershire, England, buried 3 Jul 1776, in Bitton, Gloucestershire, England. He was the son of Dennis Rogers and Mary Brayne. He married Silvester Stone[491] 10 Feb 1750, in Bitton, Gloucestershire, England. She was the daughter of William Stone and Ann Palmer.
Notes for Isaac Rogers:

England Births and Christenings, 1538-1975 residence: Bristol, Gloucester, England parents: Dennis Rogers record title: England Births and Christenings, 1538-1975 name: Isaac Rogers gender: Male baptism/christening date: 02 Oct 1727 baptism/christening place: Bitton, Gloucester, England father's name: Dennis Rogers indexing project (batch) number: I03618-9 system origin: England. source film number: 1595499 England Deaths and Burials, 1538-1991 burial: 03 Jul 1776 Bitton, Gloucester, England record title: England Deaths and Burials, 1538-1991 name: Isaac Rogers gender: Male burial date: 03 Jul 1776 burial place: Bitton, Gloucester, England indexing project (batch) number: I03618-9 system origin: England. source film number: 1595499

Children of Isaac Rogers and Silvester Stone:

    i.   **Leonard Rogers**, born Jun 1759, in Bristol, Gloucestershire, England, died before 1841, in England.

    ii.   **Ann Rogers**, born Jun 1759, in Bitton, Gloucestershire, England, christened 4 Jun 1759, in Bitton, Gloucestershire, England.
            Ann

    iii.   **James Rogers**, born Nov 1760, in Bitton, Gloucestershire, England, christened 30 Nov 1760, in Bitton, Gloucestershire, England.
            England Births and Christenings, 1538-1975 residence: Bristol, Gloucester, England parents: Isaac Rogers, Mary record title: England Births and Christenings, 1538-1975 name: James Rogers gender: Male baptism/christening date: 30 Nov 1760 baptism/christening place: Bitton, Gloucester, England father's name: Isaac Rogers mother's name: Mary indexing project (batch) number: I03618-9 system origin: England. source film number: 1595499

167. Silvester Stone was born Jan 1736, in Bristol, Gloucestershire, England, christened 9 Jan 1736, in Bristol, Gloucestershire, England, died Dec 1795, in Bitton, Gloucestershire, England, buried 11 Dec 1795, in Bitton, Gloucestershire, England. She was the daughter of William Stone and Ann Palmer. She

married Isaac Rogers[492] 10 Feb 1750, in Bitton, Gloucestershire, England. He was the son of Dennis Rogers and Mary Brayne.
Notes for Silvester Stone:

Silvestra pronounced Sylvester in English and often spelt Silvester a.k.a. Hester England Births and Christenings, 1538-1975 residence: Bristol, Gloucester, England parents: William Stone record title: England Births and Christenings, 1538-1975 Aged 14 years when married England Deaths and Burials, 1538-1991 burial: 11 Dec 1795 Bitton, Gloucester, England record title: England Deaths and Burials, 1538-1991 name: Hester Rogers gender: Female burial date: 11 Dec 1795 burial place: Bitton, Gloucester, England indexing project (batch) number: I03618-9 system origin: England. source film number:

168. Ebenezer Burges was born Nov 1738, in Bristol, Gloucestershire, England, christened 6 Nov 1738, in Bristol, Gloucestershire, England, died Sep 1789, in Bristol, Gloucestershire, England, buried 11 Sep 1789, in Bristol, Gloucestershire, England. He was the son of John Burges and Susanna Goby. He married Diana Reynolds[493] 13 Aug 1764, in Bristol, Gloucestershire, England. She was the daughter of George Reynolds and Mary Or Ann Sednel.
Notes for Ebenezer Burges:

England Births and Christenings, 1538-1975 residence: Bristol, Gloucestershire, England parents: John Burgess, Susanna record title: England Births and Christenings, 1538-1975 name: Ebenezer Burgess gender: Male baptism/christening date: 06 Nov 1738 baptism/christening place: Lewin'sMeadSocietyofProtestantDissenters, Bristol, Gloucester, England father's name: John Burgess mother's name: Susanna indexing project (batch) number: C17091-1 system origin: England-VR source film number: 1597323 England and Wales, Non-Conformist Record Indexes (RG4-8) parents: John Burgess, Susanna Burgess record title: England and Wales, Non-Conformist Record Indexes (RG4-8) name: Ebenezer Burgess event type: Baptism christening date: 06 Nov 1738 christening place: Bristol, Somerset father's name: John Burgess mother's name: Susanna Burgess record set: RG4_1830 England Marriages, 15381973 marriage: 13 Aug 1764 St. George, Bristol, Gloucester, England spouse: Dianna Reynold record title: England Marriages, 15381973 groom's name: Ebenezer Burges bride's name: Dianna Reynold marriage date: 13 Aug 1764 marriage place: St. George, Bristol, Gloucester, England indexing project (batch) number: I03976-8 system origin: England. source film number: 1595532 England and Wales, Non-Conformist Record Indexes (RG4-8) burial: 11 Sep 1789 Bristol, Somerset record title: England and Wales, Non-Conformist Record Indexes (RG4-8) name: ? Burges event type: Burial burial date: 11 Sep 1789 burial place: Bristol, Somerset record set: RG4_2871

Children of Ebenezer Burges and Diana Reynolds:

       i.   **Ann Burges,**[311] born Oct 1766, in Bristol, Gloucestershire, England, died before 1860, in England.

169. Diana Reynolds was born 1746, in Gloucestershire, England, christened 1746, in Bristol, Gloucestershire, England, died Dec 1806, in Bristol, Gloucestershire, England, buried 18 Dec 1806, in

Bristol, Gloucestershire, England. She was the daughter of George Reynolds and Mary Or Ann Sednel. She married Ebenezer Burges[494] 13 Aug 1764, in Bristol, Gloucestershire, England. He was the son of John Burges and Susanna Goby.
Notes for Diana Reynolds:

England Births and Christenings, 1538-1975 residence: Gloucester, England parents: George Reynolds, Ann record title: England Births and Christenings, 1538-1975 name: Diana Reynolds gender: Female baptism/christening date: 1746 baptism/christening place: Bristol, Gloucester, England father's name: George Reynolds mother's name: Ann indexing project (batch) number: I04146-2 system origin: England-ODM source film number: 1595986 England Marriages, 15381973 marriage: 13 Aug 1764 St. George, Bristol, Gloucester, England spouse: Dianna Reynold record title: England Marriages, 15381973 groom's name: Ebenezer Burges bride's name: Dianna Reynold marriage date: 13 Aug 1764 marriage place: St. George, Bristol, Gloucester, England indexing project (batch) number: I03976-8 system origin: England. source film number: 1595532 England Deaths and Burials, 1538-1991 burial: 18 Dec 1806 St. Werburgh'S Church, Bristol, Gloucester, England record title: England Deaths and Burials, 1538-1991 name: Diana Burges gender: Female burial date: 18 Dec 1806 burial place: St. Werburgh'S Church, Bristol, Gloucester, England indexing project (batch) number: I03218-5 system origin: England. source film number: 1595994

170. Joseph Ellerd was born about 1765, in Hertfordshire, England. He was the son of William Ellard and Catherine Spooner. He married Lydia Mealing[495,496] 7 Aug 1787, in Harpenden, Hertfordshire, England. She was the daughter of William Mealing and Rebecca Messider.

Children of Joseph Ellerd and Lydia Mealing:

      i.   **Joseph Elleston**,[314] born 27 Jan 1788, in Harpenden, Hertfordshire, England, died 3 Jun 1854, in Greenwich, Kent, England.

      ii.   **James Ellerd**,[497] born May 1789, in Harpenden, Hertfordshire, England, christened 31 May 1789, in Harpenden, Hertfordshire, England.

171. Lydia Mealing was born May 1769, in Houghton Regis, Bedfordshire, England, christened 28 May 1769, in Houghton Regis, Bedfordshire, England. She was the daughter of William Mealing and Rebecca Messider. She married Joseph Ellerd[495] 7 Aug 1787, in Harpenden, Hertfordshire, England. He was the son of William Ellard and Catherine Spooner.
Notes for Lydia Mealing:

aka Malein

172. Stephen Jennings was born Dec 1752, in Mitcham, Surrey, England, christened 23 Dec 1752, in Mitcham, Surrey, England. He was the son of Thomas Jennings and Ann Roberts. He married Elizabeth Taylor[498,499] 26 May 1777, in Bromley, Kent, England. She was the daughter of Grove Taylor and Sarah Smith.

Children of Stephen Jennings and Elizabeth Taylor:

    i.   **Elizabeth Jennings**, born Feb 1781, in Bromley, Kent, England, christened 27 Feb 1781, in Bromley, Kent, England, died Mar 1781, in Bromley, Kent, England, buried 30 Mar 1781, in Bromley, Kent, England.

    ii.   **Mary Jennings**, born Jul 1783, in Bromley, Kent, England, christened 18 Jul 1783, in Bromley, Kent, England.

    iii.   **Stephen Jennings**, born May 1785, in Bromley, Kent, England, christened 1 Jun 1785, in Bromley, Kent, England.

    iv.   **Richard Jennings**, born Nov 1786, in Bromley, Kent, England, christened 26 Nov 1786, in Bromley, Kent, England.

    v.   **Elizabeth Jennings**,[312,313] born Jan 1790, in Greenwich, Kent, England, died Jul 1848, in Greenwich, Kent, England.

    vi.   **Silus Jennings**, born 16 Mar 1795, in Southwark, Surrey, England, christened 26 Apr 1795, in Southwark, Surrey, England.

    vii.   **Ann Jellic Jennings**, born 3 Nov 1800, in Southwark, Surrey, England, christened 30 Nov 1800, in Southwark, Surrey, England.

173. Elizabeth Taylor was born Nov 1762, in Bromley, Kent, England, christened 12 Nov 1762, in Bromley, Kent, England. She was the daughter of Grove Taylor and Sarah Smith. She married Stephen Jennings[498,500] 26 May 1777, in Bromley, Kent, England. He was the son of Thomas Jennings and Ann Roberts.

174. Isaac Langley was born Feb 1762, in Suffolk, England, christened 9 Mar 1762, in Suffolk, England. He was the son of Isaac Langley and Anna Smith. He married Elizabeth Day[501,502] 8 Dec 1786, in Marylebone, London, England. She was the daughter of Charles Day and Elizabeth Darby.
Notes for Isaac Langley:

father: Isaac Lungley mother: Anne Lungley

Children of Isaac Langley and Elizabeth Day:

    i.   **Abraham Langley**,[316,317] born 25 Feb 1789, in Marylebone, London, England, died before 1880, in England.

    ii.   **Sarah Langley**,[503] born 6 Jan 1795, in Marylebone, London, England, christened 15 Jul 1795, in St Marylebone, London, England.

175. Elizabeth Day was born Dec 1763, in Stepney, Middlesex, England, christened 25 Dec 1763, in St George in The East, Stepney, London, England. She was the daughter of Charles Day and Elizabeth Darby. She married Isaac Langley[504,505] 8 Dec 1786, in Marylebone, London, England. He was the son of Isaac Langley and Anna Smith.

176. Frederick Bayse was born about 1760, in Middlesex, England, died Oct 1809, in Grays Inn Lane

Workhouse, London, England, buried 31 Oct 1809, in St Andrew, Holborn, London, England. He was the son of Thomas Bawhse and Elizabeth Martin. He married Mary Diman Pike[506,507,508,509] 27 May 1787, in St George in The East, Stepney, London, England. She was the daughter of Thomas Pike and Catharine Lamb.

Notes for Frederick Bayse:

Burial Name: Frederick Bayce Burial Date: 31 Oct 1809 Parish: St Andrew, Holborn County: London Borough: Camden Record Type: Burial Register Type: Parish Register

Children of Frederick Bayse and Mary Diman Pike:

       i.   **Elizabeth Bayse,**[315] born Nov 1789, in London, England, died before 1880, in England.

177. Mary Diman Pike was born Sep 1768, in Whitechapel, London, England, christened 11 Sep 1768, in Whitechapel, London, England, died Nov 1849, in Hendon, Middlesex, England. She was the daughter of Thomas Pike and Catharine Lamb. She married Frederick Bayse[506,509,510] 27 May 1787, in St George in The East, Stepney, London, England. He was the son of Thomas Bawhse and Elizabeth Martin.

Notes for Mary Diman Pike:

Baptism at St Mary, Whitechapel, Towert Hamlets, London Living at Great Garden Street 1841 census - Mary BAYS. (widow) born abt 1766 in Middlesex, England Living in Cannon Street, St Swithin London Stone, Middlesex, England.

178. Joseph Humber was born 1751, in Litton Cheney, Dorset, England, christened 12 May 1751, in Cattistock, Dorset, England, died 24 Jul 1829, in Litton Cheney, Dorset, England. He was the son of Hugh Humber and Mary Frampton. He married Margaret Tidby[325] 10 Apr 1776, in Litton Cheney, Dorset, England. She was the daughter of Joseph Tidby and Mary Talbot.

Children of Joseph Humber and Margaret Tidby:

       i.   **Thomas Humber,**[325,326] born Jul 1793, in Kingston Russell, Dorset, England, died 4 Feb 1865, in Litton Cheney, Dorset, England.

179. Margaret Tidby was born 1750, in Litton Cheney, Dorset, England, christened 5 Jun 1750, in Litton Cheney, Dorset, England, died 8 Aug 1836, in Litton Cheney, Dorset, England. She was the daughter of Joseph Tidby and Mary Talbot. She married Joseph Humber[511] 10 Apr 1776, in Litton Cheney, Dorset, England. He was the son of Hugh Humber and Mary Frampton.

180. John Churchill was born Mar 1764, in Long Bredy, Dorset, England, christened 8 Apr 1764, in Long Bredy, Dorset, England. He was the son of Samuell Churchill and Ann Tiber. He married Elizabeth Jacob[512,513] 12 Jul 1784, in Litton Cheney, Dorset, England. She was the daughter of Henry

Jacob and Mary Poage.

Children of John Churchill and Elizabeth Jacob:

> i. **Elizabeth Churchill**,[318,319] born Aug 1791, in Litton Cheney, Dorset, England, died about 1834, in Bridport, Dorset, England.

181. Elizabeth Jacob was born Oct 1766, in Winterbourne St Martin, Dorset, England, christened 29 Oct 1766, in Winterbourne St Martin, Dorset, England. She was the daughter of Henry Jacob and Mary Poage. She married John Churchill[512,514] 12 Jul 1784, in Litton Cheney, Dorset, England. He was the son of Samuell Churchill and Ann Tiber.

182. John Hunt was born Feb 1767, in Dorset, England, christened 15 Feb 1767, in Leigh, Dorset, England, died 11 May 1843, in Yetminster, Dorset, England, buried 11 May 1843, in Yetminster, Yetminster, Dorset, England. He was the son of Thomas Hunt and Mary Zebedee. He married Grace Burt[515] 12 May 1806, in Yetminster, Dorset, England. She was the daughter of William Burt and Joan Morris.
Notes for John Hunt:

In 1784 John Hunt

Children of John Hunt and Grace Burt:

> i. **William Hunt**, born 1807, in Leigh, Dorset, England, died 1851, in Thornford, Dorset, England.

183. Grace Burt was born 1774, in Dorset, England, died before 1870, in England. She was the daughter of William Burt and Joan Morris. She married John Hunt[515,516] 12 May 1806, in Yetminster, Dorset, England. He was the son of Thomas Hunt and Mary Zebedee.

184. John Matthews was born Jun 1782, in Whitchurch, Dorset, England, christened 16 Jun 1782, in Whitchurch, Dorset, England, died Sep 1841, in Shaftsbury, Dorset, England, buried 8 Oct 1841, in Shaftsbury, Dorset, England. He was the son of John Matthews and Ann Hodder. He married Sarah Fowler[518,519] 13 May 1800, in Charmouth, Dorset, England.[517] She was the daughter of John Fowler and Jane Culverwell.

Children of John Matthews and Sarah Fowler:

> i. **Sarah Matthews**,[327] born Jun 1803, in Leigh, Dorset, England, died 8 Nov 1854, in Thornford, Dorset, England.

185. Sarah Fowler was born 6 Apr 1784, in Charmouth, Dorset, England, christened 9 Jun 1784, in Charmouth, Dorset, England, died Feb 1858, in Dorset, England, buried 17 Feb 1858, in Dorset,

England. She was the daughter of John Fowler and Jane Culverwell. She married John Matthews[518,520,521,522] 13 May 1800, in Charmouth, Dorset, England.[517] He was the son of John Matthews and Ann Hodder.

186. William Humphry was born Jul 1750, in Hinton in the Hedges, Northamptonshire, England, christened 22 Jul 1750, in Hinton in the Hedges, Northamptonshire, England, died 1827, in Greatworth, Northamptonshire, England, buried 28 Mar 1827, in Greatworth, Northamptonshire, England. He was the son of Thomas Humphrey and Mary Linnelin. He married Ann Basely 20 Jan 1773, in Greatworth, Northamptonshire, England. She was the daughter of Nathaniel Bazley and Sarah Collison.

Children of William Humphry and Ann Basely:

> i. **Thomas Humphry**, born 1773, in Greatworth, Northamptonshire, England, christened 4 Jul 1773, in Greatworth, Northamptonshire, England, died 1847, in Greatworth, Northamptonshire, England, buried 21 Jul 1847, in Greatworth, Northamptonshire, England. He married Mrs Hannah Humphry 2 Aug 1796, in Greatworth, Northamptonshire, England. Mrs Hannah Humphry was born about 1780, in Greatworth, Northamptonshire, England, died 27 Oct 1813, in Greatworth, Northamptonshire, England, buried 27 Oct 1813, in Greatworth, Northamptonshire, England.
> ii. **Hannah Humphry**, born 1775, in Greatworth, Northamptonshire, England, christened 2 Apr 1775, in Greatworth, Northamptonshire, England. She married Thomas Franklin 24 Nov 1805, in Greatworth, Northamptonshire, England. Thomas Franklin was born 1782, in Greatworth, Northamptonshire, England, christened 4 Aug 1782, in Wappenham, Northamptonshire, England.
> iii. **William Humphry**, born 1777, in Greatworth, Northamptonshire, England, died 1834, in Marston St Lawrence, Northamptonshire, England.
> iv. **John Humphry**, born 1780, in Greatworth, Northamptonshire, England, christened 16 Jul 1780, in Greatworth, Northamptonshire, England, died 1833, in Greatworth, Northamptonshire, England, buried 17 Mar 1833, in Greatworth, Northamptonshire, England.

187. Ann Basely was born 1755, in Islip, Oxfordshire, England, christened 20 Jul 1755, in Islip, Oxfordshire, England, died 1783, in Greatworth, Northamptonshire, England, buried 15 Nov 1783, in Greatworth, Northamptonshire, England. She was the daughter of Nathaniel Bazley and Sarah Collison. She married William Humphry 20 Jan 1773, in Greatworth, Northamptonshire, England. He was the son of Thomas Humphrey and Mary Linnelin.

188. John Coleman was born Dec 1747, in Potterspury with Yardley Gobion, Northamptonshire, England, christened 26 Dec 1747, in Potterspury with Yardley Gobion, Northamptonshire, England. He was the son of Thomas Coleman Or Coalman and Ann Bitchens. He married Elizabeth Franklin[523] 4 Dec 1769, in Rushton All Saints and St Peter, Northamptonshire, England. She was the daughter of John Franklin and Anne Smith.

Notes for John Coleman:

christening: 26 Dec 1747 - INDEPENDENT, POTTERSPURY AND YARDLEY GOBION, NORTHAMPTON, ENGLAND parents:Thomas Coleman, Ann`

Children of John Coleman and Elizabeth Franklin:

 i. **John Coleman**,[524] born 13 Mar 1772, in Rushton, Northamptonshire, England, christened 13 Mar 1772, in Rushton, Northamptonshire, England.
 ii. **Elizabeth Coleman**,[525] born 9 Apr 1773, in Rushton, Northamptonshire, England, christened 9 Apr 1773, in Rushton, Northamptonshire, England.
 iii. **Charles Coleman**,[526] born 19 Feb 1775, in Rushton, Northamptonshire, England, christened 19 Feb 1775, in Rushton, Northamptonshire, England.
 iv. **Ann Coleman**,[328] born 1 Nov 1778, in Rushton, Northamptonshire, England, died Aug 1842, in Marston St Lawrence, Northamptonshire, England.
 v. **Mary Coleman**,[527] born 12 Dec 1779, in Rushton, Northamptonshire, England, christened 12 Dec 1779, in Rushton, Northamptonshire, England.
 vi. **Thomas Coleman**,[528] born 15 Jun 1783, in Rushton, Northamptonshire, England, christened 15 Jun 1783, in Rushton, Northamptonshire, England.
 vii. **Susannah Coleman**,[529] born 3 Feb 1788, in Rushton, Northamptonshire, England, christened 3 Feb 1788, in Rushton, Northamptonshire, England.
 viii. **Martha Coleman**,[530] born 18 Apr 1790, in Rushton, Northamptonshire, England, christened 18 Apr 1790, in Rushton, Northamptonshire, England.

189. Elizabeth Franklin was born Aug 1754, in Yardley Gobion, Northamptonshire, England, christened 12 Aug 1754, in Yardley Gobion, Northamptonshire, England. She was the daughter of John Franklin and Anne Smith. She married John Coleman[531,532] 4 Dec 1769, in Rushton All Saints and St Peter, Northamptonshire, England. He was the son of Thomas Coleman Or Coalman and Ann Bitchens. Notes for Elizabeth Franklin:

groom's name: John Colman bride's name: Elizabeth Franklin marriage date: 04 Dec 1769 marriage place: All Saints And Saint Peter,Rushton,Northampton,England indexing project (batch) number: M01717-1 system origin: England-ODM source film number: 1441052

190. William Chester was born Mar 1748, in Southam, Warwickshire, England, christened 20 Mar 1748, in Southam, Warwickshire, England. He was the son of John Chester and Mary Ladbrook. He married Susannah Calloway 25 Oct 1770, in Southam, Warwickshire, England. She was the daughter of William Calloway and Susannah Walker.

Children of William Chester and Susannah Calloway:

 i. **Dinah Chester**, born Mar 1774, in Southam, Warwickshire, England, christened 2 Apr 1774, in Southam, Warwickshire, England.

ii.   **Edward Chester**,[238,332,333] born 1779, in Marston St Lawrence, Northamptonshire, England, died Oct 1842, in Brackley, Northamptonshire, England.

iii.   **Richard Chester**, born 1781, in Marston St Lawrence, Northamptonshire, England.

191. Susannah Calloway was born Apr 1756, in Birdingbury, Warwickshire, England, christened 11 Apr 1756, in Birdingbury, Warwickshire, England. She was the daughter of William Calloway and Susannah Walker. She married William Chester[533,534] 25 Oct 1770, in Southam, Warwickshire, England. He was the son of John Chester and Mary Ladbrook.

192. Samuel Savage was born May 1739, in Green's Norton, Northamptonshire, England, christened 5 Jun 1739, in Pattishall, Northamptonshire, England, died 29 Mar 1802, in Green's Norton, Northamptonshire, England, buried 1 Apr 1802, in Bugbrooke, Northamptonshire, England. He was the son of Samuel Savage and Mary Hicks. He married Sarah Bodily[330] 1 Mar 1769, in Bugbrooke, Northamptonshire, England. She was the daughter of Richard Bodily and Mary Collins.
Notes for Samuel Savage:

Buried in Quaker ground - Bugbrooke

Children of Samuel Savage and Sarah Bodily:

i.   **Mary Savage**,[535] born 1 Jun 1769, in Green's Norton, Northamptonshire, England, christened 18 Nov 1823, in Blakesley, Northamptonshire, England, died Nov 1823, in Blakesley, Northamptonshire, England, buried 24 Nov 1823, in Blakesley, Northamptonshire, England.

ii.   **John Savage**,[536] born 20 Apr 1772, in Green's Norton, Northamptonshire, England, christened 21 Mar 1832, in Green's Norton, Northamptonshire, England, died Mar 1832, in Green's Norton, Northamptonshire, England, buried 25 Mar 1832, in Green's Norton, Northamptonshire, England.
Baptised on his death bed

iii.   **Ann Savage**,[537] born 14 Apr 1779, in Green's Norton, Northamptonshire, England, died Jan 1827, in Tiffield, Northamptonshire, England, buried 7 Jan 1827, in Green's Norton, Northamptonshire, England.

iv.   **Sarah Savage**,[538] born 12 Mar 1781, in Green's Norton, Northamptonshire, England, died 26 Mar 1808, in Green's Norton, Northamptonshire, England, buried 30 Mar 1808, in Bugbrooke, Northamptonshire, England.

v.   **Lydia Savage**,[329,330,331] born 9 Jan 1783, in Green's Norton, Northamptonshire, England, died before 1861, in England.

vi.   **Samuel Savage**,[539] born 8 Jul 1785, in Green's Norton, Northamptonshire, England, died 26 May 1848, in Scipio, Cayuga, New York, United States.

vii.   **William Savage**,[540] born 8 Sep 1788, in Green's Norton, Northamptonshire, England, died 22 May 1792, in Green's Norton, Northamptonshire, England, buried 25 May 1792, in Bugbrooke, Northamptonshire, England.

193. Sarah Bodily was born 1747, in Green's Norton, Northamptonshire, England, died 16 Feb 1797, in Green's Norton, Northamptonshire, England, buried 19 Feb 1797, in Bugbrooke, Northamptonshire, England. She was the daughter of Richard Bodily and Mary Collins. She married Samuel Savage[330,541] 1 Mar 1769, in Bugbrooke, Northamptonshire, England. He was the son of Samuel Savage and Mary Hicks.

194. Thomas Lucas was born Sep 1732, in Royston, Hertfordshire, England, christened 17 Sep 1732, in Royston, Hertfordshire, England, died before 1820, in England. He was the son of William Lucas and Ann Or Susanna Chambers. He married Mary Broyors[542] 7 Apr 1755, in Bygrave, Hertfordshire, England. She was the daughter of Thomas Broyors Or Bryars Or Bryers and Ann Squires.

Children of Thomas Lucas and Mary Broyors:

       i.   **Thomas Lucas,**[334,336,337,338,339] born 21 Dec 1757, in Bygrave, Hertfordshire, England, died 20 Dec 1862, in Wanstead, Essex, England.

195. Mary Broyors was born Feb 1728, in Baldock, Hertfordshire, England, christened 14 Feb 1728, in Baldock, Hertfordshire, England, died 1825, in Broxbourne, Hertfordshire, England, buried 20 Mar 1825, in Broxbourne, Hertfordshire, England. She was the daughter of Thomas Broyors Or Bryars Or Bryers and Ann Squires. She married Thomas Lucas[543] 7 Apr 1755, in Bygrave, Hertfordshire, England. He was the son of William Lucas and Ann Or Susanna Chambers.

196. Nathaniel Mayes was born about 1740, in Essex, England, died before 1840, in England. He was the son of Nathaniel Mayes Or May and Mary Lawn. He married Jane Stevens[544,545,546] 11 Oct 1763, in Hornchurch, Essex, England. She was the daughter of William Stevens and Jane Setch.

Children of Nathaniel Mayes and Jane Stevens:

       i.   **Susanna Mayes,**[547,548] born Sep 1764, in Hornchurch, Essex, England, christened 21 Sep 1764, in Hornchurch, Essex, England, died Jun 1765, in Hornchurch, Essex, England, buried 14 Jun 1765, in Hornchurch, Essex, England.

      ii.   **Nathaniel Mayes,**[549] born Oct 1766, in Hornchurch, Essex, England, christened 13 Oct 1766, in Hornchurch, Essex, England.

     iii.   **Jane Mayes,**[334,335] born Mar 1769, in Hornchurch, Essex, England, died 1843, in West Ham, Essex, England.

     iv.   **Susan Mayes,**[550] born Mar 1771, in Hornchurch, Essex, England, christened 26 Mar 1771, in Hornchurch, Essex, England.

197. Jane Stevens was born Apr 1742, in Great Warley, Essex, England, christened 2 May 1742, in Great Warley, Essex, England, died Sep 1772, in Hornchurch, Essex, England, buried 4 Oct 1772, in Hornchurch, Essex, England. She was the daughter of William Stevens and Jane Setch. She married Nathaniel Mayes[545] 11 Oct 1763, in Hornchurch, Essex, England. He was the son of Nathaniel Mayes Or May and Mary Lawn.

198. Richard Young was born Oct 1729, in Bishopsgate, London, England, christened 30 Oct 1729, in St Botolph, Bishopsgate, London, England. He was the son of Richard Young and Hester Frances Johnson. He married Elizabeth Merigest[341,552] 4 Dec 1760, in London, England.[551] She was the daughter of Jean Merigest and Elizabeth Fozeau.

Children of Richard Young and Elizabeth Merigest:

      i.   **William Young**,[340,341] born Mar 1763, in Wanstead, Essex, England, died before 1851, in England.

199. Elizabeth Merigest was born about 1735, in London, England. She was the daughter of Jean Merigest and Elizabeth Fozeau. She married Richard Young[341,552,553] 4 Dec 1760, in London, England.[551] He was the son of Richard Young and Hester Frances Johnson.

200. Francis Turner was born 11 Nov 1740, in Clerkenwell, London, England, christened 26 Nov 1740, in Clerkenwell, London, England, died before 1840, in England. He was the son of Francis Turner and Anne Norriss. He married Anne Horsley[554] 23 Oct 1763, in Cripplegate, London, England. She was the daughter of John Horsley and Mary Outfield.

Children of Francis Turner and Anne Horsley:

      i.   **Ann Elizabeth Turner**,[340] born 1765, in West Ham, Essex, England, died before 1865, in England.

201. Anne Horsley was born Sep 1740, in London, England, christened 15 Sep 1740, in St Martin in the Fields, Westminster, London, England, died before 1840, in England. She was the daughter of John Horsley and Mary Outfield. She married Francis Turner[555] 23 Oct 1763, in Cripplegate, London, England. He was the son of Francis Turner and Anne Norriss.

202. Charles Stringer was born Oct 1749, in Shipley, Sussex, England, christened 22 Oct 1749, in Shipley, Sussex, England, died 1802, in Sussex, England. He was the son of William Stringer and Sarah Williams. He married Martha Blandford about 1768, in Essex, England. She was the daughter of Mathew Blandford and Martha Watson.

Children of Charles Stringer and Martha Blandford:

      i.   **James Stringer**,[344,345,346] born 1770, in Barking, Essex, England, died 7 Jun 1853, in Barking, Essex, England.

203. Martha Blandford was born about 1754, in Essex, England. She was the daughter of Mathew Blandford and Martha Watson. She married Charles Stringer[556] about 1768, in Essex, England. He was the son of William Stringer and Sarah Williams.
Notes for Martha Blandford:

aka: Mary

204. William Witton was born 2 Jan 1754, in Clerkenwell, London, England, christened 20 Jan 1754, in Clerkenwell, London, England. He was the son of James Whitton Or Witton and Ann Ells Or Ellis. He married Elizabeth Mayor[557,558] 6 Jul 1778, in London St Botolph without Aldgate, London, England. She was the daughter of John Mayor and Margaret Norbury.

Children of William Witton and Elizabeth Mayor:

> i. **Elizabeth Sarah Wyten,**[342,343] born 3 Sep 1781, in Barking, Essex, England, died May 1855, in Barking, Essex, England.

205. Elizabeth Mayor was born 5 Dec 1750, in London, England, christened 25 Dec 1750, in London St Michael Royal with St Martin Vintry, London, England, died before 1840, in England. She was the daughter of John Mayor and Margaret Norbury. She married William Witton[557] 6 Jul 1778, in London St Botolph without Aldgate, London, England. He was the son of James Whitton Or Witton and Ann Ells Or Ellis.

206. Richard Hyde was born about 1755, in Cripplegate, London, England. He was the son of John Hyde and Mary Elizabeth Roach. He married Ann Rainbird[559,560] 16 Nov 1775, in Stepney, Middlesex, England.[559] She was the daughter of Thomas Rainbird Or Raynbird and Mary Baker.
Notes for Richard Hyde:

aka: RICHARD HEATH Christening: St Giles Cripplegate, London, England

Children of Richard Hyde and Ann Rainbird:

> i. **Richard Hyde,**[348,349,350] born about 1778, in Barking, Essex, England, died before 1840, in England.

207. Ann Rainbird was born Mar 1750, in Pakenham, Suffolk, England, christened 13 Mar 1750, in Pakenham, Suffolk, England. She was the daughter of Thomas Rainbird Or Raynbird and Mary Baker. She married Richard Hyde[559,561] 16 Nov 1775, in Stepney, Middlesex, England.[559] He was the son of John Hyde and Mary Elizabeth Roach.

208. John Briggs was born Nov 1744, in Stepney, Middlesex, England, christened 4 Nov 1744, in St Mary Whitechapel, Stepney, London, England, died May 1793, in Westminster, London, England, buried 7 May 1793, in St Margaret, Westminster, London, England. He was the son of John Briggs and Jane Rice. He married Sarah Timbrell[562,563] about 1772, in London, England. She was the daughter of William Timbrell and Sarah Crew.

Children of John Briggs and Sarah Timbrell:

      i.   **Sarah Briggs**,[347] born 21 Jan 1773, in Shoreditch, London, England, died before 1840, in England.

209. Sarah Timbrell was born Mar 1754, in London, England, christened 27 Mar 1754, in St John Zacary, London, England, died Mar 1788, in Soho, London, England, buried 7 Apr 1788, in St Anne Soho, London, England. She was the daughter of William Timbrell and Sarah Crew. She married John Briggs[564,565] about 1772, in London, England. He was the son of John Briggs and Jane Rice.

210. George Giles was born Dec 1742, in Lamberhurst, Kent, England, christened 9 Dec 1742, in Lamberhurst, Kent, England, died 12 Jul 1812, in Goudhurst, Kent, England. He was the son of George Giles and Hannah Lasshan. He married Martha Stevens[568] 3 Nov 1767, in Lamberhurst, Kent, England.[566,567] She was the daughter of John Stevens and Sarah Hayward.
Notes for George Giles:

Source Information: Batch No.: Dates: Source Call No.: Type: Printout Call No.: Type: 1563 - 1844 0992526 Film 6906607 Parish registers - Kent : Marriages at Lamberhurst, 1564 to 1837; Vol: 3 George Giles

Children of George Giles and Martha Stevens:

      i.   **Thomas Giles**,[351] born 1772, in Dover, Kent, England, died Nov 1859, in Kent, England.

211. Martha Stevens was born Sep 1746, in Marden, Kent, England, christened 29 Sep 1746, in Marden, Kent, England, died before 1840, in England. She was the daughter of John Stevens and Sarah Hayward. She married George Giles 3 Nov 1767, in Lamberhurst, Kent, England.[566,567] He was the son of George Giles and Hannah Lasshan.

212. William Holmes was born 22 Dec 1744, in Dover, Kent, England, died 1803, in Dover, Kent, England. He was the son of James Holmes and Ann Collyer. He married Elizabeth Read 6 Aug 1776, in Dover, Kent, England. She was the daughter of Andrew Read and Sarah Hawkes.

Children of William Holmes and Elizabeth Read:

      i.   **James Holmes**,[569] born 10 May 1777, in Dover, Kent, England. He married Maria Burvill[569] 19 Sep 1800, in Walmer, Kent, England.[570] Maria Burvill was born 1776, in Kent, England, christened 1 Dec 1776, in St Margaret at Cliffe, Kent, England. Plumber in Lewisham

      ii.   **Sarah Holmes**,[351] born 5 Oct 1779, in Dover, Kent, England, died 1870, in Hollingbourne, Kent, England.

      iii.   **Ann Holmes**, born 5 Apr 1782, in Dover, Kent, England, christened 26 May 1782,

in Dover, Kent, England, died Jan 1783, in Dover, Kent, England, buried 15 Jan 1783, in Dover, Kent, England.
WARNING: This is the first child in the family called Ann -she died as an infant. The second Ann went to Australia and died there as Ann Hamilton. Lived at 119 Snargate Street, Dover

iv. **William Read Holmes**,[571,572,573] born 25 Dec 1783, in Dover, Kent, England, christened 11 Jan 1784, in Dover, Kent, England, died 27 Dec 1836, in Dover, Kent, England, buried 3 Jan 1837, in Dover, Kent, England. He married Elizabeth Barber 8 Nov 1819, in Dover, Kent, England.[574] Elizabeth Barber was born 1 Jul 1792, in Dover, Kent, England, christened 22 Jul 1792, in Dover, Kent, England. William Read Holmes - 25 Dec 1783 Occupation - Cinque Port Pilot Married - Elizabeth Barber - 8 Nov 1819 Died - 27 Dec 1836 Burried - January 1837 William died in the Great Snow Storm just after Christmas,Dec 1836.He was in the Dover Straights. There's lots of info on William Holmes at the Dover Museum. The Kentish Observer of 28th Dec 1836 reported as follows: An express from Payne's Hotel Dover arrived in Canterbury last night at about eight o'clock. The boy, a light lad did it in six hours having had to walk from Bridge. We regret to say he brought the account of the wreck of the brig Harriet a timber vessel bound to London from Quebec which went to pieces under Shakespeare's Cliff. The pilot William Read Holmes was drowned and his body afterwards was picked up at Folkestone. The Canterbury Weekly Journal reported as follows in it's edition of 31st Dec 1836: We regret to state that fourteen or fifteen persons perished on board the brig Harriet which went tp pieces under Shakespeare's Cliff. The vessel was near enough to hear the voices of the unfortunate crew on land, although it was found impossible to render them any assistance. Part of the wreck floated ashore with a live cat on it... The Essex, Herts. and Kent Mercury reports as follows in its edition of 10th January 1837: "It is remarkable that the two vessels totally wrecked here, belonging to London, from foreign parts, the Prince Frederick from Rotterdam and the Harriet from Quebec, were commanded by Folkestone men, who had a narrow escape from being drowned in sight of their native place; Captain Stephenson, seventy years old, of the former, and Captain John Warman, of the Harriet. The funeral of the respected pilot,. Mr. W.R.Holmes, of this port, who, with several of the crew was drowned, took place on Tuesday and was attended by a long procession of friends and relatives of the deceased, the brother of James, a plumber from Lewisham. He leaves a widow and eight children.

v. **Ann Holmes**, born 13 Sep 1789, in Dover, Kent, England, christened 14 Oct 1789, in Dover, Kent, England, died 13 Apr 1886, in Willunga, South Australia, Australia, buried 30 Apr 1886, in Marion, South Australia, Australia. She married Richard Hamilton 8 Nov 1813, in Dover, Kent, England. Richard Hamilton was born 18 Feb 1792, in Dover, Kent, England, christened 7 Mar 1792, in Dover, Kent, England, died 13 Aug 1852, in Marion, South Australia, Australia, buried 30 Aug 1852, in Adelaide, South Australia, Australia.
WARNING: This is the second child in the family called Ann - first one died as an

infant. Lived at 119 Snargate Street, Dover

Notes for Richard Hamilton: HAMILTON Richard, Ann n HOLMES, Eliz C/Kath, John, Sarah, Hy, Anne Jane, Rbt, Alf arrived 1837-10-17 on Katherine Stewart Forbes from London [Source:2,7(also H NELL, A BARREAU),23(7),28] Register of Emigrant Labourers Applying for a Free Passage to South Australia 1836-1841, PRO CO 386/149-151 Katherine Stewart Forbes - Gravesend to Adelaide. She sailed from Gravesend on 27 July 1837 and arrived at Holdfast Bay on October 17th, 1837 under the command of Captain Alfred Fell. On this trip she brought 222 passengers with her. History In 1835 Richard Hamilton Jnr arrived in South Australia as a seaman aboard the brigantine "Duke of York" carrying settlers for the fledgling colony and due to meet up with HMS Buffalo sailing to South Australia via Buenos Aires. Richard Jnr returned to England full of tales of the potential of South Australia convincing his father of the merits of emigrating with his entire family. On June 7, 1837 Richard Hamilton (snr) took out Land Order 449 in London for the Province of South Australia. He arrived with his wife and five of his children aboard the "Katherine Stewart Forbes" on October 7, 1837. His eldest child, Henry, remained in England to complete his schooling. Initially the family lived in a camp on the banks of the River Torrens before the local Aboriginal Karuna tribe burnt it out. This forced the family to move down to the land they had secured on the banks of the Sturt River, in the Marion district 8 miles from what is today Adelaide's G.P.O where they set about establishing a farm. This marked the beginning of Hamilton's Ewell Vineyards. It became apparent to Richard that before the farm could support his family he would run short of money. Therefore he wrote to a friend in South Africa describing his predicament and requested that he send some vines to plant 'as the health of the family requires a little wine-'. Circa 1880s. The original Hamilton Ewell Vineyards, Gleneg, South Australia at vintage time. The vines, which were Pedro Ximenez, Shiraz and Grenache, arrived three months later and Richard planted them in the winter of 1838. The plants thrived in the deep alluvial soil and sunny climate helped by the annual flooding of the Sturt River much like the Bremer River does in the Langhorne Creek wine region, in South Australia. In 1841 Richard made his first and South Australia's first wine, which he subsequently loaded onto a horse and cart and sold to nearby farmers. The eldest son, Henry, joined the rest of the family after completing schooling and then spending two years on a sheep station near Burra. Gradually Henry and the family purchased surrounding land. In 1854 Henry planted two acres of vines on a section of 10 acres, which was named Ewell after a village in Surrey. Some of these vines were still bearing in 1980. This was where Henry was to build his wine cellars that became known as Hamilton's Ewell Vineyards. Henry ran a mixed farm with hard work and good management. In 1890 and 1891 he won the Angus Award for agricultural farms presented by the Royal Agricultural and Horticultural Society. At that stage he had 140 acres of farm with 40 acres of vineyard. Richard Hamilton's widow, Anne, died in 1886 aged 97 and in accordance with her husband's will the original property was divided equally amongst the nine children. Henry and his son

Frank set about buying the land back from the other members of the family. Circa 1930s. A bird's eye view of Hamilton's Ewell Vineyards original vineyard first planted by Richard Hamilton in 1838 near Glenelg, South Australia. Under the management of Frank Hamilton the vineyard expanded to 156 acres and amongst other wines they produced a "Chablis" dry white wine made from Pedro. In 1928 Frank's son, Sydney, blended Pedro with Verdelho to produce Hamilton's Ewell Moselle, a semi sweet white which went on to be Hamilton's and Australia's biggest selling wine. At the same time Hamilton's started picking the grapes early to retain some natural acidity and fermenting them in closed wooden vats rather than open concrete tanks, as was the norm. Hamilton's Ewell Vineyards developed a reputation for fine wines through the efforts of winemakers Sydney Hamilton, Russian born John A. Seeck, and Frenchman Maurice Ou. In 1945 a temperature controlled cellar was built which greatly helped the quality of the white wines. Circa 1930s. Filling 65 gallon (300 litre) hogsheads with wine in the original Hamilton's Ewell Vineyards winery near Glenelg, South Australia. Under the stewardship of managing director Eric Hamilton, the company flourished. Eric was a pioneer in exporting Australian wines spending up to six months of the year overseas promoting Hamilton's Ewell Vineyards and Australian wines, mainly in the UK and Canada. He even went to the length of shipping his Rolls Royce with him on occasions. During the 60s and 70s Hamilton's Ewell Vineyards had lost much of its vineyards at Ewell through urban expansion and compulsory acquisition although there is one small section of vineyard still alive today. When Hamilton's Ewell Vineyards was sold to Mildara (now Beringer Blass) in 1979 the company had vineyards in the Eden Valley, Nildottie and Wood Wood near Swan Hill in Victoria and wineries at Ewell, Eden Valley Nildottie and Nyah in Victoria. Mark Hamilton was horrified as a young board member in 1979, hoping to one day take over the reigns, when Hamilton's Ewell Vineyards was sold to Mildara. In 1982 Mark Hamilton's father, Robert, bought the winery and vineyard in the Eden Valley back from Mildara. Hamilton's Ewell Vineyards in turn purchased this from Robert in 1993 and named it Stonegarden. Mark, a lawyer, was determined to revive his interest in the wine industry so he and his wife Deborah began purchasing premium mature vineyards in the Barossa Valley in the 1990's. Circa 1960. The Bridgewater Mill used as a Whisky and Brandy Store by Hamilton's Ewell Vineyards in the 60s and 70s until the sale of the company to Mildara in 1979. Now a restaurant and sparkling wine cellar owned by Petaluma Winery. Mark spent a lot of time in the 90s seeking out and purchasing the right vineyards in the Barossa Valley; purchasing an old winery and vineyard called Stonegarden near Springton in the Eden Valley previously owned by Hamilton's Ewell Vineyards, and searching for the ideal piece of land for a premium vineyard in the South East of SA. At the same time Mark Hamilton took the opportunity to regain the name and associated trademarks of Hamilton's Ewell Vineyards. Hamilton's Ewell vineyards have developed a new, high quality 100-acre vineyard named Limestone Quarry Vineyard in the Wrattonbully region near Coonawarra in South

Australia's South East on predominantly terra rossa soil. Under the stewardship of chairman Eric Hamilton in the 60s and 70s, Hamilton's Ewell Vineyards became one of the biggest exporters of Australian wine. Eric spent up to six months overseas each year promoting Australian wines, even shipping his Rolls Royce with him to drive round Canada and the United Kingdom. It is with this long heritage in mind that Mark and Deborah are proud to have relaunched Hamilton's Ewell Vineyards.

213. Elizabeth Read was born 31 Jul 1752, in Dover, Kent, England, christened 4 Oct 1752, in Dover, Kent, England, died 1833, in Charlton, Kent, England. She was the daughter of Andrew Read and Sarah Hawkes. She married William Holmes 6 Aug 1776, in Dover, Kent, England. He was the son of James Holmes and Ann Collyer.

214. Henry Baldwin was born Jan 1739, in London, England, christened 7 Feb 1739, in St Sepulchre, London, England. He was the son of Heny "Henry" Baldwin and Elizabeth Laurence. He married Rebecca Smith[575,576] 24 Jan 1754, in Aldersgate, London, England. She was the daughter of Robert Smith and Susanna Browes.

Children of Henry Baldwin and Rebecca Smith:

     i.   **John Baldwin,**[353] born 2 Mar 1767, in Whitechapel, London, England, died before 1860, in England.

215. Rebecca Smith was born May 1725, in Aldgate, London, England, christened 4 Jun 1725, in Aldgate, London, England. She was the daughter of Robert Smith and Susanna Browes. She married Henry Baldwin[575,577,578] 24 Jan 1754, in Aldersgate, London, England. He was the son of Heny "Henry" Baldwin and Elizabeth Laurence.
Notes for Rebecca Smith:

aka REBEKAH

216. William Scofield Dixon was born Nov 1740, in Stepney, London, England, christened 19 Nov 1740, in Stepney, London, England. He was the son of Thomas Dixon and Mary Empey. He married Mary Ann Miller[579,580] 8 Dec 1761, in Aldgate, London, England.[579] She was the daughter of Thomas Miller and Margaret Buxton.

Children of William Scofield Dixon and Mary Ann Miller:

     i.   **Rebecca Dixon,**[352] born Apr 1770, in Whitechapel, London, England, died before 1860, in England.

217. Mary Ann Miller was born Jan 1742, in London, England, christened 9 Jan 1742, in Aldgate, London, England. She was the daughter of Thomas Miller and Margaret Buxton. She married William

Scofield Dixon[581,582] 8 Dec 1761, in Aldgate, London, England.[579] He was the son of Thomas Dixon and Mary Empey.

218. William Wine was born 9 Apr 1761, in Shoreditch, London, England, christened 28 Apr 1765, in Shoreditch, London, England, died 1829, in Stepney, Middlesex, England. He was the son of Henry Wine and Mary Smith. He married Martha Vennor[583] 25 Dec 1781, in Stepney, Middlesex, England.[583] She was the daughter of Charles Venner and Martha Wie Or Way.

Children of William Wine and Martha Vennor:

    i.   **William Wine**,[354,355] born 13 Oct 1782, in Bethnal Green, London, England,[354] died before 1880, in England.

    ii.   **Henry Wine**, born 17 May 1787, in Shoreditch, London, England, christened 3 Jun 1787, in Bethnal Green, London, England.

219. Martha Vennor was born 27 Jul 1760, in Shoreditch, London, England, christened 17 Aug 1760, in Shoreditch, London, England, died before 1860, in England. She was the daughter of Charles Venner and Martha Wie Or Way. She married William Wine[584] 25 Dec 1781, in Stepney, Middlesex, England.[583] He was the son of Henry Wine and Mary Smith.

220. William Richardson was born Oct 1756, in Stepney, London, England, christened 17 Apr 1757, in Stepney, London, England. He was the son of James Richardson and Elizabeth Jones. He married Ann Yeates[586] 4 Oct 1781, in St Sepulchre, London, England.[585] She was the daughter of William Yates and Mary Jones.

Children of William Richardson and Ann Yeates:

    i.   **Sarah Richardson**,[355,356,357] born 11 Nov 1782, in Westminster, London, England, died 15 Oct 1854, in Hackney, Middlesex, England.

221. Ann Yeates was born Jun 1762, in St Andrew, Holborn, London, England, christened 13 Jun 1762, in St Andrew, Holborn, London, England. She was the daughter of William Yates and Mary Jones. She married William Richardson[587,588] 4 Oct 1781, in St Sepulchre, London, England.[585] He was the son of James Richardson and Elizabeth Jones.

222. Thomas Rapley was born 12 Nov 1756, in Westminster, London, England, christened 8 Dec 1756, in St Marylebone, London, England, died 14 Sep 1806, in Limehouse, Middlesex, England, buried 28 Sep 1806, in Limehouse, Middlesex, England. He was the son of Jeremiah Rapley and Mary Graham. He married Mary Ann Roberts[589] 9 Jun 1783, in Stepney, Middlesex, England. She was the daughter of Benjamin Roberts and Sarah Or Sara Hawkins.

Children of Thomas Rapley and Mary Ann Roberts:

     i.   **William Thomas Rapley**,[367] born Jan 1784, in Rotherhithe, London, England, died Mar 1852, in Stepney, Middlesex, England.

     ii.   **Mary Rap**,[590] born 21 May 1786, in Shoreditch, London, England, christened 4 Jun 1786, in St Leonard's Shoreditch, London, England, died 10 Jun 1787, in London, England.

     iii.   **Thomas Rap**,[591] born 3 May 1788, in Shoreditch, London, England, christened 29 Jun 1788, in St Leonard's Shoreditch, London, England.

     iv.   **John Rap**,[592,593] born 12 Sep 1790, in Shoreditch, London, England, christened 4 Dec 1790, in St Leonard's Shoreditch, London, England, buried 25 Dec 1790, in St Leonard's Shoreditch, London, England.

     v.   **Sarah Rap**,[594] born 13 Nov 1791, in Shoreditch, London, England, christened 12 Feb 1792, in St Leonard's Shoreditch, London, England.

     vi.   **Henry Rap**,[595] born 21 Jan 1794, in Shoreditch, London, England, christened 4 May 1794, in St Leonard's Shoreditch, London, England.

223. Mary Ann Roberts was born 17 Feb 1758, in Westminster, London, England, christened 19 Feb 1758, in St James, Westminster, London, England, died before 1840, in England. She was the daughter of Benjamin Roberts and Sarah Or Sara Hawkins. She married Thomas Rapley[596,597,598] 9 Jun 1783, in Stepney, Middlesex, England. He was the son of Jeremiah Rapley and Mary Graham.
Notes for Mary Ann Roberts:

Name: Mary Ann Roberts Gender: Female Baptism/Christening Date: 19 Feb 1758 Baptism/Christening Place: St. James, Westminster, Middlesex, England Birth Date: 17 Feb 1758 Father's Name: Benjamin Roberts Mother's Name: Sarah

224. Stephen Mott was born 28 Jun 1750, in London, England, christened 20 Jul 1750, in London St Dionis Backchurch, London, England. He was the son of Samuel Mott and Mary Purviss. He married Ann Steel[599,600] about 1777, in London, England. She was the daughter of John Steel and Hannah Or Sarah Collings.

Children of Stephen Mott and Ann Steel:

     i.   **Martha Steel Mott**,[361,362] born 18 Jan 1779, in Rotherhithe, London, England, died 1842, in Stepney, Middlesex, England.

     ii.   **Sarah Steel Mott**, born Feb 1785, in Rotherhithe, London, England, christened 13 Feb 1785, in St Mary, Rotherhithe, London, England.

225. Ann Steel was born Sep 1745, in Putney, London, England, christened 10 Sep 1745, in St Mary Putney, London, England. She was the daughter of John Steel and Hannah Or Sarah Collings. She married Stephen Mott[601] about 1777, in London, England. He was the son of Samuel Mott and Mary Purviss.

Generation No. 9

226. William Aldesworth was born Oct 1701, in Eaton, Oxfordshire, England, christened 22 Oct 1701, in Appleton, Berkshire, England, died 31 May 1762, in Stanton Harcourt, Oxfordshire, England, buried 31 May 1762, in Stanton Harcourt, Oxfordshire, England. He was the son of Thomas Aldworth and Martha Collings. He married Mary Baker[602,603,604] 25 Apr 1728, in Wantage, Berkshire, England. She was the daughter of John Baker and Frances Slade.
Notes for William Aldesworth:

Surname - on Appleton parish reg - ALDWORTH Residence: Berkshire, England parents: Thomas Aldworth record title: England Births and Christenings, 1538-1975 name: William Aldworth gender: Male baptism/christening date: 22 Oct 1701 baptism/christening place: APPLETON WITH EATON,BERKSHIRE,ENGLAND father's name: Thomas Aldworth indexing project (batch) number: C02175-1 system origin: England-ODM Marriage: 25 Apr 1728 Wantage, Berkshire, England spouse: Mary Baker record title: England Marriages, 15381973 groom's name: William Aldworth bride's name: Mary Baker marriage date: 25 Apr 1728 marriage place: Wantage,Berkshire,England indexing project (batch) number: M02198-4 system origin: England-ODM source film number: 88469

Children of William Aldesworth and Mary Baker:

    i.   **Mary Aldesworth**,[605] born 1731, in Stanton Harcourt, Oxfordshire, England, died May 1803, in Stanton Harcourt, Oxfordshire, England, buried 16 May 1803, in Stanton Harcourt, Oxfordshire, England. She married Thomas Clack[606] 10 May 1756, in Stanton Harcourt, Oxfordshire, England. Thomas Clack was born about 1734, in Stanton Harcourt, Oxfordshire, England.

    ii.   **William Aldesworth**,[377] born about 1736, in Stanton Harcourt, Oxfordshire, England, died Feb 1781, in Stanton Harcourt, Oxfordshire, England.

    iii.   **Joseph Aldesworth**, born about 1737, in Stanton Harcourt, Oxfordshire, England, died before 1830, in England. He married Mrs Elizabeth Aldesworth about 1758, in Stanton Harcourt, Oxfordshire, England. Mrs Elizabeth Aldesworth was born about 1738, in Stanton Harcourt, Oxfordshire, England, died before 1800, in England. Butcher by trade

227. Mary Baker was born Dec 1709, in Appleford, Berkshire, England, christened 11 Dec 1709, in Appleford, Berkshire, England, died 1759, in Stanton Harcourt, Oxfordshire, England. She was the daughter of John Baker and Frances Slade. She married William Aldesworth[607] 25 Apr 1728, in Wantage, Berkshire, England. He was the son of Thomas Aldworth and Martha Collings.
Notes for Mary Baker:

M02198-4; system origin: England-ODM; source film number: 88469

228. Nathaniel Tindal was born about 1714, in Beckley, Oxfordshire, England, died before 1800, in England. He was the son of Tindal and Tindal. He married Mary Hanzel[608] 17 Apr 1734, in Oxford, Oxfordshire, England. She was the daughter of Hanzel and Hanzel.

Children of Nathaniel Tindal and Mary Hanzel:

    i.   **Mary Tynedall**,[368,369] born about 1738, in Stanton Harcourt, Oxfordshire, England, died Aug 1781, in Stanton Harcourt, Oxfordshire, England.

    ii.   **Nathaniel Trindal**,[609] born Dec 1748, in Beckley, Oxfordshire, England, christened 5 Jan 1749, in Beckley, Oxfordshire, England.

229. Mary Hanzel was born about 1717, in Beckley, Oxfordshire, England, died before 1800, in England. She was the daughter of Hanzel and Hanzel. She married Nathaniel Tindal[608] 17 Apr 1734, in Oxford, Oxfordshire, England. He was the son of Tindal and Tindal.

230. Henry Townshend was born Dec 1700, in Witney, Oxfordshire, England, christened 19 Dec 1700, in Witney, Oxfordshire, England. He was the son of William Townshend and Mary Carter. He married Sarah Tewksbury[610] 23 May 1721, in Shipton under Wychwood, Oxfordshire, England. She was the daughter of Tewksbury and Tewksbury.
Notes for Henry Townshend:

Son of William the Innekeeper (sic)

Children of Henry Townshend and Sarah Tewksbury:

    i.   **William Townshend**,[611] born Sep 1722, in Witney, Oxfordshire, England, christened 12 Sep 1722, in Witney, Oxfordshire, England.

    ii.   **John Townshend**,[612] born Oct 1727, in Witney, Oxfordshire, England, christened 1 Nov 1727, in Witney, Oxfordshire, England.

    iii.   **John Townshend**,[378] born Apr 1733, in Witney, Oxfordshire, England, died before 1820, in England.

    iv.   **Harry Townshend**,[613] born Jan 1737, in Witney, Oxfordshire, England, christened 2 Feb 1737, in Witney, Oxfordshire, England.
        Twin of Nanny

    v.   **Nanny Townshend**,[613] born Jan 1737, in Witney, Oxfordshire, England, christened 2 Feb 1737, in Witney, Oxfordshire, England.
        Twin of Harry

231. Sarah Tewksbury was born about 1702, in Potters Hill, Langley, Oxfordshire, England. She was the daughter of Tewksbury and Tewksbury. She married Henry Townshend[610,614] 23 May 1721, in Shipton under Wychwood, Oxfordshire, England. He was the son of William Townshend and Mary Carter.

Contents

232. Robert Hopcraft was born about 1717, in Bicester, Oxfordshire, England. He was the son of Hopcraft and Hopcraft. He married Mary Barton[615] 10 Aug 1740, in Bicester, Oxfordshire, England. She was the daughter of Barton and Barton.

Children of Robert Hopcraft and Mary Barton:

    i.   **Elizabeth Hopcraft,**[378] born about 1742, in Bucknell, Oxfordshire, England, died before 1821, in England.

233. Mary Barton was born about 1720, in Blackthorn, Oxfordshire, England. She was the daughter of Barton and Barton. She married Robert Hopcraft[615] 10 Aug 1740, in Bicester, Oxfordshire, England. He was the son of Hopcraft and Hopcraft.

234. Thomas Turner was born Oct 1690, in Ascott Under Wychwood, Oxfordshire, England, christened 6 Oct 1690, in Witney, Oxfordshire, England. He was the son of Thomas Turner and Mary Bird. He married Joane Hix[616] 17 Sep 1712, in Shipton under Wychwood, Oxfordshire, England. She was the daughter of Richard Hix and Hix.

Children of Thomas Turner and Joane Hix:

    i.   **Charles Turner,**[383,384,395] born Dec 1720, in Hailey, Oxfordshire, England, died Jan 1769, in Witney, Oxfordshire, England.

235. Joane Hix was born 1694, in Ascott Under Wychwood, Oxfordshire, England. She was the daughter of Richard Hix and Hix. She married Thomas Turner[617] 17 Sep 1712, in Shipton under Wychwood, Oxfordshire, England. He was the son of Thomas Turner and Mary Bird.

236. Thomas Cox was born about 1680, in Ramsden, Oxfordshire, England. He was the son of Cox and Cox. He married Rose Ebsworth[618,619] 11 Oct 1712, in Shipton under Wychwood, Oxfordshire, England. She was the daughter of Thomas Rose and Mary Ebsworth.

Children of Thomas Cox and Rose Ebsworth:

    i.   **Ann Cox,**[383,384] born about 1718, in Ramsden, Oxfordshire, England, died Nov 1769, in Witney, Oxfordshire, England.

237. Rose Ebsworth was born Feb 1680, in Ramsden, Oxfordshire, England, christened 14 Feb 1680, in Ramsden, Oxfordshire, England. She was the daughter of Thomas Rose and Mary Ebsworth. She married Thomas Cox[619] 11 Oct 1712, in Shipton under Wychwood, Oxfordshire, England. He was the son of Cox and Cox.

238. George Tims was born about 1675, in Ascott Under Wychwood, Oxfordshire, England, died Sep 1746, in Ascott Under Wychwood, Oxfordshire, England, buried 29 Sep 1746, in Ascott Under

Wychwood, Oxfordshire, England. He was the son of Tims and Tims. He married Elizabeth Ferrimen[620,621] 14 Dec 1704, in Shipton under Wychwood, Oxfordshire, England. She was the daughter of William Ferryman and Elizabeth Gryme.

Children of George Tims and Elizabeth Ferrimen:

 i. **John Timms**,[396] born Dec 1705, in Ascott Under Wychwood, Oxfordshire, England, died Nov 1777, in Ascott Under Wychwood, Oxfordshire, England.

 ii. **George Tims**,[622] born Mar 1709, in Ascott Under Wychwood, Oxfordshire, England, christened 30 Mar 1709, in Ascott Under Wychwood, Oxfordshire, England.

 iii. **Samuel Tims**,[623] born Nov 1712, in Ascott Under Wychwood, Oxfordshire, England, christened 9 Nov 1712, in Ascott Under Wychwood, Oxfordshire, England, died Aug 1714, in Ascott Under Wychwood, Oxfordshire, England, buried 14 Aug 1714, in Ascott Under Wychwood, Oxfordshire, England.

 iv. **Samuel Tims**,[624] born Sep 1715, in Ascott Under Wychwood, Oxfordshire, England, christened 3 Oct 1715, in Ascott Under Wychwood, Oxfordshire, England. He married Mary Clarridge[624,625] 17 Nov 1739, in Shipton under Wychwood, Oxfordshire, England. Mary Clarridge was born about 1719, in Ascott Under Wychwood, Oxfordshire, England, died Jun 1758, in Ascott Under Wychwood, Oxfordshire, England, buried 4 Jul 1758, in Ascott Under Wychwood, Oxfordshire, England.

 v. **William Tims**, born Oct 1721, in Ascott Under Wychwood, Oxfordshire, England, christened 5 Nov 1721, in Ascott Under Wychwood, Oxfordshire, England.

239. Elizabeth Ferrimen was born about 1682, in Ascott Under Wychwood, Oxfordshire, England, died Nov 1752, in Ascott Under Wychwood, Oxfordshire, England, buried 17 Nov 1752, in Ascott Under Wychwood, Oxfordshire, England. She was the daughter of William Ferryman and Elizabeth Gryme. She married George Tims[620,626] 14 Dec 1704, in Shipton under Wychwood, Oxfordshire, England. He was the son of Tims and Tims.

240. John Cockins was born Mar 1656, in Upper Heyford, Oxfordshire, England, christened 6 Apr 1656, in Upper Heyford, Oxfordshire, England, died May 1737, in Upper Heyford, Oxfordshire, England, buried 23 May 1737, in Upper Heyford, Oxfordshire, England. He was the son of Anthony Cockins and Elizabeth Howse. He married Elizabeth Vennimore[627,628] 6 Apr 1684, in Hampton Poyle, Oxfordshire, England. She was the daughter of Christopher Vennimore and Margery Watts.

Children of John Cockins and Elizabeth Vennimore:

 i. **Elenor Cockins**,[396] born 13 Oct 1699, in Upper Heyford, Oxfordshire, England, died Jun 1759, in Steeple Aston, Oxfordshire, England.

241. Elizabeth Vennimore was born Mar 1656, in Kirtlington, Oxfordshire, England, christened 20

Mar 1656, in Kirtlington, Oxfordshire, England, died May 1729, in Upper Heyford, Oxfordshire, England, buried 2 Jun 1729, in Upper Heyford, Oxfordshire, England. She was the daughter of Christopher Vennimore and Margery Watts. She married John Cockins[627,629] 6 Apr 1684, in Hampton Poyle, Oxfordshire, England. He was the son of Anthony Cockins and Elizabeth Howse.
Notes for Elizabeth Vennimore:

aka: Fennimore

242. John Drinkwater was born 1694, in Oxfordshire, England, died Mar 1768, in Bampton, Oxfordshire, England, buried 25 Mar 1768, in Bampton, Oxfordshire, England. He was the son of John Drinkwater and Mrs Hannah Drinkwater. He married Ann Lapper[630] 18 May 1730, in Bampton, Oxfordshire, England. She was the daughter of Richard Lapper and Elizabeth Panting.

Children of John Drinkwater and Ann Lapper:

    i.   **Elizabeth Drinkwater**, born Jul 1731, in Bampton, Oxfordshire, England, christened 11 Jul 1731, in Bampton, Oxfordshire, England.

    ii.   **John Drinkwater**,[401] born Apr 1733, in Bampton, Oxfordshire, England.

    iii.   **William Drinkwater**, born Feb 1737, in Bampton, Oxfordshire, England, christened 27 Feb 1737, in Bampton, Oxfordshire, England.

243. Ann Lapper was born about 1707, in Oxfordshire, England, died Nov 1766, in Bampton, Oxfordshire, England, buried 4 Dec 1766, in Bampton, Oxfordshire, England. She was the daughter of Richard Lapper and Elizabeth Panting. She married John Drinkwater[630] 18 May 1730, in Bampton, Oxfordshire, England. He was the son of John Drinkwater and Mrs Hannah Drinkwater.

244. William Windows was born Sep 1689, in Bampton, Oxfordshire, England, christened 13 Sep 1689, in Bampton, Oxfordshire, England, died Apr 1758, in Bampton, Oxfordshire, England, buried 9 Apr 1758, in Bampton, Oxfordshire, England. He was the son of John Windows and Windows. He married Mary Grimsher 12 Nov 1714, in Bampton, Oxfordshire, England. She was the daughter of Bartholemew Grimsher and Mary Linzy.

Children of William Windows and Mary Grimsher:

    i.   **Elizabeth Windows**,[631] born Sep 1715, in Bampton, Oxfordshire, England, christened 11 Sep 1715, in Bampton, Oxfordshire, England.

    ii.   **Mary Windows**,[632] born Mar 1717, in Bampton, Oxfordshire, England, christened 20 Mar 1717, in Bampton, Oxfordshire, England.

    iii.   **Mary Windows**,[633] born Apr 1718, in Bampton, Oxfordshire, England, christened 19 Apr 1718, in Bampton, Oxfordshire, England.

    iv.   **Ann Windows**, born Jul 1725, in Bampton, Oxfordshire, England, died Jun 1768, in Bampton, Oxfordshire, England.

245. Mary Grimsher was born Oct 1692, in Bampton, Oxfordshire, England, christened 4 Nov 1692, in Bampton, Oxfordshire, England, died Nov 1738, in Bampton, Oxfordshire, England, buried 20 Nov 1738, in Bampton, Oxfordshire, England. She was the daughter of Bartholemew Grimsher and Mary Linzy. She married William Windows[634] 12 Nov 1714, in Bampton, Oxfordshire, England. He was the son of John Windows and Windows.
Notes for Mary Grimsher:

aka GRIMSHAW

246. Edward Hawkins was born Apr 1704, in Little Coxwell, Berkshire, England, christened 16 Apr 1704, in Little Coxwell, Berkshire, England. He was the son of John Hawkins and Ann Webb. He married Mary Cockhead[635,636] 10 Jun 1728, in Faringdon, Berkshire, England. She was the daughter of Cockhead and Cockhead.

Children of Edward Hawkins and Mary Cockhead:

    i.   **John Hawkins**,[402,404,405] born 13 Dec 1733, in Faringdon, Berkshire, England, died about 1789.

247. Mary Cockhead was born about 1706, in Berkshire, England. She was the daughter of Cockhead and Cockhead. She married Edward Hawkins[635,636] 10 Jun 1728, in Faringdon, Berkshire, England. He was the son of John Hawkins and Ann Webb.

248. John Alder was born Apr 1706, in Wantage, Berkshire, England, christened 30 Apr 1706, in Wantage, Berkshire, England, died Sep 1740, in Great Coxwell, Berkshire, England, buried 22 Sep 1740, in Great Coxwell, Berkshire, England. He was the son of William Alder and Mary Morley. He married Ann Phelps[637] 8 Aug 1725, in Chisledon, Wiltshire, England. She was the daughter of David Phelps and Phelps.
Notes for John Alder:

aka: ALDWORTH

Children of John Alder and Ann Phelps:

    i.   **John Alder**, born Apr 1727, in Childrey, Berkshire, England, christened 22 Apr 1727, in Childrey, Berkshire, England.
        aka ALDWORTH
    ii.   **Margaret Alder**, born Jul 1731, in Childrey, Berkshire, England, christened 18 Jul 1731, in Childrey, Berkshire, England.
    iii.   **Elizabeth Alder**,[638] born Nov 1734, in Great Coxwell, Berkshire, England, christened 9 Nov 1734, in Great Coxwell, Berkshire, England.
    iv.   **Mary Alder**,[402,403] born Feb 1736, in Great Coxwell, Berkshire, England, died Apr 1782, in Little Coxwell, Berkshire, England.

    v.   **Thomas Alder**, born May 1737, in Great Coxwell, Berkshire, England, christened 22 May 1737, in Great Coxwell, Berkshire, England.

249. Ann Phelps was born Sep 1695, in Swindon, Wiltshire, England, christened 16 Sep 1695, in Swindon, Wiltshire, England, died Jan 1790, in Great Coxwell, Berkshire, England, buried 2 Feb 1790, in Great Coxwell, Berkshire, England. She was the daughter of David Phelps and Phelps. She married John Alder[639] 8 Aug 1725, in Chisledon, Wiltshire, England. He was the son of William Alder and Mary Morley.

250. Richard Heydon was born 1685, in Witney, Oxfordshire, England. He was the son of William Heydon and Mrs Anne Heydon. He married Eleanor Young[640] 18 May 1708, in Witney, Oxfordshire, England. She was the daughter of Edward Young and Mrs Edward Young.
Notes for Richard Heydon:

IMPORTANT: Coleshill registry - page 21 Baptisms - 24 July 1726 copy: HAYDON Richard s Ric.d (corrected from Joss.p for every entry) aka: HEYDON Marriage: 1708 18 Jun HEYDON Richard maltster of Witney, s. William of Witney YOUNG Eleanor sp., Witney, d. Edward late of Milton

Children of Richard Heydon and Eleanor Young:

    i.   **Anne Heydon**, born Jul 1709, in Witney, Oxfordshire, England, christened 28 Jul 1709, in Witney, Oxfordshire, England, died before 1721, in Witney, Oxfordshire, England.

    ii.   **Mary Heydon**, born 12 Aug 1711, in Witney, Oxfordshire, England, christened 12 Oct 1711, in Witney, Oxfordshire, England, died before 1719, in Witney, Oxfordshire, England.

    iii.   **Sarah Haydon**,[641] born Dec 1717, in Coleshill, Oxfordshire, England, christened 27 Dec 1717, in Coleshill, Oxfordshire, England.

    iv.   **Mary Haydon**,[642] born Jul 1719, in Coleshill, Oxfordshire, England, christened 26 Jul 1719, in Coleshill, Oxfordshire, England.

    v.   **John Haydon**,[643] born Jan 1721, in Coleshill, Oxfordshire, England, christened 14 Jan 1721, in Coleshill, Oxfordshire, England, died Nov 1773, in Buckland, Oxfordshire, England, buried 14 Nov 1773, in Buckland, Oxfordshire, England. TWIN

    vi.   **Ann Haydon**,[644] born Jan 1721, in Coleshill, Oxfordshire, England, died Mar 1721, in Coleshill, Oxfordshire, England. TWIN

    vii.   **Elizabeth Haydon**,[645] born Oct 1723, in Coleshill, Oxfordshire, England, christened 6 Oct 1723, in Coleshill, Oxfordshire, England. She married Joseph Preston 1 Oct 1748, in Faringdon, Berkshire, England. Joseph Preston was born about 1720, in Berkshire, England.

    viii.   **Richard Haydon**,[407,417] born Jul 1726, in Coleshill, Oxfordshire, England, died Mar 1785, in Buckland, Oxfordshire, England.

251. Eleanor Young was born 1690, in Witney, Oxfordshire, England. She was the daughter of Edward Young and Mrs Edward Young. She married Richard Heydon[646,647,648] 18 May 1708, in Witney, Oxfordshire, England. He was the son of William Heydon and Mrs Anne Heydon.
Notes for Eleanor Young:

aka: Sarah

252. Richard Smith was born Dec 1695, in Eton, Buckinghamshire, England, christened 29 Dec 1695, in Eton, Buckinghamshire, England. He was the son of James Smith and Smith. He married Mary Newton[649,650] 22 May 1716, in Iver, Buckinghamshire, England. She was the daughter of Newton and Newton.

Children of Richard Smith and Mary Newton:

    i.   **Mary Smith**,[651] born Jul 1717, in Iver, Buckinghamshire, England, christened 27 Jul 1717, in Iver, Buckinghamshire, England.
    ii.   **Sarah Smith**,[406,407,408,409] born Nov 1720, in Iver, Buckinghamshire, England, died Feb 1785, in Buckland, Oxfordshire, England.
    iii.   **Elizabeth Smith**,[652] born Feb 1722, in Iver, Buckinghamshire, England, christened 2 Mar 1722, in Iver, Buckinghamshire, England, died before 1725, in Iver, Buckinghamshire, England.
    iv.   **Elizabeth Smith**,[653] born Aug 1726, in Iver, Buckinghamshire, England, christened 20 Aug 1726, in Iver, Buckinghamshire, England.
    v.   **Susannah Smith**,[654] born Mar 1732, in Iver, Buckinghamshire, England, christened 10 Mar 1732, in Iver, Buckinghamshire, England.

253. Mary Newton was born about 1698, in England. She was the daughter of Newton and Newton. She married Richard Smith[649,655,656] 22 May 1716, in Iver, Buckinghamshire, England. He was the son of James Smith and Smith.

254. Hugh Hawkyns was born about 1660, in Northmoor, Oxfordshire, England, died before 1760, in England. He was the son of Hawkins and Hawkins. He married Martha Fairbeard[657,658] 29 May 1679, in Oxford, Oxfordshire, England. She was the daughter of Henrie Fairbeard and Mrs Frances Fairbeard.
Notes for Hugh Hawkyns:

A Yeoman

Children of Hugh Hawkyns and Martha Fairbeard:

    i.   **Elizabeth Hawkins**, born Nov 1685, in Northmoor, Oxfordshire, England, christened 22 Nov 1685, in Northmoor, Oxfordshire, England.
    ii.   **Mabel Hawkins**, born Apr 1689, in Northmoor, Oxfordshire, England, christened 28 Apr 1689, in Northmoor, Oxfordshire, England.

  iii. **Henry Hawkins**, born Feb 1691, in Northmoor, Oxfordshire, England, christened 25 Feb 1691, in Northmoor, Oxfordshire, England.

  iv. **William Hawkins**,[418,420] born Nov 1694, in Northmoor, Oxfordshire, England, died Oct 1779, in Northmoor, Oxfordshire, England.

  v. **Martha Hawkins**, born 21 Sep 1696, in Northmoor, Oxfordshire, England, christened 27 Sep 1696, in Northmoor, Oxfordshire, England.

  vi. **Hannah Hawkins**, born 1 Sep 1699, in Northmoor, Oxfordshire, England, christened 10 Sep 1699, in Northmoor, Oxfordshire, England, died Oct 1705, in Northmoor, Oxfordshire, England, buried 1 Nov 1705, in Northmoor, Oxfordshire, England.

255. Martha Fairbeard was born 15 Apr 1658, in Northmoor, Oxfordshire, England, christened 4 May 1658, in Northmoor, Oxfordshire, England, died before 1750, in England. She was the daughter of Henrie Fairbeard and Mrs Frances Fairbeard. She married Hugh Hawkyns[659] 29 May 1679, in Oxford, Oxfordshire, England. He was the son of Hawkins and Hawkins.
Notes for Martha Fairbeard:

aka: Mabill or Martha - Mabil on birth reg

256. Ambrose Gee was born 1692, in Chipping Norton, Oxfordshire, England, died 1773, in Chipping Norton, Oxfordshire, England. He was the son of Gee and Gee. He married Mary Ekley[660] 28 Nov 1717, in Chipping Norton, Oxfordshire, England. She was the daughter of John Eckley and Ann Bell.

Children of Ambrose Gee and Mary Ekley:

  i. **Mary Gee**,[418] born 8 Feb 1718, in Chipping Norton, Oxfordshire, England, died Oct 1784, in Northmoor, Oxfordshire, England.

  ii. **Richard Gee**, born 10 May 1720, in Chipping Norton, Oxfordshire, England, died 1761, in Chipping Norton, Oxfordshire, England.

  iii. **Bety Gee**, born 25 Nov 1723, in Chipping Norton, Oxfordshire, England, christened 25 Nov 1723, in Chipping Norton, Oxfordshire, England.

  iv. **Catherine Gee**, born 21 Oct 1725, in Chipping Norton, Oxfordshire, England, christened 21 Oct 1725, in Chipping Norton, Oxfordshire, England.

  v. **Anne Gee**, born Sep 1727, in Chipping Norton, Oxfordshire, England, christened 3 Sep 1727, in Chipping Norton, Oxfordshire, England.

  vi. **Ambrose Gee**, born Nov 1731, in Chipping Norton, Oxfordshire, England, christened 7 Nov 1731, in Chipping Norton, Oxfordshire, England.

257. Mary Ekley was born 1696, in Chipping Norton, Oxfordshire, England. She was the daughter of John Eckley and Ann Bell. She married Ambrose Gee[660] 28 Nov 1717, in Chipping Norton, Oxfordshire, England. He was the son of Gee and Gee.

258. William Morgan was born Aug 1657, in Waltham Saint Lawrence, Berkshire, England, christened

11 Aug 1657, in Waltham Saint Lawrence, Berkshire, England, died about 1695, in Berkshire, England, buried about 1695, in Berkshire, England. He was the son of John Morgan and Mrs Mary Morgan. He married Allenora Adkin Or Adkyn[661] 16 Sep 1680, in Waltham Saint Lawrence, Berkshire, England. She was the daughter of Adkin Or Adkyn and Adkin Or Adkyn.

Children of William Morgan and Allenora Adkin Or Adkyn:

    i.   **Mary Morgan**,[662] born Aug 1679, in South Hinksey, Berkshire, England, christened 21 Aug 1679, in South Hinksey, Berkshire, England.

    ii.   **John Morgan**,[663] born Mar 1681, in South Hinksey, Berkshire, England, christened 28 Mar 1681, in South Hinksey, Berkshire, England.

    iii.   **Joane Morgan**,[664] born Jun 1683, in South Hinksey, Berkshire, England, christened 15 Jul 1683, in South Hinksey, Berkshire, England.

    iv.   **Anne Morgan**,[665] born May 1684, in South Hinksey, Berkshire, England.

    v.   **Jane Morgan**,[666] born Apr 1685, in South Hinksey, Berkshire, England, christened 10 May 1685, in South Hinksey, Berkshire, England.

    vi.   **Elizabeth Morgan**,[667] born Mar 1689, in South Hinksey, Berkshire, England, christened 15 Apr 1689, in South Hinksey, Berkshire, England.

    vii.   **William Morgan**,[421,422] born Jan 1690, in South Hinksey, Berkshire, England, died Oct 1719, in Standlake, Oxfordshire, England.

    viii.   **Richard Morgan**,[668] born Apr 1693, in South Hinksey, Berkshire, England, christened 7 May 1693, in South Hinksey, Berkshire, England.

259. Allenora Adkin Or Adkyn was born about 1659, in Berkshire, England, died about 1700, in Berkshire, England. She was the daughter of Adkin Or Adkyn and Adkin Or Adkyn. She married William Morgan[661,669,670] 16 Sep 1680, in Waltham Saint Lawrence, Berkshire, England. He was the son of John Morgan and Mrs Mary Morgan.

260. Richard Veasy was born about 1655, in Oxfordshire, England. He was the son of Veasy and Veasy. He married Ann Hunt[671] 29 Oct 1676, in Witney, Oxfordshire, England. She was the daughter of Hunt and Hunt.

Children of Richard Veasy and Ann Hunt:

    i.   **Catherine Veasy**,[421] born about 1692, in Shifford, Oxfordshire, England.

261. Ann Hunt was born about 1658, in Oxfordshire, England. She was the daughter of Hunt and Hunt. She married Richard Veasy[671] 29 Oct 1676, in Witney, Oxfordshire, England. He was the son of Veasy and Veasy.

262. Richard Stone was born 24 Mar 1646, in Longworth, Berkshire, England, christened 24 Mar 1646, in Longworth, Berkshire, England, died before 1740, in England. He was the son of Richard Stone and Sibil Green. He married Ann Browne[672,673] 6 Oct 1672, in Standlake, Oxfordshire, England. She was the daughter of Browne and Browne.

Children of Richard Stone and Ann Browne:

  i.   **Richard Stone**, born Sep 1675, in Duckland, Oxfordshire, England, christened 16 Sep 1675, in Standlake, Oxfordshire, England, died Oct 1727, in Standlake, Oxfordshire, England, buried 24 Oct 1727, in Standlake, Oxfordshire, England. He married Sarah Hollowway 19 Jan 1705, in Standlake, Oxfordshire, England. Sarah Hollowway was born about 1684, in Fulbrook, Oxfordshire, England.
  ii. **Elizabeth Stone**, born Apr 1679, in Standlake, Oxfordshire, England, christened 14 Apr 1679, in Standlake, Oxfordshire, England.
  iii. **William Stone**,[280,424,425] born Mar 1681, in Standlake, Oxfordshire, England, died Jul 1725, in Standlake, Oxfordshire, England.
  iv. **Mary Stone**, born Jan 1684, in Standlake, Oxfordshire, England, christened 9 Jan 1684, in Standlake, Oxfordshire, England, died Jan 1699, in Standlake, Oxfordshire, England, buried 24 Jan 1699, in Standlake, Oxfordshire, England.

263. Ann Browne was born about 1650, in Standlake, Oxfordshire, England, died Mar 1708, in Standlake, Oxfordshire, England, buried 29 Mar 1708, in Standlake, Oxfordshire, England. She was the daughter of Browne and Browne. She married Richard Stone[672,674] 6 Oct 1672, in Standlake, Oxfordshire, England. He was the son of Richard Stone and Sibil Green.

264. Thomas Onion was born about 1652, in Berkshire, England, died Sep 1689, in Hinton Waldrist, Berkshire, England, buried Sep 1689, in Hinton Waldrist, Berkshire, England. He was the son of Thomas Onion Or Anyon and Mrs Elizabeth Onion. He married Anne Umberstone[423,675] about 1671, in Berkshire, England. She was the daughter of Thomas Umberstone and Diana Newbery.

Children of Thomas Onion and Anne Umberstone:

  i.   **Massey Onion**,[676] born Apr 1672, in Hinton Waldrist, Berkshire, England, christened 26 Apr 1672, in Hinton Waldrist, Berkshire, England.
  ii. **Martha Onion**,[280,423,424] born Mar 1675, in Hinton Waldrist, Berkshire, England, died before 1750, in England.
  iii. **Mary Onion**,[677] born Dec 1678, in Hinton Waldrist, Berkshire, England, christened 15 Dec 1678, in Hinton Waldrist, Berkshire, England, died Jun 1709, in Hinton Waldrist, Berkshire, England, buried 19 Jun 1709, in Hinton Waldrist, Berkshire, England.
  iv. **Thomas Onion**,[678,679] born Apr 1682, in Hinton Waldrist, Berkshire, England, christened 25 Apr 1682, in Hinton Waldrist, Berkshire, England, died Sep 1686, in Hinton Waldrist, Berkshire, England, buried 21 Sep 1686, in Hinton Waldrist, Berkshire, England.
       aka THOMAS OINION
  v.   **Anne Onion**,[680] born Sep 1684, in Hinton Waldrist, Berkshire, England, christened

21 Sep 1684, in Hinton Waldrist, Berkshire, England.

    vi.   **Jane Onion**,[681] born Apr 1687, in Hinton Waldrist, Berkshire, England, christened 22 Apr 1687, in Hinton Waldrist, Berkshire, England.

    vii.   **Richard Onion**,[682] born Oct 1689, in Hinton Waldrist, Berkshire, England, christened 15 Oct 1689, in Hinton Waldrist, Berkshire, England.
aka OINION

265. Anne Umberstone was born 1649, in Hurst, Berkshire, England, christened 2 Dec 1649, in Hurst, Berkshire, England, died 1700, in Berkshire, England. She was the daughter of Thomas Umberstone and Diana Newbery. She married Thomas Onion[423,675] about 1671, in Berkshire, England. He was the son of Thomas Onion Or Anyon and Mrs Elizabeth Onion.

266. Richard Hartlett was born about 1680, in Oxfordshire, England. He was the son of James Hartlett and Hartlett. He married Mary Stone[683] 18 Apr 1705, in Banbury, Oxfordshire, England. She was the daughter of Stone and Stone.

Children of Richard Hartlett and Mary Stone:

    i.   **Richard Hartlett**,[289,426] born about 1708, in Deddington, Oxfordshire, England.

267. Mary Stone was born about 1684, in Oxfordshire, England. She was the daughter of Stone and Stone. She married Richard Hartlett[684] 18 Apr 1705, in Banbury, Oxfordshire, England. He was the son of James Hartlett and Hartlett.

268. Richard King was born 4 Mar 1660, in South Newington, Oxfordshire, England. He was the son of Henry King and Margaret Claridge. He married Elizabeth Barris[685,686] 19 Oct 1689, in Byfield, Northamptonshire, England. She was the daughter of Barris and Barris.

Children of Richard King and Elizabeth Barris:

    i.   **Richard King**,[687,688] born 28 May 1691, in Banbury, Oxfordshire, England, christened 28 Aug 1691, in Banbury, Oxfordshire, England.

    ii.   **Hannah King**,[689] born 20 Jun 1693, in Banbury, Oxfordshire, England.

    iii. **Humphrey King**,[690] born 11 Mar 1695, in Banbury, Oxfordshire, England.

    iv. **Mary King**,[691] born 3 Oct 1696, in South Newington, Oxfordshire, England.

    v.   **John King**,[692] born 2 Oct 1700, in South Newington, Oxfordshire, England, christened 6 Oct 1700, in South Newington, Oxfordshire, England.

    vi.   **Sarah King**,[693] born 2 Dec 1701, in Banbury, Oxfordshire, England.

    vii. **Esther King**,[694] born 15 Nov 1703, in Banbury, Oxfordshire, England.

    viii. **Edith King**,[695] born 22 Aug 1706, in Banbury, Oxfordshire, England.

    ix. **Elizabeth King**,[289,426,427] born 3 Mar 1709, in Banbury, Oxfordshire, England.

269. Elizabeth Barris was born about 1670, in Byfield, Northamptonshire, England. She was the daughter of Barris and Barris. She married Richard King[686,696] 19 Oct 1689, in Byfield, Northamptonshire, England. He was the son of Henry King and Margaret Claridge.

270. John Gilkes was born 16 Mar 1666, in Banbury, Oxfordshire, England, died Jul 1764, in Banbury, Oxfordshire, England, buried 10 Jul 1764, in Banbury, Oxfordshire, England. He was the son of Stephen Gilkes Or Jelkes and Margaret Basely Or Bazely. He married Mary Swift[697,698] 16 Oct 1695, in Banbury, Oxfordshire, England. She was the daughter of Robert Swifte and Joyce Poulton.

Children of John Gilkes and Mary Swift:

    i.   **Tobias Gilkes**,[430] born about 1718, in Oxfordshire, England, died May 1747, in Chipping Norton, Oxfordshire, England.

271. Mary Swift was born 12 Nov 1673, in Adderbury, Oxfordshire, England. She was the daughter of Robert Swifte and Joyce Poulton. She married John Gilkes[699,700,701] 16 Oct 1695, in Banbury, Oxfordshire, England. He was the son of Stephen Gilkes Or Jelkes and Margaret Basely Or Bazely.

272. Thomas Price was born about 1675, in Chipping Norton, Oxfordshire, England. He was the son of Price and Price. He married Bridget Berry[702,703] 28 Oct 1699, in Chipping Norton, Oxfordshire, England. She was the daughter of Berry and Berry.

Children of Thomas Price and Bridget Berry:

    i.   **Bridget Price**,[704] born Feb 1701, in Chipping Norton, Oxfordshire, England, christened 2 Mar 1701, in Chipping Norton, Oxfordshire, England.
    ii.   **Sarah Price**,[430] born about 1720, in Oxfordshire, England.

273. Bridget Berry was born about 1677, in Chipping Norton, Oxfordshire, England. She was the daughter of Berry and Berry. She married Thomas Price[702,703] 28 Oct 1699, in Chipping Norton, Oxfordshire, England. He was the son of Price and Price.

274. John Foster was born about 1700, in Oxfordshire, England, died Apr 1744, in South Leigh, Oxfordshire, England, buried 12 Apr 1744, in South Leigh, Oxfordshire, England. He was the son of John Foster and Mrs Sarah Foster. He married Mary Spier[705] 3 Jan 1722, in Oxford, Oxfordshire, England. She was the daughter of Yeoman John Spier and Hannah Clinch.

Children of John Foster and Mary Spier:

    i.   **Mary Foster**,[706] born Jun 1722, in South Leigh, Oxfordshire, England, christened 22 Jun 1722, in South Leigh, Oxfordshire, England, died Dec 1739, in South Leigh, Oxfordshire, England, buried 2 Jan 1740, in South Leigh, Oxfordshire, England.
    ii.   **Sarah Foster**,[707] born Mar 1724, in South Leigh, Oxfordshire, England, christened 29 Mar 1724, in South Leigh, Oxfordshire, England.

iii. **Ann Foster**,[708] born Sep 1728, in South Leigh, Oxfordshire, England, christened 5 Oct 1728, in South Leigh, Oxfordshire, England.

iv. **Yeoman John Foster**,[443,444,445] born Apr 1731, in South Leigh, Oxfordshire, England, died Mar 1822, in Standlake, Oxfordshire, England.

275. Mary Spier was born about 1702, in South Leigh, Oxfordshire, England. She was the daughter of Yeoman John Spier and Hannah Clinch. She married John Foster[705] 3 Jan 1722, in Oxford, Oxfordshire, England. He was the son of John Foster and Mrs Sarah Foster.

276. John Harris was born 28 Jul 1697, in Standlake, Oxfordshire, England, christened 22 Aug 1697, in Standlake, Oxfordshire, England, died before 1790, in England. He was the son of William Harris and Elizabeth Andrews. He married Catherine Brooks 1729, in Standlake, Oxfordshire, England. She was the daughter of Brooks and Brooks.

Children of John Harris and Catherine Brooks:

i. **John Harris**,[709] born 1 Jan 1731, in Standlake, Oxfordshire, England.

ii. **Sarah Harris**,[431,432,433] born 25 Apr 1736, in Standlake, Oxfordshire, England, died Mar 1804, in Standlake, Oxfordshire, England.

iii. **William Harris**,[710] born 4 Feb 1739, in Standlake, Oxfordshire, England.

iv. **Joseph Harris**,[711] born 4 Oct 1741, in Standlake, Oxfordshire, England.

277. Catherine Brooks was born about 1700, in Oxfordshire, England, died before 1800, in England. She was the daughter of Brooks and Brooks. She married John Harris[712] 1729, in Standlake, Oxfordshire, England. He was the son of William Harris and Elizabeth Andrews.

278. John Duffen was born about 1680, in Berkshire, England. He was the son of Thomas Duffen and Mrs Mary Duffin. He married Alice Ludler[713] 22 Aug 1705, in West Hanney, Berkshire, England. She was the daughter of Ludler and Ludler.

Children of John Duffen and Alice Ludler:

i. **John Duffen**,[446,447] born about 1725, in Abingdon, Berkshire, England, died Nov 1787, in Abingdon, Berkshire, England.

279. Alice Ludler was born about 1682, in Berkshire, England. She was the daughter of Ludler and Ludler. She married John Duffen[713] 22 Aug 1705, in West Hanney, Berkshire, England. He was the son of Thomas Duffen and Mrs Mary Duffin.

280. Robert Clark was born 1681, in Longworth, Berkshire, England. He was the son of Thomas Clark and Mary Knapp. He married Mary Smith[714,715,716] 13 Jan 1718, in Cumnor, Berkshire, England. She was the daughter of Thomas Smith and Martha Smith.

Children of Robert Clark and Mary Smith:

    i.   **Sarah Clark**,[446,447] born Dec 1725, in South Hinksey, Berkshire, England, died Dec 1772, in Abingdon, Berkshire, England.

281. Mary Smith was born about 1697, in Berkshire, England. She was the daughter of Thomas Smith and Martha Smith. She married Robert Clark[715,716,717] 13 Jan 1718, in Cumnor, Berkshire, England. He was the son of Thomas Clark and Mary Knapp.

282. Wiliam King was born about 1690, in Witney, Oxfordshire, England. He was the son of William King and Rebecka Burcut. He married Elizabeth Ewin[718] 28 Jul 1709, in Witney, Oxfordshire, England. She was the daughter of John Ewin and Ewin.

Children of Wiliam King and Elizabeth Ewin:

    i.   **John King**,[719] born Mar 1712, in Witney, Oxfordshire, England, christened 12 Mar 1712, in Witney, Oxfordshire, England.
    ii.   **Mary King**,[720] born Mar 1713, in Witney, Oxfordshire, England, christened 14 Mar 1713, in Witney, Oxfordshire, England, buried 2 Apr 1719, in Witney, Oxfordshire, England.
    iii. **William King**,[721] born Feb 1715, in Witney, Oxfordshire, England, christened 13 Feb 1715, in Witney, Oxfordshire, England, died before Dec 1715, in Witney, Oxfordshire, England.
    iv.   **William King**,[298,454] born Feb 1716, in Witney, Oxfordshire, England, died before 1800, in England.
    v.   **Joseph King**,[722] born Aug 1720, in Witney, Oxfordshire, England, christened 5 Sep 1720, in Witney, Oxfordshire, England.

283. Elizabeth Ewin was born about 1690, in Witney, Oxfordshire, England. She was the daughter of John Ewin and Ewin. She married Wiliam King[718] 28 Jul 1709, in Witney, Oxfordshire, England. He was the son of William King and Rebecka Burcut.

284. Carew Bartlet was born about 1700, in Witney, Oxfordshire, England. He was the son of Bartlet and Bartlet. He married Elizabeth Casey[723] 14 May 1722, in Swinbrook, Oxfordshire, England. She was the daughter of Casey and Casey.

Children of Carew Bartlet and Elizabeth Casey:

    i.   **Elizabeth Bartlet**,[298] born about 1730, in Witney, Oxfordshire, England, died before 1830, in England.

285. Elizabeth Casey was born about 1701, in Cogges, Oxfordshire, England. She was the daughter of Casey and Casey. She married Carew Bartlet[724] 14 May 1722, in Swinbrook, Oxfordshire, England. He was the son of Bartlet and Bartlet.

286. John Probatts was born about 1680, in Berkshire, England. He was the son of Probatts and Probatts. He married Elizabeth Wilson[725,726] 13 Dec 1703, in Speen, Berkshire, England. She was the daughter of Wilson and Wilson.
Notes for John Probatts:

Married at Speen, St Mary, Berkshire, England. 13 Dec 1703 - 1st child born 1 month later.

Children of John Probatts and Elizabeth Wilson:

     i.   **John Probatts**,[727] born Jan 1704, in Ashbury, Berkshire, England, christened 7 Feb 1704, in Ashbury, Berkshire, England, died before 1708, in Ashbury, Berkshire, England.

    ii.   **William Probatts**,[456] born 12 Dec 1705, in Ashbury, Berkshire, England.

    iii.   **John Probatts**,[728] born Mar 1708, in Ashbury, Berkshire, England, christened 17 Apr 1708, in Ashbury, Berkshire, England.

    iv.   **Samuel Probatts**,[729] born Jan 1711, in Ashbury, Berkshire, England, christened 7 Feb 1711, in Ashbury, Berkshire, England.

287. Elizabeth Wilson was born about 1682, in Berkshire, England. She was the daughter of Wilson and Wilson. She married John Probatts[725,726] 13 Dec 1703, in Speen, Berkshire, England. He was the son of Probatts and Probatts.

288. William Bayly was born about 1690, in Berkshire, England. He was the son of Edward Bayly and Hannah Meredith. He married Susannah Lancaster[730] 9 Jun 1712, in New Windsor, Berkshire, England. She was the daughter of Lancaster and Lancaster.

Children of William Bayly and Susannah Lancaster:

     i.   **Sarah Bayly**,[455] born Apr 1724, in Faringdon, Berkshire, England.

289. Susannah Lancaster was born about 1692, in Berkshire, England. She was the daughter of Lancaster and Lancaster. She married William Bayly[730] 9 Jun 1712, in New Windsor, Berkshire, England. He was the son of Edward Bayly and Hannah Meredith.

290. Henry Newell was born about 1680, in Oxfordshire, England, died before 1780, in England. He was the son of John Newell and Ellizabeth Fettiplace. He married Anne Hunt[731] 1701, in Oxford, Oxfordshire, England. She was the daughter of Hunt and Hunt.
Notes for Henry Newell:

Parish Records Collection 1538-2005 marriage Year of Marriage: 1701 Last Name: Newell First Name: Henry Supplied First Name: Hen Spouse's Last Name: Hunt Spouse's First Name: Anne Spouse's

Supplied First Name: An Vicar General Marriage Licences Place: S Aug

Children of Henry Newell and Anne Hunt:

> i.   **Henry Newell**,[458] born 1708, in Oxfordshire, England, died 1745, in England.

291. Anne Hunt was born about 1680, in Oxfordshire, England, died before 1780, in England. She was the daughter of Hunt and Hunt. She married Henry Newell[732] 1701, in Oxford, Oxfordshire, England. He was the son of John Newell and Ellizabeth Fettiplace.

292. William Oxlade was born Feb 1690, in Great Marlow, Buckinghamshire, England, christened 8 Feb 1690, in Great Marlow, Buckinghamshire, England, died Feb 1744, in Bisham, Berkshire, England, buried 7 Feb 1744, in Bisham, Berkshire, England. He was the son of John Oxlade and Ann Hollier. He married (1) Mary Salter[733] 21 Dec 1710, in Great Marlow, Buckinghamshire, England. She was the daughter of William Salter and Mrs Mary Salter. He married (2) Margaret Langley 22 Oct 1719, in Hughenden, Buckinghamshire, England.

Children of William Oxlade and Mary Salter:

> i.   **William Oxlade**, born 1713, in Great Marlow, Buckinghamshire, England, christened 17 Dec 1713, in Great Marlow, Buckinghamshire, England, died 1807, in England. He married Elizabeth Jones about 1735, in Great Marlow, Buckinghamshire, England. Elizabeth Jones was born 1705, in Great Marlow, Buckinghamshire, England, died 1743, in Great Marlow, Buckinghamshire, England.
> ii.   **Ann Oxlade**,[458] born Jun 1716, in Great Marlow, Buckinghamshire, England, died before 1800, in England.
> iii. **John Oxlade**, born 1717, in Great Marlow, Buckinghamshire, England, christened 16 Jan 1717, in Great Marlow, Buckinghamshire, England.

Children of William Oxlade and Margaret Langley:

> i.   **William Oxlade**, born 1722, in Great Marlow, Buckinghamshire, England, christened 22 Dec 1722, in Great Marlow, Buckinghamshire, England.

293. Mary Salter was born 1685, in Great Marlow, Buckinghamshire, England, died about 1717, in Berkshire, England. She was the daughter of William Salter and Mrs Mary Salter. She married William Oxlade[733] 21 Dec 1710, in Great Marlow, Buckinghamshire, England. He was the son of John Oxlade and Ann Hollier.

294. John Broadway was born 1683, in Cuxham, Oxfordshire, England, christened 2 Mar 1683, in Cuxham, Oxfordshire, England, died Feb 1719, in Cuxham, Oxfordshire, England, buried 2 Mar 1719, in Cuxham, Oxfordshire, England. He was the son of John Broadway and Martha Pritchard. He married

Alice Bolter[735] 23 Jun 1700, in Cuxham, Oxfordshire, England.[734] She was the daughter of Robert Bolter and Bolter.

Notes for John Broadway:

Taken from parish records

Children of John Broadway and Alice Bolter:

    i.   **John Broadway**,[460] born 6 Sep 1702, in Cuxham, Oxfordshire, England, died 10 Mar 1768, in Cuxham, Oxfordshire, England.

    ii.   **Thomas Broadway**, born 30 Apr 1704, in Cuxham, Oxfordshire, England, died 7 Aug 1704, in England.

    iii.   **Edward Broadway**, born 1707, in Cuxham, Oxfordshire, England, christened 9 Apr 1707, in Cuxham, Oxfordshire, England, died 1 Oct 1766, in Cuxham, Oxfordshire, England. He married Elizabeth Costard 19 Apr 1731, in Cuxham, Oxfordshire, England. Elizabeth Costard was born 1707, in Chalgrove, Oxfordshire, England.

    iv.   **Joseph Broadway**, born 1709, in Cuxham, Oxfordshire, England, died after 1755, in Oxfordshire, England. He married Hannah King 27 Jan 1733, in Oxford, Oxfordshire, England. Hannah King was born about 1710, in Oxfordshire, England, died after 1755, in Oxfordshire, England.

295. Alice Bolter was born Mar 1684, in Bicester, Oxfordshire, England, christened 25 Mar 1684, in Bicester, Oxfordshire, England, died 25 Feb 1735, in Cuxham, Oxfordshire, England, buried 26 Feb 1735, in Cuxham, Oxfordshire, England. She was the daughter of Robert Bolter and Bolter. She married John Broadway 23 Jun 1700, in Cuxham, Oxfordshire, England.[734] He was the son of John Broadway and Martha Pritchard.

Notes for Alice Bolter:

Taken from parish records burial record - Cuxham parish records

296. Michael Hinde was born Jul 1676, in Benson, Oxfordshire, England, christened 9 Jul 1676, in Benson, Oxfordshire, England, died before 1770, in England. He was the son of Mickell Hine and Hine. He married Elizabeth Scholes[736] 4 Nov 1703, in Cuxham, Oxfordshire, England. She was the daughter of William Scoles and Jane Belson.

Notes for Michael Hinde:

aka: MICKELL HINE

Children of Michael Hinde and Elizabeth Scholes:

    i.   **Jane Hinde**,[459,460] born May 1709, in Cuxham, Oxfordshire, England, died 1 Sep 1801, in Cuxham, Oxfordshire, England.

297. Elizabeth Scholes was born about 1673, in Cuxham, Oxfordshire, England, christened 27 Oct 1673, in Lewknor, Oxfordshire, England, died before 1755, in England. She was the daughter of William Scoles and Jane Belson. She married Michael Hinde[737,738] 4 Nov 1703, in Cuxham, Oxfordshire, England. He was the son of Mickell Hine and Hine.

298. William Jones was born about 1698, in Oxfordshire, England. He was the son of Jones and Jones. He married Elizabeth Cligdale[739] 1 Feb 1718, in Oxford, Oxfordshire, England. She was the daughter of Cligdale and Cligdale.

Children of William Jones and Elizabeth Cligdale:

      i.   **Richard Jones,**[461,462] born Dec 1722, in Oxford, Oxfordshire, England.

299. Elizabeth Cligdale was born about 1700, in Oxfordshire, England. She was the daughter of Cligdale and Cligdale. She married William Jones[739] 1 Feb 1718, in Oxford, Oxfordshire, England. He was the son of Jones and Jones.

300. Thomas Green was born 11 Aug 1702, in Headington, Oxfordshire, England, christened 16 Aug 1702, in Headington, Oxfordshire, England. He was the son of John Green and Elizabeth Dudley. He married Elizabeth Snow[740,741] 23 Sep 1723, in Oxford, Oxfordshire, England. She was the daughter of Gregory Snow and Elizabeth Boyse.

Children of Thomas Green and Elizabeth Snow:

      i.   **Mary Green,**[461] born about 1735, in Headington, Oxfordshire, England, died about 1810, in England.

301. Elizabeth Snow was born Nov 1702, in Headington, Oxfordshire, England, christened 15 Nov 1702, in Headington, Oxfordshire, England. She was the daughter of Gregory Snow and Elizabeth Boyse. She married Thomas Green[741,742] 23 Sep 1723, in Oxford, Oxfordshire, England. He was the son of John Green and Elizabeth Dudley.

302. Richard Giles was born about 1716, in Islip, Oxfordshire, England. He was the son of Giles and Mary Webb. He married Susannah Allen[743] 14 Apr 1737, in Enstone, Oxfordshire, England. She was the daughter of Richard Allen and Susannah Hart.

Children of Richard Giles and Susannah Allen:

      i.   **Richard Giles,**[465,466] born Jun 1739, in Islip, Oxfordshire, England.

303. Susannah Allen was born about 1716, in Enstone, Oxfordshire, England. She was the daughter of Richard Allen and Susannah Hart. She married Richard Giles[744] 14 Apr 1737, in Enstone, Oxfordshire, England. He was the son of Giles and Mary Webb.

304. Joseph Jackson was born Feb 1705, in Bicester, Oxfordshire, England, christened 19 Feb 1705, in Bicester, Oxfordshire, England. He was the son of John Jackson and Jackson. He married Sarah Howse[745] 23 Sep 1729, in Bicester, Oxfordshire, England. She was the daughter of William Howse and Howse.

Children of Joseph Jackson and Sarah Howse:

      i.   **Mary Jackson**,[463,464] born Oct 1738, in Bicester, Oxfordshire, England.

305. Sarah Howse was born Aug 1703, in Bicester, Oxfordshire, England, christened 23 Aug 1703, in Bicester, Oxfordshire, England, died May 1779, in Bicester, Oxfordshire, England, buried 17 May 1779, in Bicester, Oxfordshire, England. She was the daughter of William Howse and Howse. She married Joseph Jackson[745,746] 23 Sep 1729, in Bicester, Oxfordshire, England. He was the son of John Jackson and Jackson.

306. William Hinton was born about 1685, in Great Haseley, Oxfordshire, England. He was the son of Hinton and Hinton. He married Hannah Latham[747] 20 Oct 1707, in Oxford, Oxfordshire, England. She was the daughter of Latham and Latham.

Children of William Hinton and Hannah Latham:

      i.   **Thomas Hinton**,[467,473] born about 1711, in Denton, Oxfordshire, England, died 1790, in England.

307. Hannah Latham was born about 1687, in Little Haseley, Oxfordshire, England. She was the daughter of Latham and Latham. She married William Hinton[747] 20 Oct 1707, in Oxford, Oxfordshire, England. He was the son of Hinton and Hinton.

308. Edward Slaughter was born about 1685, in Thame, Oxfordshire, England. He was the son of John Slaughter and Joane Kinge. He married Mary Holyman[748] 17 Nov 1717, in Oxford, Oxfordshire, England. She was the daughter of Holyman and Holyman.

Children of Edward Slaughter and Mary Holyman:

      i.   **Mary Slaughter**,[467] born 1718, in Cuddesdon, Oxfordshire, England, died Oct 1795, in Cuddesdon, Oxfordshire, England.

309. Mary Holyman was born about 1688, in Tetsworth, Oxfordshire, England. She was the daughter of Holyman and Holyman. She married Edward Slaughter[748] 17 Nov 1717, in Oxford, Oxfordshire, England. He was the son of John Slaughter and Joane Kinge.

310. Henry Kirby was born about 1700, in Charlton on Otmoor, Oxfordshire, England, died before 1800, in England. He was the son of John Kirby and Alice Grace Richardson. He married Mabel

West[304] 2 Jun 1720, in Oxford, Oxfordshire, England. She was the daughter of Jeremiah West and Mable Raymond.

Children of Henry Kirby and Mabel West:

    i.   **Henry Kirby,**[304] born 10 Jun 1722, in Charlton on Otmoor, Oxfordshire, England, christened 8 Jul 1722, in Charlton on Otmoor, Oxfordshire, England.

    ii.   **Ralph Kirby,**[304] born Dec 1724, in Charlton on Otmoor, Oxfordshire, England, died Nov 1800, in Charlton on Otmoor, Oxfordshire, England.

311. Mabel West was born about 1701, in Charlton on Otmoor, Oxfordshire, England, died before 1800, in England. She was the daughter of Jeremiah West and Mable Raymond. She married Henry Kirby[304] 2 Jun 1720, in Oxford, Oxfordshire, England. He was the son of John Kirby and Alice Grace Richardson.

312. Robert Howlett was born Jul 1694, in Murcot, Oxfordshire, England, christened 7 Jul 1694, in Charlton on Otmoor, Oxfordshire, England, died 18 Jan 1759, in Charlton on Otmoor, Oxfordshire, England, buried 18 Jan 1759, in Charlton on Otmoor, Oxfordshire, England. He was the son of John Howlet and Ann Dennett. He married Mary King[749,750] 17 Dec 1719, in Charlton on Otmoor, Oxfordshire, England. She was the daughter of Walter King and Mrs Elizabeth King.

Children of Robert Howlett and Mary King:

    i.   **Martha Howlett,**[474] born 11 Jun 1722, in Charlton on Otmoor, Oxfordshire, England, died Sep 1805, in Charlton on Otmoor, Oxfordshire, England.

313. Mary King was born Jan 1696, in Grendon Underwood, Buckinghamshire, England, christened 13 Jan 1696, in Grendon Underwood, Buckinghamshire, England, died 16 Aug 1773, in Buckinghamshire, England. She was the daughter of Walter King and Mrs Elizabeth King. She married Robert Howlett[751,752] 17 Dec 1719, in Charlton on Otmoor, Oxfordshire, England. He was the son of John Howlet and Ann Dennett.

314. Richard Clarcke was born 1670, in Dinton, Buckinghamshire, England. He was the son of Henry Clark and Elizabeth Williams. He married Ester Hallon[753] 1696, in Dinton, Buckinghamshire, England. She was the daughter of Hallon and Hallon.
Notes for Richard Clarcke:

aka: CLARK, CLARCK, CLARCKE

Children of Richard Clarcke and Ester Hallon:

    i.   **William Clark,**[475,478] born 1710, in Dinton, Buckinghamshire, England, died before 1810, in England.

315. Ester Hallon was born about 1675, in Buckinghamshire, England. She was the daughter of Hallon and Hallon. She married Richard Clarcke[753] 1696, in Dinton, Buckinghamshire, England. He was the son of Henry Clark and Elizabeth Williams.

316. Thomas Rogers was born Dec 1671, in Great Missenden, Buckinghamshire, England, christened 6 Jan 1672, in Great Missenden, Buckinghamshire, England. He was the son of William Rogers and Mrs Elizabeth Rogers[754,755]. He married Mary Clark 4 Aug 1706, in Great Missenden, Buckinghamshire, England. She was the daughter of Edward Clarke and Katherine Wright.

Children of Thomas Rogers and Mary Clark:

> i.   **Sarah Rogers,**[309,475] born Jan 1717, in Dinton, Buckinghamshire, England, died before 1800, in England.

317. Mary Clark was born Aug 1675, in Great Missenden, Buckinghamshire, England, christened 10 Aug 1675, in Great Missenden, Buckinghamshire, England. She was the daughter of Edward Clarke and Katherine Wright. She married Thomas Rogers[754,756] 4 Aug 1706, in Great Missenden, Buckinghamshire, England. He was the son of William Rogers and Mrs Elizabeth Rogers.

318. Edvardi Grant was born about 1685, in Buckinghamshire, England. He was the son of Grant and Grant. He married Mariae Hawes[757,758,759] 15 Jan 1709, in Worminghall, Buckinghamshire, England. She was the daughter of Rodulphi Hawes and Hawes.
Notes for Edvardi Grant:

aka EDUARDUS GRANT

Children of Edvardi Grant and Mariae Hawes:

> i.   **Johannes Grant,**[479,489] born 11 Nov 1716, in Worminghall, Buckinghamshire, England, died before 1800, in England.
> ii.   **Maria Grant,**[760] born 25 Jan 1718, in Worminghall, Buckinghamshire, England.
> iii. **Thomas Grant,**[761] born 17 Jan 1724, in Worminghall, Buckinghamshire, England.
> iv.   **Elizabetha Grant,**[762] born 17 Sep 1727, in Worminghall, Buckinghamshire, England.

319. Mariae Hawes was born 2 Oct 1690, in Worminghall, Buckinghamshire, England. She was the daughter of Rodulphi Hawes and Hawes. She married Edvardi Grant[757,763] 15 Jan 1709, in Worminghall, Buckinghamshire, England. He was the son of Grant and Grant.
Notes for Mariae Hawes:

aka HAWS, HAWES

320. John Yong was born Jan 1679, in Chalvey, Buckinghamshire, England, christened 25 Jan 1679, in

Chalvey, Buckinghamshire, England, died Dec 1730, in Beaconsfield, Buckinghamshire, England, buried 19 Dec 1730, in Beaconsfield, Buckinghamshire, England. He was the son of John Yong and Mrs Elizabeth Young. He married Martha Stevens[764,765] 27 Apr 1699, in Cookham, Berkshire, England. She was the daughter of Thomas Steevens and Katrigne Spott.
Notes for John Yong:

Beaconsfield, Buckingham parish records. Burial 19 Dec 1730 John YOUNG, affidavit made

Children of John Yong and Martha Stevens:

    i.   **John Young**, born 4 Sep 1700, in Beaconsfield, Buckinghamshire, England, christened 4 Sep 1700, in Beaconsfield, Buckinghamshire, England, died 10 Oct 1701, in Beaconsfield, Buckinghamshire, England, buried 10 Oct 1701, in Beaconsfield, Buckinghamshire, England.
        Beaconsfield, Buckingham parish records. Baptism 4 Sep 1700 John born 4 Sep 1700 son of John & Martha YOUNG Burial 10 Oct 1701 John YOUNG son of John, affidavit made

    ii.   **William Young**, born 14 Aug 1703, in Beaconsfield, Buckinghamshire, England, christened 19 Aug 1703, in Beaconsfield, Buckinghamshire, England.
        Beaconsfield, Buckingham parish records. Baptism 19 Aug 1703 William born 14 Aug 1703 son of John & Martha YOUNG

    iii.   **John Young**, born 5 Apr 1708, in Beaconsfield, Buckinghamshire, England, christened 10 Apr 1708, in Beaconsfield, Buckinghamshire, England, died May 1770, in Beaconsfield, Buckinghamshire, England, buried 13 May 1770, in Beaconsfield, Buckinghamshire, England.
        Beaconsfield, Buckingham parish records. Baptism 10 Apr 1708 John born 5 Apr 1708 son of John & Martha YOUNG

    iv.   **Thomas Young**, born Feb 1713, in Beaconsfield, Buckinghamshire, England, christened 2 Mar 1713, in Beaconsfield, Buckinghamshire, England.
        Beaconsfield, Buckingham parish records.

    v.   **Martha Young**,[480] born about 1717, in Buckinghamshire, England, died before 1800, in England.

321. Martha Stevens was born Dec 1680, in Bray, Berkshire, England, christened 31 Dec 1680, in Bray, Berkshire, England, died Jan 1745, in Beaconsfield, Buckinghamshire, England, buried 12 Jan 1745, in Beaconsfield, Buckinghamshire, England. She was the daughter of Thomas Steevens and Katrigne Spott. She married John Yong[764,766] 27 Apr 1699, in Cookham, Berkshire, England. He was the son of John Yong and Mrs Elizabeth Young.
Notes for Martha Stevens:

Beaconsfield, Buckingham parish records. Burial   12 Jan 1745   Martha YOUNG, widow

322. William Rowland was born 24 Sep 1699, in Fairford, Gloucestershire, England, died 1746, in

Gloucestershire, England, buried 22 Nov 1746, in Fairford, Gloucestershire, England. He was the son of Rowland and Rowland. He married Martha Bowles[767,768] 24 Dec 1722, in Fairford, Gloucestershire, England. She was the daughter of John Bowles and Martha Loveday.

Children of William Rowland and Martha Bowles:

i. **George Rowland**,[490] born Nov 1723, in Fairford, Gloucestershire, England, died before 1820, in England.

ii. **John Bowles Rowland**, born Jan 1734, in Fairford, Gloucestershire, England, christened 21 Jan 1734, in Fairford, Gloucestershire, England, buried in Fairford, Gloucestershire, England. He married Mrs. Elizabeth Rowland before 1769, in Fairford, Gloucestershire, England. Mrs. Elizabeth Rowland was born about 1739, in Fairford, Gloucestershire, England, christened about 1739, in Fairford, Gloucestershire, England, died Mar 1825, buried 15 Mar 1825, in Fairford, Gloucestershire, England.
"England Births and Christenings, 1538-1975," database, FamilySearch (https://familysearch.org/ark:/61903/1:1:NBM7-PF5 : accessed 28 November 2015), William Rowland in entry for John Bowls Rowland, 21 Jan 1734; citing FAIRFORD,GLOUCESTER,ENGLAND, reference ; FHL microfilm 856,942.

iii. **Mary Rowland**, born Nov 1726, in Fairford, Gloucestershire, England, christened 7 Nov 1726, in Fairford, Gloucestershire, England.
"England Births and Christenings, 1538-1975," database, FamilySearch (https://familysearch.org/ark:/61903/1:1:JW68-T4R : accessed 28 November 2015), William Rowland in entry for Mary Rowland, 07 Nov 1726; citing FAIRFORD,GLOUCESTER,ENGLAND, reference ; FHL microfilm 856,942.

iv. **Martha Rowland**, born Apr 1730, in Fairford, Gloucestershire, England, christened 14 Apr 1730, in Fairford, Gloucestershire, England.
"England Births and Christenings, 1538-1975," database, FamilySearch (https://familysearch.org/ark:/61903/1:1:JMLR-N8Y : accessed 28 November 2015), William Rowland in entry for Martha Rowland, 14 Apr 1730; citing FAIRFORD,GLOUCESTER,ENGLAND, reference ; FHL microfilm 856,942.

v. **Ann Rowland**, born Oct 1732, in Fairford, Gloucestershire, England, christened 11 Oct 1732, in Fairford, Gloucestershire, England, died 7 Oct 1735, in Fairford, Gloucestershire, England.
"England Births and Christenings, 1538-1975," database, FamilySearch (https://familysearch.org/ark:/61903/1:1:NPRM-LFM : accessed 28 November 2015), William Rowland in entry for Ann Rowland, 11 Oct 1732; citing , reference ; FHL microfilm 856,942.

vi. **Ann Rowland**, born Jan 1737, in Fairford, Gloucestershire, England, christened 15 Jan 1737, in Fairford, Gloucestershire, England.
England Births and Christenings, 1538-1975," database, FamilySearch (https://familysearch.org/ark:/61903/1:1:JW68-RXY : accessed 28 November 2015), William Rowland in entry for Ann Rowland, 15 Jan 1737; citing

FAIRFORD,GLOUCESTER,ENGLAND, reference ; FHL microfilm 856,942.

vii. **Elizabeth Rowland**, born Sep 1741, in Fairford, Gloucestershire, England, christened 10 Sep 1741, in Fairford, Gloucestershire, England.
England Births and Christenings, 1538-1975," database, FamilySearch (https://familysearch.org/ark:/61903/1:1:JMLR-N22 : accessed 28 November 2015), William Rowland in entry for Elizabeth Rowland, 10 Sep 1741; citing FAIRFORD,GLOUCESTER,ENGLAND, reference ; FHL microfilm 856,942.

323. Martha Bowles was born Sep 1699, in Fairford, Gloucestershire, England, christened 24 Sep 1699, in Fairford, Gloucestershire, England, died before 1790, in England. She was the daughter of John Bowles and Martha Loveday. She married William Rowland[768] 24 Dec 1722, in Fairford, Gloucestershire, England. He was the son of Rowland and Rowland.
Notes for Martha Bowles:

aka: BOWLS

324. Edward Skinner was born 1688, in Kempsford, Gloucestershire, England, christened 11 Nov 1688, in Kempsford, Gloucestershire, England, died before 1770, in England. He was the son of Humphry Skinner and Mrs Elizabeth Skinner. He married Elizabeth Tarrant 3 Oct 1716, in Kempsford, Gloucestershire, England. She was the daughter of William Tarrant and Ann Bouy.
Notes for Edward Skinner:

residence: Gloucester, England parents: Humphry Skinner, Elizabeth record title: England Births and Christenings, 1538-1975 name: Edward Skinner gender: Male baptism/christening date: 11 Nov 1688 baptism/christening place: KEMPSFORD,GLOUCESTER,ENGLAND father's name: Humphry Skinner mother's name: Elizabeth indexing project (batch) number: C00828-2 system origin: England-ODM source film number: 956946

Children of Edward Skinner and Elizabeth Tarrant:

i. **Jane Skinner**,[490] born 1719, in Kempsford, Gloucestershire, England, died before 1800, in England.

325. Elizabeth Tarrant was born 1686, in Marlborough, Wiltshire, England, christened 18 May 1686, in Marlborough, Wiltshire, England, died before 1780, in England. She was the daughter of William Tarrant and Ann Bouy. She married Edward Skinner 3 Oct 1716, in Kempsford, Gloucestershire, England. He was the son of Humphry Skinner and Mrs Elizabeth Skinner.
Notes for Elizabeth Tarrant:

residence: Wiltshire, England parents: Wm Tarrant record title: England Births and Christenings, 1538-1975 name: Elizabeth Tarrant gender: Female baptism/christening date: 18 May 1686 baptism/christening place: SAINT MARY,MARLBOROUGH,WILTSHIRE,ENGLAND father's name: Wm Tarrant indexing project (batch) number: C02292-2 system origin: England-ODM source film number: 97837

326. William Watkins was born 18 Jan 1694, in Bristol, Gloucestershire, England, christened 15 Mar 1694, in Bristol, Gloucestershire, England, died before 1760, in England. He was the son of William Watkins and Sarah Gunning. He married Sarah Watkins[769] 7 Apr 1730, in Bristol, Gloucestershire, England. She was the daughter of Watkins and Watkins.

Children of William Watkins and Sarah Watkins:

i. **Eliza Watkins**, born 1731, in Bristol, Gloucestershire, England, christened 8 Apr 1731, in Bristol, Gloucestershire, England, died about 1735, in Bristol, Gloucestershire, England.
residence: Bristol, Gloucester, England parents: Willm. Watkins, Sarah record title: England Births and Christenings, 1538-1975 name: Eliza. Watkins gender: Female baptism/christening date: 08 Apr 1731 baptism/christening place: Bristol, Gloucester, England father's name: Willm. Watkins mother's name: Sarah indexing project (batch) number: I04146-2 source film number: 1595986

ii. **Sarah Watkins**, born 1732, in Bristol, Gloucestershire, England, christened 15 Oct 1732, in Bristol, Gloucestershire, England.
residence: Gloucester, England parents: Willm. Watkins, Sarah record title: England Births and Christenings, 1538-1975 name: Sarah Watkins gender: Female baptism/christening date: 15 Oct 1732 baptism/christening place: Bristol, Gloucester, England father's name: Willm. Watkins mother's name: Sarah indexing project (batch) number: I04146-2 system origin: England-ODM source film number: 1595986

iii. **John Watkins**, born 1734, in Bristol, Gloucestershire, England, christened 24 Nov 1734, in Bristol, Gloucestershire, England, died about 1737, in Bristol, Gloucestershire, England.

iv. **Sarah Watkins**, born 1736, in Bristol, Gloucestershire, England, christened 25 Apr 1736, in Bristol, Gloucestershire, England.
residence: Bristol, Gloucester, England parents: William, Sarah record title: England Births and Christenings, 1538-1975 name: Sarah Watkins gender: Female baptism/christening date: 25 Apr 1736 baptism/christening place: St. Nicholas, Bristol, Gloucester, England father's name: William mother's name: Sarah indexing project (batch) number: I05747-0 source film number: 1595889

v. **Elizabeth Watkins**, born 1738, in Bristol, Gloucestershire, England, christened 3 Sep 1738, in Bristol, Gloucestershire, England.
residence: Bristol, Gloucester, England record title: England Births and Christenings, 1538-1975 name: Elizabeth Watkins gender: Female baptism/christening date: 03 Sep 1738 baptism/christening place: St. Nicholas, Bristol, Gloucester, England indexing project (batch) number: I05747-0 source film number: 1595889

vi. **John Watkins**, born 1739, in Bristol, Gloucestershire, England, died before 1820, in England.

327. Sarah Watkins was born about 1710, in Bristol, Gloucestershire, England, died before 1810, in England. She was the daughter of Watkins and Watkins. She married William Watkins[769,770] 7 Apr 1730, in Bristol, Gloucestershire, England. He was the son of William Watkins and Sarah Gunning.

328. Martin Kelly was born about 1710, in Gloucestershire, England, died before 1800, in England. He was the son of Kelly and Kelly. He married Anne Parry[771,772] 29 Jan 1736, in Bristol, Gloucestershire, England. She was the daughter of William Perry and Mary Heaven.

Children of Martin Kelly and Anne Parry:

     i.   **Mary Kelly**, born 1738, in Bristol, Gloucestershire, England, died before 1820, in England.

329. Anne Parry was born 1717, in Bristol, Gloucestershire, England, christened 22 Dec 1717, in Bristol, Gloucestershire, England, died before 1800, in England. She was the daughter of William Perry and Mary Heaven. She married Martin Kelly[772] 29 Jan 1736, in Bristol, Gloucestershire, England. He was the son of Kelly and Kelly.
Notes for Anne Parry:

residence: Bristol, Gloucester, England parents: Wm. Parry record title: England Births and Christenings, 1538-1975 name: Anne Parry gender: Female baptism/christening date: 22 Dec 1717 baptism/christening place: St. Philip and St. Jacob's, Bristol, Gloucester, England father's name: Wm. Parry Batch: C01716-1; film:1596656

330. Dennis Rogers was born Nov 1684, in Tetbury, Gloucestershire, England, christened 9 Nov 1684, in Tetbury, Gloucestershire, England, died Feb 1776, in Bitton, Gloucestershire, England, buried 9 Feb 1776, in Bitton, Gloucestershire, England. He was the son of Samuel Rogers and Sarah Rogers. He married Mary Brayne[773] 19 Nov 1725, in Bitton, Gloucestershire, England. She was the daughter of William Brain and Mrs Esther Brayne.
Notes for Dennis Rogers:

England Births and Christenings, 1538-1975 residence: Gloucester, England parents: Samvell Rogers record title: England Births and Christenings, 1538-1975 name: Denns Rogers gender: Male baptism/christening date: 09 Nov 1684 baptism/christening place: TETBURY,GLOUCESTER,ENGLAND father's name: Samvell Rogers indexing project (batch) number: C05486-1 system origin: England-ODM source film number: 856949 England Marriages, 1538-1973 marriage: 19 Nov 1725 -Bitton, Gloucester, England spouse: Mary Brayne

Children of Dennis Rogers and Mary Brayne:

     i.   **Isaac Rogers**,[492] born Sep 1727, in Bitton, Gloucestershire, England, died Jul 1776, in Bitton, Gloucestershire, England.

    ii.   **Denis Rogers**, born Mar 1730, in Bitton, Gloucestershire, England, christened 7 Mar 1730, in Bitton, Gloucestershire, England, died 1741, in Bitton, Gloucestershire, England, buried 7 Aug 1741, in Bitton, Gloucestershire, England. England Deaths and Burials, 1538-1991 burial: 09 Feb 1776 Bitton, Gloucester, England record title: England Deaths and Burials, 1538-1991 name: Denis Rogers gender: Male burial date: 09 Feb 1776 burial place: Bitton, Gloucester, England indexing project (batch) number: I03618-9 system origin: England. source film number: 1595499

    iii.   **Mary Rogers**, born 4 Jul 1734, in Bitton, Gloucestershire, England, christened 1 Aug 1734, in Oldland, Gloucestershire, England.

    iv.   **William Rogers**, born 21 Mar 1736, in Bitton, Gloucestershire, England, christened 21 Mar 1736, in Oldland, Gloucestershire, England.

    v.   **Henry Rogers**, born 18 Feb 1740, in Bitton, Gloucestershire, England.

    vi.   **Thos Rogers**, born 19 Oct 1741, in Bitton, Gloucestershire, England.

    vii.   **Hannah Rogers**, born 23 Oct 1743, in Oldland, Gloucestershire, England, christened 23 Oct 1743, in Oldland, Gloucestershire, England.

331. Mary Brayne was born about 1700, in Gloucestershire, England, died Jun 1784, in Bitton, Gloucestershire, England, buried 11 Jun 1784, in Bitton, Gloucestershire, England. She was the daughter of William Brain and Mrs Esther Brayne. She married Dennis Rogers[774] 19 Nov 1725, in Bitton, Gloucestershire, England. He was the son of Samuel Rogers and Sarah Rogers.
Notes for Mary Brayne:

England Deaths and Burials, 1538-1991 burial: 11 Jun 1784 Bitton, Gloucester, England record title: England Deaths and Burials, 1538-1991 name: Amey Rogers gender: Female burial date: 11 Jun 1784 burial place: Bitton, Gloucester, England indexing project (batch) number: I03618-9 system origin: England. source film number: 1595499

332. William Stone was born about 1700, in Bristol, Gloucestershire, England, died before 1800, in England. He was the son of Thomas Stone and Mary Hiyet. He married Ann Palmer[775] 2 Feb 1734, in Bitton, Gloucestershire, England. She was the daughter of Palmer and Palmer.

Children of William Stone and Ann Palmer:

    i.   **Silvester Stone**,[491] born Jan 1736, in Bristol, Gloucestershire, England, died Dec 1795, in Bitton, Gloucestershire, England.

    ii.   **Ann Stone**, born about 1740, in Bitton, Gloucestershire, England, christened 18 Apr 1740, in Bitton, Gloucestershire, England.

333. Ann Palmer was born about 1714, in Bitton, Gloucestershire, England, died before 1800, in England. She was the daughter of Palmer and Palmer. She married William Stone[776] 2 Feb 1734, in Bitton, Gloucestershire, England. He was the son of Thomas Stone and Mary Hiyet.

Notes for Ann Palmer:

England Marriages, 15381973 marriage: 02 Feb 1734 Bitton, Gloucester, England spouse: Ann Palmer

334. John Burges was born 17 Apr 1711, in Bristol, Gloucestershire, England, died before 1800, in England. He was the son of John Burges and Burges. He married Susanna Goby[494,777] 22 Jan 1733, in Spetisbury, Dorset, England. She was the daughter of Goby and Goby.

Children of John Burges and Susanna Goby:

i. **Hester Burges**,[778] born Sep 1734, in Bristol, Gloucestershire, England, christened 23 Sep 1734, in Bristol, Gloucestershire, England.

ii. **William Burges**,[779] born Mar 1736, in Bristol, Gloucestershire, England, christened 21 Mar 1736, in Bristol, Gloucestershire, England.

iii. **Ebenezer Burges**,[494] born Nov 1738, in Bristol, Gloucestershire, England, died Sep 1789, in Bristol, Gloucestershire, England.

335. Susanna Goby was born about 1712, in Spetisbury, Dorset, England, died before 1812, in England. She was the daughter of Goby and Goby. She married John Burges[780,781] 22 Jan 1733, in Spetisbury, Dorset, England. He was the son of John Burges and Burges.

336. George Reynolds was born Jan 1708, in Bristol, Gloucestershire, England, christened 5 Jan 1708, in St. Augustine, Bristol, Gloucester, England, died before 1800, in England. He was the son of Thomas Reynolds and Sarah Smith. He married Mary Or Ann Sednel[782] 14 Dec 1736, in Bristol, Gloucestershire, England. She was the daughter of Sednel and Sednel.
Notes for George Reynolds:

England Births and Christenings, 1538-1975 residence: Bristol, Gloucester, England parents: Tho. Reynolds, Sarah AKA - Renalds record title: England Births and Christenings, 1538-1975 name: Geo. Reynolds gender: Male baptism/christening date: 05 Jan 1708 baptism/christening place: St. Augustine, Bristol, Gloucester, England father's name: Tho. Reynolds mother's name: Sarah indexing project (batch) number: C00911-9 system origin: film number: 1596310 England marriages, 1538-1973 shows name as Rannolds, George & Mary (Ann) Sednel 14 Dec 1736

Children of George Reynolds and Mary Or Ann Sednel:

i. **George Reynolds**,[783] born Oct 1738, in Bristol, Gloucestershire, England, christened 8 Oct 1738, in Bristol, Gloucestershire, England, died Feb 1739, in Bristol, Gloucestershire, England.
England Births and Christenings, 1538-1975 residence: Bristol, Gloucester, England parents: George Renalds, Ann record title: England Births and Christenings, 1538-1975 name: George Renalds gender: Male baptism/christening date: 08 Oct 1738 baptism/christening place: Bristol, Gloucester, England father's

name: George Renalds mother's name: Ann indexing project (batch) number: I04146-2 system origin: film number: 1595986

    ii.   **Mary Reynolds**,[784] born Nov 1740, in Bristol, Gloucestershire, England, christened 17 Nov 1740, in Bristol, Gloucestershire, England.

    iii.   **Diana Reynolds**,[493] born 1746, in Gloucestershire, England, died Dec 1806, in Bristol, Gloucestershire, England.

337. Mary Or Ann Sednel was born about 1719, in Bristol, Gloucestershire, England, died before 1800, in England. She was the daughter of Sednel and Sednel. She married George Reynolds[782,785] 14 Dec 1736, in Bristol, Gloucestershire, England. He was the son of Thomas Reynolds and Sarah Smith.

338. William Ellard was born Sep 1735, in Preston Bisset, Buckinghamshire, England, christened 28 Sep 1735, in Preston Bisset, Buckinghamshire, England. He was the son of Thomas Ellard and Elizabeth Ellard. He married Catherine Spooner[786,787] 1762, in Cublington, Buckinghamshire, England. She was the daughter of Spooner and Spooner.

Children of William Ellard and Catherine Spooner:

    i.   **Joseph Ellerd**,[495] born about 1765, in Hertfordshire, England.

339. Catherine Spooner was born Nov 1738, in Cublington, Buckinghamshire, England, christened 12 Nov 1738, in Cublington, Buckinghamshire, England. She was the daughter of Spooner and Spooner. She married William Ellard[786,788] 1762, in Cublington, Buckinghamshire, England. He was the son of Thomas Ellard and Elizabeth Ellard.

340. William Mealing was born Feb 1733, in Houghton Regis, Bedfordshire, England, christened 3 Mar 1733, in Houghton Regis, Bedfordshire, England. He was the son of William Mealing and Mealing. He married Rebecca Messider about 1760, in Hertfordshire, England. She was the daughter of Michael Messider and Mrs Elizabeth Messider.

Children of William Mealing and Rebecca Messider:

    i.   **William Mealing**,[789] born Mar 1761, in Houghton Regis, Bedfordshire, England, christened 5 Apr 1761, in Houghton Regis, Bedfordshire, England.

    ii.   **Joseph Mealing**,[790] born Oct 1762, in Houghton Regis, Bedfordshire, England, christened 17 Oct 1762, in Houghton Regis, Bedfordshire, England.

    iii.   **Sarah Mealing**,[791] born Sep 1764, in Houghton Regis, Bedfordshire, England, christened 16 Sep 1764, in Houghton Regis, Bedfordshire, England, died 3 Jun 1766, in Houghton Regis, Bedfordshire, England.

    iv.   **John Mealing**,[792] born Jun 1766, in Houghton Regis, Bedfordshire, England, christened 6 Jul 1766, in Houghton Regis, Bedfordshire, England.

    v.   **Lydia Mealing**,[495,496] born May 1769, in Houghton Regis, Bedfordshire, England.

341. Rebecca Messider was born Jun 1736, in Houghton Regis, Bedfordshire, England, christened 24 Jun 1736, in Houghton Regis, Bedfordshire, England. She was the daughter of Michael Messider and Mrs Elizabeth Messider. She married William Mealing[793] about 1760, in Hertfordshire, England. He was the son of William Mealing and Mealing.

342. Thomas Jennings was born 19 May 1722, in Southwark, Surrey, England, christened 20 May 1722, in Southwark, Surrey, England. He was the son of Thomasin Jennings and Elizabeth Jennings. He married Ann Roberts[794] 2 Aug 1740, in Southwark, Surrey, England. She was the daughter of Thomas Roberts and Elizabeth Roberts.

Children of Thomas Jennings and Ann Roberts:

     i.   **Stephen Jennings**,[498,500] born Dec 1752, in Mitcham, Surrey, England.

343. Ann Roberts was born 25 Dec 1722, in Croydon, Surrey, England, christened 15 Jan 1723, in Croydon, Surrey, England. She was the daughter of Thomas Roberts and Elizabeth Roberts. She married Thomas Jennings[795] 2 Aug 1740, in Southwark, Surrey, England. He was the son of Thomasin Jennings and Elizabeth Jennings.

344. Grove Taylor was born about 1730, in Kent, England. He was the son of Taylor and Taylor. He married Sarah Smith[499,796,797] 4 Nov 1760, in Bromley, Kent, England. She was the daughter of Stephen Smith and Elizabeth Hills.

Children of Grove Taylor and Sarah Smith:

     i.   **Elizabeth Taylor**,[498,499] born Nov 1762, in Bromley, Kent, England.

345. Sarah Smith was born Oct 1738, in Bromley, Kent, England, christened 6 Oct 1738, in Bromley, Kent, England. She was the daughter of Stephen Smith and Elizabeth Hills. She married Grove Taylor[499,798] 4 Nov 1760, in Bromley, Kent, England. He was the son of Taylor and Taylor.

346. Isaac Langley was born about 1730, in England. He was the son of Langley and Langley. He married Anna Smith[799,800] 4 Aug 1752, in Polstead, Suffolk, England. She was the daughter of Benjamini Smith and Annae Smith.

Children of Isaac Langley and Anna Smith:

     i.   **Isaac Langley**,[504,505] born Feb 1762, in Suffolk, England.

347. Anna Smith was born Oct 1730, in Glemsford, Suffolk, England, christened 21 Oct 1730, in Glemsford, Suffolk, England. She was the daughter of Benjamini Smith and Annae Smith. She married Isaac Langley[799] 4 Aug 1752, in Polstead, Suffolk, England. He was the son of Langley and Langley. Notes for Anna Smith:

father: Benjamini Smith mother: Annae

348. Charles Day was born about 1732, in London, England. He was the son of Day and Day. He married Elizabeth Darby[801,802] 6 Apr 1762, in Stepney, Middlesex, England. She was the daughter of Darby and Darby.

Children of Charles Day and Elizabeth Darby:

      i.   **Elizabeth Day**,[501,502] born Dec 1763, in Stepney, Middlesex, England.

349. Elizabeth Darby was born 24 Nov 1735, in Stepney, Middlesex, England, christened 14 Dec 1735, in St Dunstan, Stepney, London, England. She was the daughter of Darby and Darby. She married Charles Day[801] 6 Apr 1762, in Stepney, Middlesex, England. He was the son of Day and Day.

350. Thomas Bawhse was born about 1730, in Middlesex, England. He was the son of Bawhse and Bawhse. He married Elizabeth Martin[803,804] 22 Oct 1752, in Westminster, Middlesex, England. She was the daughter of Thomas Martin and Mrs Katherine Martin.

Children of Thomas Bawhse and Elizabeth Martin:

      i.   **Frederick Bayse**,[506,509,510] born about 1760, in Middlesex, England, died Oct 1809, in Grays Inn Lane Workhouse, London, England.

351. Elizabeth Martin was born 25 Dec 1722, in Westminster, Middlesex, England, christened 6 Jan 1723, in Westminster, Middlesex, England. She was the daughter of Thomas Martin and Mrs Katherine Martin. She married Thomas Bawhse[803] 22 Oct 1752, in Westminster, Middlesex, England. He was the son of Bawhse and Bawhse.

352. Thomas Pike was born about 1740, in Middlesex, England. He was the son of Pike and Pike. He married Catharine Lamb[805] 12 Nov 1759, in St Alphege Greenwich, London, England. She was the daughter of Lamb and Lamb.

Children of Thomas Pike and Catharine Lamb:

      i.   **Mary Diman Pike**,[506,507,508,509] born Sep 1768, in Whitechapel, London, England, died Nov 1849, in Hendon, Middlesex, England.

353. Catharine Lamb was born about 1744, in Middlesex, England. She was the daughter of Lamb and Lamb. She married Thomas Pike[805] 12 Nov 1759, in St Alphege Greenwich, London, England. He was the son of Pike and Pike.
Notes for Catharine Lamb:

aka Katharine

354. Hugh Humber was born about 1720, in Cattistock, Dorset, England, died 13 Dec 1775, in Cattistock, Dorset, England. He was the son of Humber and Humber. He married Mary Frampton 4 Jan 1740, in Cattistock, Dorset, England. She was the daughter of Frampton and Frampton.

Children of Hugh Humber and Mary Frampton:

    i.   **Joseph Humber,**[511] born 1751, in Litton Cheney, Dorset, England, died 24 Jul 1829, in Litton Cheney, Dorset, England.

355. Mary Frampton was born about 1719, in Cattistock, Dorset, England, died 14 Jun 1761, in Dorset, England. She was the daughter of Frampton and Frampton. She married Hugh Humber 4 Jan 1740, in Cattistock, Dorset, England. He was the son of Humber and Humber.

356. Joseph Tidby was born 1724, in Litton Cheney, Dorset, England. He was the son of Tidby and Tidby. He married Mary Talbot 22 May 1749, in Litton Cheney, Dorset, England. She was the daughter of Talbot and Talbot.

Children of Joseph Tidby and Mary Talbot:

    i.   **Margaret Tidby,**[325] born 1750, in Litton Cheney, Dorset, England, died 8 Aug 1836, in Litton Cheney, Dorset, England.

357. Mary Talbot was born 1728, in Litton Cheney, Dorset, England. She was the daughter of Talbot and Talbot. She married Joseph Tidby 22 May 1749, in Litton Cheney, Dorset, England. He was the son of Tidby and Tidby.

358. Samuell Churchill was born Oct 1731, in Toller Porcorum, Dorset, England, christened 17 Oct 1731, in Toller Porcorum, Dorset, England. He was the son of Samuel Churchill and Mrs Elizabeth Churchill. He married Ann Tiber[806] 14 Jul 1763, in Long Bredy, Dorset, England. She was the daughter of Tiber and Tiber.

Children of Samuell Churchill and Ann Tiber:

    i.   **John Churchill,**[512,514] born Mar 1764, in Long Bredy, Dorset, England.

359. Ann Tiber was born about 1733, in Dorset, England. She was the daughter of Tiber and Tiber. She married Samuell Churchill[806,807] 14 Jul 1763, in Long Bredy, Dorset, England. He was the son of Samuel Churchill and Mrs Elizabeth Churchill.

360. Henry Jacob was born Oct 1736, in Winterbourne St Martin, Dorset, England, christened 17 Oct 1736, in Winterbourne St Martin, Dorset, England. He was the son of Lewis Jacob and Elizabeth Lake. He married Mary Poage[808] 30 Jun 1761, in Winterbourne St Martin, Dorset, England. She was the daughter of Poage and Poage.

Children of Henry Jacob and Mary Poage:

     i.   **Elizabeth Jacob**,[512,513] born Oct 1766, in Winterbourne St Martin, Dorset, England.

361. Mary Poage was born about 1740, in Dorset, England. She was the daughter of Poage and Poage. She married Henry Jacob[808,809] 30 Jun 1761, in Winterbourne St Martin, Dorset, England. He was the son of Lewis Jacob and Elizabeth Lake.

362. Thomas Hunt was born 13 May 1733, in Compton Abbas, Dorset, England, died before 1833, in England. He was the son of Thomas Hunt and Mrs Katherine Hunt. He married Mary Zebedee[810,811] 16 Oct 1757, in Cranborne, Dorset, England. She was the daughter of Timothy Zebedee and Zebedee.

Children of Thomas Hunt and Mary Zebedee:

     i.   **Molly Hunt**, born 1758, in Leigh, Dorset, England, christened 19 Mar 1758, in Leigh, Dorset, England.

    ii.   **Sarah Hunt**, born 1763, in Leigh, Dorset, England, christened 8 Jan 1764, in Leigh, Dorset, England.

   iii.   **Thomas Hunt**, born 1764, in Leigh, Dorset, England, christened 17 Mar 1765, in Leigh, Dorset, England. He married Grace Read 12 May 1788, in Yetminster, Dorset, England. Grace Read was born about 1766, in England, christened 23 Mar 1766, in Yetminster, Dorset, England.

    iv.   **Rachel Hunt**, born 1765, in Leigh, Dorset, England, christened 29 Sep 1765, in Leigh, Dorset, England.

     v.   **John Hunt**,[515,516] born Feb 1767, in Dorset, England, died 11 May 1843, in Yetminster, Dorset, England.

    vi.   **William Hunt**, born 1774, in Leigh, Dorset, England, christened 13 Feb 1774, in Leigh, Dorset, England. He married Ann Incledon 25 May 1797, in Yetminster, Dorset, England. Ann Incledon was born about 1777, in Yetminster, Dorset, England.

   vii.   **Daniel Hunt**, born 1778, in Dorset, England. Residence: 1841, Leigh, Dorsetshire, England.

  viii.   **Ann Hunt**, born 1779, in Leigh, Dorset, England, christened 7 Feb 1779, in Leigh, Dorset, England.

    ix.   **Simon Hunt**, born 1781, in Leigh, Dorset, England, christened 4 Feb 1781, in Leigh, Dorset, England, died 22 Sep 1843, in Dorset, England. He married Martha Burt 6 Apr 1808, in Yetminster, Dorset, England. She was the daughter of William Burt and Joan Morris. Martha Burt was born about 1782, in Dorset, England, christened 24 Mar 1782, in Hermitage, Dorset, England.

363. Mary Zebedee was born Jan 1736, in Bradpole, Dorset, England, christened 21 Jan 1736, in Cranborne, Dorset, England, died before 1830, in England. She was the daughter of Timothy Zebedee and Zebedee. She married Thomas Hunt[811,812,813] 16 Oct 1757, in Cranborne, Dorset, England. He was the

son of Thomas Hunt and Mrs Katherine Hunt.
Notes for Mary Zebedee:

aka: ZEBEDY

364. William Burt was born 1745, in Yetminster, Dorset, England, died before 1840, in England. He was the son of John Burt and Sarah Stokes. He married Joan Morris 1773, in Yetminster, Dorset, England. She was the daughter of George Morris and Mary Davis.

Children of William Burt and Joan Morris:

    i.   **Grace Burt**,[515] born 1774, in Dorset, England, died before 1870, in England.
    ii.   **Sarah Burt**, born 1775, in Yetminster, Dorset, England.
    iii.   **William Burt**, born 1779, in Yetminster, Dorset, England.
    iv.   **James Burt**, born 28 Jul 1780, in Marnhull, Dorset, England, died about 1860, in England.
    v.   **Susannah Burt**, born 1781, in Minterne Magna, Dorset, England, christened 2 Dec 1781, in Minterne Magna, Dorset, England.
    vi.   **Martha Burt**, born about 1782, in Dorset, England, christened 24 Mar 1782, in Hermitage, Dorset, England. She married Simon Hunt 6 Apr 1808, in Yetminster, Dorset, England. He was the son of Thomas Hunt and Mary Zebedee. Simon Hunt was born 1781, in Leigh, Dorset, England, christened 4 Feb 1781, in Leigh, Dorset, England, died 22 Sep 1843, in Dorset, England.

365. Joan Morris was born 16 Dec 1750, in Chard, Somerset, England, christened 16 Dec 1750, in Chard, Somerset, England, died before 1850, in England. She was the daughter of George Morris and Mary Davis. She married William Burt 1773, in Yetminster, Dorset, England. He was the son of John Burt and Sarah Stokes.

366. John Matthews was born about 1750, in Dorset, England. He was the son of Matthews and Matthews. He married Ann Hodder[814] 12 Nov 1777, in Whitchurch-Canonicorum, Dorset, England. She was the daughter of Hodder and Hodder.

Children of John Matthews and Ann Hodder:

    i.   **John Matthews**,[518,520,521,522] born Jun 1782, in Whitchurch, Dorset, England, died Sep 1841, in Shaftsbury, Dorset, England.

367. Ann Hodder was born Apr 1757, in Whitchurch-Canonicorum, Dorset, England, christened 11 Apr 1757, in Whitchurch-Canonicorum, Dorset, England. She was the daughter of Hodder and Hodder. She married John Matthews[814] 12 Nov 1777, in Whitchurch-Canonicorum, Dorset, England. He was the son of Matthews and Matthews.

368. John Fowler was born Jul 1749, in Hawkchurch, Dorset, England, christened 6 Aug 1749, in Broadwindsor, Dorset, England, died before 1830, in Dorset, England. He was the son of George Fowler and Jemima Guppy. He married Jane Culverwell[815] 21 Oct 1782, in Exeter, Devon, England. She was the daughter of Culverwell and Culverwelll.

Children of John Fowler and Jane Culverwell:

     i.   **Sarah Fowler**,[518,519] born 6 Apr 1784, in Charmouth, Dorset, England, died Feb 1858, in Dorset, England.

    ii.   **Mary Fowler**,[816] born 24 Nov 1785, in Charmouth, Dorset, England, christened 9 Feb 1786, in Charmouth, Dorset, England.

   iii.   **Robert Fowler**,[817] born Sep 1787, in Charmouth, Dorset, England, christened 9 Oct 1787, in Charmouth, Dorset, England.

   iv.   **William Fowler**,[818] born Nov 1789, in Charmouth, Dorset, England, christened 1 Dec 1789, in Charmouth, Dorset, England.

369. Jane Culverwell was born about 1757, in Dorset, England, died 1843, in England. She was the daughter of Culverwell and Culverwelll. She married John Fowler[815,819] 21 Oct 1782, in Exeter, Devon, England. He was the son of George Fowler and Jemima Guppy.

370. Thomas Humphrey was born May 1721, in Brackley, Northamptonshire, England, christened 31 May 1721, in Brackley, Northamptonshire, England, died Jun 1797, in Hinton in the Hedges, Northamptonshire, England, buried 10 Jun 1797, in Hinton in the Hedges, Northamptonshire, England. He was the son of Josiah Humphrey and Elizabeth Tims. He married Mary Linnelin about 1747, in Northamptonshire, England. She was the daughter of Linnelin and Linnelin.

Children of Thomas Humphrey and Mary Linnelin:

     i.   **Elizabeth Humphrey**, born 1749, in Hinton in the Hedges, Northamptonshire, England, christened 23 May 1749, in Hinton in the Hedges, Northamptonshire, England, died 1824, in Hinton in the Hedges, Northamptonshire, England, buried Jul 1824, in Hinton in the Hedges, Northamptonshire, England.

    ii.   **William Humphry**, born Jul 1750, in Hinton in the Hedges, Northamptonshire, England, died 1827, in Greatworth, Northamptonshire, England.

   iii.   **Thomas Humphrey**, born 1752, in Hinton in the Hedges, Northamptonshire, England, christened 26 Jan 1752, in Hinton in the Hedges, Northamptonshire, England.

   iv.   **Samuel Humphrey**, born 1753, in Hinton in the Hedges, Northamptonshire, England, christened 15 Jul 1753, in Hinton in the Hedges, Northamptonshire, England.

    v.   **Mary Humphrey**, born 1755, in Hinton in the Hedges, Northamptonshire, England, christened 2 Feb 1755, in Hinton in the Hedges, Northamptonshire, England.

vi.   **Jonathon Humphrey**, born 1756, in Hinton in the Hedges, Northamptonshire, England, christened 19 Dec 1756, in Hinton in the Hedges, Northamptonshire, England.

vii. **Sarah Humphrey**, born 1759, in Hinton in the Hedges, Northamptonshire, England, christened 22 Apr 1759, in Hinton in the Hedges, Northamptonshire, England, died 24 May 1759, in Hinton in the Hedges, Northamptonshire, England, buried 27 May 1759, in Hinton in the Hedges, Northamptonshire, England.

viii. **Ann Humphrey**, born 1760, in Hinton in the Hedges, Northamptonshire, England, christened 13 Jul 1760, in Hinton in the Hedges, Northamptonshire, England, died 1761, in Hinton in the Hedges, Northamptonshire, England, buried 6 Mar 1761, in Hinton in the Hedges, Northamptonshire, England.

ix.   **Hannah Humphries**, born May 1761, in Brington, Northamptonshire, England, christened 11 May 1761, in Brington, Northamptonshire, England.

x.   **Josiah Humphrey**, born 1762, in Hinton in the Hedges, Northamptonshire, England, christened 27 Jun 1762, in Hinton in the Hedges, Northamptonshire, England.

xi.   **Richard Humphrey**, born 1763, in Hinton in the Hedges, Northamptonshire, England, christened 20 Nov 1763, in Hinton in the Hedges, Northamptonshire, England, died 1836, in Helmdon with Stuchbury, Northamptonshire, England.

371. Mary Linnelin was born about 1724, in Northamptonshire, England, died Apr 1784, in Hinton in the Hedges, Northamptonshire, England, buried 21 Apr 1784, in Hinton in the Hedges, Northamptonshire, England. She was the daughter of Linnelin and Linnelin. She married Thomas Humphrey about 1747, in Northamptonshire, England. He was the son of Josiah Humphrey and Elizabeth Tims.

372. Nathaniel Bazley was born 12 Nov 1727, in Greatworth, Northamptonshire, England, christened 15 Nov 1727, in Greatworth, Northamptonshire, England, died before 1825, in England. He was the son of Robert Bazley and Alice Lilford. He married Sarah Collison 26 Jul 1747, in Noke, Oxfordshire, England. She was the daughter of William Collison and Mary Brimly.
Notes for Nathaniel Bazley:

aka: Nathanael Beesly

Children of Nathaniel Bazley and Sarah Collison:

i.   **William Bazley**, born 1748, in Greatworth, Northamptonshire, England.
ii.   **Mary Bazley**, born 1749, in Islip, Oxfordshire, England, christened 17 Dec 1749, in Islip, Oxfordshire, England.
iii. **Sarah Bazley**, born 1752, in Islip, Oxfordshire, England, christened 15 Mar 1752, in Islip, Oxfordshire, England.
iv.   **Ann Basely**, born 1755, in Islip, Oxfordshire, England, died 1783, in Greatworth, Northamptonshire, England.

v. **Thomas Bazley**, born Jul 1758, in Islip, Oxfordshire, England, christened 13 Aug 1758, in Islip, Oxfordshire, England. He married Elizabeth Hawkins 1776, in Ansty, Warwickshire, England. Elizabeth Hawkins was born 16 Nov 1755, in Ansty, Warwickshire, England, died 12 Nov 1812, in Warwickshire, England. Thomas and Elizabeh had three children. Elizabeth born about 1798, Mary christened 23 September 1787 and Thomas June 1793 all christened at Mollington,Oxfordshire.

vi. **John Bazley**, born 1762, in Islip, Oxfordshire, England, christened 18 Jul 1762, in Islip, Oxfordshire, England.

vii. **Ephraim Bazley**, born Jun 1770, in Greatworth, Northamptonshire, England, christened 1 Jul 1770, in Greatworth, Northamptonshire, England, died Feb 1836, in Greatworth, Northamptonshire, England, buried 24 Feb 1836, in Greatworth, Northamptonshire, England. He married Amelia Adams 20 Jul 1790, in Whittlebury, Northamptonshire, England. Amelia Adams was born about 1770, in Greatworth, Northamptonshire, England, christened 11 Feb 1770, in Whittlebury, Northamptonshire, England, died before 1870, in Greatworth, Northamptonshire, England.

373. Sarah Collison was born 4 Nov 1728, in Woodeaton, Oxfordshire, England, christened 1 Dec 1728, in Woodeaton, Oxfordshire, England, died Jul 1787, in Greatworth, Northamptonshire, England, buried 15 Jul 1787, in Greatworth, Northamptonshire, England. She was the daughter of William Collison and Mary Brimly. She married Nathaniel Bazley 26 Jul 1747, in Noke, Oxfordshire, England. He was the son of Robert Bazley and Alice Lilford.

374. Thomas Coleman Or Coalman was born Jul 1726, in Kettering, Northamptonshire, England, christened 23 Jul 1726, in Kettering, Northamptonshire, England. He was the son of Robert Coleman Or Coalman and Mary Fennimore. He married Ann Bitchens[820] 9 Nov 1740, in Paulerspury, Northamptonshire, England. She was the daughter of Bitchens and Bitchens.

Children of Thomas Coleman Or Coalman and Ann Bitchens:

i. **John Coleman**,[531,532] born Dec 1747, in Potterspury with Yardley Gobion, Northamptonshire, England.

ii. **Mary Coleman**,[821] born Aug 1750, in Potterspury, Northamptonshire, England, christened 31 Aug 1750, in Potterspury with Yardley Gobion, Northamptonshire, England.

375. Ann Bitchens was born about 1720, in England. She was the daughter of Bitchens and Bitchens. She married Thomas Coleman Or Coalman[820,822,823] 9 Nov 1740, in Paulerspury, Northamptonshire, England. He was the son of Robert Coleman Or Coalman and Mary Fennimore.

376. John Franklin was born Oct 1730, in Quainton, Buckinghamshire, England, christened 25 Oct 1730, in Quainton, Buckinghamshire, England. He was the son of John Franklin and Mrs Sarah Franklin.

He married Anne Smith 2 Jan 1752, in Quainton, Buckinghamshire, England. She was the daughter of Joseph Smith and Anne Seir.

Children of John Franklin and Anne Smith:

      i.   **Elizabeth Franklin**,[523] born Aug 1754, in Yardley Gobion, Northamptonshire, England.

377. Anne Smith was born Sep 1736, in Quainton, Buckinghamshire, England, christened 23 Sep 1736, in Quainton, Buckinghamshire, England. She was the daughter of Joseph Smith and Anne Seir. She married John Franklin 2 Jan 1752, in Quainton, Buckinghamshire, England. He was the son of John Franklin and Mrs Sarah Franklin.

378. John Chester was born about 1700, in Southam, Warwickshire, England. He was the son of John Chester and Chester. He married Mary Ladbrook[824] 24 Mar 1724, in Southam, Warwickshire, England. She was the daughter of Joseph Ladbrook and Elizabeth Falkner.

Children of John Chester and Mary Ladbrook:

      i.   **William Chester**,[533,534] born Mar 1748, in Southam, Warwickshire, England.

379. Mary Ladbrook was born Jul 1703, in Stoneleigh, Warwickshire, England, christened 17 Jul 1703, in Stoneleigh, Warwickshire, England. She was the daughter of Joseph Ladbrook and Elizabeth Falkner. She married John Chester 24 Mar 1724, in Southam, Warwickshire, England. He was the son of John Chester and Chester.

380. William Calloway was born about 1730, in Birdingbury, Warwickshire, England. He was the son of Calloway and Calloway. He married Susannah Walker 21 May 1755, in Birdingbury, Warwickshire, England. She was the daughter of Edward Walker and Elizabeth Mumforr.
Notes for William Calloway:

1730 (1730) 1730 (1730) (1730) 1730 (1730) child: Ann chr 26 Nov 1756 According to Warwickshire, England, Marriages and Banns, marriage banns for this couple were published multiple times in May (including the 18th and 21st - see other marriage dates); but the actual marriage was completed on 20 Sep 1755; (note that the index lists 18 September, but the handwritten date is clearly 20 September). Also note that on the same register page for the marriage between William and Susannah is listed a banns for Thomas Calloway and Susanna Hinks (which has probably contributed to the confusion with names and combined records); this later couple published additional banns in November and were married 29 Dec 1755.

Children of William Calloway and Susannah Walker:

      i.   **Susannah Calloway**, born Apr 1756, in Birdingbury, Warwickshire, England.

381. Susannah Walker was born about 1731, in Birdingbury, Warwickshire, England. She was the daughter of Edward Walker and Elizabeth Mumforr. She married William Calloway 21 May 1755, in Birdingbury, Warwickshire, England. He was the son of Calloway and Calloway.

382. Samuel Savage was born Apr 1704, in Pattishall, Northamptonshire, England, christened 30 Apr 1704, in Pattishall, Northamptonshire, England, buried 17 Feb 1755, in Pattishall, Northamptonshire, England. He was the son of Paul Savage and Mrs Jane Savage. He married Mary Hicks[825] 4 Sep 1735, in Tiffield, Northamptonshire, England. She was the daughter of Hicks and Hicks.

Children of Samuel Savage and Mary Hicks:

> i. **Samuel Savage**,[330,541] born May 1739, in Green's Norton, Northamptonshire, England, died 29 Mar 1802, in Green's Norton, Northamptonshire, England.

383. Mary Hicks was born about 1705, in Pattishall, Northamptonshire, England, died Sep 1792, in Pattishall, Northamptonshire, England, buried 24 Sep 1792, in Pattishall, Northamptonshire, England. She was the daughter of Hicks and Hicks. She married Samuel Savage[825] 4 Sep 1735, in Tiffield, Northamptonshire, England. He was the son of Paul Savage and Mrs Jane Savage.

384. Richard Bodily was born 27 Jul 1712, in Alderton, Northamptonshire, England, christened 27 Jul 1712, in Alderton, Northamptonshire, England, died 1765, in Green's Norton, Northamptonshire, England, buried in Green's Norton, Northamptonshire, England. He was the son of John Bodily and Katherine Wright. He married Mary Collins Oct 1734, in Green's Norton, Northamptonshire, England. She was the daughter of Richard Collins and Alice Ashby.

Children of Richard Bodily and Mary Collins:

> i. **Sarah Bodily**,[330] born 1747, in Green's Norton, Northamptonshire, England, died 16 Feb 1797, in Green's Norton, Northamptonshire, England.

385. Mary Collins was born 24 Sep 1714, in Heyford, Northamptonshire, England, died 22 Dec 1792, in Green's Norton, Northamptonshire, England, buried 27 Dec 1792, in Bugbrooke, Northamptonshire, England. She was the daughter of Richard Collins and Alice Ashby. She married Richard Bodily Oct 1734, in Green's Norton, Northamptonshire, England. He was the son of John Bodily and Katherine Wright.
Notes for Mary Collins:

Quaker

386. William Lucas was born 8 Nov 1710, in Hitchin, Hertfordshire, England, died before 1800, in England. He was the son of Wiliam Lucas and Sarah Rud. He married Ann Or Susanna Chambers[826,827,828] 24 Jun 1728, in Gamlingay, Hertfordshire, England. She was the daughter of George Chambers and Elizabeth Deny.

Children of William Lucas and Ann Or Susanna Chambers:

> i. **Thomas Lucas**,[543] born Sep 1732, in Royston, Hertfordshire, England, died before 1820, in England.

387. Ann Or Susanna Chambers was born Aug 1712, in Yaxley, Huntingdonshire, England, christened 14 Sep 1712, in Yaxley, Huntingdonshire, England, died before 1800, in England. She was the daughter of George Chambers and Elizabeth Deny. She married William Lucas[826,827,829] 24 Jun 1728, in Gamlingay, Hertfordshire, England. He was the son of Wiliam Lucas and Sarah Rud.

388. Thomas Broyors Or Bryars Or Bryers was born Mar 1699, in Baldock, Hertfordshire, England, died before 1760, in England. He was the son of Edward Bryers Or Bryars and Ann Lieginton. He married Ann Squires[830,831,832] 22 Jul 1722, in Ardeley, Hertfordshire, England. She was the daughter of John Squire and Mary Smith.

Children of Thomas Broyors Or Bryars Or Bryers and Ann Squires:

> i. **Mary Broyors**,[542] born Feb 1728, in Baldock, Hertfordshire, England, died 1825, in Broxbourne, Hertfordshire, England.

389. Ann Squires was born Aug 1697, in Yaxley, Huntingdonshire, England, christened 15 Aug 1697, in Yaxley, Huntingdonshire, England, died before 1760, in England. She was the daughter of John Squire and Mary Smith. She married Thomas Broyors Or Bryars Or Bryers[830,831,833] 22 Jul 1722, in Ardeley, Hertfordshire, England. He was the son of Edward Bryers Or Bryars and Ann Lieginton.

390. Nathaniel Mayes Or May was born about 1710, in Essex, England. He was the son of Mayes Or May and Mayes Or May. He married Mary Lawn 1732, in Harwich, Essex, England. She was the daughter of Lawn and Lawn.

Children of Nathaniel Mayes Or May and Mary Lawn:

> i. **Nathaniel Mayes**,[545] born about 1740, in Essex, England, died before 1840, in England.

391. Mary Lawn was born about 1712, in Essex, England. She was the daughter of Lawn and Lawn. She married Nathaniel Mayes Or May 1732, in Harwich, Essex, England. He was the son of Mayes Or May and Mayes Or May.

392. William Stevens was born about 1710, in Essex, England, died 7 Jan 1787, in Great Warley, Essex, England. He was the son of Stevens and Stevens. He married Jane Setch[834] 1738, in Great Warley, Essex, England. She was the daughter of Setch and Setch.

Children of William Stevens and Jane Setch:

     i.   **Elizabeth Stevens,**[835] born Apr 1740, in Great Warley, Essex, England, christened 16 Apr 1740, in Great Warley, Essex, England.

    ii.   **Jane Stevens,**[544,545,546] born Apr 1742, in Great Warley, Essex, England, died Sep 1772, in Hornchurch, Essex, England.

   iii.   **Susanna Stevens,**[836] born Sep 1744, in Great Warley, Essex, England, christened 13 Sep 1744, in Great Warley, Essex, England, died 1761, in Great Warley, Essex, England, buried 9 Apr 1761, in Great Warley, Essex, England.

   iv.   **William Stevens,**[837] born Feb 1746, in Great Warley, Essex, England, christened 13 Feb 1746, in Great Warley, Essex, England.

    v.   **John Stevens,**[838] born Nov 1749, in Great Warley, Essex, England, christened 3 Dec 1749, in Great Warley, Essex, England, died May 1763, in Great Warley, Essex, England, buried 30 May 1763, in Great Warley, Essex, England.

   vi.   **Rachel Stevens,**[839] born Nov 1753, in Great Warley, Essex, England, christened 11 Nov 1753, in Great Warley, Essex, England.

  vii.   **George Stevens,**[840] born Jun 1755, in Great Warley, Essex, England, christened 14 Jun 1755, in Great Warley, Essex, England, died 1804, in Great Warley, Essex, England, buried 27 Feb 1804, in Great Warley, Essex, England.

393. Jane Setch was born about 1712, in Essex, England, died 25 Aug 1774, in Great Warley, Essex, England. She was the daughter of Setch and Setch. She married William Stevens[841] 1738, in Great Warley, Essex, England. He was the son of Stevens and Stevens.

394. Richard Young was born Sep 1707, in Bishopsgate, London, England, christened 9 Sep 1707, in St Botolph, Bishopsgate, London, England, died Aug 1759, in Herne, Kent, England, buried 14 Aug 1759, in Herne, Kent, England. He was the son of William Young and An Ayling. He married Hester Frances Johnson[842] 16 Aug 1727, in London St Bride, London, England. She was the daughter of Francis Johnson and Mary Gerford.

Children of Richard Young and Hester Frances Johnson:

     i.   **Richard Young,**[341,552,553] born Oct 1729, in Bishopsgate, London, England.

    ii.   **Sarah Young,**[843] born May 1734, in Bishopsgate, London, England, christened 9 May 1734, in Bishopsgate, London, England.

   iii.   **Ann Young,**[844] born Feb 1739, in Benenden, Kent, England, christened 2 Mar 1739, in Benenden, Kent, England.

   iv.   **Elizabeth Young,**[845] born Feb 1740, in Hadlow, Kent, England, christened 19 Feb 1740, in Hadlow, Kent, England.

395. Hester Frances Johnson was born 2 Oct 1714, in Shadwell, London, England, christened 17 Oct 1714, in St Paul, Shadwell, London, England. She was the daughter of Francis Johnson and Mary Gerford. She married Richard Young[846,847,848] 16 Aug 1727, in London St Bride, London, England. He was

the son of William Young and An Ayling.
Notes for Hester Frances Johnson:

1st name spelled as   FRANCES & FRANCIS in various documents

396. Jean Merigest was born May 1702, in Westminster, London, England, christened 14 May 1702, in French Huguwest, Westminster, London, England. He was the son of Pierre Merigest Or Merignan and Marie Coudere. He married Elizabeth Fozeau[849] about 1724, in England. She was the daughter of Fozeau and Fozeau.
Notes for Jean Merigest:

Christening: GLASSHOUSE STREET AND LEICESTER FIELDS, FRENCH HUGUWEST, WESTMINSTER, LONDON, ENGLAND

Children of Jean Merigest and Elizabeth Fozeau:

    i.   **Jean Merigest**,[849] born Mar 1724, in London, England, christened 15 Mar 1724, in London, England.
    ii.   **Judith Merigest**,[850] born 18 Mar 1732, in Stepney, London, England, christened 16 Apr 1732, in Stepney, London, England.
    iii.   **Elizabeth Merigest**,[341,552] born about 1735, in London, England.

397. Elizabeth Fozeau was born about 1705, in England. She was the daughter of Fozeau and Fozeau. She married Jean Merigest[849,851] about 1724, in England. He was the son of Pierre Merigest Or Merignan and Marie Coudere.

398. Francis Turner was born 20 Jul 1696, in Westminster, London, England, christened 2 Aug 1696, in Westminster, London, England. He was the son of Francis Turner and Ann Turner. He married Anne Norriss[555,852] 9 Jun 1723, in St Martin in the Fields, Westminster, London, England. She was the daughter of Norriss and Norriss.

Children of Francis Turner and Anne Norriss:

    i.   **Francis Turner**,[555] born 11 Nov 1740, in Clerkenwell, London, England, died before 1840, in England.

399. Anne Norriss was born about 1702, in England. She was the daughter of Norriss and Norriss. She married Francis Turner[555,852,853] 9 Jun 1723, in St Martin in the Fields, Westminster, London, England. He was the son of Francis Turner and Ann Turner.

400. John Horsley was born Aug 1716, in Westminster, London, England, christened 22 Aug 1716, in St Martin in the Fields, Westminster, London, England, died 27 Nov 1777, buried in Thorley, Hertfordshire, England. He was the son of Peter Horsley and Mrs Hannah Horsley. He married Mary

Outfield[554,854] 1 Oct 1742, in Saint Dunstan, Canterbury, Kent, England. She was the daughter of Henry Outfield and Mrs Jane Outfield.
Notes for John Horsley:

Appears to have married after 1st two children were born in London

Children of John Horsley and Mary Outfield:

     i.   **Anne Horsley**,[554] born Sep 1740, in London, England, died before 1840, in England.

    ii.   **John Horsley**,[855] born Mar 1742, in Westminster, London, England, christened 31 Mar 1742, in Westminster, London, England.

   iii.   **Sarah Horsley**,[856] born Mar 1743, in Westminster, London, England, christened 31 Mar 1743, in St Martin in the Fields, Westminster, London, England.

   iv.   **George Zachary Horsley**,[857] born Jan 1745, in Westminster, London, England, christened 14 Jan 1745, in St Martin in the Fields, Westminster, London, England.

    v.   **Mary Horsley**,[858] born Jun 1747, in Westminster, London, England, christened 20 Jun 1747, in St Martin in the Fields, Westminster, London, England, died 3 Jul 1824, in Nazeing, Essex, England, buried 10 Jul 1834, in Nazeing, Essex, England.

   vi.   **Elizabeth Horsley**,[859] born Jun 1748, in Westminster, London, England, christened 23 Jun 1748, in St Martin in the Fields, Westminster, London, England, died 23 Jan 1799.

401. Mary Outfield was born May 1718, in Canterbury, Kent, England, christened 1 Jun 1718, in Holy Chross, Canterbury, Kent, England. She was the daughter of Henry Outfield and Mrs Jane Outfield. She married John Horsley[554,860] 1 Oct 1742, in Saint Dunstan, Canterbury, Kent, England. He was the son of Peter Horsley and Mrs Hannah Horsley.

402. William Stringer was born May 1726, in Woodmancote, Sussex, England, christened 25 May 1726, in Woodmancote, Sussex, England. He was the son of William Stringer and Elizabeth Lassiter. He married Sarah Williams[861,862,863] 30 Oct 1748, in Pulborough, Sussex, England. She was the daughter of John Williams and Sarah Wease.

Children of William Stringer and Sarah Williams:

     i.   **Charles Stringer**,[556] born Oct 1749, in Shipley, Sussex, England, died 1802, in Sussex, England.

    ii.   **John Stringer**, born May 1751, in Shipley, Sussex, England, christened 2 Jun 1751, in Shipley, Sussex, England.

   iii.   **Edward Stringer**, born Dec 1752, in Shipley, Sussex, England, christened 31 Dec 1752, in Shipley, Sussex, England, died 2 Sep 1802, in Sussex, England.

   iv.   **Sarah Stringer**, born Apr 1754, in Shipley, Sussex, England, christened 7 Apr 1754, in Shipley, Sussex, England, died 24 Jan 1844, in Shipley, Sussex, England.

v.   **Ann Stringer**, born 27 Feb 1756, in Shipley, Sussex, England, christened 29 Feb 1756, in Shipley, Sussex, England, died Dec 1802, in Shipley, Sussex, England.

vi.   **James Stringer**, born Mar 1757, in Shipley, Sussex, England, christened 27 Mar 1757, in Shipley, Sussex, England, died 1800, in Sussex, England.

403. Sarah Williams was born Feb 1731, in Arundel, Sussex, England, christened 19 Feb 1731, in Arundel, Sussex, England. She was the daughter of John Williams and Sarah Wease. She married William Stringer[861,864] 30 Oct 1748, in Pulborough, Sussex, England. He was the son of William Stringer and Elizabeth Lassiter.

404. Mathew Blandford was born Apr 1724, in Chrishall, Essex, England, christened 9 May 1724, in Chrishall, Essex, England. He was the son of Mathew Blandford and Mary Blandford. He married Martha Watson[865,866] 2 May 1754, in Chrishall, Essex, England. She was the daughter of Richard Watson and Watson.

Children of Mathew Blandford and Martha Watson:

i.   **Martha Blandford**, born about 1754, in Essex, England.

405. Martha Watson was born Apr 1727, in Broomfield, Essex, England, christened 30 Apr 1727, in Broomfield, Essex, England. She was the daughter of Richard Watson and Watson. She married Mathew Blandford[865,867] 2 May 1754, in Chrishall, Essex, England. He was the son of Mathew Blandford and Mary Blandford.

406. James Whitton Or Witton was born Dec 1722, in London England, christened 23 Dec 1722, in London, England. He was the son of William Witton and Elizabeth Brashee. He married Ann Ells Or Ellis[868] 2 Jan 1750, in St Leonard, Shoreditch, England. She was the daughter of Thomas Ellis and Ann Bishop.
Notes for James Whitton Or Witton:

Name: James Whitton Baptism Date: 23 Dec 1722 Parish: St Mary Somerset County: London Borough: City of London Parent(s):   William Whitton, Elizabeth Whitton Record Type: Christening Register Type: ParisR hegister Name: James Whitton Marriage Date: 2 Jan 1750 Parish: St Leonard, Shoreditch County: Middlesex Borough: Hackney Spouse: Ann Ells Record Type: Marriage Register Type: Parish Register

Children of James Whitton Or Witton and Ann Ells Or Ellis:

i.   **Mary Witton**, born 21 Jun 1752, in Shoreditch, London, England, christened 12 Jul 1752, in St Leonard's Shoreditch, London, England.

ii.   **William Witton**,[557] born 2 Jan 1754, in Clerkenwell, London, England.

407. Ann Ells Or Ellis was born Jun 1727, in Bishopgate, London, England, christened 21 Jun 1727, in

St Botolph, Bishopgate, London, England. She was the daughter of Thomas Ellis and Ann Bishop. She married James Whitton Or Witton[868,869] 2 Jan 1750, in St Leonard, Shoreditch, England. He was the son of William Witton and Elizabeth Brashee.

Notes for Ann Ells Or Ellis:

Name: Ann Ellis Baptism Date: 21 Jun 1727 Parish: St Botolph, Bishopsgate County: Parent(s):   Thomas Ellis, Ann Ellis Record Type: Christening Register Type: Parish Register Name: James Whitton Marriage Date: 2 Jan 1750 Parish: St Leonard, Shoreditch County: Middlesex Borough: Hackney Spouse: Ann Ells Record Type: Marriage Register

408. John Mayor was born Jan 1719, in London, England, christened 17 Jan 1719, in St Dunstan, Stepney, London, England. He was the son of John Maier Or Mayor and An Jones. He married Margaret Norbury 12 Aug 1750, in St Katherine by the Tower, London, England. She was the daughter of Norbury and Norbury.

Notes for John Mayor:

Birth: Name: John Mayor Gender: Male Baptism Date: 17 Jan 1719 Baptism Place: Saint Dunstan,Stepney,London,England Father: John Mayor Mother: Ann FHL Film Number5:95419 Marriage: Name: John Mayer Gender: Male Marriage Date: 12 Aug 1750 Marriage Place: Saint Katherine By The Tower,London,London,England Spouse: Margaret Norbury FHL Film Number: 3744593,74460 Marriage Bonds & Allegations: Name: John Mayer Age: 28 Birth Year: abt 1722 Event Date: 12 Aug 1750 Parish: St Stephen Walbrook County: London Spouse's Name: Margaret Norbury Spouse's Age: 23 Spouse's Parish: St Mary Ratherluth Spouse's County: Surrey Event Type: Allegation Reference Number: CLC/199/D/011/MS09772/044

Children of John Mayor and Margaret Norbury:

 i. **Elizabeth Mayor**,[557,558] born 5 Dec 1750, in London, England, died before 1840, in England.

409. Margaret Norbury was born about 1727, in St Mary Ratherluth, Surrey, England. She was the daughter of Norbury and Norbury. She married John Mayor[870] 12 Aug 1750, in St Katherine by the Tower, London, England. He was the son of John Maier Or Mayor and An Jones.

Notes for Margaret Norbury:

Marriage: Name: John Mayer Gender: Male Marriage Date: 12 Aug 1750 Marriage Place: Saint Katherine By The Tower,London,London,England Spouse: Margaret Norbury FHL Film Number: 3744593,74460 Marriage Bonds & Allegations: Name: John Mayer Age: 28 Birth Year: abt 1722 Event Date: 12 Aug 1750 Parish: St Stephen Walbrook County: London Spouse's Name: Margaret Norbury Spouse's Age: 23 Spouse's Parish: St Mary Ratherluth Spouse's County: Surrey Event Type: Allegation Reference Number: CLC/199/D/011/MS09772/044

410. John Hyde was born 28 Oct 1737, in London, England, christened 20 Nov 1737, in London St

Botolph Aldersgate, London, England. He was the son of John Hyde and Hyde. He married Mary Elizabeth Roach[871,872] 11 Dec 1754, in Marylebone, London, England. She was the daughter of John Roach and Jane Gall.

Children of John Hyde and Mary Elizabeth Roach:

    i.   **Richard Hyde,**[559,561] born about 1755, in Cripplegate, London, England.

411. Mary Elizabeth Roach was born Sep 1735, in Stepney, London, England, christened 14 Sep 1735, in Stepney, St Dunstan, London, England. She was the daughter of John Roach and Jane Gall. She married John Hyde[871,872,873] 11 Dec 1754, in Marylebone, London, England. He was the son of John Hyde and Hyde.

412. Thomas Rainbird Or Raynbird was born Jul 1719, in Walsham Le Willows, Suffolk, England, christened 9 Aug 1719, in Walsham Le Willows, Suffolk, England. He was the son of Thomas Rainbird Or Raynbard and Ann Bedwall. He married Mary Baker[874,875,876] 11 Sep 1735, in Woolpit, Suffolk, England. She was the daughter of William Baker and Mary Goodchild.

Children of Thomas Rainbird Or Raynbird and Mary Baker:

    i.   **Mary Rainbird Or Raynbird,**[877] born Dec 1735, in Suffolk, England, christened 2 Feb 1736, in Suffolk, England, died before Jun 1740, in Suffolk, England.

    ii.   **Ann Rainbird Or Raynbird,**[878] born Sep 1736, in Wilverton, Suffolk, England, christened 29 Sep 1736, in Wilverton, Suffolk, England, died before Mar 1749, in Wilverton, Suffolk, England.

    iii.   **Martha Rainbird Or Raynbird,**[879] born Mar 1738, in Wilverton, Suffolk, England, christened 23 Mar 1738, in Wilverton, Suffolk, England.

    iv.   **Mary Rainbird Or Raynbird,**[880] born Jun 1740, in Wilverton, Suffolk, England, christened 16 Jun 1740, in Wilverton, Suffolk, England.

    v.   **Thomas Rainbird Or Raynbird,**[881] born Apr 1742, in Pakenham, Suffolk, England, christened 3 May 1742, in Pakenham, Suffolk, England.

    vi.   **Robert Rainbird Or Raynbird,**[882] born Mar 1744, in Pakenham, Suffolk, England, christened 2 Apr 1744, in Pakenham, Suffolk, England.

    vii.   **Sarah Rainbird Or Raynbird,**[883] born May 1746, in Pakenham, Suffolk, England, christened 29 May 1746, in Pakenham, Suffolk, England.

    viii.   **John Rainbird Or Raynbird,**[884] born Jul 1748, in Pakenham, Suffolk, England, christened 2 Aug 1748, in Pakenham, Suffolk, England.

    ix.   **Ann Rainbird,**[559,560] born Mar 1750, in Pakenham, Suffolk, England.

413. Mary Baker was born May 1714, in Tostock, Suffolk, England, christened 2 Jun 1714, in Tostock, Suffolk, England. She was the daughter of William Baker and Mary Goodchild. She married Thomas Rainbird Or Raynbird[875,885,886] 11 Sep 1735, in Woolpit, Suffolk, England. He was the son of Thomas Rainbird Or Raynbard and Ann Bedwall.

414. John Briggs was born 5 Nov 1682, in Stepney, London, England, christened 6 Nov 1682, in St Dunstan, Stepney, London, England. He was the son of John Briggs and Mrs Anne Briggs. He married Jane Rice[887,888,889] 26 Mar 1731, in Westminster, London, England.[887] She was the daughter of Thomas Rice and Martha Rice.

Notes for John Briggs:

Parish Record Collection - Marriage Record Print Close Year: 1731 Supplied Surname: RICE Surname: RICE Full First name: Jane Supplied First Name: Jane Spouse Surname: BRIGGS Spouse Full First name: John Spouse First Name: Jn Place: WESTMINSTER (GROSVENOR CHAPEL, MAYFAIR) County: London Record source: Boyd's Marriage Index 1538-1840

Children of John Briggs and Jane Rice:

     i.   **John Briggs**,[564,565] born Nov 1744, in Stepney, Middlesex, England, died May 1793, in Westminster, London, England.

415. Jane Rice was born 9 Jan 1696, in Stepney, London, England, christened 24 Jan 1696, in St Dunstan, Stepney, London, England. She was the daughter of Thomas Rice and Martha Rice. She married John Briggs[887,890,891] 26 Mar 1731, in Westminster, London, England.[887] He was the son of John Briggs and Mrs Anne Briggs.

416. William Timbrell was born 22 Oct 1728, in London, England, christened 18 Nov 1728, in St James, Westminster, London, England, died 1774, in London, England, buried 1774, in London, England. He was the son of William Timbrell and Mary Timbrell. He married Sarah Crew[802,803,804] 23 Jan 1749, in Fleet, London, England. She was the daughter of Hezekiah Crew and Ann Capling.

Children of William Timbrell and Sarah Crew:

     i.   **William Timbrell**,[895] born Apr 1752, in London, England, christened 10 Apr 1752, in St John Zacary, London, England.

    ii.   **Sarah Timbrell**,[562,563] born Mar 1754, in London, England, died Mar 1788, in Soho, London, England.

417. Sarah Crew was born Apr 1732, in Westminster, London, England, christened 7 Apr 1732, in St Martin in the Fields, Westminster, London, England, died Nov 1788, in Whitechapel, Middlesex, England, buried 21 Nov 1788, in Whitechapel, Middlesex, England. She was the daughter of Hezekiah Crew and Ann Capling. She married William Timbrell[892,896,897,898] 23 Jan 1749, in Fleet, London, England. He was the son of William Timbrell and Mary Timbrell.

418. George Giles was born 1702, in Pembury, Kent, England, christened 28 Feb 1702, in Pembury, Kent, England, died 22 May 1778, in Kent, England. He was the son of Edward Giles and Elizabeth Foreman. He married Hannah Lasshan[899] 8 Jul 1739, in Pembury, Kent, England.[899] She was the daughter of Lasshan and Lasshan.

Notes for George Giles:

George GILES was married twice. George was the son of Edward and Elizabeth GILES (nee FOREMAN). George first married Mary BUTCHER or BELCHER on 22 Oct 1728 in Pembury, Kent, England with whom he had five children, all christened in Pembury, Kent : George (1729), Mary (1730), Elizabeth (1732), Susan (1734) and Sarah (1737). He buried his first wife on 11 Apr 1738 and wife a young family to raise, he then married Hannah LAFFHAM on 8 Jul 1739 and they had four children : Hannah (1740), Anne (1741), George (1742), and Edward (1745). Their first born Hannah was christened in Pembury and the other three children in Church of England Parish Church of Lamberhurst (Kent).

Children of George Giles and Hannah Lasshan:

  i.   **Hannah Giles**, born 20 Jan 1740, in Pembury, Kent, England, christened 20 Jan 1740, in Pembury, Kent, England, died 1784, in Lamberhurst, Kent, England. She married Bridger Marsh 19 Oct 1760, in Lamberhurst, Kent, England. Bridger Marsh was born 1729, in Lamberhurst, Kent, England, died 1805, in Lamberhurst, Kent, England.
  ii.   **Ann Giles**, born 6 Sep 1741, in Pembury, Kent, England, christened 6 Sep 1741, in Lamberhurst, Kent, England, buried 25 Jan 1819, in Brenchley, Kent, England. She married John Botten 10 Oct 1762, in Pembury, Kent, England. John Botten was born 1735, in Pembury, Kent, England, christened 8 Jun 1735, in Brenchley, Kent, England, buried 13 Oct 1808, in Brenchley, Kent, England.
  iii. **George Giles**, born Dec 1742, in Lamberhurst, Kent, England, died 12 Jul 1812, in Goudhurst, Kent, England.
  iv.   **Edward Giles**, born 9 Jun 1745, in Lamberhurst, Kent, England, christened 9 Jun 1745, in Lamberhurst, Kent, England.

419. Hannah Lasshan was born 1718, in Pembury, Kent, England, died 22 May 1778, in Kent, England. She was the daughter of Lasshan and Lasshan. She married George Giles[899] 8 Jul 1739, in Pembury, Kent, England.[899] He was the son of Edward Giles and Elizabeth Foreman.
Notes for Hannah Lasshan:

aka: LAFFHAM (batch) number:M16509-1; system origin:England-VR; source film number:1469265

420. John Stevens was born 6 Jun 1718, in Ramsgate, Kent, England. He was the son of John Stevens and Elizabeth Deverson. He married Sarah Hayward[568] 19 Nov 1736, in Marden, Kent, England. She was the daughter of Jacob Hayward and Elizabeth Tanner.

Children of John Stevens and Sarah Hayward:

  i.   **Elizabeth Stevens**, born Mar 1740, in Chatham, Kent, England, christened 8 Mar 1740, in Chatham, Kent, England.

ii. **Stephen Stevens**, born Oct 1744, in Marden, Kent, England, christened 31 Oct 1744, in Marden, Kent, England.

iii. **Martha Stevens**,[568] born Sep 1746, in Marden, Kent, England, died before 1840, in England.

iv. **Mary Stevens**, born Aug 1750, in Marden, Kent, England, christened 14 Aug 1750, in Marden, Kent, England.

v. **Anne Stevens**, born Oct 1752, in Marden, Kent, England, christened 27 Oct 1752, in Marden, Kent, England.

421. Sarah Hayward was born Apr 1709, in Marden, Kent, England, christened 24 Apr 1709, in Marden, Kent, England. She was the daughter of Jacob Hayward and Elizabeth Tanner. She married John Stevens 19 Nov 1736, in Marden, Kent, England. He was the son of John Stevens and Elizabeth Deverson.

422. James Holmes was born 16 Jul 1710, in Dover, Kent, England, christened 16 Jul 1710, in Canterbury, Kent, England, died before 1800, in England. He was the son of Edward Holmes and Mary Bennett. He married Ann Collyer[900] 30 Sep 1736, in Dover, Kent, England. She was the daughter of Robert Collyer and Deborah Epse.

Children of James Holmes and Ann Collyer:

i. **William Holmes**, born 22 Dec 1744, in Dover, Kent, England, died 1803, in Dover, Kent, England.

423. Ann Collyer was born 1713, in Dover, Kent, England, christened 10 Dec 1713, in Dover, Kent, England, died before 1810, in England. She was the daughter of Robert Collyer and Deborah Epse. She married James Holmes 30 Sep 1736, in Dover, Kent, England. He was the son of Edward Holmes and Mary Bennett.
Notes for Ann Collyer:

Christening: 10 Dec 1713 St Mary The Virgin, Dover, Kent, England C03656-1 system origin: England-ODM source film number: 355633

424. Andrew Read was born 1720, in Dover, Kent, England, died before 1820, in England. He was the son of Read and Read. He married Sarah Hawkes 28 Apr 1748, in Dover, Kent, England. She was the daughter of Thomas Hawkes and Mrs Mary Hawkes.
Notes for Andrew Read:

Customs officer Andrew b. ca 1720 was a Customs Officer at the port of Dover, KEN. He married Sarah HAWKES 1748 at St. Mary, Dover. Their daughter Elizabeth b. 1718 at Dover, married William HOLMES 1776 at St. Mary, Dover.

Children of Andrew Read and Sarah Hawkes:

    i.   **Sarah Read**, born 1748, in Dover, Kent, England, christened 24 Mar 1748, in Dover, Kent, England.

    ii.   **Thomas Read**, born 1750, in Dover, Kent, England, christened 28 Dec 1750, in Dover, Kent, England.

    iii.   **Elizabeth Read**, born 31 Jul 1752, in Dover, Kent, England, died 1833, in Charlton, Kent, England.

    iv.   **Mary Read**, born 1754, in Dover, Kent, England, christened 4 Sep 1754, in Dover, Kent, England.

    v.   **Helen Read**, born 1757, in Dover, Kent, England, christened 13 Feb 1757, in Dover, Kent, England.

    vi.   **William Read**, born 1759, in Dover, Kent, England, christened 12 Jan 1759, in Dover, Kent, England.

    vii.   **Richard Read**, born 1761, in Dover, Kent, England, christened 8 Aug 1761, in Dover, Kent, England, died 16 Jun 1768, in Dover, Kent, England, buried Jul 1768, in Dover, Kent, England.

425. Sarah Hawkes was born 1718, in Dover, Kent, England, christened 10 Jan 1718, in Folkestone, Kent, England, died before 1800, in England. She was the daughter of Thomas Hawkes and Mrs Mary Hawkes. She married Andrew Read 28 Apr 1748, in Dover, Kent, England. He was the son of Read and Read.

426. Heny "Henry" Baldwin was born Apr 1703, in Southwark, Surrey, England, christened 11 Apr 1703, in Bishopsgate, London, England. He was the son of Baldwin and Baldwin. He married Elizabeth Laurence[901,902,903] about 1730, in England. She was the daughter of Daniel Laurence and Mrs Elizabeth Laurence.
Notes for Heny "Henry" Baldwin:

ref: page 142 in Parish register of St Anthonlin, Budge Row, London Named as BALLWIN of St Olive's,

Children of Heny "Henry" Baldwin and Elizabeth Laurence:

    i.   **Henry Baldwin**,[575,577,578] born Jan 1739, in London, England.

427. Elizabeth Laurence was born Jul 1704, in London, England, christened 23 Jul 1704, in St Sepulchre, London, England. She was the daughter of Daniel Laurence and Mrs Elizabeth Laurence. She married Heny "Henry" Baldwin[901,902,904] about 1730, in England. He was the son of Baldwin and Baldwin.

428. Robert Smith was born 5 Jan 1690, in Westminster, London, England, christened 18 Jan 1690, in Westminster, London, England. He was the son of John Smith and Mrs Alice Smith. He married Susanna Browes[905] 26 Aug 1714, in Westminster, London, England. She was the daughter of Browes and

Browes.

Children of Robert Smith and Susanna Browes:

    i.   **Rebecca Smith**,[575,576] born May 1725, in Aldgate, London, England.

    ii.   **Hannah Smith**,[906] born Dec 1726, in Aldgate, London, England, christened 28 Dec 1726, in Aldgate, London, England, died 10 May 1733.

    iii.   **Sarah Smith**,[907] born Apr 1731, in Aldgate, London, England, christened 7 May 1731, in Aldgate, London, England, died 5 Sep 1732.

429. Susanna Browes was born about 1690, in London, England. She was the daughter of Browes and Browes. She married Robert Smith[905] 26 Aug 1714, in Westminster, London, England. He was the son of John Smith and Mrs Alice Smith.

430. Thomas Dixon was born Feb 1710, in Edmonton, Middlesex, England, christened 20 Feb 1710, in Edmonton, Middlesex, England. He was the son of Thomas Dixon and Mrs Elizabeth Dixon. He married Mary Empey[908,909] Nov 1732, in Fleet, London, England. She was the daughter of Elijah Empey and Mary Empey.

Children of Thomas Dixon and Mary Empey:

    i.   **Thomas Dixon**,[910] born Sep 1737, in Holborn, London, England, christened 2 Oct 1737, in Holborn, London, England.

    ii.   **William Scofield Dixon**,[581,587] born Nov 1740, in Stepney, London, England.

431. Mary Empey was born Feb 1711, in Westminster, London, England, christened 21 Feb 1711, in Westminster, London, England. She was the daughter of Elijah Empey and Mary Empey. She married Thomas Dixon[908,911] Nov 1732, in Fleet, London, England. He was the son of Thomas Dixon and Mrs Elizabeth Dixon.
Notes for Mary Empey:

aka IMPY

432. Thomas Miller was born about 1720, in England. He was the son of Miller and Miller. He married Margaret Buxton[912] 18 Apr 1742, in Westminster, London, England. She was the daughter of Buxton and Buxton.

Children of Thomas Miller and Margaret Buxton:

    i.   **Mary Ann Miller**,[579,580] born Jan 1742, in London, England.

433. Margaret Buxton was born about 1722, in England. She was the daughter of Buxton and Buxton. She married Thomas Miller[912] 18 Apr 1742, in Westminster, London, England. He was the son of Miller and Miller.

434. Henry Wine was born Nov 1737, in Stepney, Middlesex, England, christened 20 Nov 1737, in Stepney, Middlesex, England, died before 1820, in England. He was the son of John Wine and Elizabeth Hill. He married Mary Smith[913] 30 Apr 1763, in Finsbury, London, England. She was the daughter of Smith and Smith.

Children of Henry Wine and Mary Smith:

    i.   **William Wine**,[584] born 9 Apr 1761, in Shoreditch, London, England, died 1829, in Stepney, Middlesex, England.

    ii.   **Henry Wine**, born 31 May 1769, in Stepney, Middlesex, England, christened 31 May 1769, in Stepney, Middlesex, England.

    iii.   **John Wine**, born 13 Aug 1771, in Shoreditch, London, England, christened 26 Aug 1771, in Shoreditch, London, England.

    iv.   **Mary Wine**, born 6 Nov 1777, in Bethnal Green, London, England, christened 23 Nov 1777, in Bethnal Green, London, England.

435. Mary Smith was born about 1740, in England, died before 1840, in England. She was the daughter of Smith and Smith. She married Henry Wine[913,914] 30 Apr 1763, in Finsbury, London, England. He was the son of John Wine and Elizabeth Hill.

436. Charles Venner was born about 1737, in London, England, died before 1820, in London, England. He was the son of Charles Vanner and Vanner. He married Martha Wie Or Way[915,916] 1755, in London, England. She was the daughter of John Wie Or Way and Wie Or Way.

Children of Charles Venner and Martha Wie Or Way:

    i.   **Martha Vennor**,[583] born 27 Jul 1760, in Shoreditch, London, England, died before 1860, in England.

    ii.   **Charles Vanner**, born 9 Feb 1763, in Shoreditch, London, England, christened 24 Apr 1763, in Shoreditch, London, England.

    iii.   **Ann Vanner**, born 18 Jan 1766, in Shoreditch, London, England, christened 9 Mar 1766, in Shoreditch, London, England.

    iv.   **Thomas Vanner**, born 1769, in Bethnal Green, London, England, christened 25 Dec 1769, in Bethnal Green, London, England.

437. Martha Wie Or Way was born Apr 1724, in London, England, christened 10 Apr 1724, died before 1800, in London, England. She was the daughter of John Wie Or Way and Wie Or Way. She married Charles Venner[915] 1755, in London, England. He was the son of Charles Vanner and Vanner.

438. James Richardson was born Dec 1734, in Stepney, London, England, christened 10 Dec 1734, in St Dunstan, Stepney, London, England. He was the son of William Richardson and Mrs Mary

Richardson. He married Elizabeth Jones[917,918] 23 Jun 1753, in St Dunstan, Stepney, London, England. She was the daughter of Hugh Jones and Elizabeth Debell.

Children of James Richardson and Elizabeth Jones:

    i.   **William Richardson,**[587,588] born Oct 1756, in Stepney, London, England.

439. Elizabeth Jones was born May 1735, in London, England, christened 12 May 1735, in Spitalfields Christ Church, Stepney, London, England. She was the daughter of Hugh Jones and Elizabeth Debell. She married James Richardson[919] 23 Jun 1753, in St Dunstan, Stepney, London, England. He was the son of William Richardson and Mrs Mary Richardson.

440. William Yates was born 6 Jan 1735, in Westminster, London, England, christened 15 Jan 1735, in St James, Westminster, London, England. He was the son of John Yeates and Mrs Elizabeth Yeates. He married Mary Jones[920] 30 Aug 1758, in Westminster, London, England. She was the daughter of Jones and Jones.
Notes for William Yates:

father: John Yates mother: Elizabeth

Children of William Yates and Mary Jones:

    i.   **Sarah Yeates,**[921] born Jan 1761, in Stepney, London, England, christened 14 Jan 1761, in St Mary Whitechapel, Stepney, London, England.
    ii.   **Ann Yeates,**[586] born Jun 1762, in St Andrew, Holborn, London, England.

441. Mary Jones was born about 1742, in London, England. She was the daughter of Jones and Jones. She married William Yates[920,921,922] 30 Aug 1758, in Westminster, London, England. He was the son of John Yeates and Mrs Elizabeth Yeates.

442. Jeremiah Rapley was born about 1725, in England. He was the son of Rapley and Rapley. He married Mary Graham[923,924,925] 20 Nov 1745, in Westminster, London, England. She was the daughter of John Graham and Mary Partridge.

Children of Jeremiah Rapley and Mary Graham:

    i.   **Richard Rapley,**[926] born 27 Nov 1748, in Marylebone, London, England, christened 18 Dec 1748, in Marylebone, London, England.
    ii.   **Charles Rapley,**[927] born 1 Nov 1750, in Marylebone, London, England, christened 15 Nov 1750, in Marylebone, London, England.
    iii.   **Jeremiah Rapley,**[928] born 16 Oct 1752, in Marylebone, London, England, christened 19 Oct 1752, in Marylebone, London, England.
    iv.   **Perter Rene Rapley,**[929] born 24 Oct 1754, in Marylebone, London, England,

christened 9 Nov 1754, in Marylebone, London, England.

v. **Thomas Rapley**,[596,597,598] born 12 Nov 1756, in Westminster, London, England, died 14 Sep 1806, in Limehouse, Middlesex, England.

vi. **Mary Rapley**,[930] born 10 Nov 1758, in Marylebone, London, England, christened 8 Dec 1758, in Marylebone, London, England.

vii. **Ann Rebecca Rapley**,[931] born 3 Mar 1760, in Marylebone, London, England, christened 8 Apr 1760, in Marylebone, London, England.

443. Mary Graham was born Jul 1723, in Westminster, London, England, christened 28 Jul 1723, in Westminster, London, England. She was the daughter of John Graham and Mary Partridge. She married Jeremiah Rapley[923,932] 20 Nov 1745, in Westminster, London, England. He was the son of Rapley and Rapley.

444. Benjamin Roberts was born Apr 1734, in Saint Mary Somerset, London, England, christened 28 Apr 1734, in Saint Mary Somerset, London, England. He was the son of John Roberts and Ann Rumboll. He married Sarah Or Sara Hawkins[933] 1756, in Westminster, London, England. She was the daughter of Hawkins and Hawkins.

Children of Benjamin Roberts and Sarah Or Sara Hawkins:

i. **Mary Ann Roberts**,[589] born 17 Feb 1758, in Westminster, London, England, died before 1840, in England.

ii. **Elizabeth Roberts**,[934] born 18 Nov 1759, in Westminster, London, England, christened 2 Dec 1759, in Westminster, London, England.

iii. **Maria Ann Roberts**,[935] born May 1761, in Westminster, London, England, christened 8 May 1761, in Westminster, London, England.

iv. **John Roberts**,[936] born Nov 1762, in Westminster, London, England, christened 27 Nov 1762, in Westminster St James the Less, London, England.

v. **William Roberts**,[937] born Mar 1764, in Westminster, London, England, christened 13 Mar 1764, in Westminster St James the Less, London, England.

vi. **George Roberts**,[938] born May 1765, in Westminster, London, England, christened 12 May 1765, in Westminster St James the Less, London, England.

445. Sarah Or Sara Hawkins was born about 1735, in Westminster, London, England. She was the daughter of Hawkins and Hawkins. She married Benjamin Roberts[939,940] 1756, in Westminster, London, England. He was the son of John Roberts and Ann Rumboll.

446. Samuel Mott was born 25 Apr 1726, in St Sepulchre, London, England, christened 9 May 1726, in St Sepulchre, London, England. He was the son of Milford Mott and Elizabeth Hubbard. He married Mary Purviss[941,942,943] 12 Aug 1749, in Fleet, London, England. She was the daughter of Richard Purviss and Margaret Purviss.

Children of Samuel Mott and Mary Purviss:

  i.   **Stephen Mott**,[601] born 28 Jun 1750, in London, England.

447. Mary Purviss was born Jan 1727, in Blackfriers, London, England, christened 5 Feb 1727, in Blackfriers, London, England. She was the daughter of Richard Purviss and Margaret Purviss. She married Samuel Mott[941,944,945] 12 Aug 1749, in Fleet, London, England. He was the son of Milford Mott and Elizabeth Hubbard.

448. John Steel was born 16 Aug 1707, in London, England, christened 24 Aug 1707, in St Sepulchre, London, England. He was the son of John Steel and Mrs Sarah Steel. He married Hannah Or Sarah Collings[946,947] 31 Dec 1734, in Fleet, London, England. She was the daughter of Collings and Collings.

Children of John Steel and Hannah Or Sarah Collings:

  i.   **Elizabeth Mary Steel**,[948] born Feb 1735, in Putney, London, England, christened 26 Feb 1735, in Putney, London, England.
  ii. **John Steel**,[949] born May 1736, in Putney, London, England, christened 12 May 1736, in Putney, London, England.
  iii. **Joseph Steel**,[950] born Aug 1737, in Putney, London, England, christened 25 Aug 1737, in Putney, London, England.
  iv. **Edward Steel**,[951] born Jan 1739, in Putney, London, England, christened 24 Jan 1739, in Putney, London, England.
  v.   **George Steel**,[952] born Apr 1740, in Putney, London, England, christened 8 Apr 1740, in Putney, London, England, died before Mar 1741, in Putney, London, England.
  vi. **George Steel**,[953] born Apr 1741, in Putney, London, England, christened 22 Apr 1741, in Putney, London, England.
  vii. **Sarah Steel**,[954] born Feb 1743, in Putney, London, England, christened 6 Mar 1743, in Putney, London, England.
  viii. **Susanah Steel**,[955] born May 1744, in Putney, London, England, christened 13 May 1744, in Putney, London, England.
  ix. **Ann Steel**,[599,600] born Sep 1745, in Putney, London, England.

449. Hannah Or Sarah Collings was born about 1716, in England. She was the daughter of Collings and Collings. She married John Steel[946,956] 31 Dec 1734, in Fleet, London, England. He was the son of John Steel and Mrs Sarah Steel.

Generation No. 10

450. Thomas Aldworth was born Aug 1677, in Drayton, Berkshire, England, christened 22 Aug 1677, in Drayton, Berkshire, England, died Jul 1710, in Tubney, Berkshire, England, buried 8 Jul 1710, in Appleton, Berkshire, England. He was the son of Thomas Aldworth and Katherine Tyrrald. He married Martha Collings 29 Jun 1697, in South Hinksey, Berkshire, England. She was the daughter of Thomas Collings and Collings.

Notes for Thomas Aldworth:

residence: Drayton, Berkshire, England parents: Thomas Aldworth, Katherine record title: England Births and Christenings, 1538-1975 name: Thomas Aldworth gender: Male baptism/christening date: 22 Aug 1677 baptism/christening place: Drayton, Berkshire, England father's name: Thomas Aldworth mother's name: Katherine indexing project (batch) number: C16078-1 system origin: England. source film number: 1279456 marriage: 29 Jun 1697 -South Hinksey, Berkshire, England spouse: Martha Collins record title: England Marriages, 1538-1973 groom's name: Thomas Aldworth bride's name: Martha Collins marriage date: 29 Jun 1697 marriage place: South Hinksey,Berkshire,England indexing project (batch) number: M07320-1 system origin: England-ODM source film number: 887488

Children of Thomas Aldworth and Martha Collings:

    i.   **Robert Aldworth**, born Jan 1699, in Tubney, Berkshire, England, christened 9 Jan 1699, in Appleton, Berkshire, England. He married Susan Rolfe 18 Nov 1716, in Hungerford, Berkshire, England. Susan Rolfe was born about 1696, in Berkshire, England.
          Notes for Robert Aldworth and Susan Rolfe: Berkshire marriages 2nd edition Aldworth, Richard Susan Rolfe 18 nov 1716 Hungerford - St Lawrence

    ii.   **William Aldesworth**,[607] born Oct 1701, in Eaton, Oxfordshire, England, died 31 May 1762, in Stanton Harcourt, Oxfordshire, England.

    iii.   **Elizabeth Aldworth**, born Dec 1703, in Tubney, Berkshire, England, christened 16 Dec 1703, in Appleton, Berkshire, England.

    iv.   **John Aldworth**, born Dec 1705, in Tubney, Berkshire, England, christened 20 Dec 1705, in Appleton, Berkshire, England, died Mar 1765, in Appleton, Berkshire, England, buried 19 Mar 1765, in Appleton, Berkshire, England.
          John was a schoolmaster

    v.   **Ann Aldworth**, born Nov 1707, in Tubney, Berkshire, England, christened 18 Nov 1707, in Appleton, Berkshire, England.

    vi.   **James Aldworth**, born Feb 1709, in Tubney, Berkshire, England, christened 24 Feb 1709, in Appleton, Berkshire, England, died Aug 1729, in Tubney, Berkshire, England, buried 15 Aug 1729, in Appleton, Berkshire, England.

451. Martha Collings was born May 1680, in East Hanney, Berkshire, England, christened 23 May

1680, in Clewer, Berkshire, England, died Aug 1710, in Tubney, Berkshire, England, buried 17 Aug 1710, in Appleton, Berkshire, England. She was the daughter of Thomas Collings and Collings. She married Thomas Aldworth 29 Jun 1697, in South Hinksey, Berkshire, England. He was the son of Thomas Aldworth and Katherine Tyrrald.

Notes for Martha Collings:

residence: Berkshire, England parents: Thomas Collings record title: England Births and Christenings, 1538-1975 name: Martha Collings gender: Female baptism/christening date: 23 May 1680 baptism/christening place: CLEWER,BERKSHIRE,ENGLAND father's name: Thomas Collings indexing project (batch) number: C01767-2 system origin: England-ODM source film number: 88232. Marriage: 29 Jun 1697 -South Hinksey, Berkshire, England spouse: Martha Collins record title: England Marriages, 1538-1973 groom's name: Thomas Aldworth bride's name: Martha Collins marriage date: 29 Jun 1697 marriage place: South Hinksey,Berkshire,England indexing project (batch) number: M07320-1 system origin: England-ODM source film number: 887488

452. John Baker was born 16 Oct 1667, in Appleford, Berkshire, England, christened 16 Oct 1667, in Appleford, Berkshire, England, died before 1766, in England. He was the son of Richard Baker and Mrs Jane Baker. He married Frances Slade[957] 2 Jun 1700, in Sutton Courtenay, Berkshire, England.

Children of John Baker and Frances Slade:

       i.   **Mary Baker,**[602,603,604] born Dec 1709, in Appleford, Berkshire, England, died 1759, in Stanton Harcourt, Oxfordshire, England.

453. Frances Slade was born about 1682, in Berkshire, England, died before 1780, in England. She married John Baker[957] 2 Jun 1700, in Sutton Courtenay, Berkshire, England. He was the son of Richard Baker and Mrs Jane Baker.

454. _____Tindal was born about 1685, in England. He married Tindal about 1710, in England.

Children of Tindal and Tindal:

       i.   **Nathaniel Tindal,**[608] born about 1714, in Beckley, Oxfordshire, England, died before 1800, in England.

455. _____Tindal was born about 1688, in England. She married Tindal about 1710, in England.

456. _____Hanzel was born about 1690, in England. He married Hanzel about 1712, in England.

Children of Hanzel and Hanzel:

       i.   **Mary Hanzel,**[608] born about 1717, in Beckley, Oxfordshire, England, died before 1800, in England.

Contents

457. ____**Hanzel** was born about 1692, in England. She married Hanzel about 1712, in England.

458. William Townshend was born Dec 1672, in Standlake, Oxfordshire, England, christened 1 Jan 1673, in Standlake, Oxfordshire, England. He was the son of Thomas Townshend and Mrs Elizabeth Townsend. He married Mary Carter 1696, in Oxfordshire, England. She was the daughter of John Carter and Carter.
Notes for William Townshend:

Inn Keeper

Children of William Townshend and Mary Carter:

       i.   **Henry Townshend,**[610,614] born Dec 1700, in Witney, Oxfordshire, England.

459. Mary Carter was born Aug 1666, in Woodstock, Oxfordshire, England, christened 26 Aug 1666, in Woodstock, Oxfordshire, England. She was the daughter of John Carter and Carter. She married William Townshend 1696, in Oxfordshire, England. He was the son of Thomas Townshend and Mrs Elizabeth Townsend.

460. ____**Tewksbury** was born about 1670, in Oxfordshire, England. He married Tewksbury about 1690, in Oxfordshire, England.

Children of Tewksbury and Tewksbury:

       i.   **Sarah Tewksbury,**[610] born about 1702, in Potters Hill, Langley, Oxfordshire, England.

461. ____**Tewksbury** was born about 1672, in Oxfordshire, England. She married Tewksbury about 1690, in Oxfordshire, England.

462. ____**Hopcraft** was born about 1690, in Oxfordshire, England. He married Hopcraft about 1710, in England.

Children of Hopcraft and Hopcraft:

       i.   **Robert Hopcraft,**[615] born about 1717, in Bicester, Oxfordshire, England.

463. ____**Hopcraft** was born about 1692, in Oxfordshire, England. She married Hopcraft about 1710, in England.

464. ____**Barton** was born about 1680, in Oxfordshire, England. He married Barton about 1705, in Oxfordshire, England.

Children of Barton and Barton:

      i.   **Mary Barton**,[615] born about 1720, in Blackthorn, Oxfordshire, England.

465. ____Barton was born about 1685, in Oxfordshire, England. She married Barton about 1705, in Oxfordshire, England.

466. Thomas Turner was born Sep 1656, in Witney, Oxfordshire, England, christened 21 Sep 1656, in Witney, Oxfordshire, England. He was the son of Thomas Turner and Turner. He married Mary Bird[958] 20 Nov 1689, in Witney, Oxfordshire, England.

Children of Thomas Turner and Mary Bird:

      i.   **Thomas Turner**,[617] born Oct 1690, in Ascott Under Wychwood, Oxfordshire, England.

467. Mary Bird was born about 1670, in Oxfordshire, England. She married Thomas Turner[958,959] 20 Nov 1689, in Witney, Oxfordshire, England. He was the son of Thomas Turner and Turner.

468. Richard Hix was born about 1670, in Oxfordshire, England. He married Hix about 1690, in Oxfordshire, England.

Children of Richard Hix and Hix:

      i.   **Joane Hix**,[616] born 1694, in Ascott Under Wychwood, Oxfordshire, England.

469. ____Hix was born about 1672, in Oxfordshire, England. She married Richard Hix about 1690, in Oxfordshire, England.

470. ____Cox was born about 1650, in Oxfordshire, England. He married Cox about 1678, in Oxfordshire, England.

Children of Cox and Cox:

      i.   **Thomas Cox**,[619] born about 1680, in Ramsden, Oxfordshire, England.

471. ____Cox was born about 1652, in Oxfordshire, England. She married Cox about 1678, in Oxfordshire, England.

472. Thomas Rose was born about 1655, in Mickleton, Oxfordshire, England. He married Mary Ebsworth about 1675, in England.

Children of Thomas Rose and Mary Ebsworth:

     i.   **Rose Ebsworth**,[618,619] born Feb 1680, in Ramsden, Oxfordshire, England.

473. Mary Ebsworth was born about 1655, in Shipton under Wychwood, Oxfordshire, England. She married Thomas Rose[960] about 1675, in England.

474. ____Tims was born about 1640, in Oxfordshire, England. He married Tims about 1672, in Oxfordshire, England.

Children of Tims and Tims:

     i.   **George Tims**,[620,626] born about 1675, in Ascott Under Wychwood, Oxfordshire, England, died Sep 1746, in Ascott Under Wychwood, Oxfordshire, England.

475. ____Tims was born about 1642, in Oxfordshire, England. She married Tims about 1672, in Oxfordshire, England.

476. William Ferryman was born about 1660, in Oxfordshire, England. He married Elizabeth Gryme[961,962] 29 Aug 1681, in Oxford, Oxfordshire, England. She was the daughter of Edward Gryme and Gryme.
Notes for William Ferryman:

aka FERRIMAN

Children of William Ferryman and Elizabeth Gryme:

     i.   **Elizabeth Ferrimen**,[620,621] born about 1682, in Ascott Under Wychwood, Oxfordshire, England, died Nov 1752, in Ascott Under Wychwood, Oxfordshire, England.

477. Elizabeth Gryme was born Sep 1657, in Bicester, Oxfordshire, England, christened 26 Sep 1657, in Bicester, Oxfordshire, England. She was the daughter of Edward Gryme and Gryme. She married William Ferryman[961] 29 Aug 1681, in Oxford, Oxfordshire, England.

478. Anthony Cockins was born May 1633, in Upper Heyford, Oxfordshire, England, christened 12 May 1633, in Upper Heyford, Oxfordshire, England, died Jun 1705, in Tackley, Oxfordshire, England, buried 20 Jun 1705, in Tackley, Oxfordshire, England. He was the son of Stephen Cockin and Susan Haynes. He married Elizabeth Howse[963] 3 Oct 1654, in Deddington, Oxfordshire, England. She was the daughter of Robert Howse and Bridget Jelks.

Children of Anthony Cockins and Elizabeth Howse:

> i. **John Cockins**,[627,629] born Mar 1656, in Upper Heyford, Oxfordshire, England, died May 1737, in Upper Heyford, Oxfordshire, England.
>
> ii. **Stephen Cockins**, born Dec 1658, in Upper Heyford, Oxfordshire, England, christened 13 Dec 1658, in Upper Heyford, Oxfordshire, England, died 21 Feb 1723, in Oxfordshire, England, buried 24 Feb 1723, in Shipton under Wychwood, Oxfordshire, England.
>
> iii. **Thomas Cockins**, born May 1661, in Upper Heyford, Oxfordshire, England, christened 20 May 1661, in Upper Heyford, Oxfordshire, England.
>
> iv. **Elizabeth Cockins**, born about 1665, in England, christened 30 Oct 1665, in Upper Heyford, Oxfordshire, England.
>
> v. **Ann Cockins**, born 17 Mar 1668, in Upper Heyford, Oxfordshire, England, christened 29 Mar 1668, in Upper Heyford, Oxfordshire, England, buried 9 May 1697, in Tackley, Oxfordshire, England.

479. Elizabeth Howse was born Aug 1638, in Upper Heyford, Oxfordshire, England, christened 8 Aug 1638, in Upper Heyford, Oxfordshire, England, died Mar 1702, in Oxfordshire, England, buried 3 Apr 1702, in Tackley, Oxfordshire, England. She was the daughter of Robert Howse and Bridget Jelks. She married Anthony Cockins[963] 3 Oct 1654, in Deddington, Oxfordshire, England. He was the son of Stephen Cockin and Susan Haynes.

480. Christopher Vennimore was born Feb 1596, in Wendlebury, Oxfordshire, England, christened 9 Mar 1596, in Wendlebury, Oxfordshire, England. He was the son of Roger Venimore and Mrs Marian Venimore. He married Margery Watts[964] 29 Oct 1636, in Kirtlington, Oxfordshire, England. She was the daughter of Anthonie Watt and Alice Ginkins.
Notes for Christopher Vennimore:

aka VENEMORE on marriage records

Children of Christopher Vennimore and Margery Watts:

> i. **Elizabeth Vennimore**,[627,628] born Mar 1656, in Kirtlington, Oxfordshire, England, died May 1729, in Upper Heyford, Oxfordshire, England.

481. Margery Watts was born Aug 1614, in Kirtlington, Oxfordshire, England, christened 14 Aug 1614, in Kirtlington, Oxfordshire, England, died Apr 1682, in Kirtlington, Oxfordshire, England, buried 22 Apr 1682, in Kirtlington, Oxfordshire, England. She was the daughter of Anthonie Watt and Alice Ginkins. She married Christopher Vennimore[964,965] 29 Oct 1636, in Kirtlington, Oxfordshire, England. He was the son of Roger Venimore and Mrs Marian Venimore.

482. John Drinkwater was born about 1672, in Oxfordshire, England, died before 1730, in Oxfordshire, England. He married Mrs Hannah Drinkwater about 1693, in Oxfordshire, England.

Children of John Drinkwater and Mrs Hannah Drinkwater:

     i.   **John Drinkwater**,[630] born 1694, in Oxfordshire, England, died Mar 1768, in Bampton, Oxfordshire, England.

483. Mrs Hannah Drinkwater was born about 1673, in Oxfordshire, England, died Feb 1730, in Bampton, Oxfordshire, England, buried 19 Feb 1730, in Bampton, Oxfordshire, England. She married John Drinkwater about 1693, in Oxfordshire, England.

484. Richard Lapper was born about 1680, in Westwell, Oxfordshire, England. He married Elizabeth Panting 25 Jan 1702, in Westwell, Oxfordshire, England.

Children of Richard Lapper and Elizabeth Panting:

     i.   **Ann Lapper**,[630] born about 1707, in Oxfordshire, England, died Nov 1766, in Bampton, Oxfordshire, England.

485. Elizabeth Panting was born about 1682, in Westwell, Oxfordshire, England. She married Richard Lapper 25 Jan 1702, in Westwell, Oxfordshire, England.

486. John Windows was born about 1660, in Oxfordshire, England. He was the son of Windows and Windows. He married Windows about 1681, in Oxfordshire, England.

Children of John Windows and Windows:

     i.   **John Windows**, born Mar 1682, in Bampton, Oxfordshire, England, christened 12 Mar 1682, in Bampton, Oxfordshire, England.
     ii. **William Windows**,[634] born Sep 1689, in Bampton, Oxfordshire, England, died Apr 1758, in Bampton, Oxfordshire, England.

487. ____Windows was born about 1661, in Oxfordshire, England. She married John Windows[966] about 1681, in Oxfordshire, England. He was the son of Windows and Windows.

488. Bartholemew Grimsher was born Aug 1667, in Bampton, Oxfordshire, England, christened 1 Sep 1667, in Bampton, Oxfordshire, England, died Dec 1731, in Bampton, Oxfordshire, England, buried 20 Dec 1731, in Bampton, Oxfordshire, England. He was the son of Richard Grimsher and Mrs Ann Grimsher. He married Mary Linzy 4 Apr 1687, in Clanfield, Oxfordshire, England.
Notes for Bartholemew Grimsher:

aka GRIMSHOR

Children of Bartholemew Grimsher and Mary Linzy:

  i.   **Mary Grimsher**, born Oct 1692, in Bampton, Oxfordshire, England, died Nov 1738, in Bampton, Oxfordshire, England.
  ii. **Richard Grimsher**, born 1694, in Bampton, Oxfordshire, England, died Mar 1763, in Bampton, Oxfordshire, England, buried 31 Mar 1763, in Bampton, Oxfordshire, England.

489. Mary Linzy was born about 1669, in Clanfield, Oxfordshire, England, died May 1749, in Bampton, Oxfordshire, England, buried 11 May 1749, in Bampton, Oxfordshire, England. She married Bartholemew Grimsher[967] 4 Apr 1687, in Clanfield, Oxfordshire, England. He was the son of Richard Grimsher and Mrs Ann Grimsher.

490. John Hawkins was born 1679, in Shellingford, Berkshire, England, christened 6 Mar 1679, in Shellingford, Berkshire, England, died 1747, in Little Coxwell, Berkshire, England. He was the son of Robert Hawkins and Eleanor Tubbs. He married Ann Webb 12 Jan 1698, in Little Coxwell, Berkshire, England. She was the daughter of Francis Webb and Ann Boyce.

Children of John Hawkins and Ann Webb:

  i.   **John Hawkins**, born 1699, in Shrivenham, Berkshire, England, christened 7 Nov 1699, in Little Coxwell, Berkshire, England.
  ii. **Robert Hawkins**, born 1701, in Little Coxwell, Berkshire, England, christened 9 Jan 1701, in Little Coxwell, Berkshire, England.
  iii. **Edward Hawkins**,[635,636] born Apr 1704, in Little Coxwell, Berkshire, England.
  iv. **Thomas Hawkins**, born Sep 1706, in Little Coxwell, Berkshire, England, christened 15 Sep 1706, in Watlington, Oxfordshire, England.
       Watlington parish record - baptism 1706
  v.   **Mary Hawkins**, born 1714, in Little Coxwell, Berkshire, England, christened 5 Feb 1714, in Faringdon, Berkshire, England.
  vi. **Francis Hawkins**, born 1717, in Little Coxwell, Berkshire, England, christened 31 Jul 1717, in Little Coxwell, Berkshire, England.

491. Ann Webb was born Jun 1678, in Little Coxwell, Berkshire, England, christened 16 Jun 1678, in Little Coxwell, Berkshire, England. She was the daughter of Francis Webb and Ann Boyce. She married John Hawkins 12 Jan 1698, in Little Coxwell, Berkshire, England. He was the son of Robert Hawkins and Eleanor Tubbs.

492. ____Cockhead was born about 1680, in Berkshire, England. He married Cockhead about 1702, in Oxfordshire, England.

Children of Cockhead and Cockhead:

    i.   **Mary Cockhead**,[635,636] born about 1706, in Berkshire, England.

493. ____Cockhead was born about 1683, in Berkshire, England. She married Cockhead about 1702, in Oxfordshire, England.

494. William Alder was born Aug 1683, in Denchworth, Berkshire, England, christened 26 Aug 1683, in Denchworth, Berkshire, England. He was the son of William Alder and Katherine Wythers. He married Mary Morley[968] 14 Jul 1703, in Thatcham, Berkshire, England.

Children of William Alder and Mary Morley:

    i.   **John Alder**,[639] born Apr 1706, in Wantage, Berkshire, England, died Sep 1740, in Great Coxwell, Berkshire, England.

495. Mary Morley was born about 1685, in Berkshire, England. She married William Alder[968,969] 14 Jul 1703, in Thatcham, Berkshire, England. He was the son of William Alder and Katherine Wythers.

496. David Phelps was born about 1670, in England. He married Phelps about 1694, in England.

Children of David Phelps and Phelps:

    i.   **Ann Phelps**,[637] born Sep 1695, in Swindon, Wiltshire, England, died Jan 1790, in Great Coxwell, Berkshire, England.

497. ____Phelps was born about 1675, in England. She married David Phelps about 1694, in England.

498. William Heydon was born about 1655, in Oxfordshire, England. He married Mrs Anne Heydon about 1680, in Oxfordshire, England.

Children of William Heydon and Mrs Anne Heydon:

    i.   **Richard Heydon**,[646,647,648] born 1685, in Witney, Oxfordshire, England.
    ii.   **William Heydon**, born Jan 1695, in Witney, Oxfordshire, England, christened 26 Jan 1695, in Witney, Oxfordshire, England.
    iii. **Robert Heydon**, born Jun 1699, in Witney, Oxfordshire, England, christened 6 Jul 1699, in Witney, Oxfordshire, England, died Jul 1720, in Witney, Oxfordshire, England, buried 27 Jul 1720, in Witney, Oxfordshire, England.

499. Mrs Anne Heydon was born about 1660, in Oxfordshire, England. She married William Heydon[970] about 1680, in Oxfordshire, England.

500. Edward Young was born about 1660, in Milton, Oxfordshire, England. He married Mrs Edward Young about 1685, in Oxfordshire, England.

Children of Edward Young and Mrs Edward Young:

      i.   **Eleanor Young**,[640] born 1690, in Witney, Oxfordshire, England.

501. Mrs Edward Young was born about 1666, in Oxfordshire, England. She married Edward Young[970] about 1685, in Oxfordshire, England.

502. James Smith was born about 1670, in Buckinghamshire, England. He married Smith about 1695, in Buckinghamshire, England.

Children of James Smith and Smith:

      i.   **Richard Smith**,[649,655,656] born Dec 1695, in Eton, Buckinghamshire, England.

503. ____Smith was born about 1672, in Buckinghamshire, England. She married James Smith[971] about 1695, in Buckinghamshire, England.

504. ____Newton was born about 1670, in England. He married Newton about 1695, in Buckinghamshire, England.

Children of Newton and Newton:

      i.   **Mary Newton**,[649,650] born about 1698, in England.

505. ____Newton was born about 1673, in England. She married Newton about 1695, in Buckinghamshire, England.

506. ____Hawkins was born about 1635, in Oxfordshire, England. He married Hawkins about 1657, in Oxfordshire, England.

Children of Hawkins and Hawkins:

      i.   **Hugh Hawkyns**,[659] born about 1660, in Northmoor, Oxfordshire, England, died before 1760, in England.

507. ____Hawkins was born about 1637, in Oxfordshire, England. She married Hawkins about 1657, in Oxfordshire, England.

508. Henrie Fairbeard was born about 1630, in Northmoor, Oxfordshire, England, died Nov 1681, in Northmoor, Oxfordshire, England, buried 27 Nov 1681, in Northmoor, Oxfordshire, England. He was the son of John Fairbeard and Mrs Mabell Fairbeard. He married Mrs Frances Fairbeard about 1654, in Northmoor, Oxfordshire, England.

Children of Henrie Fairbeard and Mrs Frances Fairbeard:

    i.   **Frances Fairbeard**,[972,973] born 11 Nov 1656, in Northmoor, Oxfordshire, England, christened 11 Dec 1656, in Northmoor, Oxfordshire, England, died Apr 1657, in Northmoor, Oxfordshire, England, buried 9 Apr 1657, in Northmoor, Oxfordshire, England.

    ii.   **Martha Fairbeard**,[657,658] born 15 Apr 1658, in Northmoor, Oxfordshire, England, died before 1750, in England.

    iii.   **Un-Named Fairbeard**,[974] born 3 Feb 1659, in Northmoor, Oxfordshire, England, christened 3 Feb 1659, in Northmoor, Oxfordshire, England, died 3 Feb 1659, in Northmoor, Oxfordshire, England, buried 3 Feb 1659, in Northmoor, Oxfordshire, England.

    iv.   **John Fairbeard**,[975,976] born 12 Apr 1661, in Northmoor, Oxfordshire, England, christened 10 May 1661, in Northmoor, Oxfordshire, England, died Oct 1730, in Northmoor, Oxfordshire, England, buried 28 Oct 1730, in Northmoor, Oxfordshire, England.

    v.   **Maria Fairbeard**,[977] born 9 Aug 1663, in Northmoor, Oxfordshire, England, christened 25 Aug 1663, in Northmoor, Oxfordshire, England.

    vi.   **Frances Fairbeard**,[978] born 26 Feb 1666, in Northmoor, Oxfordshire, England, christened 25 Mar 1666, in Northmoor, Oxfordshire, England.

    vii.   **Henrie Fairbeard**,[979] born 15 Feb 1668, in Northmoor, Oxfordshire, England, christened 18 Mar 1668, in Northmoor, Oxfordshire, England.

    viii.   **Elizabeth Fairbeard**,[980,981] born 16 Feb 1671, in Northmoor, Oxfordshire, England, christened 26 Feb 1671, in Northmoor, Oxfordshire, England. She married Charles Greenway[981] 20 Feb 1700, in Northmoor, Oxfordshire, England. Charles Greenway was born about 1670, in Eynsham, Oxfordshire, England.

509. Mrs Frances Fairbeard was born about 1632, in Oxford, Oxfordshire, England, died Dec 1710, in Northmoor, Oxfordshire, England, buried 24 Dec 1710, in Northmoor, Oxfordshire, England. She married Henrie Fairbeard about 1654, in Northmoor, Oxfordshire, England. He was the son of John Fairbeard and Mrs Mabell Fairbeard.

510. ____Gee was born about 1665, in Oxfordshire, England. He married Gee about 1687, in Oxfordshire, England.

Children of Gee and Gee:

    i.   **Ambrose Gee**,[660] born 1692, in Chipping Norton, Oxfordshire, England, died 1773, in Chipping Norton, Oxfordshire, England.

511. ____Gee was born about 1667, in Oxfordshire, England. She married Gee about 1687, in Oxfordshire, England.

512. John Eckley was born about 1665, in Brize Norton, Oxfordshire, England. He married Ann Bell[982] 15 Apr 1688, in Burford, Oxfordshire, England.

Children of John Eckley and Ann Bell:

      i.   **Mary Ekley**,[660] born 1696, in Chipping Norton, Oxfordshire, England.

513. Ann Bell was born about 1670, in Burford, Oxfordshire, England. She married John Eckley[982] 15 Apr 1688, in Burford, Oxfordshire, England.

514. John Morgan was born about 1630, in Berkshire, England, died about 1700, in Berkshire, England. He married Mrs Mary Morgan about 1655, in England.

Children of John Morgan and Mrs Mary Morgan:

      i.   **William Morgan**,[661,669,670] born Aug 1657, in Waltham Saint Lawrence, Berkshire, England, died about 1695, in Berkshire, England.

515. Mrs Mary Morgan was born about 1632, in Berkshire, England, died about 1695, in Berkshire, England. She married John Morgan about 1655, in England.

516. ____Adkin Or Adkyn was born about 1630, in Berkshire, England, died about 1690, in Berkshire, England. He married Adkin Or Adkyn about 1658, in Berkshire, England.

Children of Adkin Or Adkyn and Adkin Or Adkyn:

      i.   **Allenora Adkin Or Adkyn**,[661] born about 1659, in Berkshire, England, died about 1700, in Berkshire, England.

517. ____Adkin Or Adkyn was born about 1632, in Berkshire, England, died about 1690, in Berkshire, England, buried 3 Apr 1694, in Marcham, Berkshire, England. She married Adkin Or Adkyn about 1658, in Berkshire, England.

518. ____Veasy was born about 1630, in Oxfordshire, England. He married Veasy about 1652, in Oxfordshire, England.

Children of Veasy and Veasy:

      i.   **Richard Veasy**,[671] born about 1655, in Oxfordshire, England.

519. ____Veasy was born about 1632, in Oxfordshire, England. She married Veasy about 1652, in Oxfordshire, England.

520. ____Hunt was born about 1630, in Oxfordshire, England. He married Hunt about 1653, in Oxfordshire, England.

Children of Hunt and Hunt:

    i.   **Ann Hunt**,[671] born about 1658, in Oxfordshire, England.

521. ____Hunt was born about 1632, in Oxfordshire, England. She married Hunt about 1653, in Oxfordshire, England.

522. Richard Stone was born 3 Apr 1617, in Longworth, Berkshire, England, christened 3 Apr 1617, in Longworth, Berkshire, England, died before 1700, in England. He was the son of Richard Stone and Ann Banner. He married Sibil Green[983] 28 Apr 1646, in Standlake, Oxfordshire, England. She was the daughter of William Green and Marie Doe.

Children of Richard Stone and Sibil Green:

    i.   **Richard Stone**,[672,674] born 24 Mar 1646, in Longworth, Berkshire, England, died before 1740, in England.
    ii.   **John Stone**, born 17 Dec 1650, in Longworth, Berkshire, England, christened 17 Dec 1650, in Longworth, Berkshire, England, died Jul 1657, in Standlake, Oxfordshire, England, buried 16 Jul 1657, in Standlake, Oxfordshire, England.

523. Sibil Green was born about 1625, in Longworth, Berkshire, England, died before 1725, in England. She was the daughter of William Green and Marie Doe. She married Richard Stone[983] 28 Apr 1646, in Standlake, Oxfordshire, England. He was the son of Richard Stone and Ann Banner.

524. ____Browne was born about 1620, in Oxfordshire, England. He married Browne about 1645, in Oxfordshire, England.

Children of Browne and Browne:

    i.   **Ann Browne**,[672,673] born about 1650, in Standlake, Oxfordshire, England, died Mar 1708, in Standlake, Oxfordshire, England.

525. ____Browne was born about 1622, in Oxfordshire, England. She married Browne about 1645, in Oxfordshire, England.

526. Thomas Onion Or Anyon was born Aug 1633, in Standlake, Oxfordshire, England, christened 1 Sep 1633, in Standlake, Oxfordshire, England, died Sep 1686, in Hinton Waldrist, Berkshire, England,

buried 21 Sep 1686, in Hinton Waldrist, Berkshire, England. He was the son of Thomas Onion and Mrs Elizabeth Onion. He married Mrs Elizabeth Onion about 1651, in Berkshire, England.
Notes for Thomas Onion Or Anyon:

Standlake parish records

Children of Thomas Onion Or Anyon and Mrs Elizabeth Onion:

> i. **Thomas Onion,**[423,675] born about 1652, in Berkshire, England, died Sep 1689, in Hinton Waldrist, Berkshire, England.

527. Mrs Elizabeth Onion was born about 1633, in Berkshire, England. She married Thomas Onion Or Anyon about 1651, in Berkshire, England. He was the son of Thomas Onion and Mrs Elizabeth Onion.

528. Thomas Umberstone was born 1616, in Berkshire, England, died 1669, in Berkshire, England. He married Diana Newbery Diana, in Newbery.

Children of Thomas Umberstone and Diana Newbery:

> i. **Anne Umberstone,**[423,675] born 1649, in Hurst, Berkshire, England, died 1700, in Berkshire, England.

529. Diana Newbery was born 1614, in Waltham Saint Lawrence, Berkshire, England, christened 10 Jan 1614, in Waltham Saint Lawrence, Berkshire, England, died 1688, in Hurst, Berkshire, England, buried 9 Jan 1688, in Hurst, Berkshire, England. She married Thomas Umberstone Diana, in Newbery.

530. James Hartlett was born about 1650, in Oxfordshire, England. He married Hartlett about 1675, in England.

Children of James Hartlett and Hartlett:

> i. **Richard Hartlett,**[684] born about 1680, in Oxfordshire, England.

531. ____Hartlett was born about 1653, in England. She married James Hartlett[984] about 1675, in England.

532. ____Stone was born about 1650, in England. He married Stone about 1675, in England.

Children of Stone and Stone:

> i. **Mary Stone,**[683] born about 1684, in Oxfordshire, England.

533. ____Stone was born about 1655, in England. She married Stone about 1675, in England.

534. Henry King was born Apr 1628, in Steeple Aston, Oxfordshire, England, christened 21 Apr 1628, in Steeple Aston, Oxfordshire, England. He married Margaret Claridge[985] 2 Mar 1654, in Banbury, Oxfordshire, England.

Children of Henry King and Margaret Claridge:

     i.   **Richard King,**[686,696] born 4 Mar 1660, in South Newington, Oxfordshire, England.

535. Margaret Claridge was born about 1637, in Oxfordshire, England. She married Henry King[985,986,987] 2 Mar 1654, in Banbury, Oxfordshire, England.

536. ____Barris was born about 1642, in Oxfordshire, England. He married Barris about 1662, in Oxfordshire, England.

Children of Barris and Barris:

     i.   **Elizabeth Barris,**[685,686] born about 1670, in Byfield, Northamptonshire, England.

537. ____Barris was born about 1645, in Oxfordshire, England. She married Barris about 1662, in Oxfordshire, England.

538. Stephen Gilkes Or Jelkes was born Jan 1635, in Bloxham, Oxfordshire, England, christened 3 Feb 1635, in Banbury, Oxfordshire, England. He was the son of William Gilkes and Mary Cooke Or Crooke. He married Margaret Basely Or Bazely[988] 17 Jun 1654, in Oxford, Oxfordshire, England.
Notes for Stephen Gilkes Or Jelkes:

Parish records for Banbury, Oxfordshire, England Vicar wrote - Steven Gylkes son of William Christening 3 Feb 1635 Name appears as Steven or Stephen - Jelkes or Gilkes as recorded on various registers Steven and Margaret were married at St Michael Oxford by the MAYOR, a civil marriage performed during the period of Oliver Cromwell and known as 'Commonwealth Marriages.' Record reads: 17 June 1654 - Gilkes, Stephen lab. of Bloxham, Oxon and Basely, Margaret spinster of Hepton parish, Deddington, Oxon by Thomas Williams, Mai(y)or

Children of Stephen Gilkes Or Jelkes and Margaret Basely Or Bazely:

     i.   **William Gilkes Or Jelkes**, born Nov 1654, in Deddington, Oxfordshire, England, christened 16 Nov 1654, in Deddington, Oxfordshire, England.
              Parish records for Deddington, Oxfordshire, England
     ii.   **Anthony Gilkes Or Jelkes**, born 9 Jun 1655, in Deddington, Oxfordshire, England, christened 9 Jun 1655, in Deddington, Oxfordshire, England.
              Parish records for Deddington, Oxfordshire, England show he was baptised on day of birth
     iii. **John Gilkes,**[699,700,701] born 16 Mar 1666, in Banbury, Oxfordshire, England, died Jul

1764, in Banbury, Oxfordshire, England.

539. Margaret Basely Or Bazely was born about 1636, in Hempton, Oxfordshire, England. She married Stephen Gilkes Or Jelkes[988] 17 Jun 1654, in Oxford, Oxfordshire, England. He was the son of William Gilkes and Mary Cooke Or Crooke.
Notes for Margaret Basely Or Bazely:

Born before baptism were recorded inj church. Parish records for Banbury, Oxfordshire, England. show the Int of Marriage to Steven (Jelkes)Gilkes. Given in church 18 May 1654 at Banbury. Later married at St Michaels in Oxford by the Mayor in a commonwealth marriage.

540. Robert Swifte was born 21 Aug 1632, in Adderbury, Oxfordshire, England, christened 2 Sep 1632, in Adderbury, Oxfordshire, England. He was the son of Martyn Swifte and Ann Ripingale. He married Joyce Poulton[989,990] 13 Jan 1670, in Adderbury, Oxfordshire, England. She was the daughter of Timothy Poulton and Mrs Joyce Poulton.

Children of Robert Swifte and Joyce Poulton:

    i.   **Mary Swift**,[697,698] born 12 Nov 1673, in Adderbury, Oxfordshire, England.

541. Joyce Poulton was born Oct 1646, in Adderbury, Oxfordshire, England, christened 27 Oct 1646, in Adderbury, Oxfordshire, England. She was the daughter of Timothy Poulton and Mrs Joyce Poulton. She married Robert Swifte[990,991,992] 13 Jan 1670, in Adderbury, Oxfordshire, England. He was the son of Martyn Swifte and Ann Ripingale.

542. ____Price was born about 1650, in Oxfordshire, England. He married Price about 1670, in Oxfordshire, England.

Children of Price and Price:

    i.   **Thomas Price**,[702,703] born about 1675, in Chipping Norton, Oxfordshire, England.

543. ____Price was born about 1652, in Oxfordshire, England. She married Price about 1670, in Oxfordshire, England.

544. ____Berry was born about 1630, in Oxfordshire, England. He married Berry about 1650, in Oxfordshire, England.

Children of Berry and Berry:

    i.   **Bridget Berry**,[702,703] born about 1677, in Chipping Norton, Oxfordshire, England.

545. ____Berry was born about 1632, in Oxfordshire, England. She married Berry about 1650, in

Oxfordshire, England.

546. John Foster was born about 1680, in Oxfordshire, England, died Apr 1731, in South Leigh, Oxfordshire, England, buried 7 Apr 1731, in South Leigh, Oxfordshire, England. He married Mrs Sarah Foster about 1699, in Oxfordshire, England.

Children of John Foster and Mrs Sarah Foster:

    i.   **John Foster**,[705] born about 1700, in Oxfordshire, England, died Apr 1744, in South Leigh, Oxfordshire, England.

547. Mrs Sarah Foster was born about 1682, in Oxfordshire, England, died Feb 1732, in South Leigh, Oxfordshire, England, buried 16 Feb 1732, in South Leigh, Oxfordshire, England. She married John Foster about 1699, in Oxfordshire, England.

548. Yeoman John Spier was born about 1675, in South Leigh, Oxfordshire, England, died Jul 1739, in South Leigh, Oxfordshire, England, buried 16 Jul 1739, in South Leigh, Oxfordshire, England. He was the son of John Spier and Spier. He married Hannah Clinch[993] 8 Feb 1700, in South Leigh, Oxfordshire, England.

Children of Yeoman John Spier and Hannah Clinch:

    i.   **Mary Spier**,[705] born about 1702, in South Leigh, Oxfordshire, England.
    ii.   **Ann Spier**,[994] born 19 Sep 1703, in South Leigh, Oxfordshire, England.
    iii.   **John Spier**,[995] born 14 May 1708, in South Leigh, Oxfordshire, England.
    iv.   **Thomas Spier**,[996] born 28 Mar 1710, in South Leigh, Oxfordshire, England.

549. Hannah Clinch was born about 1677, in Bampton, Oxfordshire, England. She married Yeoman John Spier[993] 8 Feb 1700, in South Leigh, Oxfordshire, England. He was the son of John Spier and Spier.

550. William Harris was born about 1664, in Oxfordshire, England, died before 1760, in England. He married Elizabeth Andrews[997] 11 Apr 1686, in Chipping Norton, Oxfordshire, England. She was the daughter of William Andrews and Mrs Katherine Andrews.

Children of William Harris and Elizabeth Andrews:

    i.   **Dorkas Harris**,[998] born 15 May 1687, in Standlake, Oxfordshire, England.
    ii.   **William Harris**,[999] born 7 Jun 1692, in Standlake, Oxfordshire, England.
    iii.   **Samuel Harris**,[1000] born 5 Feb 1694, in Standlake, Oxfordshire, England.
    iv.   **John Harris**,[712] born 28 Jul 1697, in Standlake, Oxfordshire, England, died before 1790, in England.
    v.   **Sara Harris**,[1001] born 4 Mar 1698, in Standlake, Oxfordshire, England.
    vi.   **Robert Harris**,[1002] born 25 Jun 1700, in Standlake, Oxfordshire, England.

vii.   **Thomas Harris**,[1003] born 9 Nov 1701, in Standlake, Oxfordshire, England.

551. Elizabeth Andrews was born Aug 1665, in Longworth, Berkshire, England, christened 13 Aug 1665, in Longworth, Berkshire, England, died before 1760, in England. She was the daughter of William Andrews and Mrs Katherine Andrews. She married William Harris[997] 11 Apr 1686, in Chipping Norton, Oxfordshire, England.

552. ____Brooks was born about 1675, in Oxfordshire, England. He married Brooks about 1698, in Oxfordshire, England.

Children of Brooks and Brooks:

       i.   **Catherine Brooks**, born about 1700, in Oxfordshire, England, died before 1800, in England.

553. ____Brooks was born about 1677, in Oxfordshire, England. She married Brooks about 1698, in Oxfordshire, England.

554. Thomas Duffen was born about 1650, in Berkshire, England. He married Mrs Mary Duffin about 1675, in Berkshire, England.

Children of Thomas Duffen and Mrs Mary Duffin:

       i.   **John Duffen**,[713] born about 1680, in Berkshire, England.
      ii.   **Ann Duffen**, born about 1684, in Abingdon, Berkshire, England.
            Abingdon, St Helen's church baptism records

555. Mrs Mary Duffin was born about 1652, in Berkshire, England, died Apr 1685, in Abingdon, Berkshire, England, buried 14 Apr 1685, in Abingdon, Berkshire, England. She married Thomas Duffen about 1675, in Berkshire, England.
Notes for Mrs Mary Duffin:

St Helen's records - burial

556. ____Ludler was born about 1650, in Berkshire, England. He married Ludler about 1675, in Berkshire, England.

Children of Ludler and Ludler:

       i.   **Alice Ludler**,[713] born about 1682, in Berkshire, England.

557. ____Ludler was born about 1653, in Berkshire, England. She married Ludler about 1675, in Berkshire, England.

558. Thomas Clark was born about 1658, in North Hinksey, Berkshire, England. He was the son of Thomas Clark and Sarah Clark. He married Mary Knapp[1004,1005] 5 Jun 1679, in North Hinksey, Berkshire, England. She was the daughter of John Knapp and Alice Knapp.

Children of Thomas Clark and Mary Knapp:

      i.   **Robert Clark**,[715,716,717] born 1681, in Longworth, Berkshire, England.

559. Mary Knapp was born Sep 1660, in Childrey, Berkshire, England, christened 1 Oct 1660, in Childrey, Berkshire, England. She was the daughter of John Knapp and Alice Knapp. She married Thomas Clark[1004] 5 Jun 1679, in North Hinksey, Berkshire, England. He was the son of Thomas Clark and Sarah Clark.

560. Thomas Smith was born about 1670, in Abingdon, Berkshire, England. He married Martha Smith about 1695, in Berkshire, England.

Children of Thomas Smith and Martha Smith:

      i.   **Mary Smith**,[714,715,716] born about 1697, in Berkshire, England.

561. Martha Smith was born about 1672, in Berkshire, England. She married Thomas Smith about 1695, in Berkshire, England.

562. William King was born about 1665, in Oxfordshire, England. He married Rebecka Burcut[1006] 4 May 1689, in Witney, Oxfordshire, England.

Children of William King and Rebecka Burcut:

      i.   **Wiliam King**,[718] born about 1690, in Witney, Oxfordshire, England.

563. Rebecka Burcut was born about 1667, in Oxfordshire, England. She married William King[1006] 4 May 1689, in Witney, Oxfordshire, England.

564. John Ewin was born about 1660, in Oxfordshire, England. He married Ewin about 1683, in Oxfordshire, England.

Children of John Ewin and Ewin:

      i.   **Elizabeth Ewin**,[718] born about 1690, in Witney, Oxfordshire, England.
     ii.   **Sarah Ewin**,[1007] born Oct 1687, in Witney, Oxfordshire, England, christened 1 Nov 1689, in Witney, Oxfordshire, England.

565. ____Ewin was born about 1663, in Oxfordshire, England. She married John Ewin about 1683, in

Oxfordshire, England.

566. ____Bartlet was born about 1660, in Oxfordshire, England. He married Bartlet about 1685, in Oxfordshire, England.

Children of Bartlet and Bartlet:

      i.   **Carew Bartlet**,[724] born about 1700, in Witney, Oxfordshire, England.

567. ____Bartlet was born about 1662, in Oxfordshire, England. She married Bartlet about 1685, in Oxfordshire, England.

568. ____Casey was born about 1660, in Oxfordshire, England. He married Casey about 1695, in Oxfordshire, England.

Children of Casey and Casey:

      i.   **Elizabeth Casey**,[723] born about 1701, in Cogges, Oxfordshire, England.

569. ____Casey was born about 1662, in Oxfordshire, England. She married Casey about 1695, in Oxfordshire, England.

570. ____Probatts was born about 1650, in Berkshire, England. He married Probatts about 1678, in Berkshire, England.

Children of Probatts and Probatts:

      i.   **John Probatts**,[725,726] born about 1680, in Berkshire, England.
     ii.   **Elizabeth Probatts**,[1008] born about 1694, in Berkshire, England. She married John Duckett[1008] 23 Apr 1714, in Ashbury, Berkshire, England. John Duckett was born about 1692, in Berkshire, England.
    iii.   **Anne Probatts**,[1008] born about 1696, in Berkshire, England. She married Robert Hawkins[1008] 3 Oct 1717, in Ashbury, Berkshire, England. Robert Hawkins was born about 1694, in Berkshire, England.

571. ____Probatts was born about 1662, in Berkshire, England. She married Probatts about 1678, in Berkshire, England.

572. ____Wilson was born about 1650, in Berkshire, England. He married Wilson about 1678, in Berkshire, England.

Children of Wilson and Wilson:

    i.   **Elizabeth Wilson**,[725,726] born about 1682, in Berkshire, England.

573. ____Wilson was born about 1652, in Berkshire, England. She married Wilson about 1678, in Berkshire, England.

574. Edward Bayly was born about 1660, in Berkshire, England. He was the son of Bayly and Bayly. He married Hannah Meredith[1009] 15 Oct 1685, in Nuffield, Oxfordshire, England.

Children of Edward Bayly and Hannah Meredith:

    i.   **William Bayly**,[730] born about 1690, in Berkshire, England.

575. Hannah Meredith was born about 1662, in Benson, Oxfordshire, England. She married Edward Bayly[1009] 15 Oct 1685, in Nuffield, Oxfordshire, England. He was the son of Bayly and Bayly.

576. ____Lancaster was born about 1660, in Berkshire, England. He married Lancaster about 1685, in Berkshire, England.

Children of Lancaster and Lancaster:

    i.   **Susannah Lancaster**,[730] born about 1692, in Berkshire, England.

577. ____Lancaster was born about 1663, in Berkshire, England. She married Lancaster about 1685, in Berkshire, England.

578. John Newell was born about 1650, in Lewknor, Oxfordshire, England. He married Ellizabeth Fettiplace 25 Sep 1679, in Oxfordshire, England.

Children of John Newell and Ellizabeth Fettiplace:

    i.   **Henry Newell**,[732] born about 1680, in Oxfordshire, England, died before 1780, in England.
    ii.   **Elizabeth Newell**,[1010] born Feb 1691, in Lewknor, Oxfordshire, England, christened 9 Mar 1691, in Lewknor, Oxfordshire, England.
    iii.   **Mary Newell**,[1011] born Mar 1694, in Lewknor, Oxfordshire, England, christened 13 Mar 1694, in Lewknor, Oxfordshire, England.
    iv.   **Hester Newell**,[1012] born Feb 1698, in Lewknor, Oxfordshire, England, christened 15 Feb 1698, in Lewknor, Oxfordshire, England.

579. Ellizabeth Fettiplace was born about 1652, in Lewknor, Oxfordshire, England. She married John Newell 25 Sep 1679, in Oxfordshire, England.

580. ____Hunt was born about 1651, in Oxfordshire, England. He married Hunt about 1675, in Oxfordshire, England.

Children of Hunt and Hunt:

      i.   **Anne Hunt**,[731] born about 1680, in Oxfordshire, England, died before 1780, in England.

581. ____Hunt was born about 1653, in Oxfordshire, England. She married Hunt about 1675, in Oxfordshire, England.

582. John Oxlade was born Feb 1652, in Great Marlow, Buckinghamshire, England, christened 21 Feb 1652, in Great Marlow, Buckinghamshire, England, died 1703, in Great Marlow, Buckinghamshire, England. He was the son of John Oxlade and Mrs Mary Oxlade. He married Ann Hollier[1013] 13 Dec 1680, in Hughenden, Buckinghamshire, England. She was the daughter of John Hollier and Hollier. Notes for John Oxlade:

residence: Buckingham, England parents: John Oxlade, Ann record title: England Births and Christenings, 1538-1975 name: Ann Oxlade gender: Female baptism/christening date: 25 Apr 1681 baptism/christening place: WEST WYCOMBE,BUCKINGHAM,ENGLAND father's name: John Oxlade mother's name: Ann indexing project (batch) number: C07380-1 system origin: England-ODM source film number: 919260 Event: Legal Document LAW sold tree to ROBINSON for (4/10) pounds but didn't pay John OXLAD Event: Legal Document MAR 1683 With John LAW of G.M.(Mourer ?) bought From Mrs BAKER a Walnut Tree for (4) pounds Event: Legal Document 1685 SEE Notes put in Stocks by John LAW because John OXLADE had sued him for trespass Occupation: Barber Chirurgeon

Children of John Oxlade and Ann Hollier:

      i.   **Ann Oxlade**,[1014] born 1681, in Great Marlow, Buckinghamshire, England, christened 25 Apr 1681, in West Wycombe, Buckinghamshire, England, died 1695, in Great Marlow, Buckinghamshire, England.
residence: Buckingham, England parents: John Oxlade, Ann record title: England Births and Christenings, 1538-1975 name: Ann Oxlade gender: Female baptism/christening date: 25 Apr 1681 baptism/christening place: WEST WYCOMBE,BUCKINGHAM,ENGLAND father's name: John Oxlade mother's name: Ann indexing project (batch) number: C07380-1 system origin: England-ODM source film number: 919260

     ii.   **Mary Oxlade**, born 1683, in Great Marlow, Buckinghamshire, England, christened 22 Mar 1683, in Great Marlow, Buckinghamshire, England.

    iii.   **John Oxlade**, born 1686, in Great Marlow, Buckinghamshire, England, christened 27 Jun 1686, in Great Marlow, Buckinghamshire, England, died 7 Sep 1774, in Great Marlow, Buckinghamshire, England. He married Elizabeth Neal about 1710, in Great Marlow, Buckinghamshire, England. Elizabeth Neal was born about 1688, in Great Marlow, Buckinghamshire, England, died 16 Aug 1732, in Fingest, Buckinghamshire, England.

- iv. **Robert Oxlade**, born Jan 1688, in Great Marlow, Buckinghamshire, England, christened 22 Jan 1688, in Great Marlow, Buckinghamshire, England, died 1761, in England.
- v. **William Oxlade**,[733] born Feb 1690, in Great Marlow, Buckinghamshire, England, died Feb 1744, in Bisham, Berkshire, England.
- vi. **Elizabeth Oxlade**, born 1693, in Great Marlow, Buckinghamshire, England, christened 23 Oct 1693, in Great Marlow, Buckinghamshire, England, died 1728, in England.
- vii. **Sarah Oxlade**, born 1695, in Great Marlow, Buckinghamshire, England, christened 14 Jul 1695, in Great Marlow, Buckinghamshire, England.
- viii. **Ann Oxlade**, born 1697, in Great Marlow, Buckinghamshire, England, christened 5 Dec 1697, in Great Marlow, Buckinghamshire, England, died 1725, in Great Marlow, Buckinghamshire, England.

583. Ann Hollier was born 1656, in Great Marlow, Buckinghamshire, England, died Apr 1701, in Great Marlow, Buckinghamshire, England, buried 17 Apr 1701, in Great Marlow, Buckinghamshire, England. She was the daughter of John Hollier and Hollier. She married John Oxlade[1013] 13 Dec 1680, in Hughenden, Buckinghamshire, England. He was the son of John Oxlade and Mrs Mary Oxlade. Notes for Ann Hollier:

residence: Buckingham, England parents: John Oxlade, Ann record title: England Births and Christenings, 1538-1975 name: Ann Oxlade gender: Female baptism/christening date: 25 Apr 1681 baptism/christening place: WEST WYCOMBE,BUCKINGHAM,ENGLAND father's name: John Oxlade mother's name: Ann indexing project (batch) number: C07380-1 system origin: England-ODM source film number: 919260

584. William Salter was born Jul 1659, in Bisham, Berkshire, England, christened 31 Jul 1659, in Bisham, Berkshire, England, died before 1740, in England. He was the son of William Salter and Mrs Jone Salter. He married Mrs Mary Salter about 1684, in Buckinghamshire, England.

Children of William Salter and Mrs Mary Salter:

- i. **Mary Salter**,[733] born 1685, in Great Marlow, Buckinghamshire, England, died about 1717, in Berkshire, England.

585. Mrs Mary Salter was born about 1664, in Buckinghamshire, England, died before 1750, in England. She married William Salter[1015] about 1684, in Buckinghamshire, England. He was the son of William Salter and Mrs Jone Salter.

586. John Broadway was born Jun 1651, in Cuxham, Oxfordshire, England, christened 28 Jun 1651, in Cuxham, Oxfordshire, England, died 2 Mar 1719, in Cuxham, Oxfordshire, England, buried 2 Mar 1719,

in Cuxham, Oxfordshire, England. He was the son of Thomas Broadway and Mrs Mary Broadway. He married Martha Pritchard 30 Jun 1673, in Brightwell Baldwin, Oxfordshire, England.[734]
Notes for John Broadway:

Taken from parish records

Children of John Broadway and Martha Pritchard:

> i. **John Broadway**, born 1683, in Cuxham, Oxfordshire, England, died Feb 1719, in Cuxham, Oxfordshire, England.

587. Martha Pritchard was born 18 Mar 1659, in Oxfordshire, England, died 1699, in Cuxham, Oxfordshire, England. She married John Broadway 30 Jun 1673, in Brightwell Baldwin, Oxfordshire, England.[734] He was the son of Thomas Broadway and Mrs Mary Broadway.
Notes for Martha Pritchard:

Taken from parish records

588. Robert Bolter was born about 1650, in Oxfordshire, England. He married Bolter about 1672, in England.

Children of Robert Bolter and Bolter:

> i. **Alice Bolter**,[133] born Mar 1684, in Bicester, Oxfordshire, England, died 25 Feb 1735, in Cuxham, Oxfordshire, England.

589. ____Bolter was born about 1652, in England. She married Robert Bolter[735] about 1672, in England.

590. Mickell Hine was born about 1655, in Oxfordshire, England. He married Hine about 1675, in England.

Children of Mickell Hine and Hine:

> i. **Michael Hinde**,[737,738] born Jul 1676, in Benson, Oxfordshire, England, died before 1770, in England.

591. ____Hine was born about 1656, in England. She married Mickell Hine[737] about 1675, in England.

592. William Scoles was born about 1645, in Lewknor, Oxfordshire, England, died 17 Mar 1706, in Lewknor, Oxfordshire, England, buried 17 Mar 1706, in Lewknor, Oxfordshire, England. He was the son of William Scholes and Ursual Munday. He married Jane Belson 1 Jun 1670, in Aston Rowant, Oxfordshire, England. She was the daughter of Richard Belson and Alicia Pottes.

Children of William Scoles and Jane Belson:

    i.   **Elizabeth Scholes**,[736] born about 1673, in Cuxham, Oxfordshire, England, died before 1755, in England.

593. Jane Belson was born Oct 1640, in Aston Rowant, Oxfordshire, England, christened 15 Oct 1640, in Aston Rowant, Oxfordshire, England, died Jan 1710, in Lewknor, Oxfordshire, England, buried 2 Feb 1710, in Lewknor, Oxfordshire, England. She was the daughter of Richard Belson and Alicia Pottes. She married William Scoles 1 Jun 1670, in Aston Rowant, Oxfordshire, England. He was the son of William Scholes and Ursual Munday.

594. ____Jones was born about 1675, in Oxfordshire, England. He married Jones about 1696, in Oxfordshire, England.

Children of Jones and Jones:

    i.   **William Jones**,[739] born about 1698, in Oxfordshire, England.

595. ____Jones was born about 1678, in Oxfordshire, England. She married Jones about 1696, in Oxfordshire, England.

596. ____Cligdale was born about 1680, in Oxfordshire, England. He married Cligdale about 1699, in Oxfordshire, England.

Children of Cligdale and Cligdale:

    i.   **Elizabeth Cligdale**,[739] born about 1700, in Oxfordshire, England.

597. ____Cligdale was born about 1680, in Oxfordshire, England. She married Cligdale about 1699, in Oxfordshire, England.

598. John Green was born about 1678, in Oxfordshire, England. He married Elizabeth Dudley[1016] 21 Jan 1698, in Oxfordshire, England.

Children of John Green and Elizabeth Dudley:

    i.   **Thomas Green**,[741,742] born 11 Aug 1702, in Headington, Oxfordshire, England.

599. Elizabeth Dudley was born about 1680, in Oxford, Oxfordshire, England. She married John Green[1017] 21 Jan 1698, in Oxfordshire, England.

600. Gregory Snow was born 1677, in Headington, Oxfordshire, England, died 1754, in Headington, Oxfordshire, England. He was the son of Thomas Snow and Mrs. Mary Snow. He married Elizabeth

Boyse[1018] 27 Feb 1697, in Oxford, Oxfordshire, England.

Children of Gregory Snow and Elizabeth Boyse:

> i. **Elizabeth Snow**,[740,741] born Nov 1702, in Headington, Oxfordshire, England.

601. Elizabeth Boyse was born 1677, in Headington, Oxfordshire, England, died 1759. She married Gregory Snow[1018] 27 Feb 1697, in Oxford, Oxfordshire, England. He was the son of Thomas Snow and Mrs. Mary Snow.

602. ____Giles was born about 1690, in Oxfordshire, England. He married Mary Webb about 1715, in Oxfordshire, England.

Children of Giles and Mary Webb:

> i. **Richard Giles**,[744] born about 1716, in Islip, Oxfordshire, England.

603. Mary Webb was born about 1692, in Boddington, Northamptonshire, England, christened 8 Apr 1692, in Boddington, Northamptonshire, England. She married Giles about 1715, in Oxfordshire, England.

604. Richard Allen was born Dec 1677, in Standlake, Oxfordshire, England, christened 26 Dec 1677, in Standlake, Oxfordshire, England,[1019] died Sep 1746, in Standlake, Oxfordshire, England, buried 1 Oct 1746, in Standlake, Oxfordshire, England.[1020] He married (1) Susannah Hart 1716, in Oxfordshire, England.

Children of Richard Allen and Susannah Hart:

> i. **Susannah Allen**,[743] born about 1716, in Enstone, Oxfordshire, England.

605. Susannah Hart was born 2 Sep 1698, in Standlake, Oxfordshire, England, christened 28 Sep 1698, in Standlake, Oxfordshire, England,[1022] died Nov 1716, in Standlake, Oxfordshire, England,[1023] buried 5 Nov 1716, in Standlake, Oxfordshire, England.[1024] She married Richard Allen[1025] 1716, in Oxfordshire, England.

606. John Jackson was born about 1672, in Bicester, Oxfordshire, England. He married Jackson about 1699, in Oxfordshire, England.

Children of John Jackson and Jackson:

> i. **Joseph Jackson**,[745,746] born Feb 1705, in Bicester, Oxfordshire, England.

607. ____Jackson was born 1675, in Bicester, Oxfordshire, England, christened 7 Jun 1675, in

Bicester, Oxfordshire, England, died Sep 1727, in Bicester, Oxfordshire, England. She married John Jackson about 1699, in Oxfordshire, England.

608. William Howse was born about 1685, in Oxfordshire, England, died 21 Apr 1736, in Bicester, Oxfordshire, England. He married Howse about 1703, in Oxfordshire, England.

Children of William Howse and Howse:

      i.   **Sarah Howse**,[745] born Aug 1703, in Bicester, Oxfordshire, England, died May 1779, in Bicester, Oxfordshire, England.

609. ____Howse was born about 1688, in Oxfordshire, England, died 17 Sep 1738, in Bicester, Oxfordshire, England. She married William Howse about 1703, in Oxfordshire, England.

610. ____Hinton was born about 1650, in Oxfordshire, England. He married Hinton about 1675, in Oxfordshire, England.

Children of Hinton and Hinton:

      i.   **William Hinton**,[747] born about 1685, in Great Haseley, Oxfordshire, England.

611. ____Hinton was born about 1657, in Oxfordshire, England. She married Hinton about 1675, in Oxfordshire, England.

612. ____Latham was born about 1655, in Oxfordshire, England. He married Latham about 1680, in Oxfordshire, England.

Children of Latham and Latham:

      i.   **Hannah Latham**,[747] born about 1687, in Little Haseley, Oxfordshire, England.

613. ____Latham was born about 1657, in Oxfordshire, England. She married Latham about 1680, in Oxfordshire, England.

614. John Slaughter was born about 1650, in Oxfordshire, England. He married Joane Kinge 1 Dec 1672, in Thame, Oxfordshire, England.
Notes for John Slaughter:

Thame parish records 1 dec 1672

Children of John Slaughter and Joane Kinge:

      i.   **Edward Slaughter**,[748] born about 1685, in Thame, Oxfordshire, England.

615. Joane Kinge was born about 1653, in Tetsworth, Oxfordshire, England. She married John Slaughter 1 Dec 1672, in Thame, Oxfordshire, England.
Notes for Joane Kinge:

Thame parish records 1 dec 1672

616. ____Holyman was born about 1660, in Oxfordshire, England. He married Holyman about 1682, in Oxfordshire, England.

Children of Holyman and Holyman:

      i.   **Mary Holyman**,[748] born about 1688, in Tetsworth, Oxfordshire, England.

617. ____Holyman was born about 1662, in Oxfordshire, England. She married Holyman about 1682, in Oxfordshire, England.

618. John Kirby was born Sep 1670, in Charlton on Otmoor, Oxfordshire, England, christened 9 Oct 1670, in Charlton on Otmoor, Oxfordshire, England. He was the son of John Kirby and Anne Walker. He married Alice Grace Richardson 31 Oct 1690, in Oxford, Oxfordshire, England.

Children of John Kirby and Alice Grace Richardson:

      i.   **Henry Kirby**,[304] born about 1700, in Charlton on Otmoor, Oxfordshire, England, died before 1800, in England.

619. Alice Grace Richardson was born about 1672, in Charlton on Otmoor, Oxfordshire, England. She married John Kirby 31 Oct 1690, in Oxford, Oxfordshire, England. He was the son of John Kirby and Anne Walker.

620. Jeremiah West was born about 1670, in Fencott, Oxfordshire, England. He married Mable Raymond 26 Oct 1696, in Charlton on Otmoor, Oxfordshire, England.

Children of Jeremiah West and Mable Raymond:

      i.   **Mabel West**,[304] born about 1701, in Charlton on Otmoor, Oxfordshire, England, died before 1800, in England.

621. Mable Raymond was born about 1672, in Fencott, Oxfordshire, England. She married Jeremiah West 26 Oct 1696, in Charlton on Otmoor, Oxfordshire, England.

622. John Howlet was born Mar 1655, in Charlton on Otmoor, Oxfordshire, England, christened 4 Apr 1655, in Charlton on Otmoor, Oxfordshire, England, died Jan 1695, in Charlton on Otmoor, Oxfordshire, England, buried 13 Jan 1695, in Charlton on Otmoor, Oxfordshire, England. He was the son of John Howlett and Howlett. He married Ann Dennett[1026] 14 May 1691, in Oxfordshire, England. She was the daughter of Robert Dennett and Alice Blackwell.

Children of John Howlet and Ann Dennett:

     i.   **Robert Howlett**,[751,752] born Jul 1694, in Murcot, Oxfordshire, England, died 18 Jan 1759, in Charlton on Otmoor, Oxfordshire, England.

623. Ann Dennett was born Jan 1663, in Combe, Oxfordshire, England, christened 24 Jan 1663, in Combe, Oxfordshire, England, died 17 Jan 1716, in Merton, Oxfordshire, England, buried 20 Jan 1716, in Charlton on Otmoor, Oxfordshire, England. She was the daughter of Robert Dennett and Alice Blackwell. She married John Howlet[1027] 14 May 1691, in Oxfordshire, England. He was the son of John Howlett and Howlett.

624. Walter King was born about 1660, in Buckinghamshire, England. He married Mrs Elizabeth King[750] about 1680, in Oxfordshire, England.

Children of Walter King and Mrs Elizabeth King:

     i.   **Mary King**,[749,750] born Jan 1696, in Grendon Underwood, Buckinghamshire, England, died 16 Aug 1773, in Buckinghamshire, England.

625. Mrs Elizabeth King was born about 1661, in Buckinghamshire, England. She married Walter King[750] about 1680, in Oxfordshire, England.

626. Henry Clark was born Feb 1644, in Waddesdon, Buckinghamshire, England, christened 20 Feb 1644, in Waddesdon, Buckinghamshire, England. He was the son of Ralph Clark and Clarke. He married Elizabeth Williams[1028] 1665, in Dinton, Buckinghamshire, England.
Notes for Henry Clark:

aka: HENNERY CLARCKE / CLARCK

Children of Henry Clark and Elizabeth Williams:

     i.   **Richard Clarcke**,[753] born 1670, in Dinton, Buckinghamshire, England.

627. Elizabeth Williams was born about 1646, in Buckinghamshire, England. She married Henry Clark[1028,1029] 1665, in Dinton, Buckinghamshire, England. He was the son of Ralph Clark and Clarke.

628. ____Hallon was born about 1650, in Buckinghamshire, England. He married Hallon about 1673, in Buckinghamshire, England.

Children of Hallon and Hallon:

      i.   **Ester Hallon**,[753] born about 1675, in Buckinghamshire, England.

629. ____Hallon was born about 1653, in Buckinghamshire, England. She married Hallon about 1673, in Buckinghamshire, England.

630. William Rogers was born about 1650, in Buckinghamshire, England. He married Mrs Elizabeth Rogers[1030] about 1670, in Buckinghamshire, England.

Children of William Rogers and Mrs Elizabeth Rogers:

      i.   **Thomas Rogers**,[754,756] born Dec 1671, in Great Missenden, Buckinghamshire, England.

631. Mrs Elizabeth Rogers was born about 1652, in Buckinghamshire, England. She married William Rogers[1030] about 1670, in Buckinghamshire, England.

632. Edward Clarke was born 9 Aug 1649, in Great Missenden, Buckinghamshire, England, christened 9 Aug 1649, in Great Missenden, Buckinghamshire, England. He was the son of Clarke and Clarke. He married Katherine Wright[1031,1032] about 1670, in Buckinghamshire, England. She was the daughter of George Wright and Jane Wright.

Children of Edward Clarke and Katherine Wright:

      i.   **Mary Clark**,[754,755] born Aug 1675, in Great Missenden, Buckinghamshire, England.

633. Katherine Wright was born Aug 1645, in Great Missenden, Buckinghamshire, England, christened 10 Aug 1645, in Great Missenden, Buckinghamshire, England. She was the daughter of George Wright and Jane Wright. She married Edward Clarke[1031,1033] about 1670, in Buckinghamshire, England. He was the son of Clarke and Clarke.

634. ____Grant was born about 1655, in England. He married Grant about 1677, in England.

Children of Grant and Grant:

      i.   **Edvardi Grant**,[757,763] born about 1685, in Buckinghamshire, England.

635. ____Grant was born about 1657, in England. She married Grant about 1677, in England.

636. Rodulphi Hawes was born about 1665, in England. He married Hawes about 1683, in England.

Children of Rodulphi Hawes and Hawes:

     i.   **Elizabeth Hawes**,[1034] born 10 Jan 1685, in Worminghall, Buckinghamshire, England.

    ii.   **Johannes Hawes**,[1035] born 9 Feb 1688, in Worminghall, Buckinghamshire, England.

    iii.   **Mariae Hawes**,[757,758,759] born 2 Oct 1690, in Worminghall, Buckinghamshire, England.

637. ____Hawes was born about 1667, in England. She married Rodulphi Hawes[1036] about 1683, in England.

638. John Yong was born about 1652, in Buckinghamshire, England. He married Mrs Elizabeth Young about 1671, in Buckinghamshire, England.

Children of John Yong and Mrs Elizabeth Young:

     i.   **Sary Yong**,[1037] born Jul 1672, in Chalvey, Buckinghamshire, England, christened 28 Jul 1672, in Chalvey, Buckinghamshire, England.

    ii.   **Elizabeth Yong**,[1038] born Dec 1673, in Chalvey, Buckinghamshire, England, christened 26 Dec 1673, in Chalvey, Buckinghamshire, England.

    iii.   **Frannces Yong**,[1039] born Jan 1675, in Chalvey, Buckinghamshire, England, christened 2 Feb 1675, in Chalvey, Buckinghamshire, England.

    iv.   **Mary Yong**,[1040] born Dec 1677, in Chalvey, Buckinghamshire, England, christened 23 Dec 1677, in Chalvey, Buckinghamshire, England.

    v.   **John Yong**,[764,766] born Jan 1679, in Chalvey, Buckinghamshire, England, died Dec 1730, in Beaconsfield, Buckinghamshire, England.

639. Mrs Elizabeth Young was born about 1653, in Buckinghamshire, England. She married John Yong about 1671, in Buckinghamshire, England.

640. Thomas Steevens was born about 1650, in England. He was the son of Isacc Steevens and Steevens. He married Katrigne Spott[1041,1042] 19 Sep 1672, in Bray, Berkshire, England.
Notes for Thomas Steevens:

aka Thomas Steeuens, Steevens, Stevens

Children of Thomas Steevens and Katrigne Spott:

     i.   **Katerine Steevens**,[1043] born Apr 1673, in Bray, Berkshire, England, christened 9 Apr 1673, in Bray, Berkshire, England.

    ii.   **Martha Stevens**,[764,765] born Dec 1680, in Bray, Berkshire, England, died Jan 1745, in Beaconsfield, Buckinghamshire, England.

    iii.   **Thomas Steevens**,[1044] born Mar 1685, in Bray, Berkshire, England, christened 3 Apr 1685, in Bray, Berkshire, England, died 9 Aug 1685, in Bray, Berkshire, England.

    iv.   **Richard Steevens**,[1045] born Oct 1688, in Bray, Berkshire, England, christened 11 Oct 1688, in Bray, Berkshire, England.

641. Katrigne Spott was born about 1652, in England. She married Thomas Steevens[1041,1046] 19 Sep 1672, in Bray, Berkshire, England. He was the son of Isacc Steevens and Steevens.
Notes for Katrigne Spott:

aka Cath, Catherine, Katherine

642. ____Rowland was born about 1670, in Gloucestershire, England. He married Rowland about 1695, in Gloucestershire, England.

Children of Rowland and Rowland:

    i.   **William Rowland**,[768] born 24 Sep 1699, in Fairford, Gloucestershire, England, died 1746, in Gloucestershire, England.

643. ____Rowland was born about 1672, in Gloucestershire, England. She married Rowland about 1695, in Gloucestershire, England.

644. John Bowles was born Jan 1670, in Fairford, Gloucestershire, England, christened 5 Feb 1670, in Fairford, Gloucestershire, England, died Dec 1714, in Fairford, Gloucestershire, England, buried 14 Dec 1714, in Fairford, Gloucestershire, England. He was the son of Thomas Bowles and Mrs Mary Bowles. He married Martha Loveday[767] about 1695, in Gloucestershire, England. She was the daughter of Thomas Loveday and Martha Hedges.

Children of John Bowles and Martha Loveday:

    i.   **Martha Bowles**,[767,768] born Sep 1699, in Fairford, Gloucestershire, England, died before 1790, in England.

645. Martha Loveday was born Oct 1670, in Wanborough, Wiltshire, England, christened 28 Oct 1670, in Wanborough, Wiltshire, England, died Nov 1758, in Fairford, Gloucestershire, England, buried 14 Nov 1758, in Fairford, Gloucestershire, England. She was the daughter of Thomas Loveday and Martha Hedges. She married John Bowles[1047] about 1695, in Gloucestershire, England. He was the son of Thomas Bowles and Mrs Mary Bowles.

646. Humphry Skinner was born 1657, in Quenington, Gloucestershire, England, christened Sep 1657, in Quenington, Gloucestershire, England, died before 1740, in England. He was the son of Edward Skinner and Mrs Sybella Skinner. He married Mrs Elizabeth Skinner about 1685, in Gloucestershire,

England.

Children of Humphry Skinner and Mrs Elizabeth Skinner:

> i.   **Edward Skinner**, born 1688, in Kempsford, Gloucestershire, England, died before 1770, in England.

647. Mrs Elizabeth Skinner was born about 1666, in Gloucestershire, England, died before 1760, in England. She married Humphry Skinner about 1685, in Gloucestershire, England. He was the son of Edward Skinner and Mrs Sybella Skinner.

648. William Tarrant was born Apr 1650, in Burbage, Wiltshire, England, christened 4 Apr 1650, in Burbage, Wiltshire, England, died before 1750, in England. He was the son of Thomas Tarrant and Mrs Elizabeth Tarrant. He married Ann Bouy 20 Oct 1677, in Salisbury, Wiltshire, England.
Notes for William Tarrant:

residence: Burbage, Wiltshire, England parents: Thomas Tarrant, Elizabeth record title: England Births and Christenings, 1538-1975 name: William Tarrant gender: Male baptism/christening date: 04 Apr 1650 baptism/christening place: Burbage, Wiltshire, England father's name: Thomas Tarrant mother's name: Elizabeth indexing project (batch) number: C15302-1 system origin: England-VR source film number: 1279365

Children of William Tarrant and Ann Bouy:

> i.   **William Tarrant**, born 1681, in Marlborough, Wiltshire, England, christened 11 Sep 1681, in Marlborough, Wiltshire, England.
> residence: Wiltshire, England parents: William Tarrant record title: England Births and Christenings, 1538-1975 name: William Tarrant gender: Male baptism/christening date: 11 Sep 1681 baptism/christening place: SAINT MARY,MARLBOROUGH,WILTSHIRE,ENGLAND father's name: William Tarrant indexing project (batch) number: C02292-2 system origin: England-ODM source film number: 97837
>
> ii. **James Tarrant**, born 1682, in Marlborough, Wiltshire, England, christened 4 Sep 1682, in Marlborough, Wiltshire, England.
> residence: Wiltshire, England parents: William Tarrant record title: England Births and Christenings, 1538-1975 name: James Tarrant gender: Male baptism/christening date: 04 Sep 1682 baptism/christening place: SAINT MARY,MARLBOROUGH,WILTSHIRE,ENGLAND father's name: William Tarrant indexing project (batch) number: C02292-2 system origin: England-ODM source film number: 97837
>
> iii. **Elizabeth Tarrant**, born 1683, in Marlborough, Wiltshire, England, christened 2 Jan 1683, in Marlborough, Wiltshire, England, died 26 Mar 1684, in Marlborough, Wiltshire, England.

death: 26 Mar 1684 residence: Wiltshire, England parents: William Tarrant record title: England Births and Christenings, 1538-1975 name: Elizebeth Tarrant gender: Female baptism/christening date: 02 Jan 1683 baptism/christening place: SAINT MARY,MARLBOROUGH,WILTSHIRE,ENGLAND death date: 26 Mar 1684 father's name: William Tarrant indexing project (batch) number: C02292-2 system origin: England-ODM source film number: 97837

iv. **John Tarrant**, born 1684, in Marlborough, Wiltshire, England, christened 9 Dec 1684, in Marlborough, Wiltshire, England, died 6 Jun 1685, in Marlborough, Wiltshire, England.

death: 06 Jun 1685 residence: Wiltshire, England parents: Wm Tarrant record title: England Births and Christenings, 1538-1975 name: John Tarrant gender: Male baptism/christening date: 09 Dec 1684 baptism/christening place: SAINT MARY,MARLBOROUGH,WILTSHIRE,ENGLAND death date: 06 Jun 1685 father's name: Wm Tarrant indexing project (batch) number: C02292-2 system origin: England-ODM source film number: 97837

v. **Elizabeth Tarrant**, born 1686, in Marlborough, Wiltshire, England, died before 1780, in England.

vi. **John Tarrant**, born 1687, in Marlborough, Wiltshire, England, christened 6 May 1687, in Marlborough, Wiltshire, England.

residence: Wiltshire, England parents: Wm Tarrant record title: England Births and Christenings, 1538-1975 name: John Tarrant gender: Male baptism/christening date: 06 May 1687 baptism/christening place: SAINT MARY,MARLBOROUGH,WILTSHIRE,ENGLAND father's name: Wm Tarrant indexing project (batch) number: C02292-2 system origin: England-ODM source film number: 97837

vii. **Susanna Tarrant**, born 1691, in Marlborough, Wiltshire, England, christened 28 Feb 1691, in Marlborough, Wiltshire, England.

residence: Wiltshire, England parents: Will Tarrant record title: England Births and Christenings, 1538-1975 name: Susanna Tarrant gender: Female baptism/christening date: 28 Feb 1691 baptism/christening place: SAINT MARY,MARLBOROUGH,WILTSHIRE,ENGLAND father's name: Will Tarrant indexing project (batch) number: C02292-2 system origin: England-ODM source film number: 97837

649. Ann Bouy was born about 1652, in Burbage, Wiltshire, England, died before 1750, in England. She married William Tarrant 20 Oct 1677, in Salisbury, Wiltshire, England. He was the son of Thomas Tarrant and Mrs Elizabeth Tarrant.

650. William Watkins was born about 1670, in Bristol, Gloucestershire, England. He married Sarah Gunning[770,1048] 16 Apr 1691, in St Phillip and St Jacob, Bristol, Gloucester, England. She was the daughter of Edward Gunning and Gunning.

Children of William Watkins and Sarah Gunning:

i.   **Sarah Watkins**,[1049] born 7 Dec 1691, in Bristol, Gloucestershire, England.
ii. **William Watkins**,[769,770] born 18 Jan 1694, in Bristol, Gloucestershire, England, died before 1760, in England.
iii. **Mary Watkins**,[1050] born 22 May 1696, in Bristol, Gloucestershire, England, christened 22 Jul 1696, in Bristol, Gloucestershire, England.

651. Sarah Gunning was born about 1672, in Bristol, Gloucestershire, England. She was the daughter of Edward Gunning and Gunning. She married William Watkins[770,1048] 16 Apr 1691, in St Phillip and St Jacob, Bristol, Gloucester, England.

652. ____Watkins was born about 1678, in Bristol, Gloucestershire, England. He married Watkins about 1705, in Bristol, Gloucestershire, England.

Children of Watkins and Watkins:

i.   **Sarah Watkins**,[769] born about 1710, in Bristol, Gloucestershire, England, died before 1810, in England.

653. ____Watkins was born about 1680, in Bristol, Gloucestershire, England. She married Watkins about 1705, in Bristol, Gloucestershire, England.

654. ____Kelly was born about 1685, in Gloucestershire, England. He married Kelly about 1705, in Gloucestershire, England.

Children of Kelly and Kelly:

i.   **Martin Kelly**,[772] born about 1710, in Gloucestershire, England, died before 1800, in England.

655. ____Kelly was born about 1687, in Gloucestershire, England. She married Kelly about 1705, in Gloucestershire, England.

656. William Perry was born 1672, in Uley, Gloucestershire, England, christened 30 May 1672, in Uley, Gloucestershire, England, died before 1770, in England. He married Mary Heaven 4 Mar 1700, in Wotton under Edge, Gloucestershire, England.
Notes for William Perry:

residence: Gloucester, England parents: Wm Perry record title: England Births and Christenings, 1538-1975 name: William Perry gender: Male baptism/christening date: 30 May 1672 baptism/christening place: ULEY,GLOUCESTER,ENGLAND father's name: Wm Perry indexing project (batch) number: C03267-2 system origin: England-ODM source film number: 855625

Children of William Perry and Mary Heaven:

> i. **Anne Parry**,[771,772] born 1717, in Bristol, Gloucestershire, England, died before 1800, in England.

657. Mary Heaven was born about 1675, in Gloucestershire, England, died before 1775, in England. She married William Perry 4 Mar 1700, in Wotton under Edge, Gloucestershire, England.

658. Samuel Rogers was born Sep 1658, in Bristol, Gloucestershire, England, christened 5 Sep 1658, in Bristol, Gloucestershire, England, died 29 Apr 1748, in Bitton, Gloucestershire, England. He was the son of Thomas Rogers and Mrs Susana Rogers. He married Sarah Rogers about 1680, in Gloucestershire, England.
Notes for Samuel Rogers:

England Births and Christenings, 1538-1975 residence: Bristol, Gloucester, England parents: Thomas Rogers, Susana record title: England Births and Christenings, 1538-1975 name: Samuell Rogers gender: Male baptism/christening date: 05 Sep 1658 baptism/christening place: St. Michael, Bristol, England father's name: Thomas Rogers mother's name: Susana Batch: C03917-1; film: 1849446

Children of Samuel Rogers and Sarah Rogers:

> i. **Dennis Rogers**,[774] born Nov 1684, in Tetbury, Gloucestershire, England, died Feb 1776, in Bitton, Gloucestershire, England.

659. Sarah Rogers was born about 1660, in Gloucestershire, England, died 12 Jan 1734, in Bitton, Gloucestershire, England. She married Samuel Rogers[1051] about 1680, in Gloucestershire, England. He was the son of Thomas Rogers and Mrs Susana Rogers.

660. William Brain was born 1670, in Blakeney, Gloucestershire, England, christened 6 Mar 1670, in Hanham, Gloucestershire, England. He married Mrs Esther Brayne about 1700, in Gloucestershire, England.

Children of William Brain and Mrs Esther Brayne:

> i. **Mary Brayne**,[773] born about 1700, in Gloucestershire, England, died Jun 1784, in Bitton, Gloucestershire, England.
> ii. **Elizabeth Brain**, born Jun 1702, in Blakeney, Gloucestershire, England, christened 26 Jun 1702, in Blakeney, Gloucestershire, England.

661. Mrs Esther Brayne was born about 1674, in Blakeney, Gloucestershire, England. She married William Brain about 1700, in Gloucestershire, England.

662. Thomas Stone was born about 1670, in Bitton, Gloucestershire, England, died before 1770, in

England. He married Mary Hiyet 28 May 1699, in Bitton, Gloucestershire, England.
Notes for Thomas Stone:

England Marriages, 15381973 marriage: 28 May 1699 Bitton, Gloucester, England spouse: Thomas Stone record title: England Marriages, 15381973 groom's name: Thomas Stone bride's name: Mary Hiyet marriage date: 28 May 1699 marriage place: Bitton, Gloucester, England indexing project (batch) number: I09520-2 system origin: England. source film number: 1597036

Children of Thomas Stone and Mary Hiyet:

       i.   **William Stone**,[776] born about 1700, in Bristol, Gloucestershire, England, died before 1800, in England.

663. Mary Hiyet was born 1676, in Bitton, Gloucestershire, England, died 1735, in Gloucestershire, England. She married Thomas Stone 28 May 1699, in Bitton, Gloucestershire, England.
Notes for Mary Hiyet:

Last name also: HYETT, HIETT England Marriages, 1538-1973 marriage: 28 May 1699 -Bitton, Gloucester, England spouse: Thomas Stone record title: England Marriages, 1538-1973 groom's name: Thomas Stone bride's name: Mary Hiyet marriage date: 28 May 1699 marriage place: Bitton, Gloucester, England indexing project (batch) number: I09520-2 system origin: England. source film number: 1597036

664. ____Palmer was born about 1690, in Gloucestershire, England. He married Palmer about 1714, in England.

Children of Palmer and Palmer:

       i.   **Ann Palmer**,[775] born about 1714, in Bitton, Gloucestershire, England, died before 1800, in England.

665. ____Palmer was born about 1692, in Gloucestershire, England. She married Palmer about 1714, in England.

666. John Burges was born about 1685, in Gloucestershire, England. He married Burges about 1706, in Gloucestershire, England.

Children of John Burges and Burges:

       i.   **John Burges**,[780,781] born 17 Apr 1711, in Bristol, Gloucestershire, England, died before 1800, in England.

667. ____Burges was born about 1687, in Gloucestershire, England. She married John Burges[780] about

1706, in Gloucestershire, England.

668. ____Goby was born 1685, in Dorset, England. He married Goby about 1708, in Dorset, England.

Children of Goby and Goby:

> i. **Susanna Goby**,[494,777] born about 1712, in Spetisbury, Dorset, England, died before 1812, in England.

669. ____Goby was born about 1687, in Dorset, England. She married Goby about 1708, in Dorset, England.

670. Thomas Reynolds was born Dec 1681, in Bristol, Gloucestershire, England, christened 1 Jan 1682, in Bristol, Gloucestershire, England, died before 1780, in England. He married Sarah Smith 1695, in Bristol, Gloucestershire, England.
Notes for Thomas Reynolds:

Boyd's marriage index, 1538-1850

Children of Thomas Reynolds and Sarah Smith:

> i. **Sarah Reynolds**, born Jul 1700, in Bristol, Gloucestershire, England, christened 11 Jul 1700, in St Augustine the Less, Bristol, Gloucestershire, England, died before Sep 1701, in Bristol, Gloucestershire, England.
> England Births and Christenings, 1538-1975
> ii. **Sarah Reynolds**, born Sep 1701, in Bristol, Gloucestershire, England, christened 16 Sep 1701, in St Augustine the Less, Bristol, Gloucestershire, England.
> England Births and Christenings, 1538-1975
> iii. **Elizabeth Reynolds**, born Jan 1703, in Bristol, Gloucestershire, England, christened 6 Feb 1703, in St Augustine the Less, Bristol, Gloucestershire, England.
> England Births and Christenings, 1538-1975
> iv. **Maria Reynolds**, born Mar 1706, in Bristol, Gloucestershire, England, christened 20 Mar 1706, in Newland, Gloucestershire, England.
> England Births and Christenings, 1538-1975
> v. **George Reynolds**,[782,785] born Jan 1708, in Bristol, Gloucestershire, England, died before 1800, in England.
> vi. **Hester Reynolds**, born Jan 1711, in Bristol, Gloucestershire, England, christened 13 Jan 1711, in St Augustine the Less, Bristol, Gloucestershire, England.
> England Births and Christenings, 1538-1975
> vii. **Johnes Reynolds**, born Jun 1715, in Bristol, Gloucestershire, England, christened 16 Jun 1715, in Newland, Gloucestershire, England, died 5 Mar 1720, in Bristol, Gloucestershire, England.
> England Births and Christenings, 1538-1975

671. Sarah Smith was born about 1675, in Gloucestershire, England, died before 1760, in England. She married Thomas Reynolds[1052] 1695, in Bristol, Gloucestershire, England.
Notes for Sarah Smith:

Boyd's marriage index, 1538-1850

672. ____Sednel was born about 1690, in Gloucestershire, England. He married Sednel about 1716, in Gloucestershire, England.

Children of Sednel and Sednel:

      i.   **Mary Or Ann Sednel,**[782] born about 1719, in Bristol, Gloucestershire, England, died before 1800, in England.

673. ____Sednel was born about 1692, in Gloucestershire, England. She married Sednel about 1716, in Gloucestershire, England.

674. Thomas Ellard was born Jul 1701, in Preston Bisset, Buckinghamshire, England, christened 27 Jul 1701, in Preston Bisset, Buckinghamshire, England. He was the son of Henry Ellard and Mary Ellard. He married Elizabeth Ellard about 1728, in Buckinghamshire, England.

Children of Thomas Ellard and Elizabeth Ellard:

      i.   **William Ellard,**[786,788] born Sep 1735, in Preston Bisset, Buckinghamshire, England.

675. Elizabeth Ellard was born about 1702, in Buckinghamshire, England. She married Thomas Ellard[1053] about 1728, in Buckinghamshire, England. He was the son of Henry Ellard and Mary Ellard.

676. ____Spooner was born about 1705, in Buckinghamshire, England. He married Spooner about 1730, in Buckinghamshire, England.

Children of Spooner and Spooner:

      i.   **Catherine Spooner,**[786,787] born Nov 1738, in Cublington, Buckinghamshire, England.

677. ____Spooner was born about 1708, in Buckinghamshire, England. She married Spooner about 1730, in Buckinghamshire, England.

678. William Mealing was born about 1700, in England. He married Mealing about 1730, in England.

Children of William Mealing and Mealing:

      i.   **William Mealing,**[793] born Feb 1733, in Houghton Regis, Bedfordshire, England.

679. ____Mealing was born about 1705, in England. She married William Mealing about 1730, in England.

680. Michael Messider was born about 1700, in Bedfordshire, England. He married Mrs Elizabeth Messider about 1734, in Bedfordshire, England.

Children of Michael Messider and Mrs Elizabeth Messider:

      i.   **Rebecca Messider**, born Jun 1736, in Houghton Regis, Bedfordshire, England.

681. Mrs Elizabeth Messider was born about 1702, in Bedfordshire, England. She married Michael Messider about 1734, in Bedfordshire, England.

682. Thomasin Jennings was born Aug 1700, in Bletchingley, Surrey, England, christened 1 Sep 1700, in Bletchingley, Surrey, England. He was the son of William Jennings and Elisabeth Jennings. He married Elizabeth Jennings about 1720, in England.

Children of Thomasin Jennings and Elizabeth Jennings:

      i.   **Thomas Jennings,**[793] born 19 May 1722, in Southwark, Surrey, England.

683. Elizabeth Jennings was born about 1701, in England. She married Thomasin Jennings[1054] about 1720, in England. He was the son of William Jennings and Elisabeth Jennings.

684. Thomas Roberts was born about 1695, in England. He married Elizabeth Roberts about 1718, in England.

Children of Thomas Roberts and Elizabeth Roberts:

      i.   **Ann Roberts,**[794] born 25 Dec 1722, in Croydon, Surrey, England.

685. Elizabeth Roberts was born about 1698, in England. She married Thomas Roberts about 1718, in England.

686. ____Taylor was born about 1700, in Kent, England. He married Taylor about 1725, in Kent, England.

Children of Taylor and Taylor:

  i. **Grove Taylor**,[499,798] born about 1730, in Kent, England.

687. ____Taylor was born about 1705, in Kent, England. She married Taylor about 1725, in Kent, England.

688. Stephen Smith was born about 1700, in Kent, England. He was the son of Smith and Smith. He married Elizabeth Hills[1055,1056] 1728, in Kingsdown, Kent, England. She was the daughter of William Hills and Hills.

Children of Stephen Smith and Elizabeth Hills:

  i. **Sarah Smith**,[499,796,797] born Oct 1738, in Bromley, Kent, England.

689. Elizabeth Hills was born Jun 1710, in Ditton, Kent, England, christened 1 Jul 1710, in Ditton, Kent, England. She was the daughter of William Hills and Hills. She married Stephen Smith[1055,1057] 1728, in Kingsdown, Kent, England. He was the son of Smith and Smith.

690. ____Langley was born about 1700, in Suffolk, England. He married Langley about 1725, in Suffolk, England.

Children of Langley and Langley:

  i. **Isaac Langley**,[799] born about 1730, in England.

691. ____Langley was born about 1702, in Suffolk, England. She married Langley about 1725, in Suffolk, England.

692. Benjamini Smith was born about 1700, in Suffolk, England. He married Annae Smith[1058] about 1722, in Suffolk, England.

Children of Benjamini Smith and Annae Smith:

  i. **Anna Smith**,[799,800] born Oct 1730, in Glemsford, Suffolk, England.

693. Annae Smith was born about 1702, in Suffolk, England. She married Benjamini Smith[1058] about 1722, in Suffolk, England.

694. ____Day was born about 1700, in England. He married Day about 1727, in London, England.

Children of Day and Day:

       i.   **Charles Day**,[801] born about 1732, in London, England.

695. ____Day was born about 1702, in London, England. She married Day about 1727, in London, England.

696. ____Darby was born about 1700, in London, England. He married Darby about 1725, in London, England.

Children of Darby and Darby:

       i.   **Elizabeth Darby**,[801,802] born 24 Nov 1735, in Stepney, Middlesex, England.

697. ____Darby was born about 1705, in London, England. She married Darby about 1725, in London, England.

698. ____Bawhse was born about 1700, in England. He married Bawhse about 1725, in England.

Children of Bawhse and Bawhse:

       i.   **Thomas Bawhse**,[803] born about 1730, in Middlesex, England.

699. ____Bawhse was born about 1702, in England. She married Bawhse about 1725, in England.

700. Thomas Martin was born about 1700, in England. He married Mrs Katherine Martin about 1722, in England.

Children of Thomas Martin and Mrs Katherine Martin:

       i.   **Elizabeth Martin**,[803,804] born 25 Dec 1722, in Westminster, Middlesex, England.

701. Mrs Katherine Martin was born about 1702, in England. She married Thomas Martin about 1722, in England.

702. ____Pike was born about 1720, in England. He married Pike about 1740, in Middlesex, England.

Children of Pike and Pike:

       i.   **Thomas Pike**,[805] born about 1740, in Middlesex, England.

703. ____Pike was born about 1722, in Middlesex, England. She married Pike about 1740, in Middlesex, England.

704. _____Lamb was born about 1720, in Middlesex, England. He married Lamb about 1744, in Middlesex, England.

Children of Lamb and Lamb:

     i.   **Catharine Lamb**,[805] born about 1744, in Middlesex, England.

705. _____Lamb was born about 1722, in Middlesex, England. She married Lamb about 1744, in Middlesex, England.

706. _____Humber was born about 1690, in England. He married Humber about 1720, in Dorset, England.

Children of Humber and Humber:

     i.   **Hugh Humber**, born about 1720, in Cattistock, Dorset, England, died 13 Dec 1775, in Cattistock, Dorset, England.

707. _____Humber was born about 1692, in England. She married Humber about 1720, in Dorset, England.

708. _____Frampton was born about 1690, in Dorset, England. He married Frampton about 1712, in Dorset, England.

Children of Frampton and Frampton:

     i.   **Mary Frampton**, born about 1719, in Cattistock, Dorset, England, died 14 Jun 1761, in Dorset, England.

709. _____Frampton was born about 1692, in Dorset, England. She married Frampton about 1712, in Dorset, England.

710. _____Tidby was born about 1700, in Dorset, England. He married Tidby about 1721, in Dorset, England.

Children of Tidby and Tidby:

     i.   **Joseph Tidby**, born 1724, in Litton Cheney, Dorset, England.

711. _____Tidby was born about 1702, in Dorset, England. She married Tidby about 1721, in Dorset, England.

712. _____Talbot was born about 1700, in Dorset, England. He married Talbot about 1725, in Dorset,

England.

Children of Talbot and Talbot:

       i.   **Mary Talbot**, born 1728, in Litton Cheney, Dorset, England.

713. ____Talbot was born about 1702, in Dorset, England. She married Talbot about 1725, in Dorset, England.

714. Samuel Churchill was born about 1700, in Dorset, England. He married Mrs Elizabeth Churchill about 1722, in Dorset, England.

Children of Samuel Churchill and Mrs Elizabeth Churchill:

       i.   **Samuell Churchill**,[806,807] born Oct 1731, in Toller Porcorum, Dorset, England.

715. Mrs Elizabeth Churchill was born about 1702, in Dorset, England, died 1770, in Stratton, Dorset, England. She married Samuel Churchill about 1722, in Dorset, England.

716. ____Tiber was born about 1705, in Dorset, England. He married Tiber about 1726, in Dorset, England.

Children of Tiber and Tiber:

       i.   **Ann Tiber**,[806] born about 1733, in Dorset, England.

717. ____Tiber was born about 1707, in Dorset, England. She married Tiber about 1726, in Dorset, England.

718. Lewis Jacob was born about 1700, in Dorset, England, christened about 1700, in Dorset, England. He married Elizabeth Lake[1059,1060] 15 Jul 1732, in Winterbourne St Martin, Dorset, England. She was the daughter of John Lake and Magdalen Lake.

Children of Lewis Jacob and Elizabeth Lake:

       i.   **Mary Jacob**,[1061] born May 1733, in Winterbourne St Martin, Dorset, England, christened 14 May 1733, in Winterbourne St Martin, Dorset, England.
      ii.   **Henry Jacob**,[808,809] born Oct 1736, in Winterbourne St Martin, Dorset, England.
     iii.   **Lewis Jacob**,[1062] born Mar 1737, in Winterbourne St Martin, Dorset, England, christened 12 Mar 1737, in Winterbourne St Martin, Dorset, England.

719. Elizabeth Lake was born Aug 1708, in Winterbourne St Martin, Dorset, England, christened 22 Aug 1708, in Winterbourne St Martin, Dorset, England. She was the daughter of John Lake and

Magdalen Lake. She married Lewis Jacob[1059] 15 Jul 1732, in Winterbourne St Martin, Dorset, England.

720. ____Poage was born about 1710, in Dorset, England. He married Poage about 1730, in Dorset, England.

Children of Poage and Poage:

    i.   **Mary Poage**,[808] born about 1740, in Dorset, England.

721. ____Poage was born about 1712, in Dorset, England. She married Poage about 1730, in Dorset, England.

722. Thomas Hunt was born 17 Oct 1704, in Compton Abbas, Dorset, England, died 2 Feb 1784, in Compton Abbas, Dorset, England. He was the son of Thomas Hunt and Hunt. He married Mrs Katherine Hunt about 1725, in Dorset, England.
Notes for Thomas Hunt:

1530-1906, Source Information: Shown as father to Thomas Hunt born: 1733 Ancestry.com. England

Children of Thomas Hunt and Mrs Katherine Hunt:

    i.   **Thomas Hunt**,[811,812,813] born 13 May 1733, in Compton Abbas, Dorset, England, died before 1833, in England.
    ii.   **Elizabeth Hunt**,[1063] born Apr 1735, in Compton Abbas, Dorset, England, christened 20 Apr 1735, in Compton Abbas, Dorset, England, died 8 Mar 1795, in West Knoyle, Wiltshire, England.
        aka - Bette

723. Mrs Katherine Hunt was born about 1702, in Dorset, England, died before 1800, in England. She married Thomas Hunt about 1725, in Dorset, England. He was the son of Thomas Hunt and Hunt.

724. Timothy Zebedee was born about 1699, in Dorset, England, died before 1780, in England. He married Zebedee about 1725, in England.

Children of Timothy Zebedee and Zebedee:

    i.   **Mary Zebedee**,[810,811] born Jan 1736, in Bradpole, Dorset, England, died before 1830, in England.

725. ____Zebedee was born about 1702, in England, died before 1800, in England. She married Timothy Zebedee about 1725, in England.

726. John Burt was born about 1700, in Yetminster, Dorset, England, died before 1800, in England. He married Sarah Stokes[1064] 8 Sep 1744, in Stock Gaylard, Dorset, England. She was the daughter of Thomas Stokes and Susannah Richards.

Children of John Burt and Sarah Stokes:

> i. **William Burt**, born 1745, in Yetminster, Dorset, England, died before 1840, in England.

727. Sarah Stokes was born 26 Jul 1720, in Evercreech, Somerset, England, christened 26 Jul 1720, in Evercreech, Somerset, England, died before 1820, in England. She was the daughter of Thomas Stokes and Susannah Richards. She married John Burt 8 Sep 1744, in Stock Gaylard, Dorset, England.

728. George Morris was born 1720, in Somerset, England, died before 1820, in England. He married Mary Davis 25 Jun 1750, in Lopen, Somerset, England.

Children of George Morris and Mary Davis:

> i. **Joan Morris**, born 16 Dec 1750, in Chard, Somerset, England, died before 1850, in England.

729. Mary Davis was born about 1722, in Somerset, England, died before 1820, in England. She married George Morris 25 Jun 1750, in Lopen, Somerset, England.

730. ____Matthews was born about 1715, in Dorset, England. He married Matthews about 1740, in Dorset, England.

Children of Matthews and Matthews:

> i. **John Matthews**,[814] born about 1750, in Dorset, England.

731. ____Matthews was born about 1720, in Dorset, England. She married Matthews about 1740, in Dorset, England.

732. ____Hodder was born about 1725, in Dorset, England. He married Hodder about 1750, in Dorset, England.

Children of Hodder and Hodder:

> i. **Ann Hodder**,[814] born Apr 1757, in Whitchurch-Canonicorum, Dorset, England.

733. ____Hodder was born about 1727, in Dorset, England. She married Hodder about 1750, in Dorset, England.

734. George Fowler was born 1703, in Hawkchurch, Dorset, England, died Nov 1761, in Hawkchurch, Dorset, England, buried 8 Nov 1761, in Hawkchurch, Dorset, England. He married Jemima Guppy[1065] 18 Jul 1732, in Hawkchurch, Dorset, England.

Children of George Fowler and Jemima Guppy:

    i.   **John Fowler,**[1066] born Dec 1747, in Hawkchurch, Dorset, England, christened 20 Dec 1747, in Hawkchurch, Dorset, England, died before Jul 1749, in Hawkchurch, Dorset, England.

    ii.   **John Fowler,**[815,819] born Jul 1749, in Hawkchurch, Dorset, England, died before 1830, in Dorset, England.

735. Jemima Guppy was born about 1713, in Hawkchurch, Dorset, England, died 8 Nov 1761, in Hawkchurch, Dorset, England, buried 8 Nov 1761, in Hawkchurch, Dorset, England. She married George Fowler[1065] 18 Jul 1732, in Hawkchurch, Dorset, England.

736. ____Culverwell was born about 1725, in England. He married Culverwelll about 1750, in England.

Children of Culverwell and Culverwelll:

    i.   **Jane Culverwell,**[815] born about 1757, in Dorset, England, died 1843, in England.

737. ____Culverwelll was born about 1727, in England. She married Culverwell about 1750, in England.

738. Josiah Humphrey was born Sep 1696, in Sulgrave, Northamptonshire, England, christened 20 Sep 1696, in Sulgrave, Northamptonshire, England, died Feb 1769, in Sulgrave, Northamptonshire, England, buried 6 Feb 1769, in Sulgrave, Northamptonshire, England. He was the son of John Humphrey and Mary Wake. He married Elizabeth Tims 17 Feb 1718, in Brackley, Northamptonshire, England. She was the daughter of William Tims and Elizabeth Naylor.

Children of Josiah Humphrey and Elizabeth Tims:

    i.   **Thomas Humphrey**, born May 1721, in Brackley, Northamptonshire, England, died Jun 1797, in Hinton in the Hedges, Northamptonshire, England.

739. Elizabeth Tims was born Apr 1691, in Farthinghoe, Northamptonshire, England, christened 17 Apr 1691, in Farthinghoe, Northamptonshire, England, died before 1790, in England. She was the daughter of William Tims and Elizabeth Naylor. She married Josiah Humphrey 17 Feb 1718, in Brackley, Northamptonshire, England. He was the son of John Humphrey and Mary Wake.

740. ____Linnelin was born about 1700, in Northamptonshire, England. He married Linnelin about

1722, in Northamptonshire, England.

Children of Linnelin and Linnelin:

> i. **Mary Linnelin**, born about 1724, in Northamptonshire, England, died Apr 1784, in Hinton in the Hedges, Northamptonshire, England.

741. ____Linnelin was born about 1702, in Northamptonshire, England. She married Linnelin about 1722, in Northamptonshire, England.

742. Robert Bazley was born 1695, in Greatworth, Northamptonshire, England, died before 1734, in England. He married Alice Lilford 10 Feb 1716, in Evenley, Northamptonshire, England.
Notes for Robert Bazley:

aka: BAZELY

Children of Robert Bazley and Alice Lilford:

> i. **Nathaniel Bazley**, born 12 Nov 1727, in Greatworth, Northamptonshire, England, died before 1825, in England.

743. Alice Lilford was born about 1696, in Northamptonshire, England, died before 1795, in England. She married Robert Bazley 10 Feb 1716, in Evenley, Northamptonshire, England.

744. William Collison was born 1690, in Woodeaton, Oxfordshire, England, christened 1690, in Woodeaton, Oxfordshire, England, died before 1785, in England. He was the son of William Collison and Mrs Mary Collison. He married Mary Brimly 17 Apr 1721, in Woodeaton, Oxfordshire, England. She was the daughter of Benjamin Brimly and Mrs Mary Brimly.

Children of William Collison and Mary Brimly:

> i. **Sarah Collison**, born 4 Nov 1728, in Woodeaton, Oxfordshire, England, died Jul 1787, in Greatworth, Northamptonshire, England.

745. Mary Brimly was born 1690, in Woodeaton, Oxfordshire, England, christened 2 Jan 1691, in Woodeaton, Oxfordshire, England, died Jan 1730, in England, buried 4 Feb 1730, in Woodeaton, Oxfordshire, England. She was the daughter of Benjamin Brimly and Mrs Mary Brimly. She married William Collison 17 Apr 1721, in Woodeaton, Oxfordshire, England. He was the son of William Collison and Mrs Mary Collison.

746. Robert Coleman Or Coalman was born about 1700, in Kettering, Northamptonshire, England. He married Mary Fennimore[1067] 14 Dec 1720, in Radstone, Northamptonshire, England.

Children of Robert Coleman Or Coalman and Mary Fennimore:

      i.   **Thomas Coleman Or Coalman**,[820,822,823] born Jul 1726, in Kettering, Northamptonshire, England.

     ii.   **Mary Coleman Or Coalman**,[1068,1069] born Aug 1729, in Kettering, Northamptonshire, England, christened 18 Aug 1729, in Kettering, Northamptonshire, England.

    iii.   **John Coleman Or Coalman**,[1070,1071] born Oct 1732, in Kettering, Northamptonshire, England, christened 18 Oct 1732, in Kettering, Northamptonshire, England.

    iv.   **Jonathan Coleman Or Coalman**,[1072,1073] born Aug 1735, in Kettering, Northamptonshire, England, christened 8 Sep 1735, in Kettering, Northamptonshire, England.

747. Mary Fennimore was born about 1702, in Northamptonshire, England. She married Robert Coleman Or Coalman[1074] 14 Dec 1720, in Radstone, Northamptonshire, England.

748. ____Bitchens was born about 1695, in England. He married Bitchens about 1715, in England.

Children of Bitchens and Bitchens:

      i.   **Ann Bitchens**,[820] born about 1720, in England.

749. ____Bitchens was born about 1697, in England. She married Bitchens about 1715, in England.

750. John Franklin was born about 1700, in Buckinghamshire, England, christened 13 Jul 1701, in Quainton, Buckinghamshire, England. He married Mrs Sarah Franklin about 1728, in Buckinghamshire, England.

Children of John Franklin and Mrs Sarah Franklin:

      i.   **John Franklin**, born Oct 1730, in Quainton, Buckinghamshire, England.

751. Mrs Sarah Franklin was born about 1702, in Buckinghamshire, England. She married John Franklin about 1728, in Buckinghamshire, England.

752. Joseph Smith was born about 1700, in Buckinghamshire, England. He married Anne Seir 30 Dec 1729, in Maids Moreton, Buckinghamshire, England.

Children of Joseph Smith and Anne Seir:

      i.   **Anne Smith**, born Sep 1736, in Quainton, Buckinghamshire, England.

753. Anne Seir was born about 1702, in Buckinghamshire, England. She married Joseph Smith 30 Dec

1729, in Maids Moreton, Buckinghamshire, England.

754. John Chester was born about 1670, in Warwickshire, England. He married Chester about 1695, in Warwickshire, England.

Children of John Chester and Chester:

      i.   **John Chester**, born about 1700, in Southam, Warwickshire, England.

755. ____Chester was born about 1672, in Warwickshire, England. She married John Chester about 1695, in Warwickshire, England.

756. Joseph Ladbrook was born about 1666, in Warwickshire, England, died Nov 1725, in Stoneleigh, Warwickshire, England, buried 23 Nov 1725, in Stoneleigh, Warwickshire, England. He married Elizabeth Falkner[824,1075,1076] 11 Apr 1697, in Stoneleigh, Warwickshire, England.

Children of Joseph Ladbrook and Elizabeth Falkner:

      i.   **Mary Ladbrook**,[824] born Jul 1703, in Stoneleigh, Warwickshire, England.

757. Elizabeth Falkner was born Mar 1667, in Coventry, Warwickshire, England, christened 4 Mar 1667, in Coventry, Warwickshire, England, died about 1760. She married Joseph Ladbrook[824,1075,1077] 11 Apr 1697, in Stoneleigh, Warwickshire, England.

758. ____Calloway was born about 1700, in Warwickshire, England. He married Calloway about 1722, in Warwickshire, England.

Children of Calloway and Calloway:

      i.   **William Calloway**, born about 1730, in Birdingbury, Warwickshire, England.

759. ____Calloway was born about 1702, in Warwickshire, England. She married Calloway about 1722, in Warwickshire, England.

760. Edward Walker was born 1700, in Frankton, Warwickshire, England, christened about 1700, died 1763, in Frankton, Warwickshire, England, buried 3 Feb 1763, in Frankton, Warwickshire, England. He married Elizabeth Mumforr 18 Oct 1725, in Warwickshire, England.

Children of Edward Walker and Elizabeth Mumforr:

      i.   **Susannah Walker**, born about 1731, in Birdingbury, Warwickshire, England.

761. Elizabeth Mumforr was born 1700, in Warwickshire, England, christened about 1700, died 1762, in Warwickshire, England, buried 17 Mar 1762, in Frankton, Warwickshire, England. She married Edward Walker 18 Oct 1725, in Warwickshire, England.

762. Paul Savage was born 1671, in Pattishall, Northamptonshire, England, christened 1671, in Pattishall, Northampton, England, died 1739, in Pattishall, Northamptonshire, England, buried 10 Jul 1739, in Pattishall, Northamptonshire, England. He married Mrs Jane Savage about 1699, in Northamptonshire, England.

Children of Paul Savage and Mrs Jane Savage:

     i.   **Samuel Savage**,[825] born Apr 1704, in Pattishall, Northamptonshire, England.

763. Mrs Jane Savage was born about 1677, in Northamptonshire, England. She married Paul Savage about 1699, in Northamptonshire, England.

764. ____Hicks was born about 1680, in England. He married Hicks about 1700, in England.

Children of Hicks and Hicks:

     i.   **Mary Hicks**,[825] born about 1705, in Pattishall, Northamptonshire, England, died Sep 1792, in Pattishall, Northamptonshire, England.

765. ____Hicks was born about 1682, in England. She married Hicks about 1700, in England.

766. John Bodily was born about 1685, in Northamptonshire, England, died 24 Jun 1723, in Alderton, Northamptonshire, England, buried 24 Jun 1723, in Alderton, Northamptonshire, England. He was the son of John Bodily and Rebeca Squire. He married Katherine Wright 30 Nov 1706, in Alderton, Northamptonshire, England.

Children of John Bodily and Katherine Wright:

     i.   **Richard Bodily**, born 27 Jul 1712, in Alderton, Northamptonshire, England, died 1765, in Green's Norton, Northamptonshire, England.

767. Katherine Wright was born about 1685, in Alderton, Northamptonshire, England, died 16 May 1723, in Alderton, Northamptonshire, England, buried 16 May 1723, in Alderton, Northamptonshire, England. She married John Bodily 30 Nov 1706, in Alderton, Northamptonshire, England. He was the son of John Bodily and Rebeca Squire.

768. Richard Collins was born about 1685, in Upper Heyford, Oxfordshire, England. He was the son of John Collins and Lydia Checkley. He married Alice Ashby[1078] 17 Feb 1711, in Flore, Northamptonshire, England. She was the daughter of John Ashby and Mary Gammage.

Children of Richard Collins and Alice Ashby:

> i. **Mary Collins**, born 24 Sep 1714, in Heyford, Northamptonshire, England, died 22 Dec 1792, in Green's Norton, Northamptonshire, England.

769. Alice Ashby was born 1689, in Bugbrooke, Northamptonshire, England, died after 1723. She was the daughter of John Ashby and Mary Gammage. She married Richard Collins 17 Feb 1711, in Flore, Northamptonshire, England. He was the son of John Collins and Lydia Checkley.
Notes for Alice Ashby:

Quaker

770. Wiliam Lucas was born about 1680, in England, died before 1760, in England. He married Sarah Rud[1079] 21 Oct 1709, in Hertford, Hertfordshire, England.

Children of Wiliam Lucas and Sarah Rud:

> i. **William Lucas**,[826,827,829] born 8 Nov 1710, in Hitchin, Hertfordshire, England, died before 1800, in England.

771. Sarah Rud was born about 1682, in England, died before 1760, in England. She married Wiliam Lucas[1079] 21 Oct 1709, in Hertford, Hertfordshire, England.

772. George Chambers was born about 1683, in England, died before 1750, in England. He married Elizabeth Deny[1080] 13 Jan 1707, in Yaxley, Huntingdonshire, England.

Children of George Chambers and Elizabeth Deny:

> i. **Ann Or Susanna Chambers**,[826,827,828] born Aug 1712, in Yaxley, Huntingdonshire, England, died before 1800, in England.

773. Elizabeth Deny was born about 1684, in England, died about 1750, in England. She married George Chambers[1080] 13 Jan 1707, in Yaxley, Huntingdonshire, England.

774. Edward Bryers Or Bryars was born about 1655, in England, died before 1750, in England. He married Ann Lieginton[1081] 1 Apr 1678, in Linton, Cambridgeshire, England.

Children of Edward Bryers Or Bryars and Ann Lieginton:

> i. **Thomas Broyors Or Bryars Or Bryers**,[830,831,833] born Mar 1699, in Baldock, Hertfordshire, England, died before 1760, in England.

775. Ann Lieginton was born about 1657, in England, died before 1750, in England. She married

Edward Bryers Or Bryars[1081,1082] 1 Apr 1678, in Linton, Cambridgeshire, England.

776. John Squire was born Oct 1658, in Redbourn, Hertfordshire, England, christened 5 Nov 1658, in Redbourn, Hertfordshire, England, died before 1740, in England. He was the son of George Squier and Mrs Ann Squier. He married Mary Smith[1083] 1680, in Redbourn, Hertfordshire, England.

Children of John Squire and Mary Smith:

     i.   **Ann Squires**,[830,831,832] born Aug 1697, in Yaxley, Huntingdonshire, England, died before 1760, in England.

777. Mary Smith was born about 1663, in England, died before 1740, in England. She married John Squire[1083,1084,1085] 1680, in Redbourn, Hertfordshire, England. He was the son of George Squier and Mrs Ann Squier.

778. ____Mayes Or May was born about 1680, in England. He married Mayes Or May about 1705, in England.

Children of Mayes Or May and Mayes Or May:

     i.   **Nathaniel Mayes Or May**, born about 1710, in Essex, England.

779. ____Mayes Or May was born about 1682, in England. She married Mayes Or May about 1705, in England.

780. ____Lawn was born about 1685, in England. He married Lawn about 1705, in England.

Children of Lawn and Lawn:

     i.   **Mary Lawn**, born about 1712, in Essex, England.

781. ____Lawn was born about 1687, in England. She married Lawn about 1705, in England.

782. ____Stevens was born about 1680, in Essex, England. He married Stevens about 1705, in England.

Children of Stevens and Stevens:

     i.   **William Stevens**,[841] born about 1710, in Essex, England, died 7 Jan 1787, in Great Warley, Essex, England.

783. ____Stevens was born about 1682, in Essex, England. She married Stevens about 1705, in England.

784. ____Setch was born about 1690, in Essex, England. He married Setch about 1709, in Essex, England.

Children of Setch and Setch:

      i.   **Jane Setch**,[834] born about 1712, in Essex, England, died 25 Aug 1774, in Great Warley, Essex, England.

785. ____Setch was born about 1691, in Essex, England. She married Setch about 1709, in Essex, England.

786. William Young was born 1678, in England, buried 3 Sep 1727, in Chislet, Kent, England. He married An Ayling[1086,1087] 12 Oct 1706, in Monkton, Kent, England.

Children of William Young and An Ayling:

      i.   **Richard Young**,[846,847,848] born Sep 1707, in Bishopsgate, London, England, died Aug 1759, in Herne, Kent, England.

     ii.   **Anne Young**,[1088] born 10 Dec 1708, in Chislet, Kent, England, christened 28 Dec 1708, in Chislet, Kent, England, died 12 Jul 1780, in Chislet, Kent, England, buried 18 Jul 1780, in Chislet, Kent, England.

787. An Ayling was born May 1682, in Monkton, Kent, England, christened 10 May 1682, in Monkton, Kent, England. She married William Young[1086] 12 Oct 1706, in Monkton, Kent, England.

788. Francis Johnson was born about 1673, in London, England. He married Mary Gerford 5 Sep 1693, in Saint James Dukes Place, London, England.

Children of Francis Johnson and Mary Gerford:

      i.   **Hester Frances Johnson**,[842] born 2 Oct 1714, in Shadwell, London, England.

789. Mary Gerford was born about 1675, in England. She married Francis Johnson 5 Sep 1693, in Saint James Dukes Place, London, England.

790. Pierre Merigest Or Merignan was born about 1670, in England. He married Marie Coudere[1089] about 1693, in England.

Children of Pierre Merigest Or Merignan and Marie Coudere:

      i.   **Ester Merignac Or Merigest Or Merignan**,[1090] born 26 Oct 1694, in Westminster, London, England, christened 4 Nov 1694, in French Huguwest, Westminster, London, England.

    ii.   **Jean Merigest Or Merignan Or Merignac,**[1091] born 19 Nov 1695, in Westminster, London, England, christened 24 Nov 1695, in French Huguwest, Westminster, London, England, died before 1702, in Westminster, London, England, buried before 1702, in Westminster, London, England.

    iii.   **Tanneguy Merignacq Or Merigest Or Merignan,**[1092] born 14 Nov 1698, in Stepney, Middlesex, England, christened 17 Nov 1698, in Stepney, Middlesex, England.

    iv.   **Jean Merigest,**[849,851] born May 1702, in Westminster, London, England.

791. Marie Coudere was born about 1673, in England. She married Pierre Merigest Or Merignan[1093] about 1693, in England.

792. ____Fozeau was born about 1680, in England, died before 1750, in England. He married Fozeau about 1702, in England.

Children of Fozeau and Fozeau:

    i.   **Elizabeth Fozeau,**[849] born about 1705, in England.

793. ____Fozeau was born about 1682, in England, died about 1755, in England. She married Fozeau about 1702, in England.

794. Francis Turner was born about 1670, in London, England. He married Ann Turner[853] about 1692, in London, England.

Children of Francis Turner and Ann Turner:

    i.   **Francis Turner,**[555,852,853] born 20 Jul 1696, in Westminster, London, England.

795. Ann Turner was born about 1672, in London, England. She married Francis Turner[853] about 1692, in London, England.

796. ____Norriss was born about 1680, in England. He married Norriss about 1700, in England.

Children of Norriss and Norriss:

    i.   **Anne Norriss,**[555,852] born about 1702, in England.

797. ____Norriss was born about 1681, in England. She married Norriss about 1700, in England.

798. Peter Horsley was born about 1685, in London, England. He married Mrs Hannah Horsley[1094] about 1710, in London, England.

Children of Peter Horsley and Mrs Hannah Horsley:

     i.   **John Horsley**,[554,860] born Aug 1716, in Westminster, London, England, died 27 Nov 1777.

799. Mrs Hannah Horsley was born about 1688, in London, England. She married Peter Horsley[1094] about 1710, in London, England.

800. Henry Outfield was born about 1695, in England. He married Mrs Jane Outfield[854] about 1717, in England.

Children of Henry Outfield and Mrs Jane Outfield:

     i.   **Mary Outfield**,[554,854] born May 1718, in Canterbury, Kent, England.

801. Mrs Jane Outfield was born about 1697, in England. She married Henry Outfield[854] about 1717, in England.

802. William Stringer was born 22 Jul 1694, in Shipley, Sussex, England, died Apr 1741, in West Grinstead, Sussex, England. He married Elizabeth Lassiter 1725, in Steyning, Sussex, England.

Children of William Stringer and Elizabeth Lassiter:

     i.   **William Stringer**,[861,864] born May 1726, in Woodmancote, Sussex, England.

803. Elizabeth Lassiter was born 1697, in Findon, Sussex, England, died 1741, in West Grinstead, Sussex, England. She married William Stringer 1725, in Steyning, Sussex, England.

804. John Williams was born about 1694, in Sussex, England. He married Sarah Wease[1095,1096] 3 Dec 1730, in Arundel, Sussex, England.

Children of John Williams and Sarah Wease:

     i.   **Sarah Williams**,[861,862,863] born Feb 1731, in Arundel, Sussex, England.

805. Sarah Wease was born Dec 1695, in South Stoke, Sussex, England, christened 11 Dec 1695, in South Stoke, Sussex, England. She married John Williams[1095] 3 Dec 1730, in Arundel, Sussex, England.

806. Mathew Blandford was born about 1700, in Essex, England. He married Mary Blandford about 1720, in Essex, England.

Children of Mathew Blandford and Mary Blandford:

  i.   **Mathew Blandford**,[865,867] born Apr 1724, in Chrishall, Essex, England.

807. Mary Blandford was born about 1701, in Essex, England. She married Mathew Blandford about 1720, in Essex, England.

808. Richard Watson was born about 1705, in Essex, England. He married Watson about 1725, in Essex, England, Great Britain.

Children of Richard Watson and Watson:

  i.   **Martha Watson**,[865,866] born Apr 1727, in Broomfield, Essex, England.

809. ____Watson was born about 1707, in Essex, England, Great Britain. She married Richard Watson about 1725, in Essex, England, Great Britain.

810. William Witton was born Mar 1692, in London, England, christened 12 Mar 1692, in London St Botolph without Bishopsgate, London, England. He married Elizabeth Brashee[869,1097] 6 Aug 1719, in Westminster, London, England.

Children of William Witton and Elizabeth Brashee:

  i.   **James Whitton Or Witton**,[868,869] born Dec 1722, in London England.

811. Elizabeth Brashee was born about 1702, in London, England. She married William Witton[869,1097,1098] 6 Aug 1719, in Westminster, London, England.

812. Thomas Ellis was born Sep 1706, in London, England, christened 26 Sep 1706, in St Stephen. Coleman Street, London, England. He married Ann Bishop 1 Jul 1726, in St Stephen, Walbrook, London, England.
Notes for Thomas Ellis:

Name: Thomas Ellis Baptism Date: 26 Sep 1706 Parish: St Stephen, Coleman Street County: London Borough: City of London Parent(s):   Thomas Ellis, Elizabeth Ellis Record Type:Christening Register Type: ParisRhegister Name: Thomas Ellis Marriage Date: 1 Jul 1726 Parish: St Stephen, Walbrook County: London Borough: City of London Spouse: Ann Bishop Record Type: Marriage Register Type: ParisRhegister Name: Ann Ellis Baptism Date: 21 Jun 1727 Parish: St Botolph, Bishopsgate County: London Borough: City of London Parent(s):   Thomas Ellis, Ann Ellis Record Type: Christening Register Type: ParisRegister

Children of Thomas Ellis and Ann Bishop:

> i. **Ann Ells Or Ellis**,[868] born Jun 1727, in Bishopgate, London, England.

813. Ann Bishop was born 2 May 1704, in Clarkenwell, London, England, christened 14 May 1704, in St James, Clarkenwell, London, England. She married Thomas Ellis 1 Jul 1726, in St Stephen, Walbrook, London, England.
Notes for Ann Bishop:

Name: Ann Bishop Gender: Female Birth Date: 2 May 1704 Baptism Date: 14 May 1704 Baptism Place: Saint James,Clerkenwell,London,England Father: John Bishop Mother: Mary FHL Film Number: 08452290,476868 Name: Thomas Ellis Marriage Date: 1 Jul 1726 Parish: St Stephen, Walbrook County: London Borough: City of London Spouse: Ann Bishop Record Type: Marriage Register Type: Parish Register Name: Ann Ellis Baptism Date: 21 Jun 1727 Parish: St Botolph, Bishopsgate County: London Borough: City of London Parent(s):   Thomas Ellis, Ann Ellis Record Type: Christening Register Type: Parish Register

814. John Maier Or Mayor was born about 1695, in London, England. He married An Jones[870,1099] 1717, in St Dunstan, Stepney, London, England.

Children of John Maier Or Mayor and An Jones:

> i. **John Mayor**,[870] born Jan 1719, in London, England.
> ii. **Mary Mayor**,[1100] born Oct 1726, in Stepney, London, England, christened 25 Oct 1726, in Stepney, London, England.

815. An Jones was born about 1698, in London, England. She married John Maier Or Mayor[870,1101] 1717, in St Dunstan, Stepney, London, England.

816.   Norbury was born about 1700, in England. He married Norbury about 1722, in England.

Children of Norbury and Norbury:

> i. **Margaret Norbury**, born about 1727, in St Mary Ratherluth, Surrey, England.

817.   Norbury was born about 1702, in England. She married Norbury about 1722, in England.

818. John Hyde was born about 1700, in London, England. He married Hyde[1102] about 1725, in London, England.

Children of John Hyde and Hyde:

> i. **John Hyde**,[871,872,873] born 28 Oct 1737, in London, England.

819. ____Hyde was born about 1703, in London, England. She married John Hyde[1102] about 1725, in London, England.

820. John Roach was born about 1710, in London, England. He married Jane Gall[1103,1104] 16 Dec 1733, in St Dunstan, Stepney, London, England.

Children of John Roach and Jane Gall:

     i.   **Mary Elizabeth Roach,**[871,872] born Sep 1735, in Stepney, London, England.

821. Jane Gall was born about 1712, in London, England. She married John Roach[1103,1104] 16 Dec 1733, in St Dunstan, Stepney, London, England.

822. Thomas Rainbird Or Raynbard was born May 1699, in Walsham Le Willows, Suffolk, England, christened 28 May 1699, in Walsham Le Willows, Suffolk, England. He married Ann Bedwall[1105] 8 Mar 1718, in Groton, Suffolk, England.
Notes for Thomas Rainbird Or Raynbard:

father: Robart Rainbard mother: Ann

Children of Thomas Rainbird Or Raynbard and Ann Bedwall:

     i.   **Thomas Rainbird Or Raynbird,**[875,885,886] born Jul 1719, in Walsham Le Willows, Suffolk, England.

823. Ann Bedwall was born Mar 1699, in Walsham Le Willows, Suffolk, England, christened 10 Mar 1699, in Walsham Le Willows, Suffolk, England. She married Thomas Rainbird Or Raynbard[1106,1107] 8 Mar 1718, in Groton, Suffolk, England.
Notes for Ann Bedwall:

father: Thomas Bedwall mother: Ann

824. William Baker was born Mar 1690, in Tostock, Suffolk, England, christened 1 Apr 1690, in Tostock, Suffolk, England. He married Mary Goodchild[1108,1109,1110] 6 May 1713, in Tostock, Suffolk, England.
Notes for William Baker:

father: Will. Baker mother: Jane

Children of William Baker and Mary Goodchild:

     i.   **Mary Baker,**[874,875,876] born May 1714, in Tostock, Suffolk, England.

825. Mary Goodchild was born Mar 1692, in Pakenham, Suffolk, England, christened 20 Mar 1692, in Pakenham, Suffolk, England. She married William Baker[1108,1111] 6 May 1713, in Tostock, Suffolk, England.
Notes for Mary Goodchild:

father: Robt. Goodchild mother: Hannah

826. John Briggs was born Apr 1656, in Bishopsgate, London, England, christened 20 Apr 1656, in Bishopsgate, London, England. He was the son of Richard Briggs and Mrs Marie Briggs. He married Mrs Anne Briggs[891] about 1675, in London, England.
Notes for John Briggs:

Framework knitter

Children of John Briggs and Mrs Anne Briggs:

     i.   **John Briggs**,[887,890,891] born 5 Nov 1682, in Stepney, London, England.

827. Mrs Anne Briggs was born about 1655, in London, England. She married John Briggs[891,1112] about 1675, in London, England. He was the son of Richard Briggs and Mrs Marie Briggs.

828. Thomas Rice was born about 1670, in London, England. He married Martha Rice[1113] about 1690, in London, England.
Notes for Thomas Rice:

On daughter's baptism record shown as a carpenter

Children of Thomas Rice and Martha Rice:

     i.   **Jane Rice**,[887,888,889] born 9 Jan 1696, in Stepney, London, England.

829. Martha Rice was born about 1672, in London, England. She married Thomas Rice[1113] about 1690, in London, England.

830. William Timbrell was born about 1700, in London, England. He married Mary Timbrell[1114] about 1722, in London, England.

Children of William Timbrell and Mary Timbrell:

     i.   **William Timbrell**,[892,896,897,898] born 22 Oct 1728, in London, England, died 1774, in London, England.

831. Mary Timbrell was born about 1700, in London, England. She married William Timbrell[1114] about

1722, in London, England.

832. Hezekiah Crew was born about 1700, in England, died Jan 1773, in Westminster, London, England, buried 27 Jan 1773, in Westminster, London, England. He was the son of Crew and Crew. He married Ann Capling[1115,1116,1117] 15 Apr 1723, in Westminster, London, England. She was the daughter of David Capling and Mrs Mary Capling.

Children of Hezekiah Crew and Ann Capling:

      i.   **Sarah Crew**,[892,893,894] born Apr 1732, in Westminster, London, England, died Nov 1788, in Whitechapel, Middlesex, England.

833. Ann Capling was born 1 Nov 1700, in Westminster, London, England, christened 1 Nov 1700, in St Martin in the Fields, Westminster, London, England, died Dec 1788, in Westminster, London, England, buried 23 Dec 1788, in St James, Westminster, London, England. She was the daughter of David Capling and Mrs Mary Capling. She married Hezekiah Crew[1115,1118] 15 Apr 1723, in Westminster, London, England. He was the son of Crew and Crew.

834. Edward Giles was born 1662, in Pembury, Kent, England, christened 4 May 1662, in Lamberhurst, Kent, England, died 25 Oct 1711, in Pembury, Kent, England. He was the son of Thomas Giles and Elizabeth Streater. He married Elizabeth Foreman[1120] 3 Oct 1695, in Hadlow, Kent, England.[1119] She was the daughter of Dunston Foreman and Jane Chamberlaine.
Notes for Edward Giles:

aka: GYLES

Children of Edward Giles and Elizabeth Foreman:

      i.   **George Giles**,[899] born 1702, in Pembury, Kent, England, died 22 May 1778, in Kent, England.

835. Elizabeth Foreman was born 1675, in Kent, England, died before 1775, in England. She was the daughter of Dunston Foreman and Jane Chamberlaine. She married Edward Giles[1121] 3 Oct 1695, in Hadlow, Kent, England.[1119] He was the son of Thomas Giles and Elizabeth Streater.
Notes for Elizabeth Foreman:

Edward and Elizabeth christened four children in Pembury, Kent England : Elizabeth (1698), Susannah (1701 who died 1714), George (1702) who married twice, firstly to Mary BUTCHER or BELCHER then secondly to Hannah LAFFAM; and Mary (1705).

836. ____Lasshan was born about 1690, in Kent, England. He married Lasshan about 1712, in Kent, England.

Contents

Children of Lasshan and Lasshan:

     i.   **Hannah Lasshan**,[899] born 1718, in Pembury, Kent, England, died 22 May 1778, in Kent, England.

837. ____Lasshan was born about 1692, in Kent, England. She married Lasshan about 1712, in Kent, England.

838. John Stevens was born about 1690, in Kent, England. He married Elizabeth Deverson 14 Aug 1715, in Ramsgate, Kent, England. She was the daughter of John Deverson and Ann Wilson.

Children of John Stevens and Elizabeth Deverson:

     i.   **Daniel Stephens**, born 1715, in Ramsgate, Kent, England, christened 31 Jul 1715, in Ramsgate, Kent, England, died 11 Mar 1804, in Ramsgate, Kent, England, buried 11 Mar 1804, in Ramsgate, Kent, England.

     ii.   **Peter Stevens**,[568] born 13 Oct 1717, in Boxley, Kent, England, christened 19 Oct 1717, in Boxley, Kent, England, died Dec 1717, in Boxley, Kent, England, buried 25 Dec 1717, in Boxley, Kent, England.

     iii. **John Stevens**, born 6 Jun 1718, in Ramsgate, Kent, England.

839. Elizabeth Deverson was born about 1692, in Kent, England, christened 22 Aug 1692, in Ramsgate, Kent, England. She was the daughter of John Deverson and Ann Wilson. She married John Stevens 14 Aug 1715, in Ramsgate, Kent, England.

840. Jacob Hayward was born about 1671, in Kent, England, christened 19 Mar 1671, in Cranbrook, Kent, England. He was the son of James Hayward and Mrs Susan Hayward. He married Elizabeth Tanner[1122] 8 Feb 1697, in Marden, Kent, England.[1122] She was the daughter of James Tanner and Ann Bowden.

Children of Jacob Hayward and Elizabeth Tanner:

     i.   **Jacob Hayward**, born Dec 1698, in Marden, Kent, England, christened 25 Dec 1698, in Marden, Kent, England.

     ii.   **Elizabeth Hayward**, born May 1702, in Marden, Kent, England, christened 10 May 1702, in Marden, Kent, England.

     iii. **Sarah Hayward**,[568] born Apr 1709, in Marden, Kent, England.

841. Elizabeth Tanner was born Sep 1675, in Cranbrook, Kent, England, christened 26 Sep 1675, in Cranbrook, Kent, England. She was the daughter of James Tanner and Ann Bowden. She married Jacob Hayward[1122] 8 Feb 1697, in Marden, Kent, England.[1122] He was the son of James Hayward and Mrs Susan Hayward.

842. Edward Holmes was born Sep 1669, in Canterbury, Kent, England, christened 19 Sep 1669, in Canterbury, Kent, England, died before 1760, in England. He was the son of Edward Holmes and Ann Ashman. He married Mary Bennett 12 Mar 1695, in Canterbury, Kent, England. She was the daughter of Henry Bennet and Joane Batty.

Children of Edward Holmes and Mary Bennett:

i. **Edward Holmes**, born 12 Mar 1695, in Canterbury, Kent, England, christened 12 Mar 1695, in Canterbury, Kent, England, died about 1697, in Canterbury, Kent, England.

ii. **Mary Holmes**, born 13 Apr 1696, in Canterbury, Kent, England, christened 13 Apr 1696, in Canterbury, Kent, England. She married William Cooke about 1716, in Kent, England. William Cooke was born about 1692, in Canterbury, Kent, England.

iii. **Edward Holmes**, born 13 Jun 1698, in Canterbury, Kent, England, christened 13 Jun 1698, in Canterbury, Kent, England.

iv. **Anne Holmes**, born Nov 1700, in Canterbury, Kent, England, christened 17 Nov 1700, in Canterbury, Kent, England. She married Thomas Lucas 13 May 1722, in Canterbury, Kent, England. Thomas Lucas was born about 1697, in Canterbury, Kent, England.

v. **Thomas Holmes**, born 12 Dec 1702, in Canterbury, Kent, England, christened 12 Dec 1702, in Canterbury, Kent, England, died 28 Dec 1702, in Canterbury, Kent, England.

vi. **Thomas Holmes**, born 7 Nov 1703, in Canterbury, Kent, England, christened 7 Nov 1703, in Canterbury, Kent, England. He married Ann Atkins 10 Jun 1728, in Stanford, Kent, England. Ann Atkins was born about 1707, in Stanford, Kent, England.

vii. **James Holmes**, born 16 Jul 1710, in Dover, Kent, England, died before 1800, in England.

viii. **Elizabeth Holmes**, born 24 May 1713, in Canterbury, Kent, England, christened 24 May 1713, in Canterbury, Kent, England. She married John Crisp 9 Jul 1734, in Norwich, Norfolk, England. John Crisp was born about 1709, in Norwich, Norfolk, England.

ix. **Bennet Holmes**, born 25 Sep 1715, in Canterbury, Kent, England, christened 25 Dec 1715, in Canterbury, Kent, England, died 30 Dec 1717, in Canterbury, Kent, England.

843. Mary Bennett was born about 1670, in Sturry, Kent, England, died before 1770, in England. She was the daughter of Henry Bennet and Joane Batty. She married Edward Holmes 12 Mar 1695, in Canterbury, Kent, England. He was the son of Edward Holmes and Ann Ashman.

844. Robert Collyer was born Nov 1680, in Coldred, Kent, England, christened 6 Dec 1680, in Coldred, Kent, England, died before 1770, in England. He was the son of William Collier and Susan Birch. He married Deborah Epse[1123] 30 Sep 1712, in Hougham, Kent, England. She was the daughter of

John Epse and Mrs Ann Epse.
Notes for Robert Collyer:

C03656-1 system origin: England-ODM source film number: 355633

Children of Robert Collyer and Deborah Epse:

      i.   **Ann Collyer**,[900] born 1713, in Dover, Kent, England, died before 1810, in England.

      ii.   **Robert Collyer**,[900] born Mar 1715, in Dover, Kent, England, christened 21 Mar 1715, in Dover, Kent, England.
          Christening: 21 mar 1715 St Mary The Virgin, Dover, Kent, England C03656-1 system origin: England-ODM source film number: 355633

     iii.   **William Collyer**,[900] born 1716, in Dover, Kent, England, christened 8 Feb 1716, in Dover, Kent, England.
          Christening: 8 feb 1716 St Mary The Virgin, Dover, Kent, England C03656-1 system origin: England-ODM source film number: 355633

     iv.   **Deborah Collyer**,[900] born 1719, in Dover, Kent, England, christened 27 Dec 1719, in Dover, Kent, England.
          Christening: 27 Dec 1719 St Mary The Virgin, Dover, Kent, England C03656-1 system origin: England-ODM source film number: 355633

845. Deborah Epse was born Mar 1684, in Sutton by Dover, Kent, England, christened 13 Mar 1684, in Sutton by Dover, Kent, England, died before 1770, in England. She was the daughter of John Epse and Mrs Ann Epse. She married Robert Collyer[900,1123,1124] 30 Sep 1712, in Hougham, Kent, England. He was the son of William Collier and Susan Birch.

846. _____ Read was born about 1695, in Kent, England. He married Read about 1718, in Kent, England.

Children of Read and Read:

      i.   **Andrew Read**, born 1720, in Dover, Kent, England, died before 1820, in England.

847. _____ Read was born about 1697, in Kent, England. She married Read about 1718, in Kent, England.

848. Thomas Hawkes was born 1692, in Folkestone, Kent, England, christened 1 May 1692, in Folkestone, Kent, England, died 1771, in Folkestone, Kent, England. He was the son of Issac Hawkes and Hannah Sladden. He married Mrs Mary Hawkes about 1715, in Folkestone, Kent, England.
Notes for Thomas Hawkes:

Thomas b. 1692 at Folkestone, KEN, Sailmaker. Wife Mary. Daughter Sarah b. 1718 at Folkestone married Andrew READ 1748 at St. Mary, Dover. Thomas probably son of Isaac b. ca 1665 place unknown, and Hannah.

Children of Thomas Hawkes and Mrs Mary Hawkes:

      i.   **Sarah Hawkes**, born 1718, in Dover, Kent, England, died before 1800, in England.

849. Mrs Mary Hawkes was born about 1694, in Folkestone, Kent, England, died before 1771, in Folkestone, Kent, England. She married Thomas Hawkes about 1715, in Folkestone, Kent, England. He was the son of Issac Hawkes and Hannah Sladden.

850. ____Baldwin was born about 1680, in England. He married Baldwin about 1700, in England.

Children of Baldwin and Baldwin:

      i.   **Heny "Henry" Baldwin**,[901,902,904] born Apr 1703, in Southwark, Surrey, England.

851. ____Baldwin was born about 1682, in England. She married Baldwin about 1700, in England.

852. Daniel Laurence was born about 1671, in London, England. He married Mrs Elizabeth Laurence[1125] about 1691, in London, England.

Children of Daniel Laurence and Mrs Elizabeth Laurence:

      i.   **George Lawrence**, born Oct 1692, in England, christened 9 Nov 1692, in England.
      ii.   **Richard Laurence**, born Apr 1699, in St Sepulchre, London, England, christened 30 Apr 1699, in St Sepulchre, London, England.
      iii. **Daniel Laurence**, born Feb 1701, in St Sepulchre, London, England, christened 2 Mar 1701, in St Sepulchre, London, England.
      iv. **Elizabeth Laurence**,[901,902,903] born Jul 1704, in London, England.

853. Mrs Elizabeth Laurence was born about 1672, in London, England. She married Daniel Laurence[1125] about 1691, in London, England.

854. John Smith was born about 1670, in England. He married Mrs Alice Smith[1126] about 1689, in England.

Children of John Smith and Mrs Alice Smith:

      i.   **Robert Smith**,[905] born 5 Jan 1690, in Westminster, London, England.

855. Mrs Alice Smith was born about 1672, in England. She married John Smith[1126] about 1689, in England.

856. ____Browes was born about 1665, in England. He married Browes about 1687, in England.

Children of Browes and Browes:

      i.   **Susanna Browes**,[905] born about 1690, in London, England.

857. ____Browes was born about 1668, in England. She married Browes about 1687, in England.

858. Thomas Dixon was born about 1685, in England. He married Mrs Elizabeth Dixon[1127] about 1709, in England.

Children of Thomas Dixon and Mrs Elizabeth Dixon:

      i.   **Thomas Dixon**,[908,911] born Feb 1710, in Edmonton, Middlesex, England.

859. Mrs Elizabeth Dixon was born about 1687, in London, England. She married Thomas Dixon[1128] about 1709, in England.

860. Elijah Empey was born about 1680, in England. He married Mary Empey[1129] about 1705, in London, England.

Children of Elijah Empey and Mary Empey:

      i.   **Mary Empey**,[908,909] born Feb 1711, in Westminster, London, England.

861. Mary Empey was born about 1685, in London, England. She married Elijah Empey[1129] about 1705, in London, England.

862. ____Miller was born about 1685, in London, England. He married Miller about 1708, in London, England.

Children of Miller and Miller:

      i.   **Thomas Miller**,[912] born about 1720, in England.

863. ____Miller was born about 1687, in London, England. She married Miller about 1708, in London, England.

864. ____Buxton was born about 1695, in England. He married Buxton about 1715, in England.

Children of Buxton and Buxton:

      i.   **Margaret Buxton**,[912] born about 1722, in England.

865. ____Buxton was born about 1698, in England. She married Buxton about 1715, in England.

866. John Wine was born about 1708, in Shoreditch, London, England, died before 1800, in England. He married Elizabeth Hill[1130] 2 Dec 1736, in Westminster, London, England.

Children of John Wine and Elizabeth Hill:

     i.   **Henry Wine,**[913,914] born Nov 1737, in Stepney, Middlesex, England, died before 1820, in England.

867. Elizabeth Hill was born about 1710, in Shoreditch, London, England, died before 1810, in England. She married John Wine[1130] 2 Dec 1736, in Westminster, London, England.

868. ____Smith was born about 1710, in England, christened about 1710, in England. He married Smith about 1735, in England.

Children of Smith and Smith:

     i.   **Mary Smith,**[913] born about 1740, in England, died before 1840, in England.

869. ____Smith was born about 1705, in England. She married Smith about 1735, in England.

870. Charles Vanner was born 1715, in England, christened 14 Jun 1715, in Middlesex, England, died before 1815, in England. He was the son of Jasper Venner and Mrs Mary Venner. He married Vanner about 1736, in England.

Children of Charles Vanner and Vanner:

     i.   **Charles Venner,**[915] born about 1737, in London, England, died before 1820, in London, England.

871. ____Vanner was born about 1718, in England, died before 1800, in England. She married Charles Vanner about 1736, in England. He was the son of Jasper Venner and Mrs Mary Venner.

872. John Wie Or Way was born about 1700, in England. He married Wie Or Way[1131] 11 Aug 1720, in London St Mary Somerset with St Mary Mounthaw, London, England.

Children of John Wie Or Way and Wie Or Way:

     i.   **Martha Wie Or Way,**[915,916] born Apr 1724, in London, England, died before 1800, in London, England.

873. ____Wie Or Way was born about 1702, in London, England. She married John Wie Or Way[1131] 11 Aug 1720, in London St Mary Somerset with St Mary Mounthaw, London, England.

874. William Richardson was born about 1700, in London, England. He married Mrs Mary Richardson about 1730, in London, England.

Children of William Richardson and Mrs Mary Richardson:

  i.   **James Richardson**,[919] born Dec 1734, in Stepney, London, England.

875. Mrs Mary Richardson was born about 1701, in London, England. She married William Richardson about 1730, in London, England.

876. Hugh Jones was born about 1710, in London, England. He married Elizabeth Debell[1132] 30 May 1734, in Saint Katherine By The Tower, London, England.

Children of Hugh Jones and Elizabeth Debell:

  i.   **Elizabeth Jones**,[917,918] born May 1735, in London, England.

877. Elizabeth Debell was born about 1712, in London, England. She married Hugh Jones[1132] 30 May 1734, in Saint Katherine By The Tower, London, England.

878. John Yeates was born about 1715, in England. He married Mrs Elizabeth Yeates about 1734, in England.

Children of John Yeates and Mrs Elizabeth Yeates:

  i.   **William Yates**,[920,921,922] born 6 Jan 1735, in Westminster, London, England.

879. Mrs Elizabeth Yeates was born about 1717, in England. She married John Yeates about 1734, in England.

880. ____Jones was born about 1705, in England. He married Jones about 1730, in England.

Children of Jones and Jones:

  i.   **Mary Jones**,[920] born about 1742, in London, England.

881. ____Jones was born about 1707, in England. She married Jones about 1730, in England.

882. ____Rapley was born about 1700, in London, England. He married Rapley about 1722, in England.

Children of Rapley and Rapley:

      i.   **Jeremiah Rapley**,[923,932] born about 1725, in England.

883. ____Rapley was born about 1702, in London, England. She married Rapley about 1722, in England.

884. John Graham was born Sep 1700, in Westminster, London, England, christened 13 Sep 1700, in Westminster, London, England. He was the son of Robert Graham and Barbara Graham. He married Mary Partridge[1133,1134,1135] 22 Jun 1718, in Westminster, London, England. She was the daughter of Richard Partridge and Alice Longmore.

Children of John Graham and Mary Partridge:

      i.   **Mary Graham**,[923,924,925] born Jul 1723, in Westminster, London, England.

885. Mary Partridge was born Aug 1699, in London, England, christened 6 Sep 1699, in London, England. She was the daughter of Richard Partridge and Alice Longmore. She married John Graham[1133,1136,1137] 22 Jun 1718, in Westminster, London, England. He was the son of Robert Graham and Barbara Graham.

886. John Roberts was born about 1710, in London, England. He married Ann Rumboll[1138] 5 Oct 1733, in London St Bride, London, England.

Children of John Roberts and Ann Rumboll:

      i.   **Benjamin Roberts**,[939,940] born Apr 1734, in Saint Mary Somerset, London, England.

887. Ann Rumboll was born about 1712, in London, England. She married John Roberts[1138] 5 Oct 1733, in London St Bride, London, England.

888. ____Hawkins was born about 1700, in England. He married Hawkins about 1730, in England.

Children of Hawkins and Hawkins:

      i.   **Sarah Or Sara Hawkins**,[933] born about 1735, in Westminster, London, England.

889. ____Hawkins was born about 1702, in England. She married Hawkins about 1730, in England.

890. Milford Mott was born Feb 1680, in Aldgate, London, England, christened Mar 1680, in Aldgate, London, England. He was the son of John Mott and Katherine Collins. He married Elizabeth Hubbard[1139,1140] 5 Aug 1718, in Westminster, London, England.

Children of Milford Mott and Elizabeth Hubbard:

     i.   **Samuel Mott**,[941,944,945] born 25 Apr 1726, in St Sepulchre, London, England.

891. Elizabeth Hubbard was born 1682, in London, England. She married Milford Mott[1139,1140,1141] 5 Aug 1718, in Westminster, London, England. He was the son of John Mott and Katherine Collins.

892. Richard Purviss was born about 1700, in London, England. He married Margaret Purviss[1142] about 1722, in London, England.

Children of Richard Purviss and Margaret Purviss:

     i.   **Mary Purviss**,[941,942,943] born Jan 1727, in Blackfriers, London, England.

893. Margaret Purviss was born about 1702, in London, England. She married Richard Purviss[1142] about 1722, in London, England.

894. John Steel was born about 1685, in London, England. He married Mrs Sarah Steel[1143] 15 Feb 1708, in Fleet, London, England.

Children of John Steel and Mrs Sarah Steel:

     i.   **John Steel**,[946,956] born 16 Aug 1707, in London, England.

895. Mrs Sarah Steel was born about 1687, in London, England. She married John Steel[1143] 15 Feb 1708, in Fleet, London, England.

896. ____Collings was born about 1690, in England. He married Collings about 1713, in England.

Children of Collings and Collings:

     i.   **Hannah Or Sarah Collings**,[946,947] born about 1716, in England.

897. ____Collings was born about 1692, in England. She married Collings about 1713, in England.

Generation No. 11

898. Thomas Aldworth was born Oct 1631, in Wantage, Berkshire, England, christened 10 Oct 1631, in Wantage, Berkshire, England, died 13 Oct 1681, in Wantage, Berkshire, England, buried 15 Oct 1681, in Wantage, Berkshire, England. He was the son of Robert Aldworth and Leticia Barlow. He married (1) Katherine Tyrrald[1144] 29 Apr 1669, in Sutton Courtenay, Berkshire, England. He married (2) Mrs Joane Aldworth about 1652, in Wantage, Berkshire, England.
Notes for Thomas Aldworth:

SS Peter & Paul, Wantage, buried in Chancell

Children of Thomas Aldworth and Katherine Tyrrald:

    i.   **William Aldworth**, born about 1670, in Wantage, Berkshire, England. He married Mary Coldry 6 Nov 1693, in Appleton, Berkshire, England. Mary Coldry was born about 1675, in Appleton, Berkshire, England.

    ii.   **Mary Aldworth**, born 15 Apr 1673, in Drayton, Berkshire, England, christened 15 Apr 1673, in Drayton, Berkshire, England. She married Richard Spindler 6 Oct 1692, in Berkshire, England. Richard Spindler was born about 1670, in Berkshire, England.

    iii.   **Thomas Aldworth**, born Aug 1677, in Drayton, Berkshire, England, died Jul 1710, in Tubney, Berkshire, England.

Children of Thomas Aldworth and Mrs Joane Aldworth:

    i.   **Joan Aldworth**, born 1653, in Wantage, Berkshire, England. She married Thomas Whitethorne 16 Jan 1674, in Wantage, Berkshire, England. Thomas Whitethorne was born 1645, in Berkshire, England, christened 15 Dec 1645, in Wantage, Berkshire, England, died 20 Jan 1698, in Wantage, Berkshire, England, buried 20 Jan 1698, in Wantage, Berkshire, England.
Notes for Thomas Whitethorne: aka Witehorn

    ii.   **Martha Aldworth**, born 11 Aug 1658, in Wantage, Berkshire, England, christened 28 Aug 1658, in Wantage, Berkshire, England. She married John Steevens 8 Oct 1691, in Wantage, Berkshire, England. John Steevens was born 12 Jul 1657, in Thatcham, Berkshire, England.
Notes for John Steevens: aka

    iii.   **Thomas Aldworth**, born 23 Jul 1662, in Wantage, Berkshire, England, christened 10 Aug 1662, in Wantage, Berkshire, England.

    iv.   **John Aldworth**, born 30 Dec 1664, in Wantage, Berkshire, England, christened 29 Jan 1665, in Wantage, Berkshire, England.

    v.   **Dennis Aldworth**, born 6 Jul 1669, in Wantage, Berkshire, England, christened 1

Aug 1669, in Wantage, Berkshire, England.

    vi.   **Nicholas Aldworth**, born 26 Jul 1671, in Wantage, Berkshire, England, christened 7 Aug 1671, in Wantage, Berkshire, England.

    vii.   **Jane Aldworth**, born 12 Nov 1673, in Wantage, Berkshire, England, christened 16 Nov 1673, in Wantage, Berkshire, England.

    viii.   **Sarah Aldworth**, born 14 Jun 1675, in Wantage, Berkshire, England, christened 14 Jun 1675, in Wantage, Berkshire, England.

899. Katherine Tyrrald was born about 1635, in Berkshire, England, died Dec 1683, in Grove, Wantage, Berkshire, England, buried 24 Dec 1683, in Wantage, Berkshire, England. She married Thomas Aldworth[1144,1145] 29 Apr 1669, in Sutton Courtenay, Berkshire, England. He was the son of Robert Aldworth and Leticia Barlow.

900. Thomas Collings was born about 1650, in Berkshire, England, died before 1750, in England. He married Collings about 1675, in Berkshire, England.

Children of Thomas Collings and Collings:

    i.   **Martha Collings**, born May 1680, in East Hanney, Berkshire, England, died Aug 1710, in Tubney, Berkshire, England.

901. ____Collings was born about 1654, in England. She married Thomas Collings about 1675, in Berkshire, England.

902. Richard Baker was born about 1640, in Berkshire, England, died before 1735, in England. He married Mrs Jane Baker about 1660, in Berkshire, England.

Children of Richard Baker and Mrs Jane Baker:

    i.   **John Baker**,[957] born 16 Oct 1667, in Appleford, Berkshire, England, died before 1766, in England.

903. Mrs Jane Baker was born about 1644, in Berkshire, England, died before 1744, in England. She married Richard Baker about 1660, in Berkshire, England.

904. Thomas Townshend was born about 1645, in Standlake, Oxfordshire, England. He married Mrs Elizabeth Townsend about 1670, in Witney, Oxfordshire, England.

Children of Thomas Townshend and Mrs Elizabeth Townsend:

    i.   **William Townshend**, born Dec 1672, in Standlake, Oxfordshire, England.

905. Mrs Elizabeth Townsend was born about 1647, in Oxfordshire, England. She married Thomas

Townshend about 1670, in Witney, Oxfordshire, England.

906. John Carter was born about 1640, in Oxfordshire, England, died before 1700, in Northmoor, Oxfordshire, England. He was the son of Carter and Carter. He married Carter[1146,1147] about 1662, in Oxfordshire, England.

Children of John Carter and Carter:

      i.   **Mary Carter**, born Aug 1666, in Woodstock, Oxfordshire, England.

907. ____Carter was born about 1640, in Northmoor, Berkshire, England, United Kingdom, died Dec 1700, in Northmoor, Oxfordshire, England, buried 19 Dec 1700, in Northmoor, Oxfordshire, England. She married John Carter[1146,1148] about 1662, in Oxfordshire, England. He was the son of Carter and Carter.

908. Thomas Turner was born about 1630, in Oxfordshire, England. He married Turner about 1653, in Oxfordshire, England.

Children of Thomas Turner and Turner:

      i.   **Thomas Turner,**[958,959] born Sep 1656, in Witney, Oxfordshire, England.
      ii.   **Charles Turner,**[1149] born Mar 1659, in Witney, Oxfordshire, England, christened 6 Mar 1659, in Witney, Oxfordshire, England.
      iii.   **Adam Turner,**[1150] born Apr 1661, in Hailey, Oxfordshire, England, christened 14 Apr 1661, in Hailey, Oxfordshire, England.
      iv.   **William Turner,**[1151] born Sep 1667, in Witney, Oxfordshire, England, christened 29 Sep 1667, in Witney, Oxfordshire, England.
      v.   **Elizabeth Turner,**[1152] born Oct 1672, in Witney, Oxfordshire, England, christened 1 Nov 1672, in Witney, Oxfordshire, England.

909. ____Turner was born about 1632, in Oxfordshire, England. She married Thomas Turner[959] about 1653, in Oxfordshire, England.

910. Edward Gryme was born about 1630, in Oxfordshire, England, died Oct 1708, in Bicester, Oxfordshire, England, buried 27 Oct 1708, in Bicester, Oxfordshire, England. He married Gryme about 1650, in Oxfordshire, England.

Children of Edward Gryme and Gryme:

      i.   **Elizabeth Gryme,**[961,962] born Sep 1657, in Bicester, Oxfordshire, England.

911. ____Gryme was born about 1632, in Oxfordshire, England. She married Edward Gryme[962,1153] about 1650, in Oxfordshire, England.

912. Stephen Cockin was born Aug 1581, in Upper Heyford, Oxfordshire, England, christened 13 Sep 1581, in Upper Heyford, Oxfordshire, England. He was the son of Thomas Cockinges and Elena Endall. He married Susan Haynes[1154,1155] 3 Oct 1620, in Upper Heyford, Oxfordshire, England.

Children of Stephen Cockin and Susan Haynes:

    i.   **Ellen Cockens**, born Nov 1627, in Kirtlington, Oxfordshire, England, christened 11 Nov 1627, in Kirtlington, Oxfordshire, England.

    ii.   **Margaret Cockin**, born Oct 1628, in Steeple Aston, Oxfordshire, England, christened 2 Nov 1628, in Steeple Aston, Oxfordshire, England.

    iii.   **Hannah Cockin**, born Mar 1630, in Steeple Aston, Oxfordshire, England, christened 28 Mar 1630, in Steeple Aston, Oxfordshire, England.

    iv.   **Agnes Cockins**, born Jun 1631, in Upper Heyford, Oxfordshire, England, christened 29 Jun 1631, in Upper Heyford, Oxfordshire, England.

    v.   **Anthony Cockins**,[963] born May 1633, in Upper Heyford, Oxfordshire, England, died Jun 1705, in Tackley, Oxfordshire, England.

    vi.   **Stephen Cockins**, born Dec 1635, in Upper Heyford, Oxfordshire, England, christened 26 Dec 1635, in Upper Heyford, Oxfordshire, England.

913. Susan Haynes was born about 1599, in Upper Heyford, Oxfordshire, England, died Dec 1649, in Upper Heyford, Oxfordshire, England, buried 20 Dec 1649, in Upper Heyford, Oxfordshire, England. She married Stephen Cockin[1154] 3 Oct 1620, in Upper Heyford, Oxfordshire, England. He was the son of Thomas Cockinges and Elena Endall.

914. Robert Howse was born Sep 1607, in Upper Heyford, Oxfordshire, England, christened 27 Sep 1607, in Upper Heyford, Oxfordshire, England, died Jan 1682, in Upper Heyford, Oxfordshire, England, buried 7 Jan 1682, in Upper Heyford, Oxfordshire, England. He was the son of Thomas Howse and Susan Timmes. He married Bridget Jelks[1156] 23 Feb 1632, in Oxford, Oxfordshire, England.

Children of Robert Howse and Bridget Jelks:

    i.   **Elizabeth Howse**,[963] born Aug 1638, in Upper Heyford, Oxfordshire, England, died Mar 1702, in Oxfordshire, England.

915. Bridget Jelks was born about 1611, in Great Tew, Oxfordshire, England, died 1 Oct 1670, in Upper Heyford, Oxfordshire, England, buried 11 Oct 1670, in Upper Heyford, Oxfordshire, England. She married Robert Howse[1156] 23 Feb 1632, in Oxford, Oxfordshire, England. He was the son of Thomas Howse and Susan Timmes.

916. Roger Venimore was born about 1557, in Wendlebury, Oxfordshire, England, died 26 Mar 1619, in Wendlebury, Oxfordshire, England, buried 26 Mar 1619, in Wendlebury, Oxfordshire, England. He was the son of William Fenimore and Mrs Alice Fenimore. He married Mrs Marian Venimore before 1582, in Wendlebury, Oxfordshire, England.

Children of Roger Venimore and Mrs Marian Venimore:

    i.   **Christopher Vennimore**,[964,965] born Feb 1596, in Wendlebury, Oxfordshire, England.

917. Mrs Marian Venimore was born about 1561, in Wendlebury, Oxfordshire, England, died 27 Apr 1635, in Wendlebury, Oxfordshire, England, buried 27 Apr 1635, in Wendlebury, Oxfordshire, England. She married Roger Venimore[965] before 1582, in Wendlebury, Oxfordshire, England. He was the son of William Fenimore and Mrs Alice Fenimore.

918. Anthonie Watt was born 1588, in Kirtlington, Oxfordshire, England. He married Alice Ginkins[1157] 11 Nov 1613, in Kirtlington, Oxfordshire, England.

Children of Anthonie Watt and Alice Ginkins:

    i.   **Margery Watts**,[964] born Aug 1614, in Kirtlington, Oxfordshire, England, died Apr 1682, in Kirtlington, Oxfordshire, England.

919. Alice Ginkins was born 1592, in Kirtlington, Oxfordshire, England, died Jul 1633, in Kirtlington, Oxfordshire, England, buried 25 Jul 1633, in Kirtlington, Oxfordshire, England. She married Anthonie Watt[1157] 11 Nov 1613, in Kirtlington, Oxfordshire, England.

920. ____Windows was born about 1635, in Oxfordshire, England. He married Windows about 1659, in Oxfordshire, England.

Children of Windows and Windows:

    i.   **John Windows**,[966] born about 1660, in Oxfordshire, England.

921. ____Windows was born about 1638, in Oxfordshire, England. She married Windows about 1659, in Oxfordshire, England.

922. Richard Grimsher was born about 1640, in England, died Dec 1682, in Bampton, Oxfordshire, England, buried 3 Jan 1683, in Bampton, Oxfordshire, England. He married Mrs Ann Grimsher[1158] about 1662, in England.

Children of Richard Grimsher and Mrs Ann Grimsher:

    i.   **Bartholemew Grimsher**,[967] born Aug 1667, in Bampton, Oxfordshire, England, died Dec 1731, in Bampton, Oxfordshire, England.
    ii. **Ann Grimsher**,[1159] born Nov 1669, in Bampton, Oxfordshire, England, christened 17 Nov 1669, in Bampton, Oxfordshire, England, died Dec 1690, in Bampton, Oxfordshire, England, buried 10 Dec 1690, in Bampton, Oxfordshire, England.

    iii.   **Hannah Grimsher**,[1159] born Nov 1669, in Bampton, Oxfordshire, England, christened 17 Nov 1669, in Bampton, Oxfordshire, England, died Dec 1690, in Bampton, Oxfordshire, England, buried 10 Dec 1690, in Bampton, Oxfordshire, England.
        twin of Ann

    iv.   **Allis Grimsher**,[1160] born Sep 1674, in Bampton, Oxfordshire, England, christened 11 Sep 1674, in Bampton, Oxfordshire, England, died Dec 1682, in Bampton, Oxfordshire, England, buried Dec 1682, in Bampton, Oxfordshire, England.

    v.   **Richard Grimsher**,[1161] born Dec 1676, in Bampton, Oxfordshire, England, christened 14 Dec 1676, in Bampton, Oxfordshire, England, died Feb 1706, in Bampton, Oxfordshire, England, buried 23 Feb 1706, in Bampton, Oxfordshire, England.

923. Mrs Ann Grimsher was born about 1644, in Oxfordshire, England, died Jun 1704, in Bampton, Oxfordshire, England, buried 4 Jul 1704, in Bampton, Oxfordshire, England. She married Richard Grimsher[1162] about 1662, in England.

924. Robert Hawkins was born 1655, in Shellingford, Berkshire, England, christened 25 Feb 1655, in Shellingford, Berkshire, England, died Jun 1688, in Shellingford, Berkshire, England, buried 8 Jun 1688, in Shellingford, Berkshire, England. He was the son of John Hawkins and Joan Shepperd. He married Eleanor Tubbs 16 Jan 1675, in East Lockinge, Berkshire, England. She was the daughter of Thomas Tubbs and Eleanor Jennings.

Children of Robert Hawkins and Eleanor Tubbs:

    i.   **Elizabeth Hawkins**, born 1676, in East Lockinge, Berkshire, England, christened 2 Feb 1676, in East Lockinge, Berkshire, England.

    ii.   **John Hawkins**, born 1679, in Shellingford, Berkshire, England, died 1747, in Little Coxwell, Berkshire, England.

    iii.   **Robert Hawkins**, born 1684, in Shellingford, Berkshire, England, christened 19 Oct 1684, in Shellingford, Berkshire, England.

925. Eleanor Tubbs was born Mar 1653, in East Lockinge, Berkshire, England, christened 1 Apr 1653, in East Lockinge, Berkshire, England, died Feb 1729, in Shellingford, Berkshire, England, buried 3 Feb 1729, in Shellingford, Berkshire, England. She was the daughter of Thomas Tubbs and Eleanor Jennings. She married Robert Hawkins 16 Jan 1675, in East Lockinge, Berkshire, England. He was the son of John Hawkins and Joan Shepperd.

926. Francis Webb was born 1650, in Berkshire, England. He was the son of Francis Webb and Webb. He married Ann Boyce about 1675, in Berkshire, England. She was the daughter of Richard Boyce and Ann Iles.

Children of Francis Webb and Ann Boyce:

      i.   **Ann Webb**, born Jun 1678, in Little Coxwell, Berkshire, England.

927. Ann Boyce was born 1655, in Little Coxwell, Berkshire, England. She was the daughter of Richard Boyce and Ann Iles. She married Francis Webb about 1675, in Berkshire, England. He was the son of Francis Webb and Webb.

928. William Alder was born 6 Oct 1656, in Stanford in the Vale, Berkshire, England, christened 13 Nov 1656, in Goosey, Berkshire, England. He was the son of William Alder and Edyth Stanbrooke. He married Katherine Wythers[1163] 16 Oct 1681, in Stanford in the Vale, Berkshire, England.
Notes for William Alder:

William Alder (senior) was a widower on his marriage to Katherine Wythers 16 Oct 1681

Children of William Alder and Katherine Wythers:

      i.   **William Alder**,[968,969] born Aug 1683, in Denchworth, Berkshire, England.

929. Katherine Wythers was born about 1662, in Berkshire, England. She married William Alder[1163,1164,1165] 16 Oct 1681, in Stanford in the Vale, Berkshire, England. He was the son of William Alder and Edyth Stanbrooke.

930. John Fairbeard was born about 1600, in Oxfordshire, England, died May 1659, in Northmoor, Oxfordshire, England, buried 2 Jun 1659, in Northmoor, Oxfordshire, England. He married Mrs Mabell Fairbeard[1166] about 1625, in Oxfordshire, England.

Children of John Fairbeard and Mrs Mabell Fairbeard:

      i.   **John Fairbeard**,[1167] born about 1625, in Oxfordshire, England, died before 1668, in Oxfordshire, England. He married Fairbeard[1168] about 1650, in Oxfordshire, England. Fairbeard was born about 1626, in Oxfordshire, England, died Dec 1668, in Northmoor, Oxfordshire, England, buried 11 Dec 1668, in Northmoor, Oxfordshire, England.
      ii.   **Henrie Fairbeard**, born about 1630, in Northmoor, Oxfordshire, England, died Nov 1681, in Northmoor, Oxfordshire, England.
      iii. **Justinion Fairbeard**,[1169] born about 1632, in Oxfordshire, England, died Aug 1677, in Northmoor, Oxfordshire, England, buried 14 Aug 1677, in Northmoor, Oxfordshire, England.

931. Mrs Mabell Fairbeard was born about 1602, in Oxfordshire, England, died Dec 1658, in Northmoor, Oxfordshire, England, buried 14 Dec 1658, in Northmoor, Oxfordshire, England. She married John Fairbeard[1170] about 1625, in Oxfordshire, England.

932. Richard Stone was born about 1590, in Berkshire, England, buried 3 Nov 1616, in Longworth, Berkshire, England. He was the son of Richard Stone and Elizabeth Flexney. He married Ann Banner 22 Oct 1615, in Longworth, Berkshire, England.

Children of Richard Stone and Ann Banner:

    i.   **Jane Stone**, born Oct 1614, in Longworth, Berkshire, England, christened 9 Oct 1614, in Longworth, Berkshire, England.

    ii.   **Jone Stone**, born Feb 1615, in Longworth, Berkshire, England, christened 18 Feb 1615, in Longworth, Berkshire, England.

    iii.   **Richard Stone**,[983] born 3 Apr 1617, in Longworth, Berkshire, England, died before 1700, in England.

933. Ann Banner was born about 1592, in Berkshire, England. She married Richard Stone 22 Oct 1615, in Longworth, Berkshire, England. He was the son of Richard Stone and Elizabeth Flexney.

934. William Green was born about 1590, in Wantage, Berkshire, England. He married Marie Doe 3 Jul 1613, in Wantage, Berkshire, England.

Children of William Green and Marie Doe:

    i.   **William Green**, born Mar 1622, in Longworth, Berkshire, England, christened 16 Mar 1622, in Longworth, Berkshire, England.

    ii.   **Sibil Green**,[983] born about 1625, in Longworth, Berkshire, England, died before 1725, in England.

    iii.   **Mary Green**,[1171] born Jan 1626, in Standlake, Oxfordshire, England, christened 29 Jan 1626, in Standlake, Oxfordshire, England.

    iv.   **Henry Green**, born Nov 1628, in Kingston Bagpuize, Berkshire, England, christened 26 Nov 1628, in Kingston Bagpuize, Berkshire, England.

935. Marie Doe was born about 1591, in Berkshire, England. She married William Green 3 Jul 1613, in Wantage, Berkshire, England.

936. Thomas Onion was born Sep 1602, in Hinton Waldrist, Berkshire, England, christened 12 Sep 1602, in Hinton Waldrist, Berkshire, England, died Jul 1686, in Hinton Waldrist, Berkshire, England, buried 22 Jul 1686, in Hinton Waldrist, Berkshire, England. He was the son of Thomas Onion and Agnes Kimber. He married (1) Jane Southby 22 Jan 1626, in Longworth, Berkshire, England. He married (2) Mrs Elizabeth Onion about 1631, in Berkshire, England.

Children of Thomas Onion and Jane Southby:

    i.   **Hannah Onion Or Verinon**, born Sep 1630, in Longworth, Berkshire, England, christened 12 Sep 1630, in Longworth, Berkshire, England.

longworth parish records

Children of Thomas Onion and Mrs Elizabeth Onion:

> i. **Thomas Onion Or Anyon**, born Aug 1633, in Standlake, Oxfordshire, England, died Sep 1686, in Hinton Waldrist, Berkshire, England.
>
> ii. **Richard Onion Or Anyon**, born Aug 1636, in Standlake, Oxfordshire, England, christened 4 Sep 1636, in Standlake, Oxfordshire, England.
> Standlake parish records
>
> iii. **Katherine Onion Or Anyon**, born Oct 1637, in Standlake, Oxfordshire, England, christened 5 Nov 1637, in Standlake, Oxfordshire, England.
> Standlake parish records

937. Mrs Elizabeth Onion was born about 1610, in Berkshire, England. She married Thomas Onion[1172] about 1631, in Berkshire, England. He was the son of Thomas Onion and Agnes Kimber.

938. William Gilkes was born about 1611, in Banbury, Oxfordshire, England, died Sep 1643, in Banbury, Oxfordshire, England, buried 23 Sep 1643, in Banbury, Oxfordshire, England. He married Mary Cooke Or Crooke 28 Jan 1632, in Banbury, Oxfordshire, England.
Notes for William Gilkes:

Parish records for Banbury, Oxfordshire, England show his as a Mercer (a specialist in silks and expensive material) - name spelled GYLKS He died when his 2nd son named william was born.

Children of William Gilkes and Mary Cooke Or Crooke:

> i. **William Gilkes**, born Apr 1633, in Banbury, Oxfordshire, England, christened 28 Apr 1633, in Banbury, Oxfordshire, England, died Feb 1642, in Banbury, Oxfordshire, England, buried 26 Feb 1642, in Banbury, Oxfordshire, England.
> Parish records for Banbury, Oxfordshire, England died 1 month before 10th birthday
>
> ii. **Stephen Gilkes Or Jelkes**,[988] born Jan 1635, in Bloxham, Oxfordshire, England.
>
> iii. **Mary Gilkes**, born Sep 1637, in Banbury, Oxfordshire, England, christened 5 Sep 1637, in Banbury, Oxfordshire, England. She married Richard Calcot 10 Nov 1664, in Deddingtony, Oxfordshire, England. Richard Calcot was born 28 Mar 1641, in Wigginton, Oxfordshire, England, christened 28 Mar 1641, in Wigginton, Oxfordshire, England.
> Parish records for Banbury, Oxfordshire, England
> Notes for Richard Calcot: Parish records for Deddington, Oxfordshire (Marriages) Shown as living in Wigington (WIGGINTON) 6 miles from Deddington Baptism record Parish records for Wigginton, Oxfordshire - Richard CALCOTT son of James and Margaret 28 Mar 1641 rest of siblings shown as CALCOT
>
> iv. **Thomas Gilkes**, born Aug 1639, in Banbury, Oxfordshire, England, christened 6

Aug 1639, in Banbury, Oxfordshire, England.
Parish records for Banbury, Oxfordshire, England

v. **Martha Gilkes**, born Jun 1641, in Banbury, Oxfordshire, England, christened 29 Jun 1641, in Banbury, Oxfordshire, England, died Nov 1643, in Banbury, Oxfordshire, England, buried 27 Nov 1643, in Banbury, Oxfordshire, England. Parish records for Banbury, Oxfordshire, England (Named spelled GYLKES) She died just 2 months after her father died.

vi. **William Gilkes**, born Mar 1643, in Banbury, Oxfordshire, England, christened 26 Apr 1643, in Banbury, Oxfordshire, England. Parish records for Banbury, Oxfordshire, England - named spelled GYLKES

939. Mary Cooke Or Crooke was born Mar 1613, in Banbury, Oxfordshire, England, christened 14 Mar 1613, in Banbury, Oxfordshire, England. She married William Gilkes 28 Jan 1632, in Banbury, Oxfordshire, England.
Notes for Mary Cooke Or Crooke:

Parish records for Banbury, Oxfordshire, England Name recorded as COOK (E), CRO(O)KE daughter of Richard Moved to Bloxham after husbands death (shown on Parish records for Banbury, Oxfordshire, England May 1654- ref to Son's int marriage.

940. Martyn Swifte was born about 1590, in Oxfordshire, England. He was the son of Robert Swifte and Swifte. He married Ann Ripingale[1173] 29 Jun 1622, in Adderbury, Oxfordshire, England.

Children of Martyn Swifte and Ann Ripingale:

i. **Edmund Swifte**,[1174] born May 1623, in Adderbury, Oxfordshire, England.
ii. **Robert Swifte**,[1175] born Nov 1624, in Adderbury, Oxfordshire, England, christened 5 Dec 1624, in Adderbury, Oxfordshire, England.
iii. **Martine Swifte**,[1176] born Feb 1627, in Adderbury, Oxfordshire, England, christened 23 Feb 1627, in Adderbury, Oxfordshire, England.
iv. **George Swifte**,[1177] born Feb 1630, in Adderbury, Oxfordshire, England, christened 2 May 1630, in Adderbury, Oxfordshire, England.
v. **Robert Swifte**,[990,991,992] born 21 Aug 1632, in Adderbury, Oxfordshire, England.
vi. **Ann Swifte**,[1178] born Mar 1634, in Adderbury, Oxfordshire, England, christened 5 Apr 1634, in Adderbury, Oxfordshire, England.

941. Ann Ripingale was born about 1599, in Oxfordshire, England. She married Martyn Swifte[1179] 29 Jun 1622, in Adderbury, Oxfordshire, England. He was the son of Robert Swifte and Swifte.

942. Timothy Poulton was born Apr 1613, in Adderbury, Oxfordshire, England, christened 17 Apr 1613, in Adderbury, Oxfordshire, England. He was the son of William Poulton and Mable Mathewe. He married Mrs Joyce Poulton[1180] about 1640, in Adderbury, Oxfordshire, England.

Children of Timothy Poulton and Mrs Joyce Poulton:

  i. **John Poulton**,[1180] born Jul 1641, in Adderbury, Oxfordshire, England, christened 7 Jul 1641, in Adderbury, Oxfordshire, England.

  ii. **William Poulton**,[1181] born Apr 1644, in Adderbury, Oxfordshire, England, christened 14 Apr 1644, in Adderbury, Oxfordshire, England.

  iii. **Joyce Poulton**,[989,990] born Oct 1646, in Adderbury, Oxfordshire, England.

  iv. **Richard Poulton**,[1182] born Feb 1649, in Adderbury, Oxfordshire, England, christened 20 Feb 1649, in Adderbury, Oxfordshire, England.

  v. **Timothye Poulton**,[1183,1184] born Jul 1651, in Adderbury, Oxfordshire, England, christened 27 Jul 1651, in Adderbury, Oxfordshire, England, died Sep 1700, in Adderbury, Oxfordshire, England, buried 27 Sep 1700, in Adderbury, Oxfordshire, England.

  vi. **Thomas Poulton**,[1185] born Mar 1654, in Adderbury, Oxfordshire, England, christened 12 Mar 1654, in Adderbury, Oxfordshire, England.

  vii. **Robert Poulton**,[1186] born Jun 1659, in Adderbury, Oxfordshire, England, christened 12 Jun 1659, in Adderbury, Oxfordshire, England.

943. Mrs Joyce Poulton was born about 1622, in Adderbury, Oxfordshire, England. She married Timothy Poulton[1187] about 1640, in Adderbury, Oxfordshire, England. He was the son of William Poulton and Mable Mathewe.

944. John Spier was born about 1635, in Oxfordshire, England. He married Spier about 1660, in Oxfordshire, England.

Children of John Spier and Spier:

  i. **Thomas Spier**,[1188] born 5 Nov 1661, in South Leigh, Oxfordshire, England.

  ii. **William Spier**,[1189] born 25 Nov 1669, in South Leigh, Oxfordshire, England.

  iii. **Edward Spier**,[1190] born 10 Feb 1672, in South Leigh, Oxfordshire, England.

  iv. **George Spier**,[1191] born 15 Jan 1674, in South Leigh, Oxfordshire, England.

  v. **Yeoman John Spier**,[993] born about 1675, in South Leigh, Oxfordshire, England, died Jul 1739, in South Leigh, Oxfordshire, England.

945. ____Spier was born about 1638, in Oxfordshire, England. She married John Spier about 1660, in Oxfordshire, England.

946. William Andrews was born about 1635, in Berkshire, England. He married Mrs Katherine Andrews about 1660, in Berkshire, England.

Children of William Andrews and Mrs Katherine Andrews:

  i. **Katherine Andrews**, born 10 Apr 1662, in Longworth, Berkshire, England, christened 10 Apr 1662, in Longworth, Berkshire, England.

    ii.   **Elizabeth Andrews**,[997] born Aug 1665, in Longworth, Berkshire, England, died before 1760, in England.

    iii.   **William Andrews**, born 11 Jun 1669, in Kingston Bagpuize, Berkshire, England, christened 11 Jun 1669, in Kingston Bagpuize, Berkshire, England.

    iv.   **Mary Andrews**, born 16 Feb 1672, in Kingston Bagpuize, Berkshire, England, christened 16 Feb 1672, in Kingston Bagpuize, Berkshire, England.

    v.   **Jane Andrews**, born 4 Aug 1678, in Kingston Bagpuize, Berkshire, England.

947. Mrs Katherine Andrews was born about 1638, in Berkshire, England. She married William Andrews about 1660, in Berkshire, England.

948. Thomas Clark was born about 1630, in Berkshire, England. He married Sarah Clark[1005] about 1655, in Berkshire, England.

Children of Thomas Clark and Sarah Clark:

    i.   **Thomas Clark**,[1004] born about 1658, in North Hinksey, Berkshire, England.

949. Sarah Clark was born about 1632, in Berkshire, England. She married Thomas Clark[1005] about 1655, in Berkshire, England.

950. John Knapp was born about 1635, in Berkshire, England. He married Alice Knapp[1005] about 1658, in Berkshire, England.

Children of John Knapp and Alice Knapp:

    i.   **Mary Knapp**,[1004,1005] born Sep 1660, in Childrey, Berkshire, England.

951. Alice Knapp was born about 1636, in Berkshire, England. She married John Knapp[1005] about 1658, in Berkshire, England.

952. ____Bayly was born about 1625, in Oxfordshire, England. He married Bayly about 1650, in Oxfordshire, England.

Children of Bayly and Bayly:

    i.   **Edward Bayly**,[1009] born about 1660, in Berkshire, England.

953. ____Bayly was born about 1627, in Oxfordshire, England. She married Bayly about 1650, in Oxfordshire, England.

954. John Oxlade was born Mar 1630, in Great Marlow, Buckinghamshire, England, christened 30 Mar

1630, in Fingest, Buckinghamshire, England, died 25 Sep 1667, in Great Marlow, Buckinghamshire, England. He was the son of John Oxlade and Frances Munday. He married Mrs Mary Oxlade about 1651, in Great Marlow, Buckinghamshire, England.

Notes for John Oxlade:

Fingest, Buckingham parish records.

Children of John Oxlade and Mrs Mary Oxlade:

> i. **John Oxlade**,[1013] born Feb 1652, in Great Marlow, Buckinghamshire, England, died 1703, in Great Marlow, Buckinghamshire, England.
> ii. **Mary Oxlade**, born 1653, in Great Marlow, Buckinghamshire, England, christened 27 Feb 1653, in Great Marlow, Buckinghamshire, England.
> iii. **Elizabeth Oxlade**, born 1662, in Brightwell Baldwin, Oxfordshire, England, died 1662, in Brightwell Baldwin, Oxfordshire, England.

955. Mrs Mary Oxlade was born 1635, in Great Marlow, Buckinghamshire, England, died 1667, in Great Marlow, Buckinghamshire, England. She married John Oxlade about 1651, in Great Marlow, Buckinghamshire, England. He was the son of John Oxlade and Frances Munday.

956. John Hollier was born about 1630, in Buckinghamshire, England. He married Hollier about 1650, in Buckinghamshire, England.

Children of John Hollier and Hollier:

> i. **Ann Hollier**,[1013] born 1656, in Great Marlow, Buckinghamshire, England, died Apr 1701, in Great Marlow, Buckinghamshire, England.

957. ____Hollier was born about 1634, in Buckinghamshire, England. She married John Hollier about 1650, in Buckinghamshire, England.

958. William Salter was born 1633, in Bisham, Berkshire, England, died 21 Oct 1669, in Bisham, Berkshire, England, buried Oct 1669, in Bisham, Berkshire, England. He was the son of Salter and Salter. He married Mrs Jone Salter about 1657, in England.

Children of William Salter and Mrs Jone Salter:

> i. **William Salter**,[1015] born Jul 1659, in Bisham, Berkshire, England, died before 1740, in England.

959. Mrs Jone Salter was born about 1637, in Bisham, Berkshire, England, christened about 1637, in Bisham, Berkshire, England, died Dec 1664, in Bisham, Berkshire, England, buried 20 Dec 1664, in Bisham, Berkshire, England. She married William Salter about 1657, in England. He was the son of

Salter and Salter.

960. Thomas Broadway was born 1 Jan 1621, in Cuxham, Oxfordshire, England, christened 1 Jan 1621, in Cuxham, Oxfordshire, England, died 25 Jun 1709, in Cuxham, Oxfordshire, England, buried 25 Jun 1709, in Cuxham, Oxfordshire, England. He was the son of Thomas Broadway and Agnes Fritwell. He married Mrs Mary Broadway about 1645, in England.
Notes for Thomas Broadway:

data - Cuxham parish records

Children of Thomas Broadway and Mrs Mary Broadway:

i. **Thomas Broadway**, born Jan 1645, in Cuxham, Oxfordshire, England, christened 16 Jan 1645, in Cuxham, Oxfordshire, England. He married Mrs Elizabeth Broadway about 1669, in Cuxham, Oxfordshire, England. Mrs Elizabeth Broadway was born 1650, in England, died 1683, in Cuxham, Oxfordshire, England.

ii. **Jane Broadway**, born 21 Dec 1647, in Cuxham, Oxfordshire, England. She married Richard Hazeley 18 Jul 1669, in Cuxham, Oxfordshire, England. Richard Hazeley was born about 1645, in Oxfordshire, England.

iii. **John Broadway**, born Jun 1651, in Cuxham, Oxfordshire, England, died 2 Mar 1719, in Cuxham, Oxfordshire, England.

iv. **Mary Broadway**, born 1654, in Cuxham, Oxfordshire, England, died 1656, in Cuxham, Oxfordshire, England.

v. **Mary Broadway**, born 1656, in Cuxham, Oxfordshire, England, died 1657, in Cuxham, Oxfordshire, England.

vi. **Edward Broadway**, born 1660, in Cuxham, Oxfordshire, England, died 1747, in Oxfordshire, England. He married Mrs Elizabeth Broadway about 1683, in England. Mrs Elizabeth Broadway was born 1665, in England, died 1735, in England.
May also had been known as Edmond

vii. **Joseph Broadway**, born 1664, in Cuxham, Oxfordshire, England. He married Mrs Elizabeth Broadway about 1688, in England. Mrs Elizabeth Broadway was born 1670, in England, died 1713, in England.

961. Mrs Mary Broadway was born 1626, in Cuxham, Oxfordshire, England, died Dec 1679, in Cuxham, Oxfordshire, England, buried 17 Dec 1679, in Cuxham, Oxfordshire, England. She married Thomas Broadway about 1645, in England. He was the son of Thomas Broadway and Agnes Fritwell.
Notes for Mrs Mary Broadway:

Cuxham parish records

962. William Scholes was born about 1615, in Lewknor, Oxfordshire, England, died 21 Apr 1664, buried 21 Apr 1664, in Lewknor, Oxfordshire, England. He was the son of William Scholes and Mrs

William Scholes. He married Ursual Munday about 1637, in Lewknor, Oxfordshire, England. She was the daughter of Robert Munday and Munday.

Children of William Scholes and Ursual Munday:

    i.   **William Scoles**, born about 1645, in Lewknor, Oxfordshire, England, died 17 Mar 1706, in Lewknor, Oxfordshire, England.

963. Ursual Munday was born about 1619, in Lewknor, Oxfordshire, England, christened 11 Mar 1620, in Aston Rowant, Oxfordshire, England. She was the daughter of Robert Munday and Munday. She married William Scholes about 1637, in Lewknor, Oxfordshire, England. He was the son of William Scholes and Mrs William Scholes.

964. Richard Belson was born 21 Dec 1601, in Aston Rowant, Oxfordshire, England, christened 21 Dec 1601, in Aston Rowant, Oxfordshire, England, died Apr 1686, in Aston Rowant, Oxfordshire, England, buried 10 Apr 1686, in Aston Rowant, Oxfordshire, England. He was the son of Richard Belson and Edith Dutton. He married Alicia Pottes[1192] 14 Jul 1628, in Aston Rowant, Oxfordshire, England. She was the daughter of Gualteri Potts and Anna Potts.

Children of Richard Belson and Alicia Pottes:

    i.   **Alicia Belson**,[1193] born Sep 1629, in Aston Rowant, Oxfordshire, England, christened 27 Sep 1629, in Aston Rowant, Oxfordshire, England, died about 1700, in Oxfordshire, England.

    ii.   **Thomas Belson**,[1194] born Sep 1631, in Aston Rowant, Oxfordshire, England, christened 11 Sep 1631, in Aston Rowant, Oxfordshire, England, buried 6 Oct 1633.

    iii.   **Edith Belson**,[1195] born Oct 1633, in Aston Rowant, Oxfordshire, England, christened 28 Oct 1633, in Aston Rowant, Oxfordshire, England, died DEAD.

    iv.   **Elizabeth Belson**,[1196] born Nov 1635, in Aston Rowant, Oxfordshire, England, christened 21 Nov 1635, in Aston Rowant, Oxfordshire, England, died Jan 1710, in Lewknor, Oxfordshire, England, buried 2 Feb 1710, in Lewknor, Oxfordshire, England.

    v.   **Richard Belson**,[1197] born Apr 1638, in Aston Rowant, Oxfordshire, England, christened 12 Apr 1638, in Aston Rowant, Oxfordshire, England.

    vi.   **Jane Belson**, born Oct 1640, in Aston Rowant, Oxfordshire, England, died Jan 1710, in Lewknor, Oxfordshire, England.

965. Alicia Pottes was born Oct 1605, in Aston Rowant, Oxfordshire, England, christened 13 Oct 1605, in Aston Rowant, Oxfordshire, England, died Apr 1678, in Aston Rowant, Oxfordshire, England, buried 8 Apr 1678, in Aston Rowant, Oxfordshire, England. She was the daughter of Gualteri Potts and Anna Potts. She married Richard Belson[1192] 14 Jul 1628, in Aston Rowant, Oxfordshire, England. He was the son of Richard Belson and Edith Dutton.

Notes for Alicia Pottes:

aka POTT

966. Thomas Snow was born about 1650, in Headington, Oxfordshire, England. He married Mrs. Mary Snow about 1670, in England.

Children of Thomas Snow and Mrs. Mary Snow:

    i.   **Gregory Snow**,[1018] born 1677, in Headington, Oxfordshire, England, died 1754, in Headington, Oxfordshire, England.

967. Mrs. Mary Snow was born about 1650, in Headington, Oxfordshire, England. She married Thomas Snow about 1670, in England.

968. John Kirby was born 27 Apr 1642, in Arncott, Oxfordshire, England, christened 1 May 1642, in Charlton on Otmoor, Oxfordshire, England, died Aug 1690, in Charlton on Otmoor, Oxfordshire, England, buried 14 Aug 1690, in Charlton on Otmoor, Oxfordshire, England. He was the son of John Kirby and Bridget Marsh. He married Anne Walker[1198] 20 May 1667, in Noke, Oxfordshire, England. She was the daughter of John Walker and Elizabeth Croxton.

Children of John Kirby and Anne Walker:

    i.   **Elizabeth Kirby**, born Apr 1668, in Charlton on Otmoor, Oxfordshire, England, christened 5 May 1668, in Charlton on Otmoor, Oxfordshire, England.

    ii.   **John Kirby**, born Jun 1669, in Charlton on Otmoor, Oxfordshire, England, christened 16 Jun 1669, in Charlton on Otmoor, Oxfordshire, England, died 29 Dec 1669, in Charlton on Otmoor, Oxfordshire, England, buried 29 Dec 1669, in Charlton on Otmoor, Oxfordshire, England.

    iii.   **John Kirby**, born Sep 1670, in Charlton on Otmoor, Oxfordshire, England.

    iv.   **Ralph Kirby**, born Sep 1671, in Charlton on Otmoor, Oxfordshire, England, christened 9 Oct 1671, in Charlton on Otmoor, Oxfordshire, England, died 19 Oct 1671, in Charlton on Otmoor, Oxfordshire, England, buried 19 Oct 1671, in Charlton on Otmoor, Oxfordshire, England.

    v.   **Anne Kirby**, born May 1673, in Charlton on Otmoor, Oxfordshire, England, christened 10 May 1673, in Charlton on Otmoor, Oxfordshire, England.

    vi.   **William Kirby**, born Nov 1674, in Charlton on Otmoor, Oxfordshire, England, christened 23 Nov 1674, in Charlton on Otmoor, Oxfordshire, England, died 21 Dec 1674, in Charlton on Otmoor, Oxfordshire, England, buried 21 Dec 1674, in Charlton on Otmoor, Oxfordshire, England.

    vii.   **Bridget Kirby**, born Dec 1675, in Charlton on Otmoor, Oxfordshire, England, christened 19 Dec 1675, in Charlton on Otmoor, Oxfordshire, England, buried 20 Oct 1737, in Charlton on Otmoor, Oxfordshire, England.

Contents

viii. **Henry Kirby**, born Sep 1677, in Charlton on Otmoor, Oxfordshire, England, christened 22 Sep 1677, in Charlton on Otmoor, Oxfordshire, England, died 19 Oct 1742, in Charlton on Otmoor, Oxfordshire, England. He married Ann Cooper 10 Feb 1700, in Charlton on Otmoor, Oxfordshire, England. Ann Cooper was born Apr 1676, in Fencot, Oxfordshire, England, christened 7 May 1676, in Fencot, Oxfordshire, England.

969. Anne Walker was born 1646, in Noke, Oxfordshire, England, died Nov 1679, in Charlton on Otmoor, Oxfordshire, England, buried 25 Nov 1679, in Charlton on Otmoor, Oxfordshire, England. She was the daughter of John Walker and Elizabeth Croxton. She married John Kirby[1199] 20 May 1667, in Noke, Oxfordshire, England. He was the son of John Kirby and Bridget Marsh.

970. John Howlett was born Jan 1626, in Charlton on Otmoor, Oxfordshire, England, christened 29 Jan 1626, in Charlton on Otmoor, Oxfordshire, England. He was the son of John Howlett and Elizabeth Sharpe. He married Howlett about 1653, in Oxfordshire, England.

Children of John Howlett and Howlett:

i. **John Howlet**,[1027] born Mar 1655, in Charlton on Otmoor, Oxfordshire, England, died Jan 1695, in Charlton on Otmoor, Oxfordshire, England.
ii. **Elizabeth Howlett**,[1200] born Sep 1657, in Charlton on Otmoor, Oxfordshire, England, christened 13 Sep 1657, in Charlton on Otmoor, Oxfordshire, England.
iii. **Elizabeth Howlett**,[1201] born Sep 1658, in Charlton on Otmoor, Oxfordshire, England, christened 22 Sep 1658, in Charlton on Otmoor, Oxfordshire, England.
iv. **Un-Named Howlett**,[1202] born Jan 1661, in Charlton on Otmoor, Oxfordshire, England, christened 28 Jan 1661, in Charlton on Otmoor, Oxfordshire, England.

971. ____Howlett was born about 1628, in Oxfordshire, England. She married John Howlett[1203] about 1653, in Oxfordshire, England. He was the son of John Howlett and Elizabeth Sharpe.

972. Robert Dennett was born about 1630, in Oxfordshire, England, died before 1730, in England. He married Alice Blackwell 23 Oct 1656, in Oxford, Oxfordshire, England.

Children of Robert Dennett and Alice Blackwell:

i. **Ann Dennett**,[1026] born Jan 1663, in Combe, Oxfordshire, England, died 17 Jan 1716, in Merton, Oxfordshire, England.

973. Alice Blackwell was born about 1631, in Oxfordshire, England, died before 1730, in England. She married Robert Dennett 23 Oct 1656, in Oxford, Oxfordshire, England.

974. Ralph Clark was born about 1622, in Buckinghamshire, England. He was the son of Ralph Clark and Katherine Longe. He married Clarke about 1642, in Buckinghamshire, England.

Children of Ralph Clark and Clarke:

      i.   **Henry Clark**,[1028,1029] born Feb 1644, in Waddesdon, Buckinghamshire, England.

975. ____Clarke was born about 1624, in Buckinghamshire, England. She married Ralph Clark[1204] about 1642, in Buckinghamshire, England. He was the son of Ralph Clark and Katherine Longe.

976. ____Clarke was born about 1622, in Buckinghamshire, England. He married Clarke about 1645, in Buckinghamshire, England.

Children of Clarke and Clarke:

      i.   **Edward Clarke**,[1031,1033] born 9 Aug 1649, in Great Missenden, Buckinghamshire, England.

977. ____Clarke was born about 1625, in Buckinghamshire, England. She married Clarke about 1645, in Buckinghamshire, England.

978. George Wright was born about 1620, in Buckinghamshire, England. He married Jane Wright[1205] about 1642, in Buckinghamshire, England.

Children of George Wright and Jane Wright:

      i.   **Katherine Wright**,[1031,1032] born Aug 1645, in Great Missenden, Buckinghamshire, England.

979. Jane Wright was born about 1622, in Buckinghamshire, England. She married George Wright[1205] about 1642, in Buckinghamshire, England.

980. Isacc Steevens was born about 1625, in England, died before 1715, in England. He married Steevens about 1650, in England.

Children of Isacc Steevens and Steevens:

      i.   **Thomas Steevens**,[1041,1046] born about 1650, in England.

981. ____Steevens was born about 1626, in England, died before 1720, in England. She married Isacc Steevens about 1650, in England.

982. Thomas Bowles was born Aug 1643, in Fairford, Gloucestershire, England, christened 13 Aug 1643, in Fairford, Gloucestershire, England, died before 1740, in England. He was the son of Thomas Bowles and Ann Mowsdale. He married Mrs Mary Bowles[1206] about 1668, in Gloucestershire, England.

Children of Thomas Bowles and Mrs Mary Bowles:

    i.   **John Bowles**,[1047] born Jan 1670, in Fairford, Gloucestershire, England, died Dec 1714, in Fairford, Gloucestershire, England.

    ii.   **Thomas Bowles**, born 18 Apr 1677, in Fairford, Gloucestershire, England, christened 18 May 1677, in Fairford, Gloucestershire, England, died 24 Dec 1689, in Gloucestershire, England, buried 24 Dec 1689, in Gloucestershire, England.

983. Mrs Mary Bowles was born about 1646, in Fairford, Gloucestershire, England, died Feb 1711, in Fairford, Gloucestershire, England, buried 16 Feb 1711, in Fairford, Gloucestershire, England. She married Thomas Bowles[1206] about 1668, in Gloucestershire, England. He was the son of Thomas Bowles and Ann Mowsdale.

984. Thomas Loveday was born Dec 1635, in Wanborough, Wiltshire, England, christened 6 Jan 1636, in Wanborough, Wiltshire, England, died May 1699, in Wanborough, Wiltshire, England, buried 25 May 1699, in Wanborough, Wiltshire, England. He was the son of Thomas Loveday and Emma Grundy. He married Martha Hedges[1207] 1 Oct 1665, in Wanborough, Wiltshire, England. She was the daughter of Henry Hedges and Margery Pleydall.

Children of Thomas Loveday and Martha Hedges:

    i.   **Margreatt Loveday**,[1208] born Apr 1666, in Wanborough, Wiltshire, England, christened 17 Apr 1666, in Wanborough, Wiltshire, England.

    ii.   **Thomas Loveday**,[1209] born Nov 1667, in Wanborough, Wiltshire, England, christened 14 Nov 1667, in Wanborough, Wiltshire, England, died about 30 Jan 1743, in Wanborough, Wiltshire, England, buried about 30 Jan 1743, in Wanborough, Wiltshire, England.

    iii.   **Martha Loveday**,[767] born Oct 1670, in Wanborough, Wiltshire, England, died Nov 1758, in Fairford, Gloucestershire, England.

    iv.   **Henry Loveday**,[1210] born Apr 1673, in Wanborough, Wiltshire, England, christened 6 May 1673, in Wanborough, Wiltshire, England.

    v.   **Elizabeth Loveday**,[1211] born Nov 1677, in Wanborough, Wiltshire, England, christened 18 Nov 1677, in Wanborough, Wiltshire, England, buried 22 Mar 1756, in Wanborough, Wiltshire, England.

    vi.   **Mary Loveday**,[1212] born Apr 1680, in Wanborough, Wiltshire, England, christened 30 Apr 1680, in Wanborough, Wiltshire, England.

    vii.   **John Loveday**,[1213] born May 1681, in Wanborough, Wiltshire, England, christened 23 May 1681, in Wanborough, Wiltshire, England, buried 11 Nov 1743, in Wanborough, Wiltshire, England.

985. Martha Hedges was born 27 Dec 1638, in Bishopstone, Wiltshire, England, christened 3 Mar 1639, in Bishopstone, Wiltshire, England, died Feb 1725, in Wanborough, Wiltshire, England, buried 28 Feb 1725, in Wanborough, Wiltshire, England. She was the daughter of Henry Hedges and Margery

Pleydall. She married Thomas Loveday[1214] 1 Oct 1665, in Wanborough, Wiltshire, England. He was the son of Thomas Loveday and Emma Grundy.

986. Edward Skinner was born about 1630, in Gloucestershire, England, died about 1730, in England. He married Mrs Sybella Skinner about 1655, in Gloucestershire, England.

Children of Edward Skinner and Mrs Sybella Skinner:

> i.   **Humphry Skinner**, born 1657, in Quenington, Gloucestershire, England, died before 1740, in England.

987. Mrs Sybella Skinner was born about 1632, in Gloucestershire, England, died before 1730, in England. She married Edward Skinner about 1655, in Gloucestershire, England.

988. Thomas Tarrant was born about 1620, in Wiltshire, England, died before 1720, in England. He married Mrs Elizabeth Tarrant about 1641, in Wiltshire, England.
Notes for Thomas Tarrant:

residence: Burbage, Wiltshire, England parents: Thomas Tarrant, Elizabeth record title: England Births and Christenings, 1538-1975 name: William Tarrant gender: Male baptism/christening date: 04 Apr 1650 baptism/christening place: Burbage, Wiltshire, England father's name: Thomas Tarrant mother's name: Elizabeth indexing project (batch) number: C15302-1 system origin: England-VR source film number: 1279365

Children of Thomas Tarrant and Mrs Elizabeth Tarrant:

> i.   **Georgius Tarrant**, born Apr 1641, in Burbage, Wiltshire, England, christened 25 Apr 1641, in Burbage, Wiltshire, England.
> residence: Burbage, Wiltshire, England parents: Thomae Tarrant, Elizabeth record title: England Births and Christenings, 1538-1975 name: Georgius Tarrant gender: Male baptism/christening date: 25 Apr 1641 baptism/christening place: Burbage, Wiltshire, England father's name: Thomae Tarrant mother's name: Elizabeth indexing project (batch) number: C15302-1 system origin: England-VR source film number: 1279365
> ii. **William Tarrant**, born Aug 1647, in Burbage, Wiltshire, England, christened 24 Aug 1647, in Burbage, Wiltshire, England, died Jun 1648, in Burbage, Wiltshire, England, buried 3 Jul 1648, in Burbage, Wiltshire, England.
> residence: Burbage, Wiltshire, England parents: Thomas Tarrant, Elizabeth record title: England Births and Christenings, 1538-1975 name: William Tarrant gender: Male baptism/christening date: 24 Aug 1647 baptism/christening place: Burbage, Wiltshire, England father's name: Thomas Tarrant mother's name: Elizabeth indexing project (batch) number: C15302-1 system origin: England-VR source film number: 1279365 burial: 03 Jul 1648 Wiltshire, England parents: Thos. Tarrant,

Elizabeth record title: England Deaths and Burials, 1538-1991 name: William gender: Male burial date: 03 Jul 1648 burial place: Wiltshire, England father's name: Thos. Tarrant mother's name: Elizabeth indexing project (batch) number: B15302-1 system origin: England. source film number: 1279365

 iii. **William Tarrant**, born Apr 1650, in Burbage, Wiltshire, England, died before 1750, in England.

989. Mrs Elizabeth Tarrant was born about 1622, in Wiltshire, England, died before 1722, in England. She married Thomas Tarrant about 1641, in Wiltshire, England.

990. Edward Gunning was born Jun 1637, in Westbury-on-Trym, Gloucestershire, England, christened Jun 1637, died Nov 1672, in Bristol, Gloucestershire, England, buried 23 Nov 1672, in Bristol, Gloucestershire, England. He married Gunning about 1665, in Gloucestershire, England.

Children of Edward Gunning and Gunning:

 i. **Sarah Gunning**,[770,1048] born about 1672, in Bristol, Gloucestershire, England.

991. ____Gunning was born about 1640, in Gloucestershire, England. She married Edward Gunning about 1665, in Gloucestershire, England.

992. Thomas Rogers was born about 1622, in Gloucestershire, England, christened 1622, in Gloucester, Gloucestershire, England, died before 1720, in England. He was the son of Thomas Rogers and Anne Finche. He married Mrs Susana Rogers about 1655, in Gloucestershire, England.

Children of Thomas Rogers and Mrs Susana Rogers:

 i. **Samuel Rogers**,[1051] born Sep 1658, in Bristol, Gloucestershire, England, died 29 Apr 1748, in Bitton, Gloucestershire, England.

993. Mrs Susana Rogers was born about 1635, in Gloucestershire, England, died before 1730, in England. She married Thomas Rogers about 1655, in Gloucestershire, England. He was the son of Thomas Rogers and Anne Finche.

994. Henry Ellard was born about 1670, in Buckinghamshire, England. He married Mary Ellard about 1695, in Buckinghamshire, England.

Children of Henry Ellard and Mary Ellard:

 i. **Thomas Ellard**,[1053] born Jul 1701, in Preston Bisset, Buckinghamshire, England.

995. Mary Ellard was born about 1672, in Buckinghamshire, England. She married Henry Ellard about 1695, in Buckinghamshire, England.

996. William Jennings was born about 1675, in England. He married Elisabeth Jennings about 1697, in England.

Children of William Jennings and Elisabeth Jennings:

      i.   **Thomasin Jennings**,[1054] born Aug 1700, in Bletchingley, Surrey, England.

997. Elisabeth Jennings was born about 1677, in England. She married William Jennings about 1697, in England.

998. ____Smith was born about 1670, in Kent, England. He married Smith about 1690, in Kingsdown, Kent, England.

Children of Smith and Smith:

      i.   **Stephen Smith**,[1055,1057] born about 1700, in Kent, England.

999. ____Smith was born about 1673, in Kent, England. She married Smith about 1690, in Kingsdown, Kent, England.

1000. William Hills was born about 1680, in Kent, England. He married Hills[1215] about 1705, in Kent, England.

Children of William Hills and Hills:

      i.   **Elizabeth Hills**,[1055,1056] born Jun 1710, in Ditton, Kent, England.

1001.____Hills was born about 1681, in Kent, England. She married William Hills[1056] about 1705, in Kent, England.

1002. John Lake was born about 1680, in Dorset, England. He married Magdalen Lake[1216] 1 Jul 1701, in Winterbourne St Martin, Dorset, England.

Children of John Lake and Magdalen Lake:

      i.   **Elizabeth Lake**,[1059,1060] born Aug 1708, in Winterbourne St Martin, Dorset, England.

1003. Magdalen Lake was born about 1682, in Dorset, England. She married John Lake[1216] 1 Jul 1701, in Winterbourne St Martin, Dorset, England.

1004. Thomas Hunt was born 1668, in Compton Abbas, Dorset, England, died before 1750, in England. He was the son of Thomas Hunt and Mrs Joan Hunt. He married Hunt about 1690, in England. Notes for Thomas Hunt:

Shown as father to Thomas Hunt born 17 Oct 1704:- Name: Birth/Christening; Death/Burial; Date Place Date Place Hunt, Thomas: 17 Oct 1704 Dorset, England; 2 Feb 1784 Compton Abbas,Dorset,England Father: Thomas Hunt Spouse: Katherine Hunt?

Children of Thomas Hunt and Hunt:

    i.   **Thomas Hunt**, born 17 Oct 1704, in Compton Abbas, Dorset, England, died 2 Feb 1784, in Compton Abbas, Dorset, England.

1005.____Hunt was born about 1670, in England, died before 1769, in England. She married Thomas Hunt about 1690, in England. He was the son of Thomas Hunt and Mrs Joan Hunt.

1006. Thomas Stokes was born about 1690, in Somerset, England, died before 1790, in England. He married Susannah Richards[1064] 9 Apr 1714, in Evercreech, Somerset, England.

Children of Thomas Stokes and Susannah Richards:

    i.   **Thomas Stokes**, born 6 Jan 1714, in Evercreech, Somerset, England, christened 6 Jan 1714, in Evercreech, Somerset, England.

    ii.   **Sarah Stokes**,[1064] born 26 Jul 1720, in Evercreech, Somerset, England, died before 1820, in England.

1007. Susannah Richards was born about 1695, in Somerset, England, died before 1780, in England. She married Thomas Stokes[1064] 9 Apr 1714, in Evercreech, Somerset, England.

1008. John Humphrey was born 1661, in Plumpton, Northamptonshire, England, christened 19 Jul 1661, in Piddington, Northamptonshire, England, died 1714, in Piddington, Northamptonshire, England. He married Mary Wake about 1682, in Northamptonshire, England.

Children of John Humphrey and Mary Wake:

    i.   **William Humphrey**, born 1683, in Sulgrave, Northamptonshire, England, christened 29 Dec 1683, in Sulgrave, Northamptonshire, England, buried 20 Feb 1684, in Sulgrave, Northamptonshire, England.

    ii.   **Mary Humphrey**, born 1685, in Sulgrave, Northamptonshire, England, christened 23 Aug 1685, in Sulgrave, Northamptonshire, England.

    iii.   **Thomas Humphrey**, born 1686, in Sulgrave, Northamptonshire, England, christened 13 Feb 1686, in Sulgrave, Northamptonshire, England.

    iv.   **Anne Humphrey**, born Feb 1689, in Sulgrave, Northamptonshire, England, christened 12 Feb 1689, in Sulgrave, Northamptonshire, England, died May 1689, in Sulgrave, Northamptonshire, England, buried 12 May 1689, in Sulgrave, Northamptonshire, England.

    v.   **Grace Humphrey**, born 1690, in Sulgrave, Northamptonshire, England, christened

4 Nov 1690, in Sulgrave, Northamptonshire, England, buried 21 Mar 1693, in Sulgrave, Northamptonshire, England.

  vi. **John Humphrey**, born 1691, in Sulgrave, Northamptonshire, England, christened 25 Feb 1691, in Sulgrave, Northamptonshire, England, buried 23 May 1693, in Sulgrave, Northamptonshire, England.

  vii. **John Humphrey**, born 1693, in Sulgrave, Northamptonshire, England, christened 18 Jun 1693, in Sulgrave, Northamptonshire, England, buried 11 Oct 1694, in Sulgrave, Northamptonshire, England.

  viii. **Richard Humphrey**, born 1694, in Sulgrave, Northamptonshire, England, christened 2 Mar 1694, in Sulgrave, Northamptonshire, England, buried 4 Mar 1695, in Sulgrave, Northamptonshire, England.

  ix. **Josiah Humphrey**, born Sep 1696, in Sulgrave, Northamptonshire, England, died Feb 1769, in Sulgrave, Northamptonshire, England.

  x. **Susanna Humphrey**, born Apr 1700, in Sulgrave, Northamptonshire, England, christened 21 Apr 1700, in Sulgrave, Northamptonshire, England, died Aug 1701, in Sulgrave, Northamptonshire, England, buried 21 Aug 1701, in Sulgrave, Northamptonshire, England.

  xi. **William Humphrey**, born Oct 1701, in Sulgrave, Northamptonshire, England, christened 12 Oct 1701, in Sulgrave, Northamptonshire, England, died Apr 1716, in Sulgrave, Northamptonshire, England, buried 24 Apr 1716, in Sulgrave, Northamptonshire, England.

1009. Mary Wake was born 1662, in Sulgrave, Northamptonshire, England, christened 15 Aug 1662, in Plumpton, Northamptonshire, England, died before 1760, in England. She married John Humphrey about 1682, in Northamptonshire, England.
Notes for Mary Wake:

Mary Wake is NOT related to Sir William Wake - they are different families. I ha ve the correct Wake family tree from the Wake family their selves and certify they are NOT related. Please stop others adding her to his tree.

1010. William Tims was born 1665, in Farthinghoe, Northamptonshire, England, christened 12 Nov 1665, in Farthinghoe, Northamptonshire, England, died before 1750, in England. He was the son of Peter Times and Mary Turland. He married Elizabeth Naylor 28 May 1688, in Farthinghoe, Northamptonshire, England. She was the daughter of William Naylor and Mrs Jane Naylor.

Children of William Tims and Elizabeth Naylor:

  i. **William Tims**, born 1689, in Farthinghoe, Northamptonshire, England, christened 10 May 1689, in Farthinghoe, Northamptonshire, England.

  ii. **Elizabeth Tims**, born Apr 1691, in Farthinghoe, Northamptonshire, England, died before 1790, in England.

  iii. **Mary Tims**, born 1693, in Farthinghoe, Northamptonshire, England, christened 16

Apr 1693, in Farthinghoe, Northamptonshire, England.

    iv.   **Peter Tims**, born 1695, in Farthinghoe, Northamptonshire, England, christened 8 Mar 1695, in Farthinghoe, Northamptonshire, England.

    v.   **John Tims**, born 1698, in Farthinghoe, Northamptonshire, England, christened 16 Oct 1698, in Farthinghoe, Northamptonshire, England.

1011. Elizabeth Naylor was born 1667, in Farthinghoe, Northamptonshire, England, christened 2 Feb 1667, in Farthinghoe, Northamptonshire, England, died before 1750, in England. She was the daughter of William Naylor and Mrs Jane Naylor. She married William Tims 28 May 1688, in Farthinghoe, Northamptonshire, England. He was the son of Peter Times and Mary Turland.

1012. William Collison was born Aug 1661, in Woodeaton, Oxfordshire, England, christened 11 Aug 1661, in Woodeaton, Oxfordshire, England, died 1730, in Woodeaton, Oxfordshire, England, buried 7 Mar 1730, in Woodeaton, Oxfordshire, England. He was the son of Thomas Collison and Mary Cox. He married Mrs Mary Collison 1685, in Woodeaton, Oxfordshire, England.

Children of William Collison and Mrs Mary Collison:

    i.   **Thomas Collison**, born 1686, in Woodeaton, Oxfordshire, England, christened 23 Jan 1686, in Woodeaton, Oxfordshire, England.

    ii.   **Mary Collison**, born 1688, in Woodeaton, Oxfordshire, England, christened 7 Nov 1688, in Woodeaton, Oxfordshire, England.

    iii.   **William Collison**, born 1690, in Woodeaton, Oxfordshire, England, died before 1785, in England.

1013. Mrs Mary Collison was born about 1666, in Woodeaton, Oxfordshire, England, died 1729, in Woodeaton, Oxfordshire, England, buried 4 Feb 1729, in Woodeaton, Oxfordshire, England. She married William Collison 1685, in Woodeaton, Oxfordshire, England. He was the son of Thomas Collison and Mary Cox.

1014. Benjamin Brimly was born about 1665, in Woodeaton, Oxfordshire, England, died 1730, in Woodeaton, Oxfordshire, England, buried 27 Apr 1730, in Woodeaton, Oxfordshire, England. He married Mrs Mary Brimly about 1689, in Woodeaton, Oxfordshire, England.

Children of Benjamin Brimly and Mrs Mary Brimly:

    i.   **Mary Brimly**, born 1690, in Woodeaton, Oxfordshire, England, died Jan 1730, in England.

    ii.   **Thomas Brimly**, born 1694, in Woodeaton, Oxfordshire, England, christened 16 Dec 1694, in Woodeaton, Oxfordshire, England.

1015. Mrs Mary Brimly was born about 1667, in Oxfordshire, England, died 1714, in Woodeaton, Oxfordshire, England, buried 9 Nov 1714, in Woodeaton, Oxfordshire, England. She married Benjamin

Brimly about 1689, in Woodeaton, Oxfordshire, England.

1016. John Bodily was born 20 Jan 1649, in Crediton, Devonshire, England, christened 20 Jan 1649, in Crediton, Devonshire, England, died 1723, in Alderton, Northamptonshire, England, buried 24 Jun 1723, in Alderton, Northamptonshire, England. He was the son of William Bodily and Mrs Alice Bodily. He married Rebeca Squire 1675, in Exeter, Devonshire, England.

Children of John Bodily and Rebeca Squire:

> i.   **John Bodily**, born about 1685, in Northamptonshire, England, died 24 Jun 1723, in Alderton, Northamptonshire, England.

1017. Rebeca Squire was born about 1654, in Exeter, Devonshire, England. She married John Bodily 1675, in Exeter, Devonshire, England. He was the son of William Bodily and Mrs Alice Bodily.

1018. John Collins was born about 1648, in England. He married Lydia Checkley 1673, in Heyford, Northamptonshire, England.

Children of John Collins and Lydia Checkley:

> i.   **Richard Collins**, born about 1685, in Upper Heyford, Oxfordshire, England.

1019. Lydia Checkley was born about 1652, in England. She married John Collins 1673, in Heyford, Northamptonshire, England.

1020. John Ashby was born about 1645, in Bugbrooke, Northamptonshire, England, died 1 Sep 1728, in Bugbrooke, Northamptonshire, England, buried 3 Sep 1728, in Bugbrooke, Northamptonshire, England. He was the son of Robert Ashby and Jane Stephenson. He married Mary Gammage 1671, in Bugbrooke, Northamptonshire, England. She was the daughter of Joseph Gammage and Gammage.

Children of John Ashby and Mary Gammage:

> i.   **Alice Ashby**,[1078] born 1689, in Bugbrooke, Northamptonshire, England, died after 1723.

1021. Mary Gammage was born 19 Sep 1653, in Bugbrooke, Northamptonshire, England, christened 16 Nov 1653, in Bugbrooke, Northamptonshire, England, died 19 Jan 1736, in Bugbrooke, Northamptonshire, England, buried Jan 1736, in Bugbrooke, Northamptonshire, England. She was the daughter of Joseph Gammage and Gammage. She married John Ashby[1217,1218,1219] 1671, in Bugbrooke, Northamptonshire, England. He was the son of Robert Ashby and Jane Stephenson.
Notes for Mary Gammage:

Quaker

1022. George Squier was born about 1630, in England, died before 1700, in England. He married Mrs Ann Squier about 1650, in England.

Children of George Squier and Mrs Ann Squier:

    i.   **John Squire**,[1083,1084,1085] born Oct 1658, in Redbourn, Hertfordshire, England, died before 1740, in England.

1023. Mrs Ann Squier was born about 1631, in England, died before 1699, in England. She married George Squier about 1650, in England.

1024. Richard Briggs was born about 1630, in London, England. He was the son of Brigges and Briggs. He married Mrs Marie Briggs about 1650, in London, England.

Children of Richard Briggs and Mrs Marie Briggs:

    i.   **John Briggs**,[891,1112] born Apr 1656, in Bishopsgate, London, England.

1025. Mrs Marie Briggs was born about 1632, in London, England. She married Richard Briggs[1220] about 1650, in London, England. He was the son of Brigges and Briggs.

1026. _____Crew was born about 1675, in England. He married Crew about 1695, in England.

Children of Crew and Crew:

    i.   **Hezekiah Crew**,[1115,1118] born about 1700, in England, died Jan 1773, in Westminster, London, England.

1027. _____Crew was born about 1677, in England. She married Crew about 1695, in England.

1028. David Capling was born about 1675, in England. He married Mrs Mary Capling[1221] about 1695, in England.

Children of David Capling and Mrs Mary Capling:

    i.   **Ann Capling**,[1115,1116,1117] born 1 Nov 1700, in Westminster, London, England, died Dec 1788, in Westminster, London, England.

1029. Mrs Mary Capling was born about 1677, in England. She married David Capling[1221] about 1695, in England.

1030. Thomas Giles was born 1630, in Pembury, Kent, England. He married Elizabeth Streater 12 May 1657, in Lamberhurst, Kent, England.

Children of Thomas Giles and Elizabeth Streater:

      i.   **Edward Giles**,[1121] born 1662, in Pembury, Kent, England, died 25 Oct 1711, in Pembury, Kent, England.

1031. Elizabeth Streater was born 1635, in Kent, England. She married Thomas Giles 12 May 1657, in Lamberhurst, Kent, England.

1032. Dunston Foreman was born Oct 1618, in Brenchley, Kent, England, christened 4 Oct 1618, in Brenchley, Kent, England. He was the son of Dunston Foreman and Lettice Barram. He married Jane Chamberlaine[1222] about 1654, in Kent, England. She was the daughter of James Chamberlaine and Chamberlaine.

Children of Dunston Foreman and Jane Chamberlaine:

      i.   **Elizabeth Foreman**,[1120] born 1675, in Kent, England, died before 1775, in England.

1033. Jane Chamberlaine was born May 1632, in Hadlow, Kent, England, christened 22 May 1632, in Hadlow, Kent, England, died after 1675, in Kent, England. She was the daughter of James Chamberlaine and Chamberlaine. She married Dunston Foreman[1223] about 1654, in Kent, England. He was the son of Dunston Foreman and Lettice Barram.

1034. John Deverson was born about 1667, in Kent, England. He married Ann Wilson about 1690, in England.

Children of John Deverson and Ann Wilson:

      i.   **Elizabeth Deverson**, born about 1692, in Kent, England.

1035. Ann Wilson was born 1670, in Kent, England. She married John Deverson about 1690, in England.

1036. James Hayward was born about 1640, in England. He married Mrs Susan Hayward about 1670, in England.

Children of James Hayward and Mrs Susan Hayward:

      i.   **Jacob Hayward**,[1122] born about 1671, in Kent, England.

1037. Mrs Susan Hayward was born about 1642, in England. She married James Hayward about 1670, in England.

1038. James Tanner was born Sep 1638, in Marden, Kent, England, christened 16 Sep 1638, in

Contents

Marden, Kent, England. He was the son of Edward Tanner and Mrs Margaret Tanner. He married Ann Bowden 9 Feb 1670, in Cranbrook, Kent, England. She was the daughter of Hugh Bowden and Mrs Susan Bowden.

Children of James Tanner and Ann Bowden:

    i.   **Elizabeth Tanner**,[1122] born Sep 1675, in Cranbrook, Kent, England.

1039. Ann Bowden was born Jan 1635, in Sandwich, Kent, England, christened 10 Jan 1635, in Sandwich, Kent, England. She was the daughter of Hugh Bowden and Mrs Susan Bowden. She married James Tanner 9 Feb 1670, in Cranbrook, Kent, England. He was the son of Edward Tanner and Mrs Margaret Tanner.

1040. Edward Holmes was born 28 Nov 1641, in Canterbury, Kent, England, christened 29 Nov 1641, in Canterbury, Kent, England, died after 1686, in Canterbury, Kent, England. He was the son of Henry Holmes and Ann Kingsland. He married Ann Ashman 25 Oct 1663, in Canterbury, Kent, England.[1224]

Children of Edward Holmes and Ann Ashman:

    i.   **Willmat Holmes**, born 30 Sep 1666, in Canterbury, Kent, England, christened 30 Sep 1666, in Canterbury, Kent, England, died 5 May 1668, in Canterbury, Kent, England.
        also known as Willmouth
    ii.   **Edward Holmes**, born Sep 1669, in Canterbury, Kent, England, died before 1760, in England.
    iii.   **Sarah Holmes**, born 24 Mar 1672, in Canterbury, Kent, England, christened 24 Mar 1672, in Canterbury, Kent, England, died 3 May 1672, in Canterbury, Kent, England.
    iv.   **William Holmes**, born 12 Oct 1673, in Canterbury, Kent, England, christened 12 Oct 1673, in Canterbury, Kent, England, died 23 Apr 1677, in Canterbury, Kent, England.
    v.   **Henry Holmes**, born 3 Dec 1676, in Canterbury, Kent, England, christened 3 Dec 1676, in Canterbury, Kent, England, died 12 Dec 1676, in Canterbury, Kent, England.
    vi.   **Judith Holmes**, born 29 Feb 1680, in Canterbury, Kent, England, christened 29 Feb 1680, in Canterbury, Kent, England.
    vii.   **Thomas Holmes**, born 16 Dec 1683, in Canterbury, Kent, England, christened 29 Dec 1685, in Canterbury, Kent, England, died before 29 Dec 1685, in Canterbury, Kent, England.
    viii.   **Thomas Holmes**, born 29 Dec 1685, in Canterbury, Kent, England, christened 29 Dec 1685, in Canterbury, Kent, England, died 30 Dec 1685, in Canterbury, Kent, England.

1041. Ann Ashman was born 1640, in Canterbury, Kent, England, died before 1735, in England. She married Edward Holmes[1225] 25 Oct 1663, in Canterbury, Kent, England.[1224] He was the son of Henry Holmes and Ann Kingsland.

1042. Henry Bennet was born about 1645, in Kent, England. He married Joane Batty 29 Oct 1667, in Blean, Kent, England.
Notes for Henry Bennet:

Bennet/Bennett

Children of Henry Bennet and Joane Batty:

      i.   **Mary Bennett**, born about 1670, in Sturry, Kent, England, died before 1770, in England.

1043. Joane Batty was born about 1646, in Kent, England. She married Henry Bennet 29 Oct 1667, in Blean, Kent, England.

1044. William Collier was born about 1642, in Kent, England, died before 1740, in England. He married Susan Birch[1226,1227,1228] 31 Oct 1669, in Shepherdswell, Kent, England.[1226] She was the daughter of Thomas Birch and Elizabeth Stuppell.

Children of William Collier and Susan Birch:

      i.   **William Collyer**,[1226] born Feb 1670, in Shepherdswell, Kent, England, christened 19 Feb 1670, in Shepherdswell, Kent, England.
     ii.   **Robert Collyer**,[1227] born Jan 1672, in Coldred, Kent, England, christened 16 Feb 1672, in Coldred, Kent, England, died before 1680, in Coldred, Kent, England. C02161-5 system origin: England-source film number: 1751813
   iii.   **Thomas Collyer**,[1227,1229] born 12 Apr 1674, in Coldred, Kent, England, christened 22 Apr 1674, in Coldred, Kent, England.
I06879-3 system origin: England- source film number: 1736631
   iv.   **Elizabeth Collyer**,[1229] born Apr 1676, in Coldred, Kent, England, christened 23 Apr 1676, in Coldred, Kent, England.
    v.   **Robert Collyer**,[900,1123,1124] born Nov 1680, in Coldred, Kent, England, died before 1770, in England.
   vi.   **Richard Collyer**,[1124] born Sep 1684, in Coldred, Kent, England, christened 28 Sep 1684, in Coldred, Kent, England.

1045. Susan Birch was born 1642, in Coldred, Kent, England, christened 1642, in Coldred, Kent, England, died before 1740, in England. She was the daughter of Thomas Birch and Elizabeth Stuppell. She married William Collier[1226,1227] 31 Oct 1669, in Shepherdswell, Kent, England.[1226]

1046. John Epse was born about 1660, in Kent, England, died before 1750, in England. He married Mrs Ann Epse about 1680, in Kent, England.

Children of John Epse and Mrs Ann Epse:

     i.   **Deborah Epse**,[1123] born Mar 1684, in Sutton by Dover, Kent, England, died before 1770, in England.

1047. Mrs Ann Epse was born about 1660, in Kent, England, died before 1760, in England. She married John Epse about 1680, in Kent, England.

1048. Issac Hawkes was born 1666, in Folkestone, Kent, England, died 31 Mar 1741, in Folkestone, Kent, England. He married Hannah Sladden 6 Jul 1691, in Folkestone, Kent, England.

Children of Issac Hawkes and Hannah Sladden:

     i.   **Thomas Hawkes**, born 1692, in Folkestone, Kent, England, died 1771, in Folkestone, Kent, England.

1049. Hannah Sladden was born 1670, in Folkestone, Kent, England, died 23 Feb 1742, in Folkestone, Kent, England. She married Issac Hawkes 6 Jul 1691, in Folkestone, Kent, England.

1050. Jasper Venner was born 1669, in Middlesex, England, christened 11 Jun 1669, in Middlesex, England, died before 1750, in England. He was the son of Allexander Venner and Elizabeth Chadwick. He married Mrs Mary Venner about 1695, in England.

Children of Jasper Venner and Mrs Mary Venner:

     i.   **Isaak Venner**, born 1698, in Stepney, Middlesex, England, christened 28 Aug 1698, in Stepney, Middlesex, England.
     ii.   **Jasper Venner**, born 1700, in Stepney, Middlesex, England, christened 26 Jul 1700, in Stepney, Middlesex, England, died before 18 Oct 1702, in Stepney, Middlesex, England.
     iii.   **Alexander Venner**, born 1704, in Stepney, Middlesex, England, christened 15 Oct 1704, in Stepney, Middlesex, England, died before 7 Oct 1705, in Stepney, Middlesex, England.
     iv.   **Solomon Venner**, born 1707, in Stepney, Middlesex, England, christened 1 Jun 1707, in Stepney, Middlesex, England.
     v.   **Mary Venner**, born 1714, in Stepney, Middlesex, England, christened 23 Aug 1714, in Stepney, Middlesex, England.
     vi.   **Charles Vanner**, born 1715, in England, died before 1815, in England.

1051. Mrs Mary Venner was born about 1672, in England, died before 1770, in England. She married

Jasper Venner about 1695, in England. He was the son of Allexander Venner and Elizabeth Chadwick.

1052. Robert Graham was born about 1670, in London, England. He married Barbara Graham[1230] about 1694, in London, England.

Children of Robert Graham and Barbara Graham:

    i.   **William Graham**,[1231] born Jul 1695, in Westminster, London, England, christened 31 Jul 1695, in Covent Garden, London, England.

    ii.   **Richard Graham**,[1232] born Nov 1697, in Westminster, London, England, christened 27 Nov 1697, in Covent Garden, London, England.

    iii.   **Mary Graham**,[1233] born Jun 1699, in Westminster, London, England, christened 4 Jul 1699, in Covent Garden, London, England.

    iv.   **John Graham**,[1133,1136,1137] born Sep 1700, in Westminster, London, England.

    v.   **James Graham**,[1234] born Jun 1702, in Westminster, London, England, christened 27 Jun 1702, in Covent Garden, London, England.

1053. Barbara Graham was born about 1672, in London, England. She married Robert Graham[1230] about 1694, in London, England.

1054. Richard Partridge was born Apr 1668, in Cripplegate, London, England, christened 26 Apr 1668, in Cripplegate, London, England. He was the son of Richard Partridge and Margaret Partridge. He married Alice Longmore[1235,1236,1237] 10 Jun 1690, in London, England. She was the daughter of William Langmore and Mrs Alice Langmore.

Children of Richard Partridge and Alice Longmore:

    i.   **Mary Partridge**,[1133,1134,1135] born Aug 1699, in London, England.

1055. Alice Longmore was born Mar 1666, in London, England, christened 23 Mar 1666, in London, England. She was the daughter of William Langmore and Mrs Alice Langmore. She married Richard Partridge[1235,1236,1238] 10 Jun 1690, in London, England. He was the son of Richard Partridge and Margaret Partridge.
Notes for Alice Longmore:

aka LANGMORE

1056. John Mott was born about 1650, in London, England. He married Katherine Collins[1239] 9 Oct 1679, in Aldgate, London, England.

Children of John Mott and Katherine Collins:

    i.   **Milford Mott**,[1139,1140,1141] born Feb 1680, in Aldgate, London, England.

1057. Katherine Collins was born about 1652, in London, England. She married John Mott[1239] 9 Oct 1679, in Aldgate, London, England.

Generation No. 12

1058. Robert Aldworth was born 14 Mar 1599, in Wantage, Berkshire, England, christened 15 Apr 1599, in Wantage, Berkshire, England, died 1641, in Wantage, Berkshire, England. He was the son of Thomas Aldworth and Martha Daniell. He married Leticia Barlow[1240,1241,1242] 5 Apr 1624, in Abingdon, Berkshire, England. She was the daughter of Geoffry Barlow and Barlow.
Notes for Robert Aldworth:

Will Bond

Children of Robert Aldworth and Leticia Barlow:

      i.   **Thomas Aldworth,**[1144,1145] born Oct 1631, in Wantage, Berkshire, England, died 13 Oct 1681, in Wantage, Berkshire, England.

     ii.   **John Aldworth,**[1144,1243] born 10 Jun 1633, in Wantage, Berkshire, England, christened 10 Jun 1633, in Wantage, Berkshire, England. He married Amy Riggins 28 Apr 1661, in Cumnor, Berkshire, England. Amy Riggins was born about 1641, in Berkshire, England.
           Notes for John Aldworth and Amy Riggins: Berekshire marriages 2nd edition 28 Apr 1661 Cumnor - St Michael

   iii.   **Robert Aldworth,**[1144,1244] born 26 Apr 1635, in Wantage, Berkshire, England, christened 26 Apr 1635, in Wantage, Berkshire, England. He married Allsworth about 1658, in Berkshire, England. Allsworth was born about 1637, in Derkshire, England.

   iv.   **Margaret Aldworth,**[1144,1245] born 3 Jun 1638, in Wantage, Berkshire, England, christened 3 Jun 1638, in Wantage, Berkshire, England. She married Thomas Seymor 12 Jul 1660, in West Challow, Berkshire, England. Thomas Seymor was born about 1635, in Hailey, Oxfordshire, England.
           Notes for Thomas Seymor: aka "Seimor"

1059. Leticia Barlow was born 3 Oct 1605, in East Hendred, Berkshire, England, christened 3 Oct 1605, in East Hendred, Berkshire, England, died before 1700, in England. She was the daughter of Geoffry Barlow and Barlow. She married Robert Aldworth[1144,1246] 5 Apr 1624, in Abingdon, Berkshire, England. He was the son of Thomas Aldworth and Martha Daniell.
Notes for Leticia Barlow:

aka: Lettice inherited 215 15s 6d on 6 October 1641 - husband's will

1060.____Carter was born about 1620, in Oxfordshire, England. He married Carter about 1639, in Oxfordshire, England.

Children of Carter and Carter:

     i.   **John Carter**,[1146,1148] born about 1640, in Oxfordshire, England, died before 1700, in Northmoor, Oxfordshire, England.

1061._____Carter was born about 1622, in Oxfordshire, England. She married Carter about 1639, in Oxfordshire, England.

1062. Thomas Cockinges was born about 1546, in Lower Heyford, Oxfordshire, England, died Jun 1618, in Oxfordshire, England, buried 23 Jun 1618, in Upper Heyford, Oxfordshire, England. He married Elena Endall[1247] 4 May 1567, in Lower Heyford, Oxfordshire, England. She was the daughter of William Endal and Anna Fox.

Children of Thomas Cockinges and Elena Endall:

     i.   **John Cockinges**,[1248] born Jun 1568, in Lower Heyford, Oxfordshire, England, christened 28 Jun 1568, in Lower Heyford, Oxfordshire, England.
     ii.   **William Cockinges**,[1249] born May 1573, in Upper Heyford, Oxfordshire, England, christened 21 May 1573, in Upper Heyford, Oxfordshire, England.
     iii. **Thomas Cockinges**,[1250] born Feb 1575, in Upper Heyford, Oxfordshire, England, christened 13 Mar 1575, in Upper Heyford, Oxfordshire, England.
     iv. **George Cockinges**,[1251] born 1577, in Upper Heyford, Oxfordshire, England, christened Feb 1577, in Upper Heyford, Oxfordshire, England, buried 3 Nov 1577, in Upper Heyford, Oxfordshire, England.
     v.   **Stephen Cockin**,[1154] born Aug 1581, in Upper Heyford, Oxfordshire, England.

1063. Elena Endall was born Sep 1545, in Lower Heyford, Oxfordshire, England, christened 8 Oct 1545, in Lower Heyford, Oxfordshire, England, died Dec 1621, in Lower Heyford, Oxfordshire, England, buried 14 Dec 1621, in Lower Heyford, Oxfordshire, England. She was the daughter of William Endal and Anna Fox. She married Thomas Cockinges[1247] 4 May 1567, in Lower Heyford, Oxfordshire, England.

1064. Thomas Howse was born Jan 1578, in Upper Heyford, Oxfordshire, England, christened 24 Jan 1578, in Upper Heyford, Oxfordshire, England, died 3 Dec 1627, in Upper Heyford, Oxfordshire, England, buried 13 Dec 1627, in Upper Heyford, Oxfordshire, England. He was the son of Robert Howse and Joan Lever. He married Susan Timmes[1252,1253] 24 Jan 1604, in Upper Heyford, Oxfordshire, England.
Notes for Thomas Howse:

incorrectly shown as HOUSE in marriage records

Children of Thomas Howse and Susan Timmes:

      i.   **Robert Howse,**[1156] born Sep 1607, in Upper Heyford, Oxfordshire, England, died Jan 1682, in Upper Heyford, Oxfordshire, England.

1065. Susan Timmes was born about 1583, in Upper Heyford, Oxfordshire, England, died Feb 1667, in Upper Heyford, Oxfordshire, England, buried 7 Feb 1667, in Upper Heyford, Oxfordshire, England. She married Thomas Howse[1254,1255,1256] 24 Jan 1604, in Upper Heyford, Oxfordshire, England. He was the son of Robert Howse and Joan Lever.

1066. William Fenimore was born about 1531, in Wendlebury, Oxfordshire, England, died about 1582, in Oxfordshire, England. He married Mrs Alice Fenimore about 1556, in Wendlebury, Oxfordshire, England.

Children of William Fenimore and Mrs Alice Fenimore:

      i.   **Roger Venimore,**[965] born about 1557, in Wendlebury, Oxfordshire, England, died 26 Mar 1619, in Wendlebury, Oxfordshire, England.

1067. Mrs Alice Fenimore was born about 1535, in Wendlebury, Oxfordshire, England. She married William Fenimore about 1556, in Wendlebury, Oxfordshire, England.

1068. John Hawkins was born 1618, in Shellingford, Berkshire, England, buried 25 Apr 1688, in Shellingford, Berkshire, England. He married Joan Shepperd 11 Oct 1640, in Stanford in the Vale, Berkshire, England.

Children of John Hawkins and Joan Shepperd:

      i.   **Robert Hawkins**, born 1655, in Shellingford, Berkshire, England, died Jun 1688, in Shellingford, Berkshire, England.

1069. Joan Shepperd was born 1618, in Stanford in the Vale, Berkshire, England, died 1658, in Stanford in the Vale, Berkshire, England, buried 1 Mar 1658, in Shellingford, Berkshire, England. She married John Hawkins 11 Oct 1640, in Stanford in the Vale, Berkshire, England.

1070. Thomas Tubbs was born Jun 1621, in Wantage, Berkshire, England, christened 10 Jun 1631, in Wantage, Berkshire, England. He was the son of Thomas Tubb and Mrs Elizabeth Tubb. He married Eleanor Jennings 27 Dec 1652, in East Lockinge, Berkshire, England.

Children of Thomas Tubbs and Eleanor Jennings:

      i.   **Eleanor Tubbs**, born Mar 1653, in East Lockinge, Berkshire, England, died Feb 1729, in Shellingford, Berkshire, England.

ii. **Thomas Tubbs**, born May 1655, in East Lockinge, Berkshire, England, christened 15 May 1655, in East Lockinge, Berkshire, England.

iii. **Esther Tubbs**, born May 1656, in East Lockinge, Berkshire, England, christened 28 May 1656, in East Lockinge, Berkshire, England.

iv. **John Tubbs**, born Mar 1657, in East Lockinge, Berkshire, England, christened 19 Mar 1657, in East Lockinge, Berkshire, England.

v. **Mary Tubbs**, born Mar 1663, in East Lockinge, Berkshire, England, christened 4 Apr 1663, in East Lockinge, Berkshire, England.

vi. **Francis Tubbs**, born Jun 1665, in East Lockinge, Berkshire, England, christened 24 Jun 1665, in East Lockinge, Berkshire, England.

vii. **Elizabeth Tubbs**, born Aug 1673, in East Lockinge, Berkshire, England, christened 11 Aug 1673, in East Lockinge, Berkshire, England.

1071. Eleanor Jennings was born 1634, in Wantage, Berkshire, England. She married Thomas Tubbs 27 Dec 1652, in East Lockinge, Berkshire, England. He was the son of Thomas Tubb and Mrs Elizabeth Tubb.

1072. Francis Webb was born 1621, in Wantage, Berkshire, England, christened 18 Oct 1621, in Wantage, Berkshire, England. He was the son of John Webb and Joanne Hicks. He married Webb about 1645, in Berkshire, England.

Children of Francis Webb and Webb:

i. **Francis Webb**, born 1650, in Berkshire, England.

1073.____Webb was born about 1625, in Berkshire, England. She married Francis Webb about 1645, in Berkshire, England. He was the son of John Webb and Joanne Hicks.

1074. Richard Boyce was born 1628, in Berkshire, England, died 1694, in Berkshire, England. He married Ann Iles about 1652, in Berkshire, England. She was the daughter of Ralph Iles and Ann Gale.

Children of Richard Boyce and Ann Iles:

i. **Ann Boyce**, born 1655, in Little Coxwell, Berkshire, England.

1075. Ann Iles was born 1628, in Little Coxwell, Berkshire, England, christened 18 May 1628, in Little Coxwell, Berkshire, England, died 1710, in Berkshire, England. She was the daughter of Ralph Iles and Ann Gale. She married Richard Boyce about 1652, in Berkshire, England.

1076. William Alder was born Jun 1618, in Goosey, Berkshire, England, christened 1 Jul 1618, in Stanford in the Vale, Berkshire, England. He was the son of Thomas Alder and Elizabeth Yarley. He married Edyth Stanbrooke[1164,1257,1258] 29 Sep 1640, in Goosey, Berkshire, England. She was the daughter of William Stanbrooke and Mrs Alice Stanbrooke.

Children of William Alder and Edyth Stanbrooke:

> i. **William Alder**,[1163,1164,1165] born 6 Oct 1656, in Stanford in the Vale, Berkshire, England.

1077. Edyth Stanbrooke was born May 1615, in Denchworth, Berkshire, England, christened 3 Jun 1615, in Denchworth, Berkshire, England. She was the daughter of William Stanbrooke and Mrs Alice Stanbrooke. She married William Alder[1164,1257,1259,1260,1261] 29 Sep 1640, in Goosey, Berkshire, England. He was the son of Thomas Alder and Elizabeth Yarley.
Notes for Edyth Stanbrooke:

aka: EDYETH STAMBROOKE

1078. Richard Stone was born about 1560, in Longworth, Berkshire, England, died Aug 1607, in Longworth, Berkshire, England, buried 7 Aug 1607, in Longworth, Berkshire, England. He was the son of William Stone and Mrs William Stone. He married Elizabeth Flexney 13 Nov 1582, in Stanton Harcourt, Oxfordshire, England. She was the daughter of Flaxnei and Flaxnei.

Children of Richard Stone and Elizabeth Flexney:

> i. **Dorytie Stone**, born Apr 1588, in Longworth, Berkshire, England, christened 1 May 1588, in Longworth, Berkshire, England.
> ii. **Thomas Stone**, born Oct 1589, in Longworth, Berkshire, England, christened 1 Nov 1589, in Longworth, Berkshire, England.
> iii. **Richard Stone**, born about 1590, in Berkshire, England.
> iv. **John Stone**, born Dec 1593, in Longworth, Berkshire, England, christened 20 Dec 1593, in Longworth, Berkshire, England.
> v. **Elizabeth Stone**, born Aug 1596, in Longworth, Berkshire, England, christened 31 Aug 1596, in Longworth, Berkshire, England.

1079. Elizabeth Flexney was born about 1560, in Stanton Harcourt, Oxfordshire, England, died 7 Aug 1614, in Longworth, Berkshire, England, buried 7 Aug 1614, in Longworth, Berkshire, England. She was the daughter of Flaxnei and Flaxnei. She married Richard Stone 13 Nov 1582, in Stanton Harcourt, Oxfordshire, England. He was the son of William Stone and Mrs William Stone.
Notes for Elizabeth Flexney:

aka FLAXNEY, FLAXNEI, FLEXNEI

1080. Thomas Onion was born about 1573, in Berkshire, England, died May 1613, in Hinton Waldrist, Berkshire, England, buried 24 May 1613, in Hinton Waldrist, Berkshire, England. He was the son of Thomas Onion and Mrs Jone Onion. He married Agnes Kimber 6 Jul 1592, in Hinton Waldrist, Berkshire, England.

Children of Thomas Onion and Agnes Kimber:

    i.   **Elizabeth Onion Or Vuyon**, born Feb 1592, in Hinton Waldrist, Berkshire, England, christened 6 Feb 1592, in Hinton Waldrist, Berkshire, England. She married William Mansfield 4 Oct 1612, in Hinton Waldrist, Berkshire, England. William Mansfield was born about 1590, in Berkshire, England.
1. Berkshire Parish Registers, . "1612, 4 Oct, Mansfield, William and Onion, Elizabeth."
Notes for William Mansfield: 1. Berkshire Parish Registers, . "1612, 4 Oct, Mansfield, William and Onion, Elizabeth."

    ii.   **Jone Onion**, born Mar 1594, in Hinton Waldrist, Berkshire, England, christened 16 Mar 1594, in Hinton Waldrist, Berkshire, England.

    iii.   **Robertus Onion**, born Nov 1597, in Hinton Waldrist, Berkshire, England, christened 23 Nov 1597, in Hinton Waldrist, Berkshire, England. He married Elizabeth Perris 9 Oct 1621, in Welford, Berkshire, England. Elizabeth Perris was born about 1600, in Welford, Berkshire, England.

    iv.   **William Onyon**, born Nov 1600, in Appleton With Eaton, Berkshire, England, christened 2 Nov 1600, in Appleton With Eaton, Berkshire, England.[1262] He married Catharine Bead 30 Jan 1633, in Longworth, Berkshire, England. Catharine Bead was born about 1605, in Berkshire, England.
First name(s)   William Last name   O'Yon (ONION) Baptism year   1600 Baptism date   02 Nov 1600 Parish   Appleton Church   St Laurence County   Berkshire Country   England Record set   Berkshire Baptisms Category   Birth, Marriage, Death & Parish Records Subcategory   Births & baptisms Collections from   Gr Battain

    v.   **Thomas Onion,**[1172] born Sep 1602, in Hinton Waldrist, Berkshire, England, died Jul 1686, in Hinton Waldrist, Berkshire, England.

    vi.   **Henry Onion,**[1263,1264] born Nov 1604, in Hinton Waldrist, Berkshire, England, christened 1 Dec 1604, in Hinton Waldrist, Berkshire, England, died Nov 1607, in Hinton Waldrist, Berkshire, England, buried 12 Nov 1607, in Hinton Waldrist, Berkshire, England.
appears in Hinton Wladrist, Berkshire, England parish burial record

    vii.   **Mary Onion,**[1265,1266] born Feb 1608, in Hinton Waldrist, Berkshire, England, christened 24 Feb 1608, in Hinton Waldrist, Berkshire, England, died Jun 1613, in Hinton Waldrist, Berkshire, England, buried 17 Jun 1613, in Hinton Waldrist, Berkshire, England.
appears in Hinton Wladrist, Berkshire, England parish burial record

1081. Agnes Kimber was born about 1571, in Hinton Waldrist, Berkshire, England, died 1616, in Hinton Waldrist, Berkshire, England, buried 13 Mar 1616, in Hinton Waldrist, Berkshire, England. She married Thomas Onion[1267] 6 Jul 1592, in Hinton Waldrist, Berkshire, England. He was the son of Thomas Onion and Mrs Jone Onion.
Notes for Agnes Kimber:

Death : Shown as Agneta - Hinton Waldrist parish records - burials

1082. Robert Swifte was born about 1555, in Oxfordshire, England, died Dec 1602, in Adderbury, Oxfordshire, England, buried 20 Dec 1602, in Adderbury, Oxfordshire, England. He married Swifte about 1575, in Oxfordshire, England.

Children of Robert Swifte and Swifte:

     i.   **Richard Swifte**,[1268] born about 1575, in Oxfordshire, England. He married Mrs Alice Swifte about 1598, in Oxfordshire, England. Mrs Alice Swifte was born about 1576, in Oxfordshire, England, christened 3 May 1603, in Adderbury, Oxfordshire, England.
Notes for Mrs Alice Swifte: Had been married for about 4 years before she was christened - Adderbury parish records 3 may 1603

    ii.   **Edward Swifte**,[1269,1270] born about 1577, in Oxfordshire, England, died Mar 1649, in Adderbury, Oxfordshire, England, buried 23 Mar 1649, in Adderbury, Oxfordshire, England. He married Margaret Wright[1269] 16 May 1598, in Adderbury, Oxfordshire, England. Margaret Wright was born about 1579, in Oxfordshire, England.

   iii.   **William Swifte**,[1269,1271] born about 1578, in Oxfordshire, England, died Jan 1609, in Adderbury, Oxfordshire, England, buried 13 Jan 1609, in Adderbury, Oxfordshire, England. He married Katheren Gibbs[1269,1272,1273] 16 Oct 1598, in Adderbury, Oxfordshire, England. Katheren Gibbs was born about 1579, in Oxfordshire, England, died Feb 1648, in Adderbury, Oxfordshire, England, buried 17 Feb 1648, in Adderbury, Oxfordshire, England

    iv.   **Michael Swifte**,[1274,1275] born about 1580, in Oxfordshire, England, died Mar 1613, in Adderbury, Oxfordshire, England, buried 24 Mar 1613, in Adderbury, Oxfordshire, England. He married Alice Turner[1274] 9 May 1603, in Adderbury, Oxfordshire, England. Alice Turner was born about 1582, in Oxfordshire, England, christened 3 May 1603, in Adderbury, Oxfordshire, England.

    v.   **Thomas Swifte**,[1276,1277] born about 1585, in Oxfordshire, England, died Mar 1612, in Adderbury, Oxfordshire, England, buried 14 Mar 1612, in Adderbury, Oxfordshire, England. He married Julian Sconce[1278] 20 Jan 1612, in Adderbury, Oxfordshire, England. Julian Sconce was born about 1590, in Oxfordshire, England.

    vi.   **Martyn Swifte**,[1179] born about 1590, in Oxfordshire, England.

1083.____Swifte was born about 1556, in Oxfordshire, England. She married Robert Swifte[1279] about 1575, in Oxfordshire, England.

1084. William Poulton was born about 1580, in Adderbury, Oxfordshire, England. He married Mable Mathewe[1280] 3 Feb 1607, in Adderbury, Oxfordshire, England.

Children of William Poulton and Mable Mathewe:

     i.   **Elizabeth Poulton**,[1281] born Oct 1607, in Adderbury, Oxfordshire, England, christened 13 Oct 1607, in Adderbury, Oxfordshire, England.

    ii.   **Mabell Poulton**,[1282] born Mar 1609, in Adderbury, Oxfordshire, England, christened 18 Mar 1609, in Adderbury, Oxfordshire, England.

   iii.   **Timothy Poulton**,[1187] born Apr 1613, in Adderbury, Oxfordshire, England.

   iv.   **Mathew Poulton**,[1283] born Jul 1620, in Adderbury, Oxfordshire, England, christened 29 Jul 1620, in Adderbury, Oxfordshire, England.

    v.   **Ann Poulton**,[1174] born Mar 1623, in Adderbury, Oxfordshire, England, christened 26 Mar 1623, in Adderbury, Oxfordshire, England.

   vi.   **Dorothie Poulton**,[1284] born Aug 1628, in Adderbury, Oxfordshire, England, christened 1 Sep 1628, in Adderbury, Oxfordshire, England.

1085. Mable Mathewe was born about 1582, in Adderbury, Oxfordshire, England. She married William Poulton[1280] 3 Feb 1607, in Adderbury, Oxfordshire, England.

1086. John Oxlade was born 1598, in Fingest, Buckinghamshire, England, died 30 Jan 1661, in Great Marlow, Buckinghamshire, England. He was the son of John Oxlade and Elizabeth Plumridge. He married Frances Munday 1 Nov 1627, in Fingest, Buckinghamshire, England.
Notes for John Oxlade:

Known as John Oxlade The younger Made his will 10 May 1652 proved 17 Apr 1662

Children of John Oxlade and Frances Munday:

     i.   **Mary Oxlade**, born 1628, in Great Marlow, Buckinghamshire, England, christened 9 Nov 1628, in Little Hampden, Buckinghamshire, England.
Fingest, Buckingham parish records.

    ii.   **John Oxlade**, born Mar 1630, in Great Marlow, Buckinghamshire, England, died 25 Sep 1667, in Great Marlow, Buckinghamshire, England.

   iii.   **Robert Oxlade**, born 1633, in Great Marlow, Buckinghamshire, England, christened 2 Jun 1633, in Fingest, Buckinghamshire, England.
Fingest, Buckingham parish records.

   iv.   **Amelia Oxlade**, born 1635, in Great Marlow, Buckinghamshire, England, christened 10 Jan 1635, in Great Marlow, Buckinghamshire, England.

    v.   **William Oxlade**, born 1637, in Great Marlow, Buckinghamshire, England, died 27 Oct 1727, in Lane End, Buckinghamshire, England. He married Mrs Dorothy Oxlade about 1670, in Berkshire, England. Mrs Dorothy Oxlade was born about 1638, in Buckinghamshire, England.

   vi.   **Elizabeth Oxlade**,[1285] born 1638, in Brightwell Baldwin, Oxfordshire, England, christened 4 Jul 1638, in Great Marlow, Buckinghamshire, England.

   vii.   **Joan Oxlade**, born 1641, in Brightwell Baldwin, Oxfordshire, England, christened

13 Jul 1641, in Great Marlow, Buckinghamshire, England.

viii. **George Oxlade**, born 1643, in Brightwell Baldwin, Oxfordshire, England, christened 17 Dec 1643, in Great Marlow, Buckinghamshire, England, died 1711, in England.

1087. Frances Munday was born 1600, in Fingest, Buckinghamshire, England, died before 1700, in England. She married John Oxlade 1 Nov 1627, in Fingest, Buckinghamshire, England. He was the son of John Oxlade and Elizabeth Plumridge.
Notes for Frances Munday:

aka: FRANNCES

1088.____Salter was born 1611, in Bisham, Berkshire, England. He married Salter about 1631, in Berkshire, England.

Children of Salter and Salter:

i. **William Salter**, born 1633, in Bisham, Berkshire, England, died 21 Oct 1669, in Bisham, Berkshire, England.

1089.____Salter was born about 1612, in Berkshire, England. She married Salter about 1631, in Berkshire, England.

1090. Thomas Broadway was born 1590, in Cuxham, Oxfordshire, England, died 26 Jun 1667, in Cuxham, Oxfordshire, England, buried 27 Jun 1667, in Cuxham, Oxfordshire, England. He was the son of Broadway and Broadway. He married Agnes Fritwell 2 Nov 1618, in Cuxham, Oxfordshire, England.[734] She was the daughter of John Fritwell and Mrs Isabell Druse.
Notes for Thomas Broadway:

taken from parish records

Children of Thomas Broadway and Agnes Fritwell:

i. **Elizabeth Broadway**, born 1619, in Cuxham, Oxfordshire, England.
ii. **Thomas Broadway**, born 1 Jan 1621, in Cuxham, Oxfordshire, England, died 25 Jun 1709, in Cuxham, Oxfordshire, England.
iii. **William Broadway**, born 1624, in Cuxham, Oxfordshire, England, died 1624, in Cuxham, Oxfordshire, England.
iv. **Jane Broadway**, born 1629, in Cuxham, Oxfordshire, England, christened 21 Feb 1629, in Cuxham, Oxfordshire, England, died 1 Nov 1639, in Cuxham, Oxfordshire, England.
v. **John Broadway**, born 1631, in Cuxham, Oxfordshire, England.

1091. Agnes Fritwell was born 1594, in Cuxham, Oxfordshire, England, christened 4 Oct 1594, in Cuxham, Oxfordshire, England, died May 1665, in Cuxham, Oxfordshire, England, buried May 1665, in Cuxham, Oxfordshire, England. She was the daughter of John Fritwell and Mrs Isabell Druse. She married Thomas Broadway 2 Nov 1618, in Cuxham, Oxfordshire, England.[734] He was the son of Broadway and Broadway.

Notes for Agnes Fritwell:

exact date of burial not given in parish record only the month May 1665

1092. William Scholes was born 1572, in Lewknor, Oxfordshire, England, died Feb 1650, in Lewknor, Oxfordshire, England, buried 20 Feb 1650, in Lewknor, Oxfordshire, England. He was the son of William Scholes and Mrs Ellenor Scholes. He married Mrs William Scholes about 1592, in Oxfordshire, England.

Children of William Scholes and Mrs William Scholes:

    i.   **William Scholes**, born about 1615, in Lewknor, Oxfordshire, England, died 21 Apr 1664.

1093. Mrs William Scholes was born about 1572, in Lewknor, Oxfordshire, England. She married William Scholes about 1592, in Oxfordshire, England. He was the son of William Scholes and Mrs Ellenor Scholes.

1094. Robert Munday was born Mar 1589, in Oxfordshire, England, christened 15 Mar 1589, in Chinnor, Oxfordshire, England, died Feb 1668, in Chalford, Oxfordshire, England, buried 13 Feb 1668, in Aston Rowant, Oxfordshire, England. He was the son of Robert Munday and Margery Floyd. He married Munday about 1619, in Aston Rowant, Oxfordshire, England.

Children of Robert Munday and Munday:

    i.   **Ursual Munday**, born about 1619, in Lewknor, Oxfordshire, England.
    ii.   **William Munday**, born Aug 1624, in Aston Rowant, Oxfordshire, England, christened 1 Sep 1624, in Aston Rowant, Oxfordshire, England, buried 29 Aug 1684, in Aston Rowant, Oxfordshire, England.
    iii.   **Robert Munday**, born Nov 1622, in Aston Rowant, Oxfordshire, England, christened 30 Nov 1622, in Aston Rowant, Oxfordshire, England, buried 27 Jan 1697, in Aston Rowant, Oxfordshire, England.

1095. Munday was born 1586, in Aston Rowant, Oxfordshire, England, christened 2 Jan 1587, in Aston Rowant, Oxfordshire, England, buried 23 Jul 1681, in Aston Rowant, Oxfordshire, England. She married Robert Munday about 1619, in Aston Rowant, Oxfordshire, England. He was the son of Robert Munday and Margery Floyd.

1096. Richard Belson was born about 1578, in Aston Rowant, Oxfordshire, England, died Nov 1631, in Aston Rowant, Oxfordshire, England, buried 18 Nov 1631, in Aston Rowant, Oxfordshire, England. He was the son of Thomas Belson and Elizabeth Lechpole. He married Edith Dutton about 1598, in Aston Rowant, Oxfordshire, England. She was the daughter of Leonard Dutton and Mrs Leonard Dutton.

Children of Richard Belson and Edith Dutton:

    i.   **Richard Belson**,[1192] born 21 Dec 1601, in Aston Rowant, Oxfordshire, England, died Apr 1686, in Aston Rowant, Oxfordshire, England.

1097. Edith Dutton was born about 1579, in Crowell, Oxfordshire, England. She was the daughter of Leonard Dutton and Mrs Leonard Dutton. She married Richard Belson about 1598, in Aston Rowant, Oxfordshire, England. He was the son of Thomas Belson and Elizabeth Lechpole.

1098. Gualteri Potts was born about 1563, in Aston Rowant, Oxfordshire, England, died Jan 1628, in Aston Rowant, Oxfordshire, England, buried 7 Jan 1628, in Aston Rowant, Oxfordshire, England. He married Anna Potts about 1586, in Aston Rowant, Oxfordshire, England.

Children of Gualteri Potts and Anna Potts:

    i.   **Alicia Pottes**,[1192] born Oct 1605, in Aston Rowant, Oxfordshire, England, died Apr 1678, in Aston Rowant, Oxfordshire, England.

1099. Anna Potts was born about 1567, in Aston Rowant, Oxfordshire, England, died Dec 1653, in Aston Rowant, Oxfordshire, England, buried 5 Dec 1653, in Aston Rowant, Oxfordshire, England. She married Gualteri Potts[1286] about 1586, in Aston Rowant, Oxfordshire, England.

1100. John Kirby was born Jan 1612, in Charlton on Otmoor, Oxfordshire, England, christened 24 Jan 1612, in Charlton on Otmoor, Oxfordshire, England, died Oct 1670, in Charlton on Otmoor, Oxfordshire, England, buried 22 Oct 1670, in Charlton on Otmoor, Oxfordshire, England. He was the son of Peter Kirbe and Jayne Allye Leyveret. He married Bridget Marsh[1287] 11 Oct 1638, in Charlton on Otmoor, Oxfordshire, England. She was the daughter of Jefferedi Marsh and Marshe.

Children of John Kirby and Bridget Marsh:

    i.   **Elizabeth Kerbie**,[1288] born Jan 1641, in Arncott, Oxfordshire, England, christened 21 Jan 1641, in Charlton on Otmoor, Oxfordshire, England.
    ii.   **John Kirby**,[1199] born 27 Apr 1642, in Arncott, Oxfordshire, England, died Aug 1690, in Charlton on Otmoor, Oxfordshire, England.

1101. Bridget Marsh was born May 1613, in Blackthorn, Oxfordshire, England, christened 20 May 1613, in Ambrosden, Oxfordshire, England, died Sep 1692, in Charlton on Otmoor, Oxfordshire, England, buried 22 Sep 1692, in Charlton on Otmoor, Oxfordshire, England. She was the daughter of

Jefferedi Marsh and Marshe. She married John Kirby[1287,1289] 11 Oct 1638, in Charlton on Otmoor, Oxfordshire, England. He was the son of Peter Kirbe and Jayne Allye Leyveret.

1102. John Walker was born about 1616, in Oxfordshire, England, died 1680, in Murcot, Oxfordshire, England. He was the son of Thomas Walker and Anne Bourne. He married Elizabeth Croxton[1290] about 1636, in Oxfordshire, England. She was the daughter of Thomas Croxton and Anna Bourne.

Children of John Walker and Elizabeth Croxton:

    i.   **John Walker**, born May 1638, in Charlton on Otmoor, Oxfordshire, England, christened 3 Jun 1638, in Islip, Oxfordshire, England.

    ii.   **Thomas Walker**, born about 1640, in Charlton on Otmoor, Oxfordshire, England.

    iii.   **William Walker**, born about 1642, in Charlton on Otmoor, Oxfordshire, England.

    iv.   **Elizabeth Walker**, born about 1644, in Murcot, Oxfordshire, England.

    v.   **Anne Walker**,[1198] born 1646, in Noke, Oxfordshire, England, died Nov 1679, in Charlton on Otmoor, Oxfordshire, England.

1103. Elizabeth Croxton was born Dec 1616, in Blackthorn, Oxfordshire, England, christened 1 Jan 1617, in Ambrosden, Oxfordshire, England. She was the daughter of Thomas Croxton and Anna Bourne. She married John Walker about 1636, in Oxfordshire, England. He was the son of Thomas Walker and Anne Bourne.

1104. John Howlett was born 5 Oct 1595, in Murcot, Oxfordshire, England, christened 5 Oct 1595, in Charlton on Otmoor, Oxfordshire, England, died May 1633, in Charlton on Otmoor, Oxfordshire, England, buried 13 May 1633, in Charlton on Otmoor, Oxfordshire, England. He was the son of Robart Howlett and Elizabeth Quenton. He married Elizabeth Sharpe[1291] 25 Nov 1619, in Charlton on Otmoor, Oxfordshire, England. She was the daughter of Christopher Sharpe and Annas Kirby.

Children of John Howlett and Elizabeth Sharpe:

    i.   **Anne Howlett**,[1292] born Mar 1621, in Charlton on Otmoor, Oxfordshire, England, christened 4 Mar 1621, in Charlton on Otmoor, Oxfordshire, England, died Oct 1665, in Charlton on Otmoor, Oxfordshire, England, buried 12 Oct 1665, in Charlton on Otmoor, Oxfordshire, England. She married John Wiat 24 Jun 1641, in Charlton on Otmoor, Oxfordshire, England. John Wiat was born about 1614, in Oxfordshire, England, christened 5 Mar 1614, in Charlton on Otmoor, Oxfordshire, England, buried 25 Nov 1680, in Charlton on Otmoor, Oxfordshire, England. Notes for John Wiat: Charlton on Otmoor, Oxford, England - chr. 1614 Mar 5 John s Willm - Will of William Wyatt, Murcott, Charlton, Oxford, (his father) Oxford Arch Ct Ser 11 Vol 8 p. 372 SLFHL film # 095,069 W.D.- W.P. 11 Apr 1640 to my son John all the rest - my copyhold in Murcott accordiing to Manor of Islip (to be paid by William my oldest son which beareth date of 29 Sept 14th year of King Charles) John, my youngest sonne to be extor

    ii.   **Robert Howlett**,[1293] born Dec 1622, in Oddington, Oxfordshire, England, christened 15 Dec 1622, in Charlton on Otmoor, Oxfordshire, England, died 11 Apr 1689, in Charlton on Otmoor, Oxfordshire, England, buried 11 Apr 1689, in Charlton on Otmoor, Oxfordshire, England. He married Mrs Ann Heulett 1654, in Charlton on Otmoor, Oxfordshire, England. Mrs Ann Heulett was born about 1633, in Charlton on Otmoor, Oxfordshire, England, died before 1733, in England.

    iii.   **Christopher Howlett**,[1294] born Jan 1625, in Charlton on Otmoor, Oxfordshire, England, christened 23 Jan 1625, in Charlton on Otmoor, Oxfordshire, England.

    iv.   **John Howlett**,[1203] born Jan 1626, in Charlton on Otmoor, Oxfordshire, England.

    v.   **Elizabeth Howlett**,[1295,1296] born Sep 1628, in Oddington, Oxfordshire, England, christened 14 Sep 1628, in Charlton on Otmoor, Oxfordshire, England, died Sep 1629, in Charlton on Otmoor, Oxfordshire, England, buried 4 Oct 1629, in Charlton on Otmoor, Oxfordshire, England.

    vi.   **Elizabeth Howlett**,[1297] born Aug 1630, in Charlton on Otmoor, Oxfordshire, England, christened 15 Aug 1630, in Charlton on Otmoor, Oxfordshire, England.

1105. Elizabeth Sharpe was born Jul 1595, in Charlton on Otmoor, Oxfordshire, England, christened 11 Jul 1595, in Charlton on Otmoor, Oxfordshire, England, died before 1680, in England. She was the daughter of Christopher Sharpe and Annas Kirby. She married John Howlett[1291,1298,1299] 25 Nov 1619, in Charlton on Otmoor, Oxfordshire, England. He was the son of Robart Howlett and Elizabeth Quenton.

1106. Ralph Clark was born Nov 1606, in Waddesdon, Buckinghamshire, England, christened 7 Dec 1606, in Waddesdon, Buckinghamshire, England. He was the son of William Clark and Clark. He married Katherine Longe[1301] 8 Jul 1621, in Waddesdon, Buckinghamshire, England.[1300]
Notes for Ralph Clark:

May have only been 15 years old at marriage

Children of Ralph Clark and Katherine Longe:

    i.   **Ralph Clark**,[1204] born about 1622, in Buckinghamshire, England.

    ii.   **Peter Clark**, born Aug 1625, in Waddesdon, Buckinghamshire, England, christened 7 Aug 1625, in Waddesdon, Buckinghamshire, England.

1107. Katherine Longe was born about 1600, in Buckinghamshire, England. She married Ralph Clark[1301,1302] 8 Jul 1621, in Waddesdon, Buckinghamshire, England.[1300] He was the son of William Clark and Clark.

1108. Thomas Bowles was born about 1600, in Gloucestershire, England, died before 1700, in England. He was the son of Roberte Bowles and Bowles. He married Ann Mowsdale[1303] 30 Jul 1626, in Fairford, Gloucestershire, England.
Notes for Thomas Bowles:

marriage: 30 Jul 1626 Fairford, Gloucester, England spouse: Ann Mowsdale record title: England Marriages, 15381973 groom's name: Thomas Bowles bride's name: Ann Mowsdale marriage date: 30 Jul 1626 marriage place: Fairford,Gloucester,England indexing project (batch) number: M04514-1 system origin: England-ODM source filmnumber: 856942

Children of Thomas Bowles and Ann Mowsdale:

    i.   **Thomas Bowles**,[1206] born Aug 1643, in Fairford, Gloucestershire, England, died before 1740, in England.

1109. Ann Mowsdale was born about 1603, in Gloucestershire, England, christened about 1603, in Fairford, Gloucestershire, England, died before 1700, in England. She married Thomas Bowles[1304,1305,1306,1307,1308,1309] 30 Jul 1626, in Fairford, Gloucestershire, England. He was the son of Roberte Bowles and Bowles.

1110. Thomas Loveday was born Apr 1601, in Wanborough, Wiltshire, England, christened 21 Apr 1601, in Wanborough, Wiltshire, England, died about 1671, in Wanborough, Wiltshire, England, buried 23 Apr 1671, in Wanborough, Wiltshire, England. He was the son of Edmond Loveday and Elizabeth Smith. He married Emma Grundy[1310,1311] 21 Oct 1624, in Wanborough, Wiltshire, England. She was the daughter of John Grundy and Grundy.

Children of Thomas Loveday and Emma Grundy:

    i.   **Thomas Loveday**,[1312] born May 1626, in Wanborough, Wiltshire, England, christened 4 Jun 1626, in Wanborough, Wiltshire, England, died before 1635, in Wanborough, Wiltshire, England.

    ii.   **Eleabeth Loveday**,[1313] born Jul 1629, in Wanborough, Wiltshire, England, christened 20 Jul 1629, in Wanborough, Wiltshire, England, died 20 Jul 1629, in Wanborough, Wiltshire, England, buried 20 Jul 1629, in Wanborough, Wiltshire, England.

    iii.   **Thomas Loveday**,[1214] born Dec 1635, in Wanborough, Wiltshire, England, died May 1699, in Wanborough, Wiltshire, England.

1111. Emma Grundy was born about 1605, in Stratton St Margaret, Wiltshire, England, christened about 1605, in Stratton St Margaret, Wiltshire, England, died Jan 1649, in Wanborough, Wiltshire, England, buried 28 Jan 1649, in Wanborough, Wiltshire, England. She was the daughter of John Grundy and Grundy. She married (1) Thomas Loveday[1314] 21 Oct 1624, in Wanborough, Wiltshire, England. He was the son of Edmond Loveday and Elizabeth Smith. She married (2) Thomas Loveday[1315] 1624, in Wanborough, Wiltshire, England. He was the son of John Loveday and Agness Brynd.

1112. Henry Hedges was born about 1613, in Hinton Parva, Wiltshire, England, died Mar 1671, in Wanborough, Wiltshire, England, buried 10 Mar 1671, in Little Hinton, Wiltshire, England. He was the son of Robert Hedges and Mrs. Dorothy Hedges. He married Margery Pleydall about 1637, in Little

Hinton, Wiltshire, England.

Children of Henry Hedges and Margery Pleydall:

> i. **Martha Hedges**,[1207] born 27 Dec 1638, in Bishopstone, Wiltshire, England, died Feb 1725, in Wanborough, Wiltshire, England.

1113. Margery Pleydall was born after 1617, in Hinton Parva, Wiltshire, England, died about Aug 1699, in Little Hinton, Wiltshire, England, buried Aug 1699, in Little Hinton, Wiltshire, England. She married Henry Hedges about 1637, in Little Hinton, Wiltshire, England. He was the son of Robert Hedges and Mrs. Dorothy Hedges.

1114. Thomas Rogers was born Jun 1602, in Tewkesbury, Gloucestershire, England, christened 27 Jun 1602, in Tewkesbury, Gloucestershire, England. He married Anne Finche[1316] 2 Apr 1621, in Cirencester, Gloucestershire, England.

Children of Thomas Rogers and Anne Finche:

> i. **Thomas Rogers**, born about 1622, in Gloucestershire, England, died before 1720, in England.

1115. Anne Finche was born about 1603, in Gloucestershire, England, died before 1700, in England. She married Thomas Rogers[1316,1317] 2 Apr 1621, in Cirencester, Gloucestershire, England.

1116. Thomas Hunt was born about 1630, in Compton Abbas, Dorset, England, died before 1728, in Compton Abbas, Dorset, England. He married Mrs Joan Hunt about 1660, in Compton Abbas, Dorset, England.

Children of Thomas Hunt and Mrs Joan Hunt:

> i. **George Hunt**, born 1663, in Compton Abbas, Dorset, England.
> ii. **Joan Hunt**, born 1664, in Compton Abbas, Dorset, England.
> iii. **Thomas Hunt**, born 1668, in Compton Abbas, Dorset, England, died before 1750, in England.

1117. Mrs Joan Hunt was born about 1633, in Compton Abbas, Dorset, England, died before 1731, in Compton Abbas, Dorset, England. She married Thomas Hunt about 1660, in Compton Abbas, Dorset, England.

1118. Peter Times was born 1619, in Farthinghoe, Northamptonshire, England, christened 11 Feb 1619, in Farthinghoe, Northamptonshire, England, died before 1700, in England. He was the son of Lawrence Tims and Marie Newman. He married Mary Turland 7 Aug 1651, in Newbottle with Charlton, Northamptonshire, England.

Children of Peter Times and Mary Turland:

    i.   **Peter Tims**, born 1652, in Newbottle with Charlton, Northamptonshire, England, christened 28 Dec 1652, in Newbottle with Charlton, Northamptonshire, England.

    ii.   **Margaret Timms**, born 1654, in Newbottle with Charlton, Northamptonshire, England.

    iii.   **Susanna Timms**, born 1657, in Newbottle with Charlton, Northamptonshire, England.

    iv.   **George Timms**, born 1661, in Aynho, Northamptonshire, England, christened 10 Nov 1661, in Aynho, Northamptonshire, England.

    v.   **William Tims**, born 1665, in Farthinghoe, Northamptonshire, England, died before 1750, in England.

    vi.   **John Timms**, born 1666, in Farthinghoe, Northamptonshire, England, christened 1 Mar 1666, in Farthinghoe, Northamptonshire, England.

    vii.   **Alice Timms**, born 1668, in Newbottle with Charlton, Northamptonshire, England.

1119. Mary Turland was born 1630, in Newbottle with Charlton, Northamptonshire, England, died before 1730, in England. She married Peter Times 7 Aug 1651, in Newbottle with Charlton, Northamptonshire, England. He was the son of Lawrence Tims and Marie Newman.

1120. William Naylor was born about 1630, in Northamptonshire, England, died before 1730, in England. He married Mrs Jane Naylor about 1660, in England.

Children of William Naylor and Mrs Jane Naylor:

    i.   **Elizabeth Naylor**, born 1667, in Farthinghoe, Northamptonshire, England, died before 1750, in England.

1121. Mrs Jane Naylor was born about 1635, in England, died before 1735, in England. She married William Naylor about 1660, in England.

1122. Thomas Collison was born 1623, in Woodeaton, Oxfordshire, England, died 1672, in Woodeaton, Oxfordshire, England, buried 11 Mar 1672, in Woodeaton, Oxfordshire, England. He married Mary Cox 1 Aug 1648, in Kidlington, Oxfordshire, England. She was the daughter of Richard Cox and Mrs Isabel Cox.

Children of Thomas Collison and Mary Cox:

    i.   **Jane Collison**, born 1648, in Woodeaton, Oxfordshire, England, christened 4 Feb 1648, in Woodeaton, Oxfordshire, England.

    ii.   **Anne Collison**, born 1654, in Woodeaton, Oxfordshire, England, christened 10 Sep 1654, in Woodeaton, Oxfordshire, England.

    iii.   **Thomas Collison**, born 1657, in Woodeaton, Oxfordshire, England, christened 27

Sep 1657, in Woodeaton, Oxfordshire, England, died 1662, in Woodeaton, Oxfordshire, England.

iv. **William Collison**, born Aug 1661, in Woodeaton, Oxfordshire, England, died 1730, in Woodeaton, Oxfordshire, England.

v. **John Collison**, born 23 Feb 1663, in Woodeaton, Oxfordshire, England, christened 28 Feb 1663, in Woodeaton, Oxfordshire, England.

vi. **Elizabeth Collison**, born 7 Jun 1667, in Woodeaton, Oxfordshire, England, christened 9 Jun 1667, in Woodeaton, Oxfordshire, England, died Feb 1675, in Woodeaton, Oxfordshire, England, buried 17 Feb 1675, in Woodeaton, Oxfordshire, England.

1123. Mary Cox was born 1625, in Woodeaton, Oxfordshire, England, christened 29 Jan 1625, in Woodeaton, Oxfordshire, England, died 1670, in Woodeaton, Oxfordshire, England, buried 7 Oct 1670, in Woodeaton, Oxfordshire, England. She was the daughter of Richard Cox and Mrs Isabel Cox. She married Thomas Collison 1 Aug 1648, in Kidlington, Oxfordshire, England.

1124. William Bodily was born 1625, in Whittlebury, Northamptonshire, England. He married Mrs Alice Bodily about 1648, in Northamptonshire, England.

Children of William Bodily and Mrs Alice Bodily:

i. **John Bodily**, born 20 Jan 1649, in Crediton, Devonshire, England, died 1723, in Alderton, Northamptonshire, England.

1125. Mrs Alice Bodily was born about 1627, in Whittlebury, Northamptonshire, England. She married William Bodily about 1648, in Northamptonshire, England.

1126. Robert Ashby was born about 1607, in Bugbrooke, Northamptonshire, England, christened 15 Jan 1608, in Bugbrooke, Northamptonshire, England, died 1689, in Bugbrooke, Northamptonshire, England, buried Jul 1689, in Bugbrooke, Northamptonshire, England. He was the son of John Ashby and Mrs Agnis Ashby. He married Jane Stephenson 1636, in Bugbrooke, Northamptonshire, England. She was the daughter of Richard Stevenson and Stevenson.
Notes for Robert Ashby:

Became a Quaker about 1651-1663 Sent to prison 1663 for refusing to pay tithes at the suit of one Whitfield priest of Bugbrooke who made great spoil on his effects at home taking away sometimes whole fields of corn and whole loads of grain and hay far exceeding any legal claim. Robert Ashby was still in prison when his wife died The sufferings of the Friends at this time were very great. It was one of their tenets that "No further support should be expected by their Ministers than what is authorised by Christ and was practiced by his Apostles, so that not feeling themselves required to provide for their own ministers whose Ministry they approve. Friends deem themselves fully warranted in declining to contribute for the support of others, from which they conscientiously dissent; and more especially they feel called upon to protest against that most objectionable and anti-Christian mode of support by tithes."

This together with their refusal to pay Church Rates; their absence from public worship at church; and their meetings together contrary to law, brought many of them into trouble. They were frequently imprisoned and in many cases cruelly ill treated. During this time that Robert Ashby was in prison, five persons were convicted of holding an illegal meeting at his house. The proceedings are recorded in a tract with an enormous title printed in 1665. According to this tract the indictments charged that William Robinson, Richard Parsons, John Cory and Elizabeth Harris and every of them were unlawfully assembled at Robert Ashby's house situate and being in Bugbrooke in the County of Northamptonshire with divers other malefactors contrary to the liturgy or practice of the Church of England in contempt of the King his laws and against his crown and dignity

Children of Robert Ashby and Jane Stephenson:

     i.   **John Ashby**,[1217,1218,1219] born about 1645, in Bugbrooke, Northamptonshire, England, died 1 Sep 1728, in Bugbrooke, Northamptonshire, England.

1127. Jane Stephenson was born about 1609, in Bugbrooke, Northamptonshire, England, died 14 Apr 1664, in Bugbrooke, Northamptonshire, England, buried Apr 1664, in Bugbrooke, Northamptonshire, England. She was the daughter of Richard Stevenson and Stevenson. She married Robert Ashby[1318,1319] 1636, in Bugbrooke, Northamptonshire, England. He was the son of John Ashby and Mrs Agnis Ashby.

1128. Joseph Gammage was born May 1625, in Bugbrooke, Northamptonshire, England, christened 8 May 1625, in Bugbrooke, Northamptonshire, England, died 2 Apr 1664, in Bugbrooke, Northamptonshire, England, buried Apr 1664, in Bugbrooke, Northamptonshire, England. He was the son of Richard Gammage and Gammage. He married Gammage about 1650, in Northamptonshire, England.

Children of Joseph Gammage and Gammage:

     i.   **Mary Gammage**, born 19 Sep 1653, in Bugbrooke, Northamptonshire, England, died 19 Jan 1736, in Bugbrooke, Northamptonshire, England.

1129.____Gammage was born about 1628, in Bugbrooke, Northamptonshire, England. She married Joseph Gammage about 1650, in Northamptonshire, England. He was the son of Richard Gammage and Gammage.

1130.____Brigges was born about 1600, in London, England. He married Briggs about 1625, in London, England.

Children of Brigges and Briggs:

     i.   **Richard Briggs**,[1220] born about 1630, in London, England.

1131.____Briggs was born about 1602, in London, England. She married Brigges about 1625, in London, England.

1132. Dunston Foreman was born Sep 1573, in Brenchley, Kent, England, christened 23 Sep 1573, in Brenchley, Kent, England, died May 1623, in Brenchley, Kent, England, buried 26 May 1623, in Brenchley, Kent, England. He was the son of Robert Foreman and Jane Terry. He married Lettice Barram[1320] 27 Apr 1600, in Brenchley, Kent, England.
Notes for Dunston Foreman:

aka: Donstone

Children of Dunston Foreman and Lettice Barram:

- i. **Richard Foreman**,[1321] born Mar 1601, in Brenchley, Kent, England, christened 14 Apr 1601, in Brenchley, Kent, England.
- ii. **Mary Foreman**,[1322] born Jan 1602, in Brenchley, Kent, England, christened 31 Jan 1602, in Brenchley, Kent, England.
- iii. **Robert Foreman**,[1323] born Aug 1603, in Brenchley, Kent, England, christened 7 Aug 1603, in Brenchley, Kent, England.
- iv. **Margaret Foreman**,[1324] born Oct 1605, in Brenchley, Kent, England, christened 20 Oct 1605, in Brenchley, Kent, England, died before 27 Oct 1605, in Brenchley, Kent, England, buried 27 Oct 1605, in Brenchley, Kent, England.
- v. **Elizabeth Foreman**,[1325] born Sep 1608, in Brenchley, Kent, England, christened 7 Sep 1608, in Brenchley, Kent, England.
- vi. **Francis Foreman**,[1326] born Nov 1611, in Brenchley, Kent, England, christened 24 Nov 1611, in Brenchley, Kent, England.
- vii. **Ann Foreman**,[1327] born Dec 1614, in Brenchley, Kent, England, christened 25 Dec 1614, in Brenchley, Kent, England.
- viii. **Dunston Foreman**,[1223] born Oct 1618, in Brenchley, Kent, England.

1133. Lettice Barram was born about 1579, in Brenchley, Kent, England. She married Dunston Foreman[1320,1328] 27 Apr 1600, in Brenchley, Kent, England. He was the son of Robert Foreman and Jane Terry.
Notes for Lettice Barram:

aka Barham

1134. James Chamberlaine was born Sep 1588, in Cranbrook, Kent, England, christened 15 Sep 1588, in Cranbrook, Kent, England. He married Chamberlaine about 1628, in Kent, England.

Children of James Chamberlaine and Chamberlaine:

- i. **Jane Chamberlaine**,[1222] born May 1632, in Hadlow, Kent, England, died after

1675, in Kent, England.

    ii.   **James Chamberlaine**,[1329] born 13 Jun 1637, in Hadlow, Kent, England, christened 13 Jun 1637, in Hadlow, Kent, England.

1135.____Chamberlaine was born about 1605, in Kent, England. She married James Chamberlaine[1330] about 1628, in Kent, England.

1136. Edward Tanner was born about 1610, in Kent, England. He married Mrs Margaret Tanner about 1635, in Kent, England.

Children of Edward Tanner and Mrs Margaret Tanner:

    i.   **James Tanner**, born Sep 1638, in Marden, Kent, England.

1137. Mrs Margaret Tanner was born about 1612, in Kent, England. She married Edward Tanner about 1635, in Kent, England.

1138. Hugh Bowden was born about 1605, in Kent, England. He married Mrs Susan Bowden about 1633, in Kent, England.

Children of Hugh Bowden and Mrs Susan Bowden:

    i.   **Ann Bowden**, born Jan 1635, in Sandwich, Kent, England.

1139. Mrs Susan Bowden was born about 1608, in Kent, England. She married Hugh Bowden about 1633, in Kent, England.

1140. Henry Holmes was born 1618, in Dover, Kent, England, died 20 Jul 1672, in Kent, England, buried Jul 1672, in Canterbury, Kent, England. He was the son of Henry Holmes and Alice Edmer. He married Ann Kingsland 5 Feb 1636, in Canterbury, Kent, England.

Children of Henry Holmes and Ann Kingsland:

    i.   **Mary Holmes**, born Mar 1638, in Canterbury, Kent, England, christened 17 Mar 1638, in Canterbury, Kent, England.

    ii.   **Edward Holmes**,[1225] born 28 Nov 1641, in Canterbury, Kent, England, died after 1686, in Canterbury, Kent, England.

    iii.   **Jeames Holmes**, born May 1644, in Canterbury, Kent, England, christened 5 May 1644, in Canterbury, Kent, England.

    iv.   **Joane Holmes**, born 1648, in Kent, England, died 27 Nov 1737, in England. She married Richard Hills about 1668, in Kent, England. Richard Hills was born about 1644, in Bearsted, Kent, England, died before 20 May 1670, in England.

Contents

1141. Ann Kingsland was born 1620, in Kent, England, died before 1720, in England. She married Henry Holmes 5 Feb 1636, in Canterbury, Kent, England. He was the son of Henry Holmes and Alice Edmer.
Notes for Ann Kingsland:

aka: Ann Kingslane, Ann Kingslare,

1142. Thomas Birch was born 6 Jul 1607, in Eythorne, Kent, England, christened 26 Jul 1607, in Eythorne, Kent, England, died before 1700, in England. He was the son of John Birch and Dime Kingsforde. He married Elizabeth Stuppell[1228,1331,1332] 14 Oct 1634, in Whitfield, Kent, England.[1331] She was the daughter of Michaell Stuppell and Elizabeth Marsh.

Children of Thomas Birch and Elizabeth Stuppell:

   i.   **Susan Birch**,[1226,1227,1228] born 1642, in Coldred, Kent, England, died before 1740, in England.

1143. Elizabeth Stuppell was born Mar 1611, in Waldershare, Kent, England, christened 22 Mar 1611, in Waldershare, Kent, England, died before 1700, in England. She was the daughter of Michaell Stuppell and Elizabeth Marsh. She married Thomas Birch[1228,1331] 14 Oct 1634, in Whitfield, Kent, England.[1331] He was the son of John Birch and Dime Kingsforde.

1144. Allexander Venner was born 1640, in Cripplegate, London, England, christened 28 Oct 1640, in Cripplegate, London, England, died before 1740, in England. He was the son of Alexander Venner and Mrs Elizabeth Venner. He married Elizabeth Chadwick 23 Apr 1660, in Cripplegate, London, England.

Children of Allexander Venner and Elizabeth Chadwick:

   i.   **Mary Venner**, born 15 Nov 1661, in Cripplegate, London, England, christened 1 Dec 1661, in Cripplegate, London, England.
   ii.   **Allexander Venner**, born 1663, in Cripplegate, London, England, christened 29 May 1663, in London, England.
   iii. **Richard Venner**, born 25 Feb 1665, in Cripplegate, London, England, christened 12 Mar 1665, in Cornhill, Middlesex, England.
   iv.   **George Venner**, born 28 Oct 1666, in Cripplegate, London, England, christened 11 Nov 1666, in Cripplegate, London, England, died 3 Sep 1670, in Cripplegate, London, England.
   v.   **Will Venner**, born 1668, in Cripplegate, London, England, christened Mar 1668, in Cripplegate, London, England.
         Christening: St Giles, Cripplegate, London, England
   vi.   **Jasper Venner**, born 1669, in Middlesex, England, died before 1750, in England.

1145. Elizabeth Chadwick was born about 1645, in England, died before 1740, in England. She married Allexander Venner 23 Apr 1660, in Cripplegate, London, England. He was the son of Alexander Venner and Mrs Elizabeth Venner.

1146. Richard Partridge was born Oct 1650, in London, England, christened 20 Oct 1650, in Colechurch, London, England. He was the son of John Partridge and Partridge. He married Margaret Partridge[1333] about 1668, in London, England.

Children of Richard Partridge and Margaret Partridge:

    i.   **Richard Partridge,**[1235,1236,1238] born Apr 1668, in Cripplegate, London, England.

1147. Margaret Partridge was born about 1642, in London, England. She married Richard Partridge[1333,1334] about 1668, in London, England. He was the son of John Partridge and Partridge.

1148. William Langmore was born about 1640, in London, England. He married Mrs Alice Langmore[1335] about 1664, in London, England.

Children of William Langmore and Mrs Alice Langmore:

    i.   **William Langmere,**[1336] born May 1664, in London, England, christened 5 Jun 1664, in Bishopsgate, London, England.
    ii. **Alice Longmore,**[1235,1236,1237] born Mar 1666, in London, England.

1149. Mrs Alice Langmore was born about 1642, in London, England. She married William Langmore[1337] about 1664, in London, England.

Generation No. 13

1150. Thomas Aldworth was born Feb 1571, in Wantage, Berkshire, England, christened 28 Feb 1571, in Wantage, Berkshire, England, died Jun 1633, in Wantage, Berkshire, England, buried 21 Jun 1633, in Wantage, Berkshire, England. He was the son of John Aldworth and Margaret Dyer. He married Martha Daniell[1339,1340] 9 May 1591, in Wantage, Berkshire, England.[1338]

Children of Thomas Aldworth and Martha Daniell:

 i. **Margrett Aldworth**,[1341,1342] born Aug 1592, in Wantage, Berkshire, England, christened 14 Aug 1592, in Wantage, Berkshire, England. She married Edward Cotterell 5 Dec 1610, in Wantage, Berkshire, England. Edward Cotterell was born about 1590, in Berkshire, England.

 ii. **Mary Aldworth**,[1341,1343] born 2 Feb 1594, in Wantage, Berkshire, England, christened 14 Feb 1594, in Wantage, Berkshire, England.

 iii. **Robert Aldworth**,[1144,1246] born 14 Mar 1599, in Wantage, Berkshire, England, died 1641, in Wantage, Berkshire, England.

 iv. **Martha Aldworth**,[1144,1344] born Aug 1602, in Wantage, Berkshire, England, christened 22 Aug 1602, in Wantage, Berkshire, England.

 v. **Cicelie Aldworth**,[1144,1345] born Nov 1608, in Wantage, Berkshire, England, christened 13 Nov 1608, in Wantage, Berkshire, England. She married Francis Slade 4 Nov 1630, in Wantage, Berkshire, England. Francis Slade was born about 1605, in Berkshire, England.

1151. Martha Daniell was born about 1570, in Wantage, Berkshire, England, died Mar 1635, in Wantage, Berkshire, England, buried 19 Mar 1635, in Wantage, Berkshire, England. She married Thomas Aldworth[1144,1346,1347] 9 May 1591, in Wantage, Berkshire, England.[1338] He was the son of John Aldworth and Margaret Dyer.

1152. Geoffry Barlow was born about 1568, in Berkshire, England. He married Barlow about 1589, in Berkshire, England.

Children of Geoffry Barlow and Barlow:

 i. **Joane Barlow**,[1348] born 10 Jun 1590, in East Hendred, Berkshire, England, christened 10 Jun 1590, in East Hendred, Berkshire, England.

 ii. **Mary Barlow**,[1349] born 27 Feb 1593, in East Hendred, Berkshire, England, christened 27 Feb 1593, in East Hendred, Berkshire, England.

 iii. **Jane Barlow**,[1350] born 10 Aug 1596, in East Hendred, Berkshire, England, christened 10 Aug 1596, in East Hendred, Berkshire, England.

 iv. **Laurence Barlow**,[1351] born 15 Aug 1598, in East Hendred, Berkshire, England, christened 22 Aug 1598, in East Hendred, Berkshire, England.

    v.   **Leticia Barlow**,[1240,1241,1242] born 3 Oct 1605, in East Hendred, Berkshire, England, died before 1700, in England.

1153.____Barlow was born about 1569, in Berkshire, England. She married Geoffry Barlow[1241] about 1589, in Berkshire, England.

1154. William Endal was born about 1523, in Lower Heyford, Oxfordshire, England, died Dec 1607, in Lower Heyford, Oxfordshire, England, buried 24 Dec 1607, in Lower Heyford, Oxfordshire, England. He married Anna Fox[1352] 7 Nov 1544, in Lower Heyford, Oxfordshire, England.

Children of William Endal and Anna Fox:

    i.   **Elena Endall**,[1247] born Sep 1545, in Lower Heyford, Oxfordshire, England, died Dec 1621, in Lower Heyford, Oxfordshire, England.

    ii.   **Friswith Endal**,[1353] born Dec 1548, in Lower Heyford, Oxfordshire, England, christened 27 Dec 1548, in Lower Heyford, Oxfordshire, England, buried 25 Sep 1617, in Lower Heyford, Oxfordshire, England.

1155. Anna Fox was born about 1523, in Lower Heyford, Oxfordshire, England, died Oct 1607, in Lower Heyford, Oxfordshire, England, buried 20 Oct 1607, in Lower Heyford, Oxfordshire, England. She married William Endal[1352] 7 Nov 1544, in Lower Heyford, Oxfordshire, England.

1156. Robert Howse was born about 1535, in Upper Heyford, Oxfordshire, England, died Apr 1597, in Upper Heyford, Oxfordshire, England, buried 19 Apr 1597, in Upper Heyford, Oxfordshire, England. He married Joan Lever[1354,1355] 10 Jul 1556, in Warborough, Oxfordshire, England.

Children of Robert Howse and Joan Lever:

    i.   **Agnes Howse**,[1356,1357] born Nov 1571, in Upper Heyford, Oxfordshire, England, christened 13 Dec 1571, in Upper Heyford, Oxfordshire, England, died about 24 Dec 1571, in Upper Heyford, Oxfordshire, England, buried 31 Dec 1571, in Upper Heyford, Oxfordshire, England.

    ii.   **Elizabeth Howse**,[1358] born Nov 1573, in Upper Heyford, Oxfordshire, England, christened 8 Dec 1573, in Upper Heyford, Oxfordshire, England.

    iii.   **Margerie Howse**,[1359] born Feb 1576, in Upper Heyford, Oxfordshire, England, christened 29 Feb 1576, in Upper Heyford, Oxfordshire, England.

    iv.   **Thomas Howse**,[1254,1255,1256] born Jan 1578, in Upper Heyford, Oxfordshire, England, died 3 Dec 1627, in Upper Heyford, Oxfordshire, England.

    v.   **John Howse**,[1360,1361] born Aug 1580, in Upper Heyford, Oxfordshire, England, christened 3 Sep 1580, in Upper Heyford, Oxfordshire, England, died Apr 1631, in Upper Heyford, Oxfordshire, England, buried 24 Apr 1631, in Upper Heyford, Oxfordshire, England.

vi. **George Howse**,[1362] born Oct 1582, in Upper Heyford, Oxfordshire, England, christened 16 Nov 1582, in Upper Heyford, Oxfordshire, England.
vii. **William Howse**,[1363] born Dec 1585, in Upper Heyford, Oxfordshire, England, christened 1 Jan 1586, in Upper Heyford, Oxfordshire, England.

1157. Joan Lever was born about 1537, in Upper Heyford, Oxfordshire, England, died Oct 1615, in Upper Heyford, Oxfordshire, England, buried 9 Oct 1615, in Upper Heyford, Oxfordshire, England. She married Robert Howse[1354] 10 Jul 1556, in Warborough, Oxfordshire, England.

1158. Thomas Tubb was born 13 Nov 1597, in Wantage, Berkshire, England, christened 19 Nov 1597, in Wantage, Berkshire, England. He was the son of Thomas Tubb and Margret Clark. He married Mrs Elizabeth Tubb about 1620, in Wantage, Berkshire, England.

Children of Thomas Tubb and Mrs Elizabeth Tubb:

i. **Thomas Tubbs**, born Jun 1621, in Wantage, Berkshire, England.

1159. Mrs Elizabeth Tubb was born about 1600, in Wantage, Berkshire, England. She married Thomas Tubb about 1620, in Wantage, Berkshire, England. He was the son of Thomas Tubb and Margret Clark.

1160. John Webb was born 1598, in Wantage, Berkshire, England, christened 17 Apr 1598, in Wantage, Berkshire, England. He was the son of William Webb and Dorathe Aldworth. He married Joanne Hicks 17 Jun 1621, in Wantage, Berkshire, England. She was the daughter of Thomas Hicks and Fridlsweede Mason.

Children of John Webb and Joanne Hicks:

i.   **Francis Webb**, born 1621, in Wantage, Berkshire, England.
ii. **Joanne Webb**, born 1625, in Wantage, Berkshire, England, christened 5 Dec 1625, in Wantage, Berkshire, England.
iii. **John Webb**, born 1628, in Wantage, Berkshire, England, christened 4 May 1628, in Wantage, Berkshire, England.

1161. Joanne Hicks was born 1592, in Great Coxwell, Berkshire, England, christened 9 Sep 1592, in Great Coxwell, Berkshire, England, died 18 Nov 1691, in Berkshire, England. She was the daughter of Thomas Hicks and Fridisweede Mason. She married John Webb 17 Jun 1621, in Wantage, Berkshire, England. He was the son of William Webb and Dorathe Aldworth.

1162. Ralph Iles was born 1602, in Lydiard Millicent, Wiltshire, England, died 1669, in Lydiard Millicent, Wiltshire, England. He married Ann Gale 1622, in Salisbury, Wiltshire, England. She was the daughter of William Gale and Gale.

Children of Ralph Iles and Ann Gale:

    i.   **Farncis Iles**, born 1622, in Little Coxwell, Berkshire, England.
    ii.   **Edward Iles**, born 1626, in Little Coxwell, Berkshire, England.
   iii. **Ann Iles**, born 1628, in Little Coxwell, Berkshire, England, died 1710, in Berkshire, England.
   iv. **Joane Iles**, born 1630, in Little Coxwell, Berkshire, England, christened 24 Apr 1630, in Little Coxwell, Berkshire, England.
    v.   **Rosse Iles**, born 1634, in Little Coxwell, Berkshire, England.

1163. Ann Gale was born 1593, in Christian Malford, Wiltshire, England, christened 6 May 1593, in Lacock, Wiltshire, England, died 1680, in Berkshire, England, buried 1699, in Berkshire, England. She was the daughter of William Gale and Gale. She married Ralph Iles 1622, in Salisbury, Wiltshire, England.

1164. Thomas Alder was born about 1595, in Stanford in the Vale, Berkshire, England. He married Elizabeth Yarley[1364,1365] 28 Oct 1617, in Stanford in the Vale, Berkshire, England. She was the daughter of Thomas Yardley and Mabell Jenever.

Children of Thomas Alder and Elizabeth Yarley:

    i.   **William Alder**,[1164,1257,1259,1260,1261] born Jun 1618, in Goosey, Berkshire, England.

1165. Elizabeth Yarley was born Mar 1591, in Stanford in the Vale, Berkshire, England, christened 7 Apr 1591, in Stanford in the Vale, Berkshire, England. She was the daughter of Thomas Yardley and Mabell Jenever. She married Thomas Alder[1366] 28 Oct 1617, in Stanford in the Vale, Berkshire, England. Notes for Elizabeth Yarley:

aka - Earley / Yearley / Yeardley / Yardley

1166. William Stanbrooke was born about 1590, in Berkshire, England. He married Mrs Alice Stanbrooke[1367] about 1612, in Berkshire, England.

Children of William Stanbrooke and Mrs Alice Stanbrooke:

    i.   **Edyth Stanbrooke**,[1164,1257,1258] born May 1615, in Denchworth, Berkshire, England.
    ii.   **George Stanbrooke**,[1368] born Feb 1620, in Stanford in the Vale, Berkshire, England, christened 12 Mar 1620, in Stanford in the Vale, Berkshire, England.

1167. Mrs Alice Stanbrooke was born about 1592, in Berkshire, England. She married William Stanbrooke[1258] about 1612, in Berkshire, England.

1168. William Stone was born about 1525, in Berkshire, England, died Feb 1605, in Longworth,

Berkshire, England, buried 13 Feb 1605, in Longworth, Berkshire, England. He married Mrs William Stone about 1550, in Berkshire, England.
Notes for William Stone:

Parish Guardian Died of the plague

Children of William Stone and Mrs William Stone:

    i.   **William Stone**, born about 1552, in Berkshire, England, died 15 Mar 1605, in Longworth, Berkshire, England, buried 15 Mar 1605, in Longworth, Berkshire, England. He married Mrs Jane Stone about 1576, in Berkshire, England. Mrs Jane Stone was born about 1555, in Berkshire, England, buried 19 Jul 1610, in Longworth, Berkshire, England.
        Died of the plague

    ii.   **Henry Stone**, born about 1554, in Berkshire, England, buried 4 May 1614, in Longworth, Berkshire, England. He married Stone about 1580, in Berkshire, England. Stone was born about 1558, in Berkshire, England, died about 1640, in England.

    iii.   **Richard Stone**, born about 1560, in Longworth, Berkshire, England, died Aug 1607, in Longworth, Berkshire, England.

    iv.   **John Stone**, born about 1570, in Berkshire, England. He married Mrs Agnes Stone 7 Nov 1596, in Longworth, Berkshire, England. Mrs Agnes Stone was born about 1573, in Berkshire, England.

1169. Mrs William Stone was born about 1528, in Berkshire, England. She married William Stone about 1550, in Berkshire, England.

1170.____Flaxnei was born about 1515, in Oxfordshire, England. He married Flaxnei about 1540, in Oxfordshire, England.

Children of Flaxnei and Flaxnei:

    i.   **Justinian Flaxnei**, born about 1545, in Stanton Harcourt, Oxfordshire, England. He married Flaxnei about 1570, in Stanton Harcourt, Oxfordshire, England. Flaxnei was born about 1551, in Stanton Harcourt, Oxfordshire, England.

    ii.   **Wenefred Flaxnei**, born about 1553, in Oxfordshire, England. She married Richard Smytheard 21 Feb 1573, in Stanton Harcourt, Oxfordshire, England. Richard Smytheard was born about 1550, in Oxfordshire, England.

    iii.   **Edmund Flaxnei**, born about 1554, in Oxfordshire, England. He married Mrs Edmund Flaxnei about 1575, in Stanton Harcourt, Oxfordshire, England. Mrs Edmund Flaxnei was born about 1555, in Oxfordshire, England.

    iv.   **John Flaxnei**, born about 1557, in Oxfordshire, England. He married Mrs Elizabeth Flaxeni about 1577, in Oxfordshire, England. Mrs Elizabeth Flaxeni was born about 1558, in Stanton Harcourt, Oxfordshire, England, died 16 Oct 1582, in Stanton Harcourt, Oxfordshire, England, buried 26 Oct 1582, in Stanton Harcourt, Oxfordshire, England.

    v.   **Elizabeth Flexney**, born about 1560, in Stanton Harcourt, Oxfordshire, England, died 7 Aug 1614, in Longworth, Berkshire, England.

1171.____Flaxnei was born about 1516, in Oxfordshire, England. She married Flaxnei about 1540, in Oxfordshire, England.

1172. Thomas Onion was born about 1540, in Berkshire, England. He married Mrs Jone Onion about 1560, in Berkshire, England.

Children of Thomas Onion and Mrs Jone Onion:

    i.   **Briget Onions**, born Aug 1562, in Thatcham, Berkshire, England, christened 14 Aug 1562, in Thatcham, Berkshire, England.
"England Births and Christenings, 1538-1975," database, FamilySearch (https://familysearch.org/ark:/61903/1:1:N15X-6H7 : accessed 17 November 2015), Briget Onions, 14 Aug 1562; citing THATCHAM,BERKSHIRE,ENGLAND, reference ; FHL microfilm unknown.

    ii.   **Thomas Onion**,[1267] born about 1573, in Berkshire, England, died May 1613, in Hinton Waldrist, Berkshire, England.

    iii.   **John Onion Or Unyon**, born Sep 1580, in Hinton Waldrist, Berkshire, England, christened 11 Sep 1580, in Hinton Waldrist, Berkshire, England, died before Mar 1582, in Hinton Waldrist, Berkshire, England.
Hinton Wladrist, Berkshire, England parish record

    iv.   **John Onion Or Unyon**, born Mar 1582, in Hinton Waldrist, Berkshire, England, christened 15 Mar 1582, in Hinton Waldrist, Berkshire, England.
Hinton Waldrist parish record

    v.   **William Onion Or Vinon**, born Aug 1585, in Hinton Waldrist, Berkshire, England, christened 8 Aug 1585, in Hinton Waldrist, Berkshire, England, died May 1607, in Hinton Waldrist, Berkshire, England, buried 29 May 1607, in Hinton Waldrist, Berkshire, England.
Hinton Wladrist, Berkshire, England parish burial record

1173. Mrs Jone Onion was born about 1542, in Berkshire, England, died Sep 1591, in Burgage, Berkshire, England, buried 29 Sep 1591, in Hinton Waldrist, Berkshire, England. She married Thomas Onion about 1560, in Berkshire, England.
Notes for Mrs Jone Onion:

appears in Hinton Wladrist, Berkshire, England parish burial record

1174. John Oxlade was born 29 Nov 1558, in Brightwell Baldwin, Oxfordshire, England, christened 9

Dec 1558, in Brightwell Baldwin, Oxfordshire, England, died Oct 1615, in Oxfordshire, England, buried 20 Oct 1615. He was the son of Henry Oxlade and Oxlade. He married Elizabeth Plumridge[1369] 25 Jun 1582, in Reading, Berkshire, England. She was the daughter of Plumridge and Plumridge.

Children of John Oxlade and Elizabeth Plumridge:

     i.   **John Oxlade**, born 1598, in Fingest, Buckinghamshire, England, died 30 Jan 1661, in Great Marlow, Buckinghamshire, England.

1175. Elizabeth Plumridge was born about 1560, in Buckinghamshire, England, died before 1660, in England. She was the daughter of Plumridge and Plumridge. She married John Oxlade[1369] 25 Jun 1582, in Reading, Berkshire, England. He was the son of Henry Oxlade and Oxlade.
Notes for Elizabeth Plumridge:

aka: PLOMBRIGE

1176.____Broadway was born about 1565, in Oxfordshire, England, died before 1660, in Oxfordshire, England. He married Broadway about 1585, in England.

Children of Broadway and Broadway:

     i.   **Thomas Broadway**, born 1590, in Cuxham, Oxfordshire, England, died 26 Jun 1667, in Cuxham, Oxfordshire, England.

1177.____Broadway was born about 1566, in England, died before 1660, in England. She married Broadway about 1585, in England.

1178. John Fritwell was born 1559, in Cuxham, Oxfordshire, England, died 1633, in Cuxham, Oxfordshire, England, buried 12 Jul 1633, in Cuxham, Oxfordshire, England. He was the son of William Fritwell and Mrs Maude Fritwell. He married Mrs Isabell Druse 28 Dec 1579, in Cuxham, Oxfordshire, England.

Children of John Fritwell and Mrs Isabell Druse:

     i.   **Agnes Fritwell**, born 1594, in Cuxham, Oxfordshire, England, died May 1665, in Cuxham, Oxfordshire, England.

1179. Mrs Isabell Druse was born 1560, in Oxfordshire, England, died 1 Jul 1636, in Cuxham, Oxfordshire, England. She married John Fritwell 28 Dec 1579, in Cuxham, Oxfordshire, England. He was the son of William Fritwell and Mrs Maude Fritwell.
Notes for Mrs Isabell Druse:

Parish records state name at marriage as 'DRUSE alias WHYT'

1180. William Scholes was born about 1538, in Lewknor, Oxfordshire, England, died about Aug 1572, in Lewknor, Oxfordshire, England, buried wp 30 September 1572, in Lewknor, Oxfordshire, England. He was the son of Richard Scholes and Mrs Agnes Scholes. He married Mrs Ellenor Scholes about 1560, in Lewknor, Oxfordshire, England.

Children of William Scholes and Mrs Ellenor Scholes:

      i.   **William Scholes**, born 1572, in Lewknor, Oxfordshire, England, died Feb 1650, in Lewknor, Oxfordshire, England.

1181. Mrs Ellenor Scholes was born about 1542, in Lewknor, Oxfordshire, England, died 25 Jan 1623, buried 25 Jan 1623, in Lewknor, Oxfordshire, England. She married William Scholes about 1560, in Lewknor, Oxfordshire, England. He was the son of Richard Scholes and Mrs Agnes Scholes.

1182. Robert Munday was born about 1558, in Chinnor, Oxfordshire, England, died about Sep 1602, in Chinnor, Oxfordshire, England. He was the son of Edmund Munday and Isabel Belson. He married Margery Floyd about 1584, in Chinnor, Oxfordshire, England.

Children of Robert Munday and Margery Floyd:

      i.   **Robert Munday**, born Mar 1589, in Oxfordshire, England, died Feb 1668, in Chalford, Oxfordshire, England.
      ii.   **John Munday**, born Mar 1585, in Chinnor, Oxfordshire, England, christened 10 Apr 1585, in Chinnor, Oxfordshire, England.
      iii.   **Ann Munday**, born Dec 1586, in Chinnor, Oxfordshire, England, christened 25 Dec 1586, in Chinnor, Oxfordshire, England.
      iv.   **Mary Munday**, born Jun 1591, in Chinnor, Oxfordshire, England, christened 11 Jun 1591, in Chinnor, Oxfordshire, England.
      v.   **Martha Munday**, born Feb 1594, in Chinnor, Oxfordshire, England, christened 2 Mar 1594, in Chinnor, Oxfordshire, England.
      vi.   **Ann Munday**, born Aug 1596, in Chinnor, Oxfordshire, England, christened 29 Aug 1596, in Chinnor, Oxfordshire, England.
      vii.   **Henry Munday**, born Aug 1599, in Chinnor, Oxfordshire, England, christened 2 Sep 1599, in Chinnor, Oxfordshire, England, died Feb 1626, in Oxfordshire, England, buried 5 Feb 1626, in Chinnor, Oxfordshire, England.

1183. Margery Floyd was born about 1560, in Chinnor, Oxfordshire, England. She married Robert Munday about 1584, in Chinnor, Oxfordshire, England. He was the son of Edmund Munday and Isabel Belson.

1184. Thomas Belson was born May 1557, in Aston Rowant, Oxfordshire, England, christened 24 May 1557, in Aston Rowant, Oxfordshire, England. He was the son of William Belson and Mrs Margaret Belson. He married Elizabeth Lechpole about 1577, in Oxfordshire, England.

Children of Thomas Belson and Elizabeth Lechpole:

      i.   **Richard Belson**, born about 1578, in Aston Rowant, Oxfordshire, England, died Nov 1631, in Aston Rowant, Oxfordshire, England.

1185. Elizabeth Lechpole was born about 1559, in Aston Rowant, Oxfordshire, England. She married Thomas Belson[1370] about 1577, in Oxfordshire, England. He was the son of William Belson and Mrs Margaret Belson.

1186. Leonard Dutton was born about 1551, in Bampton Lew, Oxfordshire, England, died Aug 1611, in Crowell, Oxfordshire, England, buried 18 Aug 1611, in Crowell, Oxfordshire, England. He was the son of William Dytton and Dytton. He married Mrs Leonard Dutton about 1575, in Crowell, Oxfordshire, England.

Children of Leonard Dutton and Mrs Leonard Dutton:

      i.   **Edith Dutton**, born about 1579, in Crowell, Oxfordshire, England.

1187. Mrs Leonard Dutton was born about 1554, in Crowell, Oxfordshire, England. She married Leonard Dutton[1371] about 1575, in Crowell, Oxfordshire, England. He was the son of William Dytton and Dytton.

1188. Peter Kirbe was born about 1584, in Charlton on Otmoor, Oxfordshire, England, died Jun 1625, in Charlton on Otmoor, Oxfordshire, England, buried 19 Jun 1625, in Charlton on Otmoor, Oxfordshire, England. He was the son of John Kirby and Mrs. Ellen Kirby. He married Jayne Allye Leyveret[1372] 6 May 1604, in Charlton on Otmoor, Oxfordshire, England. She was the daughter of John Allye and Allye.

Children of Peter Kirbe and Jayne Allye Leyveret:

      i.   **Peter Kirbie**,[1373] born Jun 1605, in Charlton on Otmoor, Oxfordshire, England, christened 30 Jun 1605, in Charlton on Otmoor, Oxfordshire, England.

     ii.   **Nathanael Kyerbye**,[1374] born Apr 1607, in Charlton on Otmoor, Oxfordshire, England, christened 6 May 1607, in Charlton on Otmoor, Oxfordshire, England. He married Mariane Mynne 20 Feb 1637, in Charlton on Otmoor, Oxfordshire, England. Mariane Mynne was born about 1619, in Charlton on Otmoor, Oxfordshire, England.

    iii.   **Jane Kyrbye**,[1375] born Jul 1610, in Charlton on Otmoor, Oxfordshire, England, christened 31 Jul 1610, in Charlton on Otmoor, Oxfordshire, England.

    iv.   **John Kirby**,[1287,1289] born Jan 1612, in Charlton on Otmoor, Oxfordshire, England, died Oct 1670, in Charlton on Otmoor, Oxfordshire, England.

     v.   **Richarde Kirbye**,[1376] born Sep 1617, in Charlton on Otmoor, Oxfordshire, England, christened 14 Sep 1617, in Charlton on Otmoor, Oxfordshire, England.

    vi.   **Anne Kerby**,[1377] born May 1620, in Charlton on Otmoor, Oxfordshire, England, christened 1 Jun 1620, in Charlton on Otmoor, Oxfordshire, England.

vii.   **Robert Kirby**,[1378] born Oct 1622, in Charlton on Otmoor, Oxfordshire, England, christened 27 Oct 1622, in Charlton on Otmoor, Oxfordshire, England.

viii.   **Joane Kerby**,[1379] born Dec 1624, in Charlton on Otmoor, Oxfordshire, England, christened 1 Jan 1625, in Charlton on Otmoor, Oxfordshire, England.

1189. Jayne Allye Leyveret was born Sep 1587, in Charlton on Otmoor, Oxfordshire, England, christened 24 Sep 1587, in Charlton on Otmoor, Oxfordshire, England. She was the daughter of John Allye and Allye. She married Peter Kirbe[1372] 6 May 1604, in Charlton on Otmoor, Oxfordshire, England. He was the son of John Kirby and Mrs. Ellen Kirby.

1190. Jefferedi Marsh was born about 1592, in Oxford, Oxfordshire, England. He was the son of Marsh and March. He married Marshe about 1613, in Oxfordshire, England.

Children of Jefferedi Marsh and Marshe:

i.   **Bridget Marsh**,[1287] born May 1613, in Blackthorn, Oxfordshire, England, died Sep 1692, in Charlton on Otmoor, Oxfordshire, England.

ii.   **Joan Marsh**,[1290] born Aug 1616, in Blackthorn, Oxfordshire, England, christened 3 Sep 1616, in Ambrosden, Oxfordshire, England.

iii.   **Thomas Marsh**,[1380] born Nov 1618, in Blackthorn, Oxfordshire, England, christened 30 Nov 1618, in Ambrosden, Oxfordshire, England.

1191. ____Marshe was born about 1592, in Ambrosden, Oxfordshire, England. She married Jefferedi Marsh about 1613, in Oxfordshire, England. He was the son of Marsh and March.

1192. Thomas Walker was born about 1590, in Blackthorn, Oxfordshire, England, died before 1628, in Blackthorn, Oxfordshire, England. He married Anne Bourne 25 Jan 1611, in Ambrosden, Oxfordshire, England.

Children of Thomas Walker and Anne Bourne:

i.   **John Walker**, born about 1616, in Oxfordshire, England, died 1680, in Murcot, Oxfordshire, England.

1193. Anne Bourne was born about 1592, in Merton, Oxfordshire, England, died 8 Aug 1628, in Blackthorn, Oxfordshire, England, buried 8 Aug 1628, in Ambrosden, Oxfordshire, England. She married Thomas Walker 25 Jan 1611, in Ambrosden, Oxfordshire, England.

1194. Thomas Croxton was born about 1580, in Blackthorn, Oxfordshire, England, died 7 Aug 1668, in Oxfordshire, England, buried 7 Aug 1668, in Ambrosden, Oxfordshire, England. He was the son of Croxton and Mrs Anne Croxton. He married Anna Bourne[1381] 25 Jan 1611, in Ambrosden, Oxfordshire, England. She was the daughter of John Bourne and Elizabeth Kerbye.

Children of Thomas Croxton and Anna Bourne:

    i.   **John Croxton**, born Jul 1613, in Ambrosden, Oxfordshire, England, christened 22 Jul 1613, in Ambrosden, Oxfordshire, England.

    ii.   **Elizabeth Croxton**, born Dec 1615, in Ambrosden, Oxfordshire, England, christened 1 Jan 1616, in Ambrosden, Oxfordshire, England, died before Nov 1616, in Ambrosden, Oxfordshire, England.

    iii.   **Elizabeth Croxton**,[1290] born Dec 1616, in Blackthorn, Oxfordshire, England.

    iv.   **William Croxton**, born Nov 1619, in Blackthorn, Oxfordshire, England, christened 30 Nov 1619, in Ambrosden, Oxfordshire, England, died 5 Oct 1685, in Blackthorn, Oxfordshire, England, buried 5 Oct 1685, in Ambrosden, Oxfordshire, England.

    v.   **Richard Croxton**, born Feb 1622, in Blackthorn, Oxfordshire, England, christened 24 Feb 1622, in Ambrosden, Oxfordshire, England, died before Jul 1625, in Blackthorn, Oxfordshire, England.

    vi.   **Thomas Croxton**, born Dec 1622, in Blackthorn, Oxfordshire, England, christened 4 Dec 1622, in Ambrosden, Oxfordshire, England.

    vii.   **Richard Croxton**, born Jul 1625, in Blackthorn, Oxfordshire, England, christened 31 Jul 1625, in Ambrosden, Oxfordshire, England.

    viii.   **Nicholas Croxton**, born Sep 1628, in Blackthorn, Oxfordshire, England, christened 28 Sep 1628, in Ambrosden, Oxfordshire, England.

    ix.   **Anne Croxton**, born Nov 1629, in Blackthorn, Oxfordshire, England, christened 8 Nov 1629, in Ambrosden, Oxfordshire, England.

1195. Anna Bourne was born about 1595, in Merton, Oxfordshire, England, died 1678, in Blackthorn, Oxfordshire, England. She was the daughter of John Bourne and Elizabeth Kerbye. She married Thomas Croxton[1381] 25 Jan 1611, in Ambrosden, Oxfordshire, England. He was the son of Croxton and Mrs Anne Croxton.

1196. Robart Howlett was born 1569, in Charlton on Otmoor, Oxfordshire, England, died Jul 1609, in Charlton on Otmoor, Oxfordshire, England, buried 11 Jul 1609, in Charlton on Otmoor, Oxfordshire, England. He was the son of John Howlett and Mrs John Howlett. He married Elizabeth Quenton[1382] 22 Jul 1594, in Charlton on Otmoor, Oxfordshire, England.

Children of Robart Howlett and Elizabeth Quenton:

    i.   **John Howlett**,[1291,1298,1299] born 5 Oct 1595, in Murcot, Oxfordshire, England, died May 1633, in Charlton on Otmoor, Oxfordshire, England.

    ii.   **Elizabeth Howlett**, born 1597, in Charlton on Otmoor, Oxfordshire, England.

    iii.   **Sarah Howlett**, born 1598, in Charlton on Otmoor, Oxfordshire, England.

    iv.   **Anne Howlett**,[1383] born 1599, in Charlton on Otmoor, Oxfordshire, England, christened 7 Sep 1600, in Charlton on Otmoor, Oxfordshire, England, died 6 Aug 1677, in Charlton on Otmoor, Oxfordshire, England, buried 6 Aug 1677, in

Charlton on Otmoor, Oxfordshire, England. She married Thomas Sharpe[1383] 29 Jan 1621, in Charlton on Otmoor, Oxfordshire, England. He was the son of Christopher Sharpe and Annas Kirby. Thomas Sharpe was born about 1600, in Charlton on Otmoor, Oxfordshire, England, christened 4 May 1600, in Charlton on Otmoor, Oxfordshire, England, died about 1649.

    v.   **Johan Howlett**, born Sep 1600, in Charlton on Otmoor, Oxfordshire, England, christened 7 Sep 1600, in Charlton on Otmoor, Oxfordshire, England, buried 6 Aug 1677, in Charlton on Otmoor, Oxfordshire, England.

    vi.   **Jone Howlett**, born Sep 1600, in Charlton on Otmoor, Oxfordshire, England, christened 7 Sep 1600, in Charlton on Otmoor, Oxfordshire, England, died 6 Aug 1677, in Charlton on Otmoor, Oxfordshire, England, buried 6 Aug 1677, in Charlton on Otmoor, Oxfordshire, England.

    vii.   **Thomas Howlett**,[1384,1385] born Jan 1606, in Charlton on Otmoor, Oxfordshire, England, christened 9 Jan 1606, in Charlton on Otmoor, Oxfordshire, England, died Apr 1634, in Charlton on Otmoor, Oxfordshire, England, buried 21 Apr 1634, in Charlton on Otmoor, Oxfordshire, England.

1197. Elizabeth Quenton was born about 1573, in Charlton on Otmoor, Oxfordshire, England, died 6 Jun 1626, in Charlton on Otmoor, Oxfordshire, England, buried 6 Jun 1626, in Charlton on Otmoor, Oxfordshire, England. She married Robart Howlett[1382] 22 Jul 1594, in Charlton on Otmoor, Oxfordshire, England. He was the son of John Howlett and Mrs John Howlett.

1198. Christopher Sharpe was born 1566, in Charlton on Otmoor, Oxfordshire, England, died 28 Mar 1629, in Charlton on Otmoor, Oxfordshire, England, buried 28 Mar 1629, in Charlton on Otmoor, Oxfordshire, England. He married Annas Kirby[1386] 15 Jan 1587, in Charlton on Otmoor, Oxfordshire, England. She was the daughter of William Kirby and Mrs Joan Kirby.

Children of Christopher Sharpe and Annas Kirby:

    i.   **William Sharpe**, born Nov 1588, in Charlton on Otmoor, Oxfordshire, England, christened 17 Nov 1588, in Charlton on Otmoor, Oxfordshire, England.

    ii.   **Elizabeth Sharpe**,[1291] born Jul 1595, in Charlton on Otmoor, Oxfordshire, England, died before 1680, in England.

    iii.   **Thomas Sharpe**,[1383] born about 1600, in Charlton on Otmoor, Oxfordshire, England, christened 4 May 1600, in Charlton on Otmoor, Oxfordshire, England, died about 1649. He married Anne Howlett[1383] 29 Jan 1621, in Charlton on Otmoor, Oxfordshire, England. She was the daughter of Robart Howlett and Elizabeth Quenton. Anne Howlett was born 1599, in Charlton on Otmoor, Oxfordshire, England, christened 7 Sep 1600, in Charlton on Otmoor, Oxfordshire, England, died 6 Aug 1677, in Charlton on Otmoor, Oxfordshire, England, buried 6 Aug 1677, in Charlton on Otmoor, Oxfordshire, England.

1199. Annas Kirby was born 1566, in Charlton on Otmoor, Oxfordshire, England, died before 1650, in

England. She was the daughter of William Kirby and Mrs Joan Kirby. She married Christopher Sharpe[1386] 15 Jan 1587, in Charlton on Otmoor, Oxfordshire, England.

1200. William Clark was born May 1568, in Waddesdon, Buckinghamshire, England, christened 22 May 1568, in Waddesdon, Buckinghamshire, England. He was the son of Thomas Clark and Elizabeth Good. He married Clark about 1595, in England.

Children of William Clark and Clark:

    i.   **John Clark**, born Feb 1597, in Waddesdon, Buckinghamshire, England, christened 15 Feb 1597, in Waddesdon, Buckinghamshire, England, died before 1598, in Waddesdon, Buckinghamshire, England.

    ii.   **John Clark**, born Feb 1598, in Waddesdon, Buckinghamshire, England, christened 12 Feb 1598, in Waddesdon, Buckinghamshire, England, died before 1599, in Waddesdon, Buckinghamshire, England.

    iii.   **William Clark**,[1301] born 6 Sep 1601, in Adstock, Buckinghamshire, England, christened 30 Oct 1601, in Waddesdon, Buckinghamshire, England, died before Dec 1605, in Waddesdon, Buckinghamshire, England.

    iv.   **Thomas Clark**, born Aug 1604, in Waddesdon, Buckinghamshire, England, christened 26 Aug 1604, in Waddesdon, Buckinghamshire, England.

    v.   **Ralph Clark**,[1301,1302] born Nov 1606, in Waddesdon, Buckinghamshire, England.

    vi.   **William Clark**, born Jan 1609, in Waddesdon, Buckinghamshire, England, christened 21 Jan 1609, in Waddesdon, Buckinghamshire, England.

1201.____Clark was born about 1573, in Buckinghamshire, England. She married William Clark[1301] about 1595, in England. He was the son of Thomas Clark and Elizabeth Good.

1202. Roberte Bowles was born about 1570, in Gloucestershire, England. He married Bowles about 1595, in Gloucestershire, England.

Children of Roberte Bowles and Bowles:

    i.   **Thomas Bowles**,[1304,1305,1306,1307,1308,1309] born about 1600, in Gloucestershire, England, died before 1700, in England.

1203.____Bowles was born about 1570, in Gloucestershire, England. She married Roberte Bowles about 1595, in Gloucestershire, England.

1204. Edmond Loveday was born about 1563, in Wanborough, Wiltshire, England, christened about 1563, in Wanborough, Wiltshire, England, died about 1638, in Wanborough, Wiltshire, England, buried 3 Jul 1638, in Wanborough, Wiltshire, England. He was the son of John Loveday and Mrs Agnes Loveday. He married Elizabeth Smith 29 Apr 1588, in Wanborough, Wiltshire, England.

Children of Edmond Loveday and Elizabeth Smith:

    i.   **John Loveday**,[1387] born Mar 1589, in Wanborough, Wiltshire, England, christened 2 Apr 1589, in Wanborough, Wiltshire, England. He married Katherine Elliott[1311] about 1615, in Wanborough, Wiltshire, England. Katherine Elliott was born about 1590, in Wanborough, Wiltshire, England, died Sep 1630, in Wanborough, Wiltshire, England, buried 12 Sep 1630, in Wanborough, Wiltshire, England.

    ii.   **Anne Loveday**,[1388] born Mar 1592, in Wanborough, Wiltshire, England, christened 19 Mar 1592, in Wanborough, Wiltshire, England, buried 16 Jan 1611, in Wanborough, Wiltshire, England. She married Thomas Hearringe[1389] 1609, in Wanborough, Wiltshire, England. Thomas Hearringe was born about 1590, in Wanborough, Wiltshire, England.

    iii.   **Emm Loveday**,[1390] born Aug 1596, in Wanborough, Wiltshire, England, christened 27 Aug 1596, in Wanborough, Wiltshire, England, died Sep 1607, in Wanborough, Wiltshire, England, buried 17 Sep 1607, in Wanborough, Wiltshire, England.

    iv.   **Thomas Loveday**,[1314] born Apr 1601, in Wanborough, Wiltshire, England, died about 1671, in Wanborough, Wiltshire, England.

1205. Elizabeth Smith was born about 1567, in Wanborough, Wiltshire, England, died Feb 1630, in Wanborough, Wiltshire, England, buried 20 Feb 1630, in Wanborough, Wiltshire, England. She married Edmond Loveday[1391] 29 Apr 1588, in Wanborough, Wiltshire, England. He was the son of John Loveday and Mrs Agnes Loveday.

1206. John Grundy was born about 1563, in Stratton St Margaret, Wiltshire, England, buried 1 Mar 1616, in Stratton St Margaret, Wiltshire, England. He married Grundy about 1594, in Stratton St Margaret, Wiltshire, England.

Children of John Grundy and Grundy:

    i.   **Emma Grundy**,[1310,1311] born about 1605, in Stratton St Margaret, Wiltshire, England, died Jan 1649, in Wanborough, Wiltshire, England.

1207._____Grundy was born about 1567, in Stratton St Margaret, Wiltshire, England, died before 1616, in England, buried in England. She married John Grundy about 1594, in Stratton St Margaret, Wiltshire, England.
Notes for Grundy:

Not mentioned in husband's will

1208. Robert Hedges was born about 1577, in Little Hinton, Wiltshire, England, buried 1617, in Little Hinton, Wiltshire, England. He married Mrs. Dorothy Hedges 1608, in Little Hinton, Wiltshire, England.
Notes for Robert Hedges:

Own probate 20 May 1617, (097,762), will 24 Oct 1616 Robert was a yeoman in Little Hinton

Children of Robert Hedges and Mrs. Dorothy Hedges:

> i. **Henry Hedges**, born about 1613, in Hinton Parva, Wiltshire, England, died Mar 1671, in Wanborough, Wiltshire, England.

1209. Mrs. Dorothy Hedges was born about 1581, in Little Hinton, Wiltshire, England. She married Robert Hedges 1608, in Little Hinton, Wiltshire, England.

1210. Lawrence Tims was born 1594, in Newbottle with Charlton, Northamptonshire, England, christened Mar 1594, in Farthinghoe, Northamptonshire, England, died before 1690, in England. He was the son of Peter Tims and Mrs Anne Tims. He married Marie Newman 29 Jul 1618, in Farthinghoe, Northamptonshire, England.

Children of Lawrence Tims and Marie Newman:

> i. **Peter Times**, born 1619, in Farthinghoe, Northamptonshire, England, died before 1700, in England.
> ii. **Marie Tims**, born 1624, in Farthinghoe, Northamptonshire, England, christened 29 Sep 1624, in Farthinghoe, Northamptonshire, England.
> iii. **Anne Times**, born 1627, in Farthinghoe, Northamptonshire, England, christened 28 Sep 1627, in Farthinghoe, Northamptonshire, England.
> iv. **Walter Times**, born 1629, in Farthinghoe, Northamptonshire, England, christened 14 Jun 1629, in Farthinghoe, Northamptonshire, England.
> v. **Patience Tims**, born 1632, in Farthinghoe, Northamptonshire, England, christened 16 May 1632, in Farthinghoe, Northamptonshire, England.
> vi. **Thomas Times**, born 1635, in Farthinghoe, Northamptonshire, England, christened 11 Oct 1635, in Farthinghoe, Northamptonshire, England.
> vii. **Alce Tims**, born 1638, in Farthinghoe, Northamptonshire, England, christened 9 May 1638, in Farthinghoe, Northamptonshire, England.

1211. Marie Newman was born 1597, in Farthinghoe, Northamptonshire, England, died before 1690, in England. She married Lawrence Tims 29 Jul 1618, in Farthinghoe, Northamptonshire, England. He was the son of Peter Tims and Mrs Anne Tims.

1212. Richard Cox was born 1599, in Woodeaton, Oxfordshire, England, died 1669, in Woodeaton, Oxfordshire, England, buried 8 Aug 1669, in Woodeaton, Oxfordshire, England. He was the son of Cox and Cox. He married Mrs Isabel Cox 1622, in Woodeaton, Oxfordshire, England.

Children of Richard Cox and Mrs Isabel Cox:

> i. **Frances Cox**, born 1623, in Woodeaton, Oxfordshire, England, christened 9 Feb

1623, in Woodeaton, Oxfordshire, England.

    ii.   **Mary Cox**, born 1625, in Woodeaton, Oxfordshire, England, died 1670, in Woodeaton, Oxfordshire, England.

    iii.   **Richard Cox**, born 1628, in Woodeaton, Oxfordshire, England, christened 14 Dec 1628, in Woodeaton, Oxfordshire, England, died 1643, in Woodeaton, Oxfordshire, England, buried 14 Jul 1643, in Woodeaton, Oxfordshire, England.

    iv.   **Anne Cox**, born 1632, in Woodeaton, Oxfordshire, England, christened 4 Jun 1632, in Woodeaton, Oxfordshire, England, died 1643, in Woodeaton, Oxfordshire, England, buried 2 Jun 1643, in Woodeaton, Oxfordshire, England.

1213. Mrs Isabel Cox was born 1601, in Woodeaton, Oxfordshire, England, died 1662, in Woodeaton, Oxfordshire, England, buried 28 Oct 1662, in Woodeaton, Oxfordshire, England. She married Richard Cox 1622, in Woodeaton, Oxfordshire, England. He was the son of Cox and Cox.

1214. John Ashby was born 1576, in Bugbrooke, Northamptonshire, England, died 1648, in Bugbrooke, Northamptonshire, England, buried 1648, in Bugbrooke, Northamptonshire, England. He was the son of Robert Ashby and Mrs Elizabeth Ashby. He married Mrs Agnis Ashby about 1602, in England.

Children of John Ashby and Mrs Agnis Ashby:

    i.   **Robert Ashby**,[1318,1319] born about 1607, in Bugbrooke, Northamptonshire, England, died 1689, in Bugbrooke, Northamptonshire, England.

1215. Mrs Agnis Ashby was born 1581, in Bugbrooke, Northamptonshire, England, died about 1640, in Bugbrooke, Northamptonshire, England. She married John Ashby[1392,1393] about 1602, in England. He was the son of Robert Ashby and Mrs Elizabeth Ashby.
Notes for Mrs Agnis Ashby:

John Ashby's first wife.

1216. Richard Stevenson was born about 1585, in Northamptonshire, England. He married Stevenson about 1607, in Northamptonshire, England.

Children of Richard Stevenson and Stevenson:

    i.   **Jane Stephenson**, born about 1609, in Bugbrooke, Northamptonshire, England, died 14 Apr 1664, in Bugbrooke, Northamptonshire, England.

1217.____Stevenson was born about 1588, in Northamptonshire, England. She married Richard Stevenson about 1607, in Northamptonshire, England.

1218. Richard Gammage was born 1590, in Bugbrooke, Northamptonshire, England. He married Gammage about 1615, in Bugbrooke, Northamptonshire, England.

Children of Richard Gammage and Gammage:

> i. **Joseph Gammage**, born May 1625, in Bugbrooke, Northamptonshire, England, died 2 Apr 1664, in Bugbrooke, Northamptonshire, England.

1219.____Gammage was born 1594, in Bugbrooke, Northamptonshire, England. She married Richard Gammage about 1615, in Bugbrooke, Northamptonshire, England.

1220. Robert Foreman was born 1538, in Brenchley, Kent, England. He married Jane Terry 2 Feb 1562, in Kent, England.

Children of Robert Foreman and Jane Terry:

> i. **Dunston Foreman**,[1320,1328] born Sep 1573, in Brenchley, Kent, England, died May 1623, in Brenchley, Kent, England.

1221. Jane Terry was born 1542, in Brenchley, Kent, England, died Apr 1587, in Brenchley, Kent, England, buried 15 Apr 1587, in Brenchley, Kent, England. She married Robert Foreman 2 Feb 1562, in Kent, England.

1222. Henry Holmes was born about 1590, in St Mary in the Marsh, Kent, England, died before 1680, in England. He was the son of Homes and Alyce Hilton. He married Alice Edmer 21 Jan 1617, in Dover, Kent, England.[1394]
Notes for Henry Holmes:

(batch) number:I07575-7; source film number:1736692

Children of Henry Holmes and Alice Edmer:

> i. **Henry Holmes**, born 1618, in Dover, Kent, England, died 20 Jul 1672, in Kent, England.

1223. Alice Edmer was born about 1590, in Kent, England, died before 1680, in England. She married Henry Holmes[1394] 21 Jan 1617, in Dover, Kent, England.[1394] He was the son of Homes and Alyce Hilton.
Notes for Alice Edmer:

aka - Edmor

1224. John Birch was born Nov 1568, in Eythorne, Kent, England, christened 8 Dec 1568, in Eythorne, Kent, England, died before 1650, in England. He was the son of John Birch and Mrs Jone Birch. He married Dime Kingsforde[1395] 16 Oct 1599, in Eythorne, Kent, England.[1395]
Notes for John Birch:

aka: Byrch

Children of John Birch and Dime Kingsforde:

     i.   **Elizabeth Birch**,[1396] born 21 Dec 1600, in Eythorne, Kent, England, christened 21 Dec 1600, in Eythorne, Kent, England.

     ii.   **Thomas Birch**,[1228,1331] born 6 Jul 1607, in Eythorne, Kent, England, died before 1700, in England.

1225. Dime Kingsforde was born about 1570, in Kent, England, died 1623, in England, buried 22 Dec 1623, in Northbourne, Kent, England. She married John Birch[1395] 16 Oct 1599, in Eythorne, Kent, England.[1395] He was the son of John Birch and Mrs Jone Birch.

1226. Michaell Stuppell was born about 1570, in Kent, England, died before 1670, in England. He married Elizabeth Marsh[1397] 4 Feb 1610, in Ewell Manor, Kent, England.[1397] She was the daughter of Wnalther Marsh and Marsh.

Children of Michaell Stuppell and Elizabeth Marsh:

     i.   **Elizabeth Stuppell**,[1228,1331,1332] born Mar 1611, in Waldershare, Kent, England, died before 1700, in England.

1227. Elizabeth Marsh was born 1590, in Coldred, Kent, England, christened 4 Oct 1590, in Coldred, Kent, England, died before 1680, in England. She was the daughter of Wnalther Marsh and Marsh. She married Michaell Stuppell[1397] 4 Feb 1610, in Ewell Manor, Kent, England.[1397]

1228. Alexander Venner was born 1615, in London, England, died 1671, in London, England. He married Mrs Elizabeth Venner about 1636, in England.

Children of Alexander Venner and Mrs Elizabeth Venner:

     i.   **Allexander Venner**, born 1640, in Cripplegate, London, England, died before 1740, in England.

     ii.   **Sara Venner**, born 1644, in London, England, christened 30 May 1644, in London, England.

     iii.   **Mary Venner**, born 1645, in London, England, christened 16 Oct 1645, in London, England.

     iv.   **Rebecka Venner**, born 1648, in London, England, christened 1 Mar 1648, in London, England.

1229. Mrs Elizabeth Venner was born about 1618, in England, died before 1700, in England. She married Alexander Venner about 1636, in England.

1230. John Partridge was born about 1625, in London, England. He married Partridge about 1645, in London, England.

Children of John Partridge and Partridge:

     i.   **Richard Partridge,**[1333,1334] born Oct 1650, in London, England.

1231.____Partridge was born about 1627, in London, England. She married John Partridge[1398] about 1645, in London, England.

Generation No. 14

1232. John Aldworth was born 1532, in Wantage, Berkshire, England, died after 1573, in Wantage, Berkshire, England. He was the son of Robert Aldworth and Mrs Jhone Aldworth. He married Margaret Dyer[1400] 12 Dec 1554, in Wantage, Berkshire, England.[1399]

Children of John Aldworth and Margaret Dyer:

    i.   **Bridgett Aldworth**,[1401] born Dec 1558, in Wantage, Berkshire, England, christened 11 Jan 1559, in Wantage, Berkshire, England. She married Thomas Salter 25 May 1575, in Wantage, Berkshire, England. Thomas Salter was born about 1555, in Berkshire, England.

    ii.   **Sara Aldworth**, born Nov 1565, in Wantage, Berkshire, England, christened 25 Nov 1565, in Wantage, Berkshire, England.

    iii.   **Judeth Aldworth**,[1402] born Jan 1567, in Wantage, Berkshire, England, christened 29 Jan 1567, in Wantage, Berkshire, England, died Sep 1623, in Wantage, Berkshire, England, buried 19 Sep 1623, in Wantage, Berkshire, England.

    iv.   **John Aldworth**,[1403] born Oct 1568, in Wantage, Berkshire, England, christened 11 Nov 1568, in Wantage, Berkshire, England, died 2 Dec 1569, in Wantage, Berkshire, England.

    v.   **Thomas Aldworth**,[1144,1346,1347] born Feb 1571, in Wantage, Berkshire, England, died Jun 1633, in Wantage, Berkshire, England.

    vi.   **Robert Aldworth**, born Oct 1573, in Wantage, Berkshire, England, christened 21 Oct 1573, in Wantage, Berkshire, England.

1233. Margaret Dyer was born about 1536, in Berkshire, England, died Jul 1613, in Wantage, Berkshire, England, buried 13 Jul 1613, in Wantage, Berkshire, England. She married John Aldworth[1404,1405] 12 Dec 1554, in Wantage, Berkshire, England.[1399] He was the son of Robert Aldworth and Mrs Jhone Aldworth.

1234. Thomas Tubb was born 31 Dec 1566, in Wantage, Berkshire, England, christened 31 Dec 1566, in Wantage, Berkshire, England. He was the son of Peter Tubb and Elizabeth Pearne. He married Margret Clark 28 Apr 1593, in Wantage, Berkshire, England. She was the daughter of John Clark and Mrs Matheu Clark.

Children of Thomas Tubb and Margret Clark:

    i.   **Thomas Tubb**, born 13 Nov 1597, in Wantage, Berkshire, England.

1235. Margret Clark was born 16 Sep 1573, in Wantage, Berkshire, England, christened 16 Sep 1573, in Wantage, Berkshire, England. She was the daughter of John Clark and Mrs Matheu Clark. She married Thomas Tubb 28 Apr 1593, in Wantage, Berkshire, England. He was the son of Peter Tubb and Elizabeth Pearne.

1236. William Webb was born about 1555, in Wantage, Berkshire, England, christened 7 Sep 1560, in Longworth, Berkshire, England, died 23 Mar 1605. He married Dorathe Aldworth[1406] 1 Nov 1580, in Wantage, Berkshire, England.

Children of William Webb and Dorathe Aldworth:

  i.   **William Webb**, born 1582, in Wantage, Berkshire, England, christened 12 Feb 1582, in Wantage, Berkshire, England.
  ii. **Robert Webb**, born 1586, in Wantage, Berkshire, England, christened 21 Apr 1586, in Wantage, Berkshire, England.
  iii. **Richard Webb**, born 1589, in Wantage, Berkshire, England, christened 12 Dec 1589, in Wantage, Berkshire, England.
  iv. **Margaret Webb**, born 1591, in Wantage, Berkshire, England, christened 24 Mar 1591, in Wantage, Berkshire, England.
  v.   **Sarah Webb**, born 1594, in Wantage, Berkshire, England, christened 28 Jul 1594, in Wantage, Berkshire, England.
  vi. **John Webb**, born 1598, in Wantage, Berkshire, England.

1237. Dorathe Aldworth was born 1559, in Wantage, Berkshire, England, christened 15 Mar 1560, in Kintbury, Berkshire, England, died about 1624, in England. She married William Webb 1 Nov 1580, in Wantage, Berkshire, England.

1238. Thomas Hicks was born 1545, in Berkshire, England. He married Fridisweede Mason 27 Oct 1566, in Great Coxwell, Berkshire, England.

Children of Thomas Hicks and Fridisweede Mason:

  i.   **Elizabeth Hicks**, born 1572, in Great Coxwell, Berkshire, England, christened 15 Nov 1572, in Great Coxwell, Berkshire, England.
  ii. **Richard Hicks**, born 1581, in Great Coxwell, Berkshire, England, christened 12 Mar 1581, in Great Coxwell, Berkshire, England.
  iii. **Joanne Hicks**, born 1592, in Great Coxwell, Berkshire, England, died 18 Nov 1691, in Berkshire, England.

1239. Fridisweede Mason was born 1545, in Berkshire, England. She married Thomas Hicks 27 Oct 1566, in Great Coxwell, Berkshire, England.

1240. William Gale was born about 1570, in Christian Malford, Wiltshire, England. He married Gale about 1592, in Wiltshire, England.

Children of William Gale and Gale:

     i.   **Ann Gale**, born 1593, in Christian Malford, Wiltshire, England, died 1680, in Berkshire, England.

1241.____Gale was born about 1572, in Wiltshire, England. She married William Gale about 1592, in Wiltshire, England.

1242. Thomas Yardley was born about 1555, in Berkshire, England. He married Mabell Jenever[1407,1408] 19 Nov 1577, in Stanford in the Vale, Berkshire, England.

Children of Thomas Yardley and Mabell Jenever:

     i.   **Elizabeth Yarley**,[1364,1365] born Mar 1591, in Stanford in the Vale, Berkshire, England.

1243. Mabell Jenever was born about 1557, in Berkshire, England. She married Thomas Yardley[1407,1408] 19 Nov 1577, in Stanford in the Vale, Berkshire, England.

1244. Henry Oxlade was born 1528, in Aston Rowant, Oxfordshire, England, died before 1600, in England. He was the son of Oxlade and Oxlade. He married Oxlade about 1550, in England.

Children of Henry Oxlade and Oxlade:

     i.   **John Oxlade**,[1369] born 29 Nov 1558, in Brightwell Baldwin, Oxfordshire, England, died Oct 1615, in Oxfordshire, England.

1245.____Oxlade was born about 1530, in England, died before 1630, in England. She married Henry Oxlade about 1550, in England. He was the son of Oxlade and Oxlade.

1246.____Plumridge was born about 1530, in Buckinghamshire, England, died before 1630, in England. He married Plumridge about 1559, in England.

Children of Plumridge and Plumridge:

     i.   **Elizabeth Plumridge**,[1369] born about 1560, in Buckinghamshire, England, died before 1660, in England.

1247.____Plumridge was born about 1530, in England, died before 1630, in England. She married Plumridge about 1559, in England.

1248. William Fritwell was born about 1535, in Oxfordshire, England, died 1592, in Cuxham, Oxfordshire, England. He married Mrs Maude Fritwell about 1555, in Oxfordshire, England.

Children of William Fritwell and Mrs Maude Fritwell:

> i.   **John Fritwell**, born 1559, in Cuxham, Oxfordshire, England, died 1633, in Cuxham, Oxfordshire, England.

1249. Mrs Maude Fritwell was born about 1540, in Oxfordshire, England, died 1593, in Cuxham, Oxfordshire, England. She married William Fritwell about 1555, in Oxfordshire, England.

1250. Richard Scholes was born about 1510, in Lewknor, Oxfordshire, England, died Mar 1550, in Lewknor, Oxfordshire, England, buried 1 Apr 1550, in Lewknor, Oxfordshire, England. He married Mrs Agnes Scholes about 1530, in Lewknor, Oxfordshire, England.

Children of Richard Scholes and Mrs Agnes Scholes:

> i.   **William Scholes**, born about 1538, in Lewknor, Oxfordshire, England, died about Aug 1572, in Lewknor, Oxfordshire, England.

1251. Mrs Agnes Scholes was born about 1514, in Lewknor, Oxfordshire, England, died 1565, buried 11 Oct 1565, in Lewknor, Oxfordshire, England. She married Richard Scholes about 1530, in Lewknor, Oxfordshire, England.

1252. Edmund Munday was born about 1535, in Aston Rowant, Oxfordshire, England, died in Oxfordshire, England. He married Isabel Belson[1409] 30 Jan 1558, in Aston Rowant, Oxfordshire, England.

Children of Edmund Munday and Isabel Belson:

> i.   **Robert Munday**, born about 1558, in Chinnor, Oxfordshire, England, died about Sep 1602, in Chinnor, Oxfordshire, England.

1253. Isabel Belson was born about 1538, in Aston Rowant, Oxfordshire, England. She married Edmund Munday[1409] 30 Jan 1558, in Aston Rowant, Oxfordshire, England.

1254. William Belson was born about 1530, in Aston Rowant, Oxfordshire, England, died May 1571, in Aston Rowant, Oxfordshire, England, buried 12 Jun 1571, in Aston Rowant, Oxfordshire, England. He married Mrs Margaret Belson[1410] about 1550, in Oxfordshire, England.

Children of William Belson and Mrs Margaret Belson:

> i.   **William Belson**,[1411] born Jan 1554, in Aston Rowant, Oxfordshire, England, christened 6 Mar 1554, in Aston Rowant, Oxfordshire, England.
> ii. **Thomas Belson**,[1370] born May 1557, in Aston Rowant, Oxfordshire, England.

Contents

1255. Mrs Margaret Belson was born about 1532, in Aston Rowant, Oxfordshire, England, died May 1603, in Aston Rowant, Oxfordshire, England, buried 14 May 1603. She married William Belson[1412] about 1550, in Oxfordshire, England.

1256. William Dytton was born about 1518, in Bampton Lew, Oxfordshire, England, died 15 Feb 1568, in Bampton Lew, Oxfordshire, England, buried 15 Feb 1568, in Bampton Lew, Oxfordshire, England. He married Dytton 1542, in Bampton Lew, Oxfordshire, England.

Children of William Dytton and Dytton:

    i.   **Leonard Dutton,**[1371] born about 1551, in Bampton Lew, Oxfordshire, England, died Aug 1611, in Crowell, Oxfordshire, England.

1257.____Dytton was born about 1521, in Bampton Lew, Oxfordshire, England. She married William Dytton 1542, in Bampton Lew, Oxfordshire, England.

1258. John Kirby was born about 1556, in Charlton on Otmoor, Oxfordshire, England, died 14 Apr 1599, in Charlton on Otmoor, Oxfordshire, England, buried 14 Apr 1599, in Charlton on Otmoor, Oxfordshire, England. He was the son of Peter Kirby and Mrs. Agnes Kirby. He married Mrs. Ellen Kirby about 1578, in Charlton on Otmoor, Oxfordshire, England.

Children of John Kirby and Mrs. Ellen Kirby:

    i.   **Elizabeth Kerbye**, born about 1578, in Charlton on Otmoor, Oxfordshire, England. She married John Bourne 1595, in Merton, Oxfordshire, England. John Bourne was born about 1575, in Merton, Oxfordshire, England, died 20 Jan 1626, in Oxfordshire, England.
    ii.   **Yeoman John Kirby,**[1413] born about 1579, in Charlton on Otmoor, Oxfordshire, England, died Jan 1642, in Charlton on Otmoor, Oxfordshire, England, buried 11 Jan 1642, in Charlton on Otmoor, Oxfordshire, England. He married Maryan Burnan[1413] 12 Nov 1599, in Charlton on Otmoor, Oxfordshire, England. Maryan Burnan was born about 1579, in Charlton on Otmoor, Oxfordshire, England, died 4 Jun 1646, in Charlton on Otmoor, Oxfordshire, England.
    iii.   **Peter Kirbe,**[1372] born about 1584, in Charlton on Otmoor, Oxfordshire, England, died Jun 1625, in Charlton on Otmoor, Oxfordshire, England.
    iv.   **Margaret Kirby**, born about 1588, in Charlton on Otmoor, Oxfordshire, England, died Jul 1624, in Charlton on Otmoor, Oxfordshire, England, buried 3 Aug 1624, in Chesterton, Oxfordshire, England.
    v.   **Ellyn Kirby**, born Oct 1592, in Charlton on Otmoor, Oxfordshire, England, christened 5 Oct 1592, in Charlton on Otmoor, Oxfordshire, England.
    vi.   **Joane Kirby**, born Nov 1594, in Charlton on Otmoor, Oxfordshire, England, christened 25 Nov 1594, in Charlton on Otmoor, Oxfordshire, England.

1259. Mrs. Ellen Kirby was born about 1558, in Charlton on Otmoor, Oxfordshire, England, died 21 May 1614, in Charlton on Otmoor, Oxfordshire, England, buried 21 May 1614, in Charlton on Otmoor, Oxfordshire, England. She married John Kirby about 1578, in Charlton on Otmoor, Oxfordshire, England. He was the son of Peter Kirby and Mrs. Agnes Kirby.

1260. John Allye was born 1552, in Charlton on Otmoor, Oxfordshire, England. He married Allye about 1578, in Charlton on Otmoor, Oxfordshire, England.

Children of John Allye and Allye:

    i.   **Ann Allye**, born Sep 1578, in Charlton on Otmoor, Oxfordshire, England, christened 19 Sep 1578, in Charlton on Otmoor, Oxfordshire, England.

    ii.   **Richard Allye**, born May 1580, in Charlton on Otmoor, Oxfordshire, England, christened 29 May 1580, in Charlton on Otmoor, Oxfordshire, England.

    iii.   **John Allye**, born Mar 1581, in Charlton on Otmoor, Oxfordshire, England, christened 10 Mar 1581, in Charlton on Otmoor, Oxfordshire, England.

    iv.   **Jayne Allye Leyveret**,[1372] born Sep 1587, in Charlton on Otmoor, Oxfordshire, England.

1261._____Allye was born about 1557, in Charlton on Otmoor, Oxfordshire, England. She married John Allye about 1578, in Charlton on Otmoor, Oxfordshire, England.

1262._____Marsh was born about 1560, in Oxfordshire, England. He married March about 1585, in Oxfordshire, England.

Children of Marsh and March:

    i.   **Jefferedi Marsh**, born about 1592, in Oxford, Oxfordshire, England.

1263._____March was born about 1564, in Oxfordshire, England. She married Marsh about 1585, in Oxfordshire, England.

1264._____Croxton was born about 1555, in Oxfordshire, England. He married Mrs Anne Croxton about 1575, in Oxfordshire, England.

Children of Croxton and Mrs Anne Croxton:

    i.   **Thomas Croxton**,[1381] born about 1580, in Blackthorn, Oxfordshire, England, died 7 Aug 1668, in Oxfordshire, England.

    ii.   **Anne Croxton**, born about 1599, in Blackthorn, Oxfordshire, England. She married William Meades 26 Nov 1618, in Ambrosden, Oxfordshire, England. William Meades was born about 1597, in Ambrosden, Oxfordshire, England.

1265. Mrs Anne Croxton was born about 1557, in Oxfordshire, England, died Aug 1628, in Blackthorn, Oxfordshire, England, buried 8 Aug 1628, in Ambrosden, Oxfordshire, England. She married Croxton about 1575, in Oxfordshire, England.

1266. John Bourne was born about 1575, in Merton, Oxfordshire, England, died 20 Jan 1626, in Oxfordshire, England. He married Elizabeth Kerbye 1595, in Merton, Oxfordshire, England. She was the daughter of John Kirby and Mrs. Ellen Kirby.

Children of John Bourne and Elizabeth Kerbye:

> i. **Anna Bourne**,[1381] born about 1595, in Merton, Oxfordshire, England, died 1678, in Blackthorn, Oxfordshire, England.

1267. Elizabeth Kerbye was born about 1578, in Charlton on Otmoor, Oxfordshire, England. She was the daughter of John Kirby and Mrs. Ellen Kirby. She married John Bourne 1595, in Merton, Oxfordshire, England.

1268. John Howlett was born 1543, in Charlton on Otmoor, Oxfordshire, England, died 20 Sep 1597, in Charlton on Otmoor, Oxfordshire, England, buried 20 Sep 1597, in Charlton on Otmoor, Oxfordshire, England. He married Mrs John Howlett[1414] 1568, in Charlton on Otmoor, Oxfordshire, England.
Notes for John Howlett:

Birth Abt 1543

Children of John Howlett and Mrs John Howlett:

> i. **Robart Howlett**,[1382] born 1569, in Charlton on Otmoor, Oxfordshire, England, died Jul 1609, in Charlton on Otmoor, Oxfordshire, England.
> ii. **Myllysey Howlett**,[1415] born after 1570, in Charlton on Otmoor, Oxfordshire, England, christened 14 Jul 1576, in Charlton on Otmoor, Oxfordshire, England.
> iii. **Catherine Howlett**, born 1571, in Charlton on Otmoor, Oxfordshire, England.
> iv. **Annys Howlett**,[1382] born 1573, in Charlton on Otmoor, Oxfordshire, England, buried 4 Jun 1625, in Charlton on Otmoor, Oxfordshire, England. She married John Newell[1382] 8 Jul 1594, in Charlton on Otmoor, Oxfordshire, England. John Newell was born about 1570, in Oxfordshire, England.
> v. **Richard Howlett**,[1416] born 1575, in Charlton on Otmoor, Oxfordshire, England, died Jul 1609, in Charlton on Otmoor, Oxfordshire, England, buried 11 Jul 1609, in Charlton on Otmoor, Oxfordshire, England.
> vi. **Margerie Howlett**,[1417] born 1577, in Charlton on Otmoor, Oxfordshire, England, died 22 Jun 1625, in Charlton on Otmoor, Oxfordshire, England, buried 22 Jun 1625, in Charlton on Otmoor, Oxfordshire, England.
> vii. **Peter Howlett**, born Jan 1578, in Charlton on Otmoor, Oxfordshire, England, christened 1 Feb 1578, in Charlton on Otmoor, Oxfordshire, England.

Contents

1269. Mrs John Howlett was born about 1547, in Charlton on Otmoor, Oxfordshire, England, died Aug 1595, in Charlton on Otmoor, Oxfordshire, England, buried 31 Aug 1595, in Charlton on Otmoor, Oxfordshire, England. She married John Howlett[1418] 1568, in Charlton on Otmoor, Oxfordshire, England.

1270. William Kirby was born 1546, in Charlton on Otmoor, Oxfordshire, England, died 30 Aug 1584, in Charlton on Otmoor, Oxfordshire, England. He was the son of Peter Kirbye and Mrs Elyne Kirby. He married Mrs Joan Kirby 1565, in Charlton on Otmoor, Oxfordshire, England.

Children of William Kirby and Mrs Joan Kirby:

 i. **Annas Kirby**,[1386] born 1566, in Charlton on Otmoor, Oxfordshire, England, died before 1650, in England.
 ii. **William Kirby**, born Jan 1572, in Charlton on Otmoor, Oxfordshire, England, christened 17 Jan 1572, in Charlton on Otmoor, Oxfordshire, England.

1271. Mrs Joan Kirby was born 1546, in Charlton on Otmoor, Oxfordshire, England, died 17 Jul 1610, in Charlton on Otmoor, Oxfordshire, England. She married William Kirby 1565, in Charlton on Otmoor, Oxfordshire, England. He was the son of Peter Kirbye and Mrs Elyne Kirby.

1272. Thomas Clark was born about 1540, in Buckinghamshire, England. He married Elizabeth Good[1301] 5 Nov 1566, in Waddesdon, Buckinghamshire, England.[1301]

Children of Thomas Clark and Elizabeth Good:

 i. **William Clark**,[1301] born May 1568, in Waddesdon, Buckinghamshire, England.

1273. Elizabeth Good was born about 1544, in Buckinghamshire, England. She married Thomas Clark[1301] 5 Nov 1566, in Waddesdon, Buckinghamshire, England.[1301]

1274. John Loveday was born about 1540, in Wanborough, Wiltshire, England, died Sep 1585, in Wanborough, Wiltshire, England, buried 25 Sep 1585, in Wanborough, Wiltshire, England. He married Mrs Agnes Loveday about 1559, in Wanborough, Wiltshire, England.

Children of John Loveday and Mrs Agnes Loveday:

 i. **Richard Loveday**,[1419] born about 1560, in Wanborough, Wiltshire, England, died Nov 1589, in Wanborough, Wiltshire, England, buried 6 Dec 1589, in Wanborough, Wiltshire, England. He married Katheryne Smith[1420] 1584, in Wanborough, Wiltshire, England. Katheryne Smith was born about 1562, in Wanborough, Wiltshire, England, died Nov 1610, in Wanborough, Wiltshire, England, buried 13 Nov 1610, in Wanborough, Wiltshire, England.
 ii. **John Loveday**,[1421] born about 1561, in Wanborough, Wiltshire, England, died Oct 1602, in Wanborough, Wiltshire, England, buried 30 Oct 1602, in Wanborough,

Wiltshire, England. He married Agness Brynd 10 Feb 1588, in Wanborough, Wiltshire, England. Agness Brynd was born about 1561, in Wanborough, Wiltshire, England.

iii. **Edmond Loveday**,[1391] born about 1563, in Wanborough, Wiltshire, England, died about 1638, in Wanborough, Wiltshire, England.

1275. Mrs Agnes Loveday was born about 1540, in Wanborough, Wiltshire, England. She married John Loveday about 1559, in Wanborough, Wiltshire, England.

1276. Peter Tims was born 1571, in Northamptonshire, England, died before 1670, in England. He married Mrs Anne Tims 1590, in Northamptonshire, England.

Children of Peter Tims and Mrs Anne Tims:

i. **Frances Tims**, born 1591, in Farthinghoe, Northamptonshire, England, christened 27 Jan 1591, in Farthinghoe, Northamptonshire, England.
ii. **Lawrence Tims**, born 1594, in Newbottle with Charlton, Northamptonshire, England, died before 1690, in England.
iii. **Phillip Tyms**, born 1596, in Farthinghoe, Northamptonshire, England, christened 4 Apr 1596, in Farthinghoe, Northamptonshire, England.
iv. **Anne Tymes**, born Aug 1599, in Farthinghoe, Northamptonshire, England, christened 9 Oct 1599, in Farthinghoe, Northamptonshire, England.
Twin - Margaret
v. **Margaret Tymes**, born Aug 1599, in Farthinghoe, Northamptonshire, England, christened 9 Oct 1599, in Farthinghoe, Northamptonshire, England.
Twin - Anne
vi. **Nathaniel Tymmes**, born 1602, in Farthinghoe, Northamptonshire, England, christened 19 Sep 1602, in Farthinghoe, Northamptonshire, England.
vii. **Eleanor Tims**, born 1604, in Farthinghoe, Northamptonshire, England, christened 1 Jan 1605, in Farthinghoe, Northamptonshire, England.
viii. **Peter Tims**, born 1608, in Farthinghoe, Northamptonshire, England, christened 1608, in Farthinghoe, Northamptonshire, England.

1277. Mrs Anne Tims was born about 1571, in Farthinghoe, Northamptonshire, England, died before 1670, in England. She married Peter Tims 1590, in Northamptonshire, England.

1278.____Cox was born about 1575, in Oxfordshire, England. He married Cox about 1595, in Oxfordshire, England.

Children of Cox and Cox:

i. **Richard Cox**, born 1599, in Woodeaton, Oxfordshire, England, died 1669, in Woodeaton, Oxfordshire, England.

1279._____Cox was born about 1578, in Oxfordshire, England. She married Cox about 1595, in Oxfordshire, England.

1280. Robert Ashby was born 1540, in Bugbrooke, Northamptonshire, England, died 1602, in Bugbrooke, Northamptonshire, England. He was the son of John Ashby and Mrs Katherine Ashby. He married Mrs Elizabeth Ashby about 1566, in Northamptonshire, England.

Children of Robert Ashby and Mrs Elizabeth Ashby:

     i.   **John Ashby**,[1392,1393] born 1576, in Bugbrooke, Northamptonshire, England, died 1648, in Bugbrooke, Northamptonshire, England.

1281. Mrs Elizabeth Ashby was born 1545, in Northamptonshire, England, died Jul 1596, in Bugbrooke, Northamptonshire, England, buried 16 Jul 1596, in Bugbrooke, Northamptonshire, England. She married Robert Ashby[1422,1423] about 1566, in Northamptonshire, England. He was the son of John Ashby and Mrs Katherine Ashby.

1282._____Homes was born about 1555, in Kent, England, died before 1640, in England. He married Alyce Hilton 14 Feb 1581, in Mereworth, Kent, England. She was the daughter of Wyll Hilton and Hilton.

Children of Homes and Alyce Hilton:

     i.   **Henry Holmes**,[1394] born about 1590, in St Mary in the Marsh, Kent, England, died before 1680, in England.

1283. Alyce Hilton was born 30 Jan 1564, in Mereworth, Kent, England, christened 30 Jan 1564, in Mereworth, Kent, England, died before 1660, in England. She was the daughter of Wyll Hilton and Hilton. She married Homes 14 Feb 1581, in Mereworth, Kent, England.

1284. John Birch was born about 1530, in Eythorne, Kent, England, died 31 Jan 1595, in Eythorne, Kent, England. He married Mrs Jone Birch about 1565, in Eythorne, Kent, England.

Children of John Birch and Mrs Jone Birch:

     i.   **John Birch**,[1395] born Nov 1568, in Eythorne, Kent, England, died before 1650, in England.
    ii.   **Wyllm Birch**, born Nov 1573, in Eythorne, Kent, England, christened 13 Dec 1573, in Eythorne, Kent, England. He married Agnes Jarvise 29 Sep 1594, in Eythorne, Kent, England. Agnes Jarvise was born about 1577, in Eythorne, Kent, England.

1285. Mrs Jone Birch was born about 1533, in Eythorne, Kent, England, died 12 Jan 1580, in Eythorne,

Kent, England, buried 19 Jan 1580, in Eythorne, Kent, England. She married John Birch about 1565, in Eythorne, Kent, England.

1286. Wnalther Marsh was born about 1560, in Kent, England, died before 1660, in England. He married Marsh about 1586, in Kent, England.

Children of Wnalther Marsh and Marsh:

      i.   **Elizabeth Marsh**,[1397] born 1590, in Coldred, Kent, England, died before 1680, in England.

1287._____Marsh was born about 1565, in Kent, England, died before 1650, in England. She married Wnalther Marsh about 1586, in Kent, England.

Generation No. 15

1288. Robert Aldworth was born about 1510, in Wantage, Berkshire, England, died after 1564, in Wantage, Berkshire, England. He married Mrs Jhone Aldworth[1400] about 1530, in Berkshire, England.

Children of Robert Aldworth and Mrs Jhone Aldworth:

- i. **John Aldworth**,[1404,1405] born 1532, in Wantage, Berkshire, England, died after 1573, in Wantage, Berkshire, England.
- ii. **Robert Aldworth**,[1400,1424] born 16 Apr 1540, in Wantage, Berkshire, England, christened 18 Apr 1540, in Wantage, Berkshire, England.
  aka Robert ye younger
- iii. **William Aldworth**,[1400,1425,1426] born 8 Aug 1542, in Wantage, Berkshire, England, christened 8 Aug 1542, in Wantage, Berkshire, England. He married Jone Webb[1427] 13 Nov 1562, in Wantage, Berkshire, England. Jone Webb was born about 1544, in Berkshire, England.
- iv. **Jone Aldworth**,[1400] born 27 Oct 1548, in Wantage, Berkshire, England, christened 27 Oct 1548, in Wantage, Berkshire, England. She married Thomas Loder 15 Feb 1568, in Wantage, Berkshire, England. Thomas Loder was born about 1545, in Berkshire, England.
- v. **Richard Aldworth**,[1400,1428] born 25 Dec 1550, in Wantage, Berkshire, England, christened 7 Jan 1551, in Wantage, Berkshire, England, died Aug 1593, in Aldworth, Berkshire, England, buried 27 Aug 1593, in Aldworth, Berkshire, England. He married Mrs Annis Aldworth about 1565, in Wantage, Berkshire, England. Mrs Annis Aldworth was born about 1550, in Berkshire, England, died 23 Mar 1598, in Wantage, Berkshire, England.
- vi. **James Aldworth**,[1400,1429,1430] born 4 Aug 1553, in Wantage, Berkshire, England, christened 4 Aug 1553, in Wantage, Berkshire, England, died 28 May 1554, in Wantage, Berkshire, England.
- vii. **Francis Aldworth**,[1400,1431] born 13 Jun 1555, in Wantage, Berkshire, England, christened 13 Jun 1555, in Wantage, Berkshire, England.
- viii. **Margett Aldworth**,[1400,1432,1433] born 23 Dec 1557, in Wantage, Berkshire, England, christened 24 Dec 1557, in Wantage, Berkshire, England, died 5 Jan 1558, in Wantage, Berkshire, England, buried 5 Jan 1558, in Wantage, Berkshire, England.
- ix. **Thomas Aldworth**,[1400,1434] born 26 Apr 1559, in Wantage, Berkshire, England, christened 26 Apr 1559, in Wantage, Berkshire, England, died before 1560, in Wantage, Berkshire, England.
- x. **Thomas Aldworth**,[1400,1435] born 19 May 1560, in Wantage, Berkshire, England, christened 19 May 1560, in Wantage, Berkshire, England, died about 1590, in Berkshire, England. He married Ellizabeth Maynborow 5 Oct 1584, in Reading St Giles, Berkshire, England. Ellizabeth Maynborow was born about 1565, in

Berkshire, England.

Title: Master Forename: Thomas Surname: Aldworth Day Buried: 28 Month Buried: Jan Year Buried: 1577 Church Name: St Giles, Horn Street Place Name: Reading County: Berkshire Other Details: For thomas aldworth's mortuary 6s 8d "England Births and Christenings, 1538-1975," database, FamilySearch (https://familysearch.org/pal:/MM9.1.1/J3D3-HFC : accessed 2 November 2015), Robert Aldworth in entry for Thomas Aldworth, 19 May 1560; citing WANTAGE,BERKSHIRE,ENGLAND, reference ; FHL microfilm 88,468, 88,469. Notes for Thomas Aldworth and Ellizabeth Maynborow: Berkshire married 2nd ed 5 oct 1584 Reading St Giles

xi. **Henry Aldworth,**[1400,1436] born 14 May 1561, in Wantage, Berkshire, England, christened 14 May 1561, in Wantage, Berkshire, England.

xii. **Alice Aldworth,**[1400,1437] born 22 Mar 1564, in Wantage, Berkshire, England, christened 25 Dec 1564, in Wantage, Berkshire, England.

Inherited from Alexander FETIPLACE sum of 5 on her marriage ... I Alexander Fetiplace of BRK Childrey ... My body is to be buried in the aisle of St Katherine of Childrey if I happen to die there. My funeral charges and the disposition of certain money to the poor I reserve? to the discretion of my executors I give to every one of my servants being a yeoman that has stayed with me four years 6s 8d I give to Dorothy Phetiplace my wife all the following plate: the gilt goblets under a cover and a ring, two little silver goblets under a cover with a ring, one gilt bowl with a rose, one bowl of silver parcel gilt with a S ke pricked in the bottom, one standing cup bought of Edward Gline, five silver spoons tipped with acorns, one spoon gilt with a s   ke, one ale cup with a cover bought of Mr____Edmirthe of Reading, 6 silver spoons bought of the said Mr____with angels at the tips; all which plate I give to my wife for life, on condition that if she re-marries she shall find [a] sufficient surety to be bound with her before she marries to deliver the plate to my Executors for the use of my son Christopher Fetiplace. If Christopher dies before age 20 then all the above plate shall remain to my children by Dorothy. I give my wife Dorothy all the grain, corn and hay as remains at the time of my death at Letcombe Bassett or in the corn barns for her own use, also all tithes and fallows and grains sown at the time of my death. Also I give her all the grain, corn and hay or cattle as remain at the time of my death in my chantry barns, formerly Sir Edmond de Childrey's, which I purchased. I give her all the goods, chattels etc within the s   the_ of the said chantry house, moveable or unmoveable, remaining at the time of my death, without any interference from my executors. I give her twenty kine and one bull to be drawn out of my pasture of wood? for her own use. I give her 4 feather-beds, whereof one is to be my little down bed and bolster bought of my ?tenant Pegge, with a pair of fustian blankets to the same and a coverlet which I bought of Ms ?Grant; another feather-bed and bolster which she bought herself with a pair of fustians and two new pillows which she bought and one great coverlet unlined; another feather-bed with the bolster which used to lie over my buttery at Childrey with all the furniture as I used to lie in it myself; the fourth bed to be the bed which used to be in my sister's chamber, with a pair of woollen blankets, one pair of pillows and a coverlet which is with a white lion. I give my wife my great chest with the broken hasps and two locks [and] one yellow grease chest bought at London. She is to have all such jewels, goods and stuff which she brought with her to me. I give her two pairs of my finest sheets which she uses when in child-bed; also one piece of diaper which was never used. I give to Cicily Phetiplace my daughter 100 to be levied of my lands in Swinbrook immediately after my death, to be delivered to Cissie when she reaches age 18 by my trusty feoffees Edmond Plowden and [blurred] Esquires (the said feoffment annexed to my will dated 10 Jun 1554) If Cicily dies before 18 then my daughter Mary shall have the 100 over and above her own legacies. Out of the rest of the moiety to be levied out of my manor of Swinbrooke during ten years after my decease I give to Mary my daughter 100. If Mary dies before age 18 and her sister Cicily is living then I will that my feoffees shall pay the 100 to Cicily immediately after Mary's death. I give my son Anthony Fetiplace all such interest, right or title which I have in the Parsonage of Swinbrooke by virtue of a lease which I bought. I give Anthony all the grain and all my goods, chattels or implements of household as shall be found in or upon the houses or grounds of the Parsonage. If both Cicily and Mary die (god forbid) before reaching 18 then their 200 is to be evenly divided between my two sons Christopher and Anthony if both are living, else the whole 200 to the survivor. If neither of my two sons are living (god forbid) then the 200 is to be given to Alexander Phetiplace my godson and one of the sons of William Phetiplace my son and heir late deceased. I bequeath to my daughter Elizabeth 200 marks to be paid within one year after my decease unless I provide otherwise for her in my life-time. If Elizabeth dies before that year is ended, then my executors shall pay the 200 marks to my son Anthony Fettiplace when he reaches age 20. I give my wife all the household stuff in or about the house at Childrey with all the t_implements thereto belonging, ploughs and ploughshares? earth? and cart gears. I give to Alice Aldsworthe 5 at the day of marriage. I will that within four days after my decease my executors shall make with my other sheep a perfect flock or stock of 500 wether sheep after five score to every hundred on my farm of BRK Up Letcombe, if there shall not be so many sheep there pasturing in one flock the day of my decease. Dorothy my wife and her Executors etc shall have the use and occupation and profits of those sheep and farm and all the other lands and Tenements etc in Letcombe which I have for years of the Assignment of John ide gent deceased, and also of twenty acres of meadow ground in the old fields which I hold by lease of Queens College in Oxford, from the day of my decease until Christopher Phetiplace my son reaches age 21 if he survives. My wife or her Executors etc shall use part of the clear yearly issues and profits thereof to bring up my son in learning, as well at the grammar after his easement? thereof as in the study of the common laws of this realm, and the rest of the clear issues and profits thereof, the flock of sheep always maintained and other charges deducted, shall yearly [be invested] in the flock on behalf of Christopher, and which shall be delivered to him at or before age 21 if he marries, unless any good farm office or other living may be therewith obtained by my wife or her Executors etc before his said age or marriage. The said farm lands, tenements and meadows and the leases thereof for the years to come after my decease I give to Christopher. If he dies unmarried before age 21 leaving Dorothy [alive] then I will to Dorothy not only such clear issues and profits thereof as shall be received to the use of Christopher and remain unpaid, but also such farm or other living as [might have been] obtained for him as aforesaid, and my wife shall have the profits of the farm, lands, Tenements, meadows, flock of sheep etc to her own use for life if the years in the [leases etc] shall so long continue If my wife and son Christopher both die before Christopher reaches 21, or if Christopher dies before 21 whereby my wife has the profits etc for her life as above but she dies before the leases etc have expired, then the said farm, lands, Tenements and meadows shall for the remaining years of the leases, together with the said stock of sheep, go to my son and heir William Phetiplace to whom I give the farm and also the indentures of leases thereof. If William has died then the premises demised to him shall remain to the use of such of my children as shall have most need thereof. I grant to my son Christopher Phettiplace all the Indentures of Lease for term of years which I do? assign of Nicholas Weston yeoman have in the manor of Letcombe Regis with the appurtenances, and of other lands, Tenements etc in Letcombe Regis, and of the Office of the Bailiwick of the said manor, and all my estate, right, title, term of years and interest which I now have in the manor, bailiwick and [everything else mentioned in the leases], to hold to hijm and his assigns for the remaining years of the leases. If my son Christopher dies before reaching 21 or marrying then I grant the said Indenture of the manor of Letcombe Regis and [all the rest as above] to my son Anthony Fetyplace If he has died I give it to Alexannder Fettiplace my godson second son to my son William Fettiplace. For default of him, to his lawfully begotten son and heir. The rest of my goods unbequeathed, my debts, legacies and funeral charges paid, I give to my well beloved son Christopher Phetiplace and in William Wolescot of Tidmarsh whom I make my only executor. For overseers I most heartily desire my brother-in-law Mr Michael Hampden and my brother-in-law Mr Thomas Ashefeilde to take the pains. My daughter Elizabeth shall not intermingle with any of my said leases. Witnesses Robert Allen, Henrie Davies clerk, Elizabeth Fetiplace, Alice Alder with divers others

1289. Mrs Jhone Aldworth was born about 1512, in Berkshire, England, died Jun 1593, in Berkshire, England, buried 30 Jun 1593, in Reading, Berkshire, England. She married Robert Aldworth[1400] about 1530, in Berkshire, England.
Notes for Mrs Jhone Aldworth:

aka: Jone - Jhon - Jane - Yony - Joane Forename: Joane Surname: Ailworth (Aldworth) Day Buried: 30 Month Buried: Jun Year Buried: 1593 Church Name: St Giles, Horn Street Place Name: Reading County: Berkshire

1290. Peter Tubb was born about 1532, in Wantage, Berkshire, England. He married Elizabeth Pearne 20 Jul 1557, in Wantage, Berkshire, England.

Children of Peter Tubb and Elizabeth Pearne:

    i.   **Thomas Tubb**, born 31 Dec 1566, in Wantage, Berkshire, England.

1291. Elizabeth Pearne was born about 1536, in Wantage, Berkshire, England. She married Peter Tubb 20 Jul 1557, in Wantage, Berkshire, England.

1292. John Clark was born about 1546, in Wantage, Berkshire, England. He married Mrs Matheu Clark about 1571, in Wantage, Berkshire, England.

Children of John Clark and Mrs Matheu Clark:

    i.   **Margret Clark**, born 16 Sep 1573, in Wantage, Berkshire, England.

1293. Mrs Matheu Clark was born about 1550, in Wantage, Berkshire, England. She married John Clark about 1571, in Wantage, Berkshire, England.

1294.____Oxlade was born about 1499, in England, died before 1580, in England. He married Oxlade about 1522, in England.

Children of Oxlade and Oxlade:

    i.   **Henry Oxlade**, born 1528, in Aston Rowant, Oxfordshire, England, died before 1600, in England.

1295.____Oxlade was born about 1502, in England, died before 1600, in England. She married Oxlade about 1522, in England.

1296. Peter Kirby was born about 1535, in Charlton on Otmoor, Oxfordshire, England, died 11 Jun 1574, in Charlton on Otmoor, Oxfordshire, England. He was the son of John Kirby and Mrs. Agnes Kirby. He married Mrs. Agnes Kirby about 1555, in Charlton on Otmoor, Oxfordshire, England.

Children of Peter Kirby and Mrs. Agnes Kirby:

    i.   **John Kirby**, born about 1556, in Charlton on Otmoor, Oxfordshire, England, died 14 Apr 1599, in Charlton on Otmoor, Oxfordshire, England.
    ii.   **Jane Kirby**, born about 1558, in Charlton on Otmoor, Oxfordshire, England.
    iii.   **Elyne Kirby**, born about 1559, in Charlton on Otmoor, Oxfordshire, England.
    iv.   **Isabell Kirby**, born about 1561, in Charlton on Otmoor, Oxfordshire, England.
    v.   **William Kirby**, born about 1562, in Charlton on Otmoor, Oxfordshire, England.

1297. Mrs. Agnes Kirby was born about 1536, in Charlton on Otmoor, Oxfordshire, England. She married Peter Kirby about 1555, in Charlton on Otmoor, Oxfordshire, England. He was the son of John Kirby and Mrs. Agnes Kirby.

1298. Peter Kirbye was born 1515, in Charlton on Otmoor, Oxfordshire, England, died 1574, in Charlton on Otmoor, Oxfordshire, England. He married Mrs Elyne Kirby 1539, in Charlton on Otmoor, Oxfordshire, England.

Children of Peter Kirbye and Mrs Elyne Kirby:

    i.   **Elyne Kirbye**, born about 1539, in Charlton on Otmoor, Oxfordshire, England.
    ii.   **Isabell Kirby**, born 1540, in Charlton on Otmoor, Oxfordshire, England.
    iii.   **John Kirby**, born 1542, in Charlton on Otmoor, Oxfordshire, England.
    iv.   **Jane Kirby**, born 1544, in Charlton on Otmoor, Oxfordshire, England.
    v.   **William Kirby**, born 1546, in Charlton on Otmoor, Oxfordshire, England, died 30 Aug 1584, in Charlton on Otmoor, Oxfordshire, England.

1299. Mrs Elyne Kirby was born 1519, in Charlton on Otmoor, Oxfordshire, England, died 21 May 1614, in Charlton on Otmoor, Oxfordshire, England. She married Peter Kirbye 1539, in Charlton on Otmoor, Oxfordshire, England.

1300. John Ashby was born 1518, in Bugbrooke, Northamptonshire, England, died 1567, in Bugbrooke, Northamptonshire, England. He was the son of William Ashby and Mrs Alise Ashby. He married Mrs Katherine Ashby about 1537, in England.

Children of John Ashby and Mrs Katherine Ashby:

    i.   **Robert Ashby**,[1422,1423] born 1540, in Bugbrooke, Northamptonshire, England, died 1602, in Bugbrooke, Northamptonshire, England.
    ii.   **Isabelle Ashby**,[1438] born about 1543, in Bugbrooke, Northamptonshire, England.
    iii.   **Ales Ashby**,[1438] born about 1545, in Bugbrooke, Northamptonshire, England.
    iv.   **Jane Ashby**,[1438] born 1546, in Bugbrooke, Northamptonshire, England.
    v.   **Thomas Ashby**,[1438] born about 1547, in Bugbrooke, Northamptonshire, England, died 1601, in Bugbrooke, Northamptonshire, England.
    vi.   **Richard Ashby**,[1438] born about 1549, in Bugbrooke, Northamptonshire, England.

1301. Mrs Katherine Ashby was born about 1520, in England, died 1575, in England. She married John Ashby[1439,1440] about 1537, in England. He was the son of William Ashby and Mrs Alise Ashby.

1302. Wyll Hilton was born about 1535, in Kent, England, died before 1630, in England. He married Hilton about 1561, in Kent, England.

Children of Wyll Hilton and Hilton:

       i.   **Alyce Hilton**, born 30 Jan 1564, in Mereworth, Kent, England, died before 1660, in England.

1303.____Hilton was born about 1540, in Kent, England, died before 1640, in England. She married Wyll Hilton about 1561, in Kent, England.

Generation No. 16

1304. John Kirby was born about 1512, in Charlton on Otmoor, Oxfordshire, England, died about 1583, in Charlton on Otmoor, Oxfordshire, England. He married Mrs. Agnes Kirby about 1534, in Charlton on Otmoor, Oxfordshire, England.

Children of John Kirby and Mrs. Agnes Kirby:

  i. **Peter Kirby**, born about 1535, in Charlton on Otmoor, Oxfordshire, England, died 11 Jun 1574, in Charlton on Otmoor, Oxfordshire, England.
  ii. **Robert Kirby**, born about 1545, in Charlton on Otmoor, Oxfordshire, England.

1305. Mrs. Agnes Kirby was born about 1513, in Charlton on Otmoor, Oxfordshire, England. She married John Kirby about 1534, in Charlton on Otmoor, Oxfordshire, England.

1306. William Ashby was born 1475, in Northamptonshire, England, died 1530, in Bugbrooke, Northamptonshire, England. He married Mrs Alise Ashby about 1510, in Northamptonshire, England.

Children of William Ashby and Mrs Alise Ashby:

  i. **Robert Ashby**, born about 1515, in Bugbrooke, Northamptonshire, England.
  ii. **John Ashby**,[1439,1440] born 1518, in Bugbrooke, Northamptonshire, England, died 1567, in Bugbrooke, Northamptonshire, England.

1307. Mrs Alise Ashby was born about 1485, in England. She married William Ashby about 1510, in Northamptonshire, England.

1. Thomas Aldwyn "Tom"[1] Allsworth,[1441,1442] born 17 Nov 1946, in London, Middlesex, England, christened 15 Dec 1946, in Harrow, Middlesex, England. He married Janet Beasley 14 Mar 1964, in Oxford, Oxfordshire, England. Janet Beasley was born 26 Sep 1946, in Penge St John, Kent, England.

Notes for Thomas Aldwyn "Tom" Allsworth:

Personal history found in published autobiography - Boomer's Walk.

Notes for family of Thomas Aldwyn "Tom" Allsworth and Janet Beasley:

Appears in Boomer's Walk - by Toma (Thomas Aldwyn Allsworth - autobiography) Marriage cert shows two names Beasley and Busby. Correct name = Beasley. Mother lied about changing name to Busby to hide her infidelity

Children of Thomas Aldwyn "Tom" Allsworth and Janet Beasley:

2	i.	**Paula Janet Allsworth,** born 8 Mar 1965, in Oxford, Oxfordshire, England.
3	ii.	**Mark Thomas Allsworth,** born 21 Dec 1966, in Oxford, Oxfordshire, England.
4	iii.	**Aaron Paul Allsworth,** born 21 Feb 1977, in Headington, Oxfordshire, England.
5	iv.	**Rachel Anne Allsworth,** born 21 Jan 1979, in Headington, Oxfordshire, England.

2. Paula Janet² Allsworth *(Thomas Aldwyn "Tom")*, born 8 Mar 1965, in Oxford, Oxfordshire, England. She married Andrew David Rosser 31 Aug 1985, in Northampton, Northamptonshire, England. Andrew David Rosser was born 26 Sep 1965, in Gloucester, Gloucestershire, England.

Children of Paula Janet Allsworth and Andrew David Rosser:

	i.	**Rebekah Janet Rosser**, born 4 Sep 1986, in Banbury, Oxfordshire, England.
6	ii.	**Laura Caitlin Rosser**, born 17 Dec 1987, in Banbury, Oxfordshire, England.
	iii.	**Heidi Louise Rosser**, born 13 Jul 1990, in Eastleigh, Hampshire, England.
7	iv.	**Genevieve Mary Rosser**, born 5 Jan 1993, in Winchester, Hampshire, England.
	v.	**David Thomas Allsworth Rosser**, born 6 Jul 1995, in Winchester, Hampshire, England.
	vi.	**Benjamin Edward Andrew Rosser**, born 2 Jun 1999, in Stoke-on-Trent, Staffordshire, England, died 2 Jun 1999, in Stoke-on-Trent, Staffordshire, England.
	vii.	**Olivia Alice Rosser**, born 1 Sep 2000, in Stoke-on-Trent, Staffordshire, England.
	viii.	**Isobel Rachel Rosser**, born 6 Dec 2002, in Stoke-on-Trent, Staffordshire, England.

3. Mark Thomas² Allsworth *(Thomas Aldwyn "Tom")*, born 21 Dec 1966, in Oxford, Oxfordshire, England. He married (1) Michelle Holmes 23 May 2009, in Lincoln, Lincolnshire, England. Michelle Holmes was born 12 Oct 1976, in Fort Riley Township, Riley, Kansas, United States. He married (2) Rebecca Lorlen Shepard 29 Jul 1988, in Los Angeles, California, United States. Rebecca Lorlen Shepard was born 14 Jan 1968, in Long Beach, Los Angeles, California, United States.

Children of Mark Thomas Allsworth and Michelle Holmes:

	i.	**Darby Allsworth**, born 19 Aug 2010, in Grimsby, Lincolnshire, England.

Children of Mark Thomas Allsworth and Rebecca Lorlen Shepard:

	i.	**Michael Thomas Allsworth**, born 3 Jun 1990, in Los Angeles, California, United States.
	ii.	**Adam Jean Luc Allsworth**, born 28 Mar 1992, in Ventura, California, United States.
8	iii.	**Fauve-Ashleigh Allsworth**, born 15 Mar 1994, in Immingham, Lincolnshire, England.

4. Aaron Paul² Allsworth *(Thomas Aldwyn "Tom")*, born 21 Feb 1977, in Headington, Oxfordshire, England. He married Elizabeth Gail Hannah Aitchison 9 Sep 2000, in Bristol, Gloucestershire, England. Elizabeth Gail Hannah Aitchison was born 31 Jul 1975, in Bristol, Gloucestershire, England.

Children of Aaron Paul Allsworth and Elizabeth Gail Hannah Aitchison:

   i.   **Jacob David Thomas Allsworth**, born 31 Mar 2004, in Winchester, Hampshire, England.
   ii. **Amelie Eve Allsworth**, born 2 Aug 2006, in Bath, Somerset, England.
   iii. **Madeleine Grace Genevieve Allsworth**, born 25 May 2013, in Wiltshire, England.

5. Rachel Anne[2] **Allsworth** *(Thomas Aldwyn "Tom"*[1]*)*, born 21 Jan 1979, in Headington, Oxfordshire, England. She married Wayne Sanderson. Wayne Sanderson was born 12 Jan 1976, in Grimsby, Lincolnshire, England.

Notes for Rachel Anne Allsworth:

Rachel born at 7:13 am by C Section. many more details in personal family history

Notes for family of Rachel Anne Allsworth and Wayne Sanderson:

Not married

Children of Rachel Anne Allsworth and Wayne Sanderson:

   i.   **Arthur Thomas "Kismet" Sanderson**, born 10 Dec 2014, in Grimsby, Lincolnshire, England.

        Born by Cessearian section at 3 am BIRTH: Also shown as Born Grimsby, North East Lincolnshire, England.

6. Laura Caitlin³ Rosser *(Paula Janet Allsworth², Thomas Aldwyn "Tom"¹)*, born 17 Dec 1987, in Banbury, Oxfordshire, England. She married Thomas Wield 27 Jun 2009, in Stoke-on-Trent, Staffordshire, England. Thomas Wield was born 22 Feb 1988, in Hampshire, England.

Children of Laura Caitlin Rosser and Thomas Wield:

  i.   **Nathaniel Wield**, born 30 May 2011, in Portsmouth, Hampshire, England.
  ii. **Elias Wield**, born 12 Aug 2012, in Portsmouth, Hampshire, England.
  iii. **Xavier Thomas Wield**, born 30 Oct 2014, in Portsmouth, Hampshire, England.

7. Genevieve Mary³ Rosser *(Paula Janet Allsworth², Thomas Aldwyn "Tom"¹)*, born 5 Jan 1993, in Winchester, Hampshire, England. She married Tom Barber. Tom Barber was born 25 Oct (Abt) 1990, in England.

Children of Genevieve Mary Rosser and Tom Barber:

  i.   **Eliza Rose Barber**, born 11 Oct 2014, in Walsall, Stafordshire, England.

       I heard on the phone her first cry as she entered the world and a little gurgle minutes later.

8. Fauve-Ashleigh³ Allsworth *(Mark Thomas², Thomas Aldwyn "Tom"¹)*, born 15 Mar 1994, in Immingham, Lincolnshire, England. She married Jordan Christensen 21 Jan 2012, in California, United States. Jordan Christensen was born 3 Aug 1992, in California, United States.

Children of Fauve-Ashleigh Allsworth and Jordan Christensen:

  i.   **London Elizabeth Christensen**, born 20 May 2013, in California, United States.
  ii. **Thomas Christensen**, born 10 Jan 2015, in California, United States.

Sources and Endnotes

1. IGI ; Thomas William Allsworth; Male; Birth: 23 SEP 1905 Headington, Oxford, Oxford, England; Death: 12 MAY 1992 Jeffreston, Pembroke, Wales; Burial: , , Wales; Father: Walter William Allsworth; Mother: Annie Newell.
2. , Birth certificate , , , Thomas William Allsworth; YD953430; 23 September 1905.
3. <i>Parish Records Collection - Baptism</i>, page 144 (5 Nov 1905).
4. England & Wales Marriages, 1538-1940 , Harrow, Middlesex; Date: 1945.
5. COPY - Birth Certificate
6. COPY - Marriage Certificate
7. COPY - Death Certificate
8. Marriage Certificate: ; , , , Thomas William Allsworth; 23 January 1932.
9. Personal Family Records , Family bible; Date: 1967.
10. <i>1911 Census</i>
11. <i> - Oxfordshire Parish Registers</i>, Oxford; Date: 1903.
12. 1901 Census
13. 1891 Census
14. COPY - Marriage Certificate ; Date: 26 December 1903.
15. IGI ; Lydia Amy Allsworth; Female; Birth: 06 JAN 1907 2 Deans Row Coln St Aldwyns, , Oxford, England; Christening: 07 FEB 1907 St Frideswide'S, , Oxford, England; Death: Before 2000 Westergate, Sussex, England; Father: Walter William Allsworth; Mother: Annie Newell.
16. IGI ; Edith Florence Allsworth; Female; Birth: 28 OCT 1908 2 Deans, Row, Cumberland, England; Death: 26 JUN 1998 Church Walk House, , London, England; Father: Walter William Allsworth; Mother: Annie Newell.
17. IGI ; Reginald Walter Allsworth; Male; Birth: 18 AUG 1910 2 Deans, Row, Cumberland, England; Death: 17 AUG 1979 Felpham, Sussex, England; Burial: St Mary'S, Felpham, Sussex, England; Father: Walter William Allsworth; Mother: Annie Newell.
18. <i> - Oxfordshire Parish Registers</i>, Summertown - marriages; Date: 1 October 1938 Mildred Dorothy Allsworth; Female; Birth: 17 NOV 1914 , Oxford, England; Death: Before 2000 Braintree, Essex, England; Father: Walter William Allsworth; Mother: Annie Newell.
19. <i> - Oxfordshire Parish Registers</i>, Summertown - marriages; Date: 1 October 1938.
20. <i> - Oxfordshire Parish Registers</i>, Summertown - marriages; Date: 15 December 1951 Emily Grace Allsworth; Female; Birth: 28 MAR 1921 Woodbine Cottage, Headington, Oxford, England; Death: 26 JAN 2002 , , England; Burial: 04 FEB 2002 Headington, Oxford, England; Father: Walter William Allsworth; Mother: Annie Newell.
21. <i> - Oxfordshire Parish Registers</i>, Summertown - marriages; Date: 15 December 1951.
22. <i> - Oxfordshire Parish Registers</i>, Summertown - marriages; Date: 9 May 1942.
23. 1881 Census
24. COPY - Birth Certificate ; Date: 6 June 1879.
25. Free BMD Death Index, , Oxford 1969: vol 68 - page 925.
26. COPY - Death Certificate ; Date: 1938.

27. Ireland, Civil Registration Index 1845-1958 , Film number: 101575; Vol: 2; Page: 339; GS #: 4199367; Image #: 00023; Date: 1922 Name: Sarah Lucas Registration district: Dublin North Record type: MARRIAGES Registration date - quarter and year: Jan - Mar 1922 Estimated birth year: Age: Mother's surnames: Film number: 101575 Volume: 2 Page: 339 Digital GS number: 4199367 Image number: 00023 Collection: Ireland, Civil Registration Indexes 1845-1958.
28. COPY - Marriage Certificate ; Date: 4 May 1921.
29. England & Wales, Birth Index: , Devon, St Thomas reg dist; vol 5b; page 49; Date: 1901.
30. <i>England & Wales Death index</i> <i>First name(s) PAMELA Last name ALLSWORTH Gender Female Birth day 23, Taunton, Somerset reg dist; vol 23; page 1513; reg# 390; Date: 1990.
31. England & Wales Marriage Index: 1916-2005 , Surrey N.E. reg dist; vol 5g; page 1408; Date: 1958.
32. Free BMD Death Index, , Reg dist: Surrey; Vol 5g; Page: 281; Date: 1957 Name: Agnes Elizabeth Rowland Birth Date: 1 Aug 1910 Death Registration Month/Year: Jul 1990 Age at death (estimated): 79 Registration district: Surrey Mid-Eastern Inferred County: Surrey Volume: 17 Page: 294.
33. England & Wales, Birth Index: , Reg Dist -Surrey, Chertsey; Vol 2a; page 52; Date: 1910.
34. England & Wales Marriage Index: 1916-2005 , Surrey South Western reg dist - Vol 2a; page 1231; Date: 1939.
35. England & Wales, Birth Index: , Births Sep; Date: 1921.
36. England & Wales, Birth Index: , Wandsworth reg district vol 1d page 860; Date: 1922.
37. England & Wales, Birth Index: , Wandsworth district vol.1d page 777a; Date: 1924.
38. England & Wales Marriage Index: 1916-2005 , Durham NE, vol 1a, page 1283; Date: 1947.
39. International Genealogical Index, The Church of Jesus Christ of Latter-day Saints, Family History Library, 35 N. West Tem
40. Free BMD Death Index, , Reg dist: Haywards heath; reg#: 35a; District#: 781/1a; entry:66; Name: Carolyn Frances Green Birth Date: 30 Nov 1941 Death Registration Month/Year: Jan 2003 Age at death (estimated): 61 Registration district: Haywards Heath Inferred County: West Sussex Register number: 35A District and Subdistrict: 781/1A Entry number: 66.
41. Ireland, Civil Registration Index 1845-1958 , Dublin North District - Marriages - 1922 File#:101575; vol 2; page 339; Date: 1922 Name: George Rowland Registration district: Dublin North Record type: MARRIAGES Registration date - quarter and year: Jan - Mar 1922 Estimated birth year: Age: Mother's surnames: Film number: 101575 Volume: 2 Page: 339 Digital GS number: 4199367 Image number: 00032 Collection: Ireland, Civil Registration Indexes 1845-1958.
42. England & Wales, National Probate Calendar (Index of Wills and Administrations) , Rowland, George William - 1959; R; Ro; 92; page 424.
43. <i> - Oxfordshire Parish Registers</i>, Oxford; Date: 1871.

44. 1861 Census , Source Citation: Class: RG9; Piece: 896; Folio: 17; Page: 28; GSU roll: 542718.
45. 1901 Census , Class: RG13; Piece: 1386; Folio: 16; Page: 22.
46. 1881 Census , Class: RG11; Piece: 1504; Folio: 19; Page: 32; GSU roll: 1341363.
47. 1891 Census , RG12 piece 1169 folio 14 page 21.
48. <i>1871 Census</i>, RG10 piece 1440 folio 32 page 20.
49. <i>1911 Census</i>, RG14PN8150 RG78PN413 RD153 SD1 ED9 SN166.
50. <i> - Oxfordshire Parish Registers</i>, St Thomas, Oxford BMD records - Christening; Date: 1850.
51. <i> - Oxfordshire Parish Registers</i>, St Thomas - Marriage records; Date: 1871.
52. <i> - Oxfordshire Parish Registers</i>, St Thomas - Burial records; Date: 1917.
53. <i> - Oxfordshire Parish Registers</i>, HEADINGTON CEMETERY REGISTERS Burials Page 43 (Second Register); Date: 1926.
54. 1881 Census , Class: RG11; Piece: 1495; Folio: 63; Page: 8; Line: ; GSU roll: 1341361.
55. War records , REDAN RIDGE CEMETERY No. 2, BEAUMONT-HAMEL; Date: 1916.
56. <i> - Oxfordshire Parish Registers</i>, St Thomas - christening records; Date: 1874.
57. <i> - Oxfordshire Parish Registers</i>, St Frideswide, Oxford, Oxfordshire, England parish record 18 Oct 1902.
58. <i> - Oxfordshire Parish Registers</i>, Oxford - Deaths Vol:3a; page: 403; Date: 1875.
59. <i> - Oxfordshire Parish Registers</i>, St Thomas - christening records; Date: 1875.
60. <i> - Oxfordshire Parish Registers</i>, St Thomas - burial records; Date: 1875.
61. England & Wales, Birth Index: , Oxford vol:3a; page 691; Date: 1876.
62. <i> - Oxfordshire Parish Registers</i>, St Thomas - christening records; Date: 1877.
63. <i> - Oxfordshire Parish Registers</i>, St Thomas - burial records; Date: 1877.
64. <i> - Oxfordshire Parish Registers</i>, Oxford birth vol:3a page 704; Date: 1878.
65. <i> - Oxfordshire Parish Registers</i>, St Thomas - christening records; Date: 1878.
66. <i> - Oxfordshire Parish Registers</i>, St Thomas - Marriage records; Date: 1897.
67. <i><i>England & Wales Christening Records, 1530-1906</i> Ancestry.com. England & Wales Christening Records, 1530-1906 [da, Oxford Vol:3a page:735; Date: 1881.
68. <i> - Oxfordshire Parish Registers</i>, St Thomas - christening records; Date: 1881.
69. <i> - Oxfordshire Parish Registers</i>, St Thomas - burial records; Date: 1882.
70. <i> - Oxfordshire Parish Registers</i>, St Thomas - christening records; Date: 1885.
71. Free BMD Death Index, , Registration district: Oxford Inferred County: Oxfordshire Volume: 3a Page: 910; Date: 1917.
72. 1861 Census ; Name: Thomas Allsworth Age in years: 11 Gender: Male Birth place: Stanton Harcourt, Oxfordshire Relationship to head-of-household: Son Record type: Household Collection: 1861 England and Wales Census.
73. 1901 Census , Class: RG13; Piece: 1386; Folio: 16; Page: 22; Date: 1901.
74. <i>1851 Census</i>, HO107; Piece 1731; Folio 173; Page 14.
75. <i> - Oxfordshire Parish Registers</i>, Stanton Harcourt baptism; Date: 1849.

76. <i> - Oxfordshire Parish Registers</i>, St Thomas - Burial records; Date: 1908.
77. <i> - Oxfordshire Parish Registers</i>, Oxford; Date: 1874.
78. Free BMD Death Index, , ACDB-01/1904D1-N-0263.tif; Date: March 1904 Surname Given Name Age District Volume Page Transcriber Deaths Mar 1904 NEWELL Elizabeth 57 Headington 3a 602.
79. <i>1851 Census</i>, HO107 Piece 1731 Folio 173 Page 14.
80. 1861 Census , RG09 piece 733 folio 15 page 24.
81. 1881 Census , RG11 piece 1495 folio 63 page 8.
82. 1891 Census , RG12 piece 1173 folio 100 page 1.
83. 1901 Census , RG13 piece 1378 folio 72 page 23.
84. <i> - Oxfordshire Parish Registers</i>, Northmoor - Baptism; Date: 1846.
85. 1881 Census , : Class: RG11; Piece: 1504; Folio: 67; Page: 80; Line: ; GSU roll: 1341363.
86. <i>England & Wales Death index</i> <i>First name(s) PAMELA Last name ALLSWORTH Gender Female Birth day 23, Volume   6A page 379; Date1:950.
87. <i>1871 Census</i>, RG10-1433_0148.
88. 1861 Census , RG905298-088802-089201-00192A.
89. <i>1851 Census</i>, HO107 piece 1727 folio 115 page 15.
90. 1891 Census , G12 piece 1173 folio 100 page 1.
91. London, England, Births & Baptisms , London Metropolitan Archives, Christ Church, Manchester Road, Register of baptisms, P88/CT; Date: 1881.
92. Free BMD Death Index, , Registration district: Surrey South Western Inferred County: Surrey Volume: 5g Page: 837; Date: 1952.
93. 1901 Census , Class: RG13; Piece: 68; Folio: 119; Page: 29; Date: 1901 Name: Augusta Rowland Age: 19 Estimated birth year: abt 1882 Relation: Wife Spouse's name: George Stephen Gender: Female Where born: Milland, London, England Civil parish: Fulham Ecclesiastical parish: St Matthew County/Island: London Country: England Registration district: Fulham Sub-registration district: South Fulham ED, institution, or vessel: 23 Neighbors: View others on page Household schedule number: 184 Household Members: Name Age George Stephen Rowland 32 Augusta Rowland 19.
94. <i>1911 Census</i>, RG14 piece 4745 ref RG78PN203 RD69 SD2 ED15 SN501.
95. 1891 Census , RG12 piece 51 folio 160 page 20.
96. London, England, Births & Baptisms , Source Citation: London Metropolitan Archives, Christ Church, Manchester Road, Register of; Date: 1881.
97. Free BMD Death Index, , District: Hendon; Vol: 3a; Page:651; Date: 1929.
98. 1881 Census , RG number: RG11   Piece: 500   Folio: 123   Page: 55; 33, Spey St, Bromley National Archive Reference: RG number: RG11 Piece: 500 Folio: 123 Page: 55 Reg. District: Poplar Sub District: Bromley Parish: Bromley Enum. District: Ecclesiastical District: City/Municipal Borough: Address: 33, Spey St, Bromley County: Middlesex Name Relation Condition Sex Age Birth Year Occupation , Disability Where Born ROWLAND, Stephen Head Married M 39 1842 Police Inspector Henbury Gloucestershire ROWLAND, Mary Ann Wife Married F 38 1843 Greenwich Kent ROWLAND, Walter Son Single M 11 1870 Scholar Dulwich Surrey ROWLAND, Alice Daughter Single F 8 1873 Scholar West Ham Essex ROWLAND, Harry

Son Single M 4 1877 Scholar Bromley Middlesex ROWLAND, George Son Single M 2 1879 Bromley Middlesex ROWLAND, Mary Ann Daughter Single F 0 1881 Bromley Middlesex.

99. 1901 Census , Class: RG13; Piece: 68; Folio: 119; Page: 29; 1901 England Census 1901 England Census Name: George Stephen Rowland Age: 32 Estimated birth year: abt 1869 Relation: Head Spouse's name: Augusta Gender: Male Where born: Poplar, London, England Civil parish: Fulham Ecclesiastical parish: St Matthew County/Island: London Country: England Registration district: Fulham Sub-registration district: South Fulham ED, institution, or vessel: 23 Neighbors: View others on page Household schedule number: 184 Household Members: Name Age George Stephen Rowland 32 Augusta Rowland 19.

100. Free BMD Death Index,

101. 1901 Census , Class: RG13; Piece: 1585; Folio: 20; Page: 31; Name: Mary Lucas Age: 39 Estimated birth year: abt 1862 Relation: Wife Spouse's name: Charles Gender: Female Where born: Limehouse, Middlesex, England Civil parish: West Ham Ecclesiastical parish: Holy Trinity County/Island: Essex Country: England Registration district: West Ham Sub-registration district: Canning Town ED, institution, or vessel: 42 Neighbors: View others on page Household schedule number: 194 Household Members: Name Age Charles Lucas 43 Mary Lucas 39 George Lucas 13 Thomas Lucas 11 Harriet Lucas 9 Sarah Lucas 4 James Lucas 1 James Giles 30.

102. <i>1911 Census</i>, RG14 piece 9506 ref# RG78PN508 RD188 SD4 ED36 SN75.

103. 1891 Census , RG12 piece 210 folio 99 page 20.

104. 1881 Census , RG11 piece 468 folio 17 page 27.

105. <i>1871 Census</i>, RG10 piece 552 folio 23 page 40.

106. 1861 Census , RG09 piece 289 folio 16 page 38.

107. COPY - Christening Certificate , St Anne's - Limehouse; Date: 1860.

108. Free BMD Death Index, , Stepney district; Vol 1c; Page 325; Date: 1882 Name: Mary Ann Lucas Estimated birth year: abt 1882 Year of Registration: 1882 Quarter of Registration: Jul-Aug-Sep Age at Death: 0 District: Stepney (To 1921) County: London, Middlesex Volume: 1c Page: 325.

109. London, England, Births & Baptisms , St Mary's Limehouse; page 222; Date: 1882.

110. London, England, Births & Baptisms , St Anne's Limehouse; page 272; Date: 1882.

111. Free BMD Death Index, , West Ham District; Vol 4a; Page:26; Date: 1903 Name: James Lucas Estimated birth year: abt 1899 Year of Registration: 1903 Quarter of Registration: Jul-Aug-Sep Age at Death: 4 District: West Ham County: Essex, Greater London Volume: 4a Page: 26.

112. 1901 Census , RG13; Piece: 1585; Folio: 20; Page: 31; Date: 1901 Civil parish: West Ham Ecclesiastical parish: Holy Trinity County/Island: Essex Country: England Registration district: West Ham Sub-registration district: Canning Town Household schedule number: 194 Household Members: Name Age Charles Lucas 43 Mary Lucas 39 George Lucas 13 Thomas Lucas 11 Harriet Lucas 9 Sarah Lucas 4 James Lucas 1 James Giles 30.".

113. <i><i>London, England, Deaths and Burials, 1813-1980</i> London Metropolitan Archives</i> London Metropolitan Archives</i, Register of burials at Finchley Cemetery, P90/PAN1, Item 208;

Date: 1903 Name: Marie Lucas Record Type: Burial Event Date: 15 Jun 1903 Age: infant Estimated birth year: abt 1903 Parish: Saint Pancras Old Church Borough: Camden County: Middlesex.

114. London, England, Births & Baptisms ; Date: 1906 Name: Henry Jno Lucas Record Type: Births Date: 26 Apr 1906 Father's Name: Chas Lucas Mother's Name: Mary Lucas Poor Law Union: Southwark Borough: Southwark County: London.

115. England & Wales Marriage Index: 1916-2005 , Hendon District; Vol:3a; Page: 1363.

116. 1861 Census , Class: RG9; Piece: 1070; Folio: 16; Page: 28; GSU roll: 542747; Birth date: abt 1857 Birth place: Barking Side, Essex, England Residence date: 1861 Residence place: Barking, Essex, England.

117. <i>1871 Census</i>, RG10 piece 1647 folio 44 page 8.

118. 1901 Census , RG13 Piece 1585 Folio 20 Page 31.

119. 1861 Census ; Name: Ellen Allsworth Age in years: 39 Gender: Female Birth place: Brize Norton, Oxfordshire Relationship to head-of-household: Wife Record type: Household Collection: 1861 England and Wales Census.

120. <i> - Oxfordshire Parish Registers</i>, St Thomas - burial records; Date: 1899.

121. 1861 Census ; Name: Hannah Aldsworth Age in years: 18 Gender: Female Birth place: Northmoor, Oxfordshire Relationship to head-of-household: Servant Record type: Household Collection: 1861 England and Wales Census.

122. 1861 Census ; Name: Noah Allsworth Age in years: 9 Gender: Male Birth place: Stanton Harcourt, Oxfordshire Relationship to head-of-household: Son Record type: Household Collection: 1861 England and Wales Census.

123. 1861 Census ; Name: Frederick Allsworth Age in years: 6 Gender: Male Birth place: Stanton Harcourt, Oxfordshire Relationship to head-of-household: Son Record type: Household Collection: 1861 England and Wales Census.

124. 1861 Census , Class: RG9; Piece: 733; Folio: 15; Page: 24; GSU roll: 542692; Date: 1861 Name: Thomas Allsworth Age in years: 39 Gender: Male Birth place: Stanton Harcourt, Oxfordshire Relationship to head-of-household: Head Record type: Household Collection: 1861 England and Wales Census 1861 England Census about Thomas Allsworth Name: Thomas Allsworth Age: 39 Estimated Birth Year: abt 1822 Relation: Head Spouse's Name: Ellen Gender: Male Where born: Stanton Harcourt, Oxfordshire, England Civil Parish: Cumnor County/Island: Berkshire Country: England Registration district: Abingdon Sub registration district: Cumnor ED, institution, or vessel: 1 Neighbors: Household schedule number: 129 Household Members: Name Age Thomas Allsworth 39 Ellen Allsworth 39 Elizabeth Allsworth 15 Eliza Allsworth 13 Thomas Allsworth11 Noah Allsworth9 Frederick Allsworth 6.

125. 1881 Census , Class: RG11; Piece: 1504; Folio: 67; Page: 80; Line: ; GSU roll: 1341363; Date: 1881 1881 England Census about Thos. Allsworth Name: Thos. Allsworth Age: 59 Estimated Birth Year: abt 1822 Relation: Head Spouse's Name: Helen Gender: Male Where born: Stanton Harcourt, Oxfordshire, England Civil Parish: Oxford St Thomas County/Island: Oxfordshire Country: England Street address: 12 Duke St Condition as to marriage: Married Occupation: Labourer Registration district: Oxford Sub registration district: Oxford ED, institution, or vessel: 17 Household Members: Name Age Thos. Allsworth 59 Helen Allsworth 58

Walter Allsworth 17.

126. 1901 Census , Source Citation: Class: RG13; Piece: 1386; Folio: 6; Page: 2; Date: 1891 1901 England Census about Thos Allsworth Name: Thos Allsworth Age: 81 Estimated Birth Year: abt 1820 Relation: Head Gender: Male Where born: Stanton Harcourt, Oxfordshire, England Civil Parish: Oxford St Thomas Ecclesiastical parish: Oxford St Thomas County/Island: Oxfordshire Country: England Registration district: Oxford Sub registration district: Oxford ED, institution, or vessel: 17 Household schedule number: 12 Household Members: Name Age Thos Allsworth 81.

127. Free BMD Death Index, , District: Oxford County: Berkshire, Oxfordshire Volume: 3a Page: 558; Date: 1906.

128. <i> - Oxfordshire Parish Registers</i>, St Thomas - Burial records; Date: 1906.

129. Free BMD Death Index, , District: Oxford; County:Oxfordshire; Volume: 3a; Page: 458; Date: 1885.

130. 1861 Census , Source Citation: Class: RG9; Piece: 896; Folio: 17; Page: 28; GSU roll: 542718.g.

131. Pallot's Marriage Index for England: 1780 - 1837 , Name: Chas Morgan Spouse: Mary Foster Marriage Date: 1826 PARISH: Stanton Harcourt.

132. <i> - Oxfordshire Parish Registers</i>, Volume 2 .Stanton Harcourt 1570-1837; Parish Records Groom's Name - MORGAN Charles >County - Oxfordshire Parish - Stanton Harcourt Date of Marriage (dd-mm-yyyy) - 14-Oct-1826 Abbreviations - Residence - Kidlington Employment - Notes - Bride's Name - FOSTER Mary Abbreviations - Residence - Employment - Notes - Original Appearance - Charles Morgan, p. Kidlington,& Mary Foster 14 Oct. ,.

133. 1861 Census , Class: RG9; Piece: 896; Folio: 17; Page: 28; GSU roll: 542718.

134. <i> - Oxfordshire Parish Registers</i>, St Thomas, Oxford BMD records - Christening, Date. 1835.

135. <i> - Oxfordshire Parish Registers</i>, St Thomas, Oxford BMD records - Christening; Date: 1836.

136. <i> - Oxfordshire Parish Registers</i>, St Thomas, Oxford BMD records - Christening; Date: 1838.

137. <i> - Oxfordshire Parish Registers</i>, St Thomas, Oxford BMD records - Christening; Date: 1843.

138. <i> - Oxfordshire Parish Registers</i>, St Thomas, Oxford BMD records - Christening; Date: 1845.

139. <i> - Oxfordshire Parish Registers</i>, St Thomas, Oxford BMD records - Christening; Date: 1848.

140. <i> - Oxfordshire Parish Registers</i>, St Thomas, Oxford BMD records - Christening; Date: 1855.

141. 1881 Census , Class: RG11; Piece: 1504; Folio: 19; Page: 32; GSU roll: 1341363; Household Members: Name & Age Charles Morgan 79 Fredrick Morgan 35 Joseph Morgan 26 John Thomas 37.

142. Free BMD Death Index, , Reigate District, Surrey; Vol: 2a; Page: 144.

143. London, England, Marriages & Banns, 1754-1921

144. 1881 Census , RG11; Piece:500; Folio:123; Page:55; GSU roll:1341111.

145. 1901 Census , RG number: RG13 Piece: 68 Folio: 121 Page: 34; National Archive Reference: RG number: RG13 Piece: 68 Folio: 121 Page: 34 Reg. District: Fulham Sub District: South Fulham Parish: Fulham Enum. District: 23 Ecclesiastical District: St Matthew City/Municipal Borough: Address: 56, Rosebury Road, Fulham County: London Name Relation Condition Sex Age Birth Year Occupation , Disability Where Born ROWLAND, Walter Head Married M 30 1871 Police Constable E Dulwich London ROWLAND, Alice Wife Married F 31 1870 Westminster London ROWLAND, Ethel Daughter F 9 1892 Westminster London ROWLAND, Nellie Daughter F 7 1894 South Hackney London.

146. 1901 Census , RG13; Piece:864; Folio: 103; Page:15.

147. Free BMD Death Index, , Free BMD Death index - Fulhan District; Volume:1a; Page:226.

148. 1861 Census , RG9; Piece:1698; Folio:86; Page:11; GSU roll:542852; Date: 1861.

149. 1901 Census , RG13; Piece:864; Folio: 103; Page:15; Date: 1861.

150. <i><i>England & Wales Christening Records, 1530-1906</i> Ancestry.com. England & Wales Christening Records, 1530-1906 [da, Place: Yetminster, Dorset, England; Date Range: 1851 - 1860; Film Number: 1239263; Date: 1851.

151. London Metropolitian Archives - Register of Marriages , St Luke, Millwall; P88/LUK; item:008; Name: Thomas Humber Age: Full Age Estimated birth year: abt 1877 Spouse Name: Fanny Humphreys Record Type: Marriage Event Date: 23 Dec 1877 Parish: St Luke, Millwall County: Middlesex Borough: Tower Hamlets Father Name: John Humber Spouse Father Name: James Humphreys.

152. 1881 Census , Class: RG11; Piece: 511; Folio: 67; Page: 42; GSU roll: 1341114; Name: Fanny Humber Age: 27 Estimated birth year: abt 1854 Relation: Wife Spouse's name: Thomas Gender: Female Where born: Greatworth, Northamptonshire, England Civil parish: Poplar County/Island: London Country: England Street Address: 409 West Ferry Rd Condition as to marriage: Married Occupation: Labourer Wife Registration district: Poplar Sub-registration district: Poplar ED, institution, or vessel: 34 Neighbors: View others on page Household Members: Name Age Thomas Humber 29 Fanny Humber 27 John Humber 2.

153. 1861 Census , Class: RG9; Piece: 923; Folio: 101; Page: 24; GSU roll: 542722.

154. England & Wales Marriages, 1538-1940 , Chelsea, Middlesex Volume: 1a Page: 512; Name: Frances Humber Year of Registration: 1890 Quarter of Registration: Jan-Feb-Mar District: Chelsea, Middlesex Volume: 1a Page: 512.

155. 1901 Census , Class: RG13; Piece: 75; Folio: 103; Page: 10; Name: Frances Tennant Age: 47 Estimated birth year: abt 1854 Relation: Wife Spouse's name: James Gender: Female Where born: Northauts, Marston Civil parish: Chelsea Ecclesiastical parish: St Simon Zelote Upper Chelsea County/Island: London Country: England Registration district: Chelsea Sub-registration district: Chelsea, North ED, institution, or vessel: 24 Neighbors: View others on page Household schedule number: 53 Household Members: Name & Age James Tennant 44 Frances Tennant 47 Hilda Humber 16 Arthur J Tennant 10.

156. Free BMD Death Index, , Pancras, London; Vol 1b; page 121; Name: Frances Tennant Death Registration Month/Year: 1932 Age at death (estimated): 79 Registration district: Pancras Inferred County: London Volume: 1b Page: 121.

157. 1881 Census , Class: RG11; Piece: 511; Folio: 67; Page: 42; GSU roll: 1341114.; Date: 1881 Name: John Humber Age: 2 Estimated birth year: abt 1879 Relation: Son Father's Name: Thomas Mother's Name: Fanny Gender: Male Where born: Poplar, Middlesex, England Civil parish: Poplar County/Island: London Country: England Street Address: 409 West Ferry Rd Registration district: Poplar Sub-registration district: Poplar ED, institution, or vessel: 34 Neighbors: View others on page Household Members: Name Age Thomas Humber 29 Fanny Humber 27 John Humber 2.

158. London, England, Births & Baptisms , Christ Church, Manchester Road, Tower Hamlets , Middlesex; Date: 1879 Name: John Humphreys Humber Record Type: Baptism Date: 6 Apr 1879 Father's Name: Thomas Humber Mother's Name: Fanny Humber Parish: Christ Church, Manchester Road Borough: Tower Hamlets County: Middlesex.

159. <i>Parish Records Collection - Baptism</i>, Parish: St Luke, West Ferry Road, Millwall. Entry No: 466; Source Ref: X085/131; Day: 29 Month: June Year: 1884 Forename: Frances Othernames: Hilda Surname: Humber Fathers forenames: Thomas Fathers occupation: Labourer-Deceased Mothers forenames: Fanny Birth date: 02/06/1884 Address: 36 Charles Street Location of church: Millwall Parish: St Luke Church address: West Ferry Road Entry No: 466 Source Ref: X085/131.

160. 1901 Census , Class: RG13; Piece: 75; Folio: 103; Page: 10; Name: James Tennant Age: 44 Estimated birth year: abt 1857 Relation: Head Spouse's name: Frances Gender: Male Where born: Long Compton, Warwickshire, England Civil parish: Chelsea Ecclesiastical parish: St Simon Zelote Upper Chelsea County/Island: London Country: England Registration district: Chelsea Sub-registration district: Chelsea, North ED, institution, or vessel: 24 Neighbors: View others on page Household schedule number: 53 Household Members: Name & Age James Tennant 44 Frances Tennant 47 Hilda Humber 16 Arthur J Tennant 10.

161. 1881 Census , Class: RG11; Piece: 511; Folio. 67; Page: 42; GSU roll: 1341114; Name: Thomas Humber Age: 29 Estimated birth year: abt 1852 Relation: Head Spouse's name: Fanny Gender: Male Where born: Leigh, Dorset, England Civil parish: Poplar County/Island: London Country: England Street Address: 409 Westferry Rd Condition as to marriage: Married Occupation: Labourer Registration district: Poplar Sub-registration district: Poplar ED, institution, or vessel: 34 Neighbors: View others on page Household Members: Name Age Thomas Humber 29 Fanny Humber 27 John Humber 2.

162. 1861 Census , Class: RG9; Piece: 1359; Folio: 35; Page: 18; GSU roll: 542801.

163. Free BMD Death Index, , District: Poplar, Middlesex: Volume: 1c: Page: 431; Date: 1884 Name: Thomas Humber Estimated birth year: abt 1852 Year of Registration: 1884 Quarter of Registration: Apr-May-Jun Age at Death: 32 District: Poplar, Middlesex: Volume: 1c: Page: 431.

164. COPY - Death Certificate , Poplar district; Date: 20 April 1884 Died at home (36 Charles Street, Poplar, Middlesex, England.) Wife (Fanny) in attendance. Brain hemorrhage - Rupture of the Middle Meningeal Artery.

165. 1861 Census ; Source Citation: Class: RG9; Piece: 1070; Folio: 16; Page: 28; GSU roll: 542747. 1861 census Household Members: Name Age Thomas Lucas 45 Mary Lucas 35 George Lucas 16 Henry Lucas 13 Sarah Lucas 8 Thomas Lucas 6 Charles Lucas 4 Elizebeth Lucas 1.

166. 1881 Census , Class: RG11; Piece: 498; Folio: 18; Page: 30; GSU roll:

1341110; Date: 1881 Name: Mary A. Foster Age: 54 Estimated birth year: abt 1827 Relation: Wife Spouse's name: William Gender: Female Where born: Barkingside, Essex, England Civil parish: St Leonard Bromley County/Island: London Country: England Street Address: 58 Knapp Rd Condition as to marriage: Married Occupation: Carman Wife Registration district: Poplar Sub-registration district: Bromley Household Members: Name Age William Foster 55 Mary A. Foster 54 (Real name - Mary Ann Lucas) Emily Lucas 18 Eliza Lucas 16.

167. 1901 Census , Class: RG13; Piece: 1582; Folio: 69; Page: 59; Name: Mary Ann Lucas Age: 70 Estimated birth year: abt 1831 Gender: Female Where born: East Ham, Essex, England Civil parish: West Ham Ecclesiastical parish: St Luke County/Island: Essex Country: England Registration district: West Ham Sub-registration district: Canning Town ED, institution, or vessel: 26 Neighbors: View others on page Household schedule number: 342 Household Members: Name Age Frederick Dunston 38 Eliza Dunston 36 Eliza Dunston 16 Frederick Dunston 11 James Dunston 9 Thomas Dunston 6 Samuel Proudfoot 36 Mary Ann Lucas 70.

168. Free BMD Death Index, , District: Romford; Vol: 4a; Page: 297; Date: 1906 Name: Mary Ann Lucas Estimated birth year: abt 1824 Year of Registration: 1906 Quarter of Registration: Oct-Nov-Dec Age at Death: 82.

169. COPY - Death Certificate ; Date: 1901 Mary Ann Lucas Died 26 Dec 1901 132 Pond Road West Ham Middlesex Age 68 Widow of James Lucas Cause of death: Hemiplegia, Syncope.

170. 1861 Census

171. 1841 Census , RG number:HO107;Piece:323; Book/Folio:51; Page:2; Address: Newell's Corner, Barking, Ilford County: Essex Name Age, Birth Year & Where Born LUCAS, Thomas M 45 1796 Essex LUCAS, Sarah F 45 1796 Essex LUCAS, William M 25 1816 Essex LUCAS, Thomas M 25 1816 Essex LUCAS, John M 20 1821 Essex LUCAS, Sarah F 15 1826 Essex LUCAS, Jane F 13 1828 Essex LUCAS, Matilda F 10 1831 Essex LUCAS, Mary Ann F 8 1833 Essex LUCAS, Martha F 5 1836 Essex BUSH, Susannah F 25 1816 Essex BUSH, Sarah F 1 1840 Essex.

172. London, England, Marriages & Banns, 1754-1921 , London Metropolitan Archives, Saint Philip, Bethnal Green, Register of marriages, P72/PHI; Date: 1856 Name: George Giles Age: 22 Estimated birth year: abt 1834 Spouse Name: Ann Wine Spouse Age: 21 Record Type: Marriage Event Date: 14 Jan 1856 Parish: Saint Philip, Bethnal Green County: Middlesex Borough: Tower Hamlets Father Name: Thomas Giles Spouse Father Name: James Wine.

173. Free BMD Death Index, , District: Stepney; Volume: 1c; Page: 296; Date: 1882 Name: Ann Giles Estimated birth year: abt 1833 Year of Registration: 1882 Quarter of Registration: Apr-May-Jun Age at Death: 49.

174. 1881 Census , Class: RG11; Piece: 468; Folio: 120; Page: 29; GSU roll: 1341102; Date: 1881 Name: Ann Giles Age: 48 Estimated birth year: abt 1833 Relation: Wife Spouse's name: George Gender: Female Where born: Limehouse, Middlesex, England Civil parish: Linchouse County/Island: London Country: England Street Address: 17 St Anns Street Condition as to marriage: Married Registration district: Stepney Sub-registration district: Limehouse ED, institution, or vessel: 20 Household Members: Name Age George Giles 48 Ann Giles 48 George Giles 18 Sarah Giles 15 Francis Giles 14 James Giles 11 Ellen Giles 3 Elisabeth Giles 6.

175. London Metropolitian Archives - Register of Marriages , Saint Philip, Bethnal Green, P72/PHI, Item 018; Date: 1856 Name: Ann Wine Age: 21 Estimated birth year: abt 1835 Spouse Name: George Giles Spouse Age: 22 Record Type: Marriage Event Date: 14 Jan 1856 Parish: St Philip, Bethnal Green County: Middlesex Borough: Tower Hamlets Father Name: James Wine Spouse Father Name: Thomas Giles.

176. 1861 Census , Middlesex, Limehouse, District 22; image 33; Date: 1861.

177. Free BMD Death Index, , District: Stepney; Volume: 1c; Page: 408; Date: 1858 Death Reg Name: Hannah Giles Year of Registration: 1858 Quarter of Registration: Jan-Feb-Mar District: Stepney (To 1921) County: London, Middlesex Volume: 1c; Page: 408.

178. Free BMD Death Index, , West Ham Vol 4a page 165.

179. <i>1871 Census</i>, St Ann Limehouse, London, England; Date: 1871.

180. <i>1871 Census</i>, Middlesex, Limehouse, District 21; image 41; Date: 1871.

181. <i>Oxfordshire Family History Society, <i>Oxfordshire Marriages 1559-1837</i></i> </i>, page A 34.

182. Pallot's Marriage Index for England: 1780 - 1837 , Pallot's Marriage Index for England: 1780 - 1837; Date: 1805.

183. Oxfordshire, England, Extracted Parish Records , Volume 4. Marriages and Banns Register [marked No. 5.]; Date: 1805 Text: William Allsworth & Jane Turner 01 Apr 1805 Book: Volume 4. Marriages and Banns Register [marked No. 5.] (Marriage) Collection: Oxford: - Register of Marriages, 1559-1837.

184. <i>Oxfordshire Family History Society, <i>Oxfordshire Marriages 1559-1837</i></i> </i>, Marriages at Stanton Harcourt; Vol 4 (marked as 5); page 24; Date: 1834.

185. Stanton Harcourt Parish Records, Burials; Date: 1 September 1838.

186. <i>Oxfordshire Family History Society, <i>Oxfordshire Marriages 1559-1837</i></i> </i>; Text: William Alsworth & Hannah Turner 23 May 1836 Book: Volume 4. Marriages and Banns Register [marked No. 5.] (Marriage) Collection: Oxford: - Register of Marriages, 1559-1837.

187. Oxfordshire, England, Extracted Parish Records , Volume 4. Marriages and Banns Register [marked No. 5.].

188. <i>Oxfordshire Family History Society, <i>Oxfordshire Marriages 1559-1837</i></i> </i>, A 37.

189. Oxfordshire, England, Extracted Parish Records , Volume 4. Marriages and Banns Register [marked No. 5.]; Text: William Alsworth & Hannah Turner 23 May 1836 Book: Volume 4. Marriages and Banns Register [marked No. 5.] (Marriage) Collection: Oxford: - Register of Marriages, 1559-1837.

190. 1861 Census ; Name: Robert Allsworth Age in years: 42 Gender: Male Birth place: Stanton Harcourt Relationship to head-of-household: Head Record type: Household Collection: 1861 England and Wales Census.

191. <i>Oxfordshire Family History Society, <i>Oxford Marriage Index - 1538 to 1837</i></i> </i>, Index by husbands - page 34; Date: 1805.

192. <i> - Oxfordshire Parish Registers</i>, Northmoor - burials; Date: 1862.

193. <i> - Oxfordshire Parish Registers</i>, Witney Union Workhouse records.

194. <i>Oxfordshire Family History Society, <i>Oxfordshire Marriages 1559-1837</i></i> </i>, Marriages at West Hanny, 1564 - 1837; Vol: 9; Date: 1834 William Drinkwater, of Brize Norton, co. Oxon, & Rosanna Hayden, of Lyford 23 Nov 1834.

195. IGI , IGI Film Number: 0088172, Batch Number: C021751; Baptism - 15 Apr 1770 St. Lawrence Anglican Church, Appleton with Eaton, Berkshire, England.

196. <i>Berkshire Parish Registers</i>, Appleton Parish (Christening); Date: 15 April 1770.

197. <i>Oxfordshire Family History Society, <i>Oxfordshire Marriages 1559-1837</i></i> </i>, Oxford: - Register of Marriages, 1559-1837 <GR:"H3"Volume 4. Marriages and Banns Register [; Oxford: - Register of Marriages, 1559-1837.

198. <i><i>Bishops transcripts</i> Extracted from microfilm copy of bishop's transcripts on film no. 0095201 it. 1-3, 5. Batc, Batch nos. 02210-1.

199. <i>Oxfordshire Family History Society, <i>Oxfordshire Marriages 1559-1837</i></i> </i>, Marriages at Cassington, 1673 to 1837; Vol 3; Page: 12; Date: 1797.

200. Free BMD Death Index, , Oxford, Oxfordshire, Death Index, Volume 16 page 63.

201. Free BMD Death Index, , Dist: Witney; County:Oxfordshire; Vol: 16; Page:102; Date: 1845 Name: John Foster Year of Registration: 1845 Quarter of Registration: Apr-May-Jun District: Witney County: Berkshire, Gloucestershire, Oxfordshire Volume: 16 Page: 102.

202. <i>Oxfordshire Family History Society, <i>Oxfordshire Marriages 1559-1837</i></i> </i>, Oxfordshire Marriages - indexed by Husbands 1538-1837; page:42; Parish Records Groom's Name - FOSTER John County - Oxfordshire Parish - Stanton Harcourt Date of Marriage (dd-mm-yyyy) - 0-Jul-1810 Abbreviations - Residence - Employment - Notes - Bride's Name - KING Ann Abbreviations - Residence - Bletchington Employment - Notes - Original Appearance - John Foster & Ann King, p. of Bletchington Oct. 181O.

203. 1841 Census , Piece:890; Book/Folio:13/6; Page: 4; Date: 1841.

204. <i> - Oxfordshire Parish Registers</i>, Stanton Harcourt BMD records - Christening; Date: 1815.

205. Free BMD Death Index, , Dist: Witney; County:Oxfordshire; Vol: 3a; Page:419; Date: 1853 Name: Ann Foster Year of Registration: 1853 Quarter of Registration: Jan-Feb-Mar District: Witney County: Berkshire, Gloucestershire, Oxfordshire Volume: 3a Page: 419.

206. <i> - Oxfordshire Parish Registers</i>, - St Michael, Stanton Harcourt.

207. 1841 Census , Piece:890; Book/Folio:13/6; Page: 4; Date: 1841 Piece:890; Book/Folio:13/6; Page: 4 Registration District: Witney Civil Parish: Stanton Harcourt Address: Sutton, Stanton Harcourt County: Oxfordshire.

208. <i> - Oxfordshire Parish Registers</i>, Stanton Harcourt BMD records - Christening; Date: 1791.

209. <i>Oxfordshire Family History Society, <i>Oxfordshire Marriages 1559-1837</i></i> </i>, page N11 (husbands name) & page N38 (wife name).

210. <i>Oxfordshire Family History Society, <i>Oxfordshire Marriages 1559-1837</i></i> </i>, Oxfordshire Marriages 1559-1837, page N11 (husbands name) & page N38 (wife name).

211. <i> - Oxfordshire Parish Registers</i>, Charlton-on-Otmoor - christening records; Date: 1794.

212. <i> - Oxfordshire Parish Registers</i>, Great Milton, baptism; Date: 1816.

213. <i>1851 Census</i>

214. Free BMD Death Index, , Oxfordshire, Headington, Vol 3a; Page:351; Date: 1857 Name: John Hinton Year of Registration: 1857 Quarter of Registration: Jul-Aug-Sep District: Headington County: Buckinghamshire, Oxfordshire Volume: 3a Page: 351.

215. , Stanton St John Parish records; 6 sep 1857; Burial records.

216. <i>Oxfordshire Family History Society, <i>Oxford Marriage Index - 1538 to 1837</i></i> </i>, listed by husbands name; Date: 1815.

217. 1841 Census , Class: HO107; Piece 877; Book 13.

218. Free BMD Death Index, , District: Keynsham County: Gloucestershire, Somerset Volume: 5c Page:477; Date: 1874.

219. 1861 Census , RG9; Piece:1698; Folio:86; Page:11; GSU roll:542852.

220. 1881 Census , Class: RG11; Piece: 2445; Folio: 116; Page: 24; GSU roll: 1341588; Household: Name Relation Marital Status Gender Age Birthplace Occupation Disability Jabez ROWLAND Head M Male 41 Bitton, Gloucester, England Accountant Ellen ROWLAND Wife M Female 34 Walcot Bath Accountant Wife Percy ROWLAND Son Male 1 Bitton, Gloucester, England Ann ROWLAND Mother W Female 86 Bitton, Gloucester, England Sarah A. NEWPORT Servant U Female 17 St Georges, Gloucester, England Domestic Servant --- Source Information: Dwelling Hanham Census Place Bitton, Gloucester, England Family History Library Film 1341588 Public Records Office Reference RG11 Piece / Folio 2445 / 116 Page Number 24.

221. 1841 Census , Class: HO107; Piece 361; Book: 15; Civil Parish: Bitton; Date: 1841 Household Members: Name Age George Rowland 40 Ann Rowland 40 William Rowland 20 Ann Rowland 15 Luke Rowland 14 Elizabeth Rowland 9 Hannah Rowland 6 Emma Rowland 3 6 Mo Jabez Rowland 1 6 Mo.

222. Free BMD Death Index, , Barton R. District; Vol 6a; Page: 162; Date: 1899.

223. 1841 Census , 1841 Census, Class: HO107; Piece 361; Book: 15; Civil Parish: Bitton, 184; Date: 1841 Household Members: Name Age George Rowland 40 Ann Rowland 40 William Rowland 20 Ann Rowland 15 Luke Rowland 14 Elizabeth Rowland 9 Hannah Rowland 6 Emma Rowland 3 6 Mo Jabez Rowland 1 6 Mo.

224. England & Wales Marriages, 1538-1940 , Bristol, Gloucestershire, England; Collection: St Philip and St Jacob.

225. 1881 Census , Class: RG11; Piece: 2445; Folio: 116; Page: 24; GSU roll: 1341588; Date: 1881 Registration district: Keynsham Sub-registration district: Bitton ED, institution, or vessel: 7 Neighbors: View others on page Household Members: Name Age Jabez Rowland 41 Ellen Rowland 34 Percy Rowland 1 Ann Rowland 86 Sarah A. Newport.

226. 1881 Census , Class: RG11; Piece: 2445; Folio: 116; Page: 24; GSU roll: 1341588; Date: 1881 Sub-registration district: Bitton ED, institution, or vessel: 7 Neighbors: View others on page Household Members: Name Age Jabez Rowland 41 Ellen Rowland 34 Percy Rowland 1 Ann Rowland 86 Sarah A. Newport.

227. Free BMD Death Index, , Keynsham District; Vol: 5c; Page: 399; Date: 1881 Surname Given Name District Volume Page Deaths Dec 1881 Rowland, Ellen - Keynsham - 5c - 399 Aged 35.

228. COPY - Death Certificate , Personal Copy; Date: 1874.

229. London, England, Marriages & Banns, 1754-1921 , Guildhall, St Leonard Shoreditch, Register of marriages, Sep 1835 - Nov 1836, P91/LEN/A/01/.

230. London, England, Marriages & Banns, 1754-1921 , P91/LEN/A/01/Ms 7498/44; Date: 1836 Name: George Elleston Spouse Name: Mary Langley Record Type: Banns

Event Date: 28 Aug 1836 Parish: St Leonard Shoreditch County: London Borough: Hackney Source Citation: Guildhall, St Leonard Shoreditch, Register of marriages, Sep 1835 - Nov 1836, P91/LEN/A/01/Ms 7498/44.

231. 1861 Census , Class: RG9; Piece: 401; Folio: 130; Page: 22; GSU roll: 542631.

232. England & Wales Marriage Index: 1916-2005 , Sherbourne Dist; Volume #: 8; Page#: 207; Date: 1849 Husband: HUMBER, John Churchill Wife: HUNT, Julia E. Registration district: Sherborne County: Dorset Year of registration: 1849 Quarter of registration: Apr-May-Jun 10 Apr 1849.

233. <i>1851 Census</i>, RG number: HO107 Piece: 1859 Folio: 76; Page: 19; Date: 1851 1851 census transcription details for: Totnell Farm, Leigh Reg. Dist: Sherborne Name Relation Sex Age Birth Occupation Where Born HUMBER, John Head Married M 39 1812 Surveyor Litton Dorset HUMBER, Julia Wife Married F 23 1828 Leigh HUMBER, Charles Son M 1 1850 Leigh HUMBER, Harriot Daughter F 9 1842 Leigh.

234. 1881 Census , Class: RG11; Piece: 2116; Folio: 34; Page: 14; Line: ; GSU roll: 1341511.

235. England & Wales Marriage Index: 1916-2005 , Sherborne District:Volume #: 8; Page#: 207; Date: 1849 Husband: HUMBER, John Churchill Wife: HUNT, Julia E. Registration district: Sherborne County: Dorset Year of registration: 1849 Quarter of registration: Apr-May-Jun 10 Apr 1849.

236. <i>Parish Records Collection - Baptism</i>, Dorset parish registers - ref:PE/LIC; Date: 15 August 1813.

237. Free BMD Death Index, , District: Brackley, County: Northamptonshire, Volume: 3b, Page: 4; Date: 1886.

238. - Indexing Project - , Batch #: I05023-8; film #: 1999883; Date: 1814 name: Sarah Chester gender: Female baptism/christening date: 20 Mar 1814 baptism/christening place: Marston St. Lawrence, Northampton, England father's name: Edward Chester mother's name: Lydia.

239. Free BMD Death Index, , District: Brackley, County: Northamptonshire, Volume: 3b, Page: 5; Date: 1879.

240. 1881 Census , Class: RG11; Piece: 1533; Folio: 89; Page: 11; GSU roll: 1341369.

241. 1861 Census , RG9; Piece: 1063; Folio: 83; Page: 9; GSU roll: 542745; Name: Sarah Lucas Age: 72 Estimated birth year: abt 1789 Relation: Wife Spouse's name: Thomas Gender: Female Where born: Wanstead, Essex, England Civil parish: Chingford County/Island: Essex Country: England Registration district: Epping Sub-registration district: Chigwell ED, institution, or vessel: 6 Neighbors: View others on page Household schedule number: 44 Household Members: Name Age Thomas Lucas 74 Sarah Lucas 72 William Lucas 44 Thomas Lucas 5.

242. Free BMD Death Index, , West Ham Dist; Vol:4a; Page:21; Name: Sarah Lucas Year of Registration: 1861 Quarter of Registration: Jan-Feb-Mar.

243. 1861 Census , Class: RG9; Piece: 1070; Folio: 12; Page: 17; GSU roll: 542747.

244. 1841 Census ; Address: Newell's Corner, Barking, Ilford County: Essex Name Age, Birth Year & Where Born LUCAS, Thomas M 45 1796 Essex LUCAS, Sarah F 45 1796

Essex LUCAS, William M 25 1816 Essex LUCAS, Thomas M 25 1816 Essex LUCAS, John M 20 1821 Essex LUCAS, Sarah F 15 1826 Essex LUCAS, Jane F 13 1828 Essex LUCAS, Matilda F 10 1831 Essex LUCAS, Mary Ann F 8 1833 Essex LUCAS, Martha F 5 1836 Essex BUSH, Susannah F 25 1816 Essex BUSH, Sarah F 1 1840 Essex.

245. 1841 Census ; RG number:HO107;Piece:323; Book/Folio:51; Page:2 Address: Newell's Corner, Barking, Ilford County: Essex Name Age, Birth Year & Where Born LUCAS, Thomas M 45 1796 Essex LUCAS, Sarah F 45 1796 Essex LUCAS, William M 25 1816 Essex LUCAS, Thomas M 25 1816 Essex LUCAS, John M 20 1821 Essex LUCAS, Sarah F 15 1826 Essex LUCAS, Jane F 13 1828 Essex LUCAS, Matilda F 10 1831 Essex LUCAS, Mary Ann F 8 1833 Essex LUCAS, Martha F 5 1836 Essex BUSH, Susannah F 25 1816 Essex BUSH, Sarah F 1 1840 Essex.

246. 1861 Census , RG9; Piece: 1063; Folio: 83; Page: 9; GSU roll: 542745; Name: Thomas Lucas Age: 74 Estimated birth year: abt 1787 Relation: Head Spouse's name: Sarah Gender: Male Where born: Leytonstone, Essex, England Civil parish: Chingford County/Island: Essex Country: England Registration district: Epping Sub-registration district: Chigwell ED, institution, or vessel: 6 Neighbors: View others on page Household schedule number: 44 Household Members: Name Age Thomas Lucas 74 Sarah Lucas 72 William Lucas 44 Thomas Lucas 5.

247. Free BMD Death Index, , Epping, Essex reg; vol:4a; page:59; Date: 1869.

248. Free BMD Death Index, , District: Romford County: Essex Volume: 4a Page:179; Source Information: FreeBMD. England & Wales, FreeBMD Death Index: 1837-1915.

249. - Indexing Project - , Barking, Essex, England; I07195-6; film 1471843; Date: 30 November 1798.

250. Free BMD Death Index, , District: Romford County: Essex Volume: 4a Page:54; Date: 1854.

251. 1861 Census , Class: RG9; Piece: 1070; Folio: 12; Page: 17; GSU roll: 542747; 1861 England Census about James Stringer Name: James Stringer Age: 62 Estimated Birth Year: abt 1799 Relation: Father-in-law Gender: Male Where born: Barking Side, Essex, England Civil Parish: Barking Ecclesiastical parish: Barking Side County/Island: Essex Country: England Registration district: Romford Sub registration district: Ilford ED, institution, or vessel: 1 Household schedule number: 91 Household Members: Name Age John Lucas 42 Sarah Lucas 46 James Lucas 20 Thomas Lucas 17 Henry Lucas 15 John Lucas 12 Eliza Lucas 10 Sarah Lucas 8 William Lucas 4 Charlotte Lucas 1 James Stringer 62
**.

252. 1881 Census , Class: RG11; Piece: 1746; Folio: 13; Page: 19; Line: ; GSU roll: 1341420; 1881 England Census about James Stringer Name: James Stringer Age: 82 Estimated Birth Year: abt 1799 Relation: Father Gender: Male Where born: Barkingside, Essex, England Civil Parish: Barking County/Island: Essex Country: England Street address: Mossford Green Barkingside Condition as to marriage: Widow Occupation: Ag Lab Registration district: Romford Sub registration district: Ilford Household Members: Name Age Caroline Stringer 51 James Stringer 82 **.

253. Free BMD Death Index, , England & Wales, FreeBMD Death Index: 1837-1983; Name: James Stringer Estimated Birth Year: abt 1797 Year of Registration: 1887

Quarter of Registration: Oct-Nov-Dec Age at Death: 90 District: Romford County: Essex Volume: 4a.

254. 1861 Census , Class: RG9; Piece: 284; Folio: 81; Page: 55; GSU roll: 542606; 1861 England Census 1861 England Census Name: Thomas Giles Age: 61 Estimated birth year: abt 1800 Relation: Head Spouse's name: Hannah Gender: Male Where born: Dover, Kent, England Civil parish: Stepney Ecclesiastical parish: St Thomas County/Island: Middlesex Country: England Street Address: Occupation: Condition as to marriage: View image Registration district: Stepney Sub-registration district: Ratcliff ED, institution, or vessel: 2 Neighbors: View others on page Household schedule number: 314 Household Members: Name Age Thomas Giles 61 Hannah Giles 56 John M Giles 22 Ann M Giles 19 Elizabeth Giles 14.

255. - Indexing Project - , batch #:I04646-2; film: 1702587; Date: 1821 groom's name: Thomas Giles bride's name: Hannah Maria Baldwin marriage date: 13 Jun 1821 marriage place: North Shoebury, Essex, England.

256. 1861 Census , Class: RG9; Piece: 284; Folio: 81; Page: 55; GSU roll: 542606.

257. 1861 Census , Class: RG9; Piece: 284; Folio: 81; Page: 55; GSU roll: 542606; Date: 1861 Household Members: Name Age Thomas Giles 61 Hannah Giles 56 John M Giles 22 Ann M Giles 19 Elizabeth Giles 14.

258. Free BMD Death Index, , District: Stepney; Volume: 1c; Page: 346; Date: 1872 Name: Thomas Giles Estimated birth year: abt 1801 Year of Registration: 1872 Quarter of Registration: Jan-Feb-Mar Age at Death: 71.

259. <i>1851 Census</i>, Middlesex, Limehouse, District 18; image 54; Date: 1851.

260. London, England, Marriages & Banns, 1754-1921 , Saint Dunstan And All Saints, Reg of banns, P93/DUN, item:158; Date: 1834 Name: James Wine Spouse Name: Mary Ann Rapp Record Type: Banns Event Date: 18 May 1834 Parish: St Dunstan and All Saints, Stepney County: Middlesex Borough: Tower Hamlets.

261. London, England, Marriages & Banns, 1754-1921 , Saint Dunstan And All Saints, Reg of marriages, P93/DUN, Item 072; Date: 1834 Name: James Wine Spouse Name: Mary Ann Rapp Record Type: Banns Event Date: 18 May 1834 Parish: St Dunstan and All Saints, Stepney County: Middlesex Borough: Tower Hamlets.

262. London, England, Marriages & Banns, 1754-1921 , London Metropolitan Archives, Saint Dunstan And All Saints, Register of marriages, P93/DUN; Name: Mary Ann Rapp Spouse Name: James Wine Record Type: Marriage Event Date: 19 May 1834 Parish: St Dunstan and All Saints, Stepney County: Middlesex Borough: Tower Hamlets.

263. <i>England & Wales Death index</i> <i>First name(s) PAMELA Last name ALLSWORTH Gender Female Birth day 23, Stephney Dist; Vol: 2; Page: 311; Date: 1839.

264. London Metropolitian Archives - Register of Baptisms , Saint Dunstan and All Saints, Apr 1798 - Dec 1812, P93/DUN, Item 006; Date: 1811.

265. London, England, Births & Baptisms ; Date: 1817 Name: James Vanner Wine Record Type: Baptism Date: 26 Oct 1817 Father's Name: William Wine Mother's Name: Sarah Wine Parish: St Leonard, Shoreditch High Street, Shoreditch Borough: Hackney County: Middlesex.

266. Oxfordshire, England, Extracted Parish Records , Book: Volume 4. Marriages and Banns Register [marked No. 5.] (Marriage); Text: William Aldsworth & Hannah Townsend 17

Dec 1781 Book: Volume 4. Marriages and Banns Register [marked No. 5.] (Marriage) Collection: Oxford: - Register of Marriages, 1559-1837.

267. <i>Oxfordshire Family History Society, <i>Oxfordshire Marriages 1559-1837</i></i> </i>, page A 20.

268. <i> - Oxfordshire Parish Registers</i>, Bletchingdon BMD christening; Date: 1761.

269. Oxfordshire, England, Extracted Parish Records , Book: Volume 4. Marriages and Banns Register [marked No. 5.] (Marriage); Date: 1781 Text: William Aldsworth & Hannah Townsend 17 Dec 1781 Book: Volume 4. Marriages and Banns Register [marked No. 5.] (Marriage) Collection: Oxford: - Register of Marriages, 1559-1837.

270. - Indexing Project - , M02411-1 : England-ODM Source Film Number: 95203.

271. - Indexing Project - , C02411-2 system origin: England-ODM source film number: 95203.

272. Oxfordshire, England, Extracted Parish Records , Book: Volume 4. Marriages and Banns Register [marked No. 5.]; Date: 1807 Text: p. 6. Thomas Turner, p. of Ascot, Oxon., & Esther Ridge, lic. 23 Oct 1807 Book: Volume 4. Marriages and Banns Register [marked No. 5.] (Marriage) Collection: Oxford: - Register of Marriages, 1559-1837.

273. <i>Oxfordshire Family History Society, <i>Oxford Marriage Index - 1538 to 1837</i></i> </i>; Date: 1783.

274. <i> - Oxfordshire Parish Registers</i>, Bampton, Witney Dist #4; Date: 24 March 1759.

275. <i> - Oxfordshire Parish Registers</i>; 1. Parish Records Collection - Marriage, Northmoor Parish, Oxfordshire, 1778. "Parish Records Groom's Name - HAYDON William >County - Oxfordshire Parish - Northmoor Date of Marriage (dd-mm-yyyy) - 28-Sep-1778 Abbreviations - Residence - Lyford Employment - Notes - Berks. Bride's Name - HAWKINS Elizabeth Abbreviations - Residence - Employment - Notes - Original Appearance - William Haydon, of Lyford, Berks., & Elizabeth beth Hawkins,28 Sept. „..".

276. <i>Parish Records Collection - Marriage</i>, Northmoor Parish, Oxfordshire; Date: 1778 Parish Records Groom's Name - HAYDON William >County - Oxfordshire Parish - Northmoor Date of Marriage (dd-mm-yyyy) - 28-Sep-1778 Abbreviations - Residence - Lyford Employment - Notes - Berks. Bride's Name - HAWKINS Elizabeth Abbreviations - Residence - Employment - Notes - Original Appearance - William Haydon, of Lyford, Berks., & Elizabeth beth Hawkins,28 Sept. „.

277. - Indexing Project - , Batch #:C01766-3; film #:1279452; Date: 1752 name: William Haydon gender: Male baptism/christening date: 15 Mar 1752 baptism/christening place: Buckland, Berkshire, England father's name: Richard Haydon mother's name: Sarah.

278. <i> - Oxfordshire Parish Registers</i>, Buckland - christening; Date: 1752.

279. <i>Oxfordshire Family History Society, <i>Oxford Marriage Index - 1538 to 1837</i></i> </i>, Standlake Reg; Date: 1750 p. 109. William Vesey Morgan & Mary Stone ... ... 24 Apr. 1750.

280. <i> - Oxfordshire Parish Registers</i>, Standlake Baptism records; Date: 1725 1725, Apr, 4 - STONE, Mary d of Willm & Ann.

281. <i>Oxfordshire Family History Society, <i>Oxford Marriage Index - 1538 to 1837</i></i> </i>; Date: 1750 p. 109. William Vesey Morgan & Mary Stone ... ... 24 Apr. 1750.

282. <i>Oxfordshire Family History Society, <i>Oxford Marriage Index - 1538 to 1837</i></i> </i>,

H; page 71; Date: 1761 Husband: Hartley (tt) John Mid. Barton Married at Steeple Barton Wife: Gilks, Mary Year: 1761 Date: 20 Sep.

283. - Indexing Project - , batch) number: C02422-2; Source film number: 95211.

284. - Indexing Project - , C02210-2; Source film number: 95201.

285. - Indexing Project - , C03842-1 system origin: England-ODM source film number: 952335.

286. - Indexing Project - , batch) number: C03842-1; Source film number: 952335.

287. - Indexing Project - , batch) number: C02210-2; Source film number: 95201.

288. <i>Oxfordshire Family History Society, <i>Oxford Marriage Index - 1538 to 1837</i></i> </i>, H: page 71; Date: 1761 Husband: Hartley (tt) John Mid. Barton Married at Steeple Barton Wife: Gilks, Mary Year: 1761 Date: 20 Sep.

289. - Indexing Project - , Batch: P01757-1; film: 0962417 IT 2; Date: 1739 John Hartlet Christening: 4 Mar 1739 Enstone, Oxfordshire Father: Richard Mother: Elizabeth.

290. - Indexing Project - , Batch: M02037-2; film: 88220; Date: 1785 groom's name: John Foster bride's name: Elizabeth Duffen marriage date: 08 Dec 1785 marriage place: Binfield,Berkshire,England.

291. <i> - Oxfordshire Parish Registers</i>, Stanton Harcourt parish reg.

292. <i> - Oxfordshire Parish Registers</i>, Standlake reg; Christening; Date: 1757 1757 Aug 21 - Foster, John s of John & Sarah (written over Mary).

293. Oxfordshire, England, Extracted Parish Records , Oxford: - Register of Marriages, 1559-1837; Date: 1783.

294. <i>Oxfordshire Family History Society, <i>Oxfordshire Marriages 1559-1837</i></i> </i>, Volume 4. Marriages and Banns Register [marked No. 5.] (Marriage); Oxfordshire, England, Extracted Parish Records, Oxford: - Register of Marriages, 1559-1837, 1783. Text: Daniel King & Sarah Proboat 05 Oct 1783 Book: Volume 4. Marriages and Banns Register [marked No. 5.] (Marriage) Collection: Oxford: - Register of Marriages, 1559-1837.

295. <i> - Oxfordshire Parish Registers</i>, Cassington - marriages; Date: 1783.

296. - Phillimores Marriages , Cassington, Oxford, page 162; Date: 1783.

297. <i>Oxfordshire Family History Society, <i>Oxfordshire Marriages 1559-1837</i></i> </i>, Book: Volume 4. Marriages and Banns Register [marked No. 5.] (Marriage); Oxfordshire, England, Extracted Parish Records, Oxford: - Register of Marriages, 1559-1837, 1783. Text: Daniel King & Sarah Proboat 05 Oct 1783 Book: Volume 4. Marriages and Banns Register [marked No. 5.] (Marriage) Collection: Oxford: - Register of Marriages, 1559-1837.

298. - Indexing Project - , C03862-2 system origin: England-ODM source film number: 994085.

299. <i>Oxfordshire Family History Society, <i>Oxfordshire Marriages 1559-1837</i></i> </i>, page N 11.

300. <i> - Oxfordshire Parish Registers</i>, Charlton-on-Otmoor - Marriages; Date: 1788.

301. - Indexing Project - , C02437-2; film: 95226; Date: 1769 name   Ann Giles gender Female baptism/christening date 12 Feb 1769 baptism/christening place CHARLTON ON OTMOOR,OXFORD,ENGLAND father's name Richd. Giles mother's name Mary indexing project (batch) number   C02437-2; film9:5226.

302. <i> - Oxfordshire Parish Registers</i>, Headington baptism records; Date: 1762.

303. <i>Oxfordshire Family History Society, <i>Oxford Marriage Index - 1538 to 1837</i></i> </i>, Index by Husbands; page 160.

304. - Indexing Project - , C02437-2 system origin: England-ODM source film number: 95226.

305. <i>Oxfordshire Family History Society, <i>Oxfordshire Marriages 1559-1837</i></i> </i>, listed by husband name; Date: 1785.

306. - Indexing Project - , I06977-8 system origin: England-EASy source film number: 1967108.

307. <i>Oxfordshire Family History Society, <i>Oxford Marriage Index - 1538 to 1837</i></i> </i>, Indexed by wives - G; page 81; Date: 1785.

308. <i> - Oxfordshire Parish Registers</i>, Waterperry - burial; Date: 1812.

309. - Indexing Project - , C14545-1 ; System Origin: England-ODM.

310. <i> - Oxfordshire Parish Registers</i>, Waterperry - burial; Date: 1804.

311. - Indexing Project - , Batch: I03618-9; film: 1595499; Date: 1787 record title: England Marriages, 1538-1973 groom's name: Leonard Rogers bride's name: Ann Burges marriage date: 13 May 1787 marriage place: Bitton, Gloucester, England.

312. 1841 Census , HO107 piece 489 folio 8/36 page 29.

313. <i>England & Wales Death index</i> <i>First name(s) PAMELA Last name ALLSWORTH Gender Female Birth day 23, District:Greenwich, Ref:Volume 5 Page 192.

314. 1841 Census , HO107 piece 489 folio 8/36 page 29; Date: 1841 Reg. District: Greenwich Name Sex Age Birth Year Where Born
_____ELLISTON, Joseph M 50 1791 ELLISTON, Elizabeth F 50 1791 Kent ELLISTON, Samuel M 15 1826 Kent ELLISTON, Abigail F 12 1829 Kent BOLTON, Francis M 60 1781 Kent.

315. - Indexing Project - , Batch #: I04107-1; film #: 1751896; Date: 15 August 1789 name: Elizabeth Bayse gender:Female baptism/christening date:15 Nov 1789 baptism/christening place:St. George-in-the-East, Middlesex, England father's name:Frederick Bayse mother's name:Mary.

316. - Indexing Project - , # 103144-8; source film:585391.

317. - Indexing Project - , number:C03524-2; source film number:580906.

318. - Indexing Project - , digital folder - 004508373; Date: 1822.

319. <i>Parish Records Collection - Baptism</i>, Litton Cheney, Dorset parish registers - ref:PE/LIC; Date: 4 September 1791.

320. <i>Parish Records Collection - Baptism</i>, Dorset parish registers - ref:PE/LIC; Date: 16 March 1817.

321. <i>Parish Records Collection - Baptism</i>, Dorset parish registers - ref:PE/LIC; Date: 28 March 1819.

322. <i>Parish Records Collection - Baptism</i>, Dorset parish registers - ref:PE/LBY; Date: 5 June 1824.

323. <i>Parish Records Collection - Baptism</i>, Dorset parish registers - ref:PE/LBY; Date: 1 November 1829.

324. <i>Parish Records Collection - Baptism</i>, Dorset parish registers - ref:PE/LBY; Date: 1 July 1832.

325. <i>Parish Records Collection - Baptism</i>, Dorset baptisms; Date: 1793.
326. - Indexing Project - , C15815-1; film: 1279482 - baptism; Date: 28 July 1793.
327. - Indexing Project - , Christening - Sherborne, Dorset, England; batch:C00672-6; film number:1239227; Date: 11 June 1803 name:Sarah Matthews gender:Female baptism/christening date:11 Jun 1803 baptism/christening place: Sherborne, Dorset, England father's name:John Matthews mother's name:Sarah indexing project (batch) number:C00672-6 system origin:England-ODM source film number:1239227.
328. - Indexing Project - , P01717-1; film: 1441052 IT 4; Date: 9 November 1778.
329. - Indexing Project - , #: I05023-8; film #: 1999883; Date: 1814 name: Sarah Chester gender: Female baptism/christening date: 20 Mar 1814 baptism/christening place: Marston St. Lawrence, Northampton, England father's name: Edward Chester mother's name: Lydia.
330. - Indexing Project - , #: C01697-9; film: 811722; Date: 1783.
331. England and Wales, Non-Conformist Record Indexes , RG6_0773; Date: 1783.
332. Free BMD Death Index, , Brackley, Northampton District; Vol; 15; page 159; Date: 1842.
333. - Indexing Project - ; Date: 1769.
334. - Indexing Project - , Batch #: M04092-2; film #: 857062; Date: 1787 groom's name: Thomas Lucas bride's name: Jane Mayes marriage date: 28 Jan 1787 marriage place: Little Ilford,Essex,England.
335. <i>Essex Parish Registers, 1538-1900</i>, film: 857075; folder 4006318; image 11; Date: 1769.
336. <i>1851 Census</i>, Piece:1769; Folio:12; Page:16; Date: 1851 Registration District: West Ham Civil Parish: St Marys Wanstead Address: George Lane, St Marys Wanstead, Essex.
337. 1861 Census , RG number: RG09 Piece: 1060 Folio: 125 Page: 15; Date: 1861 LUCAS, Thomas - Lodger - Widower - M - age:103, born 1758, Hertfordshire - No Occupation.
338. 1851 Census , Piece:1769; Folio:12; Page:16; Date: 1851 Registration District: West Ham Civil Parish: St Marys Wanstead Address: George Lane, St Marys Wanstead, Essex.
339. - Indexing Project - , Batch #: M04092-2; film #: 857062; Date: 1787 groom's name: Thomas Lucas bride's name: Jane Mayes marriage date: 28 Jan 1787 marriage place: Little Ilford,Essex,England.
340. 1841 Census , Romford, Hornchurch reg District; Piece 330; Book 32; page 3.
341. - Indexing Project - , Batch #:C00161-6; film #:380143; Date: 1763 name: William Young gender: Male baptism/christening date: 13 Mar 1763 baptism/christening place: ST BOTOLPH BISHOPSGATE,LONDON,LONDON,ENGLAND death date: 26 Apr 1764 father's name: Richard mother's name: Elizabeth.
342. - Indexing Project - , Folder: 4047856; Date: 1799 name: James Stringer event: Marriage event date: 08 Apr 1799 event place: Barking, Essex, England gender: Male marital status: Married spouse: Elizabeth Wyten digital folder number:4047856.
343. - Indexing Project - , #: I03397-9; film #: 1702105; Date: 1855.
344. - Indexing Project - , Marriage - Barking, Essex, England; folder #: 4047856; Date: 8 April 1799 name: James Stringer event: Marriage event date: 08 Apr 1799 event place: Barking, Essex, England gender: Male marital status: Married spouse: Elizabeth Wyten digital folder number: 4047856.
345. - Indexing Project - , digital folder number: 4047856; Date: 1799 name:

James Stringer event: Intended Marriage event date: 24 Feb 1799 event place: Barking, Essex, England gender: Male marital status: Married spouse: Elizabeth Wyten digital folder number: 4047856.

346. - Indexing Project - , #: I03397-9; film #: 1702105; Date: 1853.

347. - Indexing Project - , Batch #:C04081-1; film #: 396230; Date: 1773 name: Sarah Briggs gender: Female baptism/christening date: 23 Feb 1773 baptism/christening place: SAINT LEONARDS,SHOREDITCH,LONDON,ENGLAND birth date: 21 Jan 1773 father's name: John Briggs mother's name: Sarah.

348. - Indexing Project - , Daughter's christening - Barking, Essex, England; I07195-6; film 1471843; Date: 30 November 1798.

349. - Indexing Project - , Christening; Barking, Essex, England; digital folder 4047856; Date: 21 March 1779 name: Richard Hyde event: Christening event date: 21 Mar 1779 event place: Barking, Essex, England gender: Male father: Richard Hyde mother: Ann digital folder number: 4047856.

350. - Indexing Project - , Marriage- M05576-3; film #578821, 596921, 596922, 597247; Date: 28 March 1796.

351. Canterbury Marriage Licences, 1781-1837 , Page 141; Date: 1799 Thos Giles of St Mary Dover bach & Sarah Holmes of the s (20, fath Wm H). 12 Jul 1799.

352. - Indexing Project - , (Batch) Number: M00061-7; Source Film Number: 375005; Reference Number: v 4.

353. - Indexing Project - , (batch) #:C02274-1; film number:374508, 374509, 374510; Date: 1767.

354. IGI , Film 0855938; WILLIAM WINE; Male; Birth: 13 OCT 1782; Christening: 08 DEC 1782 Saint Matthew, Bethnal Green, London, England; Father: WILLIAM WINE; Mother: MARTHA; Batch No.: C046982 Dates: 1746 - 1790 Source Call No.: 0855938 Type: Film Printout Call No.: 6900605 Type: Film Sheet: C046982 1790 0855939 Film NONE 00.

355. London, England, Marriages & Banns, 1754-1921 , Saint Dunstan And All Saints, Reg of marriages, P93/DUN, Item 052; Name: William Wine Spouse Name: Sarah Richardson Record Type: Marriage Event Date: 25 Jun 1809 Parish: St Dunstan and All Saints, Stepney County: Middlesex Borough: Tower Hamlets.

356. <i><i>London, England, Deaths and Burials, 1813-1980</i> London Metropolitan Archives</i> London Metropolitan Archives</i, Saint Mary, Haggerston, Register of burials, P91/MRY1, Item 051; Name: Sarah Wine Record Type: Burial Event Date: 15 Oct 1854 Age: 72 Estimated birth year: abt 1782 Parish: St Mary, Haggerston Borough: Hackney County: Middlesex.

357. - Indexing Project - , C04160-3; Source film#: 574266, 574267; Date: 1 December 1782.

358. IGI , Film 0396233; JOSEPH RICHARD WINE; Male; Birth: 25 OCT 1815; Christening: 24 DEC 1815 Saint Leonards, Shoreditch, London, England; Father: WILLIAM WINE; Mother: SARAH; Batch No.: C040803 Dates: 1810 - 1816 Source Call No.: 0396233 Type: Film Printout Call No.: 0933433 Type: Film Sheet: C040803 1816 - 1819 0396234 Film NONE 00.

359. IGI , Film 0396233; MARY ANN WINE; Female; Birth: 15 NOV 1819; Christening: 25 DEC 1819 Saint Leonards, Shoreditch, London, England; Father: WILLIAM

WINE; Mother: SARAH; Batch No.: C040803 Dates: 1810 - 1816 Source Call No.: 0396233 Type: Film Printout Call No.: 0933433 Type: Film Sheet: C040803 1816 - 1819 0396234 Film NONE 00.

360. - Indexing Project - , (batch) #: M04160-1; film #: 574460, 574461, 574462, 574463, 574464, 574465; Date: 1808.

361. - Indexing Project - , (batch) #: M04160-1; film #: 574460, 574461, 574462, 574463, 574464, 574465; Date: 1808 groom's name: William Rapley bride's name: Martha Mott marriage date: 14 Mar 1808 marriage place: St Clement Danes, Westminster, London, England.

362. London Metropolitian Archives - Register of Baptisms , Saint Mary, Rotherhithe; Jan 1765 - Dec 1791, P71/MRY, Item 012; Date: 1779 Name: Martha Sleel Motts Baptism Date: 14 Mar 1779 Parish: St Mary, Rotherhithe, Surrey Parent(s): Stephen Motts, Ann Motts.

363. - Indexing Project - , Batch #:C05576-1; film #:595420; Date: 1808 name: Elizabeth Rap gender: Female baptism/christening date:12 Feb 1809 baptism/christening place:SAINT DUNSTAN,STEPNEY,LONDON,ENGLAND birth date: 05 Dec 1808 father's name: William Rap mother's name: Martha.

364. - Indexing Project - , Batch #:I04825-1; film #:597604; Date: 1814 name: William Rap gender: Female baptism/christening date:16 Jan 1814 baptism/christening place:STEPNEY,LONDON,ENGLAND birth date: 15 Jan 1814 father's name: William Rap mother's name: Martha.

365. - Indexing Project - , Batch #:C05576-2; film #:596913; Date: 1817 name: Joseph Rap gender: Female baptism/christening date:6 Apr 1817 baptism/christening place:SAINT DUNSTAN,STEPNEY,LONDON,ENGLAND birth date: 29 Oct 1816 father's name: William Rap mother's name: Martha.

366. - Indexing Project - , Batch #:I04825-4; film #:597604; Date: 1818 name: Martha Rap gender: Female baptism/christening date:27 Dec 1818 baptism/christening place:SAINT DUNSTAN,STEPNEY,LONDON,ENGLAND birth date: father's name: William Rap mother's name: Martha.

367. - Indexing Project - , Batch #:C00625-1; film #:254545; Date: 1808 groom's name: William Rapley bride's name: Martha Mott marriage date: 14 Mar 1808 marriage place: St Clement Danes, Westminster, London, England.

368. Oxfordshire, England, Extracted Parish Records , Volume 4. Marriages and Banns Register [marked No. 5.]; Oxfordshire, England, Extracted Parish Records about William Aldesworth Mary Tyndall [Signs Tyndell] Text: William Aldesworth & Mary Tyndall [signs Tyndell] 19 Feb 1759 Book: Volume 4. Marriages and Banns Register [marked No. 5.] (Marriage) Collection: Oxford: - Register of Marriages, 1559-1837.

369. <i> - Oxfordshire Parish Registers</i>, Stanton Harcourt Parish - Burials; Date: 2 September 1781.

370. <i> - Oxfordshire Parish Registers</i>, Stanton Harcourt - burials; Date: 1759.

371. Oxfordshire Phillimores Marriage Parish Registers , Marriages at Northmoor, 1654-1837; Vol:3; page:1; Date: 1790 Groom's Name - ALDSWORTH John County - Oxfordshire Parish - Northmoor Date of Marriage - 15 Aug 1790 Bride's Name - WEEKS Anne Original Appearance - John ,1. John Aldsworth & Anne Weeks,15 Aug. 1790.

372. Oxfordshire Phillimores Marriage Parish Registers , Marriages at Northmoor, 1654-1837; Vol:3; page:1; Date: 1790 Groom's Name - ALDSWORTH John County - Oxfordshire Parish - Northmoor Date of Marriage - 15-Aug-1790 Bride's Name - WEEKS Anne John Aldsworth & Anne Weeks,15 Aug. 1790.

373. <i> - Oxfordshire Parish Registers</i>, Stanton Harcourt - christening; Date: 1764.

374. <i> - Oxfordshire Parish Registers</i>, Stanton Harcourt - christening; Date: 1769.

375. <i> - Oxfordshire Parish Registers</i>, Stanton Harcourt - burials; Date: 1786.

376. <i> - Oxfordshire Parish Registers</i>, Stanton Harcourt - burials; Date: 1798.

377. Oxfordshire, England, Extracted Parish Records , Volume 4. Marriages and Banns Register [marked No. 5.]; Date: 1759 Text:: William Aldesworth & Mary Tyndall [signs Tyndell] 19 Feb 1759 Book:: Volume 4. Marriages and Banns Register [marked No. 5.] (Marriage) Collection: Oxford: - Register of Marriages, 1559-1837.

378. <i>Oxfordshire Family History Society, <i>Oxford Marriage Index - 1538 to 1837</i></i> </i>; Date: 1759.

379. <i> - Oxfordshire Parish Registers</i>, Bletchingdon BMD christening; Date: 1764.

380. <i> - Oxfordshire Parish Registers</i>, Bletchingdon BMD christening; Date: 1767.

381. <i> - Oxfordshire Parish Registers</i>, Bletchingdon BMD christening; Date: 1770.

382. <i> - Oxfordshire Parish Registers</i>, Bletchingdon BMD christening; Date: 1773.

383. <i>Oxfordshire Family History Society, <i>Oxford Marriage Index - 1538 to 1837</i></i> </i>; Date: 1738.

384. <i> - Oxfordshire Parish Registers</i>, Witney burials; Date: 1769.

385. <i> - Oxfordshire Parish Registers</i>, Witney christenings; Date: 1742.

386. <i> - Oxfordshire Parish Registers</i>, Witney burials; Date: 1746.

387. <i> - Oxfordshire Parish Registers</i>, Witney christenings; Date: 1744.

388. <i> - Oxfordshire Parish Registers</i>, Witney christenings; Date: 1746.

389. <i> - Oxfordshire Parish Registers</i>, Witney burials; Date: 1760.

390. <i> - Oxfordshire Parish Registers</i>, Witney christenings; Date: 1748.

391. <i> - Oxfordshire Parish Registers</i>, Witney christenings; Date: 1750.

392. <i> - Oxfordshire Parish Registers</i>, Witney burials; Date: 1753.

393. <i> - Oxfordshire Parish Registers</i>, Witney christenings; Date: 1752.

394. <i> - Oxfordshire Parish Registers</i>, Witney christenings; Date: 1755.

395. <i> - Oxfordshire Parish Registers</i>, Witney christening; Date: 1720.

396. <i>Oxfordshire Family History Society, <i>Oxford Marriage Index - 1538 to 1837</i></i> </i>; Date: 1731.

397. <i> - Oxfordshire Parish Registers</i>, Bampton, Witney Dist #4; Date: 19 September 1754.

398. <i> - Oxfordshire Parish Registers</i>, Bampton, Witney Dist #4; Date: 1756.

399. <i> - Oxfordshire Parish Registers</i>, Bampton, Witney Dist #4; Date: 1761.

400. <i> - Oxfordshire Parish Registers</i>, Bampton, Witney Dist #4; Date: 1765.

401. <i> - Oxfordshire Parish Registers</i>, Bampton, Witney; District #4 Parish Reg; Date: 25 April 1733.

402. <i>Oxfordshire Family History Society, <i>Oxford Marriage Index - 1538 to 1837</i></i> </i>; Date: 1756.

403. <i>Berkshire Parish Registers</i>, Great Coxwell - baptisms; Date: 1726.

404. *<i>* - Indexing Project - *</i></i> </i>*, number:C00224-4;system origin:England;source film number:1279457; Date: 1733 name:John Hawkins gender:Male baptism/christening date:13 Dec 1733 baptism/christening place:Berkshire, England father's name:Edwd. Hawkins mother's name:Mary.

405. *<i>* - Indexing Project - *</i></i> </i>*, number:P01865-1;system origin:England;source film number:88260; Date: 1733 name:John Hawkins gender:Male baptism/christening date:18 Dec 1733 baptism/christening place:Berkshire, England father's name:Edwd. Hawkins mother's name:Mary.

406. *<i>* - Indexing Project - *</i></i> </i>*, Batch #:C01766-3; film #:1279452. - Shows Sarah as mother of William; Date: 1752.

407. *<i>* - Indexing Project - *</i></i> </i>*, Batch: B01766-3; film: 1279452; Date: 1785 name: Sarah Heydon gender: Female burial date: 15 Feb 1785 burial place: Buckland, Berkshire, England.

408. *<i>* - Indexing Project - *</i></i> </i>*, Batch: M01767-3; film: 1279454; Date: 1750 groom's name: Richard Hutton (Haydon) bride's name: Sarah Smith marriage date: 30 Sep 1750 marriage place: Clewer, Berkshire, England.

409. *<i>* - Indexing Project - *</i></i> </i>*, C10967-2 ; film: 919234 - birth; Date: 1720 name Sarah Smith gender   Female baptism/christening date   26 Nov 1720 baptism/christening place IVER,BUCKINGHAM,ENGLAND father's name Richard Smith mother's name Mary indexing project (batch) number   C10967-2 ; film9:19234.

410. *<i>* - Indexing Project - *</i></i> </i>*, Batch #:C01766-3; film #:1279452; Date: 1754.

411. *<i>* - Indexing Project - *</i></i> </i>*, Batch #: P01766-1; film #: 88204; Date: 1755.

412. *<i>* - Indexing Project - *</i></i> </i>*, Batch #:C01766-3; film #:1279452; Date: 1757.

413. *<i>* - Indexing Project - *</i></i> </i>*, Batch #:C01766-3; film #:1279452; Date: 1759.

414. *<i>* - Indexing Project - *</i></i> </i>*, Batch #:C01766-3; film #:1279452; Date: 1761.

415. *<i>* - Indexing Project - *</i></i> </i>*, Batch #:C01766-3; film #:1279452; Date: 1767.

416. *<i>* - Indexing Project - *</i></i> </i>*, Batch #:C01766-3; film #:1279452; Date: 1771.

417. *<i>* - Indexing Project - *</i></i> </i>*, Batch #:P00882-1; Film #:88234; Date: 1726 name: Richard Haydon gender: Male baptism/christening date: 24 Jul 1726 baptism/christening place: COLESHILL,BERKSHIRE,ENGLAND father's name: Joseph Haydon (INCORRECT) **** see attached note below **** IMPORTANT: Coleshill registry - page 21 Baptisms - 24 July 1726 copy: HAYDON Richard s Ric.d (corrected from Joss.p for every entry).

418. *<i>Oxfordshire Family History Society, <i>Oxford Marriage Index - 1538 to 1837</i></i> </i>*; Date: 1742.

419. *<i>* - Oxfordshire Parish Registers*</i>*, Northmoor - marriages; Date: 1777.

420. *<i>* - Oxfordshire Parish Registers*</i>*, Northmoor Parish Register - Baptisms; Date: 29 November 1694.

421. *<i>Oxfordshire Family History Society, <i>Oxford Marriage Index - 1538 to 1837</i></i> </i>*, Indexed by bride - V; Date: 1711.

422. *<i>* - Indexing Project - *</i></i> </i>*, C07320-3; film: 1279460; Date: 1690.

423. *<i>* - Indexing Project - *</i></i> </i>*, Batch: C01878-2; film: 88272; Date: 1675 name: Martha Onion gender: Female baptism/christening date: 01 Apr 1675 baptism/christening place: HINTON WALDRIST,BERKSHIRE,ENGLAND father's name: Thomas Onion mother's name:

Anne.

424. <i>Berkshire Parish Registers</i>, St Helen, Abingdon reg's (StH1538m); page 47; Date: 1707 1707 19 May STONE William agric., Kingston Bag. ONEUN Martha Kingston Bag.

425. <i> - Oxfordshire Parish Registers</i>, Standlake Baptism records; Date: 1681 1681, Mar, 20 - STONE, William s of Richard & Ann.

426. <i>Oxfordshire Family History Society, <i>Oxford Marriage Index - 1538 to 1837</i></i> </i>, H; page 71; Date: 1735.

427. - Indexing Project - , I02039-3; film: 813693; Date: 3 March 1709 name: Bety King gender: Female birth date: 03 Mar 1709 birthplace: Banbury, Oxford, England father's name: Richard King mother's name: ElizabKetihng.

428. <i> - Oxfordshire Parish Registers</i>, Deddington - christenings; Date: 1737.

429. <i> - Oxfordshire Parish Registers</i>, Deddington - christening; Date: 1739.

430. <i>Oxfordshire Family History Society, <i>Oxford Marriage Index - 1538 to 1837</i></i> </i>, G; page: 45; Date: 1744 Husband:GILKES, Tobias Married at Hook Norton Wife: PRICE, Sarah Year: 1744 Date: 10 Aug appear to have married 6 years after first child born.

431. <i> - Oxfordshire Parish Registers</i>, Standlake reg - Christenings; Date: 1757 1757 Aug 21 - Foster, John s of John & Sarah (written over Mary).

432. <i> - Oxfordshire Parish Registers</i>, Standlake BMD records - marriages; Date: 1756.

433. <i> - Oxfordshire Parish Registers</i>, Standlake - burial; Date: 1804.

434. <i> - Oxfordshire Parish Registers</i>, Standlake BMD records - Christening; Date: 1759.

435. <i> - Oxfordshire Parish Registers</i>, Standlake BMD records - Christening; Date: 1761.

436. <i> - Oxfordshire Parish Registers</i>, Standlake; Date: 1762.

437. <i> - Oxfordshire Parish Registers</i>, Standlake BMD records - Christening; Date: 1765.

438. <i> - Oxfordshire Parish Registers</i>, Standlake BMD records - Christening; Date: 1767.

439. <i> - Oxfordshire Parish Registers</i>, Standlake BMD records - Christening; Date: 1770.

440. <i> - Oxfordshire Parish Registers</i>, Standlake BMD records - Christening; Date: 1772.

441. <i> - Oxfordshire Parish Registers</i>, Standlake - burial; Date: 1773.

442. <i> - Oxfordshire Parish Registers</i>, Standlake BMD records - Christening; Date: 1776.

443. <i> - Oxfordshire Parish Registers</i>, Standlake Reg; Christenings; Date: 1757 1757 Aug 21 - Foster, John s of John & Sarah (written over Mary).

444. <i> - Oxfordshire Parish Registers</i>, Standlake BMD records - Christening; Date: 1756.

445. <i> - Oxfordshire Parish Registers</i>, Southleigh- christenings; Date: 1731.

446. <i>Berkshire Parish Registers</i>, Abingdon StH1685c page 131; Date: 1766 Eliz Duffin born 18 may 1766 Abingdon, Berkshire, England d of john & sarah.

447. - Indexing Project - , Batch: M01888-1; Film: 254490; Date: 1751 Groom: John Duffin Bride: Sarah Clark Marriage: 7 May 1751 Saint Nicholas,Abingdon,Berkshire,England.

448. <i>Berkshire Parish Registers</i>, Abingdon St Helen - burials; Date: 1752.

449. <i>Berkshire Parish Registers</i>, Abingdon St Helen 1685- christenings; Date: 1753.

450. <i>Berkshire Parish Registers</i>, Abingdon St Helen 1685- christenings; Date: 1756.

451. <i>Berkshire Parish Registers</i>, Abingdon St Helen 1685- christenings; Date: 1761.

452. <i>Berkshire Parish Registers</i>, Abingdon St Helen 1685- christenings; Date: 1764.

453. <i>Berkshire Parish Registers</i>, Abingdon St Helen 1685- christenings; Date: 1770.

454. <i> - Oxfordshire Parish Registers</i>, Witney - christenings; Date: 1716.

455. - Indexing Project - , Batch: P01865-1; film 88260; Date: 1724 Father: William Bayly Mother: Ann Name: Sarah Bayly Date: 8 April 1724 Christening: Faringdon,Berkshire,England.

456. - Indexing Project - , Project #: P01048-1; Film #: 88176; Date: 1705.

457. <i>Oxfordshire Family History Society, <i>Oxfordshire Marriages 1559-1837</i></i> </i>, page N 10.

458. <i>Oxfordshire Family History Society, <i>Oxford Marriage Index - 1538 to 1837</i></i> </i>, Husband index: N; page 10; Date: 1738 Husband: NEWELL, Henry Wife: OXLADE, Ann Nov 23, 1738 Lewknor, Oxfordshire.

459. FamilySearch Extraction Program - BIRTH , Call number: 0095237, Event date: , Sheet number: 00, Reference number: 0095237, Batch numb.

460. <i>Oxfordshire Archdeacon's Marriage Bond Index 1634-1849</i>, Alphabetized by Groom's names; Date: 1730 1730 - Cuxham, Oxfordshire Groom: Broadway, John Bride: Hinde, Jane Cuxham.

461. - Indexing Project - , Oxford St Giles - marriages; Date: 1754.

462. <i> - Oxfordshire Parish Registers</i>, St Thomas - bap records; Date: 1722.

463. <i>Oxfordshire Family History Society, <i>Oxford Marriage Index - 1538 to 1837</i></i> </i>, index by groom; Date: 1760.

464. - Indexing Project - , C02419-2; film: 95214; Date: 1738 name Mary Jackson gender   Female baptism/christening date   12 Oct 1738 baptism/christening place BICESTER,OXFORD,ENGLAND father's name Joseph Jackson indexing project (batch) number   C02419-2; film9:5214.

465. - Indexing Project - , J13151-1; film: 887482 - baptism; Date: 1739 name Richard Giles gender Male baptism/christening date 15 Jun 1739 baptism/christening place , ISLIP, OXFORD, ENGLAND father's name   Richard Giles mother's name   Susannah indexing project (batch) number   J13151-1; film8:87482.

466. <i>Oxfordshire Family History Society, <i>Oxford Marriage Index - 1538 to 1837</i></i> </i>, Index by groom G; Date: 1760.

467. <i> - Oxfordshire Parish Registers</i>, cuddesdon - marriages; Date: 1736.

468. <i> - Oxfordshire Parish Registers</i>, cuddesdon - baptism; Date: 1737.

469. <i> - Oxfordshire Parish Registers</i>, cuddesdon - baptism; Date: 1738.

470. <i> - Oxfordshire Parish Registers</i>, cuddesdon - baptism; Date: 1744.

471. <i> - Oxfordshire Parish Registers</i>, cuddesdon - baptism; Date: 1747.

472. <i> - Oxfordshire Parish Registers</i>, cuddesdon - baptism; Date: 1749.

473. <i> - Oxfordshire Parish Registers</i>, cuddesdon - baptism; Date: 1742.

474. <i> - Oxfordshire Parish Registers</i>, Charlton on Otmoor - baptism; Date: 1722.

475. - Indexing Project - , M10993-1 system origin: England-ODM source film number: 919247.

476. - Indexing Project - , I04450-7 system origin: England-ODM source film number: 1999420.

477. <i>Parish Records Collection - Baptism</i>, Long Crendon, Buckinghamshire. Parish records; Date: 23 December 1744.

478. - Indexing Project - , C13563-5 system origin: England-VR source film number: 1042379.
479. - Indexing Project - , Batch #:106977-8; Film #: 1967108; Date: 1738.
480. - Indexing Project - , Batch #:106977-8; Film #: 1967108 - marriage; Date: 1738.
481. - Indexing Project - , Batch #:107018-3; Film #: 1967108; Date: 1739.
482. - Indexing Project - , Batch #:106977-8; Film #: 1967108; Date: 1741.
483. - Indexing Project - , Batch #:106977-8; Film #: 1967108; Date: 1742.
484. - Indexing Project - , Batch #:106977-8; Film #: 1967108; Date: 1744.
485. - Indexing Project - , Batch #:106977-8; Film #: 1967108; Date: 1745.
486. - Indexing Project - , Batch #:106977-8; Film #: 1967108; Date: 1748.
487. - Indexing Project - , Batch #:106977-8; Film #: 1967108; Date: 1750.
488. - Indexing Project - , Batch #:106977-8; Film #: 1967108; Date: 1754.
489. - Indexing Project - , Batch #:106977-8; Film #: 1967108 - birth; Date: 11 November 1716 name: Johannes Grant gender: Male birth date: 11 Nov 1716 birthplace: Worminghall, Buckingham, England father's name: Edvardi Grant mother's name: Mariae.
490. - Indexing Project - , Batch #: I04146-2; film #: 1595986; Date: 1749 record title: England Marriages, 1538-1973 groom's name: George Rowland bride's name: Jane Skinner marriage date: 31 Mar 1749 marriage place: Bristol, Gloucester, England.
491. - Indexing Project - , Batch : C01717-1; film: 1596677; Date: 1736 name: Silvester Stone gender: Female baptism/christening date: 09 Jan 1736 baptism/christening place: St. Phillip and St. Jacob's, Bristol, Gloucester, England father's name: William Stone.
492. - Indexing Project - , Batch: I03618-9; film: 1595499; Date: 1727 name: Isaac Rogers gender: Male baptism/christening date: 02 Oct 1727 baptism/christening place: Bitton, Gloucester, England father's name: Dennis Rogers.
493. - Indexing Project - , Batchr: I03976-8; film: 1595532; Date: 1764 record title: England Marriages, 1538-1973 groom's name: Ebenezer Burges bride's name: Dianna Reynold marriage date: 13 Aug 1764 marriage place: St. George, Bristol, Gloucester, England.
494. England and Wales, Non-Conformist Record Indexes , (RG4-8); record set: RG4_1830; Date: 1738 name: Ebenezer Burgess event type: Baptism christening date: 06 Nov 1738 christening place: Bristol, Somerset father's name: John Burgess mother's name: Susanna Burgess.
495. - Indexing Project - , M07240-3; film 991403; Date: 1787.
496. - Indexing Project - , C03553-1; film: 826545; Date: 1769.
497. - Indexing Project - , C07240-2; film: 991402; Date: 1789.
498. - Indexing Project - , M14754-2; film: 1042454 - marriage; Date: 1777 groom's name: Stephen Jennings bride's name: Elizabeth Taylor marriage date: 26 May 1777 marriage place: Bromley,Kent,England.
499. - Indexing Project - , C01839-5; film: 1042453 - baptism; Date: 1762 name: Elizabeth Taylor gender: Female baptism/christening date: 12 Nov 1762 baptism/christening place: BROMLEY, KENT, ENGLAND father's name: Grove Taylor mother'sname: Sarah.
500. - Indexing Project - , C07152-2; film: 0991690, 0991691; Date: 1752.

501. <i>Parish Records Collection - Marriage</i>, Marylebone, London - Marriages 1783-1792 page 57; Date: 1786.

502. Docklands Ancestors , ref: X024/123 - Baptism; Date: 1763 25 December 1763 Baptism Forename: Elizabeth Othernames: Surname: Day Fathers forenames: Charles Fathers occupation: Smith Mothers forenames: Elizabeth Birth date: Address: Artichoke Hill.

503. - Indexing Project - , Batch #: C03524-3; film #: 580907; Date: 1795.

504. <i>Parish Records Collection - Marriage</i>, Marylebone, London - Marriages 1783-1792 page 57; Date: 1786 Supplied Surname: LANGLEY Surname: LANGLEY Full First name: Isaac Supplied First Name: Isaac Spouse Surname: DAY Spouse Full First name: Elizabeth Spouse First Name: Eliz Place: Marylebone, London.

505. - Indexing Project - , c03717-8; film 887385; Date: 9 March 1762.

506. - Indexing Project - , Batch #: I04107-1; film #: 1751896; Date: 1789 name: Elizabeth Bayse gender:Female baptism/christening date:15 Nov 1789 baptism/christening place:St. George-in-the-East, Middlesex, England father's name:Frederick Bayse mother's name:Mary.

507. 1841 Census , London; piece: 723; Book: 12; folio: 9; page 12.

508. <i>England & Wales Death index</i> <i>First name(s) PAMELA Last name ALLSWORTH Gender Female Birth day 23, Middlesex, Hendon; vol: 3; page: 168; Date: 1849.

509. London, England, Marriages & Banns, 1754-1921 , London Met Archives; St George; Marriage regs; P93/GEO, item 037; Date: 1787.

510. London, England, Baptisms, Marriages and Burials, 1538-1812 , 1802 - 1812, P69/AND2/A/010/MS06673, Item 014; Date: 31 October 1809.

511. <i>Parish Records Collection - Baptism</i>, Dorset - baptism of Thomas (son); Date: 1793.

512. <i>Parish Records Collection - Marriage</i>, Litton Cheney, Dorset; Date: 24 July 1784.

513. <i>Parish Records Collection - Baptism</i>, Dorset parish register - Winterborne St MartinPE/WSM:RE1/3; Date: 29 October 1766.

514. <i>Parish Records Collection - Baptism</i>, Longbredy, Dorset - parish registers - ref:PE/LBY; Date: 8 April 1764.

515. - Indexing Project - , Batch Number: M16031-1; film: 1239263; ref: 2:3HP1QQR; Date: 1806.

516. <i>Somerset & Dorset Family History Society, <i>Dorset Hemp and Flax growers</i></i> </i>, Table Ref 1: D3c; Orig Table Ref 2: 10 ; QS quarter: 1786. ii & iii; Date: 1875 Dorset Hemp and Flax growers Year crop grown: 1784 Forenames: John & John HUNT Surname: SLADE Fields: Ryall Parish where grown: Over Compton Abode: Over Compton County: Dorset Country: England Bounty pounds: 1 Bounty shillings: 8 Bounty pence: 4 Hemp stones: 0 Flax stones: 85 Year crop grown: 1785 Forenames: John & John HUNT Surname: SLADE Fields: Parish where grown: Abode: Over Compton County: Dorset Country: England Bounty pounds: 1 Bounty shillings: 0 Bounty pence: 4 Hemp stones: 0 Flax stones: 61 Table Ref 1: D3c; Orig Table Ref 2: 10 ; QS quarter: 1786. ii & iii.

517. - Indexing Project - , batch #: M07415-2; film#: 1279491.

518. - Indexing Project - , batch #: M07415-2; film#: 1279491; Date: 13 May 1800 groom's name: John Mathews bride's name: Sarah Fowler marriage date: 1800 marriage place: Independent, Charmouth, Dorset, England.

519. - Indexing Project - , B39039-4; film 1279498; Date: 1858.
520. - Indexing Project - , Batch #:C16006-2; film #:1239253; Date: 1782 name: John Matthews gender: Male baptism/christening date:1782 baptism/christening place:WHITCHURCH-CANONICORUM, DORSET, ENGLAND father's name: John Matthews mother's name: Ann.
521. <i>Parish Records Collection - Baptism</i>, Dorset; Date: 1782.
522. - Indexing Project - , Burial: B39039-4, film 1279498; Date: 1841.
523. - Indexing Project - , Batch: M01717-1; Film: 1441052; Date: 1769 groom's name: John Colman bride's name: Elizabeth Franklin marriage date: 04 Dec 1769 marriage place: All Saints And Saint Peter,Rushton,Northampton,England.
524. - Indexing Project - , P01717-1; film: 1441052 IT 4, 9; Date: 13 March 1772.
525. - Indexing Project - , P01717-1; film: 1441052 IT 4, 9; Date: 9 April 1773.
526. - Indexing Project - , P01717-1; film: 1441052 IT 4, 9; Date: 19 February 1775.
527. - Indexing Project - , P01717-1; film: 1441052 IT 4, 9; Date: 12 December 1779.
528. - Indexing Project - , P01717-1; film: 1441052 IT 4, 9; Date: 15 June 1783.
529. - Indexing Project - , P01717-1; film: 1441052 IT 4, 9; Date: 3 February 1788.
530. - Indexing Project - , P01717-1; film: 1441052 IT 4, 9; Date: 18 April 1790.
531. - Indexing Project - , Batch: M01717-1; Film: 1441052; Date: 4 December 1769 groom's name: John Colman bride's name: Elizabeth Franklin marriage date: 04 Dec 1769 marriage place: All Saints And Saint Peter,Rushton,Northampton,England.
532. - Indexing Project - , C07468-1; film0825344; Date: 1747.
533. - Indexing Project - , P01081-1; film 1696649 IT 6; Date: 1748.
534. - Indexing Project - , Folder 4291942; Date: 1748.
535. England and Wales, Non-Conformist Record Indexes , RG6_0502; Date: 1769.
536. England and Wales, Non-Conformist Record Indexes , RG6_0502; Date: 1772.
537. England and Wales, Non-Conformist Record Indexes , RG6_0773; Date: 1779.
538. England and Wales, Non-Conformist Record Indexes , RG6_0773; Date: 1781.
539. England and Wales, Non-Conformist Record Indexes , RG6_0773; Date: 1785.
540. England and Wales, Non-Conformist Record Indexes , RG6_0773; Date: 1788.
541. England and Wales, Non-Conformist Record Indexes , (RG4-8), record set: RG6_0773; Date: 1783.
542. - Indexing Project - , C07210-1; film 991305; Date: 14 February 1728.
543. - Indexing Project - , C07281-1; film 991320; Date: 17 September 1732.
544. <i>Essex Parish Registers, 1538-1900</i>, film: 857075; folder 4006318; image 64; Date: 4 October 1772.
545. <i>Essex Parish Registers, 1538-1900</i>, film: 857075; folder 4006318; image 180; Date: 11 October 1763.
546. <i>Essex Parish Registers, 1538-1900</i>, I05606-8; film 1526973; item 17; Date: 2 May 1742.
547. <i>Essex Parish Registers, 1538-1900</i>, film: 857075; folder 4006318; image 6; Date: 21 September 1764.

548. <i>Essex Parish Registers, 1538-1900</i>, film: 857075; folder 4006318; image 51; Date: 14 June 1765.

549. <i>Essex Parish Registers, 1538-1900</i>, film: 857075; folder 4006318; image 9; Date: 13 October 1766.

550. <i>Essex Parish Registers, 1538-1900</i>, film: 857075; folder 4006318; image 13; Date: 26 March 1771.

551. - Indexing Project - , Batch #: M00161-1; film #: 547171; Date: 1760.

552. - Indexing Project - , Batch #:M00161-1; filn #:547171; Date: 1760 groom's name: Richard Young bride's name: Elizabeth Merigest marriage date: 04 Dec 1760 marriage place: Saint Botolph Bishopsgate,London,England.

553. - Indexing Project - , Batch #: C00161-4; film #: 380143; Date: 1729 name: Richard Young gender: Male baptism/christening date: 30 Oct 1729 baptism/christening place: ST BOTOLPH BISHOPSGATE,LONDON,LONDON,ENGLAND father's name: Richd. Young mother's name: Francis.

554. - Indexing Project - , batch: C00145-7; film: 561142; Date: 1740.

555. - Indexing Project - , batch: P00141-1; film: 0845229, 0476868; Date: 1740.

556. - Indexing Project - , Project: I03630-2; film:1041562; Date: 1749 name: Charles Stringer gender: Male baptism/christening date: 22 Oct 1749 baptism/christening place: Shipley, West Sussex, England father's name: William Stringer mother's name: Sarah Stringer.

557. - Indexing Project - , M00080-2; film: 380123; Date: 1778.

558. - Indexing Project - , C02245-1; film: 374482 - baptism; Date: 25 December 1750.

559. London, England, Marriages & Banns, 1754-1921 , Saint Dunstan And All Saints, Register of marriages, P93/DUN, Item 043; Date: 1775 Name: Richard Heath Spouse Name: Ann Rainbird Record Type: Marriage Event Date: 16 Nov 1775 Parish: Stepney St Dunstan and All Saints Borough: Tower Hamlets Register Type: Parish Register.

560. - Indexing Project - , P01266-1; film: 0496823 IT 3; Date: 1750 name: Ann Raynbird gender: Female baptism/christening date: 13 Mar 1750 baptism/christening place: PAKENHAM,SUFFOLK,ENGLAND father's name: Thos. Raynbird mother's name: Mary indexing project (batch) number: P01266-1 system origin: England-ODM source film number: 0496823 IT.

561. - Indexing Project - , Batch: C02577-6; film #: 380207; Date: 1756 name: Richard Hyde gender: Male baptism/christening date: 06 Jun 1756 baptism/christening place: ST GILES CRIPPLEGATE,LONDON,LONDON,ENGLAND father's name: John Hyde mother's name: Mary.

562. - Indexing Project - , Batch #:C02246-1; film #:374455; Date: 1754 name: Sarah Timbrel gender: Female baptism/christening date: 27 Mar 1754 baptism/christening place: ST JOHN ZACHARY,LONDON,LONDON,ENGLAND father's name: William Timbrel mother's name: Sarah.

563. London, England. Westminster Burials- Transcripts , Westminster Archives page 136; Date: 7 April 1788.

564. - Indexing Project - , Batch #:C00629-5; film #: 94693; Date: 1744 name: John Briggs gender: Male baptism/christening date: 04 Nov 1744 baptism/christening place: ST

MARY WHITECHAPEL,STEPNEY,LONDON,ENGLAND father's name: John Briggs mother's name: Jane.

565. London, England. Westminster Burials- Transcripts , St Margaret, Westminster; Date: 7 May 1793.

566. Kent Parish Records ; Date: 1767 Groom's Name - GILES George County - Kent Parish - Lambershurst Date of Marriage- 3-Nov-1767 Notes - Bride's Name - STEVENS Martha Original Appearance - George Giles & Martha Stevens,3 Nov.

567. Kent, Phillimore's, Register of Marriages, 1538-1837 , Lamberhurst; Vol: 3; Date: 1767 Groom's Name - GILES George County - Kent Parish - Lambershurst Date of Marriage- 3-Nov-1767 Notes - Bride's Name - STEVENS Martha Original Appearance - George Giles & Martha Stevens,3 Nov. Groom's Name - GILES George County - Kent Parish - Lambershurst Date of Marriage- 3-Nov-1767 Notes - Bride's Name - STEVENS Martha Original Appearance - George Giles & Martha Stevens,3 Nov. Groom's Name - GILES George County - Kent Parish - Lambershurst Date of Marriage- 3-Nov-1767 Notes - Bride's Name - STEVENS Martha Original Appearance - George Giles & Martha Stevens,3 Nov. Groom's Name - GILES George County - Kent Parish - Lambershurst Date of Marriage- 3-Nov-1767 Notes - Bride's Name - STEVENS Martha Original Appearance - George Giles & Martha Stevens,3 Nov. George Giles & Martha Stevens 3 Nov 1767.

568. - Indexing Project - , 106870-0; England; source:1736878.

569. Canterbury Marriage Licences, 1781-1837 , Page 152; Date: 1800 Jas Holmes of St Mary Dover bach & Maria Burvill of Walmer sp, at W. 19 Sep 1800.

570. Canterbury Marriage Licences, 1781-1837 , page 152; Date: 1800 Jas Holmes of St Mary Dover bach & Maria Burvill of Walmer sp, at W. 19 Sep 1800.

571. FamilySearch Extraction Program - BIRTH , Call number: 6906439, Sheet #: 00, Reference #: 6906439, Batch#: C036562, Serial #: 02735; Date: 1783 William Read Homes Birth date: 25 December 1783 Place: St. Mary The Virgin, Dover, Kent County, England, Time period: 1770-1826, Sources about Gender: Male Media type: Microfilm.

572. FamilySearch Extraction Program - CHRISTENING , Call #: 6906439, Sheet #: 00, Ref #: 6906439, Batch #: C036562, Serial #: 02735; Name: William Read Homes Christening date: 11 January 1784 Place: Saint Mary The Virgin,Dover,Kent,England Time period: 1770-1826 Media type: Microfilm.

573. FamilySearch Extraction Program - DEATH ; Date: 1789 William Read Homes Birth date: 25 December 1783 Death date: 1789 Place: Dover, Kent, England, United Kingdom.

574. Canterbury Marriage Licences, 1781-1837 ; Date: 1819 Wm Read Holmes of St Mary Dover pilot bach & Eliz Barber of the s sp. 6 Nov 1819.

575. <i>Parish Records Collection - Baptism</i>, Saint Mary, Whitechapel, Reg of baptisms, Feb 1758 - Oct 1774, P93/MRY1, Item 010; Date: 1766 Name: John Baldwin Baptism Date: 11 Apr 1766 Parish: St Mary, Whitechapel County: Middlesex Borough: Tower Hamlets Parent(s): John, Rebecca.

576. - Indexing Project - , C02555-6; film: 370931 - (baptism); Date: 1725 name: Rebekah Smith gender: Female baptism/christening date: 04 Jun 1725 baptism/christening place: ST BOTOLPH WITHOUT ALDGATE,LONDON,LONDON,ENGLAND father's

name: Robt. Smith mother'nsame: Susanna.
577. - Indexing Project - , Batch: M02236-1; film: 374413; Date: 1754.
578. - Indexing Project - , project: C00633-6; Film: 370931, 370933; Date: 7 February 1739.
579. - Indexing Project - , Marriage; St. Botolph Aldgate, London, England; Batch: M00080-2; film # 380123; Date: 8 December 1761 groom's name: William Dickinson bride's name: Mary Miller marriage date: 08 Dec 1761 marriage place: St. Botolph Aldgate, London, England groom's marital status: Single bride's marital status: Single indexing project (batch) number: M00080-2 source film number: 380123.
580. - Indexing Project - , Christening; ALDGATE, LONDON, ENGLAND; batch #: C02555-7; film #: 370933; name: Mary Ann Miller gender: Female baptism/christening date: 09 Jan 1742 baptism/christening place: ST BOTOLPH WITHOUT ALDGATE,LONDON,LONDON,ENGLAND father's name: Thos. Miller mother's name: Margt. indexing project (batch) number: C02555-7 system origin: England-ODM source film number: 370933.
581. - Indexing Project - , Marriage; St. Botolph Aldgate, London, England; Batch: M00080-2; film # 380123; Date: 8 December 1761 "groom's name: William Dickinson bride's name: Mary Miller marriage date: 08 Dec 1761 marriage place: St. Botolph Aldgate, London, England groom's marital status: Single bride's marital status: Single indexing project (batch) number: M00080-2 source film number: 380123.".
582. - Indexing Project - , C00629-5; film 94692, 94693 - baptism records; Date: 1470 name: William Scofield Dixon gender: Male baptism/christening date: 19 Nov 1740 baptism/christening place: ST MARY WHITECHAPEL,STEPNEY,LONDON,ENGLAND father's name: Thomas Dixon mother'nsame: Mary.
583. London, England, Marriages & Banns, 1754-1921 , Saint Dunstan And All Saints, Register of marriages, P93/DUN, Item 045; Name: William Wine Spouse Name: Martha Vanner Record Type: Marriage Event Date: 25 Dec 1781 Parish: St Dunstan and All Saints, Stepney County: Middlesex Borough: Tower Hamlets.
584. London, England, Marriages & Banns, 1754-1921 , Saint Dunstan And All Saints, P93/DUN, Item 045; Name: William Wine Spouse Name: Martha Vanner Record Type: Marriage Event Date: 25 Dec 1781 Parish: St Dunstan and All Saints, Stepney County: Middlesex Borough: Tower Hamlets.
585. - Indexing Project - , M04160-1; England; Source: 574465.
586. - Indexing Project - , p01051-5; film 374354; Date: 13 June 1762.
587. - Indexing Project - , C05578-1; film 578786, 578787; Date: 17 April 1757.
588. - Indexing Project - , M00061-7; film#: 375005; Date: 4 October 1781 St. Sepulchre, London, England.
589. - Indexing Project - , Batch #: C13553-3; film #: 1042308; ref: 2:2GTVCPF; Date: 1758.
590. - Indexing Project - , number:C04080-1;system origin:England;source film number:396231; Date: 1786 Christening name: Mary Rap Birth date:21 may 1786 Birth place:Shoreditch, London, England Christening Date: 4 Jun 1786 Christening Place: St Leonards, Shoreditch, London, England Father's name: William Rap Mother's name: Elisabeth.

591. - Indexing Project - , number:C04080-1;system origin:England;source film number:396231; Date: 1788 Christening name: Thomas Rapp Birth date:03 May 1788 Birth place:Shoreditch, London, England Christening Date:29 Jun 1788 Christening Place: St Leonards, Shoreditch, London, England Father's name: William Rap Mother's name: Elisabeth.

592. - Indexing Project - , number:C04080-1;system origin:England;source film number:396231; Date: 1790 Christening name: John Rapp Birth date: 12 sep 1790 Birth place:Shoreditch, London, England Christening Date:4 Dec 1790 Christening Place: St Leonards, Shoreditch, London, England Father's name: William Rap Mother's name: Elisabeth.

593. London, England, Baptisms, Marriages and Burials, 1538-1812 , St Leonard Shoreditch, Register of burials, 1778 - 1792, P91/LEN/A/012/MS07499, Item 010; Name: John Rap Burial Date: 25 Dec 1790 Parish: St Leonard, Shoreditch County: Middlesex Borough: Hackney Record Type: Burial Register Type: Parish Register.

594. - Indexing Project - , number:C04080-1;system origin:England;source film number:396231; Date: 1792 Christening name: Sarah Rapp Birth date:13 Nov 1791 Birth place:Shoreditch, London, England Christening Date:12 Feb 1792 Christening Place: St Leonards, Shoreditch, London, England Father's name: William Rap Mother's name: Elisabeth.

595. - Indexing Project - , number:C04080-1;system origin:England;source film number:396231; Date: 1794 Christening name: Henry Rapp Birth date: 21 Jan 1794 Birth place:Shoreditch, London, England Christening Date: 4 May 1794 Christening Place: St Leonards, Shoreditch, London, England Father's name: William Rap Mother's name: Elisabeth.

596. - Indexing Project - , Batch #: C00625-1; film #: 254545; Date: 1784 name: William Thomas Rapley gender: Male baptism/christening date: 25 Jan 1784 baptism/christening place: SAINT Mary Rotherhithe, LONDON, ENGLAND father's name: Thomas mother's name: Mary Ann.

597. London Metropolitian Archives - Register of Baptisms , Saint Marylebone, baptisms Mar 1749 - Dec 1764, P89/MRY1, Item 004; Date: 1756 Name: Thomas Rapley Baptism Date: 8 Dec 1756 Parish: St Marylebone County: Middlesex Borough: Westminster Parent(s): Jeremiah, Mary Record Type: Baptism Register Type: Parish Register.

598. - Indexing Project - , C03524-1; film: 580904, 580905; Date: 1756 name: Thomas Rapley gender: Male baptism/christening date: 08 Dec 1756 baptism/christening place: SAINT MARY-ST MARYLEBONE ROAD,ST MARYLEBONE,LONDON,ENGLAND birth date: 12 Nov 1756 father's name: Jeremiah Rapley mother's name: Mary.

599. London Metropolitian Archives - Register of Baptisms , Saint Mary, Putney; baptisms Apr 1735 - Dec 1760, P95/MRY1, Item 367; Date: 1745 Name: Ann Steel Baptism Date: 10 Sep 1745 Parish: St Mary, Putney, Surrey Parent(s): John Steel, Hannah Steel Record Type: Baptism Register Type: Parish Register.

600. - Indexing Project - , P01749-1; film: 908518 - baptism record; Date: 1745 name: Ann Steel gender: Female baptism/christening date: 10 Sep 1745 baptism/christening place: PUTNEY,LONDON,ENGLAND father's name: John Steel mother's name: Hannah.

601. - Indexing Project - , P00140-1; film 845234; Date: 1750 name: Stephen Mott gender: Male baptism/christening date: 20 Jul 1750 baptism/christening place: SAINT DIONIS BACKCHURCH,LONDON,LONDON,ENGLAND birth date: 28 Jun 1750 father's name: Samuel Mott mother's name: Mary.

602. - Indexing Project - , M02198-4; system origin: England-ODM; source film number: 88469.

603. - Indexing Project - , C03647-1; system origin: England-ODM; source film number: 254494.

604. - Indexing Project - , C03647-2; system origin: England-VR; source film number: 1279444.

605. <i>Oxfordshire Family History Society, <i>Oxfordshire Marriages 1559-1837</i></i> </i>, Stanton Harcourt Marriages; Vol 4; page3; Date: 1756 p. 3. Thomas Clack & Mary Aldsworth 10 May 1756.

606. <i>Oxfordshire Family History Society, <i>Oxfordshire Marriages 1559-1837</i></i> </i>, Marriages at Stanton Harcourt; Vol 4 (marked 5); page 3; Date: 1756 p. 3. Thomas Clack & Mary Aldsworth 10 May 1756.

607. <i>Berkshire Parish Registers</i>, Appleton, baptism records; Date: 1701.

608. <i>Oxfordshire Family History Society, <i>Oxford Marriage Index - 1538 to 1837</i></i> </i>, Indexed by Grooms - T - (St Mary Mag Oxford); Date: 1734.

609. <i> - Oxfordshire Parish Registers</i>, Beckley baptism; Date: 1748 or 1749.

610. <i> - Oxfordshire Parish Registers</i>, Witney marriages; Date: 1721.

611. <i> - Oxfordshire Parish Registers</i>, Witney BMD christening; Date: 1722.

612. <i> - Oxfordshire Parish Registers</i>, Witney BMD christening; Date: 1727.

613. <i> - Oxfordshire Parish Registers</i>, Witney BMD christening; Date: 1737.

614. <i> - Oxfordshire Parish Registers</i>, Witney marriages; Date: 1700.

615. <i> - Oxfordshire Parish Registers</i>, Bicester marriages; Date: 1740.

616. <i> - Oxfordshire Parish Registers</i>, Shipton marriages; Date: 1712.

617. <i> - Oxfordshire Parish Registers</i>, Witney christening; Date: 1690.

618. <i> - Oxfordshire Parish Registers</i>, Shipton under Wytchwood - christening; Date: 1680.

619. <i> - Oxfordshire Parish Registers</i>, Shipton under Wytchwood - marriages; Date: 1712.

620. <i> - Oxfordshire Parish Registers</i>, Shipton Parish BMD records - Marriage; Date: 1704.

621. <i> - Oxfordshire Parish Registers</i>, Ascot BMD records - burials; Date: 1752.

622. <i> - Oxfordshire Parish Registers</i>, Upper Heyford BMD records - Ascot - baptism; Date: 1709.

623. - Indexing Project - , Ascott under Wychwood, Oxon BMD records; Date: 1714.

624. <i>Oxfordshire Family History Society, <i>Oxfordshire Marriages 1559-1837</i></i> </i>, indexed by Husband - T; Date: 1739.

625. <i> - Oxfordshire Parish Registers</i>, Ascot BMD -records - burial; Date: 1758.

626. <i> - Oxfordshire Parish Registers</i>, Ascot BMD records; Date: 1746.

627. <i>Oxfordshire Family History Society, <i>Oxford Marriage Index - 1538 to 1837</i></i> </i>, Indexed by husbands C; page 99; Date: 1684.

628. <i> - Oxfordshire Parish Registers</i>, Upper Heyford BMD records; Date: 1729.

629. <i> - Oxfordshire Parish Registers</i>, Upper Heyford BMD records - baptism; Date: 1737.

630. - Indexing Project - , number:M02208-2;system origin:England;source film number:952336; Date: 1730 Marriage name:John Drinkwater Marriage date:18 May 1730 Marriage place:Bampton, Oxfordshire, England Bride's name:Ann Lapper.

631. <i> - Oxfordshire Parish Registers</i>, Bampton parish BMD records; Date: 1715.

632. <i> - Oxfordshire Parish Registers</i>, Bampton parish BMD records; Date: 1717.

633. <i> - Oxfordshire Parish Registers</i>, Bampton parish BMD records; Date: 1718.

634. <i> - Oxfordshire Parish Registers</i>, Bampton parish BMD records; Date: 1714.

635. - Indexing Project - , number:M01865-2;system origin:England;source film number:88260; Date: 1728 Marriage name:Edward Hawkins Marriage date:10 Jun 1728 Marriage place:Berkshire, England father's name:Edwd. Hawkins Bride's name:Mary Cockhead.

636. <i>Berkshire Parish Registers</i>, Faringdon Marriages; Date: 1728.

637. <i>Berkshire Parish Registers</i>, Great Coxwell - burials; Date: 1790.

638. <i>Berkshire Parish Registers</i>, Great Coxwell - baptisms; Date: 1734.

639. <i>Berkshire Parish Registers</i>, Great Coxwell - burials; Date: 1740.

640. <i>Oxfordshire Family History Society, <i>Oxfordshire Marriages 1559-1837</i></i> </i>, Indexed by husbands - H page 135; Date: 1708 Richard Heydon, of Witney. Married at Witney Quaker. Wife: Eleanor Young, of Witney 18 Mar 1708.

641. - Indexing Project - , Batch #:P00882-2; Film #:88234; Date: 1717.

642. - Indexing Project - , Batch #:P00882-2; Film #:88234; Date: 1719.

643. - Indexing Project - , Batch #:P00882-1; Film #:88234; Date: 1721.

644. <i>Berkshire Parish Registers</i>, Coleshill, Berkshire - Burials; Date: 1721 Infant.

645. - Indexing Project - , Batch #:P00882-1; Film #:88234; Date: 1723.

646. England and Wales, Non-Conformist Record Indexes , Record set: RG6_1370; Date: 1708 Name: Richard Heydon Event Type: Marriage Birth Date: Birthplace: Christening Date: Christening Place: Marriage Date: 18 May 1708 Marriage Place: Witney, Oxfordshire Death Date: Death Place: Burial Date: Burial Place: Father's Name: William Heydon Mother's Name: Record Set: RG6_1370.

647. <i>Oxfordshire Family History Society, <i>Oxfordshire Marriages 1559-1837</i></i> </i>, Indexed by husbands - H page 135; Date: 1708 "Richard Heydon, of Witney. Married at Witney Quaker. Wife: Eleanor Young, of Witney 18 Mar 1708." Witney Quakers.

648. Oxfordshire Family History Society, Witney Quakers records , Page 8; Marriage: 1708 18 Jun HEYDON Richard maltster of Witney, s. William of Witney YOUNG Eleanor sp., Witney, d. Edward late of Milton.

649. - Indexing Project - , C10967-2 ; film: 919234 - birth of child; Date: 1717.

650. - Indexing Project - , I04449-3; film: 1999402 - marriage; Date: 22 May 1716.

651. - Indexing Project - , C10967-2 ; film: 919234 - birth; Date: 1717.

652. - Indexing Project - , C10967-2 ; film: 919234 - birth; Date: 1722.

653. - Indexing Project - , C10967-2 ; film: 919234 - birth; Date: 1726.

654. - Indexing Project - , C10967-2 ; film: 919234 - birth; Date: 1732.

655. - Indexing Project - , I04449-3; film: 1999402 - marriage; Date: 1716.

656. - Indexing Project - , C06999-1; film: 919642, 919643 - christening; Date: 1695 name Richard Smith gender Male baptism/christening date 29 Dec 1695 baptism/christening place ETON,BUCKINGHAM,ENGLAND father's name James Smith indexing project (batch) number   C06999-1; film: 9196429,19643.

657. <i>Oxfordshire Family History Society, <i>Oxfordshire Marriages 1559-1837</i></i> </i>, index by husband - H; Date: 1679.

658. <i> - Oxfordshire Parish Registers</i>, Northmoor - christenings; Date: 1658.

659. <i>Oxfordshire Family History Society, <i>Oxford Marriage Index - 1538 to 1837</i></i> </i>, index by husband - H; Date: 1679.

660. - Phillimores Marriages , Chipping Norton, Oxfordshire; Date: 1717.

661. - Indexing Project - , M02170-2; film 88466.

662. - Indexing Project - , C07320-1; film: 887488; Date: 1679.

663. - Indexing Project - , C073201; film: 887488; Date: 1681.

664. - Indexing Project - , C073201; film: 887488; Date: 1683.

665. - Indexing Project - , C073201; film: 887488; Date: 1684.

666. - Indexing Project - , C07320-3; film: 1279460; Date: 1685.

667. - Indexing Project - , C073201; film: 887488; Date: 1689.

668. <i> - Oxfordshire Parish Registers</i>, South Hinksey - christening records; Date: 1693.

669. - Indexing Project - , Index# C07320-3; film 1279460; ref# 2:2zzms89; Date: 11 August 1657.

670. <i><i>Berkshire Marriages - 2nd Edition</i> (Berkshire Family History Society)</i> (Berkshire Family History Society)</i>, page 9867.

671. - Indexing Project - , Witney St Mary - marriages; Date: 1676.

672. <i>Oxfordshire Family History Society, <i>Oxford Marriage Index - 1538 to 1837</i></i> </i>, Index (By husband) page 193; Date: 1672 Husband: Stone, Richard Wife: Browne, Ann Married at Standlake, Oxfordshire 6 October 1672.

673. - Phillimores Marriages , Standlake, Oxfordshire; page:71; Date: 1672 Richardus Stone et Anna Browne ... 6 Oct 1672.

674. - Phillimores Marriages , Standlake, Oxfordshire. P:71; Date: 1672 (Vol IV: p:7) Richardus Stone et Anna Browne ... 6 Oct 1672.

675. <i> - Oxfordshire Parish Registers</i>, Yarnton - marriage records; Date: 1 June 1663.

676. - Indexing Project - , C01878-2; film 88272; Date: 1672 name: Massey Onion gender: Female baptism/christening date: 26 Apr 1672 baptism/christening place: HINTON WALDRIST,BERKSHIRE,ENGLAND father's name: Thomas Onion mother'nsame: Anne.

677. - Indexing Project - , C01878-2; film: 88272; Date: 1678 name: Mary Onion gender: Female baptism/christening date: 15 Dec 1678 baptism/christening place: HINTON WALDRIST,BERKSHIRE,ENGLAND father's name: Thomas Onion mother'nsame: Anne.

678. - Indexing Project - , C01878-2; film 88272; Date: 1682 name: Thomas Onion gender: Male baptism/christening date: 25 Apr 1682 baptism/christening place: HINTON WALDRIST,BERKSHIRE,ENGLAND father's name: Thomas Onion mother'nsame: Anne.

679. <i>Berkshire Parish Registers</i>, Hinton Waldrist, Burials; Date: 21 September 1686.

680. - Indexing Project - , C01878-2; film: 88272; Date: 1684 name: Anne Onion gender: Female baptism/christening date: 21 Sep 1684 baptism/christening place: HINTON WALDRIST,BERKSHIRE,ENGLAND father's name: Thomas Onion mother'nsame: Anne.

681. <i>Berkshire Parish Registers</i>, Hinton Waldrist - baptism record; Date: 1687.

682. <i>Berkshire Parish Registers</i>, Hinton Waldrist - baptism record; Date: 1689.

683. - Indexing Project - , M02639-1; film: 0990430 IT 2, 1696464 IT 4-5 - marriage; Date: 1705 groom's name Richd. Hartlett bride's name Mary Stone marriage date 18 Apr 1705 marriage place Banbury,Oxford,England indexing project (batch) number M02639-1; film:

0990430 IT 2, 1696464 IT 4-5.

684. - Indexing Project - , M02639-1; film: 0990430 IT 2, 1696464 IT 4-51705 -marriage; Date: 1705 groom's name Richd. Hartlett bride's name Mary Stone marriage date 18 Apr 1705 marriage place Banbury,Oxford,England indexing project (batch) number M02639-1; film: 0990430 IT 2, 1696464 IT 4-5.

685. - Indexing Project - , I02039-3; film: 813693 - daughter's birth record.

686. - Indexing Project - , M01319-8; film: 811723; Date: 1689 groom's name Rich. King groom's birthplace Southnowton, Co. Oxford (should read SOUTH NEWINGTON) bride's name Eliz. Barris bride's birthplace Byfold - (should read BYFIELD) marriage date 19 Oct 1689 marriage place Northampton, England indexing project (batch) number M01319-8; film8:11723.

687. - Indexing Project - , I02039-3; film: 813693 - daughter's birth record; Date: 1709.

688. - Indexing Project - , I02039-3; film: 813693 - birth; Date: 1691.

689. England and Wales, Non-Conformist Record Indexes , RG6_1332; Date: 20 June 1693.

690. - Indexing Project - , I02039-3; film: 813693 - birth; Date: 11 March 1695.

691. England and Wales, Non-Conformist Record Indexes , RG6_1332; Date: 1695.

692. England and Wales, Non-Conformist Record Indexes , RG6_1332 - Birth; Date: 1700.

693. England and Wales, Non-Conformist Record Indexes , RG6_1332 - birth; Date: 1701.

694. England and Wales, Non-Conformist Record Indexes , RG6_1332 - birth; Date: 1703.

695. - Indexing Project - , I02039-3; film: 813693 - birth; Date: 1706.

696. - Indexing Project - , C02639-2; film: 942.57 B2 B4B V.9 - birth; Date: 4 March 1660 name: Richard King gender: Male birth date: 04 Mar 1660 birthplace: BANBURY,OXFORD,ENGLAND father's name: Henry King.

697. England and Wales, Non-Conformist Record Indexes , Banbury; RG6_1220; Date: 1695 SWIFT, Mary Marriage: Banbury,Oxfordshire 16 Oct 1695 Father: Joyne Swift.

698. England and Wales, Non-Conformist Record Indexes , RG7_1332; Date: 1673 Mary Swift birthdate: 12 nov 1673 Banbury, Ox father: Robert Swift Mother: Joane Swift.

699. England and Wales, Non-Conformist Record Indexes , Banbury; RG6_1332; Date: 1666 GILKES, John Birth: Banbury,Oxfordshire 16 March 1666 Father: Thomas Gilkes Mother: Mary.

700. England and Wales, Non-Conformist Record Indexes , RG6_1332; Date: 1764 John Gilkes Burial - 10 Jul 1764 Banbury Ox Mother name: Mary Gilkes.

701. England and Wales, Non-Conformist Record Indexes , RG6_1220; Date: 1695 John Gilkes marriage: 16 Oct 1695 Banbury, Ox.

702. <i> - Oxfordshire Parish Registers</i>, Chipping Norton - marriages; Date: 1699.

703. <i> - Oxfordshire Parish Registers</i>, Chipping Norton - christening of daughter; Date: 1701.

704. <i> - Oxfordshire Parish Registers</i>, Chipping Norton - christening; Date: 1701.

705. <i>Oxfordshire Family History Society, <i>Oxford Marriage Index - 1538 to 1837</i></i> </i>,

Indexed by groom - F; Date: 1722.

706. <i> - Oxfordshire Parish Registers</i>, Southleigh - christenings; Date: 1722.

707. <i> - Oxfordshire Parish Registers</i>, Southleigh - christenings; Date: 1724.

708. <i> - Oxfordshire Parish Registers</i>, Southleigh - christenings; Date: 1728.

709. <i> - Oxfordshire Parish Registers</i>, Standlake BMD records - Christening; Date: 1731.

710. <i> - Oxfordshire Parish Registers</i>, Standlake BMD records - Christening; Date: 1739.

711. <i> - Oxfordshire Parish Registers</i>, Standlake BMD records - Christening; Date: 1741.

712. <i> - Oxfordshire Parish Registers</i>, Standlake BMD records - Christening; Date: 1697.

713. - Indexing Project - , M86694-0; film:496694; Date: 1705.

714. - Indexing Project - , Batch: C07320-1; Film: 887488; Date: 1725 Father: Robert Clark Mother: Mary Clark Name: Sarah Clark Date: 12 Dec 1725 Christening: South Hinksey,Berkshire,England.

715. <i><i>Berkshire Marriages - 2nd Edition</i> (Berkshire Family History Society)</i> (Berkshire Family History Society)</i>, Indexed by grooms name - page 1058; Date: 1718.

716. - Indexing Project - , M16077-1; film: 1279456 - marriage; Date: 1717 groom's name: Robert Clark bride's name: Mary Smith marriage date: 13 Jan 1717 marriage place: Cumnor, BerkshireE,ngland.

717. - Indexing Project - , South Hinksey,Berkshire,England; Date: 1725 Father: Robert Clark Mother: Mary Clark Name: Sarah Clark Date: 12 Dec 1725 Christening: South Hinksey,Berkshire,England.

718. <i> - Oxfordshire Parish Registers</i>, Witney - marriages; Date: 1709.

719. <i> - Oxfordshire Parish Registers</i>, Witney - christenings; Date: 1712.

720. <i> - Oxfordshire Parish Registers</i>, Witney - christenings; Date: 1713.

721. <i> - Oxfordshire Parish Registers</i>, Witney - christenings; Date: 1715.

722. <i> - Oxfordshire Parish Registers</i>, Witney - christenings; Date: 1720.

723. <i>Oxfordshire Family History Society, <i>Oxford Marriage Index - 1538 to 1837</i></i> </i>, indexed by husbands, page 41; Date: 1722.

724. <i>Oxfordshire Family History Society, <i>Oxfordshire Marriages 1559-1837</i></i> </i>, indexed by husbands, page 41; Date: 1722.

725. - Indexing Project - , Project #: P01048-1; Film #: 88176.

726. <i><i>Berkshire Marriages - 2nd Edition</i> (Berkshire Family History Society)</i> (Berkshire Family History Society)</i>, Grooms By Name; Date: 1703.

727. - Indexing Project - , Project #: P01048-2; Film #: 1279444; Date: 1703.

728. - Indexing Project - , Project #: P01048-1; Film #: 88176; Date: 1708.

729. - Indexing Project - , Project #: P01048-1; Film #: 88176; Date: 1711.

730. - Indexing Project - , Batch: C07320-1; Film: 887488; Date: 1724 Father: William Bayly Mother: Ann Name: Sarah Bayly Date: 8 April 1724 Christening: Faringdon,Berkshire,England.

731. Boyd's Marriage Index 1538-1840 , 1st Misc Series,; Date: 1701 Last Name: Newell First Name: Henry Supplied First Name: Hen Spouse's Last Name: Hunt Spouse's First Name: Anne Spouse's Supplied First Name: An Vicar General Marriage Licences Place: S Aug & S Faith County: Oxfordshire Year of Marriage: 1701.

732. Boyd's Marriage Index 1538-1840 , 1st Misc Series; Date: 1701 Last Name:

Newell First Name: Henry Supplied First Name: Hen Spouse's Last Name: Hunt Spouse's First Name: Anne Spouse's Supplied First Name: An Vicar General Marriage Licences Place: S Aug & S Faith County: Oxfordshire Year of Marriage: 1701.

733. - Indexing Project - , Batch: I04452-5; film 1999444; Date: 1710 groom's name: William Oxlade bride's name: Mary Salter marriage date: 21 Dec 1710 marriage place: Great Marlow, Buckingham, England.

734. <i>Oxfordshire Family History Society, <i>Oxfordshire Marriages 1559-1837</i></i> </i>, page B 196.

735. - Indexing Project - , Batch : C02419-2; film: 95214; Date: 1684 name: Alice Bolter gender: Female baptism/christening date: 25 Mar 1684 baptism/christening place: BICESTER,OXFORD,ENGLAND father's name: Robert Bolter.

736. <i>Oxfordshire Family History Society, <i>Oxford Marriage Index - 1538 to 1837</i></i> </i>, Marriages H; page 159; Date: 1703 Husband: HINE, Michael Wife: SCOLES, Elizabeth May 4, 1703 - Cuxham, Oxfordshire.

737. - Indexing Project - , Batch: P00648-1; film 0095198, 0095213, 951980, 095213; Date: 1676 name: Mickell Hine gender: Male baptism/christening date: 09 Jul 1676 baptism/christening place: BENSON,OXFORD,ENGLAND father's name: Mickell Hine.

738. <i>Oxfordshire Family History Society, <i>Oxford Marriage Index - 1538 to 1837</i></i> </i>, Marriages H; page 159; Date: 1703 Husband: HINE, Michael Wife: SCOLES, Elizabeth May 4, 1703 - Cuxham, Oxfordshire.

739. <i> - Oxfordshire Parish Registers</i>, Oxford St Giles marriages; Date: 1718.

740. <i> - Oxfordshire Parish Registers</i>, Headington - baptism records; Date: 1702.

741. <i> - Oxfordshire Parish Registers</i>, St Mary Mag' Oxford - marriages; Date: 1723.

742. <i> - Oxfordshire Parish Registers</i>, Headington parish records - baps; Date: 1702.

743. <i> - Oxfordshire Parish Registers</i>, Enston records - baptisms; Date: 1704.

744. <i> - Oxfordshire Parish Registers</i>, Islip marriage record; Date: 1737.

745. <i>Oxfordshire Family History Society, <i>Oxford Marriage Index - 1538 to 1837</i></i> </i>, indexed by groom - J; Date: 1729.

746. - Indexing Project - , C02419-3; film: 887478; Date: 1705 name Joseph Jackson gender   Male baptism/christening date   19 Feb 1705 baptism/christening place BICESTER,OXFORD,ENGLAND father's name John Jackson indexing project (batch) number   C02419-3; film8:87478.

747. <i> - Oxfordshire Parish Registers</i>, Oxford St Peter in the East; Date: 1707.

748. <i>Oxfordshire Family History Society, <i>Oxfordshire Marriages 1559-1837</i></i> </i>, indexed by groom - S; Date: 1717.

749. <i> - Oxfordshire Parish Registers</i>, Charlton on Otmoor - marriage; Date: 1719.

750. - Indexing Project - , C07375-1; film: 919229; Date: 1696 name: Mary King gender: Female baptism/christening date: 13 Jan 1696 baptism/christening place: GRENDON UNDERWOOD,BUCKINGHAM,ENGLAND father's name: Walter King mother's name: Elizabeth.

751. <i> - Oxfordshire Parish Registers</i>, Charlton on Otmoor - baptism; Date: 1694.

752. <i> - Oxfordshire Parish Registers</i>, Charlton on Otmoor - marriages; Date: 1719.

753. - Indexing Project - , M14535-1; film 1042379; Date: 1696.

754. - Indexing Project - , M02348-2; film: 919240, 919241 - marriage; Date: 1706 groom's name Thomas Rogers bride's name Mary Clarke marriage date 04 Aug 1706 marriage place GreMt issenden,Buckingham,England.

755. - Indexing Project - , C02348-1; film: 88593 - christening; Date: 1675 name Mary Clark gender Female baptism/christening date 10 Aug 1675 baptism/christening place GREAT MISSENDEN,BUCKINGHAM,ENGLAND father's name Edward Clark mother's name Katherin indexing project (batch) number C02348-1; f8m85:93.

756. - Indexing Project - , C02348-1; film:88593 - christening; Date: 1672 name Thomas Rogers gender Male baptism/christening date 06 Jan 1672 baptism/christening place GREAT MISSENDEN,BUCKINGHAM,ENGLAND father's name William Rogers mother's name Elizabeth indexing project (batch) number C02348film; :88593.

757. - Indexing Project - , Batch #:106977-8; Film #: 1967108 - birth of son; Date: 1716.

758. - Indexing Project - , I06977-8; film: 1967108; Date: 1709 groom's name Eduardus Grant bride's name Maria Haws marriage date 15 Jan 1709 marriage place Worminghall, BuckinghamE,ngland.

759. - Indexing Project - , I06977-8; film: 1967108 - birth; Date: 2 October 1690 name Maria Hawes gender Female birth date 02 Oct 1690 birthplace Worminghall, Buckingham, England father's name RodulphHi awes.

760. - Indexing Project - , Batch #:106977-8; Film #: 1967108 - birth; Date: 1718.

761. - Indexing Project - , Batch #:106977-8; Film #: 1967108 - birth; Date: 1724.

762. - Indexing Project - , Batch #:106977-8; Film #: 1967108 - birth; Date: 1727.

763. - Indexing Project - , I06977-8; film: 1967108 - marriage; Date: 1709 groom's name Eduardus Grant bride's name Maria Haws marriage date 15 Jan 1709 marriage place Worminghall, BuckinghamE,ngland.

764. - Indexing Project - , M00865-1; film: 882; Date: 27 April 1699 groom's name John Younge bride's name Martha Stevens marriage date 27 Apr 1699 marriage place Cookham,Berkshire,England indexing project M00865-1; film8:82.

765. - Indexing Project - , C01859-2film: 88197 - birth; Date: 1680 name Martha Steevens gender Female baptism/christening date 31 Dec 1680 baptism/christening place BRAY,BERKSHIRE,ENGLAND father's name Thomas Steevens mother's name Cath indexing project (batch) number C01859-2film8:8197.

766. - Indexing Project - , C07376-1; film: 919251 - christening; Date: 1679 name John Yong gender Male baptism/christening date 25 Jan 1679 baptism/christening place UPTON CUM CHALVEY,BUCKINGHAM,ENGLAND father's name John Yong mother's name Elizabeath indexing project (batch) number C07376-1; f9ml9.251.

767. - Indexing Project - , Batch number: C04514-1; film number: 856942; Date: 1699 name: Martha Bowles gender: Female baptism/christening date: 24 Sep 1699 baptism/christening place: FAIRFORD,GLOUCESTER,ENGLAND father's name: John Bowles mother's name: Martha.

768. - Phillimores Marriages , Gloucestershire; Vol 16; page 95 (Fairford); Date: 1722 William Rowland & Martha Bowls, both of F. 24 Dec 1722.

769. - Indexing Project - , Batch #:I04146-1; film #:1595986; Date: 1730 groom's

name: Willm. Watkins bride's name: Sarah Watkins marriage date: 07 Apr 1730 marriage place: Bristol, Gloucester, England.

770. England and Wales, Non-Conformist Record Indexes , RG4-8; Date: 1694.

771. - Indexing Project - , Batch: C01716-1; film:1596656; Date: 1717 name: Anne Parry gender: Female baptism/christening date: 22 Dec 1717 baptism/christening place: St. Philip and St. Jacob's, Bristol, Gloucester, England father's name: Wm. Parry.

772. - Indexing Project - , Batch #:I04146-2; film #:1595986; Date: 1736 groom's name: Martin Kelly bride's name: Ann Perry marriage date: 29 Jan 1736 marriage place: Bristol, Gloucester, England.

773. - Indexing Project - , Batch: I09520-2 film: 1597036, 1725; Date: 1725 record title: England Marriages, 1538-1973 groom's name: Dennis Rogers bride's name: Mary Brayne marriage date: 19 Nov 1725 marriage place: Bitton, Gloucester, England.

774. - Indexing Project - , Batch: I09520-2 film: 1597036; Date: 1725 record title: England Marriages, 1538-1973 groom's name: Dennis Rogers bride's name: Mary Brayne marriage date: 19 Nov 1725 marriage place: Bitton, Gloucester, England.

775. - Indexing Project - , Batch: I09520-2   ; film: 1597036; Date: 1734 record title: England Marriages, 1538-1973 groom's name: Will. Stone bride's name: Ann Palmer marriage date: 02 Feb 1734 marriage place: Bitton, Gloucester, England.

776. - Indexing Project - , Batch: I09520-2; film: 1597036; Date: 1734 record title: England Marriages, 1538-1973 groom's name: Will. Stone bride's name: Ann Palmer marriage date: 02 Feb 1734 marriage place: Bitton, Gloucester, England.

777. <i>Parish Records Collection - Marriage</i>, Spetisbury, Dorset; Date: 1733.

778. - Indexing Project - , C09915-1; film: 0593816 (RG4 338); Date: 1734.

779. - Indexing Project - , C08347-1; film: 0825377 (RG4 1830), 0825377 (RG4 3507); Date: 1736.

780. - Indexing Project - , Batch #:C17286-2; film #:1596531; Date: 1711 name: John Burges gender: Male baptism/christening date: 17 Apr 1711 baptism/christening place: St. Jame's, Bristol, Gloucester, England father's name: John Burges.

781. England and Wales, Non-Conformist Record Indexes , (RG4-8); record set: RG4_1830, 1738; Date: 1738 "name: Ebenezer Burgess event type: Baptism christening date: 06 Nov 1738 christening place: Bristol, Somerset father's name: John Burgess mother's name: Susanna Burgess.".

782. <i><i>England & Wales Christening Records, 1530-1906</i> Ancestry.com. England & Wales Christening Records, 1530-1906 [da, Batch: I04146-2; film: 1595986; Date: 1746 name: Diana Reynolds gender: Female baptism/christening date: 1746 baptism/christening place: Bristol, Gloucester, England father's name: George Reynolds mother's name: Ann.

783. - Indexing Project - , I04146-2; film 15995986; Date: 8 October 1738.

784. - Indexing Project - , I04146-2; film:1595986; Date: 1740.

785. - Indexing Project - , C00911-9; film: 1596310; Date: 5 January 1708.

786. <i>Parish Records Collection - Marriage</i>, Cublington, Buckinghamshire -film: 1042378 - marriage; Date: 1762.

787. - Indexing Project - , C14534-1; film: 1042378; Date: 1738.

788. - Indexing Project - , C07367-1; film: 919245; Date: 1735.

789. - Indexing Project - , c03553-1; film 826545; Date: 5 April 1761.
790. - Indexing Project - , C03553-1; film: 826545; Date: 17 October 1762.
791. - Indexing Project - , C03553-1; film: 826545; Date: 16 September 1764.
792. - Indexing Project - , C03553-1; film: 826545; Date: 6 July 1766.
793. - Indexing Project - , C03553-1; film: 826545; Date: 1733.
794. - Indexing Project - , C02171-9; film: 994331; Date: 1722.
795. - Indexing Project - , C02272-5; film: 375308; Date: 1722.
796. - Indexing Project - , M14754-2; film 1042454 - marriage; Date: 1760 groom's name: Grove Taylor bride's name: Sarah Smith marriage date: 04 Nov 1760 marriage place: Bromley,Kent,England.
797. - Indexing Project - , C01839-5; film:1042453 - baptism; Date: 1738 name: Sarah Smith gender: Female baptism/christening date: 06 Oct 1738 baptism/christening place: BROMLEY, KENT, ENGLAND father's name: StephSemnith.
798. - Indexing Project - , M14754-2; film: 1042454 - marriage; Date: 1760 groom's name: Grove Taylor bride's name: Sarah Smith marriage date: 04 Nov 1760 marriage place: Bromley,Kent,England.
799. - Indexing Project - , m06302-2; film 919627; Date: 4 August 1752.
800. - Indexing Project - , c06222-4; film 950452; Date: 21 October 1730.
801. Docklands Ancestors , ref: X024/123 - Baptism record; Date: 1763 25 December 1763 Baptism Forename: Elizabeth Othernames: Surname: Day Fathers forenames: Charles Fathers occupation: Smith Mothers forenames: Elizabeth Birth date: Address: Artichoke Hill.
802. Docklands Ancestors , X024/016 - Baptism record; Date: 1735 14 December 1735 Forename:Elizabeth Surname:Darby Fathers forenames:Nath Fathers occupation:Wea Mothers forenames:Rose Birth date: Parish:St Dunstan Church address:Stepney High Street Entry No:Source Ref:X024/016 Original Note:20 Days Old.
803. - Indexing Project - , I01289-1; film 814302; Date: 22 October 1752.
804. - Indexing Project - , C32049-7, film 1042307; Date: 6 January 1722.
805. London, England, Marriages & Banns, 1754-1921 , Greenwich, Register of marriages, P78/ALF, Item 03; Date: 1759.
806. <i>Parish Records Collection - Marriage</i>, Dorset Parish Registers; Reference: PE/LBY: RE3/1; Date: 14 July 1763.
807. <i>Parish Records Collection - Baptism</i>, Dorset Parish Registers; Reference: PE/TRF: RE1/1; Date: 17 October 1731.
808. <i>Parish Records Collection - Marriage</i>, Dorset Parish Registers; Reference: PE/WSM:RE1/3; Date: 30 June 1761.
809. <i>Parish Records Collection - Baptism</i>, Dorset Parish Registers; Reference: PE/WSM:RE1/1; Date: 17 October 1736.
810. England & Wales Marriages, 1538-1940 , Place: Cranborne, Dorset, England; Date Range: 1731 - 1778; Film Number: 1279494.
811. - Indexing Project - , Batch #: M15857-1; film #: 1279494; Date: 1757.
812. England & Wales Marriages, 1538-1940 , Place: Cranborne, Dorset, England; Date Range: 1731 - 1778; Film Number: 1279494; Date: 1757.

813. <i><i>England & Wales Christening Records, 1530-1906</i> Ancestry.com. England & Wales Christening Records, 1530-1906 [da, Compton-Abbas, Dorset, England; Collection: ; BTs; Date Range: 1731 - 1755; Film Number: 12.

814. - Indexing Project - , Batch #:M16006-2; Film #:1239253; Date: 13 November 1777 groom's name: John Matthews bride's name: Ann Hodder marriage date: 13 Nov 1777 marriage place: Whitchurch-Canonicorum, Dorset, England.

815. - Indexing Project - , M05053-1; film: 916843, 916844 - marriage; Date: 21 October 1782.

816. - Indexing Project - , C07415-1; film: 0590698 (RG4 2035), 0590698 (RG4 584); Date: 1786.

817. - Indexing Project - , C07415-1; film: 0590698 (RG4 2035), 0590698 (RG4 584); Date: 1787.

818. - Indexing Project - , C07415-1; film: 0590698 (RG4 2035), 0590698 (RG4 584); Date: 1789.

819. - Indexing Project - , C15902-1; film: 1279499; Date: 1749.

820. <i>Northamptonshire Marriages</i> Northamptonshire Family History Society, Paulerspury Marriage records; Date: 9 November 1740.

821. - Indexing Project - , C07468-1; film: 0825344 (RG4 2861), 0825344 (RG4 906); Date: 31 August 1750.

822. - Indexing Project - , Co7455-2; film: 0825339 (RG4 2179); Date: 23 July 1726 parents: Robert Coalman, Mary Coalman Name: Thomas Coalman Event Type: Baptism Christening Date:23 Jul 1726 Christening Place: Great Meeting- Independent, Kettering, Northamptonshire.

823. England and Wales, Non-Conformist Record Indexes , RG4-8, RG4_2179; Date: 23 July 1726.

824. - Indexing Project - , digital folder: 4290851; Date: 1703.

825. <i>Parish Records Collection - Marriage</i>, Tiffield, Northampton -; Date: 4 September 1735.

826. - Indexing Project - , C07281-1; film 991320 (bap of son); Date: 17 September 1732.

827. - Indexing Project - , M07363-1; film 990297; Date: 24 June 1728.

828. - Indexing Project - , I02206-7; film 1040731; Date: 14 September 1712.

829. England and Wales, Non-Conformist Record Indexes , RG4-8; RG6_1419; Date: 8 November 1710.

830. - Indexing Project - , C07210-1; film 991305 (bap fo daughter); Date: 14 February 1728.

831. - Indexing Project - , M04629-2; film 1040846 IT 9-11; Date: 22 July 1722.

832. - Indexing Project - , I02206-7; film 1040731; item 13; Date: 15 August 1697.

833. - Indexing Project - , C07210-1; film 991305; Date: March 1699.

834. Boyd's Marriage Index 1538-1840 , Great Warley, Essex; Date: 1738.

835. - Indexing Project - , I05606-8; film 1526973; item 17; Date: 16 April 1740.

836. - Indexing Project - , I05606-8; film 1526973; item 17; Date: 13 September 1744.

837. - Indexing Project - , I05606-8; film 1526973; item 17; Date: 13 February

1746.

838. - Indexing Project - , 1526973; folder 4298754; image 1923; Date: 3 December 1749.

839. - Indexing Project - , I05606-8; film 1526973; item 17; Date: 11 November 1753.

840. - Indexing Project - , I05606-8; film 1526973; item 17; Date: 14 June 1755.

841. Boyd's Marriage Index 1538-1840 , Warley Great, Essex; Date: 1738.

842. - Indexing Project - , I00531-1; film 1836274; id 5-10; Date: 14 August 1759.

843. - Indexing Project - , C00161-4; film 380143; Date: 9 May 1734.

844. - Indexing Project - , I01333-0; film 1751588; Item 1; Date: 2 March 1739.

845. - Indexing Project - , C13135-1; film 992517; Date: 19 February 1740.

846. - Indexing Project - , England and Wales, Non-Conformist Record Indexes (RG4-8); record set: RG7_022; Date: 1727 name: Richard Young event type: Marriage marriage date: 16 Aug 1727 marriage place: Fleet, London record set: RG7_022.

847. - Indexing Project - , Batch #: C00161-3; film #: 380143; Date: 1707 name: Richard Young gender: Male baptism/christening date: 09 Sep 1707 baptism/christening place: ST BOTOLPH BISHOPSGATE,LONDON,LONDON,ENGLAND father's name: William Young mother's name: Ann.

848. - Indexing Project - , I00531-1; film 1836274; id 5-10; Date: 1759.

849. England and Wales, Non-Conformist Record Indexes , RG4_4646; Date: 15 March 1724.

850. - Indexing Project - , C04916-1; film 942.1B4H V.45; Date: 16 April 1732.

851. - Indexing Project - , C04921-1; film 942.1 L1 B4H V.29; Date: 14 May 1702.

852. - Indexing Project - , batch M00145-7; film: 561155; Date: 1723.

853. - Indexing Project - , batch: C00145-4; film 560371; Date: 1696.

854. - Indexing Project - , I0111-2; film 1736585; Date: 1 June 1718.

855. - Indexing Project - , batch: C00145-7; film 561142; Date: 1741.

856. - Indexing Project - , batch: C00145-7; film 561142; Date: 1743.

857. - Indexing Project - , batch: C00145-7; film 561142; Date: 1745.

858. - Indexing Project - , batch: C00145-7; film 561142; Date: 1747.

859. - Indexing Project - , batch: C00145-7; film 561142; Date: 1748.

860. - Indexing Project - , batch: C00145-6; film: 560372; Date: 22 August 1716.

861. - Indexing Project - , Project: I03630-2; film 1041562; Date: 1749 name: Charles Stringer gender: Male baptism/christening date: 22 Oct 1749 baptism/christening place: Shipley, West Sussex, England father's name: William Stringer mother's name: Sarah Stringer.

862. - Indexing Project - , M07093-1; film 0918480; Date: 30 October 1748.

863. - Indexing Project - , c07006-1; film 0918264-5; Date: 19 February 1731.

864. - Indexing Project - , batch: I03632-6; film: 1041589; Date: 1726.

865. - Indexing Project - , M04337-1; film: 857071; Date: 2 May 1754.

866. - Indexing Project - , Batch 8826530, sheet 16; serial #: 00086; Date: 30 April 1727.

867. - Indexing Project - , C04337-1; film: 857071; Date: 1724.

868. - Indexing Project - , I01009-7; film:813833; p52; Date: 1745.
869. - Indexing Project - , batch: P00149-1; film: 845245; Date: 1722.
870. - Indexing Project - , batch: 05577-3; film 595419; Date: 1719.
871. - Indexing Project - , Batch: C02577-6; film #: 380207; Date: 1756
   name: Richard Hyde gender: Male baptism/christening date: 06 Jun 1756 baptism/christening
   place: ST GILES CRIPPLEGATE,LONDON,LONDON,ENGLAND father's name: John Hyde
   mother's name: Mary indexing project (batch) number: C02577-6 system origin: England-ODM
   source film number: 380207.
872. - Indexing Project - , batch: M03524-2; film:942 B4HA V. 47, 942 B4HA
   v.48; Date: 1754.
873. - Indexing Project - , batch: C02238-1; film: 374441, 374442; Date: 1737.
874. - Indexing Project - , P01266-1; film 0496823 IT 3; Date: 1750 name: Ann
   Raynbird gender: Female baptism/christening date: 13 Mar 1750 baptism/christening
   place: PAKENHAM,SUFFOLK,ENGLAND father's name: Thos. Raynbird mother's name: Mary
   indexing project (batch) number: P01266-1; film 0496823 IT3.
875. - Indexing Project - , i03847-1; film 989984 - 79-80 P265 r9; Date: 1735.
876. - Indexing Project - , c06274-1; film 952206; Date: 2 June 1714.
877. - Indexing Project - , i03847-1; film 989984 - 79-80 P417 P4; Date: 2
   February 1736.
878. - Indexing Project - , i03847-1; film 989984 - 79-80 P417 P2; Date: 29
   September 1736.
879. - Indexing Project - , i03847-2; film 989985 - 80 P417 R5.
880. - Indexing Project - , c03145-6; film 989608; Date: 16 June 1740.
881. - Indexing Project - , Batch P01266-1; Date: 1742.
882. - Indexing Project - , P01266-1; Date: 1744.
883. - Indexing Project - , P01266-1; Date: 1746.
884. - Indexing Project - , P01266-1; Date: 1748.
885. - Indexing Project - , P01266-1; film 0496823 IT 3; Date: 1750 name: Ann
   Raynbird gender: Female baptism/christening date: 13 Mar 1750 baptism/christening
   place: PAKENHAM,SUFFOLK,ENGLAND father's name: Thos. Raynbird mother's name: Mary
   indexing project (batch) number: P01266-1 system origin: England-ODM source film
   number: 0496823 IT.
886. - Indexing Project - , c06276-2; film 952204; Date: 9 August 1719.
887. - Indexing Project - , Batch#: M14005-5; film #: 813819; Date: 1731 groom's
   name: John Briggs bride's name: Jane Rice marriage date: 26 Mar 1731 marriage place: Fleet
   Prison And Rules Of The Fleet, London, England groom's marital status: Widowed bride's marital
   status: Widowed.
888. Boyd's Marriage Index 1538-1840 , WESTMINSTER (GROSVENOR
   CHAPEL, MAYFAIR), London; Date: 1731 Parish Record Collection - Marriage Record Print
   Close Year: 1731 Supplied Surname: RICE Surname: RICE Full First name: Jane Supplied First
   Name: Jane Spouse Surname: BRIGGS Spouse Full First name: John Spouse First Name: Jn
   Place: WESTMINSTER (GROSVENOR CHAPEL, MAYFAIR) County: London Record
   source: Boyd's Marriage Index 1538-1840.

889. <i>Parish Records Collection - Baptism</i>, St Dunstan, Stepney, London; Ref:X0241-066; Date: 1696 Transcription page details Day:24 Month:1 Year:1696 Forename:Jane Othernames: Surname:Rice Fathers forenames:Thomas Fathers occupation:Carpenter Mothers forenames:Martha Birth date: Address:Ratcliffe Location of church:Stepney Parish:St Dunstan Church address:High Street Entry No: Source Ref:X0241-066 Transcriber Note: Original Note:15 days old.

890. <i>Parish Records Collection - Marriage</i>, Boyd's marriage index 1538-1840; Date: 1731 Parish Record Collection - Marriage Record Print Close Year: 1731 Supplied Surname: RICE Surname: RICE Full First name: Jane Supplied First Name: Jane Spouse Surname: BRIGGS Spouse Full First name: John Spouse First Name: Jn Place: WESTMINSTER (GROSVENOR CHAPEL, MAYFAIR) County: London Record source: Boyd's Marriage Indle5x38-1840.

891. <i>Parish Records Collection - Baptism</i>, St Dunstan, Stepney, London; Ref:X0241-066; Date: 1682 Transcription page details Day:6 Month:11 Year:1682 Forename:John Othernames: Surname:Briggs Fathers forenames:John Fathers occupation:Framework Knitter Mothers forenames:Anne Birth date: Address:St. John Street Location of church:Stepney Parish:St Dunstan Church address:High Street Entry No: Source Ref:X0241-066 Transcriber Note: Original Note:1 day old.

892. - Indexing Project - , I01204-8; film 814115 - marriage; Date: 1749 groom's name: Willm. Tunbrell bride's name: Sarah Crew marriage date: 23 Jan 1749 marriage place: Westminster, Middlesex, England indexing project (batch) number: I01204-8 source film number: 814115.

893. - Indexing Project - , C00145-7; film 561142; Date: 1732 name: Sarah Crew gender: Female baptism/christening date: Apr 1732 baptism/christening place: SAINT MARTIN IN THE FIELDS,WESTMINSTER,LONDON,ENGLAND father's name: Hezekiah Crew mother's name: Anne.

894. - Indexing Project - , B00024-0; film #: 94713; Burial Date: 21 November 1788.

895. - Indexing Project - , Batch #:C02246-1; film #:374455; Date: 1752 name: William Timbrel gender: Male baptism/christening date: 10 April 1752 baptism/christening place: ST JOHN ZACHARY,LONDON,LONDON,ENGLAND father's name: William Timbrel mother's name: Sarah.

896. - Indexing Project - , Batch #:C13551-7; film #:1042308; Date: 1728 name: William Timbrel gender: Male baptism/christening date: 18 Nov 1728 baptism/christening place: St. James, Westminster, Middlesex, England father's name: William Timbrel mother's name: Mary.

897. England and Wales, Non-Conformist Record Indexes , RG4-8; record set: RG7_250; name: William Timbrel event type: Marriage marriage date: 23 Jan 1749 marriage place: Fleet, London.

898. Boyd's London Burials 1538-1872 , Bunhill Fields, London; Date: 1774.

899. - Indexing Project - , (batch) number:M16509-1; system origin:England-VR; source film number:1469265.

900. - Indexing Project - , C03656-1 system origin: England-ODM source film number: 355633.

901. - Indexing Project - , Batch: C02323-5; film: 37500; Date: 1737 name: John

Baldwin gender: Male baptism/christening date: 25 Apr 1737 baptism/christening place: ST SEPULCHRE,LONDON,LONDON,ENGLAND father's name: John Baldwin mother's name: Elizabeth.

902. - Indexing Project - , Batch: I02503-3; film 18866581; Date: 1734.

903. - Indexing Project - , C02323-3; film: 374999 - baptism; Date: 1704 name: Elizabeth Laurence gender: Female baptism/christening date: 23 Jul 1704 baptism/christening place: ST SEPULCHRE,LONDON,LONDON,ENGLAND father's name: Daniel Laurence mother's name: Elizabeth.

904. - Indexing Project - , Batch: C00161-3; film: 380143; Date: 1703.

905. - Indexing Project - , C02555-6; film: 370931 - (daughter's baptism record); Date: 1725.

906. - Indexing Project - , C02555-6; film: 370931 - (baptism); Date: 1726.

907. - Indexing Project - , C02555-6; film: 370931 - (baptism); Date: 1731.

908. - Indexing Project - , C00629-5; film 94692, 94693 - (son's baptism records); Date: 1740.

909. - Indexing Project - , C00145-5; film 560372 - Baptism record; Date: 1711 name: Mary Impy gender: Female baptism/christening date: 21 Feb 1711 baptism/christening place: SAINT MARTIN IN THE FIELDS,WESTMINSTER,LONDON,ENGLAND father's name: Elijah Impy mother'nsame: Mary.

910. - Indexing Project - , P01051-4; film 374353; Date: 1737.

911. - Indexing Project - , I03974; film 2214228 - baptism record; Date: 1710 name: Thomas Dixon gender: Male baptism/christening date: 20 Feb 1710 baptism/christening place: Edmonton, Middlesex, England father's name: Thomas Dixon mother's name. Elizabeth Dixon.

912. - Indexing Project - , I01009-7; film: 813833 - marriage record; Date: 1742 groom's name: Thos Miller bride's name: Margt Buxton marriage date: 18 Apr 1742 marriage place: Westminster, MiddlesexE,ngland.

913. - Indexing Project - , M02069-1; film: 585446, 585447, 585448 - Marriage; Date: 1763 groom's name: Henry Wine bride's name: Mary Smith marriage date: 03 Apr 1763 marriage place: Saint Luke OlSdtreet,Finsbury,London,England.

914. - Indexing Project - , C02530-1; film: 94692; Date: 1737 name: Henry Wine gender: Male baptism/christening date: 20 Nov 1737 baptism/christening place: ST MARY WHITECHAPEL,STEPNEY,LONDON,ENGLAND father's name: John Wine mother's name: Elizabeth.

915. <i>Gentleman's Magazine</i> Boyd's 1st Misc Series 1538-1775; Date: 1755.

916. London Metropolitian Archives - Register of Marriages , St Dunstan in the West, Register of baptisms, 1707 - 1739, P69/DUN2/A/009/MS010349; Date: 10 April 1724.

917. - Indexing Project - , M00143-1; film: 396189, 942 B4HA V. 69, 942 B4HA V. 84-85, 942 B4HA V. 86-87; Date: 23 June 1753.

918. - Indexing Project - , C06969-1; film: 592621; Date: 19 May 1735.

919. - Indexing Project - , C05577-4; film: 595419, 595420; Date: 10 December 1734.

920. - Indexing Project - , m00157-1; film 942 b4ha v.35; Date: 30 August 1758.

921. - Indexing Project - , c02550-1; film 94693; Date: 14 January 1761.

922. - Indexing Project - , c13552-2; film 1042308; Date: 15 January 1735.

923. London Metropolitian Archives - Register of Baptisms , Register of Baptisms, Saint Marylebone, baptisms Mar 1749 - Dec 1764, P89/MRY1, Item 004.; Date: 1756.

924. - Indexing Project - , M01902-1; source:942 B4HA V.15; Date: 1745 groom's name: Jeremiah Rapley bride's name: Mary Grayham marriage date: 20 Nov 1745 marriage place: Saint GeorgMe ayfair,Westminster,London,England.

925. - Indexing Project - , C14750-2; film 1042308; Date: 1723 name: Mary Graham gender: Female baptism/christening date: 28 Jul 1723 baptism/christening place: SAINT JAMES, WESTMINSTER, LONDON, ENGLAND father's name: John Graham mother's name: Mary.

926. - Indexing Project - , C03524-1; film: 580904, 580905; Date: 1748 name: Richard Rapley gender: Male baptism/christening date: 18 Dec 1748 baptism/christening place: SAINT MARY-ST MARYLEBONE ROAD,ST MARYLEBONE,LONDON,ENGLAND birth date: 27 Nov 1748 father's name: Jeremiah Rapley mothexdsne: Mary.

927. - Indexing Project - , C03524-1; film: 580904, 580905; Date: 1750 name: Charles Rapley gender: Male baptism/christening date: 15 Nov 1750 baptism/christening place: SAINT MARY-ST MARYLEBONE ROAD,ST MARYLEBONE,LONDON,ENGLAND birth date: 01 Nov 1750 father's name: Jeremiah Rapley mothexdsne: Mary.

928. - Indexing Project - , C03524-1; film: 580904, 580905; Date: 1752 name: Jeremiah Rapley gender: Male baptism/christening date: 19 Oct 1752 baptism/christening place: SAINT MARY-ST MARYLEBONE ROAD,ST MARYLEBONE,LONDON,ENGLAND birth date: 16 Oct 1752 father's name: Jeremiah Rapley mothexdsne: Mary.

929. - Indexing Project - , C03524-1; film: 580904, 580905; Date: 1754 name: Peter Rene Rapley gender: Male baptism/christening date: 09 Nov 1754 baptism/christening place: SAINT MARY-ST MARYLEBONE ROAD,ST MARYLEBONE,LONDON,ENGLAND birth date: 24 Oct 1754 father's name: Jeremiah Rapley mothexdsne: Mary.

930. - Indexing Project - , C03524-1; film: 580904, 580905; Date: 1758 name: Mary Rapley gender: Female baptism/christening date: 08 Dec 1758 baptism/christening place: SAINT MARY-ST MARYLEBONE ROAD,ST MARYLEBONE,LONDON,ENGLAND birth date: 10 Nov 1758 father's name: Jeremiah Rapley mothexdsne: Mary.

931. - Indexing Project - , C03524-1; film: 580904, 580905; Date: 1760 name: Ann Rebecca Rapley gender: Female baptism/christening date: 08 Apr 1760 baptism/christening place: SAINT MARY-ST MARYLEBONE ROAD,ST MARYLEBONE,LONDON,ENGLAND birth date: 03 Mar 1760 father's name: Jeremiah Rapley mothexdsne: Mary.

932. - Indexing Project - , M01902-1; source:942 B4HA V.15; Date: 1745.

933. Boyd's Marriage Index 1538-1840

934. - Indexing Project - , batch: C13553-4; Film: 1042308; Reference ID: 2:2JQZVLM; Date: 2 December 1759.

935. - Indexing Project - , batch: C13550-5; film 1042308; Ref ID - 2:2RLCBGM; Date: 1761.

936. - Indexing Project - , batch: C13550-7; film 1042308; Ref ID: 2:3T1CGT1; Date: 1762.

937. - Indexing Project - , batch: C13550-7; film: 1042308; ref ID:2:3T1DT5W; Date: 1764.

938. - Indexing Project - , batch: C13551-2; flim: 1042308; Ref ID: 2:3VTP9FL; Date: 1765.

939. England and Wales, Non-Conformist Record Indexes , RG4-8 - marriage record; Date: 1753 name: Benjamin Robert event type: Marriage birth date: birthplace: christening date: christening place: marriage date: 23 Nov 1753 marriage place: Fleet, London death date: death place: burial date: burial place: father's name: mother's name: record set: RG7_271.

940. - Indexing Project - , batch: P00149-1; film: 845245 - Christening; Date: 28 April 1734.

941. - Indexing Project - , P00140-1; film 845234 (son's baptism record); Date: 1750.

942. - Indexing Project - , I01046-3; film 814113 Marriage record; Date: 1749 groom's name: Samuell Mott bride's name: Mary Purviss marriage date: 12 Aug 1749 marriage place: Fleet Prison And Rules Of The Fleet, LondonE,ngland.

943. - Indexing Project - , P02209-1; film 0374416, 0374417 - baptism; Date: 1727 name: Mary Purvis gender: Female baptism/christening date: 05 Feb 1727 baptism/christening place: ST ANN BLACKFRIARS,LONDON,LONDON,ENGLAND father's name: Richd. Purvis mother's name: Margaret.

944. - Indexing Project - , I01046-3; film 814113 Marriage record; Date: 1749 spouse: Mary Purviss groom's name: Samuell Mott bride's name: Mary Purviss marriage date: 12 Aug 1749 marriage place: Fleet Prison And Rules Of The Fleet, LondonE,ngland.

945. - Indexing Project - , C01074-1; film: 374999 - baptism record; Date: 1726 name: Samuel Mott gender: Male baptism/christening date: 09 May 1726 baptism/christening place: St. Sepulchre, London, England birth date: 25 Apr 1726 father's name: Milford Mott mother's name: Elizabeth.

946. - Indexing Project - , P01749-1; film: 908518 - as shown on children's baptism record; Date: from 1735 to 1745.

947. - Indexing Project - , i03117-5; film 813825; ref 135-47; Date: 31 December 1734.

948. - Indexing Project - , P01749-1; film: 908518 - baptism record; Date: 1735.

949. - Indexing Project - , P01749-1; film: 908518 - baptism record; Date: 1736.

950. - Indexing Project - , P01749-1; film: 908518 - baptism record; Date: 1737.

951. - Indexing Project - , P01749-1; film: 908518 - baptism record; Date: 1739.

952. - Indexing Project - , P01749-1; film: 908518 - baptism record; Date: 1740.

953. - Indexing Project - , P01749-1; film: 908518 - baptism record; Date: 1741.

954. - Indexing Project - , P01749-1; film: 908518 - baptism record; Date: 1743.

955. - Indexing Project - , P01749-1; film: 908518 - baptism record; Date: 1744.

956. - Indexing Project - , C01062-8; film# :374999; ref: v3p 150; Date: 16 August 1707.

957. <i>Berkshire Parish Registers</i>, Sutton Courtney - marriage records; Date: 1700.

958. <i> - Oxfordshire Parish Registers</i>, Witney marriages; Date: 1689.

959. <i> - Oxfordshire Parish Registers</i>, Witney christening; Date: 1656.

960. <i> - Oxfordshire Parish Registers</i>, Shipton under Wytchwood - Christening; Date: 1680.
961. <i>Oxfordshire Family History Society, <i>Oxfordshire Marriages 1559-1837</i></i> </i>, indexed by Husband - F; Date: 1681.
962. <i> - Oxfordshire Parish Registers</i>, Bicester 1a BMD records - christening; Date: 1657.
963. <i>Oxfordshire Family History Society, <i>Oxford Marriage Index - 1538 to 1837</i></i> </i>, Indexed by husbands C; page 99; Date: 1654.
964. <i>Oxfordshire Family History Society, <i>Oxford Marriage Index - 1538 to 1837</i></i> </i>, Indexed by husbands V; page 5; Date: 1636.
965. <i> - Oxfordshire Parish Registers</i>, Wendlebury, BMD records - christening; Date: 1597.
966. <i> - Oxfordshire Parish Registers</i>, Bampton parish BMD records; Date: 1689.
967. <i> - Oxfordshire Parish Registers</i>, Bampton parish BMD - Baptism records; Date: 1667.
968. - Indexing Project - , M15779-1; Date: 1703.
969. - Indexing Project - , P01353-1; film 599897; Date: 1683.
970. Oxfordshire Family History Society, Witney Quakers records , Page 8; Date: 1708 Marriage: 1708 18 Jun HEYDON Richard maltster of Witney, s. William of Witney YOUNG Eleanor sp., Witney, d. Edward late of Milton.
971. - Indexing Project - , C06999-1; film: 919642, 919643 - christening of son; Date: 1695.
972. <i> - Oxfordshire Parish Registers</i>, Northmoor - christenings; Date: 1656.
973. <i> - Oxfordshire Parish Registers</i>, Northmoor - burials; Date: 1657.
974. <i> - Oxfordshire Parish Registers</i>, Northmoor - christenings; Date: 1659.
975. <i> - Oxfordshire Parish Registers</i>, Northmoor - christenings; Date: 1661.
976. <i> - Oxfordshire Parish Registers</i>, Northmoor - burials; Date: 1730.
977. <i> - Oxfordshire Parish Registers</i>, Northmoor - christenings; Date: 1663.
978. <i> - Oxfordshire Parish Registers</i>, Northmoor - christenings; Date: 1666.
979. <i> - Oxfordshire Parish Registers</i>, Northmoor - christenings; Date: 1668.
980. <i> - Oxfordshire Parish Registers</i>, Northmoor - christenings; Date: 1671.
981. <i> - Oxfordshire Parish Registers</i>, Northmoor - marriages; Date: 1700.
982. <i>Oxfordshire Family History Society, <i>Oxfordshire Marriages 1559-1837</i></i> </i>, index by husband - E; Date: 1688.
983. - Phillimores Marriages , Standlake, Oxfordshire; page:69; Date: 1646 Richardus Stone et Sibilla Green, de Longworth ... 28 Aug 1646.
984. England and Wales, Non-Conformist Record Indexes , record set: RG6_1220 - marriage of son; Date: 1705 name Richard Hartley event type Marriage marriage date 18 Apr 1705 marriage place   Banbury, Oxfordshire father's name   James Hartley recosedt RG6_1220.
985. - Indexing Project - , M02639-1; film:0990430 IT 2, 1696464 IT 4-5 - Marriage; Date: 2 March 1654.
986. - Indexing Project - , C02639-2; film: 942.57 B2 B4B V.9 - birth of son; Date: 1660.
987. <i> - Oxfordshire Parish Registers</i>, Steeple Aston - Baptism records; Date: 1628.
988. <i>Oxfordshire Family History Society, <i>Oxford Marriage Index - 1538 to 1837</i></i> </i>, Indexed by husbands - G; page 44; Date: 1654.
989. <i> - Oxfordshire Parish Registers</i>, Adderbury 1 BMD - christening; Date: 1646.

990. <i> - Oxfordshire Parish Registers</i>, Adderbury - marriage; Date: 1670.

991. <i> - Oxfordshire Parish Registers</i>, Adderbury 1 BMD - christening; Date: 1641.

992. <i> - Oxfordshire Parish Registers</i>, Adderbury - christening; Date: 1632.

993. <i> - Oxfordshire Parish Registers</i>, Southleigh - Marriages; Date: 1700.

994. <i> - Oxfordshire Parish Registers</i>, Southleigh - christening; Date: 1703.

995. <i> - Oxfordshire Parish Registers</i>, Southleigh - christening; Date: 1708.

996. <i> - Oxfordshire Parish Registers</i>, Southleigh - christening; Date: 1710.

997. - Phillimores Marriages , Chipping Norton, Oxfordshire, England; Date: 1686.

998. <i> - Oxfordshire Parish Registers</i>, Standlake BMD records - Christening; Date: 1687.

999. <i> - Oxfordshire Parish Registers</i>, Standlake BMD records - Christening; Date: 1664.

1000. <i> - Oxfordshire Parish Registers</i>, Standlake BMD records - Christening; Date: 1694.

1001. <i> - Oxfordshire Parish Registers</i>, Standlake BMD records - Christening; Date: 1698.

1002. <i> - Oxfordshire Parish Registers</i>, Standlake BMD records - Christening; Date: 1700.

1003. <i> - Oxfordshire Parish Registers</i>, Standlake BMD records - Christening; Date: 1701.

1004. - Indexing Project - , M13278-3; film 1279460; Date: 1679 groom's name: Thomas Clarke bride's name: Mary Knapp marriage date: 05 Jun 1679 marriage place: North Hinksey, Berkshire, England.

1005. - Indexing Project - , C04109-1; film: 88231 - baptism; Date: 1660.

1006. <i> - Oxfordshire Parish Registers</i>, Witney - marriages; Date: 1689.

1007. <i> - Oxfordshire Parish Registers</i>, Witney - christenings; Date: 1689.

1008. - Indexing Project - , P01048-1; Film #: 88176.

1009. <i>Oxfordshire Family History Society, <i>Oxford Marriage Index - 1538 to 1837</i></i> </i>, indexed by husbands - B; page 61; Date: 1685.

1010. <i> - Oxfordshire Parish Registers</i>, Lewknor, baptism; Date: 1691.

1011. <i> - Oxfordshire Parish Registers</i>, Lewknor, baptism; Date: 1694.

1012. <i> - Oxfordshire Parish Registers</i>, Lewknor, baptism; Date: 1698.

1013. - Indexing Project - , number: C07380-1 system origin: England-ODM source film number: 919260.

1014. - Indexing Project - , indexing project (batch) number: C07380-1 system origin: England-ODM source film number: 91.

1015. Bisham & Upton Parish Register ; Date: 1659 William son of William Salter Bapt: 31 Jul 1659.

1016. <i> - Oxfordshire Parish Registers</i>, Oxford marriage records; Date: 1698.

1017. <i> - Oxfordshire Parish Registers</i>, Oxford marriages; Date: 1698.

1018. <i> - Oxfordshire Parish Registers</i>, St John, Oxford - marriage; Date: 1697.

1019. #81, 1677 Dec 26. Richard s of Phillip & Mary.

1020. <i> - Oxfordshire Parish Registers</i>, Standlake, Oxfordshire, England - Burial register: 1745, Oct 1. Richard Allen.

1021. #81, Marriages - 1702 may 25. Allen, Richard & Bullock, Elizabeth.

1022. #81, 1698 birth:2 Sep Chr: 26 Sep 1698 Susannah d of Simon Hart.

1023. #81, Standlake burials - parish reg - 5 nov 1716 - wife of Richard ALLEN.

1024. #81, Standlake burials - ALLEN, wife of Richard.

1025. <i>Oxfordshire Archdeacon's Marriage Bond Index 1634-1849</i>, Alphabetized by Groom's names. 1716 Allen, Ricd Standlake widr Hart, Susannah Standlake.

1026. <i> - Oxfordshire Parish Registers</i>, Charlton on Otmoor - marriages; Date: 1691.

1027. <i> - Oxfordshire Parish Registers</i>, Charlton on Otmoor - baptism; Date: 1655.

1028. - Indexing Project - , M14535-1; film 1042379; Date: 1665.

1029. - Indexing Project - , Batch number: C04403-1, source film number: 88596; Date: 1644 name: Henry Clark gender: Male baptism/christening date: 20 Feb 1644 baptism/christening place: WADDESDON,BUCKINGHAM,ENGLAND father's name: Ralph Clarke.

1030. - Indexing Project - , C02348-1; film:88593 - christening of son; Date: 1672.

1031. - Indexing Project - , C02348-1; film: 88593 - christening of daughter; Date: 1675.

1032. - Indexing Project - , C02348-1; film: 88593 - christening; Date: 1645 name Katherine Wright gender Female baptism/christening date 10 Aug 1645 baptism/christening place GREAT MISSENDEN,BUCKINGHAM,ENGLAND father's name George Wright mother's name   Jane.

1033. - Indexing Project - , C02348-1; film: 88593 - christening; Date: 1649 name Edward Clarke gender Male baptism/christening date 09 Aug 1649 baptism/christening place   GREAT MISSENDEN,BUCKINGHAM,ENGLAND indexing project (batch) number   C02348-1; film8:8593.

1034. - Indexing Project - , I06977-8; film: 1967108; Date: 1685.

1035. - Indexing Project - , I06977-8; film: 1967108; Date: 1688.

1036. - Indexing Project - , I06977-8; film: 1697108 - daughter's birth; Date: 1690 name Maria Hawes gender Female birth date 02 Oct 1690 birthplace Worminghall, Buckingham, England father's name   RodulphHi awes.

1037. - Indexing Project - , C07376-1; film: 919251 - christening; Date: 1672.

1038. - Indexing Project - , C07376-1; film: 919251 - christening; Date: 1673.

1039. - Indexing Project - , C07376-1; film: 919251 - christening; Date: 1675.

1040. - Indexing Project - , C07376-1; film: 919251 - christening; Date: 1677.

1041. - Indexing Project - , C01859-2film: 88197 - daughter's christening; Date: 1680.

1042. - Indexing Project - , M01859-2; film: 881; Date: 1672 groom's name Thomas Steeuens bride's name   Katrigne Spott marriage date   19 Sep 1672 marriage place   Bray,Berkshire,England indexing project (batch) number   M01859-2; fi881.

1043. - Indexing Project - , C01859-2film: 88197; Date: 1673.

1044. - Indexing Project - , C01859-2film: 88197; Date: 1685.

1045. - Indexing Project - , C01859-2film: 88197; Date: 1688.

1046. - Indexing Project - , M01859-2; film: 881; Date: 1672 groom's name Thomas Steeuens bride's name   Katrigne Spott marriage date   19 Sep 1672 marriage place   Bray,Berkshire,England.

1047. - Indexing Project - , Batch number: C04514-1; film number: 856942; Date: 1670 name: John Bowles gender: Male baptism/christening date: 05 Feb 1670 baptism/christening place: FAIRFORD,GLOUCESTER,ENGLAND father's name: Thomas Bowles mother's name: Mary.

1048. - Indexing Project - , M17287-1; film: 1596655; Date: 1691.

1049. England and Wales, Non-Conformist Record Indexes , RG6-1650; Date: 1691.

1050. England and Wales, Non-Conformist Record Indexes , RG6-1440; Date: 1696.

1051. - Indexing Project - , Batch: C03917-1; film: 1849446; Date: 1658 name: Samuell Rogers gender: Male baptism/christening date: 05 Sep 1658 baptism/christening place: St. Michael, Bristol, England father's name: Thomas Rogers mother's name: Susana.

1052. - Indexing Project - , Batch: C01721-6; film: 1596655; Date: 1672 name: Thomas Reynold gender: Male baptism/christening date: 31 Mar 1672 baptism/christening place: St. Philip and St. Jacob's, Bristol, Gloucester, England father's name: Edward Reynold.

1053. - Indexing Project - , C07367-1; film: 919245; Date: 1701.

1054. - Indexing Project - , P01710-1; film: 97133; Date: 1700.

1055. - Indexing Project - , M07335-2; film: 1469264 - marriage; Date: 1728 groom's name: Stephen Smith bride's name: Elizabeth Hills marriage date: 1728 marriage place: Kingsdown Near Sevenoaks, KentE,ngland.

1056. - Indexing Project - , C13101-1; film 992461 - baptism; Date: 1710 name: Eliz. Hill gender: Female birth date: 01 Jul 1710 birthplace: DITTON,KENT,ENGLAND father's name: William Hill mother'nsame: Eliz.

1057. - Indexing Project - , C01839-5; film:1042453 - baptism; Date: 1738.

1058. - Indexing Project - , m06302-2; film 919627; Date: 21 October 1730.

1059. <i>Parish Records Collection - Marriage</i>, Dorset Parish Registers; Reference: PE/WSM:RE1/1; Date: 15 July 1732.

1060. <i>Parish Records Collection - Baptism</i>, Dorset Parish Registers; Reference: PE/WSM:RE1/1; Date: 22 August 1708.

1061. <i>Parish Records Collection - Baptism</i>, Dorset Parish Registers; Reference: PE/WSM:RE1/1; Date: 14 May 1733.

1062. <i>Parish Records Collection - Baptism</i>, Dorset Parish Registers; Reference: PE/WSM:RE1/1; Date: 12 March 1737.

1063. <i><i>England & Wales Christening Records, 1530-1906</i> Ancestry.com. England & Wales Christening Records, 1530-1906 [da, Place: Compton-Abbas, Dorset, England; Collection: ; BTs; Date Range: 1731 - 1755; Film Num; Date: 1735.

1064. - Indexing Project - , Christening - project: C14127-2; Date: 1720.

1065. - Indexing Project - , C15902-1; film: 1279499 - christening of son; Date: 1749.

1066. - Indexing Project - , C15902-1; film: 1279499; Date: 1747.

1067. - Indexing Project - , C07455-2: film 0825339 (RG4 2179; Date: 23 July 1726 Baptism of son parents: Robert Coalman, Mary Coalman Name: Thomas Coalman Event Type: Baptism Christening Date:23 Jul 1726 Christening Place: Great Meeting- Independent, Kettering, Northamptonshire.

1068. - Indexing Project - , C07455-2; film 0825339 (RG4 2179); Date: 18 August 1729.

1069. England and Wales, Non-Conformist Record Indexes , RG4-8, RG4_2179; Date: 18 August 1729.

1070. - Indexing Project - , RG4_2179; Date: 18 October 1732 parents:Robert

Coalman, Mary Coalman NameJohn Coalman Event TypeBaptism Christening Date18 Oct 1732 Christening PlaceKettering, Northamptonshire Father's NameRobert Coalman Mother's NameMary Coalman Affiliate Publication NumberRG4_2179.

1071. England and Wales, Non-Conformist Record Indexes , RG4-8, RG4_2179; Date: 18 October 1732.

1072. - Indexing Project - , RG4_2179; Date: 8 September 1735.

1073. England and Wales, Non-Conformist Record Indexes , RG4-8, RG4_2179; Date: 8 September 1735.

1074. - Indexing Project - , C07455-2; film: 0825339 (RG4 2179); Date: 23 July 1726 Baptism of son - Thomas parents: Robert Coalman, Mary Coalman Name: Thomas Coalman Event Type: Baptism Christening Date:23 Jul 1726 Christening Place: Great Meeting-Independent, Kettering, Northamptonshire.

1075. - Indexing Project - , Marriage - digital folder 4290851; Date: 1697.

1076. - Indexing Project - , Christening - C14880-2; film: 1657254; Date: 1667.

1077. - Indexing Project - , Burial - digital folder 4290851; Date: 1725.

1078. WILL , Unproved father's will in possession of Morris Ashby, Bugbrooke; Date: 1728.

1079. - Indexing Project - , I01773-7; film 828175; ref 828175; Date: 21 October 1709.

1080. - Indexing Project - , I02207-1; film 1040731; Date: 13 January 1707.

1081. - Indexing Project - , M13824-1; film 0990399 IT 2; Date: 1 April 1678.

1082. - Indexing Project - , C07210-1; film 991305 (bap of son); Date: March 1699.

1083. - Indexing Project - , M07277-6; film 569753; id: 2:3X7FQZB; Date: 1680.

1084. - Indexing Project - , I02206-7; film 1040731; item 13 (bap of daughter); Date: 15 August 1697.

1085. - Indexing Project - , C07277-2; film 1040655; ref 2:2Z0WR3C; Date: 5 November 1658.

1086. - Indexing Project - , I04159-4; film 1736927; item 4; Date: 12 October 1706.

1087. - Indexing Project - , I04159-4; film 1736927; item 4; Date: 10 May 1682.

1088. FamilySearch Extraction Program - BIRTH , "Ancestral File," database, FamilySearch: /MM9.2.1/MZ95-CL6; Date: 10 December 1708.

1089. - Indexing Project - , C04921-1; film 942.1L1B4HV.29; Date: 1702.

1090. - Indexing Project - , C04921-1; film 942.1L1B4HV.29; Date: 26 October 1694.

1091. - Indexing Project - , C04921-1; film 942.1L1B4HV.29; Date: 24 November 1695.

1092. - Indexing Project - , I04009-4; film 1482448; id 75; Date: 17 November 1698.

1093. - Indexing Project - , C04921-1; film 942.1L1B4HV.29; Date: 14 May 1702.

1094. - Indexing Project - , batch: C00145-6; film: 560372; Date: 1716.

1095. - Indexing Project - , m07006-1; film 0918264-65; Date: 3 December 1730.

1096. - Indexing Project - , c07111-1; film 0416749; Date: 11 December 1695.

1097. - Indexing Project - , batch: I02570-2; film: 815482; Ref ID yr 1706-1728 p26; Date: 1719.

1098. - Indexing Project - , batch: C00161-2; film: 380142; Date: 1692.

1099. Boyd's Marriage Index 1538-1840 , Record collection: Marriages & divorces; Date: 1717 First name(s)   John Last name   Maier Birth year   - Marriage year   1717 Spouse's first name(s)   Jn Spouse's full first name(s)   John Spouse's last name   MAIER Supplied first name(s)   An Supplied last name JONES Place   STEPNEY (ST DUNSTAN) County   London Country   England Record set   Boyd's Marriage Index 1538-1840 Category   Birth, Marriage, Death & Parish Records Record collection   Marriages & divorces Collections from   GrBeartitain.

1100. - Indexing Project - , C05577-4; film 595419; Date: 25 October 1726.

1101. Boyd's Marriage Index 1538-1840 , Record collection: Marriages & divorces; Date: 1717 Boyd's Marriage Index 1538-1840 Transcription First name(s)   John Last name   Maier Birth year   - Marriage year   1717 Spouse's first name(s)   Jn Spouse's full first name(s)   John Spouse's last name   MAIER Supplied first name(s)   An Supplied last name   JONES Place   STEPNEY (ST DUNSTAN) County   London Country   England Record set   Boyd's Marriage Index 1538-1840 Category   Birth, Marriage, Death & Parish Records Record collection   Marriages & divorces Collections from   GreaBtritain.

1102. - Indexing Project - , batch: C02238; film: 374441, 374442; Date: 1737.

1103. - Indexing Project - , batch: C02238; film: 374441, 374442; Date: 1735.

1104. - Indexing Project - , batch: M05576-3; film:578821, 596921, 596922, 597247; Date: 1733.

1105. - Indexing Project - , c06276-2; film 952204; Date: 10 March 1699.

1106. - Indexing Project - , batch M06297-1; film 952218; Date: 1718.

1107. - Indexing Project - , batch: c06276-2; film: 952204; Date: 1699.

1108. - Indexing Project - , m06274-1; film 952206; Date: 6 May 1713.

1109. - Indexing Project - , m06274-1; film 952206; Date: 1713.

1110. - Indexing Project - , p01266-1; film 0496823 IT 3; Date: 20 March 1692.

1111. - Indexing Project - , c06274-1; film 952206; Date: 1 April 1690.

1112. - Indexing Project - , P00161-1; film#: 942.1 L1 V26BOT V1-3; name: John Briggs gender: Male baptism/christening date: 20 Apr 1656 baptism/christening place: SAINT BOTOLPH BISHOPSGATE,LONDON,LONDON,ENGLAND father's name: Richard Briggs mother's name: Marie indexing project (batch) number: P00161-1 system origin: England-ODM source film number: 942.1 L1 V26BOTV1-3.

1113. <i>Parish Records Collection - Baptism</i>, St Dunstan, Stepney, London; Ref:X0241-066; Date: 1696.

1114. - Indexing Project - , Batch #:C13551-7; film #:1042308; Date: 1728.

1115. - Indexing Project - , M00145-7; film 561155 - marriage; Date: 1723 groom's name: Hezekiah Crew bride's name: Anne Caplinn marriage date: 15 Apr 1723 marriage place: Saint Martin In The Fields,Westminster,London,England.

1116. - Indexing Project - , C00145-4; film: 560371 - baptism; Date: 1700 name: Anne Capling gender: Female baptism/christening date: 01 Nov 1700 baptism/christening place: SAINT MARTIN IN THE FIELDS,WESTMINSTER,LONDON,ENGLAND birth date: 01 Nov 1700 father's name: David Capling mother'nsame: Mary.

1117. London, England. Westminster Burials- Transcripts , St James, Piccadilly; Date: 23 December 1788.

1118. - Indexing Project - , B03493-1; film#: 1042314; Date: 27 January 1773.

1119. - Indexing Project - , M13135-1; system origin: England-ODM; source film number: 992517.

1120. IGI , Film 0992517; ELIZABETH FOREMAN; Female; Spouse: EDWARD GYLES; Marriage: 03 OCT 1695 Hadlow, Kent, England; Batch No.: M131351 Dates: 1558 - 1753 Source Call No.: 0992517 Type: Film Printout Call No.: NONE Type: Sheet:.

1121. IGI , Film 0992517; EDWARD GYLES; Male; Spouse: ELIZABETH FOREMAN; Marriage: 03 OCT 1695 Hadlow, Kent, England; Batch No.: M131351 Dates: 1558 - 1753 Source Call No.: 0992517 Type: Film Printout Call No.: NONE Type: Sheet:.

1122. - Indexing Project - , :M02063-6; source film number:1736878.

1123. - Indexing Project - , I04799-7 system origin: England; source film number: 1736836.

1124. - Indexing Project - , C02161-5 system origin: England- source film number: 1751813.

1125. - Indexing Project - , C02323-3; film: 374999 - (daughter's baptism record); Date: 1704.

1126. - Indexing Project - , Batch: C00145-4; Film number 560371 (baptism of son); Date: 1690.

1127. - Indexing Project - , I03974; film 2214228 - baptism record; Date: 1710.

1128. - Indexing Project - , I03974; film 2214228 - (son's baptism record); Date: 1710.

1129. - Indexing Project - , C00145-5; film 560372 - (on son's Baptism record); Date: 1711.

1130. - Indexing Project - , I03117-8; film: 813830 - marriage; Date: 1736 groom's name: John Wine bride's name: Eliz. Hill marriage date: 02 Dec 1736 marriage place: Westminster, Middlesex, England.

1131. London Metropolitian Archives - Register of Baptisms , St Dunstan in the West, Register of baptisms, 1707 - 1739, P69/DUN2/A/009/MS010349; Date: 10 April 1724.

1132. - Indexing Project - , M00144-2; film: 374459, 374460; Date: 30 May 1734.

1133. - Indexing Project - , C14750-2; film 1042308; Date: 1723.

1134. - Indexing Project - , I02941-0; film 814094 - marriage; Date: 1718 groom's name: John Graham bride's name: Mary Partridge marriage date: 22 Jun 1718 marriage place: Westminster, MiddlesexE,ngland.

1135. - Indexing Project - , P00156-1; film: 845228 -baptism; Date: 1699 name: Mary Partridge gender: Female baptism/christening date: 06 Sep 1699 baptism/christening place: SAINT PETER CORNHILL,LONDON,LONDON,ENGLAND father's name: Richard Partridge mother's name: Alice.

1136. - Indexing Project - , I02941-0; film 814094; Date: 1718 groom's name: John Graham bride's name: Mary Partridge marriage date: 22 Jun 1718 marriage place: Westminster, Middlesex, England.

1137. - Indexing Project - , P00157-1; film: 845241 - baptism; Date: 1700 name: John Graham gender: Male baptism/christening date: 13 Sep 1700 baptism/christening place: SAINT PAUL COVENT GARDEN,WESTMINSTER,LONDON,ENGLAND father's name: Robert Graham mother'nsame: Barbara.

1138. - Indexing Project - , batch: M14005-4; film 813818; ref ID 1728-1743; Date: 5 October 1733.

1139. - Indexing Project - , P00140-1; film 845234; Date: 1750.

1140. - Indexing Project - , M06236-5; film: 918609 - marriage; Date: 1718 groom's name: Milford Mott bride's name: Eliza. Hubbard marriage date: 05 Aug 1718 marriage place: Saint AnnSeoho,Westminster,London,England.

1141. - Indexing Project - , C02555-4; film: 370929, 370930 - baptism record; Date: 1680 name: Millford Mott gender: Male baptism/christening date: Mar 1680 baptism/christening place: ST BOTOLPH WITHOUT ALDGATE,LONDON,LONDON,ENGLAND father's name: John Mott mother'nsame: Katherin.

1142. - Indexing Project - , P02209-1; film 0374416, 0374417 - daughter's baptism record; Date: 1727.

1143. - Indexing Project - , C01062-8; film# :374999; ref: v3p 150; Son's birth and baptism Date: 16 August 1707.

1144. - Indexing Project - , (Batch) Number: C02198-1 System Origin: England-ODM Source Film Number: 88469.

1145. <i>Berkshire Parish Registers</i>, Wantage SS Peter & Paul (Christening); Date: 10 October 1631.

1146. <i> - Oxfordshire Parish Registers</i>, Northmoor marriages; Date: 1671.

1147. <i> - Oxfordshire Parish Registers</i>, Northmoor burials; Date: 1700.

1148. <i> - Oxfordshire Parish Registers</i>, Woodstock baptisms; Date: 1676.

1149. <i> - Oxfordshire Parish Registers</i>, Witney christening; Date: 1659.

1150. <i> - Oxfordshire Parish Registers</i>, Witney christening; Date: 1661.

1151. <i> - Oxfordshire Parish Registers</i>, Witney christening; Date: 1667.

1152. <i> - Oxfordshire Parish Registers</i>, Witney christening; Date: 1672.

1153. <i> - Oxfordshire Parish Registers</i>, Bicester 1a BMD records - burial; Date: 1708.

1154. <i>Oxfordshire Family History Society, <i>Oxford Marriage Index - 1538 to 1837</i></i> </i>, Indexed by husbands C; page 99; Date: 1620.

1155. <i> - Oxfordshire Parish Registers</i>, Upper Heyford BMD records - burial; Date: 1649.

1156. <i>Oxfordshire Family History Society, <i>Oxfordshire Marriages 1559-1837</i></i> </i>, indexed by Husband - H; Date: 1632.

1157. <i>Oxfordshire Family History Society, <i>Oxfordshire Marriages 1559-1837</i></i> </i>, index by husband - W; Date: 1613.

1158. <i> - Oxfordshire Parish Registers</i>, Bampton parish BMD records; Date: 1704.

1159. <i> - Oxfordshire Parish Registers</i>, Bampton parish BMD records; Date: 1669.

1160. <i> - Oxfordshire Parish Registers</i>, Bampton parish BMD records; Date: 1674.

1161. <i> - Oxfordshire Parish Registers</i>, Bampton parish BMD records; Date: 1676.

1162. <i> - Oxfordshire Parish Registers</i>, Bampton parish BMD records; Date: 1667.

1163. - Indexing Project - , M02213-2; film 88414; Date: 1681.

1164. - Indexing Project - , C02213-2; film 88414; Date: 1656.

1165. <i>Berkshire Parish Registers</i>, Stanford in the Vale - Marriages; Date: 1681.
1166. <i> - Oxfordshire Parish Registers</i>, Northmoor - burials; Date: 1658.
1167. <i> - Oxfordshire Parish Registers</i>, Northmoor - burials; Date: 1672.
1168. <i> - Oxfordshire Parish Registers</i>, Northmoor - burials; Date: 1668.
1169. <i> - Oxfordshire Parish Registers</i>, Northmoor - burials; Date: 1677.
1170. <i> - Oxfordshire Parish Registers</i>, Northmoor - burials; Date: 1659.
1171. <i> - Oxfordshire Parish Registers</i>, Standlake - baptisms; Date: 1626.
1172. <i> - Oxfordshire Parish Registers</i>, Hinton Waldrist (Berks) - christening; Date: 1602.
1173. <i> - Oxfordshire Parish Registers</i>, Adderbury - marriages; Date: 1622.
1174. <i> - Oxfordshire Parish Registers</i>, Adderbury - christening; Date: 1623.
1175. <i> - Oxfordshire Parish Registers</i>, Adderbury - christening; Date: 1624.
1176. <i> - Oxfordshire Parish Registers</i>, Adderbury - christening; Date: 1627.
1177. <i> - Oxfordshire Parish Registers</i>, Adderbury - christening; Date: 1630.
1178. <i> - Oxfordshire Parish Registers</i>, Adderbury - christening; Date: 1634.
1179. <i> - Oxfordshire Parish Registers</i>, Adderbury - marriage; Date: 1622.
1180. <i> - Oxfordshire Parish Registers</i>, Adderbury - christening; Date: 1641.
1181. <i> - Oxfordshire Parish Registers</i>, Adderbury - christening; Date: 1644.
1182. <i> - Oxfordshire Parish Registers</i>, Adderbury - christening; Date: 1649.
1183. <i> - Oxfordshire Parish Registers</i>, Adderbury - christening; Date: 1651.
1184. <i> - Oxfordshire Parish Registers</i>, Adderbury - burial; Date: 1700.
1185. <i> - Oxfordshire Parish Registers</i>, Adderbury - christening; Date: 1654.
1186. <i> - Oxfordshire Parish Registers</i>, Adderbury - christening; Date: 1659.
1187. <i> - Oxfordshire Parish Registers</i>, Adderbury 1 BMD - christening; Date: 1613.
1188. <i> - Oxfordshire Parish Registers</i>, Southleigh - christening; Date: 1661.
1189. <i> - Oxfordshire Parish Registers</i>, Southleigh - christening; Date: 1669.
1190. <i> - Oxfordshire Parish Registers</i>, Southleigh - christening; Date: 1672.
1191. <i> - Oxfordshire Parish Registers</i>, Southleigh - christening; Date: 1674.
1192. <i>Oxfordshire Family History Society, <i>Oxford Marriage Index - 1538 to 1837</i></i> </i>, Indexed by husbands - B; page 90; Date: 1628.
1193. - Indexing Project - , C03831-2; film 887477; Date: 1629.
1194. - Indexing Project - , C03831-2; film 887477; Date: 1631.
1195. - Indexing Project - , C03831-2; film 887477; Date: 1633.
1196. - Indexing Project - , C03831-2; film 887477; Date: 1635.
1197. - Indexing Project - , C03831-2; film 887477; Date: 1638.
1198. <i> - Oxfordshire Parish Registers</i>, Charlton on Otmoor BMD records - marriage; Date: 1667.
1199. <i> - Oxfordshire Parish Registers</i>, Charlton on Otmoor BMD records - christening; Date: 1642.
1200. <i> - Oxfordshire Parish Registers</i>, Charlton on Otmoor - baptism; Date: 1657.
1201. <i> - Oxfordshire Parish Registers</i>, Charlton on Otmoor - baptism; Date: 1658.
1202. <i> - Oxfordshire Parish Registers</i>, Charlton on Otmoor - baptism; Date: 1661.
1203. <i> - Oxfordshire Parish Registers</i>, Charlton on Otmoor - baptism; Date: 1626.
1204. - Indexing Project - , C04403-1; film 88596; Date: 1644.

1205. - Indexing Project - , C02348-1; film: 88593 - christening of daughter; Date: 1645.

1206. - Indexing Project - , Batch number: C04514-1; film number: 865942; Date: 1643 name: Thomas Bowles gender: Male baptism/christening date: 13 Aug 1643 baptism/christening place: FAIRFORD,GLOUCESTER,ENGLAND father's name: Thomas Bowles mother's name: Ann.

1207. <i>Wiltshire, England Parish Records</i>, Wanborough marriages; Date: 1665.

1208. <i>Wiltshire, England Parish Records</i>; Date: 1666.

1209. <i>Wiltshire, England Parish Records</i>, Wanborough; Date: 1667.

1210. <i>Wiltshire, England Parish Records</i>, Wanborough; Date: 1673.

1211. <i>Wiltshire, England Parish Records</i>, Wanborough; Date: 1677.

1212. <i>Wiltshire, England Parish Records</i>, Wanborough; Date: 1680.

1213. <i>Wiltshire, England Parish Records</i>, Wanborough; Date: 1681.

1214. <i>Wiltshire, England Parish Records</i>, Wanborough; Date: 1635.

1215. - Indexing Project - , C13101-1; film: 992461; Date: 1710 name: Eliz. Hill gender: Female birth date: 01 Jul 1710 birthplace: DITTON,KENT,ENGLAND father's name: William Hill mother'nsame: Eliz.

1216. <i>Parish Records Collection - Marriage</i>, Dorset Parish Registers; Reference: PE/WSM:RE1/1; Date: 1 July 1701.

1217. Society of Friends (Quakers) records , Death register; Date: 1728.

1218. Settlement by deed ; Date: 6 March 1713.

1219. WILL , Unproved will in possession of Morris Ashby, Bugbrooke; Date: 1724.

1220. - Indexing Project - , P00161-1; film#: 942.1 L1 V26BOT V1-3; Date: 1656 name: John Briggs gender: Male baptism/christening date: 20 Apr 1656 baptism/christening place: SAINT BOTOLPH BISHOPSGATE,LONDON,LONDON,ENGLAND father's name: Richard Briggs mother's name: Marie indexing project (batch) number: P00161-1 system origin: England-ODM source film number: 942.1 L1 V26BOVT1-3.

1221. - Indexing Project - , C00145-4; film: 560371; Date: 1700 name: Anne Capling gender: Female baptism/christening date: 01 Nov 1700 baptism/christening place: SAINT MARTIN IN THE FIELDS,WESTMINSTER,LONDON,ENGLAND birth date: 01 Nov 1700 father's name: David Capling mother'nsame: Mary.

1222. Kent Parish Records , Hadlow BMD 1558-1752; image 24; Date: 1632.

1223. Kent Parish Records , Kent, Brenchley; 1538-1911 (copy list p77); Date: C - 1618.

1224. - Indexing Project - , (batch) number: I04803-9; source film number: 1736588.

1225. - Indexing Project - , I00356-3 system origin: England-source film number: 1850994.

1226. - Indexing Project - , I04762-7 system origin: England-source film number: 1737008.

1227. - Indexing Project - , C02161-5 system origin: England-EASy source film number: 1751813.

1228. - Indexing Project - , I00358-1 system origin: England-ODM source film number: 1866544.

1229. - Indexing Project - , I06879-3 system origin: England-EASy source film number: 1736631.

1230. - Indexing Project - , P00157-1; film: 845241 - baptism; Date: 1700.

1231. - Indexing Project - , P00157-1; film: 845241 - baptism; Date: 1695 name: William Graham gender: Male baptism/christening date: 31 Jul 1695 baptism/christening place: SAINT PAUL COVENT GARDEN,WESTMINSTER,LONDON,ENGLAND father's name: Robert Graham mother'nsame: Barbara.

1232. - Indexing Project - , P00157-1; film: 845241 - baptism; Date: 1697 name: Richard Graham gender: Male baptism/christening date: 27 Nov 1697 baptism/christening place: SAINT PAUL COVENT GARDEN,WESTMINSTER,LONDON,ENGLAND father's name: Robert Graham mother'nsame: Barbara.

1233. - Indexing Project - , P00157-1; film: 845241 - baptism; Date: 1699 name: Mary Graham gender: Female baptism/christening date: 04 Jul 1699 baptism/christening place: SAINT PAUL COVENT GARDEN,WESTMINSTER,LONDON,ENGLAND father's name: Robert Graham mother'nsame: Barbara.

1234. - Indexing Project - , P00157-1; film: 845241 - baptism; Date: 1702 name: James Graham gender: Male baptism/christening date: 27 Jun 1702 baptism/christening place: SAINT PAUL COVENT GARDEN,WESTMINSTER,LONDON,ENGLAND father's name: Robert Graham mother'nsame: Barbara.

1235. - Indexing Project - , P00156-1; film: 845228 - Daughter's baptism; Date: 1699.

1236. - Indexing Project - , M00156-1; film: 374996, 942 B4HA V. 1, 942 B4HA V. 4 - Marriage; Date: 1690 groom's name: Richard Partridge bride's name: Alice Longmore marriage date: 10 Jun 1690 marriage place: Saint PeCteormhill,London,London,Englan.

1237. - Indexing Project - , P00154-1; film:845229 - baptism; Date: 1666 name: Alice Langmore gender: Female baptism/christening date: 23 Mar 1666 baptism/christening place: ST MICHAEL CORNHILL,LONDON,LONDON,ENGLAND father's name: William Langmore mother's name: Alice.

1238. - Indexing Project - , C02243-7; film: 380201, 380202 - baptism; Date: 1668 name: Richard Partridge gender: Male baptism/christening date: 26 Apr 1668 baptism/christening place: ST GILES CRIPPLEGATE,LONDON,LONDON,ENGLAND father's name: Rich. Partridge mother's name: Margt.

1239. - Indexing Project - , M00080-2; film: 380123 - marriage; Date: 1679 groom's name: John Mott bride's name: Katherine Collins marriage date: 09 Oct 1679 marriage place: St. Botolph Aldgate, London, England groom's marital status: Single bride's marital status: Single.

1240. - Indexing Project - , Number: C02198-1 System Origin: England-ODM Source Film Number: 88469.

1241. - Indexing Project - , C01751-2 system origin: England-ODM source film number: 88257.

1242. <i>Berkshire Parish Registers</i>, St. Augustine, East Hendred (Christening); Date: 3 October

1605.

1243. <i>Berkshire Parish Registers</i>, Wantage SS Peter & Paul (Christening); Date: 10 June 1633.

1244. <i>Berkshire Parish Registers</i>, Wantage SS Peter & Paul (Christening); Date: 26 April 1635.

1245. <i>Berkshire Parish Registers</i>, Wantage SS Peter & Paul (Christening); Date: 3 June 1638.

1246. <i>Berkshire Parish Registers</i>, Wantage SS Peter & Paul (Christening); Date: 15 April 1599.

1247. <i>Oxfordshire Family History Society, <i>Oxford Marriage Index - 1538 to 1837</i></i> </i>, Indexed by wife E; page 38; Date: 1567.

1248. <i> - Oxfordshire Parish Registers</i>, Upper Heyford BMD records - baptism; Date: 1568.

1249. <i> - Oxfordshire Parish Registers</i>, Upper Heyford BMD records - baptism; Date: 1573.

1250. <i> - Oxfordshire Parish Registers</i>, Upper Heyford BMD records - baptism; Date: 1575.

1251. <i> - Oxfordshire Parish Registers</i>, Upper Heyford BMD records - baptism; Date: 1577.

1252. <i>Oxfordshire Family History Society, <i>Oxfordshire Marriages 1559-1837</i></i> </i>, indexed by Husband - H; Date: 1604.

1253. <i> - Oxfordshire Parish Registers</i>, Upper Heyford BMD records - burial; Date: 1667.

1254. <i>Oxfordshire Family History Society, <i>Oxford Marriage Index - 1538 to 1837</i></i> </i>, indexed by Husband - H; Date: 1604.

1255. <i> - Oxfordshire Parish Registers</i>, Upper Heyford BMD records - Baptism; Date: 1577.

1256. <i> - Oxfordshire Parish Registers</i>, Upper Heyford BMD records - burial; Date: 1627.

1257. - Indexing Project - , M02213-2; film 88414; Date: 1640.

1258. - Indexing Project - , P01353-1; film 599897; Date: 1615.

1259. - Indexing Project - , C02213-2; film 88414; Date: 1618.

1260. <i>Berkshire Parish Registers</i>, Stanford in the Vale, Marriages; Date: 1640.

1261. <i>Berkshire Parish Registers</i>, Stanford in the Vale - Christenings; Date: 1618 William Alder sonn of Thomas Alder and Elizabeth his wife was baptised in Stanford the first of July.

1262. <i>Berkshire Parish Registers</i>

1263. <i>Berkshire Parish Registers</i>, Hinton Waldrist, - christenings; Date: 1604.

1264. <i>Berkshire Parish Registers</i>, Hinton Waldrist, Burials; Date: 12 November 1607.

1265. <i>Berkshire Parish Registers</i>, Hinton Waldrist - christenings; Date: 1608.

1266. <i>Berkshire Parish Registers</i>, Hinton Waldrist, Burials; Date: 17 June 1613.

1267. <i>Berkshire Parish Registers</i>, Hinton Waldrist, Burials; Date: 24 May 1613.

1268. <i> - Oxfordshire Parish Registers</i>, Adderbury - christening; Date: 1599.

1269. <i> - Oxfordshire Parish Registers</i>, Adderbury - marriages; Date: 1598.

1270. <i> - Oxfordshire Parish Registers</i>, Adderbury - burial; Date: 1649.

1271. <i> - Oxfordshire Parish Registers</i>, Adderbury - burial; Date: 1609.

1272. <i> - Oxfordshire Parish Registers</i>, Adderbury 1 BMD - christening; Date: 1648.

1273. <i> - Oxfordshire Parish Registers</i>, Adderbury - burial; Date: 1648.

1274. <i> - Oxfordshire Parish Registers</i>, Adderbury - marriages; Date: 1603.

1275. <i> - Oxfordshire Parish Registers</i>, Adderbury - burial; Date: 1613.

1276. <i> - Oxfordshire Parish Registers</i>, Adderbury - marriage; Date: 1612.

1277. <i> - Oxfordshire Parish Registers</i>, Adderbury - burial; Date: 1612.

1278. <i> - Oxfordshire Parish Registers</i>, Adderbury - marriages; Date: 1612.

1279. <i> - Oxfordshire Parish Registers</i>, Adderbury - burials; Date: 1602.

1280. <i> - Oxfordshire Parish Registers</i>, Adderbury - marriage; Date: 1607.

1281. <i> - Oxfordshire Parish Registers</i>, Adderbury - christening; Date: 1607.

1282. <i> - Oxfordshire Parish Registers</i>, Adderbury - christening; Date: 1609.

1283. <i> - Oxfordshire Parish Registers</i>, Adderbury - christening; Date: 1620.

1284. <i> - Oxfordshire Parish Registers</i>, Adderbury - christening; Date: 1628.

1285. - Indexing Project - , batch number:I04452-1, system origin:England, source film number:1999444.

1286. - Indexing Project - , C03831-2; film 887477; Date: 1605.

1287. <i> - Oxfordshire Parish Registers</i>, Charlton on Otmoor BMD records - marriage; Date: 1638.

1288. <i> - Oxfordshire Parish Registers</i>, Charlton on Otmoor BMD records - christening; Date: 1641.

1289. <i> - Oxfordshire Parish Registers</i>, Charlton on Otmoor BMD records - christening; Date: 1613.

1290. <i> - Oxfordshire Parish Registers</i>, Ambrosden BMD records - christening; Date: 1616.

1291. <i> - Oxfordshire Parish Registers</i>, Charlton on Otmoor - marriage; Date: 1619.

1292. <i> - Oxfordshire Parish Registers</i>, Charlton on Otmoor - baptism; Date: 1621.

1293. <i> - Oxfordshire Parish Registers</i>, Charlton on Otmoor - baptism; Date: 1622.

1294. <i> - Oxfordshire Parish Registers</i>, Charlton on Otmoor - baptism; Date: 1625.

1295. <i> - Oxfordshire Parish Registers</i>, Charlton on Otmoor - baptism; Date: 1628.

1296. <i> - Oxfordshire Parish Registers</i>, Charlton on Otmoor - burials; Date: 1629.

1297. <i> - Oxfordshire Parish Registers</i>, Charlton on Otmoor - baptism; Date: 1630.

1298. <i> - Oxfordshire Parish Registers</i>, Charlton on Otmoor - baptism; Date: 1569.

1299. <i> - Oxfordshire Parish Registers</i>, Charlton on Otmoor - burials; Date: 1633.

1300. - Indexing Project - , Batch number: C04403-1, source film number: 88596; Date: 8 July 1621.

1301. - Indexing Project - , Batch number: C04403-1, source film number: 88596.

1302. - Indexing Project - , M04403-1; film 88596; Date: 1621.

1303. - Phillimores Marriages , Gloucestershire; Vol 16; page 89; Date: 1626 Thomas Bowles & Ann Mowsdale 30 July 1626.

1304. - Phillimores Marriages , Gloucestershire; Vol 16; page 89 (Fairford); Date: 1626 Thomas Bowles & Ann Mowsdale 30 July 1626.

1305. "England Marriages, 15381973 ," database, FamilySearch (https://familysearch.org/pal:/MM9.1.1/NLSW-6YV : accessed 2 A

1306. "England Births and Christenings, 1538-1975," database, FamilySearch (https://familysearch.org/pal:/MM9.1.1/NPRM-D3D : ac

1307. "England Births and Christenings, 1538-1975," database, FamilySearch (https://familysearch.org/pal:/MM9.1.1/NPRM-5JR : ac

1308. "England Births and Christenings, 1538-1975," database, FamilySearch (https://familysearch.org/pal:/MM9.1.1/NBM7-R2T : ac

1309. "England Births and Christenings, 1538-1975," database, FamilySearch (https://familysearch.org/pal:/MM9.1.1/JMLR-J5N : ac

1310. <i>Wiltshire, England Parish Records</i>, Wanborough marriage records; Date: 1624.

1311. <i>Wiltshire, England Parish Records</i>, Wanborough.

1312. <i>Wiltshire, England Parish Records</i>, Wanborough; Date: 1626.

1313. <i>Wiltshire, England Parish Records</i>, Wanborough; Date: 1629.

1314. <i>Wiltshire, England Parish Records</i>; Date: 1601.

1315. <i>Wiltshire, England Parish Records</i>, Wanborough; Date: 1591.

1316. - Indexing Project - , Batch #:M02747-2; film #:417142; Date: 1621 groom's name: Thomas Rogers bride's name: Anne Finche marriage date: 02 Apr 1621 marriage place: Cirencester,Gloucester,England.

1317. - Indexing Project - , Batch #:C05487-1; film #:856971; Date: 1602 name: Thomas Rogers gender: Male baptism/christening date: 27 Jun 1602 baptism/christening place: TEWKESBURY,GLOUCESTER,ENGLAND father's name: Thomas Rogers.

1318. Settlement by deed , In possession of Morris Ashby, Bugbrooke, N'ton, England; Date: 29 September 1682.

1319. Society of Friends (Quakers) records , Friends' Death Registers; Date: 1689.

1320. Kent Parish Records , Kent, Brenchley; 1538-1911 (copy list p53); Date: M - 1600.

1321. Kent Parish Records , Kent, Brenchley; 1538-1911 (copy list p54); Date: C - 1601.

1322. Kent Parish Records , Kent, Brenchley; 1538-1911 (copy list p55); Date: C - 1602.

1323. Kent Parish Records , Kent, Brenchley; 1538-1911 (copy list p57); Date: C - 1603.

1324. Kent Parish Records , Kent, Brenchley; 1538-1911 (copy list p61); Date: C - 1605.

1325. Kent Parish Records , Kent, Brenchley; 1538-1911 (copy list); Date: C - 1608.

1326. Kent Parish Records , Kent, Brenchley; 1538-1911 (copy list p68); Date: C - 1611.

1327. Kent Parish Records , Kent, Brenchley; 1538-1911 (copy list p71); Date: C - 1611.

1328. Kent Parish Records , Kent, Brenchley; 1538-1911 (copy list p19); Date: C - 1573.

1329. - Indexing Project - , Kent, Hadlow; index: C13135-1; film: 992517; Date: 1637.

1330. - Indexing Project - , Kent Cranbrook; index: C03077-0; film: 2228373; Date: 1588.

1331. - Indexing Project - , I03618-0 system origin: England- source film number: 1751478.

1332. - Indexing Project - , I00388-3 system origin: England-ODM source film number: 1866580.

1333. - Indexing Project - , C02243-7; film: 380201, 380202 - Son's baptism record; Date: 1668.

1334. - Indexing Project - , C05840-2; film: 374989 - baptism; Date: 1650 name: Richard Partridge gender: Male baptism/christening date: 20 Oct 1650 baptism/christening

place: SAINT MILDRED POULTRY WITH SAINT MARY
COLECHURCH,LONDON,LONDON,ENGLAND father's name: JohnPartridge.

1335. - Indexing Project - , P00154-1; film:845229 - (daughter's baptism); Date: 1669.

1336. - Indexing Project - , P00142-1; film: 845235 - baptism; Date: 1664 name: William Langmere gender: Male baptism/christening date: 05 Jun 1664 baptism/christening place: SAINT HELEN BISHOPSGATE,LONDON,LONDON,ENGLAND father's name: William Langmere mother's name: Alse.

1337. - Indexing Project - , P00154-1; film:845229 - (daughter's baptism); Date: 1666.

1338. <i>Berkshire Parish Registers</i>, Berkshire: - Register of Marriages, 1538-1837; Date: 9 May 1591.

1339. - Indexing Project - , (M02198-1 system origin: England-ODM source film number: 88468.

1340. <i>Berkshire Parish Registers</i>, Wantage St Mary (Burial); Date: 19 March 1635.

1341. - Indexing Project - , C02198-1 system origin: England-ODM source film number: 88469.

1342. <i>Berkshire Parish Registers</i>, Wantage SS Peter & Paul (Christening); Date: 14 August 1592.

1343. <i>Berkshire Parish Registers</i>, Wantage SS Peter & Paul (Christening); Date: 14 February 1594.

1344. <i>Berkshire Parish Registers</i>, Wantage SS Peter & Paul (Christening); Date: 22 August 1602.

1345. <i>Berkshire Parish Registers</i>, Wantage SS Peter & Paul (Christening); Date: 13 November 1608.

1346. <i>Parish Records Collection - Marriage</i>, Wantage, Berkshire, England; Date: 1591.

1347. <i>Berkshire Parish Registers</i>, Wantage SS Peter & Paul (Christening); Date: 17 February 1570.

1348. <i>Berkshire Parish Registers</i>, St. Augustine, East Hendred (Christening); Date: 10 June 1591.

1349. <i>Berkshire Parish Registers</i>, St. Augustine, East Hendred (Christening); Date: 27 February 1593.

1350. <i>Berkshire Parish Registers</i>, St. Augustine, East Hendred (Christening); Date: 10 August 1596.

1351. <i>Berkshire Parish Registers</i>, St. Augustine, East Hendred (Christening); Date: 15 August 1599.

1352. <i>Oxfordshire Family History Society, <i>Oxford Marriage Index - 1538 to 1837</i></i> </i>, Indexed by husbands E; page 38; Date: 1544.

1353. <i> - Oxfordshire Parish Registers</i>, Lower Heyford, BMD records - christening; Date: 1548.

1354. <i>Oxfordshire Family History Society, <i>Oxfordshire Marriages 1559-1837</i></i> </i>, indexed by Husband - H; Date: 1556.

1355. <i> - Oxfordshire Parish Registers</i>, Upper Heyford BMD records - burial; Date: 1615.

1356. <i> - Oxfordshire Parish Registers</i>, Upper Heyford BMD records - baptism; Date: 1571.

1357. *- Oxfordshire Parish Registers*, Upper Heyford BMD records - Burial; Date: 1571.

1358. *- Oxfordshire Parish Registers*, Upper Heyford BMD records; Date: 1573.

1359. *- Oxfordshire Parish Registers*, Upper Heyford BMD records; Date: 1576.

1360. *- Oxfordshire Parish Registers*, Upper Heyford BMD records; Date: 1580.

1361. *- Oxfordshire Parish Registers*, Upper Heyford BMD records - burial; Date: 1631.

1362. *- Oxfordshire Parish Registers*, Upper Heyford BMD records; Date: 1582.

1363. *- Oxfordshire Parish Registers*, Upper Heyford BMD records; Date: 1586.

1364. *<i>Berkshire Marriages - 2nd Edition* (Berkshire Family History Society)* (Berkshire Family History Society)*, Stanford in the Vale - Marriages; Date: 1617.

1365. *Berkshire Parish Registers*, Stanford in the Vale - baptism; Date: 1591.

1366. *Berkshire Parish Registers*, Stanford in the Vale - Marriages; Date: 1617.

1367. *<i> - Indexing Project - </i>* *, 02213-2; film 88414; Date: 1620.

1368. *<i> - Indexing Project - </i>* *, C02213-2; film88414; Date: 1620.

1369. *<i>Berkshire Marriages - 2nd Edition* (Berkshire Family History Society)* (Berkshire Family History Society)*, BMv2 GroomsByName; page: 3768; Date: 1582 Husband: OXLAD(E), John Wife: PLOMBRIGE, Elizabeth 25 June 1582 Reading - St Giles.

1370. *<i> - Indexing Project - </i>* *, C03831-2; film 887477; Date: 1557.

1371. *- Oxfordshire Parish Registers*, Crowell, burials; Date: 1611.

1372. *- Oxfordshire Parish Registers*, Charlton on Otmoor BMD records - marriage; Date: 1604.

1373. *- Oxfordshire Parish Registers*, Charlton on Otmoor BMD records - christening; Date: 1605.

1374. *- Oxfordshire Parish Registers*, Charlton on Otmoor BMD records - christening; Date: 1607.

1375. *- Oxfordshire Parish Registers*, Charlton on Otmoor BMD records - christening; Date: 1610.

1376. *- Oxfordshire Parish Registers*, Charlton on Otmoor BMD records - christening; Date: 1617.

1377. *- Oxfordshire Parish Registers*, Charlton on Otmoor BMD records - christening; Date: 1620.

1378. *- Oxfordshire Parish Registers*, Charlton on Otmoor BMD records - christening; Date: 1622.

1379. *- Oxfordshire Parish Registers*, Charlton on Otmoor BMD records - christening; Date: 1625.

1380. *- Oxfordshire Parish Registers*, Ambrosden BMD records - christening; Date: 1618.

1381. *- Oxfordshire Parish Registers*, Ambrosden BMD records - marriages; Date: 1611.

1382. *- Oxfordshire Parish Registers*, Charlton on Otmoor - marriage; Date: 1594.

1383. *- Oxfordshire Parish Registers*, Charlton on Otmoor - marriage; Date: 1621.

1384. *- Oxfordshire Parish Registers*, Charlton on Otmoor - baptism; Date: 1606.

1385. *- Oxfordshire Parish Registers*, Charlton on Otmoor - burials; Date: 1634.

1386. *- Oxfordshire Parish Registers*, Oxfordshire Family History Society parish transcripts.

1387. *Wiltshire, England Parish Records*; Date: 1589.

1388. *Wiltshire, England Parish Records*; Date: 1592.

1389. <i>Wiltshire, England Parish Records</i>, Wanborough marriages; Date: 1609.
1390. <i>Wiltshire, England Parish Records</i>; Date: 1596.
1391. <i>Wiltshire, England Parish Records</i>, Wanborough (as father); Date: 1589.
1392. WILL , of of Robert Ashby (father); Date: 13 October 1602.
1393. Public Records Office - London, England , Chancery Bills and Answers
    Miscellaneous. Series 1 part 33; Date: 12 June 1621 To the Kings most Excellent Maiestie in
    highnes Court of Chancery. 12th June 1621 In all humble manner complayninge sheweth unto
    your moste Excellent Maiestie your Highnes faithful and subiecte John Ashby of Bugbrooke in
    your highnes County of Northampton Yeoman. That whereas Robert Ashby late of Bugbrooke
    aforesaid deceased and father to your subiecte was in his lyftyme lawfully possessed for div se
    (divers) yeares of and in one messuage and close and one yardeland and a quarterne in Bugbrooke
    with the appurtenance. The said Robert Ashby your subiects father being soe possessed, did in his
    lyfetyme and aboute the fourth yeare of the reigne of our late Sowiange Lady Queene Elizabeth of
    famous memory for a valuable consideration in money purchase to him and his heaires for en
    (ever) of Thomas Pagitt late of the Middle Temple London Esqre deceased and Gregory Isham
    Esqre or one of them, the said messuage, close, one yarland and a quarterne and the appurtenance,
    and was therof in his lyfetyme lawfully seized in his demesne as of fee and did as well before his
    said purchase by virtue of his said lease or tearme as afterwards by virtue of his said purchase
    dureinge his lyfetyeme peaceably holde and enjoye the same withoute any manner of disturbance
    or interrupcon of any pson or psons of which said yardlande and a quarterne one acre of pasture
    grounde conteyninge by estimacion halfe an acre or thereabouts and lyinge under a certain place
    there called the Downes in the field of Bugbrooke aforesaid ys and allwaies (tyme out of memory
    of man) hath been pcell (parcel) and accompted soe to be and was and hath been enjoyed as well
    by your subiects said father in his lyfetyme as divse (divers) other psons whoe have been farmours
    and tenants of the said yardlande and a quarterne as pcell of the same. And your subiects said
    father being so seized dyed lawfully seized and interested of and in the same after whose decease
    the same messuage close yardlande and a quartenre did as of right the same ought to do discende
    and come onto your subjiecte as sonne and heire to the said Robert his father whereupon your
    subjiecte ymmediately after the death of the said Robert his father entered into and upon all and
    singular the said premises and was therefore lawfully seized in his demesne as of fee and the rents
    yssues and pffits of the same pmisses did receive pceave and take to his own use as lawfull ytt
    was for him to doe. And your subjiecte ought in all law and equity to enjoye the said pcell of
    pasture ground being pte of the saide yardeland and a quarterne. But now soe ytt is, may itt please
    your moste excellent maiestie that Richard Wallop of Bugbrooke aforesaid Esq Thomas Steere
    and William Cowp (Cowper) Thomas Symonds Richard Johnson als Jackson and Thomas Ashby
    or some of them having purchased divse pcells of lande lyinge aboute and nere adioyninge unto
    the said pcell of pasture ground conteyninge the said halfe acre and they or some of them
    haveinge gotten into their hands and custodies all your subiects evidences and writings
    concerninge the said lande and divse ancient Terrards and deeds whereby ytt would appear and be
    manifest that the said halfe acre of meadowe lyeinge under the Downes is pcell of the said
    yardeland and a quarterne and purchased by your subiectes said father and discended unto your
    said subiecte as aforesaid and that by reason thereof your said subiecte is truly intituled unto the
    same doe sometymes give out in speeches and ptend that the said pcell of grounde is pte of the

demesnes or waste grounde of the Manor of Bugbrooke aforesaid. And sometymes doe lykewyse give oute in speeches that ytt is pcell of theire or some of theire sevall (several) freeholds and sometymes that the same is towne grounde and to that purpose they the saide Richard Wallopp Thomas Steere William Cowp Thomas Symonds Richard Johnson als Jackson and Thomas Ashby combyneigne and confederateinge together how to deprive your subiecte of the saide pcell of lande have made or some of them hath made some secret estate or estates unto the saide Thomas Steere and the said Thomas Steere by color thereof hath entered into and upon the same and the said Steere by the combynacon and confederacy aforesaid hath brought an action of trespass and lictment or some other action att the common lawe against your subiecte endeavoureinge thereby your subiecte being altogether deprived of his evidence and such ancient deeds terrars and writings as manifest your subiects title to the same and the same beinge remayninge and come to the hands of the said Steere and the rest of the confederates presently to pcede to a triall against your suiecte at lawe upon the same and thereby to putt your subiecte oute of possession of the said pcell of grounde contrary to all equite and good conscience. In tender consideracon whereof and for that your subiecte doth not knowe the certeine dates and contents of the charters evidences terras and writings aforesaide nor any other neither doth he knowe whether they are in bage or boxxe sealed or in chest locked whereby he is withoute all remedy at the Common Lawes of this realme for the same and alsoe without all other means to finde relief in this behalfe except by course in equity by obteyneinge he evidences and writings aforesaid. May it therefore please your moste excellent Maiestie the pmisses considered to grant unto your saide subiecte your highnes' gracious writ of subpoena to them the said Richard Wallop Thomas Steere Willm Cowp Thomas Symonds Richard Johnson als Jackson and Thomas Ashby and ewry (every) of them to be directed commandeinge them thereby att a certaine daye and onder a certaine peine thereon to be lymitted not only to be and psonally to appeare before your Maiestie in your highnes' saide Court of Chancery then and there to answer the pmisses oppon theire corporall oaths and plainly and truly to showe forth there estate in and to the said pcell of pasture grounde and likewise to shewe what right and tytle they or any of them have or claime in and to the same and lykwyse to pduce and sett forthe what charters evidences and writings aforesaid they or any of them have concerneinge the same pcell of ground and wch may manifest your subiects title to the same, but also to grante unto your said subiecte his Maiesties gracious letters of Injunction for staye of the said acion at lawe against your subiecte and further that they may all answere the premisses and stand to and abide such further order and direccon therein as to your highness shall seem fitt to stand with equity and good conscience. And your saide subiecte shall as in all duty bound dayly pray for your Maistie in all healthe and happiness long to reigne on us. Richard Lane (Richard Lane is the name of the barrister by whom the bill was drawn up. All Chancery Bills required counsel's signature. The reference to the bill at the Public Record Office is "Chancery Bills and Answers Miscellaneous. Series 1 part 33.").

1394. - Indexing Project - , (batch) number:I07575-7; source film number:1736692.
1395. - Indexing Project - , M01471-4 system origin: England- source film number: 1751865.
1396. - Indexing Project - , C01966-7 system origin: source film number: 1751865.
1397. - Indexing Project - , I00358-2 system origin: England-source film number: 1866545.

1398. - Indexing Project - , C05840-2; film: 374989 - (son's baptism); Date: 1650.

1399. <i>Berkshire Parish Registers</i>, Berkshire: - Register of Marriages, 1538-1837; Date: 12 October 1554.

1400. - Indexing Project - , (Batch) Number: C02198-1; System Origin: England-OD; Source film #: 88469.

1401. <i>Berkshire Parish Registers</i>, Wantage Parish Records (Christening); Date: 1 January 1558.

1402. <i>Berkshire Parish Registers</i>, Wantage parish records (christening); Date: 19 January 1567.

1403. <i>Berkshire Parish Registers</i>, Wantage Parish records (christening); Date: 1 November 1568.

1404. - Indexing Project - , (Batch) Number: C02198-1; System Origin: England-ODM; Source Film #: 88469.

1405. <i>Berkshire Parish Registers</i>, Wantage SS Peter & Paul (Marriage); Date: 12 October 1554.

1406. <i>Berkshire Parish Registers</i>, Wantage Parish (Marriage); Date: 22 October 1580.

1407. <i>Berkshire Parish Registers</i>, Stanford in the Vale - Baptism; Date: 1591.

1408. <i>Berkshire Parish Registers</i>, Stanford in the Vale - Marriages; Date: 1577.

1409. <i> - Oxfordshire Parish Registers</i>, Aston Rowant church marriage records; Date: 1557 or 1558.

1410. <i> - Oxfordshire Parish Registers</i>, Aston Rowant - burials; Date: 1603.

1411. <i> - Oxfordshire Parish Registers</i>, Aston Rowant - baptisms; Date: 1554.

1412. <i> - Oxfordshire Parish Registers</i>, Aston Rowant - burials; Date: 1571.

1413. <i> - Oxfordshire Parish Registers</i>, Charlton on Otmoor BMD records - marriage; Date: 1599.

1414. <i> - Oxfordshire Parish Registers</i>, Charlton on Otmoor - burials; Date: 1595.

1415. <i> - Oxfordshire Parish Registers</i>, Charlton on Otmoor - burials; Date: 1576.

1416. <i> - Oxfordshire Parish Registers</i>, Charlton on Otmoor - burials; Date: 1609.

1417. <i> - Oxfordshire Parish Registers</i>, Charlton on Otmoor - burials; Date: 1625.

1418. <i> - Oxfordshire Parish Registers</i>, Charlton on Otmoor - burials; Date: 1597.

1419. <i>Wiltshire, England Parish Records</i>, Wanborough (as father).

1420. <i>Wiltshire, England Parish Records</i>

1421. <i>Wiltshire, England Parish Records</i>, Wanborough (as father); Date: 1591.

1422. WILL , of John Ashby (father); Date: 12 January 1567.

1423. WILL , of Robert Ashby; Date: 13 October 1602 Copy of Robert Ashby's Will In the name of God, Amen. The 13th daie of October in the yeare of or Lord God 1602, and in the 44th yeare of the raigne of our most gratious Sovraigne Ladye Queene Elizabeth &c I Robert Ashbye of Bugbrooke in the Countie of Northt husbandman considering that all men are mortall, and the hower of death uncertain doe declare ordaine and make my last will and testment in manr and forme following. First, I comende my soule to Almightie God my maker hoping that for his sonnes sake Jesus Christ my Lorde and onlie saviour he will freelie pardon all my synnes, and receave the same to his favourable mercie. And I will my bodye to be decently buryed as the bodie of a Xrian who believeth the resurrection thereof to lyfe everlasting. Item. I give and beqth to Richard Ashbye my sonne 6 of lawful English money to be paid unto him at his age of 28 yeares. Itm. I give to Henry Ashbye my sonne 6 of lawfull English money to be paid unto him within one year after he shall come forthe of his apprentishipp. Itm. I give to Robert Ashbye my sonne 6 of currant English money to be to be paid unto him within one yeare next after he commeth forth of his apprenticeshippe. Itm. I give to Stephyn Ashbye my sonne 6 of lawfull English money to be paid unto him at his age of 24 yeares. Itm. I give to Edward Ashbye my sonne 6 of currant English money to be paid unto him at his age of 24 yeares. Itm. I give to Alice Ashbye my daughter 6.13s.4d of currant English money to be paid unto her at her age of 20 yeares. Provyded allwaise and my will is that yf anie of my children dye before their stock be paid then the porcon of money dew to them so dying shall remayne amonge the resedue of my children being alive and unmarryed. Itm. I give and bequeath to my daughtr Alice Ashbye 10 of lawful English money to be payd unto her at her age of 21 yeares so that her whole porcon of money ys 16.13s.4d. Itm. I give to Joan Ashbye my wyffe all the household stuff wch I had with her at marriage to be delivered unto her by my executors being sett out and devyded from the rest of my household stuff by my daughters Mary and Elizabeth because they know it from the rest. Itm. I give more to my wyffe tenne shillings of currant English money. All the same household stuff and money to be paid and delivered to my said wyffe within six days after ye probacon of my will. Itm. My will is that my executor shall keepe my said wyffe with competent meate and drinke and lodging at my now dwelling house at Bugbrooke aforesaid so longe as she dwelleth quyetlie with my said executor without anie trouble of lawe and keepeth herself unmarried. The residue of all other my goods, cattels, and chattels (my debts and legacies being paid, and my funeral expenses discharged) I give and bequeath to John Ashbye my sonne whom I ordayne and make sole and whole executor of this my last will and testamt. And I give to John Ashby my sonne and heire and to his heires males for ever all my messuage or tent and all my lands tents & hereditaments whatsoever with all their appurtenances in the towne and fields of Bugbrooke aforesaid, and for want of such heires males then I give all the said messuage tent lands and hereditaments to my sonne Richard Ashbye and to his heires males for ever and for want of such heires males then I give all the said messuage tent lands and hereditaments to my sonne Stephen Ashbye and to his heires males for ever, and for want of such heires males then I give all the said messuage tenements lands and hereditaments to my sonne Edward Ashbye and to his heires males for ever, and for want of such issue male, then to the right heires of me the said Robert Ashbye for ever and I appoint overseers hereof Stephen Oliver and Richard Fowke of Caldecott to whom I give 2/- a pece. In witness whereof I the testator have hereunto putt my hande and seale the daie and yeare first above written. These being witness's Robt Ashbye of Kislingbury Richard Fowke of Caldicott & Stephen Oliver of Bugbrooke & Robert Adams of Shitlanger.

1424. <i>Berkshire Parish Registers</i>, Wantage SS Peter & Paul (Christening); Date: 18 April 1540.
1425. <i>Parish Records Collection - Marriage</i>, Wantage, Berkshire, England; Date: 1562.
1426. <i>Berkshire Parish Registers</i>, Wantage SS Peter & Paul (Christening); Date: 29 July 1542.
1427. <i>Berkshire Parish Registers</i>, Wantage St Mary (Marriage); Date: 3 November 1562.
1428. <i>Berkshire Parish Registers</i>, Wantage SS Peter & Paul (Christening); Date: 28 December 1550.
1429. <i>Berkshire Parish Registers</i>, Wantage SS Peter & Paul (Christening); Date: 25 July 1553.
1430. <i>Berkshire Parish Registers</i>, Wantage SS Peter & Paul (Burial); Date: 18 May 1554.
1431. <i>Berkshire Parish Registers</i>, Wantage SS Peter & Paul (Christening); Date: 3 June 1555.
1432. <i>Berkshire Parish Registers</i>, Wantage SS Peter & Paul (Christening); Date: 14 December 1557.
1433. <i>Berkshire Parish Registers</i>, Wantage SS Peter & Paul (Burial); Date: 26 December 1557.

1434. <i>Berkshire Parish Registers</i>, Wantage SS Peter & Paul (Christening); Date: 16 April 1559.

1435. <i>Berkshire Parish Registers</i>, Wantage SS Peter & Paul (Christening); Date: 19 May 1560.

1436. <i>Berkshire Parish Registers</i>, Wantage SS Peter & Paul (Christening); Date: 4 May 1561.

1437. <i>Berkshire Parish Registers</i>, Wantage SS Peter & Paul - (Christenings); Date: 15 December 1564.

1438. WILL , of John Ashby; Date: 12 January 1567.

1439. Subsidy roll , (156 / 248) c Henry VIII; Date: about 1543.

1440. WILL , of John Ashby; Date: 12 January 1567 In the name of God, Amen. The 12thof January Anno Dei 1567 I John Ashebie of Bugbrooke in the County of Northton felinge myself feeble and sick in body and hole and pfect in remembrance providing beforehand against the hower of deathe whch unto all men is uncertain, doe ordeyn and make my testament in manner and forme followinge. First and above all things I commend my soule into the hands of Almyghtie God my maker and Redeemer, and my body to be buried in the churchyard of Bugbrooke aforesaid. Itm I give to the mother church of Peterboroughe 2d. Itm I give to the poore men's boxxe 4d. Itm I give to the mayntenance of the bells of Bugbrooke aforesaid one strike of barley Itm I bequeathe to my daughter Jane 40s and 2 shepe. Itm I bequeath to my daughter Isabell 3 strike of pease. Itm I give to my daughter Jane 40s and 2 shepe Itm I give to Ales my daughter 40s one cowe, one chaisleinge shete, 2 payre of other sheets, one coffer, one soffer and all that is in it. Itm I give to Thomas my sonne 40s 2 shepe and one heifer with calffe. Itm I give to Richard my sonne 40s 2 shepe and one yearling bullock. Itm I give to my daughter Emme 40s one cowe two shepe and two payer of sheets Itm I will that Richard my sonne and Emme my daughter shall have their cattels at the age of 16 yeares, the foresaid Thomas and Ales at the age of 18 yeares. Itm I will that these my 4 children Thoms Ales Richard and Emme shall have all their said legacies at the age of 18 yeares. Also I will that the said Richard and Emme shall be kept of my sonne Robert until they come to the age of 18 yeares. Itm I will that Robt my sonne shall kepe any of my fower children yff they fall sicke before they come to the age of 18 yeares. Itm I will that Robert my sonne shall kepe my sonne William, finding him sufficient meate, drinke, and clothinge Itm I will that if any of my children namely Thoms Ales Richard and Emme die before they come to the age of 18 yeares, there legacies shall remayne to the other portion lyke. Itm the residue off my goods after my debts paid and my legacies fulfilled I give to Robert my sonne whome I make my whole executower. These being my overseers to see this my will pformed Richard Symonds, John Preston, they having each of them 12d for their labr. These being witness, Richard Symonds, John Preston, and Edward Ashebie wth other.

1441. , Birth certificate , , , Thomas Aldwyn Allsworth; 17 November 1946.

1442. : ; , , , Thomas Aldwyn Allsworth; 14 March 1964.

Index of Names

Adams
    Amelia (about 1770 - before 1870), 148
    Phobe (1835 - about 1876), 40
Adkin Or Adkyn
    (about 1630 - about 1690), 120, 178
    (about 1632 - about 1690), 120, 178
    Allenora (about 1659 - about 1700), 81, 82, 120, 178
Aitchison
    Elizabeth Gail Hannah (31 Jul 1975 -), 332
Alder
    Elizabeth (Nov 1734 -), 116
    John (Apr 1706 - Sep 1740), 78, 116, 117, 175
    John (Apr 1727 -), 116
    Margaret (Jul 1731 -), 116
    Martha (Jun 1827 - 1886), 33
    Mary (Feb 1736 - Apr 1782), 53, 54, 78, 116
    Thomas (May 1737 -), 117
    Thomas (about 1595 -), 273, 274, 295
    William (Aug 1683 -), 116, 117, 175, 243
    William (6 Oct 1656 -), 175, 243, 274
    William (Jun 1618 -), 243, 273, 274, 295
Aldesworth
    Joseph (about 1737 - before 1830), 111
    Mary (1731 - May 1803), 111
    Mary (Jul 1759 - Jul 1759), 74
    Mrs Elizabeth (about 1738 - before 1800), 111
    William (Oct 1701 - 31 May 1762), 74, 75, 111, 167
    William (about 1736 - Feb 1781), 52, 74, 75, 111
Aldsworth
    Ann (Jan 1769 - 1850), 74
    Charlotte (1 Nov 1829 - before 1920), 34
    Hanna (14 Feb 1785 - before 1841), 52
    Hannah (Sep 1766 - Oct 1783), 74
    John (6 Oct 1762 - 10 Nov 1833), 74
    Martha (Dec 1770 - Mar 1786), 75
    Martha (23 Nov 1787 - 11 Jan 1788), 52
    Mary (Jul 1764 - 1785), 74
    Mary (1783 - before 1883), 52
    Robert (Oct 1775 - Oct 1798), 75
    William (Aug 1760 - Oct 1796), 32, 34, 52, 74
    William (Sep 1781 - Feb 1862), 21, 23, 32, 34
Aldworth
    Alice (22 Mar 1564 -), 323
    Ann (Nov 1707 -), 167
    Bridgett (Dec 1558 -), 311
    Cicelie (Nov 1608 -), 292
    Dennis (6 Jul 1669 -), 237
    Dorathe (1559 - about 1624), 294, 312

    Elizabeth (Dec 1703 -), 167
    Francis (13 Jun 1555 -), 322
    Henry (14 May 1561 -), 323
    James (4 Aug 1553 - 28 May 1554), 322
    James (Feb 1709 - Aug 1729), 167
    Jane (12 Nov 1673 -), 238
    Joan (1653 -), 237
    John (10 Jun 1633 -), 270
    John (1532 - after 1573), 292, 311, 322
    John (Dec 1705 - Mar 1765), 167
    John (Oct 1568 - 2 Dec 1569), 311
    John (30 Dec 1664 -), 237
    Jone (27 Oct 1548 -), 322
    Judeth (Jan 1567 - Sep 1623), 311
    Margaret (3 Jun 1638 -), 270
    Margett (23 Dec 1557 - 5 Jan 1558), 322
    Margrett (Aug 1592 -), 292
    Martha (11 Aug 1658 -), 237
    Martha (Aug 1602 -), 292
    Mary (15 Apr 1673 -), 237
    Mary (2 Feb 1594 -), 292
    Mrs Annis (about 1550 - 23 Mar 1598), 322
    Mrs Jhone (about 1512 - Jun 1593), 311, 322, 325
    Mrs Joane (about 1633 -), 237
    Nicholas (26 Jul 1671 -), 238
    Richard (25 Dec 1550 - Aug 1593), 322
    Robert (Jan 1699 -), 167
    Robert (16 Apr 1540 -), 322
    Robert (14 Mar 1599 - 1641), 237, 238, 270, 292
    Robert (26 Apr 1635 -), 270
    Robert (about 1510 - after 1564), 311, 322, 325
    Robert (Oct 1573 -), 311
    Sara (Nov 1565 -), 311
    Sarah (14 Jun 1675 -), 238
    Thomas (Aug 1677 - Jul 1710), 111, 167, 168, 237
    Thomas (Oct 1631 - 13 Oct 1681), 167, 168, 237, 238
    Thomas (Feb 1571 - Jun 1633), 270, 292, 311
    Thomas (26 Apr 1559 - before 1560), 322
    Thomas (19 May 1560 - about 1590), 322
    Thomas (23 Jul 1662 -), 237
    William (8 Aug 1542 -), 322
    William (about 1670 -), 237
Aldwyn-Allsworth
    Helen (9 Sep 1952 -), 5
    Joan (21 Apr 1958 -), 6
Allen
    Mary (Sep 1816 - Oct 1893), 38
    Richard (Dec 1677 - Sep 1746), 129, 192

Broadway (continued)
John (6 Sep 1702 - 10 Mar 1768), 58, 59, 87, 88
John (1683 - Feb 1719), 87, 88, 127, 128
John (Jun 1651 - 2 Mar 1719), 127, 128, 189, 190
John (21 Mar 1730 - after 1755), 87
John (1631 -), 278
Joseph (1736 -), 87
Joseph (12 Sep 1754 -), 88
Joseph (1664 -), 250
Joseph (1709 - after 1755), 128
Martha (12 Feb 1737 -), 87
Mary (1654 - 1656), 250
Mary (1656 - 1657), 250
Mary (1 Dec 1751 - 6 Jul 1830), 87
Michael (5 Dec 1742 - 6 Sep 1809), 87
Mrs Elizabeth (1650 - 1683), 250
Mrs Elizabeth (1665 - 1735), 250
Mrs Elizabeth (1670 - 1713), 250
Mrs Mary (1626 - Dec 1679), 190, 250
Thomas (1 Jan 1621 - 25 Jun 1709), 190, 250, 278
Thomas (Jan 1645 -), 250
Thomas (1590 - 26 Jun 1667), 250, 278, 279, 298
Thomas (25 Mar 1733 - 4 Jan 1803), 87
Thomas (30 Apr 1704 - 7 Aug 1704), 128
William (1624 - 1624), 278
Brooks
(about 1675 -), 124, 184
(about 1677 -), 124, 184
Catherine (about 1700 - before 1800), 83, 84, 124, 184
Browes
(about 1665 -), 161, 162, 231, 232
(about 1668 -), 161, 162, 231, 232
Susanna (about 1690 -), 108, 161, 162, 232
Browne
(about 1620 -), 121, 179
(about 1622 -), 121, 179
Ann (about 1650 - Mar 1708), 82, 120, 121, 179
Broyors
Mary (Feb 1728 - 1825), 66, 67, 101, 151
Broyors Or Bryars Or Bryers
Thomas (Mar 1699 - before 1760), 101, 151, 218
Bryers Or Bryars
Edward (about 1655 - before 1750), 151, 218
Brynd
Agness (about 1561 -), 283, 319
Burcut
Rebecka (about 1667 -), 125, 185
Burges
(about 1687 -), 139, 203
Ann (Oct 1766 - before 1860), 41, 43, 62, 63
Ebenezer (Nov 1738 - Sep 1789), 62, 63, 93, 94

Hester (Sep 1734 -), 139
John (17 Apr 1711 - before 1800), 93, 94, 139, 203
John (about 1685 -), 139, 203
William (Mar 1736 -), 139
Burnan
Maryan (about 1579 - 4 Jun 1646), 315
Burt
Grace (1774 - before 1870), 65, 97, 145
James (28 Jul 1780 - about 1860), 145
John (about 1700 - before 1800), 145, 211, 212
Martha (about 1782 -), 144, 145
Sarah (1775 -), 145
Susannah (1781 -), 145
William (1745 - before 1840), 97, 144, 145, 212
William (1779 -), 145
Burvill
Maria (1776 -), 104
Buxton
(about 1695 -), 162, 232
(about 1698 -), 162, 232
Margaret (about 1722 -), 108, 162, 232
Calcot
Richard (28 Mar 1641 -), 245
Callow
Elizabeth (1836 -), 41
Calloway
(about 1700 -), 149, 150, 216
(about 1702 -), 149, 150, 216
Susannah (Apr 1756 -), 66, 99, 100, 149
William (about 1730 -), 99, 100, 149, 150
Capling
Ann (1 Nov 1700 - Dec 1788), 158, 227, 263
David (about 1675 -), 227, 263
Mrs Mary (about 1677 -), 227, 263
Carter
(about 1640 - Dec 1700), 169, 239
(about 1620 -), 239, 270, 271
(about 1622 -), 239, 270, 271
Edith Mary (12 Jun 1908 - before 2000), 5
John (about 1640 - before 1700), 169, 239, 271
Mary (Aug 1666 -), 112, 169, 239
Cartwright
Cheryl (about 1952 -), 5
Casey
(about 1660 -), 125, 186
(about 1662 -), 125, 186
Elizabeth (about 1701 -), 85, 125, 186
Chadwick
Elizabeth (about 1645 - before 1740), 267, 268, 290
Chamberlaine
(about 1605 -), 264, 288, 289
James (Sep 1588 -), 264, 288, 289

Morgan (continued)
  Sarah (Apr 1763 -), 55
  William (1828 - 1914), 24
  William (Jan 1690 - Oct 1719), 55, 56, 81, 82
  William (Aug 1657 - about 1695), 81, 82, 119, 120
  William V. (Dec 1750 -), 55
  William Veasy (Nov 1717 - before 1817), 36, 55, 56, 81
Morley
  Mary (about 1685 -), 116, 117, 175
Morris
  George (1720 - before 1820), 145, 212
  Joan (16 Dec 1750 - before 1850), 97, 144, 145, 212
Mott
  John (about 1650 -), 235, 236, 268, 269
  Martha Steel (18 Jan 1779 - 1842), 50, 51, 72, 73
  Milford (Feb 1680 -), 165, 166, 235, 236
  Samuel (25 Apr 1726 -), 110, 165, 166, 236
  Sarah Steel (Feb 1785 -), 110
  Stephen (28 Jun 1750 -), 72, 73, 110, 166
Mowsdale
  Ann (about 1603 - before 1700), 254, 255, 282, 283
Mumforr
  Elizabeth (1700 - 1762), 149, 150, 216
Munday
  (1586 -), 251, 279
  Ann (Dec 1586 -), 299
  Ann (Aug 1596 -), 299
  Edmund (about 1535 -), 299, 314
  Frances (1600 - before 1700), 249, 277, 278
  Henry (Aug 1599 - Feb 1626), 299
  John (Mar 1585 -), 299
  Martha (Feb 1594 -), 299
  Mary (Jun 1591 -), 299
  Robert (Mar 1589 - Feb 1668), 251, 279, 299
  Robert (about 1558 - about Sep 1602), 279, 299, 314
  Robert (Nov 1622 -), 279
  Ursual (about 1619 -), 190, 191, 251, 279
  William (Aug 1624 -), 279
Mynne
  Mariane (about 1619 -), 300
Naylor
  Elizabeth (1667 - before 1750), 213, 260, 261, 285
  Mrs Jane (about 1635 - before 1735), 260, 261, 285
  William (about 1630 - before 1730), 260, 261, 285
Neal
  Elizabeth (about 1688 - 16 Aug 1732), 188
Newbery
  Diana (1614 - 1688), 121, 122, 180
Newell
  Ada (Sep 1888 - Jul 1954), 17
  Ann (1788 -), 59

  Ann (1740 -), 87
  Annie (4 Apr 1882 - 6 Aug 1969), 5, 6, 7, 9
  Annie (14 Apr 1878 - 20 Apr 1878), 17
  Arthur (May 1874 - Jan 1951), 16
  Eliseus Clark (10 May 1844 - 14 Apr 1899), 7, 9, 13, 15
  Elizabeth (Feb 1691 -), 187
  Elizabeth Ann (22 Jan 1832 - before 1911), 39
  Emily (May 1876 - Jul 1947), 13, 16
  Fredrick (Sep 1879 - Nov 1948), 17
  Henry (15 Sep 1775 - 1 Apr 1829), 58
  Henry (1708 - 1745), 58, 59, 86, 87
  Henry (1742 -), 87
  Henry (about 1680 - before 1780), 86, 87, 126, 127
  Hester (Feb 1698 -), 187
  Jane (12 Jan 1777 -), 59
  John (7 Mar 1813 - Oct 1869), 38
  John (21 Feb 1779 -), 59
  John (about 1570 -), 317
  John (about 1650 -), 126, 127, 187
  Mary (5 Apr 1772 - before 1841), 58
  Mary (Mar 1694 -), 187
  Michael (5 Jun 1811 - Aug 1878), 15, 18, 24, 25
  Michael (4 Nov 1770 - before 1841), 58
  Richard (18 May 1782 - 29 Aug 1852), 24, 25, 38, 39
  Samuel (19 Jun 1785 - Mar 1844), 59
  Samuel (1817 - Mar 1891), 38
  Thomas (23 Feb 1784 -), 59
  William (30 Aug 1885 - Nov 1941), 17
  William (Dec 1846 - Dec 1920), 25
  William (24 Jan 1739 - 1788), 38, 39, 58, 59
Newman
  George (about 1830 - after 1876), 34
  Marie (1597 - before 1690), 284, 285, 306
Newton
  (about 1670 -), 118, 176
  (about 1673 -), 118, 176
  Mary (about 1698 -), 78, 80, 118, 176
Norbury
  (about 1700 -), 156, 224
  (about 1702 -), 156, 224
  Margaret (about 1727 -), 103, 156, 224
Norriss
  (about 1680 -), 153, 221
  (about 1681 -), 153, 221
  Anne (about 1702 -), 102, 153, 221
Onion
  Anne (Sep 1684 -), 121
  Henry (Nov 1604 - Nov 1607), 275
  Jane (Apr 1687 -), 122
  Jone (Mar 1594 -), 275
  Martha (Mar 1675 - before 1750), 55, 56, 82, 121
  Mary (Dec 1678 - Jun 1709), 121

GOOD MOTHER GILES

(An adapted extract from the book: *East End Pictures: Being More Leaves from My Log of Twenty-Five Years' Christian work Among Sailors and Others* (1885) by Thomas Charles Garland. Chapter 7 "Good Mother Giles")

HANNAH BALDWIN was born at North Shoebury, in 1805, and was married in 1821 to Thomas Giles, of Dover who was at that time a coast-guard. In the year 1844 they came to London. The death of one of her children first brought her to serious thoughts about her soul. She was much impressed by a sermon preached by the Rev. George Smith, of Poplar, and shortly afterwards found peace with God in the vestry of Spitalfields Wesleyan Chapel, and at once became a member of the Society at the Seamen s Chapel Having herself found Jesus, she became anxious to do something for Him Who had done so much for her, and earnestly besought the Lord to teach her what He would have her to do. She was soon deeply impressed with the thought that she must go to the Tower and distribute tracts amongst the soldiers. This seemed no easy task; but she did not shrink from taking up the cross, and on the following Sunday went with her bag well filled, and commenced her work by giving tracts to officers and men. At first they were amused at what they called the little woman's efforts to make them" pious" but her faith never failed, and she toiled on in this field of labour alone for many years. Sometimes she was persecuted, at other times cheered by the kindness both of men and officers, who occasionally contributed towards the purchase of tracts. In all weathers she was at her post on the Sunday mornings, and many will be her crown of rejoicing at the last great day.

One case only can be here recorded. One evening she attended a Love-feast at Spitalfields Chapel. During the meeting a soldier gave his experience, and told what a wicked life he had lived for several years, till a tract given by "good Mother Giles" had led him to Christ. "Since then," he added, my dear mother has been saved through my efforts and prayers, and four of my comrades have given their hearts to God." Mother Giles sat unobserved by the speaker, her heart overflowing with joy. At length she exclaimed, "Bless the Lord? I give all the glory to His holy name." Mother Giles also offered her services to the Rev. R. Chapman, of the Thames Mission, as a tract distributer, and thus the Loan Tract Society at our Seamen s Chapel was begun. Few persons, perhaps, have suffered more for righteousness sake than she did; yet none of these things moved her, and God was pleased to crown her labours with much success. Many who have passed into the spirit-land and others still living, will have to bless God to all eternity for her gentle and persistent labours. At one time her heart was drawn out in deep concern for two tradesmen who opened their shops on thy Lord s Day. She regularly called with her tracts, and spoke faithfully to them as to the sin they were committing, and urged them again and again to close their shops on the Sabbath; but all in vain. One told her, "We cannot afford to close; it would be our ruin." On account of these refusals she would often weep in secret before the Lord. One Sunday when she called with her tracts the master said: "My dear woman, how ill you look, what is the matter with you what s your trouble?" She was silent till all the customers had left, and then she replied: "0 Sir, I am in trouble about your soul, and those of your wife and family. I have been asking the Lord to stop your Sabbath -breaking, and I have the answer. Sir, He will stop you; but how or when I cannot say," and bursting into tears, she added, "I feel sure it will be a heavy blow when it does come." The man only smiled, and began to serve another customer who had entered the shop. Next morning, very early, the cry of "Fire" was raised, and flames were seen proceeding from the baker s shop. In a short time the house was burnt down, the master, his wife and family having only time to escape with their lives. The house was not insured, and they were left utterly penniless. The other tradesman, when he heard of the calamity, said, "If it had been my house and shop, it would not have been so bad, for I am well insured. Strange to tell, however, before the week was over, the Almighty visited that family with an awful affliction and in his deep sorrow the Sabbath-breaker sent for this godly woman, urging her not to pray against him any longer, but to pray for him, and he would never open his shop again on the Lord s Day. She entreated the Lord to withdraw His hand and show mercy to the penitent. God answered her prayer; and both these men became truly converted to God.

Another case is I think more remarkable still. There lived in Limehouse a sailor James Witchell a professed infidel, and in other respects a very wicked man. He appeared to have only one good quality he was passionately fond of his mother. This man was quite a stranger to Mrs. Giles, and she only heard of his name and wickedness while taking tea at a friend s house. The good woman could not restrain her feelings, but began to weep, saying, "Poor James! Poor James! I must pray for him! The next Sabbath morning, immediately after breakfast, she left borne with her bundle of tracts, she offered one to the first person she met, but the man looked at her with contempt, saying with an oath, "Keep your tracts." "I have plenty more" was her "soft answer." "Please take and read it, it may do your soul good." "I have no soul" said the man. "There is no soul, no God, no hereafter. Why, my little woman, you don't know whom you are talking to, my name is Witchell, of Limehouse. Nobody that knows me would offer me a tract." She looked him in the face and asked, "Is your name James?" "Yes, James Witchell is my name." Placing her hand on his shoulder, she said solemnly, "Listen to the word of the Lord of Hosts, Whose servant I am: Turn ye, turn ye ... for why will ye die? James, I have heard of you, and of your wicked life, and have been asking the Lord to convince and save your soul. Once more listen to me, James. He says, "Turn ye, turn ye, for why will ye die?" The astonished sinner turned pale, his lips quivered, and he could scarcely speak. At length he inquired what place of worship she attended. "That's my chapel" she said, pointing to the Seamen's Chapel "Then I'll be there this evening." he said. James was true to his word, and became a true Christian, a zealous worker, and died a most triumphant death.

During her long Christian experience „Mother Giles never lost her sense of acceptance with God: her trials and sufferings were of no ordinary character, but she had learnt to "glory in tribulations also." For several weeks before she was laid aside, it was evident from her experience and prayers that God was preparing her for the better home. This was particularly noticed in the Class-meetings; and no one present at those meetings will ever forget the influence which came down upon us there. The last time she attended her Class, all felt that she was living as in the ante-chamber of heaven. When leaving the room, she laid down her two pence for two weeks class-money on the table, saying. "That will clear up, will it not? " Then, taking my hand, she said, "Good-bye, this is my last visit. I replied, "I hope to see you here again, and that many times" "No" she said; "no Brother Garland, never again, but we shall meet above; "and looking up to heaven, she added, "My soul is full of joy and peace. Bless His Holy Name! I can say the blood of Jesus Christ cleanseth me from all sin." This indeed proved to be her last Class-meeting. Shortly after she was seized with a slight attack of paralysis, which for a time afflicted her speech and one side of her body. In answer to prayer God restored her speech so that she could speak quite distinctly. For several weeks her sufferings were great, but not a murmur escaped her lips. The last time I saw her she said, "Praise the Lord! The race is almost over." and after speaking of a few family matters, she took my hand, saying, "Give my love to Mr. Grigg, he has been so kind to me." She then wanted to mention other names, but her strength failed. Recovering herself a little, she said, "I want you to pray for two things: first, for my speedy release, if it is God's will; if not, for perfect resignation. And I want you to pray for my family; I have done it, as you know, for many years, but I can pray no longer." Then with a significant look she whispered in my ear, "You know all about them, pray till they are all saved." She closed her eyes and lay quiet for some minutes; then raising her hands she cried out, "He is faithful, who hath promised. I do believe all, all, yes, all will be saved." In a few days her happy spirit had left the body to be forever with the Lord. She entered into rest on the 13th of January, 1883.

"Mother Giles" was one of the happiest and brightest Christians I ever knew: her prepossessing countenance, gentle manner, and loving words won many a heart, making her a favourite with all who met her. She would never listen to the words of slanderers or talebearers. The Scripture rule was her guide continually: "Do as ye would that men should do to you, do ye also to them likewise." She was a great admirer of Wesley's hymns, most of which she seemed to have committed to memory. She would repeat the Scriptures very accurately in conversation and prayer.

A remarkable interposition of Providence on my own behalf I attribute chiefly to her prayers.
During the year 1866, when the Fenian movement was at its height in London, some week-night cottage prayer-meetings were commenced in connection with our chapel. There were several bands of young men thus employed, and to one of these I belonged. One of these meetings was held in Collingwood Street, Ratcliff, the Committee having taken a house and fitted up a room for the services. In this neighbourhood a large number of Irish families resided, and many of their children came to the services. I was also well known in the district, for during the cholera epidemic I had visited and relieved hundreds of Irish families, and thought my life was as safe there as in any part of London, when on a sudden things took a different turn. A number of young men and lads, about sixty in number, had agreed on a certain evening to break up the meeting and kill the "pious men" (a nickname given to the band). By some means his had reached the ears of one of the prayer leaders, and he communicated the news to his companions, who decided not to go to the

meeting, but unfortunately they never thought to send me word. Not knowing anything of this rumour, I went as usual to the service, and found the room quite full. The people seemed much excited, and as soon as I had given out the hymn-books one of the men said, "Now teacher, what shall we sing?" The announcement of the hymn was to be the signal for a general assault. But as none of my band had yet come, and as I fully expected them, I begged them to wait patiently for a short time; but I saw at once that mischief was intended, for near the desk where I was standing one of the men dropped by accident a short dagger. He hastily took it up again, hiding it beneath his jacket.

Again the first man shouted, "Now, teacher, what hymn shall we sing?" I made no reply. Immediately an order was given to "Close the door and bolt it." Then another voice was heard "Now, lads, to business." I then saw the man near me drawing his dagger from beneath his jacket. I instantly knocked him down, and the next moment I broke the lamp which hung suspended from the ceiling. The shouts, oaths, and confusion baffle all description, and in the darkness none could distinguish friend from foe. Deliverance came from an unexpected quarter Mr. Mainprise, who was then and still is one of our stewards, came to my rescue. He reached the house about the same moment that I broke the lamp, arriving just as the noise and shouting began. He tried to open the door, but found it fastened. Being a very strong and powerful man, he burst it in, when the men and lads hurried out as quickly as possible. The reason of my friend coming to Collingwood Street was this: "Good Mother Giles " who had greatly rejoiced in these cottage-meetings - when she could not attend, would spend some time in prayer in her own closet, pleading that God would bless the services. Whilst thus engaged this evening, she felt impressed to go immediately to the Seamen's Chapel, but for what reason she could not tell. Guided by this feeling, she went, and found Mr. Mainprise standing in the lobby. Addressing him, she said: "I have a message from God to thee; you must go at once to Collingwood Street." Mr. Mainprise replied, "You are mistaken this time, it is not my appointment." But the old lady said: "Never mind whose appointment it is, you must go and that without delay." This was said with so much earnestness that he went, much wondering at the strange errand. And, thank God! He was just in time to prevent bloodshed and perhaps murder. The following day the house was examined, and it was found that pipes had been laid in order to blow up the house.

Ashbys of Bugbrooke
Wills and comments

General comments

The family of Ashby whose history for nearly four hundred years is contained in the following pages, was one of yeomen, a position which they have held at Bugbrooke in Northamptonshire from the commencement of the sixteenth century, till within a few years of the present time and during the greater part of which period (from 1561) they have occupied their own land.

The Bugbrooke Parish Registers were commenced in 1538 in which year Lord Cromwell, Henry the Eighth's Vicar General, enjoined that "every parson, vicar or curate for every Church keep one Book or register wherein he shall write the day and the year of every Wedding, Christening or Burial made within his parish... And for the safe keeping of the same Book the parish shall be bound to provide of their common charges one sure Coffer with two locks & keys whereof the one to remain with him and the other with the Wardens of the Parish wherein the said Book shall be laid up, which Book he was every Sunday to take forth and in the presence of the said Wardens or one of them write and record in the same all the Weddings, Christenings and Burials made the whole week afore."

This injunction of the Vicar general was obeyed by the Rector of Bughrooke and the register was kept, probably on paper. But many of the clergy in the kingdom neglected to keep registers and this caused further injunctions to be made at different times. A Constitution in the Convocation holden at London in 1597 in the reign of Queen Elizabeth, ordered these Registers to be written in parchment Books, and the entries in the then existing books were to be copied into the parchment ones, since the time that the law was first made so far as the ancient books could be procured, but especially since the commencement of the reign of Elizabeth. This accounts for so many of the existing Registers commencing in 1558. The Bugbrooke Registers since the year 1538 were copied into parchment Books in 1598 in pursuance of the last mentioned Order of Convocation, the first volume covering the period from 1538 to 1557. This volume has been lost. It was extant in the time of Bridges who wrote a History of the County at the end of the last century, but Baker, who also wrote a History of the County published in 1822,1830 mentions that the volume has been lost in the meantime.

-

William Ashby (1475-1530)

Will

In Die Noie Amen. The 28th daye of January the yere of o^r Lord 1530
I Willm Ashebye of Bugbrooke hole of mynde made my testament after this man^r.
First I bequeath my soule to Allmyghtie God and o^r Ladye Sainte Marye and to all
the holye Company of Heven, and my bodye to be buryed in the Churchyarde of
Bugbrooke. Allso I bequeathe for my mortueyre as the Kings Acts will require.
It. to the Mother Church of Lincolyn 4^d Allso I bequeath to the hic awlt^r 4^d Allso to
the paynteing of Sent Cuthberd 16^d. It. to the bells 8^d to the Sepulchre 8^d It.
toward the bylding of o^r Ladye Chappel a strike of Barley. It. to the Causaye of
Pegnesaife a loode of straw. Also I will that Robert my eldyst son be half ptyn of all
my outward goods and no inward goods w^t my horses doying as a good jewell
child should do to his moder or els yff the cannot agree together Robert to have
the third parte of my outward goods. Allso the resedew of my goods I guyff and
bequeathe to my wyf Alis whom I make my souls Execr to dispose for my souls
helthe as ytt pleases her and f John to be ov^{r}sear wt other and he shall have a
nobell for his laboure. Wyttnes Sr Thoms Smyth Willm Symons and Thoms
Atthkyns.

An Inquisition indented taken at ~~~~ the ~~~ day of ~~~ in the second year of the
reign of King Richard the Third before Richard Burton Esquire, Escheator of our
Lord the King in the County aforesaid (ie Northampton) by virtue of the writ of our
Lord the King to his Escheator directed by the oaths of John Cuffyn, John Russell,
Henry Hibdenham, William Brayton, William Glover, William Jones, William
Harford, William Grene, Henry John Brayton, and William Gedfrey, who say upon
their oaths that John Assheby, Gent^m in the said Writ mentioned held no land or
tenements of the said Lord the King in Capite or otherwise, nor of any one else in
his demesne as of fee nor by service in the County aforesaid on the day on which
he died. And they further say that the said William (sic) died on the 20th day of
September last past, and that John (sic) Assheby is the son and next heir of the
said William (sic) Assheby in the said Writ mentioned, and is ten years of age and
upwards. In witness &c

Robert Ashby (died 1577)

Recorded comments and financial inquisition

William Ashby left two sons Robert and John, both mentioned in his will.
Robert's wife appears from the will of one of his sons to have been named Alice.

Robert Ashby made his will on the 6th February 1576 and it was proved on the 24th March 1577 the next month (February being then the last month and March the first month of the year). In it he mentions his children William, John the Elder, Anne, Katherine, Edward, and Cuthbert. John Ashby the younger is mentioned but not as a child of the testator. A "Richard Ashby of Lytchbourowe"(about 4 miles from Bugbrooke) made his will in 1572 in which he mentions his father and mother Robert and Alice, and his brothers and sisters, Edward, John the younger, Cuthbert, Anne, Katherine, Thomas, Steven and William. On comparing the names of these latter, with the names of the children of Robert Ashby of Bugbrooke it will at once be seen that they are the same persons, and Richard Ashby of Lichborough who also mentions the Peasnalls, a family then and still resident in Bugbrooke, must therefore have been a son of Robert Ashby of Bugbrooke. His Brother Thomas also lived at Lichborough and made his will in the same year (1572) wherein he mentions his brothers and sisters Edward, Katherine, Cuthbert, and Anne.

According to the wills of Robert Ashby, and his sons Richard and Thomas, Robert has ten children William, Thomas, Edward, Steven, Cuthbert, Richard, Anne, Katherine, John the Elder, and John the younger. It may seem strange that he should have had two children of the same name (John), but it is quite clear he had, as in his own will he calls John the Elder his son, and his son Richard calls John Ashby the Younger his brother. There are several cases in the family of a child having received the same name as an elder child who had died, and very probably at the time Robert's son John the younger was baptised, his son John the elder may have been so seriously ill as not to be expected to live, and John the younger was thence christened John. Of the children of Robert Ashby of Bugbrooke, Richard and Thomas then appear to have settled at Lichborough in their father's lifetime. Thomas died in 1572 leaving two daughters Ursula and Jane, and devising his houses and lands in Lichborough to his son if one should be born after his death, and if not then to his daughters. In his will he mentions his debts to Thomas Pesnoll and Thomas Billing, and makes John Harris and his brother Steven overseers.

Robert's son Richard also died in 1572 leaving a will, but does not appear to have married. He left his houses and lands to his brother Edward and in default of Edward's heirs to his brother John Ashby the younger, and in default of John's heirs, to his brother Cuthbert. He left John Ashby the elder two sheep, and to Thomas Pesenoll, one sheep. Elizabeth Hopkins and Alice Pesenoll were also legatees. Robert Ashby the testator's father was appointed executor, and John Harris and Steven Ashby overseers.
Robert's son Edward appears to have gone to Lichborough and taken possession of his

brother Robert's property after his death. He married Margaret Wright at Bugbrooke in 1576. He is taxed for his land at Lichborough valued at £1 per annum, by a subsidy roll (157/361) of the 41st Elizabeth (1599) and paid a tax of 4/-. And again the next year (157/363) and in 1597 he paid a tax of 8/- for his goods valued at £3 (157/366) and again in 1611 he paid 5/- for his goods valued as before (157/392) and in the same year paid anther tax of 3/- (157/398).

Edward died on the 12th August 1620 and an inquisition was taken after his death by which it appears that he held a close called the West End Close and a virgate (about 16 acres) of land in Lichborough which he had purchased of Sir George Farmer and others, and settled on himself for life, then on his wife Margaret for life, and then on his daughter Anne intail. West End Close was held of Lord Burford by fealty, and at the rent of a broad arrow, and the virgate was held of the King as of his manor of East Greenwich in free socage and not in capite at the rent of 5/-. He also held a house at Lichborough in his own occupation, and a cottage and a close, and two virgates and three quarters of land which had belonged to the monastery of Saint James near Northampton dissolved in the time of Henry VIII. These lands were held by military tenure as the hundredth part of a fee at 10/- per annum. Edward Ashby left no son but three daughters.
I find no notice of Robert's son Cuthbert from the time of his father's will in 1576 till 1628 after his brother Edward's death when he is mentioned in a subsidy roll (157/411) and is taxed for lands in Lichborough valued at £1. The next year he is again taxed for the same (157/413) and this is the last notice I have of him.

They adhered to the church after the other Ashby's of Bugbrooke who were descended from William's son John had joined the Society of Friends.

-

John Ashby (died 1567)

Will

In the name of God, Amen. The 12th of January Anno Dei 1567 I John Ashebie of Bugbrooke in the County of Northton felinge myself feeble and sick in body and hole and pfect in remembrance providing beforehand against the hower of deathe wh^{ch} unto all men is uncertain, doe ordeyn and make my testament in manner and forme followinge. First and above all things I commend my soule into the hands of Almyghtie God my maker and Redeemer, and my body to be buried in the churchyard of Bugbrooke aforesaid. It^m I give to the mother church of Peterboroughe 2^d. It^m I give to the poore men's boxxe 4^d. It^m I give to the mayntenance of the bells of Bugbrooke aforesaid one strike of barley It^m I bequeathe to my daughter Jane 40s and 2 shepe. It^m I bequeath to my daughter Isabell 3 strike of pease. It^m I give to my daughter Jane 40s and 2 shepe It^m I give to Ales my daughter 40s one cowe, one chaisleinge shete, 2 payre of other sheets, one coffer, one soffer and all that is in it. It^m I give to Thomas my sonne 40s 2 shepe and one heifer with calffe. It^m I give to Richard my sonne 40s 2 shepe and one yearling bullock. It^m I give to my daughter Emme 40s one cowe two shepe and two payer of sheets It^m I will that Richard my sonne and Emme my daughter shall have their cattels at the age of 16 yeares, the foresaid Thomas and Ales at the age of 18 yeares. It^m I will that these my 4 children Thom^s Ales Richard and Emme shall have all their said legacies at the age of 18 yeares. Also I will that the said Richard and Emme shall be kept of my sonne Robert until they come to the age of 18 yeares. It^m I will that Robt my sonne shall kepe any of my fower children yff they fall sicke before they come to the age of 18 yeares. It^m I will that Robert my sonne shall kepe my sonne William, finding him sufficient meate, drinke, and clothinge It^m I will that if any of my children namely Thom^s Ales Richard and Emme die before they come to the age of 18 yeares, there legacies shall remayne to the other portion lyke. It^m the residue off my goods after my debts paid and my legacies fulfilled I give to Robert my sonne whome I make my whole executower. These being my overseers to see this my will pformed –Richard Symonds, John Preston, they having each of them 12d for their lab^r. These being witness, Richard Symonds, John Preston, and Edward Ashebie wth other.

Robert Ashby (1530-1602)

Will

In the name of God, Amen.

The 13th daie of October in the yeare of o^r Lord God 1602, and in the 44th yeare of the raigne of our most gratious Sovraigne Ladye Queene Elizabeth &c

I Robert Ashbye of Bugbrooke in the Countie of North^t husbandman considering that all men are mortall, and the hower of death uncertain doe declare ordaine and make my last will and testment in man^r and forme following. First, I comende my soule to Almightie God my maker hoping that for his sonnes sake Jesus Christ my Lorde and onlie saviour he will freelie pardon all my synnes, and receave the same to his favourable mercie. And I will my bodye to be decently buryed as the bodie of a Xrian who believeth the resurrection thereof to lyfe everlasting.

Item. I give and beqth to Richard Ashbye my sonne £6 of lawful English money to be paid unto him at his age of 28 yeares.

It^m. I give to Henry Ashbye my sonne 6£ of lawfull English money to be paid unto him within one year after he shall come forthe of his apprentishipp.

It^m. I give to Robert Ashbye my sonne 6£ of currant English money to be to be paid unto him within one yeare next after he commeth forth of his apprenticeshippe. It^m. I give to Stephyn Ashbye my sonne 6£ of lawfull English money to be paid unto him at his age of 24 yeares.

It^m. I give to Edward Ashbye my sonne 6£ of currant English money to be paid unto him at his age of 24 yeares.

It^m. I give to Alice Ashbye my daughter £6.13s.4d of currant English money to be paid unto her at her age of 20 yeares.

Provyded allwaise and my will is that yf anie of my children dye before their stock be paid then the porcon of money dew to them so dying shall remayne amonge the resedue of my children being alive and unmarryed.

It^m. I give and bequeath to my daught^r Alice Ashbye 10£ of lawful English money to be payd unto her at her age of 21 yeares so that her whole porcon of money ys 16£.13s.4d. It^m. I give to Joan Ashbye my wyffe all the household stuff wc^h I had with her at marriage to be delivered unto her by my executors being sett out and devyded from the rest of my household stuff by my daughters Mary and Elizabeth because they know it from the rest.

It^m. I give more to my wyffe tenne shillings of currant English money. All the same household stuff and money to be paid and delivered to my said wyffe within six days after ye probacon of my will.

It^m. My will is that my executor shall keepe my said wyffe with competent meate and drinke and lodging at my now dwelling house at Bugbrooke aforesaid so longe as she dwelleth quyetlie with my said executor without anie trouble of lawe and keepeth herself unmarried. The residue of all other my goods, cattels, and chattels (my debts and legacies being paid, and my funeral expenses discharged) I give and bequeath to John Ashbye my sonne whom I ordayne and make sole and whole

executor of this my last will and testam^t. And I give to John Ashby my sonne and heire and to his heires males for ever all my messuage or ten^t and all my lands tent^s & hereditaments whatsoever with all their appurtenances in the towne and fields of Bugbrooke aforesaid, and for want of such heires males then I give all the said messuage ten^t lands and hereditaments to my sonne Richard Ashbye and to his heires males for ever and for want of such heires males then I give all the said messuage ten^t lands and hereditaments to my sonne Stephen Ashbye and to his heires males for ever, and for want of such heires males then I give all the said messuage tenements lands and hereditaments to my sonne Edward Ashbye and to his heires males for ever, and for want of such issue male, then to the right heires of me the said Robert Ashbye for ever and I appoint overseers hereof Stephen Oliver and Richard Fowke of Caldecott to whom I give 2/- a pece. In witness whereof I the testator have hereunto putt my hande and seale the daie and yeare first above written.
These being witness's
Robt Ashbye of Kislingbury Richard
Fowke of Caldicott
& Stephen Oliver of Bugbrooke &
Robert Adams of Shitlanger

John Ashby (died 1648)

Will

In the name of God, Amen.

I John Ashby of Bugbrooke beinge sicke in body but of wholl and perfect remembrance doe make and ordaine this my last will and testament in manner and forme following.

First, I give and bequeath my soule to the Almighty God my maker and redeemer, and my bodie to the earth from whence it came. As for my worldly goods as followeth. I give and bequeath unto John Ashby the sone of my daughter Elizabeth ten pounds to be payde when she shall come to the age of too and twenty yeares.

It^m. I give to the four daughters of the aforesaid Elizabeth Ashby twenty shillings a pece and to be payde when they shall com to the age of one and twenty yeares. Also my will is that my sone Robert Ashby doe paye unto my daughter Elizabeth eighteen shillings yearly untell the ten pounds be payde which eighteen shillings shall be foreborne the first too yeares after my decease.

Item. I give to my daughter Hannah Stephens of Shipton in the parish of Winslow in the County of Buckingham twenty shillings to be payed too yeares after the date hereof.

It^t. I give unto Robert Ashby's children 2s6d a pece. It^t. I give to Robert Stephen's children 2s6d a pece. It^t. I give to the poore in Bugbrooke twenty shillings. It^t. I give unto Anna my wife too platters and all the bedding linen and wollon except the It^t. I give to Stephen Ashby the bedstead, the falling table, and the coffer with the rest of the trash *(sic)* which are and were lately at Northton. It^t. I give unto John Olliver my best coat.

All the rest of my goods I give unto Robert Ashby whom I make my soale and wholl executrix *(sic)* of this my last will and testament paying all my debts and bringing me sufficiently to the ground. And alsoe I doe make Stephen Ashby and John Olliver overseers of this my last will and testament in the sixth and twentyth day of July and in the four and twentyth yeare of the raigne of our sovereign Lord Charles by the grace of God King of England Scotland France and Ireland Defender of the Faith &c 1648.

In witness whereof I the testator hath set to my hand and seale in the presence of Robert Ashby The mark of
Stephen Ashby X
The mark of X Agnis Caulcott John Ashby

Robert Ashby (Died -1664)

Quaker and his persecution.

Robert Ashby was baptized in 1607 in the Church of England, and was about 30 at the time of his marriage, and about 40 at his father's death. He joined the Society of Friends around 1662, and was imprisoned for refusing to pay tithes in 1663, and his wife died in 1664 while he was still in prison, her death being recorded in the Friends Registers.

The sufferings of the Friends at this time were very great. It was one of their tenets that "No further support should be expected by their Ministers than what is authorised by Christ and was practiced by his Apostles, so that not feeling themselves required to provide for their own ministers whose Ministry they approve, Friends deem themselves fully warranted in declining to contribute for the support of others, from which they conscientiously dissent; and more especially they feel called upon to protest against that most objectionable and anti-Christian mode of support by tithes."

This together with their refusal to pay Church Rates; their absence from public worship at church; and their meetings together contrary to law, brought many of them into trouble. They were frequently imprisoned and in many cases cruelly ill treated. It is recorded in a book entitled "An Abstract of the Sufferings of the People called Quakers" that in 1660 "the number of persons together in the County Gaol at Northampton was now nearly forty put into the low gaol twelve steps under ground where they were lock^t up every night among felons, and in winter the gaoler kept the door fast sixteen hours together; and they lay so thick one by another that he who was up last could hardly set his foot between them to go to the place where he should lie. Some of them were sick for want of air, and when their friends came many miles to visit them they were not admitted. Their food and necessaries were frequently kept from them so that their sufferings were very great." The same book also states that, "about the end of of the year 1663 twenty- two friends having been long confined together with the felons and debtors in a close room, most of which was taken up with the straw on which they lodged so that they had little space to wash in, a violent fever seiz^{d}first on some of the felons to whom, as fellow creatures and fellow prisoners, though in a cause vastly different, Friends thought it a duty to be assistant in their extreme weakness; and accordingly did what they could for them till at length the air being exceedingly corrupted with the breath of the distempered, a kind of contagion spread among the prisoners, and the Friends so generally fell sick that when called over at the assizes only four of them were able to appear before the judge, who understanding their sad condition gave private orders to the gaoler to let them forth for air, by which means some recovered, but seven of them being too weak to go out or to be removed, died there, to wit (1) Wm Carr (2) Richard Ashby" &c.

"Robert Ashby was still in prison at the suit of one Whitfield priest of Bugbrooke who made great spoil on his effects at home taking away sometimes whole fields of corn and whole loads of grain and hay far exceeding any legal claim."

During this time that Robert Ashby was in prison, five persons were convicted of holding an illegal meeting at his house. The proceedings are recorded in a tract with an enormous title printed in 1665. According to this tract the indictments charged that William Robinson, Richard Parsons, John Cory and Elizabeth Harris and every of them were unlawfully assembled at Robert Ashby's house situate and being in Bugbrooke in the County of Northamptonshire with divers other malefactors contrary to the liturgy or practice of the Church of England in contempt of the King his laws and against his crown and dignity &c.

The evidence showed that, "at the meeting where the offence was committed there were about thirty persons and one of them was praying and preaching for he sometimes stood and sometimes kneeled down." It also appeared that the prisoners had been twice before convicted of the same offence and a third conviction incurring the penalty of transportation they were now sentenced to seven years transportation to Jamaica with the option however of a fine of £100 a piece.

John Ashby (1645-1728)

Will

"In the name of God, Amen. I John Ashby of Bugbrooke in the County of Northampton yeoman Being of sound mind and understanding and calling to mind the onsartanty of time in this World and the Certainty of Death I Doe Make and Ordaine this my last Will and Testament in manner following – that is to say I commend my soul to the Lord who is the disposer of all things and my Body I desire may be Buried at the discretion of my loveing Wife and the Executor of this my Last Will & Testament and as for What Worldy Goods itt hath pleased God to Bestoe Upon me I Doe give and Bequeath as underwritten:

Imprs I doe give and Bequeath to my son Robert Ashby of Quinton Grassor Five shillings.

Item. I Doe give and Bequeath to my daughter Jane Banniger of Brampton five shillings. Item. I doe give and Bequeath to my daughter Elizabeth Gray five shillings.

Item. I doe give and Bequeath to my daughter Sarah Hinson five shillings and to my daughter Hannah Johnson five shillings.

Item. I doe give and Bequeath to my son Joseph Ashby my best sute of Wareing Cloaths. Item. I doe Give and Bequeath to my daughter Sarah Hinson my Great Chest.

Item. I doe Give and Bequeath to my Grand Son John Ashby my bedstead in the Seller Chamber and furnice and Deaske and my Iron Barr.

All the rest and residue of my Goods and Chattels whatsoever I doe give and Bequeath to my Loveing wife Mary for and during her naturall Life and immediately after her decease I doe give and Bequeath all these my goods and Chattels to my son Joseph Ashby and daughters Mary Paine and Alice Collings to be equally divided between these three share and share a Like.

Lastly I doe constitute and appoint my son Joseph Ashby of Rattley Com Clackmore in the County of Bucks Executor of this my last Will and Testament and Doe hereby revoke all former Wills heretofore by me made in witness whereof I have to this my Last Will and Testament sett my hand and seal this Twentith second day of the third month called May and in the tenth year of the regne of our Sovering Lord George by the Grace of God King of Great Britten France and Ireland Defender of the Faith Anno Dony 1724. Note Hannah Johnson was enterlined.

Signed sealed puplished and declared in the Pessance of us and in the prssence of the Testator hir Mary o Lucas Marke

Sarah Adams Senr Jos

Adams

Robert Ashby (1673- 1741)

Will

I Robert Ashby of Quinton in the County of Northampton Yeoman do make this my last Will and Testament in manner and forme following (that is to say) First all that my real estate lying and being in Bugbrook and Bugbrook Parish Fields in the said County of Northampton (excepting that yardland I bought and purchased of Robert Mobbs of Bugbrook aforesaid) with all and singular the appurtenances thereunto belonging I give and devise and bequeath unto my son John Ashby and his heirs and assigns for ever.

All that my said yardland which I bought and purchased of and from Robert Mobbs lying and being in Bugbrook Fields aforesaid with the appurtenances I give to my son Robert Ashby and his heirs and assigns for ever, he my said son Robert Ashby paying out of the said yardland the sum of eight pounds a year of good and lawful money of Great Britaine unto my son Joseph Ashby yearly and ever year during the natural life of of him my said son Joseph, by four equal quarterly payments thereof to begin and to be made three Kalendar months next after my decease and so to be continued by such quarterly payments yearly and every year as aforesaid during the natural life of him my said son Joseph....(Here follows a long proviso declaring that the annuity should cease if Joseph Ashby should attempt to sell or exchange it)... I also give to my said son Joseph Ashby the further summe of twelve pounds a yeare of good and lawfull money of Great Britaine yearly and every yeare during his natural life to be paid him by my executors out of my personall estate by four equal quarterly payments in each year by three pounds every quarter of a year the first quarterly payment thereof to begin and be made three Kalendar months next after my decease ... (Here follows a similar proviso in case of attempted sale &c)... And my will further is that my Executors after named shall immediately after my decease by good and sufficient bond or Bonds under their hands and seals bind themselves their heirs executors and administrators to the payment of the said twelve pounds a year to be paid to my said son Joseph under the limitations and in manner as aforesaid. And my will further is that if he my said son Joseph Ashby shall dy leaving issue of his body lawfully begotten then my executors shall pay to such person or persons who shall have the care and bringing up of such his child or children the summe of five pounds a year for and towards the bringing up and educating such his Child or children until such his child or children (if any) shall attain unto his her or their age of one and twenty years. And further my will is that if my said son Joseph shall dye leaving such issue of his body as aforesaid who shall attaine the said age of one and twenty years then my executors shall pay unto such Child (if but one) the summe of one hundred pounds of good and lawfull money of Great Britaine, but if more than one attaining the said age then the said Hundred Pounds shall be paid by my executors to and amongst such his Children part and share alike.

I give to my sister Alice Collins the summe of twenty shillings a year, yearly and every year during her naturall life to be paid by my executors.

I give to my cousin Leonard Baringer Five pounds of lawfull money.

I give to Thomas and Hannah son and daughter of my brother William Paine
two pounds and ten shillings a piece.
I give to my kinswoman Elizabeth Hewlet wife of Daniel Hewlet of Northampton
the sum of two pounds and ten shillings.
I give the sum of two pounds and ten shillings to be equally distributed to and
amongst poor Friends belonging to the Northampton and Bugbrook Monthly
Meetings that is to say, one pound and five shillings to each Meeting.
All my goods chattels ready money and Securities for money and personall estate
whatsoever and wheresoever the same may or can be found (excepting one
twenty pound note in the hand of Joseph Coles) I give and bequeath unto my two
sons John Ashby and Robert Ashby whom I appoint executors of this my last Will
and testament they paying all my just debts legacies and funeral expenses.
And I do declare this to be my last Will and Testament. In witness whereof I
have hereunto set my hand and seale this second day of the fourth month
called June One thousand seven hundred and forty one – 1741
Signed sealed and declared By the
said Robert Ashby

William Read Holmes - Great Snow Storm 25 Dec 1783

Occupation - Cinque Port Pilot

Married – Elizabeth Barber - 8 Nov 1819

Died - 27 Dec 1836

Buried - January 1837

William died in the Great Snow Storm just after Christmas, Dec 1836. He was in the Dover Straights. There's lots of info on William Holmes at the Dover Museum.

The Kentish Observer of 28th Dec 1836 reported as follows:

An express from Payne's Hotel Dover arrived in Canterbury last night at about eight o'clock. The boy, a light lad did it in six hours having had to walk from Bridge. We regret to say he brought the account of the wreck of the brig Harriet a timber vessel bound to London from Quebec which went to pieces under Shakespeare's Cliff. The pilot William Read Holmes was drowned and his body afterwards was picked up at Folkestone.

The Canterbury Weekly Journal reported as follows in it's edition of 31st Dec 1836:

We regret to state that fourteen or fifteen persons perished on board the brig Harriet which went tp pieces under Shakespeare's Cliff. The vessel was near enough to hear the voices of the unfortunate crew on land, although it was found impossible to render them any assistance. Part of the wreck floated ashore with a live cat on it...

The Essex, Herts. and Kent Mercury reports as follows in its edition of 10th January 1837:

"It is remarkable that the two vessels totally wrecked here, belonging to London, from foreign parts, the Prince Frederick from Rotterdam and the

Harriet from Quebec, were commanded by Folkestone men, who had a narrow escape from being drowned in sight of their native place; Captain Stephenson, seventy years old, of the former, and Captain John Warman, of the Harriet.

The funeral of the respected pilot,. Mr. W.R.Holmes, of this port, who, with several of the crew was drowned, took place on Tuesday and was attended by a long procession of friends and relatives of the deceased, the brother of James, a plumber from Lewisham. He leaves a widow and eight children."

Joseph Young – Mormon Pioneer

Mormon Pioneer Overland Travel, 1847–1868 Young, Joseph Birth Date: 22 Feb. 1802
Death Date: 23 July 1875
Gender: Male Age: 64
Pioneer Information: wife - Jane (Flemming) and 2 children

Company Information: 64 Company: John D. Holladay (1866)

350 individuals and 69 wagons were in the company when it began its journey from the outfitting post at Wyoming, Nebraska (the west bank of the Missouri River about 40 miles south of Omaha)

Information: YOUNG, Joseph Birth: 2/22/1802
Place of Birth: Wanstead, Essex, England.
Death: 7/23/1875
Burial:Place of Death: Peterson, Morgan, Utah
Grave Location: Peterson Cemetery

Richard Hamilton – Australian Wine

In 1835 Richard Hamilton Jnr arrived in South Australia as a seaman aboard the brigantine "Duke of York" carrying settlers for the fledgling colony and due to meet up with HMS Buffalo sailing to South Australia via Buenos Aires.

Richard Jnr returned to England full of tales of the potential of South Australia convincing his father of the merits of emigrating with his entire family.

On June 7, 1837 Richard Hamilton (snr) took out Land Order 449 in London for the Province of South Australia. He arrived with his wife and five of his children aboard the "Katherine Stewart Forbes" on October 7, 1837. His eldest child, Henry, remained in England to complete his schooling.

Initially the family lived in a camp on the banks of the River Torrens before the local Aboriginal Karuna tribe burnt it out. This forced the family to move down to the land they had secured on the banks of the Sturt River, in the Marion district 8 miles from what is today Adelaide's G.P.O where they set about establishing a farm. This marked the beginning of Hamilton's Ewell Vineyards.

It became apparent to Richard that before the farm could support his family he would run short of money. Therefore he wrote to a friend in South Africa describing his predicament and requested that he send some vines to plant 'as the health of the family requires a little wine-'.

The vines, which were Pedro Ximenez, Shiraz and Grenache, arrived three months later and Richard planted them in the winter of 1838. The plants thrived in the deep alluvial soil and sunny climate helped by the annual flooding of the Sturt River much like the Bremer River does in the Langhorne Creek wine region, in South Australia. In 1841 Richard made his first and South Australia's first wine, which he subsequently loaded onto a horse and cart and sold to nearby farmers.

The eldest son, Henry, joined the rest of the family after completing schooling and then spending two years on a sheep station near Burra. Gradually Henry and the family purchased surrounding land. In 1854 Henry planted two acres of vines on a section of 10 acres, which was named Ewell after a village in Surrey. Some of these vines were still bearing in 1980. This was where Henry was to build his wine cellars that became known as Hamilton's Ewell Vineyards. Henry ran a mixed farm with hard work and good management. In 1890 and 1891 he won the Angus Award for agricultural farms presented by the Royal Agricultural and Horticultural Society. At that stage he had 140 acres of farm with 40 acres of vineyard.

Richard Hamilton's widow, Anne, died in 1886 aged 97 and in accordance with her husband's will the original property was divided equally amongst the nine children. Henry and his son Frank set about buying the land back from the other members of the family.

Under the management of Frank Hamilton the vineyard expanded to 156 acres and amongst other wines they produced a "Chablis" dry white wine made from Pedro. In 1928 Frank's son, Sydney, blended Pedro with Verdelho to produce Hamilton's Ewell Moselle, a semi sweet white which went on to be Hamilton's and Australia's biggest selling wine.
At the same time Hamilton's started picking the grapes early to retain some natural acidity and fermenting them in closed wooden vats rather than open concrete tanks, as was the norm. Hamilton's Ewell Vineyards developed a reputation for fine wines through the efforts of winemakers Sydney Hamilton, Russian born John A. Seeck, and Frenchman Maurice Ou. In 1945 a temperature controlled cellar was built which greatly helped the quality of the white wines.

Under the stewardship of managing director Eric Hamilton, the company flourished. Eric was a pioneer in exporting Australian wines spending up to six months of the year overseas promoting Hamilton's Ewell Vineyards and Australian wines, mainly in the UK and Canada. He even went to the length of shipping his Rolls Royce with him on occasions.
During the 60s and 70s Hamilton's Ewell Vineyards had lost much of its vineyards at Ewell through urban expansion and compulsory acquisition although there is one small section of vineyard still alive today. When Hamilton's Ewell Vineyards was sold to Mildara (now Beringer Blass) in 1979 the company had vineyards in the Eden Valley, Nildottie and Wood Wood near Swan Hill in Victoria and wineries at Ewell, Eden Valley Nildottie and Nyah in Victoria.

Mark Hamilton was horrified as a young board member in 1979, hoping to one day take over the reigns, when Hamilton's Ewell Vineyards was sold to Mildara.
In 1982 Mark Hamilton's father, Robert, bought the winery and vineyard in the Eden Valley back from Mildara. Hamilton's Ewell Vineyards in turn purchased this from Robert in 1993 and named it Stonegarden. Mark, a lawyer, was determined to revive his interest in the wine industry so he and his wife Deborah began purchasing premium mature vineyards in the Barossa Valley in the 1990's.

Mark spent a lot of time in the 90s seeking out and purchasing the right vineyards in the Barossa Valley; purchasing an old winery and vineyard called Stonegarden near Springton in the Eden Valley previously owned by Hamilton's Ewell Vineyards, and searching for the ideal piece of land for a premium vineyard in the South East of SA.

At the same time Mark Hamilton took the opportunity to regain the name and associated trademarks of Hamilton's Ewell Vineyards. Hamilton's Ewell vineyards have developed a new, high quality 100-acre vineyard named Limestone Quarry Vineyard in the Wrattonbully region near

Coonawarra in South Australia's South East on predominantly terra rossa soil.

Under the stewardship of chairman Eric Hamilton in the 60s and 70s, Hamilton's Ewell Vineyards became one of the biggest exporters of Australian wine. Eric spent up to six months overseas each year promoting Australian wines, even shipping his Rolls Royce with him to drive round Canada and the United Kingdom.

It is with this long heritage in mind that Mark and Deborah are proud to have relaunched Hamilton's Ewell Vineyards.

"The Wakes of Blisworth"

A talk given in Blisworth Village Hall [1] by Sir Hereward Wake on 28th March 2003.

Over 700 years ago my great, great, gr . . . grandfather Sir Hugh Wake of Bourne in Lincolnshire inherited in 1265 the Manor of Blisworth. He lived in a manor house, long since fallen down, just near the Church. It had a park and a warren. He already held lands at Deeping near Bourne, and in Guernsey. Due to marrying heiresses the family in the course of time owned Liddel in Cumberland, Clevedon in Somerset, Wake's Colne and Waltham Abbey and Nazeing in Essex, Clifton Reynes and Chicheley in Buckinghamshire, Riddlesworth in Suffolk and lands in Derbyshire and Kent. And not least Collingtree and Courteenhall in Northamptonshire.

But Blisworth was the family's main base. Both Sir Hugh's grandfather Baldwin and grandson Sir Thomas were Patrons of the Living of Blisworth and appointed the earliest recorded Rector in 1272. We lived there for 258 years. Sadly in 1523 Thomas Wake who had been imprisoned in the Tower of London for his misdeeds, sold Blisworth.

Over the following 475 years the family owned land at Piddington, Preston Deanery, Hartwell and Salcey Forest, finally inheriting Courteenhall which has been our home for the last 11 generations of Wakes including our son Charles aged 50 and his two sons now both at Universities.

The remarkable thing about the family is that, astonishingly, we have archives going back nearly 1000 years to the time when Hereward the Wake who owned Bourne defied William the Conqueror on the Isle of Ely, About 30 generations all succeeded through the male Wake line from father to son and all of whom were Northamptonshire or Lincolnshire Squires.

But it is about Blisworth I talk to you tonight, so I only just touch on some of the earlier Wakes before Sir Hugh. His great, great grandfather died in 1172 having founded the Abbey at Bourne and the Priory at nearby Deeping. We continued being Lords of the Manor of Bourne for about 450 years. Surprisingly we are still Lords of the Manor of Deeping.

Sir Hugh's father also named Hugh, fought alongside King Henry II in Brittany in 1230. He was the first bearer of our Wake coat of arms. Our crest then was a black lion, the Wake Knot being an even older family badge. He went on the Crusade to the Holy Land with Simon de Montford where he built a castle at Ascalon near Gaza which still bears our Coat of Arms today. He died there in 1241.

Sir Hugh died in 1315. He was a Knight of the Shire and represented

Northamptonshire in 7 Parliaments. His elder brother Baldwin, probably born at Blisworth, did not inherit. His son, the 1st Lord Blisworth, defended the Scottish frontier on behalf of the King and lived in the stronghold of Liddel Castle in Cumberland.

After Hugh there were 6 generations of Thomas Wakes all of whom owned Blisworth, all father to son nearly all of whom inherited young and died young after playing important parts in Northamptonshire.

Sir Thomas Wake I, ie. the first, married Elizabeth Cransley from Kettering. He was a Knight of the County, the Kings Chief Falconer and Sheriff in 1329 and again in 1335. He was the King's chief representative in the County. No local government e.g. County or District Councils. There were no Lords Lieutenant until Henry VIII's reign. Since 1329 there have been 12 occasions when Wakes have been Sheriffs of Northamptonshire.

While Chief Officer of the Crown, Thomas revived the appointment of Justices of the Peace which had been dormant for 45 years. He gave judgment on that important occasion In the Great Hall of Northampton Castle. He was a distinguished soldier. He took 200 Archers to France in 1345 and fought with the Black Prince son of King Edward III at Crecy. The Black Prince was married to Joan Baroness Wake the "Fair Maid of Kent". He died in 1346 during the Siege of Calais.

His son Sir Thomas Wake II married Alice, a daughter of Sir John Pattishall. He was summoned to Parliament as a baron in 1341. Amongst his duties in Northamptonshire he was a Justice of the Peace. He died in 1379. His son Thomas Wake III married Maud, sister of Sir John Pigot. He died only 4 years after his father in 1383. Thomas Wake IV married Margaret Philpot and died in 1425.

Thomas Wake V was born in 1402. Thomas was known as The Great Wake owning a huge number of Manors including Blisworth, Collingtree and Milton Malsor; and Manors in Lincolnshire, Buckinghamshire, Bedfordshire and Kent. He succeeded his father aged 23, married aged 30 Agnes Lovell of Clevedon in Somerset which remained in the family for about 170 years until about 1600 Sir Baldwin Wake, the 1st Baronet, sold it.

The Great Wake was Sheriff of Northamptonshire on 3 occasions and was a Justice of the Peace for Northamptonshire and Somerset and served in the Parliament at Winchester 1449. There is a seal of his in the British Museum, dated 1429, depicting the lion crest on his helmet together with the Wake Knot badge. He died in 1459 aged 56 and was succeeded by his son.

Thomas Wake VI was born in 1435. He too inherited aged 23 and was Sheriff on two occasions in 1461 and 1463. His cousin Richard Wake was Rector of Blisworth 1462 - 1475. Thomas died in 1476. He married Elizabeth Beauchamp, a daughter of the Earl of Warwick. She was 20 years older than him.

His son Roger Wake born 1452, was important. He inherited Blisworth from his father, aged 24, in the reign of Edward IV. He married Elizabeth Catesby of Ashby St Legers. He was Sheriff on two occasions. He founded a Free School in Blisworth; I wonder where it was?

He lived to the age of 51 during difficult times when the Yorkist and Lancastrian families were fighting the Wars of the Roses contending for the throne. King Edward IV had died in 1483 and his brother Richard, Duke of York, had his young nephews murdered in the Tower and crowned himself King Richard III. Two years later at the Battle of Bosworth Field, Henry Tudor the Lancastrian heir to the throne who had been in exile for 14 years, defeated and killed Richard. The King was supported by Roger Wake and Roger's father-in-law Richard Catesby who was Chancellor of the Exchequer and Speaker of Parliament. Catesby was subsequently beheaded at Leicester. Roger luckier than his father in law was imprisoned, and had his lands forfeited.

By Act of Parliament Roger's lands were later restored to him. He lived until 1503. His and his wife's tomb in Blisworth Church, which I restored in 1988, bears the family's shields and Wake Knots. Set in the purbeck marble top are fine brasses depicting Roger in armour with an apron of mail, spurs and a long sword. He is bare headed with long hair. Elizabeth is dressed in a flowing robe with an ornamental girdle and fur cuffs and wears a pedimental cap with a veil on her head. Their 7 sons are in loose gowns and the 3 daughters are shown with gowns and also with long hair.

The surrounding inscription is damaged but reads: "Here lyeth Roger Wake Esquyer Lord of Blisworth in the Counte of Northampton and Elizabeth his wife which Roger Decessyed the XVI day of Marche the yere of our Lord God MCCCCCIII on whose soule have mercy".

In his will land in Buckinghamshire was sold thereby endowing a priest to pray each year in the Lady Chapel at Blisworth for him and his wife Elizabeth and his many Wake forebears, previously buried there.

After the Battle of Bosworth the family's fortunes steadily declined.

Roger's son, another Thomas succeeded. He married Isobel Sapcotes from Burley on the Hill in Rutland. Shortly after his father's death "by reason of certain trespass he had done" Thomas was sent to the Tower and his life was in peril. His mother Elizabeth continued to live at Blisworth and by means of bribery managed to get him released and pardoned.

By 1515 Thomas had sold Collingtree; and 8 years later in 1523 disposed of Blisworth to Sir Richard Knightley of Fawsley, thus ended our long association with Blisworth. He died in 1536. There is a plaque on the wall of an ancient church which reads: "Here lies Sir Tom but do not think it odd. Not earth to earth but sod to sod. Surely for miscreants such as this, Hell was created bottomless". His son and then his grandson, both Thomas's continued to own Bourne and Deeping in Lincolnshire, until these two ancient Wake possessions were sold in 1574 to William Cecil Lord Burghley, at Stamford, in Queen Elizabeth's reign.

Because of Thomas' disgrace the chief of member or head of the family fell to his younger brother Richard Wake who lived at Hartwell and continued to own Clevedon in Somerset. His first wife Dorothy Dyve had 18 children. His second wife Margaret was a daughter of the Marquess of Dorset. Richard and his two wives all lie buried beneath an ancient tomb in Roade Church.

Though our Wake ownership of Blisworth had ended, the family continued to live nearby.

John Wake, born 1519, lived at Piddington, His daughter Magdalene married Richard Ousley of Courteenhall. John was in charge of Salcey and Whittlewood Forests and petitioned for extra hay for the deer. He contributed £25 towards the cost of opposing the Spanish Armada in Queen Elizabeth's reign. He is recorded by the Privy Council of settling a dispute with his neighbour John Fermor of Easton Neston. He died in 1572.

His grandson Sir Baldwin Wake was born in 1574. At the age of 40 he succeeded to Piddington and Clevedon from his father. He married at St Margaret's Westminster, Elizabeth, daughter of Sir George Digby of Warwickshire, in 1621 King James II made him one of the earliest baronets.
Finally he lived at Hartwell and died in 1628, greatly in debt. His eldest son John the 2nd Baronet had to sell Clevedon in 1630. He was lieutenant and forester of Salcey Forest and fined on several occasions for misdeeds and made insolvent. A loyal Royalist in the Civil War - the family further declined.

The next five baronets, the 2nd, 3rd, 4th, and 5th lived mostly at Hartwell and Piddington but like their predecessors married heiresses and brought additional properties to the family, including Riddlesworth in Suffolk. Then in 1672, 371 years ago, the family inherited Waltham and Nazeing in Essex and Courteenhall.

Nine succeeding Baronets 6th to 14th including me, have lived there now for over 277 years during which time we have produced Admirals, a General, an Archbishop of Canterbury, an Ambassador and High Sheriffs.

For the last five generations we have used the name 'Hereward'. My father, when a boy, used to say the Lord's Prayer thus: "Our Father who Art in Heaven, "Hereward" be Thy Name..."

EXTRODINARY CASE OF LONGEVITY –Mr Thomas Lucas

CHELMSFORD CHRONICAL – FRIDAY 2ND JANUSRY 1863

A native of Hertfordshire expired at Wanstead in this county, in his 105 year. He retained the use of all his faculties up to the period of his dissolution. His mother lived to the advanced age of 101. Deceased had been confined to his room only a few weeks previously to his demise, up to which period he enjoyed excellent health. The following interesting particulars connected with this centenarian are from the pen of Rev W.P. Wigram, rector of Wanstead, who was a very kind friend to the aged deceased for many years – Thomas Lucas was born in Bygrave in Hertfordshire and was baptised in 1762. The certificate of his baptism, obtained a few years ago. According to what his mother told him he was either 4 or 5 years old when baptised, and he assured me he remembered walking to church on that occasion when a younger brother was baptised with him.

The old man's memory was so good there seems to be no reason to doubt the accuracy of his statements. His family consider him to be 105, he was formally a Bailiff to Mr Long Wellesley at Wanstead House. Had been married and had several children of whom some at advanced age are still living. He had a remarkable healthy appetite and clear grey eyes, was of courteous manners and of a very cheerful temper and retained excellent health and the complete use of his faculties including his memory hearing and eyesight till almost the end. Until a few months of his death he chopped his own firewood, was conversational and agreeable to visitors, and was generally in full enjoyment of life.

He received much fondness from many of my parishioners which contributed doubtless to the prolongation of his days. As he died on the 20December (the day before his birthday which was 21 December) I understand that he had, in point of law, completed 105 years. He suffered considerably during the last 6 weeks but his end was tranquil and happy.